Strategies for *e*-Business

We work with leading authors to develop the strongest educational materials in business, bringing cutting-edge thinking and best learning practice to a global market

Under a range of well-known imprints, including Financial Times Prentice Hall, we craft high quality print and electronic publications which help readers to understand and apply their content, whether studying or at work.

To find out more about the complete range of our publishing, please visit us on the World Wide Web at: **www.pearsoned.co.uk**

Strategies for *e*-Business

Creating Value through Electronic and Mobile Commerce

Concepts and Cases

Second Edition

TAWFIK JELASSI

ALBRECHT ENDERS

FT Prentice Hall
FINANCIAL TIMES

An imprint of **Pearson Education**
Harlow, England • London • New York • Boston • San Francisco • Toronto
Sydney • Tokyo • Singapore • Hong Kong • Seoul • Taipei • New Delhi
Cape Town • Madrid • Mexico City • Amsterdam • Munich • Paris • Milan

Pearson Education Limited

Edinburgh Gate
Harlow
Essex CM20 2JE
England
and Associated Companies throughout the world

Visit us on the World Wide Web at:
www.pearsoned.co.uk

_____

First published 2005
Second edition published 2008

© Pearson Education Limited 2008

ISBN 978-0-273-71028-8

British Library Cataloguing-in-Publication Data
A catalogue record for this book is available from the British Library

Library of Congress Cataloging-in-Publication Data
Jelassi, Tawfik, 1957-
 Strategies for e-business : creating value through electronic and mobile commerce :
concepts and cases / Tawfik Jelassi, Albrecht Enders. -- 2nd ed.
    p. cm.
 Includes bibliographical references and index.
 ISBN 978-0-273-71028-8 (alk. paper)
 1. Electronic commerce. 2. Electronic commerce--Europe--Case studies. 3.
Industries--Technological innovations--Economic aspects. 4. Strategic planning. I.
Enders, Albrecht. II. Title.
 HF5548.32.J45 2008
 658.8'72--dc22

                                                              2008017070

10 9 8 7 6 5 4 3 2 1
13 12 11 10 09 08

Typeset in 10/12½ pt Minion by 30
Printed and bound by Rotolito Lombarda, Italy

The publisher's policy is to use paper manufactured from sustainable forests.

BRIEF CONTENTS

DETAILED CONTENTS

Part II The e-business strategy framework

Part III A roadmap for e-business strategy implementation

Part IV   Case studies

Chapter 14   Building e-business competence through concepts and cases   269

Supporting resources

Visit **www.pearsoned.co.uk/jelassi** to find valuable online resources

For instructors
- PowerPoint slides of figures and tables from the book, as well as some textual slides with key points from the chapters, to help withlecture preparation
- Teaching notes for the case studies to save valuable preparation time
- Suggested syllabi for alternative courses draw on the authors' experience of teaching the subject to a range of students in different countries

For more information please contact your local Pearson Education sales representative or visit **www.pearsoned.co.uk/jelassi**

LIST OF EXHIBITS

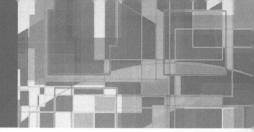

FOREWORDS

The emergence of e-business

By F. Warren McFarlan

Harvard Business School, Boston, Massachusetts

2008 is an especially good time for a thoughtful book on e-business. We are nearly a quarter of the way into the second half of the Information Age revolution. Very little of what is now accepted management practice and application opportunity today was even conceived of 13 years ago. The first half of the Information Age took place between 1955 and 1995. 1955 was the year when IBM built, in short order, its 701, 702 and 703 computers, while Univac launched its Univac I. Large, rather unreliable and with a vastly limited processing capacity in terms of today's machines, those machines and their clumsy (by today's standards) languages, nonetheless, provoked a revolution in back-office transaction processing, leading to sharp improvements in cost, quality and services. Insurance, banking, airline reservations were where some of the most exciting IT applications took place in those early days, with the structures of those industries being profoundly impacted over a long period of time (over 15 years, for example, one insurance firm's premium notice department gradually withered from 150 people to one). Additionally, a heavy focus, of course, was on financial processes relating to accounting, payroll, etc., with overall IT responsibility being most often housed in the financial function. All of this was done mostly in the context of home-grown systems, where the prevailing model was to *build* and *run*. Large IT departments, filled with highly specialized technical skills, emerged to develop and operate these systems. They made intense efforts to learn how to plan their activities, better manage projects, assess and manage risk. This work evolved in a more or less linear way over two decades, creating the great legacy systems, many of which still run today. How to cope managerially with this world was captured by the first generation of IT literature, which was heavily executional in its focus.

In the late 1970s, a sharp shift in the technology cost performance allowed the emergence of the PC with desktop computing soon becoming a standard part of corporate life. The technology rapidly spread across the desktops of the firm, causing great angst to the operators of large data centers, whose processes were severely challenged. All through the 1980s, however, much of the prevailing focus of a firm's IT activities still remained in the *build* and *run* category. Near the end of the decade, however, the first big outsourcing of IT resource deals emerged. This fact, combined with the explosion of the applications software industry (SAP, Oracle, etc.), caused the monopoly role of the in-house IT department to *build* and *deliver* systems to begin to disappear. It was increasingly replaced by the *source* and *manage* model. This resulted in a genuine revolution. Early adapters, Eastman-Kodak and General Dynamics, found fundamentally different, and more effective, corporate operating models.

Increasingly, over the next two decades, managers came to focus on how IT could deliver a competitive advantage and they worried less about the mechanics of how to build and operate systems, but turned that over to the burgeoning software and service industry. (IBM, Accenture, CSC and EDS, plus a host of smaller ones.) Conventional wisdom about how to manage IT and its impact was severely challenged, creating a new literature. For the first time, IT as a competitive weapon began to be extensively talked about.

The thunder clouds of even more dramatic changes, however, were to emerge. Tom Friedman, in his remarkable book *The World is Flat* (2005) (Farrar, Straus & Giroux), identified three dominant events that have shaped this new world. From the 1990s until today, the first was the fall of the Berlin Wall in 1989, which combined with the emergence of China effectively delivered more than 3 billion people into the world markets (this topic is not dealt with in Dr. Jelassi and Dr. Enders' book), creating new sources of supply and demand for all forms of products and services and turning the IT world inside out.

The second event was the stream of activities which were triggered by the Netscape IPO in October, 1995. This is widely seen as the beginning of the Internet I Era, the emergence of e-business, and the concurrent propulsion of the world towards open systems and widely accessible data. The third event was the massive overinvestment by telecommunications companies in fiber networks which collectively created the wide, almost zero cost highways for today's digital economy. Tom notes that these trends led to the words insourcing, outsourcing and off-shoring, supply chaining and informating, which fundamentally transformed the operation and performance of global enterprise. Dr. Jelassi and Dr. Enders' book wisely ignores the issues of where work is done globally (a separate book by itself), and chooses instead to focus on the other aspects of this revolution; namely, on how the core processes and products of a firm are shaped by these new opportunities in a world of essentially free telecommunication and Internet-enabled interconnections. In doing this, they bring enormous insight to the task. The book is a tour de force:

1 First, the book is grounded in a deep sense of history. It richly catches the forces which led to the emergence of the e-business world and to its tremendous growth that ultimately led to the Bubble. They effectively document the Bubble's collapse, the underlying reason for it, and identify the exciting opportunities beyond. As one reads about the brief existence of Webvan for example, nostalgic memories surge of an exciting, yet fundamentally flawed vision. The book captures brilliantly both the opportunities and the drivers towards excess of the early days. It provides useful warnings for today.

2 Secondly, the book has deep and informed command of the relevant literatures as they relate to company and industry competitive strategy and dynamics (Porter, *et al.*). The discussion of the opportunities and risks of new technologies are firmly rooted in value chain and other contemporary forms of strategic analysis. It is worth noting; there is not a strategic framework Dr. Jelassi and Dr. Enders use that existed before 1982. They avail themselves of the latest insights in this area. In short, the book combines the latest of strategic thinking with the opportunities posed by the new technologies.

3 The book is built on informed understanding of detailed management practice. A particular strength is the assembly of a rich collection of articles from the *Financial Times*, which illustrate the key moves made by different players during this period and, in so doing, gives useful insight on the breadth of applications. Those articles ensure that the book is as well rooted in management practice as theory and make the book as relevant to the manager as to the MBA student.

4 The book demonstrates a broad command of the general IT literature (summarized in the Appendix, now on the Companion Website, along with an appropriate set of technical definitions for those new to this area). This link between strategy, theory, IT application literatures, and the world of practice makes this a very unusual and impactful book.

5 The book reaches from the past to the absolute current leading edge of practice and application. For example, the chapter on Internet II is as good a piece as I have seen on this rapidly emerging technology.

6 Behind the articles for those readers who are interested in more applications' depth lie a series of intensively researched and comprehensive IT application case studies. Some 19 detailed, leading-edge, field-based case studies predominantly based in Europe are presented for those who need deeper insight in the issues of contemporary management practice. Combined with the chapters, these cases make the book a compelling text for MBAs.

This, however, is much more than just a book for an MBA course, although it has all the material for a first-rate course. It is also a book for the thoughtful practitioner who is trying to position his/her organization to take advantage of these fast-moving technologies. The book gives a detailed structure and guidance for how to find profitable business opportunities. It contains a panoply of practical easy-to-understand examples of applications. It also spends an appropriate amount of time on the problems of implementation.

On the negative side, the book makes no attempt to deal with the complexities of global outsourcing and coordination of services across national boundaries. The roles of India, China and other countries are hardly alluded to in the book. I do not see this as a serious omission, but rather the beginning focus of what another equally rich book on contemporary IT management might be built on.

In short, the book is rich, high impact and very well thought out.

e-Business – advancing competitive advantage

By Professor Dr. Bolko von Oetinger
Senior Vice President and Director of the Strategy Institute of The Boston Consulting Group, Munich

In 2004, in the aftermath of the dot-com bubble, I chose the French Revolution as the preferred metaphor in my Foreword to Tawfik Jelassi's and Albrecht Enders' first edition. It still holds true, but history has marched on.

Beyond all the narcissism and glamour of the early dot-com days there has been considerable change in our economic world – change which has irrevocably and fundamentally changed many businesses. In the shortest time possible, e-business offered a new opportunity for creating competitive advantage. The surprising novelty of the approach first shook up the markets, then the bubble (caused by rash extrapolations) finally burst. Now that the dust has settled, and more rapidly than many investors may have wished, it has become clear that nothing will be the same again; in fact the most fundamental ways of conducting business have been profoundly and irrevocably altered.

The reign of terror of the Jacobins, that is the irrational hype and hysteria surrounding the dot-com industries, is now history. Robespierre, and along with him hundreds of other dotcoms, have been led to the scaffold. The revolution is dead – but the revolutionary ideas have changed the world. Or, to put it in more modern terms: the excesses are over, but the guiding principles of e-businesses remain. That was what we saw happening in 2004.

In 2007, Internet businesses are part and parcel of our daily lives and we cannot imagine what it was like without them. eBay, Amazon, travel agencies, airline booking, classified ads, etc. are the most normal activities in the world of consumers; online supply chains are a fact of life for companies; social networks break into classical channels; open source systems can turn customers into competitors. e-Business strategy framework and value creation testify to the normality of e-business. Not enough? An army of Web.2 applications marches inexorably across the world, advancing and changing competitive behavior in a radical way.

Again, the new assault changes the way we do business. Web.2 is in a literal sense disruptive. The company – as we know it – dominates its markets through its size, is run by an elaborate hierarchy, and knows exactly what is in the company and what is outside the company. Web.2 is dramatically undermining these assumptions by means of user-generated content. The scale of giants in businesses with non-physical assets can easily be undercut by small attackers, growing the 'tail' of the business – a good example being Wikipedia articles written by voluntaries competing with Encyclopedia Britannica, a full-blown firm. Small businesses, even individuals, can do big things! Sometimes the consumers will not consume what they are offered but cook their meals either alone or with the help of others. The distinction of production and consumption can get blurred. The more the customer's autonomy and self-organization, the less important the firm's hierarchy.

Technological innovations can provide an attractive basis for growth strategies, new customer value, new business models, and innovative products. Of crucial importance during this early stage is the ability to determine where technological innovations meet consumer needs and allow new business models to emerge. That is what happened in the past, and that is what happens in e-business and Web.2.

If we differentiate between Internet technology and its commercial applications in e-business, we soon notice that there are two main strategic options: on the one hand, it is obvious that within e-business itself there is still massive untapped potential. The impact that e-business applications will have in the areas of health care, education or in the public sector, to name but three, is still not entirely clear. In these areas, we still find ourselves at the beginning of potentially revolutionary changes to existing business models. On the other hand, the technological innovation potential of the Internet itself is in no way yet fully exploited. A glance at the future of broadband technology, which is already being put to good use in Korea and Japan, points the way to many new applications of the high-speed Internet – television on the Internet being but one example. Consider also the possibilities that will arise from the synergies between the Internet and mobile phone technologies. These applications will not only create new business opportunities, but also fundamentally change the strategies of many companies, particularly in the communications and media industries.

Thus, technological platforms and innovations provide an important foundation for competitive advantages which, in turn, manifest themselves in commercial applications. But e-business technologies have opened up even more business opportunities: they have also changed the way we think about business strategies and sources of competitive advantage. The once self-contained value chain has been transformed into a network of value elements, and has thus made possible an organizational deconstruction of previously unimaginable extent. Those who still think in terms of value chains are not merely using the wrong term, they are also missing out on a great opportunity since an open network offers far greater opportunities than a single chain. The Internet creates the communication links that open up the creative space into which new businesses can grow.

As early as 1911, Schumpeter referred to these kinds of new combinations of different value chains in his *Theory of Economic Development*. Today, almost 100 years later, technological development is accelerating this unending succession of creative destruction and reconstruction in a way that was previously unheard of. Today, it is becoming increasingly easy to interlink the different parts of a value chain across companies and across geographical boundaries. Supported by increasingly sophisticated IT solutions in the supply chain management process, the concept of deconstruction has shaped many organizations. Thus, the world today appears as if encompassed by a single production line, allowing us to connect individual stages of production around the globe. We can also replace vertical organizational structures with horizontal layers, thereby transforming a company into one that can compete at different stages of the value structure. Those who do not include such considerations in their thinking are omitting strategic options that will influence the efficiency and effectiveness of their business. It is clear that the Internet and the accompanying structural and organizational changes have become the backbone of the economy. And yet, most likely, this is only the beginning. We are entering an era of growing economic freedom, in which the multitude of possible value chain combinations reminds us of the Lego® system. And, as the freedom to recombine different parts of the value structure increases, the space for innovations and real surprises also grows.

For the majority of businesses that adopted e-business, it has proven advantageous not to get rid of existing structures and replace everything with the new (that is, with e-business) but, rather, to skillfully merge the new with the old. This combination of tried and tested tradition with sensible innovation leads to an increase in efficiency, improvement in quality, and higher customer retention.

However, there are businesses in which merging the new (online) business with the existing one cannot be done so easily. A remarkable example of turning the threat of the online world to an existing traditional print business into a renewed competitive advantage for the incumbent is the move that *The Wall Street Journal* print version has recently made. As news today can be received online every second of every hour of every day everywhere, most of the news in the newspaper version is the previous day's news. Whereas 'The Wall Street Journal Online' deals with 'what is happening right now', the print journal has been repositioned to make 80% of the journal 'what-it-means journalism' and only 20% is the news the reader should not have missed the previous day. The result: significantly increased readership for the printed version. So, the informed reader can use *The Wall Street Journal* throughout the day, online and in printed form. e-Business is not just e-business but also a driver of innovation for non-e-businesses.

The best results have always been achieved when operational excellence, attention to the smallest details, step-by-step change, and careful experimentation over a long period of time have driven the implementation of e-business. The successful e-business companies did not fall into the trap of believing that being first in the market would be sufficient to guarantee lasting competitive advantage. They had internalized one of the most important strategic insights: it is not simply enough to be the first; you must also be the best. Many dot-coms grew faster than demand, thereby creating overcapacity which ultimately led to their demise. A more realistic appraisal of the evolution of the online market, which was slower than many of the start-ups had anticipated, could have helped to avoid many a disappointment. If there is an important lesson to be learned from this period of hype, then it is this: the integration of old and new combined with superior execution – which is more important than just speed – turns technological innovations into sustainable competitive advantages.

e-Business has also created entirely new types of innovative business models, thereby providing the strategic theme of 'disruptive innovation' with some instructive examples of strategic excellence. Business models have sprung up which would have been unthinkable before. Think of eBay, Google and Amazon, enterprises that have disruptively stirred up the market like no other. The distinctive trait that sets these three companies apart is the fact that they were not just innovative in the past, they continue to be so. Started as Web.1 companies they have adopted major Web.2 characteristics. Through peer reviews eBay certifies buyer and seller reputation. Peer-generated higher reputation translates into higher prices and is more important than the platform brand. Amazon adopted reader ratings, reviews, and recommendations. Google gave Wikipedia a free ride.

They did not just create new companies: they also built strong global brands. They were able to do this because they deliver superior customer value. There were numerous competitors who had also recognized the potential of these new business opportunities, but they were unable to act accordingly. The courage of the entrepreneur, the courage to experiment, as well as the courage to hold on to a vision when the figures don't yet add up, the courage to swim against the tide but at the same time to maintain a grasp on the economic reality are reminiscent of a classical recipe for success for laying the foundations of a successful business.

The history of the three above-mentioned companies indicates a high level of flexibility – an unmistakable sign of good strategy management. eBay began as an electronic flea market and has become one of the largest retailing companies, constantly winning new customers and expanding into new product categories. Today, Amazon is not only a general mail order company, but also a software provider that markets its own software and business processes. Both companies have realized that, at the edges of their existing business models, there often lurks a new strategic option just waiting to be discovered. In the online music industry, the story which began with Napster is now continued by Apple against Microsoft, and Sony shows just how strong the innovative will of the visionary entrepreneur has to be, the eye he/she has to have for the quality of the future business model, how much energy is required for it to be put into practice, and finally how risky the attempt to transform a business idea into an actual business really is. Through an extensive strategy framework and detailed case studies from many different industries and countries, Jelassi and Enders illustrate powerfully that a successful strategy consists of the combination of many factors rather than one single element. This is also particularly true for e-business.

The emergence and development of e-business is a chapter from that great story that deals with the question of how something new comes into being. It is a chapter from the history of innovation, and for that reason alone deserves to be examined in detail. It was not the established firms that seized the new opportunities, but rather the outsiders. The outsider as innovative strategic genius is not an unusual phenomenon. Due to the fact that venture capital for e-business start-ups was seemingly unlimited, droves of inexperienced entrepreneurs, many of them with unsustainable business plans, got themselves to the starting block and simply took off. The laws of the market have caught up with them all. Only the best have survived.

The world of e-business has become a fact of life, so it is important to have a precise understanding of the history of e-business. There is no growth, no value creation, and no employment without innovation and without entrepreneurs. And there is no innovation without advantage. e-Business in its various shapes as Web.1 and Web.2 is the story of the creation of new advantages. It is important to note that the story continues. There is more to come.

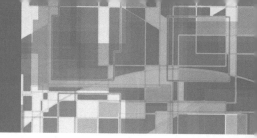

PREFACE

People tend to over-estimate new technology in the short run and under-estimate it in the long run.

Roy Amara, Institute for the Future

Context and positioning of the book

When we talked to colleagues and friends in the fall of 2003 about the writing of the first edition of our e-business book, many of them asked whether we were arriving too late with the book. They reminded us that the Internet bubble had burst three years ago and that most online companies had since gone bankrupt. Since then, the thinking has changed. Both traditional bricks-and-mortar corporations such as Tesco, Sony BMG or Mercedes-Benz and pure online companies such as Amazon, Google, or eBay have continued to develop and implement e-business strategies, albeit initially with less public attention and media coverage than before. Due to the recent rapid growth of so-called Web 2.0 applications, online companies such as Facebook, MySpace or XING once again dominate the headlines of the business press.

Similar to other important technological revolutions such as railways or steam engines, the Internet has also undergone a typical cycle of boom and bust. Following a bust, technological revolutions rebound, and it is only then – during the 'golden age' – that they show their true impact. At the time of writing of this second edition of the book, it looks as if e-business has entered this golden age.

During our research for this book, we found very few books published after the collapse of the dotcom bubble that specifically address e-business strategy issues. We also noticed that there were many excellent books on strategy and many books on e-business, yet there were relatively few books that attempted to bring the two fields together in a comprehensive and rigorous manner.

This book, as its title suggests, attempts to close this gap. It aims at providing readers with a holistic and integrated view of the realms of strategy and e-business by focusing on strategic management concepts and linking them to actual case studies of companies engaged in e-business activities. It also aims at going beyond the hype by closely analysing examples of failure as well as success in order to help readers assess the underlying drivers for a successful e-business strategy.

Target readers

Strategies for e-Business is a textbook targeted at senior managers, business strategists, entrepreneurs and consultants, as well as participants enrolled in MBA, Masters and executive education programmes and students in the final year of their undergraduate education. It should be of interest to general management programmes and seminars as well as to those specialising in e-business, electronic commerce, technology management, marketing, entrepreneurship, innovation management and business strategy.

Key features

The key differentiating features of this book include the following:

- *A comprehensive e-business strategy framework.* This framework serves as a comprehensive basis for e-business strategy formulation. It is based on rigorous and time-proven concepts from the field of strategic management, which were adapted to the specific context of e-business.

- *An e-business roadmap.* Chapter 13 of the book contains an e-business roadmap that is meant as a guide to help in the formulation and implementation process of an e-business strategy. It provides an overview of the key issues involved in this process. At the same time, extensive cross-references to the more detailed e-business strategy framework allow the reader to obtain more in-depth information when needed.

- *A detailed study approach for e-business strategy.* Creativity and analytical ability are of fundamental importance in the strategy formulation process. Chapter 14 of this book discusses how to improve these qualities through the use of concepts and case studies.

- *In-depth case studies.* The book contains 19 real-world case studies, which provide in-depth accounts of how companies in several industries and different countries (in Europe, North America and Japan) have developed and implemented e-business, electronic commerce or mobile e-commerce strategies. All the case studies result from first-hand field-based research, which the case authors have personally conducted in co-operation with executives and top-level managers of the companies involved.

- *Geographic focus on Europe.* While most of the existing e-business casebooks focus on companies that are based in the USA, this book focuses primarily on companies operating in Europe. In addition to the USA and Japan, European countries covered by the case studies contained in this book include Denmark, France, Germany, Finland, Italy, Norway, Sweden, The Netherlands and the UK. In addition to the technological aspects discussed in the case studies, the wide variety of countries that are involved helps to provide insights into the specific business environment and national culture that characterise the different countries covered.

Structure and content

Content-wise, Part I presents the broader context of the book. It introduces the key terminology and evolution of e-business and provides an historic overview of the distinct phases that technological revolutions typically go through before reaching their full potential.

Part II suggests a strategy framework for the formulation of e-business strategies. Chapter 3 discusses the external environment of e-business ventures. This includes an analysis of the macro-environment and the industry structure. Chapter 4 focuses on the internal dimension of e-business strategy formulation. Chapter 5 is concerned with generic strategy options, which determine the overall strategic direction of an e-business venture. The issue of sustaining a competitive advantage over time and the dangers that threaten to erode such advantage are discussed in Chapter 6. Chapter 7 provides a systematic approach for developing innovations that aim to make the competition irrelevant. Chapter 8 presents the value-process framework which integrates different perspectives of strategy into a holistic model. Chapters 9 to 11 address three strategic issues that are of special relevance for e-business companies. These include the internal organisation of an e-business venture (Chapter 9), its relations with suppliers (Chapter 10) and its relations with customers/users (Chapter 11). Chapter 12 presents conceptual frameworks that are specific to mobile e-commerce applications.

Part III provides a roadmap for the formulation of an e-business strategy. Through the use of cross-references, this roadmap (presented in Chapter 13) is closely linked to the e-business strategy framework presented in Part II.

Part IV first provides an introduction to case study work by discussing how the concepts and cases presented in the book can help managers and students interested in e-business strategies to expand their skills along the dimensions of creativity and analytical ability (Chapter 14). Following this, a brief synopsis section provides an overview of the key topics in the cases and is then followed by the full-length case studies.

Getting the most from *Strategies in e-Business*

In order to benefit most from this book, we recommend that you try to achieve the following when working through the book chapters:

- Thoroughly understand the theoretical concepts presented in the e-business strategy framework.
- Critically assess the strengths and weaknesses of each concept and determine the context for its appropriate use.
- Apply the concepts when analysing the case studies and make action-oriented recommendations backed up by logical reasoning and supporting arguments.
- Expand the usage of the concepts and the frameworks into other business situations that you encounter in your daily work or study.

To make your learning experience more effective and enriching, the book contains the following features:

- *Chapter at a glance* at the beginning of each chapter provides a quick overview of the most important topics discussed in the chapter.
- *Related case studies* are included at the beginning of each chapter to illustrate which cases are most relevant for the topics discussed. For more information on this, Exhibit P.1 illustrates the relationships between the case studies and specific chapters and sections of the book.
- *Learning outcomes* offer a brief description of what you should have achieved after reading the chapter.
- Different types of boxes are contained in the text body of each chapter to provide added information about the concepts that are discussed.

- *FT articles* are taken from the *Financial Times* to provide a journalistic perspective (within the timeframe context) of the issue discussed in the section.

- *Critical perspectives* present a different, if not opposing, view to the position taken in the main text of the chapter. For instance, the resource-based view is presented as a critical perspective on Porter's market-based view to strategy formulation. Weighing the merits of each view is a valuable exercise for gaining a more in-depth understanding of the concept that is presented.

- *Blog boxes* contain excerpts from blog writers who provide their opinions on current developments in the e-business world. These excerpts provide an additional and at times different perspective to the concepts discussed in the chapters.

- *Strategy in action* boxes are examples that provide additional background to the concepts discussed in the chapters.

- *Summaries* at the end of each chapter allow you to review the most important points that were discussed in the chapter.

- *Review questions* help you assess your understanding of the material presented in the chapter. In general, the answers to these questions are straightforward since they are based on the material presented in the chapter.

- *Discussion questions* help you to transfer the concepts from the chapter into different business contexts. They are also meant as a starting point for discussion with your colleagues and peers.

- *Recommended key reading* provides a select list of additional books and articles that you can read if you wish to find out more about a specific topic.

- *Useful third-party weblinks* provide additional information on some material contained in the chapter.

- Our blog at **www.jelassi-enders.com** informs you about current e-business developements and how they relate to the content of the book. In addition, the blog provides links to relevant videos and other e-business websites.

Exhibit P.1 The cases cover several industries and focus on different themes

	Case study name			Chapter 3	Chapter 4	Chapter 5	Chapter 6	Chapter 7	Chapter 8	Chapter 9	Chapter 10	Chapter 11	Chapter 12
				External analysis	Internal analysis	Strategy options	Sustaining a competitive advantage	New market spaces	Value process framework	Internal organisation	Relationship with suppliers	Relationship with users/customers	Mobile business
B2C in retailing	1	Tesco	299		●●	●●	●	●●		●●	●	●	
B2C in financial services	2	Nordea	314	●	●●	●●	●●	●●		●●		●	●
	3	ING DIRECT	330	●		●●	●	●●	●			●	
B2C in manufacturing	4	Ducati vs. Harley	343		●●		●			●●		●	
	5	Otis	356	●	●●		●●	●●		●●			
B2B e-commerce	6	Mondus	370		●		●				●●	●●	
	7	Covisint	388		●					●	●●		
	8	IBX	407				●			●	●●		
	9	eBay	423		●					●●	●●		
Corporate portals	10	Shell	437		●●					●●			
e-Government	11	e-Government	451	●●	●		●●						
P2P model	12	P2P file-sharing	468	●●			●●	●		●	●	●●	
Online communities and user-generated content	13	openBC	482	●●			●●	●				●●	
	14	Spreadshirt	505	●	●●	●●	●●	●	●	●		●●	
	15	Second Life	525	●●	●●			●●				●●	
Mobile e-commerce	16	Sony BMG	548	●●	●	●●	●●	●	●●	●			●●
	17	NTT DoCoMo	570	●				●●			●●	●	●●
	18	YOC	585	●	●			●			●	●●	●●
	19	Paybox	601							●			●●

●● Primary focus of the case study ● Secondary focus of the case study

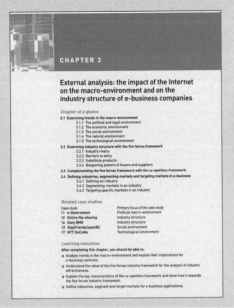

Chapter at a glance and **Learning outcomes** allow the reader to identify and review the key learning points in each chapter, and evaluate their learning.

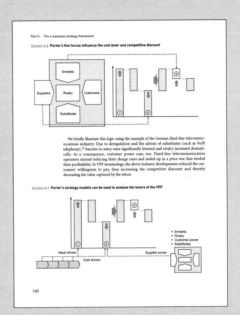

Figures and **diagrams** are used throughout to illustrate concepts and provide useful learning aids.

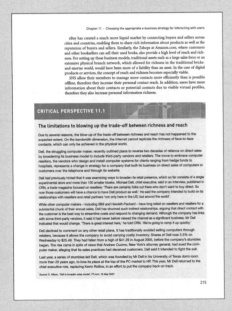

Critical perspective boxes present alternative viewpoints and encourage the reader to critically evaluate key ideas and practices.

Financial Times **articles** offer opinions and comments showing e-business strategy in practice, helping to illustrate the theory and provide a critical viewpoint.

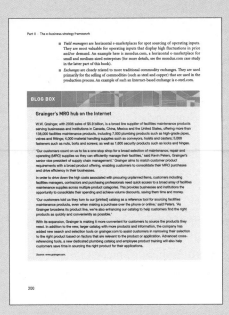

New **Blog boxes** contain excerpts from blog writers who provide their opinions on current developments in the e-business world.

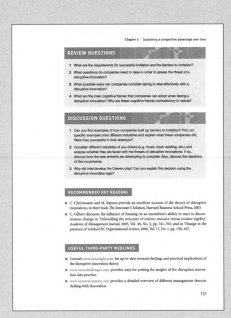

Review and **Discussion questions** at the end of each chapter help the reader to test and develop the ideas they have learned.

Recommended key reading provides a select list of books and articles for the reader to further explore specific topics.

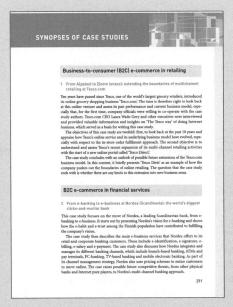

Synopses of the case studies provide an overview of each case and draw out the most important themes.

Nineteen in-depth **Case studies** provide real-world examples from a variety of industries and countries. All the cases result from first-hand field-based research which the authors have personally undertaken in co-operation with executives and top-level managers.

Author acknowledgements

Throughout the writing and publication process of this book, we have received valuable support and contributions from many people. Therefore, we would like to thank and express our gratitude to the following individuals:

- The authors who worked with us during the development of the case studies. These include Dr Stefanie Leenen (BASS, Germany), Dr Michael Müller (RWE, Germany), Dr Guus Pijpers (TiasNimbas Business School, The Netherlands), André Achtstätter, Leslie Diamond, Hans-Joachim Jost, Timothy Lennon and Morven McLean (past MBA participants at the Ecole Nationale des Ponts et Chaussées School of International Management, Paris) and Prof. Charles Waldman (INSEAD, France).

- Our colleagues and students at the Department of Management at the University of Nuremberg who conducted case study research with us. In particular we would like to thank our colleagues Prof. Harald Hungenberg and Andreas König, and our students Sebastian Bartz, Henning Blarr, Hans Denker, Fernando Endarra, Thomas Engelbertz, Sebastian Mauch, Matthias Promny and Maria Štšekotovitš.

- The authors who contributed the remaining case studies contained in the book. These include Prof. Lynda Applegate and Prof. F. Warren McFarlan (both from Harvard Business School, USA), Prof. Gary Grikscheit, Prof. Scott Newman, Prof. Rohit Verma and Vivek Malapati (all from the University of Utah, USA), Prof. Kurt Verweire and Prof. Lutgart Van den Berghe (from the Vlerick Leuven Gent Management School, Belgium).

- Prof. F. Warren McFarlan (Emeritus Professor at Harvard Business School) and Prof. Bolko von Oetinger (Senior Vice President and Director of the Strategy Institute of The Boston Consulting Group) for taking time out of their busy schedule to write forewords for the book.

- The students on several MBA programmes in different countries as well as the managers in executive education programmes and seminars at business schools, corporate universities and companies who, through their analysis and discussion of the case studies, contributed to the shaping of the book.

- The executives and managers of the companies featured in the case studies contained in the book.

- The staff at Pearson Education; in particular, we would like to thank our editors Linda Dhondy and Matthew Walker for their support throughout the whole publication process.

- The numerous reviewers who provided valuable insights through their detailed feedback on the first edition of the book. For this second edition we would like to thank: Laura Bradley, Bock Gee Woo, Mary Martin, Judith Molka-Danielsen, Ravi Seethamraju, Ken Stevens, Paula Swatman and Brian Webb.

- Last but not least, special thanks go to our families for their unlimited support and much appreciated encouragement of this book project. It is to our dear ones (Rafia, Samy, Sélim, Mehdi, Kim, Megan and Julia as well as to the larger Chadli Jelassi, Mohamed Kallala, Dietrich Enders and Charles Hicks families) that we dedicate this book.

Feedback

We are interested in hearing your comments about this book. We appreciate both critical and supportive feedback, which can help us to improve future editions of this book. You can reach us via e-mail at: jelassi@enpcmbaparis.com and albrecht.enders@wiso.uni-erlangen.de. In the spirit of the concepts and case studies presented in this book, we also encourage you to provide feedback on the Amazon.com websites so that others can find out about your opinion.

Tawfik Jelassi
Albrecht Enders
March 2008

Tawfik Jelassi (*right*) is Professor of e-Business and Information Technology and Dean of the School of International Management at the Ecole Nationale des Ponts et Chaussées (Paris). He is also Adjunct Professor of Technology Management at INSEAD (Fontainebleau). Dr Jelassi holds a PhD degree from the Stern School of Business at New York University (USA), graduate degrees from the Université de Paris-Dauphine (France) and an undergraduate degree from the Institut Supérieur de Gestion (Tunis, Tunisia). His research focuses on e-business/electronic commerce, the strategic use of IT and technology-based innovation. This research has appeared in his books: *Competing through Information Technology: Strategy and Implementation* (Prentice Hall, 1994), *Strategic Information Systems: A European Perspective* (Wiley, 1994) and *Strategies for e-Business: Creating Value through Electronic and Mobile Commerce* (Financial Times/Prentice Hall, 2005). Prof. Jelassi has also published over 80 research articles in leading academic journals and conference proceedings, and was awarded several teaching and research excellence awards. He has written over 50 field-based case studies, several of which won internatuional awards. Prof. Jelassi has taught extensively on MBA and executive education programmes for leading business schools and international corporations in over a dozen countries around the world. He has also served as an adviser to several companies and government organisations.

Albrecht Enders (*left*) is Assistant Professor of Strategic Management at the University of Nuremberg in Germany. Previously, he worked as a consultant with The Boston Consulting Group and as a Research Fellow at INSEAD (Fontainebleau) where he conducted research on electronic and mobile commerce. He has written numerous articles and case studies on e-business and strategy. Albrecht Enders holds a PhD in strategic management from the Leipzig Graduate School of Management in Germany and a BA in economics from Dartmouth College in the USA.

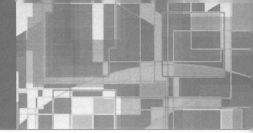

PUBLISHER'S ACKNOWLEDGEMENTS

We are grateful to the Financial Times Limited for permission to reprint the following material:

Chapter 1 Minitel proves a mixed blessing, © *Financial Times*, 8 February 2000; Chapter 1 A billion-dollar mistake: Webvan's failure has been an expensive lesson for the Internet, © *Financial Times*, 10 July 2001; Chapter 1 Netscape to the Next Big Thing: how a dotcom decade changed our lives, © *Financial Times*, 5 August 2005; Chapter 3 E-business: the odds lengthen: The Us crackdown on online gaming is forcing a rethink, © *Financial Times*, 14 November 2006; Chapter 3 Get a (second) life, © *Financial Times*, 18 November 2006; Chapter 3 All eyes on Google advertising, © *Financial Times*, 17 April 2007; Chapter 3 Men propel surge in online shopping, © *Financial Times*, 6 November 2006; Chapter 3 Sole listener is target for online radio, © *Financial Times*, 16 January 2007; Chapter 6 Why disruption can be good for business, © *Financial Times*, 3 October 2003; Chapter 7 Dell aims to stretch its way of business, © *Financial Times*, 13 November 2003; Chapter 7 Apple's sound strategy can keep the i-Pod at number one, © *Financial Times*, 2 September 2006; Chapter 9 Facebook spreads its web wider, © *Financial Times*, 29 June 2007; Chapter 9 Bertelsmann folds e-taylor into book clubs, © *Financial Times*, 16 May 2001; Chapter 11 Advertisers discover the merits of networking, © *Financial Times*, 17 July 2006; Chapter 11 Dell to broaden sales model, © *Financial Times*, 16 May 2007; Chapter 11 Lulu aims to wag 'long tail, © *Financial Times*, 25 August 2006; Chapter 12 Barcode hope for mobile advertising, © *Financial Times*, 6 March 2007; Chapter 12 Little harmony in mobile music, © *Financial Times*, 5 July 2007;

We are grateful to the following for permission to use copyright material:

Chapter 3 Take your partners for the IT square dance from *The Financial Times Limited*, 15 June 2005, © Dan Gillmor; Chapter 9 The open source movement has great promise from *The Financial Times Limited*, 1 June 2005, © Geoff Mulgan; Chapter 13 Google's algorithm of life: rejoice and be wary from *The Financial Times Limited*, 24 May 2007, © Thomas Hazlett; Exhibits 1.1, 4.7 and 10.3 adapted from *E-Business and E-Commerce Management*, Pearson Education, (Chaffey, D. 2002); Exhibits 1.3 and 1.4 adapted from *Technological Revolutions and Financial Capital: The Dynamics of Bubbles and Golden Ages*, Edward Elgar Publishing, (Perez, C. 2002); Exhibits 3.1, 4.1, 5.1, 5.2, 5.3, 5.6, 5.7 and 6.1 adapted from *Strategisches Management in Unternehmen*, Gabler Verlag, (Hungenberg, H. 2006); Exhibits 3.2 and 4.3 Adapted with the permission of The Free Press, a Division of Simon & Schuster Adult Publishing Group, from COMPETITIVE STRATEGY: Techniques for Analyzing Industries and Competitors by Michael E. Porter. Copyright © 1980, 1998 by The Free Press. All rights reserved.; Exhibits 3.3 and 4.4 Reprinted by permission of *Harvard Business Review*. From "Strategy and the Internet" by M. Porter, March 2001. Copyright © 2001 by the Harvard Business School Publishing Corporation; all rights reserved.; Exhibit 3.4 adapted from *Co-opetition*, Random House, Inc., (Brandenburger, A. & Nalebuff, B. 1998); Exhibit 3.7 Adapted from D. Abell (1977), "Strategy and Structure: Public Policy Implications," In Proceedings of Marketing and the Public Interest. Cambridge, Mass.: Marketing Science Institute.; Exhibit 4.5 adapted from e-banking to e-business at Nordea (Scandinavia): the world's biggest clicks-and-mortar bank in *Management Information Systems Quarterly Executive*, Vol. 5, No. 1, MIS Quarterly Executive and the University of Minnesota, (Enders, A. & Jelassi, T. 2006); Exhibit 4.6 Reprinted from *European Management Journal*, Vol. 15, A. Angehrn, Designing mature internet strategies: the ICDT model, p. 9, Copyright (1997), with permission from Elsevier.; Exhibit 6.2 Reprinted by permission of Harvard Business School Press. From *The Innovator's Solution* by C. Christensen & M. Raynor. Boston, MA 2004, pp. 33. Copyright © 2004 by the Harvard Business School Publishing

Corporation; all rights reserved.; Exhibit 6.3 adapted from Change in the presence of residual fit in *Organization Science*, Vol. 17, No. 1, The Institute for Operations Research and the Management Sciences, (Gilbert, C. 2006); Exhibit 7.1 Reprinted by permission of *Harvard Business Review*. From "Creating new market space" by C. Kim & R. Mauborgne, Jan–Feb 1999. Copyright © 1999 by the Harvard Business School Publishing Corporation; all rights reserved.; Exhibit 9.2 Reprinted by permission of *Harvard Business Review*. From "Get the right mix of bricks and clicks" by R. Gulati & J. Garino, May–June 2000. Copyright © 2000 by the Harvard Business School Publishing Corporation; all rights reserved.; Exhibit 9.3 and 9.4 Reprinted by permission of *Harvard Business Review*. From "Unbundling the corporation" by J. Hagel & M. Singer, March–April 1999. Copyright © 1999 by the Harvard Business School Publishing Corporation; all rights reserved.; Exhibit 10.1 Reprinted by permission of *Harvard Business Review*. From "E hubs: the new B2B marketplaces" by S. Kaplan & M. Sawhney, May–June 2000. Copyright © 2000 by the Harvard Business School Publishing Corporation; all rights reserved.; Exhibit 11.2 Reprinted by permission of Harvard Business School Press. From *Blown to Bits* by P. Evans & T. Wurster. Boston, MA 1999, pp. 24. Copyright © 1999 by the Harvard Business School Publishing Corporation; all rights reserved.; Exhibit 11.4 adapted from *Mass-Customization*, Gabler Verlag, (Piller, F. 2006); Exhibits 12.1, 12.2 and 12.3 adapted from *UMTS report – an investment perspective*, Durlacher Research, (Muller-Veerse, F. et al. 2001). Reprinted with permission of Panmure Gordon & Co; Exhibits 12.4 and 12.5 adapted from *The Mobile Revolution: The Making of Mobile Services Worldwide*, Kogan Page, (Steinbock, D. 2005).

Text extracts: 'It's too early for e-business to drop its 'e'' by David Bowen, *Financial Times*, 21 May 2002; 'Burning money at Boo: the founders of the infamous Internet company were fools rather than knaves' by Tim Jackson, *Financial Times*, 1 November 2001; 'Google acquires Internet (May 2017)' by Philipp Lenssen, http://blogoscoped.com/archive/2007-04-14-n32.html; www.tesco.com, 24 April 2007, Tesco Stores Limited; Strategy in Action 14.1 from Business thinking, B. Henderson in *Perspectives on Strategy*, C. Stern & G. Stalk (eds); Copyright © (1998 John Wiley & Sons, Inc.); Reprinted with permission of John Wiley & Sons, Inc.; Strategy in Action 14.2 from Probing, J. Isaacs in *Perspectives on Strategy*, C. Stern & G. Stalk (eds); Copyright © (1998 John Wiley & Sons, Inc.); Reprinted with permission of John Wiley & Sons, Inc.

Case studies: We are grateful to INSEAD for permission to use the following case studies: Case study 1, From A[pples] to Z[oom lenses]: Extending the boundaries of multichannel retailing at Tesco.com, Copyright © 2007 INSEAD; Case study 2, From e-banking to e-business at Nordea (Scandinavia): The world's biggest clicks-and-mortar bank, Copyright © 2004 INSEAD, Fontainebleau, France; Case study 18, YOG AG: Integrating the mobile phone into the marketing mix, Copyright © 2007 INSEAD; We are grateful to the following for permission to use their case studies: Case study 3, ING Direct: Rebel in the banking industry, reproduced by permission of Kurt Verweire and L.A.A. Van Den Berghe; Case Study 5, Otis Elevator: Accelerating business transformation with IT, Harvard Business School Case 9-305-048, Harvard Business School Publishing, (McFarlan, F.W and Delacey, B.J. 2005); Case Study 7 Covisint (A): The evolution of a B2B marketplace, Harvard Business School Case 9-805-110, Harvard Business School Publishing, (Applegate, L.M. and Collins, E.L. 2006); Case study 9, eBay customer support outsourcing, reproduced by permission of Gary M. Grikscheit and Scott A. Newman.

In some instances we have been unable to trace the owners of copyright material and we would appreciate any information that would enable us to do so.

PART I

Introduction

PART OVERVIEW

This introductory part sets up the overall context for the book. It contains the following elements:

- A definition of the key terminology used throughout the book

- An overview of the evolution of e-business over time.

The goal of this introductory part is to provide a guide and a context for the content of the book. Chapter 1 starts out with some definitions of the most important terms used in the book, such as e-business, electronic commerce and mobile e-commerce, and the concepts of strategy and value creation. It then provides an overview of the evolution of e-business over the last decade and recognises four distinct periods: (1) the 'grassroots of e-business', (2) the 'rise of the Internet', (3) the 'crash' (or the burst of the dotcom bubble) and (4) the 'synergy phase'.

CHAPTER 1

Key terminology and evolution of e-business

Chapter at a glance

Learning outcomes

After completing this chapter, you should be able to:

- Understand what the terms of 'e-business', 'electronic commerce' and 'mobile e-commerce' mean.
- Define the concept of strategy and recognise the different levels of strategy development.
- Describe the life cycle of technological revolutions and illustrate it through different examples.
- Recognise the four main periods of the e-business evolution over the past decade and explain the peculiar characteristics of each period.

INTRODUCTION

The purpose of this chapter is to set the stage for the remainder of the book. Since, due to the relative novelty of e-business, there is not yet a clear and shared view of what this domain entails, we first want to ensure a common understanding of the key terminology used throughout the book. Section 1.1 includes the definition of e-business-related terms and concepts as well as some strategy-specific perspectives. Following that, Section 1.2 provides a framework that describes the typical stages of technological revolutions and positions the evolution of electronic business during the past decade within this framework.

1.1 Key terminology

1.1.1 e-Business

The term *e-business* is defined here as the use of electronic means to conduct an organisation's business internally and/or externally.[1] Internal e-business activities include the linking of an organisation's employees with each other through an intranet to improve information sharing, facilitate knowledge dissemination and support management reporting. e-Business activities also include supporting after-sales service activities and collaborating with business partners, e.g. conducting joint research, developing a new product and formulating a sales promotion.

In spite of the distinct terminology that is used, e-business should not be viewed in isolation from the remaining activities of a firm. Instead, an organisation should integrate online e-business activities with its offline business into a coherent whole. The *Financial Times* (FT) article 'It's too early for e-business to drop its "e"', provides a further discussion of the importance of the 'e' in e-business.

1.1.2 Electronic commerce

Electronic commerce, or *e-commerce*, is more specific than e-business and can be thought of as a subset of the latter (see Exhibit 1.1). Electronic commerce deals with the facilitation of transactions and selling of products and services online, i.e. via the Internet or any other telecommunications network. This involves the electronic trading of physical and digital goods, quite often encompassing all the trading steps such as online marketing, online ordering, e-payment and, for digital goods, online distribution (i.e. for after-sales support activities). e-commerce applications with external orientation are buy-side e-commerce activities with suppliers and sell-side activities with customers.

1.1.3 Mobile e-commerce

Mobile e-commerce, or *m-commerce*, is a subset of electronic commerce. While it refers to online activities similar to those mentioned in the electronic commerce category, the

Exhibit·1.1 **Electronic business includes electronic commerce and mobile electronic commerce**

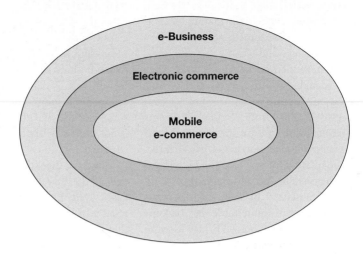

Source: Adapted from D. Chaffey, *E-Business and E-Commerce Management*, FT Prentice Hall, 2002, p. 9.

underlying technology is different since mobile commerce is limited to mobile telecommunication networks, which are accessed through wireless hand-held devices such as mobile phones, hand-held computers and personal digital assistants (PDAs).

It's too early for e-business to drop its 'e'

Jargon is used to make the banal sound enthralling, the simple sophisticated. It is often used to disguise the fact that the speaker, or writer, does not know what he is talking about, or cannot be bothered to find a more precise word. In the past five years, one letter has come to symbolize the worst of jargon. The fifth letter in the Roman alphabet, it has been used in front of business, commerce, finance, procurement, learning, enablement, government. Almost any noun you can think of has probably been an e-noun. Companies have used 'e' liberally to give themselves a buzz on the stock market.

Now, 'e' is on its way out. Yet, despite everything I have said, this is bad news. The 'e' has been chased away by the dotcom crash, which transformed it from magic drug to kiss of stock market death. But, even before that, it was going out of fashion. One

senior consultant told me in 2000 that the 'e' would be dropped by his organization within a year or two (it was). His argument – widely accepted – was that Internet-based business would become so pervasive that it would be pointless, indeed damaging, to talk about it as a separate discipline.

E-business would and should disappear into business. And so it should; but not yet. At the Richmond Events e-forum last October, several hundred senior managers from blue-chip companies gathered on a cruise ship to be assaulted by a mixture of cabernet sauvignon and hard sell from vendors of e-services of various sorts. There was a 'last days of Rome' feeling about it, as delegate after delegate let slip that he or she had either just left their e-job, or was about to.

→

What was particularly interesting was that people were revealing their 'real selves' beneath their e-titles: they were either information technology people, or they were something else. While a few could talk strategy and technology with equal fluency, most gave their backgrounds away. They were happy speaking about marketing and strategy, or about integration issues; not both. I have since received a letter from Richmond Events announcing the death of e-forum, saying that its functions would be rolled into either the IT directors or the marketing forum. The divide that was apparent at the event has been formalized.

Why does this matter? Because, even as it has crumbled, the value of the letter 'e' has become ever more clear. It is, or has been, a bridge between technical and non-technical managers.

From the earliest days of the commercial Internet, proponent after proponent of the strange new medium said the same thing: 'Don't let the IT people run it.' They believed the effective use of the Internet depended not on the technology but on a strategic understanding of what it could do. Technologists were, of course, vital for implementing the strategy, but they often knew too much about the trees to be able to see the wood. Also, most IT directors had a 'supplier' role to an organization; they were rarely involved in strategic decision-making.

As the commercial Internet became e-commerce and then e-business this view held, though there were tensions. Many companies put their trust in new media consultancies led by marketing people who loved to talk strategy. 'Leave your strategy to us; we understand it better than you can,' they would tell their open-walleted clients. They hired technical people – indeed, the real skills shortage was at the technical end – but they kept control.

Sadly, these agencies also sowed the seeds of their own destruction, because they could not match either the technical skills of systems integration specialists, or the strategic skills of the big consultancies. Meanwhile, a sizeable minority of organizations kept their e-business strategy in-house and under the control of their IT departments. Add to this the rush by boards to pour money into Internet ventures simply for the sake of tickling the share price and it is not surprising that so much was wasted so fast by so many.

How is it, then, that any companies managed to exploit the new technology effectively? How did Cisco, Dell, Electrocomponents, General Electric manage it? Largely, because people at the summit saw that the secret was in bringing technologists and non-technologists together and making them work together – and often they used the banner 'e' as a marshalling-point. The good e-business managers I have met are (or were) either technologists on the way to becoming strategists, or non-technologists with an increasing understanding of IT. On the way, I stress; rarely close to achieving fluency in both.

The new media agencies, for all their arrogance, were also attempting to master both skills. Again, they had a long way to go; so it is a shame that they have been humbled so brutally. The danger, as the e-bridge crashes into the river, is that the great unrealized possibilities of the Internet will be swept away with it. When an organization has a cadre of managers with a real understanding of both strategy and technology, fine – let the bridge collapse. But until then, some form of e-business department and function – labeled with whatever jargon – should remain essential to any intelligent group's structure.

Source: D. Bowen, 'It's too early for e-business to drop its "e"', *Financial Times*, 21 May 2002.

1.1.4 The concept of strategy

In addition to e-business, *strategy* is the second key thrust of this book. More specifically, we analyse and illustrate how firms develop and implement strategies for their e-business activities and draw lessons and guidelines from the studied practices. However, we should recognise that the term 'strategy' means different things to different people. To get a clear understanding of the meaning of strategy the way it is used in this book, let us first consider the following definitions of strategy and then suggest a common foundation.

Strategy is:

... the direction and scope of an organization over the long-term, which achieves advantage for the organization through its configuration of resources within a changing environment to the needs of markets and fulfill stakeholder expectations.

Gerry Johnson and Kevan Scholes[2]

... the determination of the basic long-term goals and objectives of an enterprise, and the adoption of courses of action and the allocation of resources necessary for carrying out theses goals.

Alfred Chandler[3]

... the deliberate search for a plan of action that will develop a business's competitive advantage and compound it.

Bruce Henderson[4]

... the strong focus on profitability not just growth, an ability to define a unique value proposition, and a willingness to make tough trade-offs in what not to do.

Michael Porter[5]

Based on the above definitions, we would like to stress the following aspects that are crucial for strategy formulation:[6]

- Strategy is concerned with the *long-term direction* of the firm.
- Strategy deals with the *overall plan for deploying the resources* that a firm possesses.
- Strategy entails the willingness to make *trade-offs*, to choose between different directions and between different ways of deploying resources.
- Strategy is about achieving *unique positioning* vis-à-vis competitors.
- The central goal of strategy is to achieve sustainable *competitive advantage* over rivals and thereby to ensure lasting profitability.

Having defined the concept of strategy, we can now differentiate it from the concept of *tactics*, a term that is often used interchangeably with strategy. Tactics are schemes for individual and specific actions that are not necessarily related to one another. In general, specific actions can be planned intuitively because of their limited complexity. A firm can, for instance, have a certain tactic when it launches a marketing campaign.

Strategy, on the other hand, deals with a more overarching formulation that affects not just one activity at one point in time but all activities of a firm over an extended time horizon. To achieve consistency between different activities over time, intuition is generally not sufficient; it also requires logical thinking. Drawing an analogy with warfare, we could say that while tactics are about winning a battle, strategy is concerned primarily with winning the war.

It has often been argued that the increasing importance of technology reduces the need for clear strategies. Firms should instead focus on getting their technology to work. This is especially true for the technology underlying e-business and electronic commerce. Yet, technology is not, and cannot be, a substitute for strategy. Overlooking strategy and how a firm can create sustainable competitive advantage is a likely recipe for failure. Just because certain activities are feasible from a technological perspective does not mean that they are sensible from a strategic perspective. Ultimately, information technology (IT) and the Internet should be used not for the sake of using them but instead to create benefit for customers in a cost-efficient way.

Formulating long-term strategies has become more difficult due to the continuously changing business environment. How long-term can a strategy be when the technological environment is permanently changing? This is obviously a difficult question that has no clear-cut answers. When a disruptive innovation emerges and redefines the basis of competition, previous strategies become all but worthless. This was the case, for instance, when Amazon.com entered the book-retailing market with its online bookstore and when Napster launched its file-sharing platform for online music distribution. Nonetheless, it is important to be aware of the trade-offs that arise when a firm gives up long-term strategy in return for short-term flexibility.

Within organisations, we typically recognise the following three different levels of strategy (see Exhibit 1.2). They are (1) *corporate-level strategy*, (2) *business unit strategy* and (3) *operational strategy*.[7] It is important to note here that most of the cases featured in this book deal primarily with issues related to the first two levels of strategy.

Corporate-level strategy

The highest strategy level, i.e. the corporate-level strategy, is concerned with the overall purpose and scope of the firm. It typically involves the chief executive officer (CEO) and top-level managers. Corporate strategy addresses issues such as how to allocate resources between different business units, mergers, acquisitions, partnerships and alliances.

Consider, for instance, the merger in 2000 between AOL and Time Warner, where the CEOs of both firms looked across all the businesses of their respective companies before deciding to merge the two corporations. Another example of corporate strategy that is important in the e-business context is the choice of distribution and sales channels. For example, the top management of Tesco plc first made the decision in 1995 about whether to use the Internet to sell groceries online and then on how to set it up organisationally (see Chapter 9 for a discussion of the different ways of organising e-commerce ventures). Only then was the responsibility delegated from the corporate level to the Tesco.com business unit.

Business unit strategy

Business unit strategy is concerned primarily with how to compete within individual markets. Dell, for instance, operates distinct business units that target large corporate customers, private households and public-sector customers. Since these are very separate markets, with differing needs and preferences, it is also necessary to formulate a distinct business unit strategy for each one of these markets (see Section 3.4 on market segmentation for e-commerce).

At a more detailed level, a business unit strategy deals with issues such as industry analysis, market positioning and value creation for customers. Furthermore, when formulating a business unit strategy, it is also necessary to think about the desired scale and scope of operations.

Exhibit 1.2 **The focus of the cases is on corporate level and business unit strategy**

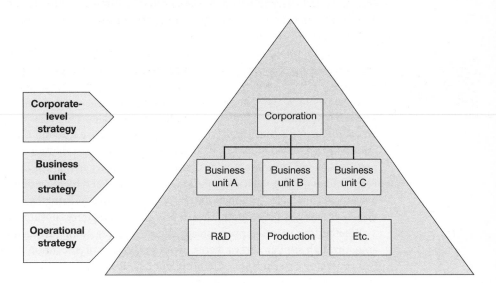

Operational strategy

Operational strategy deals with how to implement the business unit strategy with regard to resources, processes and people. In the context of e-business, this includes issues such as optimal website design, hardware and software requirements, and the management of the logistics process. Furthermore, this also includes operational effectiveness issues, which are addressed by techniques such as business process re-engineering (BPR) and total quality management (TQM).

Although these approaches are important, they do not belong intrinsically to strategy formulation, since, as stated above, strategy is about making trade-offs; that is, strategy focuses on deciding which activities a firm should perform and which ones it should *not* perform. Operational issues are of high importance for any organisation; however, they are not the primary focus of this book, and covering them in depth would overextend the scope of the book.[8]

1.1.5 The concept of value creation and capturing

The ability of a firm to create value for its customers is a prerequisite for achieving sustainable profitability. In the context of e-business strategies, the concept of *value creation* deserves special attention because many Internet start-ups that ended up in bankruptcy at the end of the Internet boom years did not pay enough attention to this issue. Instead, they were frequently concerned mainly with customer acquisition and revenue growth, which was sustainable only as long as venture capitalists and stock markets were willing to finance these firms.

Nowadays, however, in a harder and more turbulent business environment, it is imperative that strategies focus on what value to create and for whom, as well as how to create it and how to capture the value in the form of profits. In economic terms, value created is the difference between the benefit a firm provides to its consumers and the costs it incurs for doing so. The concepts of value creation and capturing are discussed in more detail in Chapter 8.

1.2 The evolution of e-business

Before discussing e-business from a structural perspective through the e-business strategy framework presented in Part II, we first want to analyse the evolution of e-business over the past decade and compare it with the life cycle of other *technological revolutions*. Carlota Perez defines a technological revolution as a 'powerful and highly visible cluster of new and dynamic technologies, products and industries, capable of bringing about an upheaval in the whole fabric of the economy and of propelling a long-term upsurge of development'.[9]

Whether the printing press, steam engine, railway or car, all such technologies have gone through similar surges. Perez divides the surge of a technological revolution into two consecutive periods: (1) the *installation period*, which consists of an *irruption* stage and a *frenzy* ('gilded age') stage, and (2) the *deployment period*, which consists of a *synergy* ('golden age') stage and a *maturity* stage. These stages are typically separated by a downturn or crash, as shown in Exhibit 1.3.

Below, we describe in more detail each stage of a typical surge of a technological revolution:[10]

- *Irruption (1)*. The irruption stage takes place right after a new technology is introduced to the market. Revolutionary new technologies, also called 'big bangs', include the mechanised cotton industry in the 1770s, railway construction in the 1830s and, more recently, Intel's first microprocessor in 1971. During the irruption stage, innovative products and services based on the new technology appear and start slowly to penetrate the economy, which is still dominated by the previous technology.

- *Frenzy (2)*. The frenzy stage, also called the 'gilded age', is characterised by a sense of exploration and exuberance as entrepreneurs, engineers and investors alike try to find the best opportunities created by the technological big bang irruption. Using a trial-and-error approach, investors fund numerous projects, which help quickly to install the new technology in the economy. However, as investors become increasingly confident and excited, they start considering themselves to be infallible. Depending on the technological revolution, they have financed digging canals from any river to any other river, building railway tracks between every city and village imaginable, and, more recently, creating online retailing websites for every conceivable product, be it pet food, medicine or furniture. This process typically continues until it reaches an unsustainable exuberance, also called 'bubble' or 'mania'. At that point, the 'paper wealth' of the stock market loses any meaningful relation with the realistic possibilities of the new technology to create wealth.

- *Crash (3)*. The gilded age is followed by a crash, when the leading players in the economy realise that the excessive investments will never be able to fulfil the high expectations. As a result, investors lose confidence and pull their funds out of the new technology. Doing so sets off a vicious cycle, and, as everyone starts to pull out of the stock market, the bubble deflates and the stock market collapses.

Exhibit 1.3 Technological revolutions move through different stages as their diffusion increases

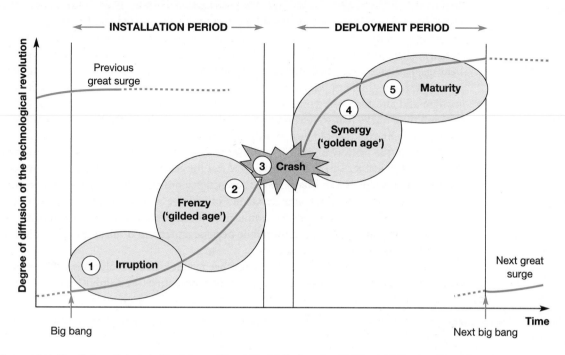

Source: Adapted from C. Perez, *Technological Revolutions and Financial Capital: The Dynamics of Bubbles and Golden Ages*, Edward Elgar, 2002, p. 48.

■ *Synergy (4)*. Following the crash, the time of quick and easy profits has passed. Now, investors prefer to put their money into the 'real' economy, and the successful firms are not the nimble start-ups but instead established incumbents. While, during the frenzy stage, there were many start-ups competing within an industry, the crash led to a shake-out where most of these ventures went out of business. During the synergy stage, a few large companies start to dominate the markets and leverage their financial strength to generate economies of scale and scope. Now, the emphasis is no longer on technological innovation but instead on how to make technology easy to use, reliable, secure and cost efficient.

In order for the synergy stage to take hold, governmental agencies need to introduce regulations to remedy the fallacies that caused the previous frenzy and the ensuing crash and, by doing so, to regain investors' confidence. For instance, following the stock market crash in 1929, the US government set up separate regulatory bodies for banks, securities, savings and insurances, and also established protective agencies including the Federal Deposit Insurance Corporation (FDIC) and the Securities and Exchange Commission (SEC).

■ *Maturity (5)*. The maturity stage is characterised by market saturation and mature technologies. Growth opportunities in new and untapped markets are becoming scarcer, and there are fewer innovations resulting from the new technology. During this stage, companies concentrate on increasing efficiency and reducing costs, for instance through mergers and acquisitions. In today's mature automobile industry, for example, large global manufacturers such as Renault and Nissan or VW and Porsche have merged or established strategic partnerships in order to generate scale effects and expand market reach.[11]

For a more extensive example of a surge of a technological revolution, consider the evolution of the railway industry in England. Railroads started to become popular in the 1830s. Many entrepreneurs, financed by eager investors, started constructing railway routes throughout the country, which culminated in an investment bubble in 1847. Initially, when building railway tracks, investors sought out those projects that showed a clear need and were easy to build. As the bubble kept growing, investors, searching desperately for investment opportunities, started to fund projects for which there was hardly any demand and that were complicated and costly. Ultimately, railway companies were even building tracks that were running parallel to one another, even though it was obvious that only one track could be operated profitably in the long term.

Inevitably, the railway bubble burst; after the dust had settled, the stocks of railway companies had lost 85% of their peak value. After the crash in 1847, when a large number of railroad companies went bankrupt, the industry bounced back, rapidly increasing mileage and passengers, and tripling revenues in just five years after the bust. After 1850, railways drove much of England's economic growth, and they continued to dominate the transportation market until the automobile became a medium of mass transportation in the middle of the twentieth century.[12]

We can observe similar evolutions with other technological revolutions, such as steel production, steam energy and, more recently, the automobile (see Exhibit 1.4).

Exhibit 1.4 Major technological revolutions during the past two centuries show similar patterns of evolution

	INSTALLATION PERIOD			DEPLOYMENT PERIOD	
	1	2	3	4	5
Technological revolution (core country)	Irruption	Frenzy	Crash	Synergy	Maturity
The Industrial Revolution (Britain)	1770s and early 1780s	Late 1780s and early 1790s	crash in 1797	1798–1812	1813–1829
Age of steam and railways (Britain, then spreading to Continental Europe and the USA)	1830s	1840s	crash in 1847	1850–1857	1857–1873
Age of steel, electricity, and heavy engineering (USA and Germany overtaking Britain)	1875–1884	1884–1893	crash in 1893	1895–1907	1908–1918
Age of oil, automobiles and mass production (USA, then spreading to Europe)	1908–1920	1920–1929	crash in 1929	1943–1959	1960–1974

Timeline

Source: Adapted from C. Perez, *Technological Revolutions and Financial Capital: The Dynamics of Bubbles and Golden Ages*, Edward Elgar, 2002, p. 57.

The above perspective illustrates that the time from the first commercial usage of a new technology to its widespread application can stretch over a period lasting up to 50 years. Within these long periods, the technology's diffusion and growth are not continuous. Instead, they are often marked by a crash, when the initial exuberance and optimism about a new technology fades.

One of the main reasons for these long gestation periods between the irruption and the synergy stages is that it is not sufficient just to have the appropriate technology in place. In addition, managers need to be willing and able to abandon previous ways of doing things and start using the new technology in such a way that it actually creates value. This takes time and requires a lot of experimenting and fine tuning.

The development of e-business has been quite similar to that described above. During the past decade, e-business has changed dramatically, evolving through the following four periods (see Exhibit 1.5), which mirror the evolution of the National Association of Securities Dealers Automated Quotations (NASDAQ)[13] during the same time period:

Exhibit 1.5 **During the past decade, e-business companies have passed through four distinct periods, as is reflected in the evolution of the NASDAQ**

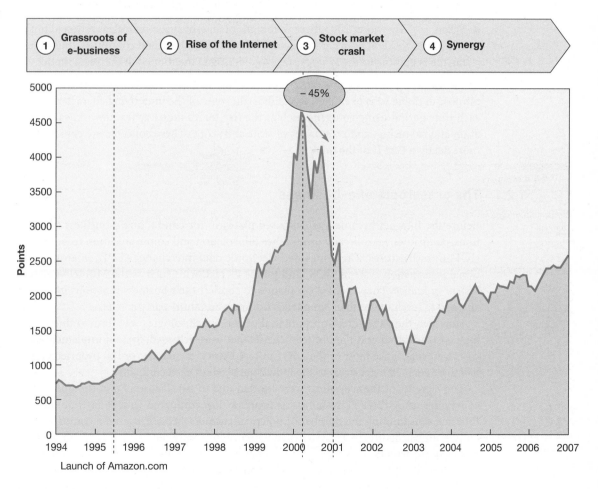

Source: NASDAQ quotes taken from Factiva.com.

■ *Grassroots of e-business (1).* Before the widespread commercial use of the Internet, the NASDAQ showed only modest increases. Between 1983 and 1993, it hardly doubled from 350 to 700 points. We refer to this period as the grassroots of e-business which corresponds to the irruption stage in the Perez model.

■ *Rise of the Internet (2).* Even though the beginning of the dotcom boom cannot be determined precisely, we chose 1995, the year when Amazon.com was launched, as the starting point of the rise of the Internet period.[14] The year 1995 also saw the going public of Netscape, the maker of the Netscape Navigator web browser, which presented the first initial public offering (IPO) of a major Internet company. This period, which corresponds to the 'gilded age', is reflected in the strong rise of the NASDAQ, especially during the late 1990s. At the peak of this frenzy stage, the NASDAQ traded at price/earning (p/e) ratios of 62, after it had not exceeded p/e ratios of 21 in the years between 1973 and 1995.[15]

■ *Crash (3).* The bubble burst in March and April of 2000, when the NASDAQ crashed. Between 10 March and 14 April 2000, the NASDAQ dropped 1727 points or 34%. By the end of 2000, it had fallen by 45%. The subsequent consolidation has been characterised by a more sober approach to e-business and a refocusing on the fundamental drivers of value creation. The NASDAQ continued its decline for another two years, albeit at much slower rates, until it bottomed out in early 2003.

■ *Synergy (4).* By winter 2003 there were signs of an e-business revival, as reflected in the rise of the NASDAQ during the second half of 2003. This trend continued, thus marking the beginning of the synergy stage ('golden age') mentioned in the Perez model.

In the following sections, the above four time periods are discussed in more detail. The purpose of doing so is to explain with hindsight some of the underlying characteristics of each time period using concepts such as the five forces industry framework, value creation and capturing, and economies of scale and scope. These concepts are explained in more detail in Part II of the book.

1.2.1 The grassroots of e-business

Before the Internet became a widely used platform for conducting e-business transactions, companies were already using other information and communication technologies (ICT) infrastructures. These included electronic data interchange (EDI), interorganisational information systems (IOS) and public IT platforms such as the Minitel videotext system in France. They enabled companies to connect their business functions internally and also to reach out to their suppliers, customers and third-party partners.

However, the value-creation potential of these technologies was limited due to the high costs involved and the limited benefits that were achieved. System implementation costs were high since most of these ICT infrastructures were more or less proprietary and had to be adapted extensively to the individual needs of each company.

The benefits of these systems were limited due to two factors. First, the number of companies using these IT systems was relatively low compared with today's ubiquitous Internet, thus limiting the number of potential partners. Second, even if a company used an ICT infrastructure, its IT systems and applications were not compatible with those of its business partners. This made it difficult at best, if not impossible, to interconnect different 'islands of technology'. As a result of the above factors, e-business existed only to a limited extent within and across companies or even beyond national boundaries (see the FT article 'Minitel proves a mixed blessing').

FT

Minitel proves a mixed blessing

When Internet service providers began to promote their services in France in 1996, France Telecom, then a state-run monopoly, immediately stepped up advertising for Minitel, the French online service, in an effort to shield it from the competition. Four years later, Wanadoo, France Telecom's Internet arm, is the country's biggest ISP and the former monopoly – now the largest market capitalisation on the Paris Bourse – is selling ADSL high-speed Internet connections to the country's households and small businesses.

'In France, you cannot dissociate the Internet from Minitel,' says Philippe Guglielmetti, chief executive of Integra, the country's pioneer in e-commerce services and infrastructure. Minitel, launched in 1983, was a rudimentary equivalent of today's net-PC. Roughly double the size of a table-top telephone set, it had no storage capabilities, a black and white screen displaying text only, and an in-built modem that was slow by today's standards. Millions of terminals were handed out free to telephone subscribers, resulting in a high penetration rate among businesses and the public. Paradoxically, Minitel is now blamed for the country's slow take-up of the Internet, and hailed as the platform from which France can leap on to the worldwide web.

'French consumers have been making online purchases for more than 15 years,' says Ramzi Nahas, managing director of Fimadex, a venture adviser. 'Minitel has played an important role in dispelling consumers' fears about making payments on a screen.' The French still feel that credit card details are more secure on a less open system. In 1995, before net access was widely available, 16% of train reservations on the SNCF national railway were made through Minitel. France Telecom estimates that almost 9m terminals – including web-enabled PCs – had access to the network at the end of last year. In the past few years, Minitel connections were stable at 100m a month plus 150m online directory inquiries, in spite of growing Internet use.

A recent survey of Wanadoo customers showed that 82% also used Minitel regularly. More significantly, 14% started logging on to Minitel after they became web users. Other surveys show that Minitel is more efficient than the net for some uses. According to France Telecom, a train reservation takes on average 3.5 minutes on Minitel, compared with 4.5 minutes on SNCF's website. Directory inquiries take 30 seconds and 1.5 minutes respectively. But there are signs that sophisticated users of Minitel are switching to the Internet.

Customers of Cortal, the online brokerage of Paribas bank, have been trading securities on Minitel since 1993. Barely a year after Cortal launched Internet trading in October 1998, two-thirds of online trades had shifted to the new service, with Minitel handling the remaining third.

France Telecom, which has invested large sums to develop Minitel, believes it will co-exist – and gradually converge – with the net in the coming years. Software to access Minitel has been embedded in the French version of the Windows 98 operating system, alongside Microsoft's Internet Explorer web browser. France Telecom is not alone in hanging on to Minitel. Most French companies are also attached to the network, partly because of the investment they have made but mainly because they have perfected the methods to generate revenues from online activities.

France Telecom charges Minitel users, at rates of up to $1 a minute, on their monthly telephone bill. It then pays back part of the sum to the companies that operate Minitel servers. In 1998, Minitel generated €832m ($824m) of revenues, of which €521m was channelled by France Telecom to service providers. Wanadoo's sales (which are not published) are 'insignificant in comparison', according to a company official.

Analysts say Minitel's structure, a monopoly operated by a governmental organisation, was a blessing and a curse. 'That it operated on a single network made it safe and allowed e-commerce to take off in France,' says Mohamed Lakhlifi, sales manager at Unilog, a Paris-listed computer services company. 'But regulatory hurdles and the absence of competition stifled innovation.' Another consultant says habits acquired in the Minitel age are tempering managers' enthusiasm for the Internet. 'Almost two-thirds of projects that start as ambitious Internet operations end up being scaled down to a website that connects users to the company's existing Minitel server,' says an IT specialist.

Mr Nahas at Fimadex says the average age of French senior managers is higher than in the US, 'which means they are less computer-literate. Most of these managers see the Internet as just another way of channelling orders for their products. Very few are aware that their whole marketing strategy must be reviewed.'

But Minitel's most important contribution to French e-business will undoubtedly be in the form of lessons learnt. Minitel provides more than 15 years of statistics about retailing and online usage habits. 'A lot of what is happening on the Internet today took place locally [in France] in the 1980s,' says an information technology consultant. 'We have known for years that sex chat rooms, dating services and financial applications are the engines of innovation and revenue generation in an online environment.'

Integra says the Minitel experience can be transposed into Internet business practices. 'Early studies in the US predicted that Internet transactions would stabilise at 1% or 1.5% of consumer goods retailing,' says Mr Guglielmetti. 'Our experience with Minitel leads us to think that e-commerce could make up some 10 per cent of sales of products adapted to distance selling.' Minitel sales in recent years accounted for almost 15% of turnover at La Redoute and Les Trois Suisses, France's biggest mail order companies. Integra estimates that Minitel represents 7–8% of all French distance selling.

One of the biggest barriers to greater Internet use is the French language. Integra, which operates web hosting services in several countries, says 90% of its servers are in the language of the country they are based in. 'This is not a problem when your language is English,' says an executive. 'It becomes a problem when your language is less widely used.' Conversely, French e-business is expected to benefit from a number of national factors. The country is more advanced than most of its neighbours – and the US – in its use of smartcards. All credit and debit cards issued in France have an embedded chip with a dedicated identification code, which makes online payments more secure.

Source: 'Minitel proves a mixed blessing', FT.com, 8 February 2000.

1.2.2 The rise of the Internet

In July 1995, the Internet boom years began with the launch of Amazon.com, one of today's best-known online retailers. The subsequent five years were characterised by great exuberance and the belief in the seemingly unlimited potential of the Internet. During that time period, the profitability and economic viability of companies and business models did not seem to matter much. Instead, metrics such as 'click-through rates', or 'number of eyeballs', i.e. the number of visitors to a site, were the main determinants for stock market success and media coverage. In the case of the fashion retailer Boo.com, the founder Ernst Malmsten did not even have to provide investors with these kinds of metrics. The mere hope of high future profits allowed Boo.com to spend $30 million of venture capital money, even before launching its website (see the FT article 'Burning money at Boo').

For a more detailed insight into this period, consider the example of Priceline.com, which allowed people to purchase airline tickets over the Internet. Priceline.com went public on 30 March 1999, and the shares that were issued at $16 each soared immediately to $85 each. At the end of the day, Priceline.com had reached a valuation of almost $10 billion, which was more than those of United Airlines, Continental Airlines and Northwest Airlines combined.[16] While these airlines had a proven business model, valuable brands and substantial physical assets, Priceline.com owned only a few computer servers and an untested business model.

In fact, the company even stated in its IPO prospectus that it did not expect to be profitable at any time in the near future, that the business model was new and unproven, and that the brand might not be able to achieve the required brand recognition. Investors ignored these warnings because they believed that they would always be able to sell the stock to someone else at an even higher price. This investment approach during the Internet boom years became known as the 'Greater Fool Theory'.[17] In the USA, some 100 million people, about half of the adult population, had invested in stocks at the peak of the bubble. As the stock market kept soaring, more and more people – who had seen their colleagues and friends get rich – also started investing in Internet stocks. This meant that the chances of finding a 'greater fool' were high – at least during the Internet boom years.

The case study on Mondus.com, which dates back to this time period, illustrates this very same spirit of almost boundless excitement and optimism.

The fundamental driver of the e-business boom was the belief that it would be possible to increase value creation manyfold because, as explained below, the Internet would lower costs while, at the same time, increasing consumer benefits. Costs were expected to decrease significantly because managers and analysts alike believed that Internet ventures would not require heavy investments in expensive bricks-and-mortar infrastructure, such as warehouses, retail outlets and delivery trucks. Instead, they believed that all physical activities could be outsourced to external providers while they focused on the technology aspect of the business and on customer interactions.

At the same time, the belief was that, compared with their more traditional bricks-and-mortar competitors, Internet 'pure-play' companies would provide far superior consumer benefits. It was thought that coupling the two-way connectivity of the Internet with database capabilities and customer relationship management (CRM) systems would create much higher benefits than traditional outlets ever could.

This still leaves us with the question of why so many companies rushed into this e-market so rapidly during the Internet boom years. Several factors can explain this new 'gold rush' (see also Chapter 7 for a more detailed discussion of early-mover advantages and disadvantages in e-business).

By entering the e-market early, companies were trying to generate scale effects through large sales volumes. They wanted to attract new customers quickly and build up a large customer base. The underlying hope was that once customers had used a website a number of times, then they would be unlikely to switch to a competitor, since they would have to get used to a new website layout and functioning. Furthermore, data-mining techniques would allow online companies to customise their offerings to the specific preferences of the individual customer. By switching to another provider, customers lose this level of customisation, at least over the short term.

Internet ventures also expected to create a customer lock-in through network effects. As more and more customers sign up and provide information about themselves, as is the case at eBay and through Amazon.com's book reviews, customers are less likely to switch to competitors unless the latter offer better (or at least similar) network effects. Because of these effects, there was a 'winner-takes-all' expectation, whereby a dominant player would outperform competitors through high-scale economies and network effects.

Finally, and probably most importantly, the peculiar investment climate pushed companies to spend and expand rapidly instead of taking a more cautious approach. In 1999,

Silicon Valley venture capitalist firms such as Sequoia Capital and Benchmark Capital invested an all-time high of $48.3 billion. This represented a 150% increase over 1998, and 90% of this money went towards high-tech and Internet companies.[18] In order to qualify for venture capital funding, companies had to convince investors that they would be able to grow big and fast and so fuel the hope of a rapid payback on investment.

These investors did not necessarily believe in the future of the start-ups they funded. Yet they knew that as long as stock markets kept going up and people kept buying Internet stocks, regardless of the underlying business model, they could not go wrong. At the same time, investment bankers and venture capitalists who refused to play this 'game' also knew that they would fall behind their less scrupulous competitors. These perverted incentives contributed significantly to the build-up of the stock market bubble.

FT

Burning money at Boo: the founders of the infamous Internet company were fools rather than knaves

When Boo.com went into liquidation on May 17 last year, barely six months after its launch, the question was not why the global online fashion retailer had closed. Rather, it was why investors had allowed the company to burn through $100m before it did so.

It takes only a few chapters of this enthralling book to realise that the answer began with the personality of Ernst Malmsten, a 6ft 5in Swede of 27, with nerdy glasses. Malmsten, the founder and chief executive of Boo, had already proved himself spectacularly skilled at getting big companies to put money behind strange ideas when he set up a festival of Nordic poetry in New York, signing up as sponsors Ericsson, Saab, Ikea, Carlsberg and Absolut. He later created and then sold a pioneering online book store in Sweden.

When Malmsten turned his attention to selling clothes online in spring 1998, his natural fluency, passion and authority became the fuse that ignited an explosive mixture of investor greed and uncertainty as to whether the web would be earth-changing or merely very big. Malmsten's partners were Kajsa Leander, a kindergarten playmate turned model turned girlfriend turned business partner, and Patrik Hedelin, an investment banker who had helped them to sell their stakes in the online book store. The three talked the investment bank JP Morgan into helping them find investors

to put up $15m for the plan – and brought in blue-chip lawyers, headhunters, technology providers and public relations and advertising agencies to add further credibility.

Despite JP Morgan's roster of contacts, they were turned away by venture capitalists with a record in backing technology start-ups. Instead, it was less expert investors who took the bait – notably a small British investment firm called Eden Capital, the luxury-goods magnate Bernard Arnault, the Benetton family and a rag-bag of Middle Eastern investors.

As the company approached its target launch date of June 1999, the glamorous young founders generated more and more positive media coverage. Given the received wisdom at that time that only funky young people understood the Internet, the investors left their dream team to get on with opening offices in cool warehouse spaces around the world and hiring hundreds of staff. But there was a problem: beneath the buzz and excitement, not one of the founders was a capable manager, let alone up to the Welchian task of getting a highly complex international launch project finished on time and on budget. Instead, they devoted their energies to talking at conferences in Venice, shooting television commercials in Los Angeles, entertaining journalists at Nobu in London and the SoHo Grand in New York, spending $10,000 ➔

on clothes at Barneys so they would look the part on the cover of *Fortune*, holding staff parties in smart nightclubs before the company even had a product, and flying around the world to investor meetings on Concorde and private jets.

As the schedule began to slip, Malmsten lost faith, one by one, in his partners and underlings. Ericsson was no good at systems integration, he concluded. Hill and Knowlton did not know how to sell the story to the media. JP Morgan was not bringing in investors fast enough. The chief technology officer was not up to his job. Even Patrik, his fellow founder, was too much of an individual to be a good chief financial officer. With five launch deadlines passed and $30m spent, Malmsten took all his staff out to lunch at the Cafe Royal in August 1999 to announce that another of his managers would create Project Launch, with a new deadline set for three months later. It was a measure of the height to which the Internet craze had grown that the company's investors, told of the delays at a board meeting three weeks later, did not fire Malmsten and his two co-founders on the spot. Instead, they accepted the assurance that the new November deadline would be met, allowing the company to go public a few months later, and agreed to put up more cash. Astonishingly, a Lebanese investment fund then put in another $15m at a price that valued the business at $390m.

Boo.com did open, as promised, in November. But only 25,000 people visited its website on day one, compared with an expected 1m, and it soon became clear that sales would be less than a 10th of the promised target of $37m in the first seven months. The conclusion seemed clear: Boo's founders had wildly overestimated the market size, their ability to penetrate it, or both. The company needed another $20m to last until February and the strategic investor that JP Morgan wanted to bring in – Federated Department Stores of the US – postponed a deal to put up $10m until it saw how Christmas sales went. Despite this, the company's investors, still driven more by greed than by fear, provided more cash in the hope of doubling their money in a forthcoming initial public offering. Their new investment valued at $285m a business that had annualised sales to date of $3m.

Not even the market crash of March 2000, which killed forever any hope of a quick exit at a profit, managed to restore sanity to investors or management. The Boo founders continued to bicker internally about the depth of the cuts they should be making, while the core investors talked seriously about putting in another $30m at a price that valued the existing shareholdings at $20m.

In Malmsten's account, the Boo story is more comic opera than tragedy and its leading characters are fools rather than knaves. The lesson, if there is one, is that the Boo people copied every detail of the fast-growing Silicon Valley start-up except for one key point. The private-jet lifestyle and global partying are what you do after becoming a billionaire. Before getting to profit, you fly economy and spend money for the benefit of customers, not staff.

Source: T. Jackson, 'Burning money at Boo: the founders of the infamous Internet company were fools rather than knaves', *Financial Times*, 1 November 2001.

1.2.3 The crash

During 1995–1999, investors and managers had artificially inflated market sizes for dotcom companies and overlooked a number of important issues that led to the subsequent end of the Internet boom years.[19]

On the one hand, revenues were artificially inflated through a number of ways. First, in order to gain market share, Internet ventures subsidised customers' purchases of their products. For instance, Internet retailers such as Amazon.com and the pet-food supplier pets.com provided free shipping and delivery to their customers – even for 20lb dog-food bags. Second, many customers bought products and services online more out of curiosity than to fulfil an actual need. After the novelty wore off, many customers reverted to their traditional buying behaviour. Third, in many instances, revenues for the Internet ventures were generated through stocks from partner companies that enjoyed equally high market valuations.

On the other hand, costs were not represented realistically, which further distorted the true state of the underlying business. In many cases, dotcom companies received subsidised inputs because suppliers were eager to do business with them, which helped them to reduce costs. More importantly, many suppliers and employees accepted equity as payment, expecting that the stock market boom would continue to rise.

The above-mentioned factors resulted in bad operating financials, which did not reflect the actual Internet ventures' business model in terms of costs and revenues. Furthermore, bank analysts, such as Mary Meeker from Morgan Stanley, who, in 1996, wrote the highly publicised *Internet Report*, had pointed out that the focus of investors should be not on current earnings but on earnings potential.[20] Instead, investors were supposed to emphasise the numbers of online customers, unique website visitors and repeat online buyers. Consequently, e-managers, trying to meet investors' expectations spent heavily on marketing and advertising to attract site visitors and customers, regardless of costs. As it turned out, however, these metrics might have been a good indicator for spectator traffic on a website, yet they did not represent a reliable indicator of profitability.

On Monday, 13 March 2000, the dotcom bubble started to burst. Within three days, the NASDAQ slid by almost 500 points. At that time, Jack Willoughby, a journalist for *Barron's*, published an article in which he calculated the 'burn-rate' of Internet companies, which measured the rate at which these companies were spending money. He concluded that most of the Internet companies would run out of money within a year:

> When will the Internet bubble burst? For scores of Net upstarts, that unpleasant popping sound is likely to be heard before the end of this year. Starved for cash, many of these companies will try to raise fresh funds by issuing more stock or bonds. But a lot of them won't succeed. As a result, they will be forced to sell out to stronger rivals or go out of business altogether. Already, many cash-strapped Internet firms are scrambling for funding.[21]

This article shattered the hope of investors that, regardless of their economic viability, Internet firms would always be able to raise more money.

Along with most other Internet firms, the stock of the above-mentioned Priceline.com started to slide from $150 at its peak down to less than $2. At this valuation level, the capitalisation of Priceline.com would not even have sufficed to purchase two Boeing 747 jets. Other Internet companies faced similar fates and either went bankrupt (see the FT article 'Webvan's billion-dollar mistake') or were acquired by a larger competitor, often a traditional bricks-and-mortar company from the so-called 'old economy'. For instance, K·B Toys, an 80-year-old, bricks-and-mortar toy retailer, purchased the intellectual property, software and warehouses of bankrupt eToys.com – once one of the most highly praised online start-ups and valued at $10 billion – and relaunched eToys.com in October 2001.

Subsequent to the burst of the Internet bubble, which took place in March and April 2000, e-business entrepreneurs, managers, investors and the media awoke to the new reality and started reflecting on what had really happened. More importantly, they tried to understand the reasons that led to the failure of so many Internet ventures, as well as the flaws in their business models.

In addition to the hysteria that had distorted valuations, many of these ventures did not create as much value as was anticipated, and they were also unable to capture the value they created in the form of profits. Let us look at each of these points in turn.

Overall, the value created by Internet ventures turned out to be lower since costs were higher and benefits were lower than it was thought throughout the boom years. The belief that e-business would be comparatively low cost stemmed mainly from the idea that it required only a couple of computer servers and a website to set up an online company. Furthermore, it was thought that doing business over the Internet would be highly scalable since it required only setting up additional computer processing capability to cater for new customers around the globe.

Yet for many online businesses the costs of developing a website turned out to be only a small fraction of the total costs. For instance, during the boom years, Amazon.com, on average, paid around $16 for buying and shipping a book. On top of that came $8 for marketing and advertising and $1 for overheads (which included the website development), raising overall costs per book to $25. Average price per book sold, however, was only $20.[22] The main reason for the high costs was that most costs, including marketing and sales, were not nearly as scale sensitive as the set-up of a website. In fact, the acquisition costs of online customers were, in general, much higher than those of traditional bricks-and-mortar companies. Internet 'pure-player' companies had first to build up their brand name and then win over the trust of online customers.

Furthermore, the notion of the unbundled corporation in which external providers manage the high fixed-cost logistical processes did not work out as expected – at least during those early years when the interfaces between e-business companies and their logistics providers had not yet been clearly defined. In order to maintain high levels of quality and reliability, online companies such as Amazon.com reverted to setting up their own warehouses and distribution centres, thereby adding significantly to overall costs.

It also turned out to be difficult for most Internet companies to establish a sustainable revenue model. As a result, they were unable to ensure a high enough return on investment to justify their stock market valuation. For instance, after starting operations in April 1998, Priceline.com managed, by the end of that year, to sell $35 million worth of airline tickets – at an overall cost of $36.5 million!

The inability of many firms to charge appropriate prices for products and services was due to the following factors. First, the Internet lowered barriers to entry (see Section 3.2). While, in the past, it was necessary to operate an extensive physical network to compete in the retailing sector, many companies from all realms, such as Boo.com and eToys.com, attempted to grab market share by leveraging the Internet. In the online market for pet food, more than half a dozen web retailers were competing for customers. This led to a price war to attract customers, with some companies giving away products or services for free.

Second, the strategic stakes that were involved further aggravated the competitive situation. Knowing that only a few online companies per sector would be able to stay in business, these companies invested heavily and sacrificed profits for market share. They also hoped that market share would translate into durable customer relationships. After all, e-business was supposed to be a winner-takes-all market. Yet, ultimately the lock-in effect created through high switching costs and network effects occurred only in a few cases (see also Section 7.4.1). As websites became user-friendlier, it also became easier for customers to switch from one provider to another.

Regarding network effects, only companies that rely heavily on consumer interactions, such as eBay, were able to leverage the power of their installed customer base. However, as long as there was no substantial interaction with other users, individual customers usually did not care much about the size of the installed user base of an e-business company.

The final dark side of the boom years was that many companies, most notably the energy trader Enron, once hailed as the model Internet-based company, and the telecom operator WorldCom, applied illegal accounting practices to boost profits. This worked out as long as the boom persisted and the stock market kept going up. However, once the market had collapsed and investors started to scrutinise accounts more closely, the extent of the criminal activities became obvious, forcing these companies and numerous others to file for bankruptcy. Just like after previous crashes, regulatory agencies also reacted this time to improve investor protection. In July 2002, President George W. Bush signed the Sarbanes–Oxley Act of 2002, which mandates a number of reforms to enhance corporate responsibility and financial disclosures and to combat corporate and accounting fraud. In addition, this Act also created the Public Company Accounting Oversight Board (PCAOB), which has the role of overseeing the activities of the auditing profession.

FT

Webvan's billion-dollar mistake

The demise of Webvan ends the hope that a business as mundane as grocery shopping could be transformed by a standalone Internet company.

Webvan was the best funded and the most hyped of the online grocers, soaring to an $8.7bn market valuation on its first day of trading in November 1999. Now it has burned through more than $1bn of cash in less than two years.

The rise and fall of Webvan is a study in the illusions of the dotcom boom and the wishful thinking of Wall Street. It is leaving little in its wake but a stain on the reputations of the blue-chip backers it attracted in its early days.

Founded in 1996 by Louis Borders of Borders Books, Webvan managed to lure George Shaheen, managing partner of Andersen Consulting, to be its chief executive. Its board was filled with some of the most revered names of the era: Christos Cotsakos of E*Trade, Tim Koogle of Yahoo and Michael Moritz of Sequoia Capital. Its money came from such Silicon Valley powerhouses as Softbank Capital Partners and Benchmark Capital and its shares were touted by Wall Street's best-known investment banks.

Goldman Sachs said in February 2000 that Webvan could become an Internet franchise to rank alongside AOL and Yahoo. 'Webvan has re-engineered the backend fulfilment system to create a scalable solution to the last-mile problem of e-commerce,' its analysts wrote. Having such names behind it ensured that Webvan was able to come to market – with Goldman as lead underwriter – after only a few months of trading in which it had managed to sell just $3.2m worth of goods.

Nonetheless, its executives assured investors it had a vast opportunity. Groceries represented a far larger market than books, videos or music – areas in which e-commerce made its first forays. The typical US household spends $5,000 a year on groceries and goes food shopping more than twice a week.

From the start, the company had big ambitions. Rather than starting off in a large city or two, learning from its mistakes and perhaps making a small profit before expanding, it decided to open in 26 markets within three years.

Each distribution centre would be 18 times the size of a typical supermarket and would cost $35m. Almost 5 miles of conveyor belts would bring products to the packers at each site and refrigerated vans fitted with sophisticated global satellite positioning systems would allow each warehouse to serve a 50-mile radius.

It soon became obvious that Webvan was overbuilding – but by then it had nine centres →

open, each bleeding cash and operating at a fraction of capacity. 'I believe they were doomed from the start because their business model was one that was predicated on reinventing the entire system rather than using any of the existing structure,' says Robert Mittelstaedt, vice-dean of executive education at the Wharton School. Webvan's profligate plan 'defied economic sense in a low-margin business,' he adds.

Groceries did not offer the prospect of fat margins that a smart new entrant could try to undercut. Kroger's return on sales in 1999 was just 2.2 per cent and Ahold achieved a 4.5 per cent operating margin in the same year. Many online retailers have got round such issues by charging above-market prices for convenience but this was always likely to be a challenge. Most families watch their weekly food bills carefully, as food manufacturers that have raised prices know to their cost.

The hope that e-tailers' gross margins could exceed those of traditional retailers was punctured not only by high fulfilment costs but also by online grocers' lack of purchasing power and the heavy discounting many had to offer to attract customers.

The cost of Webvan's infrastructure, however impressive, eventually prevented it from competing with traditional supermarkets. Mr Mittelstaedt says this problem was not unique to online grocers. 'The places you see where (e-tailers) successfully changed the business model have nothing to do with physical distribution – such as recruitment sites,' he says.

Shoppers were not crying out for an alternative way to buy groceries and it is notable that the supermarket model had not been challenged by previous innovations such as catalogues.

Whether Webvan truly offered convenience is also questionable. Although it guaranteed delivery within a 30-minute window chosen by the customer – although not the same day – this still required somebody to be at home to accept the goods.

The one factor that cannot be blamed for Webvan's failure is online competition from traditional grocers such as Safeway, Kroger and Albertson's. All were slow to the Internet and all invested only small sums in online operations.

The big retailers are slowly showing signs of learning from Webvan's mistakes. Ahold invested last year in Peapod, an online-only grocer that now picks merchandise from Ahold's US chains. Safeway last month gave up its warehouse model in favor of a partnership with Tesco, the UK retailer that has built the world's largest online grocery business by using a model whereby orders are assembled in its stores.

Meanwhile, more than 200 of Webvan's delivery vans currently sit outside its closed plant in Lawrenceville, Georgia, awaiting auction next month. They are expected to fetch a fraction of what Webvan paid for them.

Webvan's investors now face an anxious wait to see whether they can salvage anything from the physical assets left behind by this supposedly virtual business. For now, it seems, few people apart from the time-stressed technophiles who founded the company really need Webvan.

There were a few mourners yesterday. Sarah Lonsdale, a San Francisco freelance writer, was until yesterday a devoted user of the service. Now she will have to lug her two children to the grocery store. 'I'm disappointed,' she says. 'Webvan had really got its act together. The convenience of ordering was fantastic.' But in the end, that was not enough.

Source: P. Abrahams and A. Edgecliffe-Johnson, 'A billion-dollar mistake: Webvan's failure has been an expensive lesson for the Internet', *Financial Times*, 10 July 2001.

1.2.4 The synergy phase

What messages can we take away from looking at these boom and bust cycles across history? First, in order to enter the synergy phase it is essential to return to business fundamentals. This entails paying close consideration to issues such as industry structure, value creation, and ways to create profits and a sustainable competitive advantage through the Internet.

Second, just like the railway, steel and automobile industries underwent boom and bust phases before releasing their true economic potential, we are now observing a similar evolution in the e-business sector. The booming installation years of the Internet were followed by a bust. Since then, the time has come for the much more profound deployment period of e-business (see also FT article 'From Netscape to the Next Big Thing').[23]

FT

From Netscape to the Next Big Thing: how a dotcom decade changed our lives

Somewhere in the world in the next few weeks the billionth human being will sit down at a computer, log on to the Internet for the first time and join the swelling throng in cyberspace. That is quite a record for a medium that broke away from its academic roots only a decade ago. But it may be only a taste of the upheaval in store over the next 10 years.

The Internet's 10th birthday is marked next week by the anniversary of the Netscape initial public offering – an event that triggered Wall Street's dotcom mania. Netscape's browser made the Internet a more conducive place for the non-technical user and spurred the creation of companies such as e-Bay, Yahoo and Amazon.com, which have all had 10th birthday parties of their own – although most dotcom companies never made it this far.

It is worth considering the extent to which those survivors have become part of the everyday lives of their users. The $34bn of goods that changed hands on e-Bay last year is roughly equivalent to the gross domestic product of Kenya; Yahoo's 379m unique users are equal to the populations of the US and UK combined; and the average person on the planet views 10 webpages on Google each month.

Even early enthusiasts for the medium did not quite foresee how far it would work its way into popular culture. 'It was a stretch to say that niche focus newsgroups and bulletin boards about Unix would some day be newsgroups about the latest Harry Potter book or Batman movie', says Mary Meeker, the Morgan Stanley Internet analyst who was among the first on Wall Street to tout the Internet's potential.

Much of the early euphoria was of course misplaced, even if it has been proved right over the longer term. It is three years in October since the nadir of the stock market slump, which wiped more than $6,500bn from the peak value of Nasdaq stock market where many US technology companies are traded [see Exhibit 1.5]. Most of that wealth destruction reflected over-investment in telecommunications networks and the technology companies that were building the infrastructure on which the Internet depends. Overcapacity in telecoms and tech, though, has brought down prices and made the Internet more widely available, helping to fuel a new round of online innovation.

'The pace of change is accelerating,' says Ms Meeker.

It is hard to argue with the sheer weight of numbers. According to estimates by Morgan Stanley, 1bn people will be online by the end of next month, three times as many as at the beginning of the decade. Roughly one in five of those people already uses a broadband connection. And mobile access to the Internet has barely begun: sometime during the next decade, more mobile handsets than personal computers will be plugged into the global information network. Of course, eyeballs alone do not create a business – a point amply demonstrated by the experiences of many dotcom pioneers. But this time around business is following close behind.

Global online advertising hit $15bn last year, two-thirds of it in the US, and it is growing at some 30% a year as advertisers rush to keep up with the shift in their audience online. Consumer e-commerce, which reached $295bn last year, is set →

to grow by 38% this year, according to IDC. At the same time, the companies that dominate the medium have learnt from the mistakes of the past and are refining business plans that already make them some of the most valuable on the planet. 'We are doing a better job of getting more value from each click,' says Eric Schmidt, chief executive officer of Google. 'If you show better ads – which sometimes means fewer ads – business improves. That's something we've learnt over the last year.'

None of this even touches on the less visible, and potentially even more profound, impact that the web has had on how businesses are organised, how social and political life has been affected or how a country such as India has been able to join the world economy in a way that would once have seemed impossible.

If that is the story of the Internet so far, then what do the next 10 years hold in store? In two words: more upheaval, as the forces that caused consternation in many corporate boardrooms in the late-1990s are once again unleashed, this time backed by more robust business models and better technology. 'A lot of business people were very happy about the Internet market correction – that pulled a lot of resources off the Internet,' says Ms Meeker. 'But the Internet business just kept on going. The disruption to a lot of traditional businesses has only just begun.'

Many Internet businesses are probably in for an unsettling time of their own. As Meg Whitman, chief executive officer of e-Bay, warns, half of the Internet giants 10 years from now may well be companies that you have never heard of before. Internet stock valuations, including Google's price/earnings ratio of 87, once again seem to be ignoring the fact that barriers to entry in this global medium remain low and that the next disruptive idea may be just around the corner.

As with the last decade, the impact of the web in the next 10 years is likely to be felt most acutely in those fields that depend most on disseminating information: in communications, commerce and the media. While e-mail and instant messaging were the low-cost communications of the Internet's first decade, the next communications revolution may well take aim at the voice calls that account for the bulk of the telecom industry's revenues. In its first

year, more than 140m people have downloaded free software from Skype, which lets computer users talk over the Internet, making it the fastest-growing consumer technology in history.

'We will have free global communications in very short order,' says Paul Saffo, director of Institute for the Future, a California research group. Along with new low-cost communications technologies such as WiFi and WiMax, that signals a fresh threat to an industry that was hit hard during the first phase of the Internet. As the barriers online between communications, commerce and media are eroded, meanwhile, the Internet is likely to bring forth new technologies and challenge existing forms of human interaction.

Two forces, in particular, characterise this latest wave: the rise of search engines, and the many online tools that have been created to support the outpouring of what is known on the Internet as 'user-generated content'. Search engines have already established themselves as a pivotal form of distribution online. As more of the media become digitised, that role is only likely to become more significant. 'The Internet will become a very serious competitor to cable and satellite in the home, and the impact on print media is likely to be dramatic,' says Roger McNamee, a Silicon Valley financier who specialises in the media industry. 'At the end of the day, search-based technology is really how consumers will access and find that content – that's a huge deal.'

An increasing part of this content is likely to come from Internet users themselves. 'We are in the middle of a very big shift from mass media to personal media: you get to answer back and create if you want,' says Mr Saffo. Blogging, now a pastime of more than 15m people, has been an unlikely early manifestation. Other forms of self-expression and community-building are gathering force, including photo-sharing sites that let families or groups of friends see each others' pictures; podcasting (a form of audio blogging); and social networks that connect wider groups of friends. 'Blogging is a transitional form on its way to something else. It's interesting, but it isn't stable,' says Mr Saffo. The urge towards communication and self-expression, and the low-cost technology to make it possible, will give rise to new fads.

Seen from the perspective of 2015, search and blogging may look like quaint and antiquated ideas, overtaken by another Next Big Thing on the Internet: some new way of fulfilling people's desire to interact and find information, entertainment or goods to buy online. Whatever its form, though, what comes next is likely to draw on the forces manifested during the medium's first decade: a pervasive interconnectivity, aided by increasingly sophisticated software tools that uncover and make useable the ever-expanding sources of information on the open global database.

There is another lesson from the first decade that is likely to hold good for the years ahead: for clues about how the Internet will eventually change your life, look no further than the teenager sitting next to you. 'The 15- to 20-year-olds,' says Ms Meeker, 'will show and tell you where it is going.'

Jerry Yang was a student at Stanford University when he and David Filo started Yahoo as an index of Internet pages in 1994. 'When we first got together, we weren't even thinking about it as a business. It really began as a hobby – we wanted to keep track of our personal interests on the web. The Internet had been around for a long time obviously, but it's when Mosaic [the Netscape browser] and some of the other earlier tools came out that we really started to get excited about it. We knew there was a future to this whole thing but we never imagined where things would end up. Eventually, our personal interest lists for the web became too long and unmanageable, so we broke them out into categories and then sub-categories and there you had it – the core concept behind Yahoo was born. We also shared these lists with our friends but it wasn't until we saw our first million-hit day that we realised, "Hey, maybe we have something here." So when I look at where we are today, I'm amazed. The success and growth of the business has far exceeded anything I could have ever imagined.

'I think when you look back at the last 10 years, there are things that have happened much faster than we had anticipated, but also things that took a lot longer than expected, such as users making the shift from the PC to mobile devices and general access to broadband. I think if you look at users early on, people saw the web as this great outlet for publishing. For the first time, people could have an individual voice out there. That was the driver for the Internet from the beginning. But if you look at how that has evolved over the last 10 years, it's still not as sophisticated as we thought it would be. A good example of that is blogging – look how long it took before people actually embraced it. It's surprising to me how things like that took so long.

'It's always difficult to predict what's next, but I think there will definitely be a digital convergence. If you look at the people who grew up with the Internet, their media consumption and approach to technology is totally different to their parents' generation. They rely heavily on the Internet for information, personal communication, work and entertainment and they want to take this with them wherever they are. The online industry is constantly evolving and I think the Internet will continue to impact traditional business far beyond anything we've seen today. With the talent, technology and resources out there today, I think we're going to see some great things happen over the next few years.'

Meg Whitman left a job at toymaker Hasbro to become president and chief executive of e-Bay in 1998. The value of goods traded on the company's sites has risen from $740m when she joined to $34bn last year. 'I look back and say, "What were we thinking?" We quit two jobs, moved to California, put the children in new schools. I didn't think it was going to be anything like it turned out. I thought e-Bay could be a great collectibles website for the US. I thought this could be a small, quite profitable company. We began to understand that what worked in collectibles would work in other markets as well. What e-Bay does is make inefficient markets efficient. The business model is very powerful. We were able to move globally far faster than land-based companies can. The remarkable thing about e-Bay is that it's instantly local: 98% of our content is user-generated.

'The other thing I wasn't expecting was the way the market empowered small businesses. That was a big surprise. I thought this would be the home of big business. But it has levelled the playing field, and made small businesses as accessible as big ones. That was an "a-ha" moment. Some categories didn't work the way we thought they would. We look for markets where there is price and information inefficiency. It turns out that real estate is pretty darn efficient.

'I am startled by the ubiquity of the Internet today. It is one of the fastest-growing technologies ever. It's just remarkable. It has changed the way we communicate, the way we play. E-mail has changed the way business is conducted. The timing may finally be right now for mobile access. We thought it was important to have mobile access to e-Bay and the net five years ago, but nobody used it. That could be changing because of the growing power of mobile phones. In countries like China and India, you may see a shift to primary access to the Internet coming through mobile handsets. Moving to 100% broadband penetration will also make a huge difference. You will see an always-on Internet that changes the way people behave.

'There is still room for new Internet leaders to be created. Of the five biggest Internet companies 10 years from now, I can imagine that two or three of the existing leaders will stay on, but that two will be companies that haven't even been born yet. The Internet is an incredibly dynamic environment. You have to respond really fast.'

Source: R. Waters, 'From Netscape to the Next Big Thing: how a dotcom decade changed our lives', *Financial Times*, 5 August 2005.

At the time of writing the second edition of this book, almost seven years have passed since the crash. Companies with established Internet businesses such as Ducati, eBay, Google, Tesco.com or Nordea, some of which are documented in this book, confirm that if firms have consistent e-business strategies and implement them superiorly, they can create significant value for their customers while at the same time being highly profitable. As a result, the stock valuation of some highly successful Internet ventures, such as eBay and Amazon.com, have increased beyond the levels that we witnessed last during the Internet boom years.

In addition, in recent years, entrepreneurial start-ups have also had substantial success. Ironically, nowadays it seems to be the case that it really only requires a couple of computer servers and a website to set up an online company. Most of the companies that were recently acquired by large industry incumbents such as Yahoo! or Google.com were founded by young entrepreneurs out of their private homes or college dorm rooms. Companies such as Flickr, YouTube, MySpace or del.icio.us have in common that they actually have built communities around a website offering videos and photos, or enabling people to network with their friends, all of which did not require heavy investments in marketing (because users mostly took care of this) or infrastructure (because no physical goods were involved).

All these companies, however, had a different starting point than their predecessors of the dotcom period. The actual network infrastructure of the Internet has changed dramatically in the last few years. The spread of broadband Internet connections has had the effect that more people spend more time online and it has also allowed for richer content to be created and viewed, which, in turn, makes it easier for new start-ups to create new service sites around user-generated content. Furthermore, new technology standards such as RSS and AJAX have evolved which make it easier to keep track of content updates and provide a faster and more convenient web experience.

Based on these improvements, a new web-based service variety has evolved that focuses on fostering communication, sharing or collaboration. The so-called blogosphere where bloggers author their own content and comment on other bloggers' output is democratising the web by allowing individuals to engage in their personal journalistic interests, delivering articles on any possible topic. While web-based folksonomies such as YouTube or Flickr allow their members to upload, label and categorise content such as videos or photos using tags, social networking sites allow their users to create their own profiles and to connect with other people through a social network. Furthermore, there is a whole variety of services evolving on the web, such as Google's online calendar or word processing and spreadsheet applications, which are mimicking traditional desktop applications, thus posing another threat to established software industry incumbents such as Microsoft.

By functioning as platforms for its users, these software services allow participants to make various content items available and accessible for others. One common concept for understanding to what extent this new service variety creates value from a user's point of view is the concept of the 'long tail', which is discussed in more detail in Chapter 11. By allowing the individual to capitalise better on previously inaccessible market niches, the 'long tail' can be reached down. Search tools, for instance, are an integral part and are needed in order to break down a complex world of choice into reasonable pieces which can be handled by the user.

Still many of the new services have yet to prove that they have substantial revenue models. However, highly trafficked sites and high user numbers suggest that the value created by these companies is more significant than the value created by companies during the new economy era. While survivors of the dotcom bust such as eBay and Amazon.com always had community aspects in their business models, and managed to be successful hybrid retailers, companies selling solely digital content have the advantage of completely freeing themselves from the boundaries of a physical world, therefore being even more cost efficient than others.

Furthermore, investors seem to be more realistic about their protégés' future. Although Web 2.0 is all about people it is not about IPOs. Selling a successful, meaning heavily trafficked, website to one of the established incumbents on the Internet appears to be the modus operandi of exiting entrepreneurs. Google's acquisition of YouTube or the acquisition of MySpace in a $580 million deal further demonstrates that substantial value is created.

It seems that the maturity stage of e-business companies is not yet in sight. The Blog Box 'Google acquires Internet' provides a glimpse into a possible, although not likely, future.

BLOG BOX

Google acquires Internet (May 2017)

Mountain View-based search giant Google Inc today announced they've acquired the Internet for the astounding sum of $2,455.5 billion in cash. The deal had been rumored in various search blogs since the beginning of the year and was now confirmed by the company's CEO. 'This is in line with our vision to make information more accessible to end-users,' says Eric Schmidt. 'With the acquisition, we can increase the speed of indexing as everything will already be on our servers by the time it's published.'

In a conference call earlier today, Larry Page explained the strategy behind the acquisition. 'We realized it's not very cost-effective to buy the Internet in smaller portions.' During the past two decades, Google had acquired YouTube for $1.65 billion, DoubleClick for $3.1 billion, AOL for $12.5 billion, and last year, Microsoft for the record sum of $120 billion. Questioned on the first steps the company would take integrating the Internet onto their servers, Eric Schmidt announced immediate plans to redirect Yahoo.com to Google's own search engine. 'From an end user perspective, having two search engines is just bad usability, and causes confusion. While we appreciate Yahoo's recent advances in search technology, we felt this move is best aligned with the interests of our advertisers, users and shareholders.' Eric added, 'By leveraging third-generation mobile platforms in sustainable verticals, new monetization opportunities can manifest into an improved web experience, greatly benefiting investors and digerati alike – a true paradigm change synergizing the Web 6.0 framework on the enterprise level.'

Accompanying Google's acquisition revelation, privacy groups today released a paper criticizing the move. However, Larry Page argues that privacy is improved by Google's acquisition, explaining that '[the] main privacy issues for users today are data leaks to third parties. By eliminating all third parties, we closed this hole.' Eric Schmidt adds that Google intends to replace their current privacy policy with a 'privacy scale' which better balances necessary compromises. 'When you can improve the privacy of a large group of people by violating the privacy rights of a small number of people, in the end this improves overall privacy.'

The Chinese government in the meantime congratulated Google Inc. on their move. Regarding the potentials of expanded censorship, Sergey Brin told members of the press that Google would now drop all search results filtering and instead 'address the root problem from a publisher perspective' by directly blocking certain keywords the time they are entered in Google-owned tools such as Blogger, Gmail, Page Creator, Yahoo 360 and MSN Spaces. Amnesty International and Reporters Without Borders were not available for comment at this time due to temporary technical problems with their web-based email clients.

Source: Philipp Lenssen, 'Google Acquires Internet (May 2017)', www.blogoscoped.com.

SUMMARY

- This chapter first introduced the definitions of e-business-related terms, including 'e-business', 'electronic commerce' and 'mobile e-commerce', and definitions of strategy and value creation.
- Second, this chapter provided a framework that describes the typical periods of technological revolutions. It also positions within this framework the evolution of the Internet during the last decade. The four main periods that characterise this evolution are:
  - the *grassroots of e-business* period, which took place before the widespread commercial use of the Internet;
  - the *rise of the Internet* period, which started with the launch of Amazon.com in 1995 and continued until 2000;
  - the *crash* (or burst of the dotcom bubble) which took place in March and April 2000 and caused a 45% decline of the NASDAQ by the end of that year;
  - the *synergy phase*, which followed the stock market crash and continues until today.

REVIEW QUESTIONS

1 Define the terms 'e-business', 'electronic commerce' and 'mobile electronic commerce', and describe how they differ from one another.

2 Provide a definition of strategy the way it is used in this book.

3 What are the three distinctive levels of strategy that can be recognised?

4 Describe the different periods of the life cycle model, as proposed by Carlota Perez.

5 What are the four time periods of the Internet evolution? What are the peculiar characteristics of each period?

6 What are the main lessons that Jerry Yang (CEO of Yahoo!) and Meg Whitman (CEO of eBay) have drawn from the first decade of the Internet?

DISCUSSION QUESTIONS

1 Referring to the FT article 'It's too early for e-business to drop its "e"', do you think that it is sensible to still speak today of e-business strategies or to drop the 'e' from the term 'e-business'? Defend your arguments.

2 What do you think are the main elements of strategy formulation? Does the perspective chosen in this chapter correspond to your own experiences and observations?

3 Choose two technological revolutions and discuss their evolution using the Perez framework described in this chapter.

4 Have we already entered (or are we about to enter) the maturity stage of the Internet? Explain your position on this matter.

5 What specific issues does the hypothetical acquisition of the Internet by Google in May 2017 (as described at the end of Chapter 1) raise? What is your position regarding these issues?

RECOMMENDED KEY READING

- B. Henderson uses the metaphor of biological evolution to describe the essence of strategy in 'The origin of strategy', *Harvard Business Review*, 1989, November–December, pp. 139–143.

- A detailed account of different levels of strategy can be found in G. Johnson, K. Scholes and R. Whittington, *Exploring Corporate Strategy*, 7th edition, Prentice Hall, 2005.

- H. Mintzberg is one of the most prominent critics of the design or positioning school. For further reading, see *Strategy Safari – A Guided Tour Through the Wilds of Strategic Management*, Prentice Hall, 1998, pp. 114–118, which offers no less than 10 different approaches to explaining strategy. His article 'The design school: reconsidering the basic premises of strategic management', *Strategic Management Journal*, 1990, Vol. 11, No. 3, pp. 171–195, provides a more condensed criticism of the design school.

■ M. Porter's article 'Strategy and the Internet', *Harvard Business Review*, 2001, March, pp. 63–78, provides an excellent overview of the impact of the Internet on strategy formulation.

■ C. Perez developed the five-stage model of technological revolutions presented in this chapter: see *Technological Revolutions and Financial Capital: The Dynamics of Bubbles and Golden Ages*, Edward Elgar, 2002. She draws heavily on the writings of twentieth-century economist J. Schumpeter. Among his important works rank the books *Business Cycles*, Porcupine Press, 1982 and *Capitalism, Socialism and Democracy*, Harper&Rank, 1975.

■ B. Arthur builds on the insights of C. Perez in the article 'Is the information revolution dead?', *Business 2.0*, 2002, March, pp. 65–73, where he suggests that the Internet economy is undergoing the same evolutionary phases as previous technological revolutions.

■ In 'Profits and the Internet: seven misconceptions', *Sloan Management Review*, 2001, Summer, pp. 44–53, S. Rangan and R. Adner analyse why the promises of the Internet economy were not fulfilled.

■ J. Cassidy takes a critical perspective of the development of the Internet economy in *Dot.con*, Perennial, 2003.

■ E. Malmsten (the co-founder of Boo.com), E. Portanger and C. Drazin provide an account of the rise and fall of the Internet fashion retailer Boo.com in their book *Boo Hoo*, Arrow Books, 2002.

■ In *The Long Tail: Why the Future of Business is Selling Less of More*, Hyperion, 2006, C. Anderson illustrates how, by using the Internet, companies can capitalise on niche markets better to serve their customers.

USEFUL THIRD-PARTY WEBLINKS

■ The website www.tutor2u.net provides interesting background information on a number of concepts discussed in this chapter.

■ In www.thelongtail.com, Chris Anderson provides up-to-date information on the concept of the 'long tail'.

■ www.brint.com provides deep coverage of articles on e-business and e-commerce.

■ www.ecommercetimes.com is an online newspaper specific to e-commerce developments.

NOTES AND REFERENCES

1 For definitions of e-business and e-commerce, see A. Bartels, 'The difference between e-business and e-commerce', www.Computerworld.com. Accessed 30 October 2000.
2 G. Johnson, R. Whittington and K. Scholes, *Exploring Corporate Strategy*, 7th edition, Prentice Hall, 2005, p. 10.
3 A. Chandler, *Strategy and Structure in the History of the American Industrial Enterprise*, MIT Press, 1962, p. 13.
4 B. Henderson, 'The origin of strategy', *Harvard Business Review*, 1989, November–December, p. 141.
5 M. Porter, 'Strategy and the Internet', *Harvard Business Review*, 2001, March, p. 72.

6 Researchers of strategy have been engaging in a heated debate about what strategy entails. Most notably, there are two different schools of strategy. The 'design view' of strategy considers strategy as characterised by deliberate planning and objective setting. The 'experience view' suggests that strategies develop in an adaptive fashion and depend to a large extent on existing strategies. See also G. Johnson, K. Scholes and R. Whittington, *Exploring Corporate Strategy*, 7th edition, Prentice Hall, 2005. The frameworks and concepts proposed in this book focus on the design view of strategy.

7 For a detailed discussion of different levels of strategy, see G. Johnson, K. Scholes and R. Whittington, *Exploring Corporate Strategy*, 7th edition, Prentice Hall, 2005.

8 For a discussion of operational issues in e-commerce, including topics such as website design and HTML programming, see D. Chaffey, *e-Business and e-Commerce Management*, FT Prentice Hall, 2007.

9 C. Perez, *Technological Revolutions and Financial Capital: The Dynamics of Bubbles and Golden Ages*, Edward Elgar, 2002, p. 8.

10 Ibid. pp. 90–137.

11 Note that as one technology reaches maturity, the next technological revolution is about to emerge. As a result, there can be considerable overlap between two technology surges.

12 C. Perez, *Technological Revolutions and Financial Capital: The Dynamics of Bubbles and Golden Ages*, Edward Elgar, 2002, pp. 90–137.

13 The NASDAQ is the main US-based stock exchange for high-tech companies.

14 Amazon.com was the first firm to add the suffix '.com' to the end of its name, thereby establishing the expression 'dotcom', which refers to all types of Internet ventures.

15 The p/e ratio of a company's stock is calculated by dividing its stock price by its earnings per share. For instance, if a company made €5 per share in the past year and the share sells for €50, then the p/e ratio for this share is 10.

16 J. Cassidy provides a detailed account of the exuberance and hysteria during the Internet boom years in *Dot.con*, Perennial, 2003, pp. 2–5.

17 Ibid. p. 5.

18 M. Pandya, H. Singh, R. Mittelstaedt, *et al.*, *On Building Corporate Value*, John Wiley, 2002, p. 8.

19 For an excellent discussion of the flawed thinking during the boom years of the Internet, refer to M. Porter, 'Strategy and the Internet', *Harvard Business Review*, 2001, March, pp. 63–78.

20 M. Meeker and C. DePuy, *The Internet Report*, Harper Business, 1996.

21 J. Willoughby, 'Burning up: Warning: Internet companies are running out of cash', *Barron's*, 20 March 2000, p. 29.

22 J. Cassidy, *Dot.con*, Perennial, 2003, p. 148.

23 See also T. Mullaney and H. Green, 'The e-Biz surprise', *BusinessWeekOnline*, 12 May 2003.

PART II

The e-business strategy framework

PART OVERVIEW

This part proposes an e-business strategy framework that consists of the following three phases:

- Strategic analysis
- Strategy formulation
- Strategy implementation.

The goal of this part is to provide a comprehensive strategy framework that addresses the crucial elements of e-business strategy formulation. The key elements of the three phases of strategic analysis, strategy formulation and strategy implementation are as follows:

- External analysis of the macro-environment and industry structure
- Internal analysis of key resources and capabilities
- Generic strategy options
- Sustainable competitive advantage
- Exploration of new market spaces
- Creation and capturing of value
- Internal organisation
- Interaction with suppliers, customers and users
- Mobile e-commerce strategies
- Strategy implementation.

CHAPTER 2

Overview of the e-business strategy framework

Chapter at a glance

2.1 Key challenges in e-business strategy formulation
2.2 A systematic approach to e-business strategy formulation

Learning outcomes

After completing this chapter, you should be able to:

- Understand the key challenges that are involved during the e-business strategy formulation process.
- Have a broad understanding of the structure and the key elements of the e-business strategy framework.

INTRODUCTION

In Part II of this book, we propose an overarching e-business strategy framework that can serve as a comprehensive basis for e-business strategy formulation. This framework should help you address the following:

- Understand the external macro-environment and industry structure of e-business companies.
- Understand internal e-business competencies.
- Choose a specific type of Internet-enabled competitive advantage.
- Sustain the Internet-enabled competitive advantage against imitation and disruptive innovations.
- Create new market spaces through e-business initiatives.
- Link the external and internal perspectives of e-business strategies using the value process framework.
- Make decisions regarding the internal organisation of e-business initiatives.
- Interact with e-business customers, suppliers and users.
- Understand specific issues and applications of mobile e-commerce.
- Implement e-business strategies.

To do so, we believe that it is valuable to begin this part of the book by covering rigorous and time-proven concepts from the field of strategic management and then to adapt them to the specific context of e-business. This adaptation takes places in the following three ways.

First, although the conceptual chapters cover several generic strategy frameworks, they also highlight specific concepts that are important for e-business and help understand recent successes and failures in the field. These include, for instance, economies of scale and scope, switching costs, network effects and transaction cost theory.

Second, the framework presents specific e-business concepts such as the virtual value chain (see Section 4.3), the ICDT (Information, Communication, Distribution and Transaction) model (see Section 4.4) and the 'long tail' concept (see Section 11.4).

Third, all the concepts and frameworks that are presented in the conceptual chapters are illustrated through specific e-business examples and case studies. By doing so, we want to link real-world applications with theoretical and conceptual considerations, hoping to make the material more accessible to readers and useful to practising managers.

2.1 Key challenges in e-business strategy formulation

Before explaining the e-business strategy framework in more detail, let us return to Chapter 1 where we discussed the definition and goals of a strategy. There, we stated that:

- Strategy is concerned with the *long-term direction* of the firm.
- Strategy deals with the *overall plan for deploying the resources* that a firm possesses.

- Strategy entails the willingness to make *trade-offs*, to choose between different directions and between different ways of deploying resources.
- Strategy is about achieving *unique positioning* vis-à-vis competitors.
- The central goal of strategy is to achieve sustainable *competitive advantage* over rivals and thereby to ensure lasting profitability.

The bottom line of the above statements is that a strategy is concerned with overarching decisions that determine the fundamental direction of a company. In this sense, a strategy helps to determine the positioning of a firm in the marketplace and the choice of required resources. The overall goal of developing an e-business strategy is to succeed in using the Internet as an enabler for achieving a competitive advantage (see Exhibit 2.1). There are several ways of attaining a competitive advantage including, among others, having a strong and unique brand, a large and loyal customer base, innovative products and services, and low-cost production facilities.

However, making the right decisions regarding where to build up a competitive advantage is not trivial. The first challenge is that strategic decisions involve choices that might not take effect until some time in the future. Due to the high degree of uncertainty regarding future developments, especially in the e-business environment where technologies and business models change rapidly, making long-term commitments to a strategy is a difficult challenge. Furthermore, there are usually numerous, different and frequently contradicting decision criteria that need to be evaluated during strategy analysis and formulation. For instance, in the case of Tesco.com featured in the case studies section of the book, a crucial strategic issue was to choose between two different fulfilment approaches for online orders: in-store-based fulfilment versus warehouse-based fulfilment. As the case study illustrates, there were numerous arguments in favour and against each one of these two options. This ambiguity and uncertainty is typical for strategic decision making.

Exhibit 2.1 The goal of e-business strategy is to achieve (long-term) success by building up one or more sources of competitive advantage

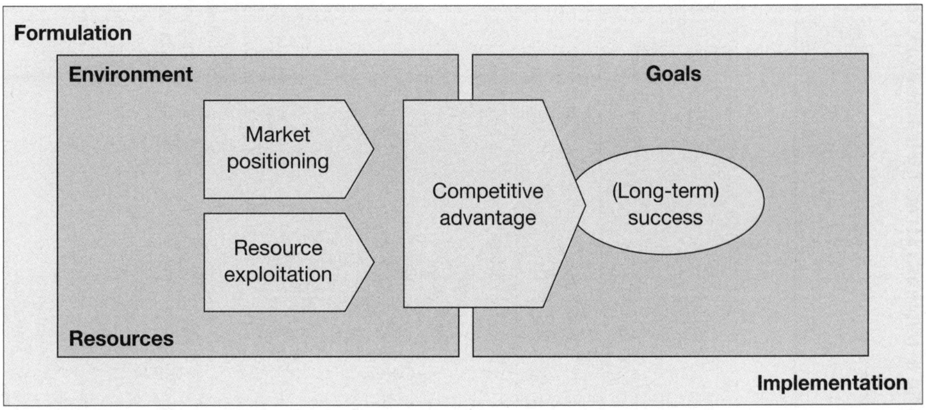

Source: Adapted from H. Hungenberg, *Strategisches Management in Unternehmen*, Gabler, 2006, p. 83.

Exhibit 2.2 **The e-business strategy framework consists of three main steps**

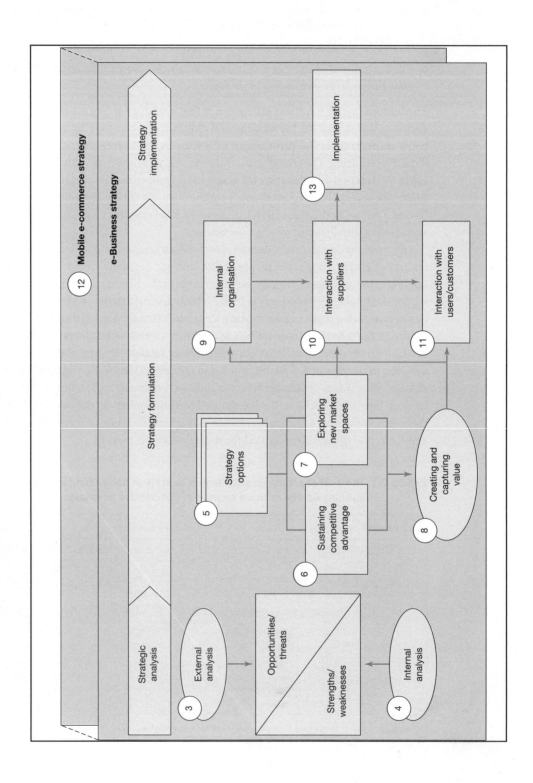

2.2 A systematic approach to e-business strategy formulation

As stated above, the goal of e-business strategy analysis and formulation lies in gaining an understanding of different strategy options and their implications, and then iteratively evaluating arguments in favour or against these options. This process does not revolve around finding the *one* right answer, but focuses more on making trade-offs apparent, making decision makers aware of the implications of different options and helping them make decisions regarding the future based on past and current developments. In this sense, strategic management can be considered to be a 'planned evolution' – the alternative to this approach would be an unguided evolution based on pure chance.[1]

This raises the question of how to go, in a systematic way, about e-business strategy development. As an anchoring point for the remainder of this book, we propose a three part e-business strategy framework consisting of: (1) strategic analysis; (2) strategy formulation; and (3) strategy implementation (see Exhibit 2.2). Note that in this exhibit, a given number (inside a circle) corresponds to the specific book chapter in which the listed issue is discussed in detail.

The first part of this framework entails the strategic analysis, which consists of two different perspectives: (1) the external analysis and (2) the internal analysis.

The goal of the external analysis, which is covered in Chapter 3, is to gain an understanding of the external developments that might have an impact on the e-business strategy of your company. On an aggregate level, the external analysis refers to developments in the broad macro-environment, which includes topics such as technological changes, overall economic developments or societal changes. On a more detailed level, it also entails an analysis of the different players within an industry, including competitors, suppliers or substitutes. The outcome of this analysis should help you gain an improved understanding of the opportunities and threats that your company might face in the future.

The goal of the internal analysis, which is discussed in detail in Chapter 4, is to understand the key resources and capabilities that a firm possesses to implement or sustain a specific e-business strategy. Resources might, for instance, refer to a large installed user base (as in the case of eBay), deep financial pockets to make targeted acquisitions (as is the case with Google), or a strong brand (as in the case of Tesco.com). e-Capabilities refer to a firm's ability through IT and the Internet to turn resources into valuable products or services. Based on the insights gained from the internal and external analyses, you should be able to gain an understanding of the strengths and weaknesses that your company possesses vis-à-vis competitors.

The overall insights from these two analyses can then be integrated into a SWOT matrix (Strengths–Weaknesses–Opportunities–Threats matrix), which raises the four key questions listed in Exhibit 2.3.

After having gained a clear understanding of a company's characteristics and the key environmental and industry developments, we come to the crucial decision of choosing a strategic direction. The primary choices are: (1) a cost leadership position where a company competes primarily on the basis of low prices, and (2) a differentiated position where a company competes on the basis of superior products and services. This topic is covered in greater detail in Chapter 5.

Obviously, a competitive advantage that a company possesses today is not necessarily sustainable over time. In the e-business world in particular, there is constant pressure from new Internet start-ups or incumbent bricks-and-mortar firms trying to imitate or otherwise outperform existing e-business companies. The issue of sustaining a competitive advantage over time and the dangers that threaten to erode such advantage are covered in Chapter 6. In particular, this chapter deals with the threats of imitation and disruptive innovations.

In addition to defending their competitive advantage against imitators, companies can also build up new sources of competitive differentiation by developing new e-business innovations, thereby creating new market spaces that hitherto have been uncontested. The value innovation framework, presented in Chapter 7, provides a systematic approach for developing these types of innovations that aim at making the competition irrelevant.

Exhibit 2.3 e-Business strategy formulation entails an internal and an external analysis to identify strengths, weaknesses, opportunities and threats

Key environmental/ industry developments		
	Opportunities	**Threats**
Strengths	• Do we have the strengths to seize possible opportunities?	• Do we have the strength to fend off possible threats?
Weaknesses	• Which opportunities do we miss because of our deficits?	• To which threats do our weaknesses expose us?

Firm characteristics

Chapter 8 presents the value-process framework (VPF) which integrates different perspectives of strategy into a holistic model. The purpose of the VPF is to show how a company's ability to create and capture value is a necessary condition for long-term success.

Following these broad considerations, Chapters 9 to 11 address three strategic issues that are of special relevance for e-business companies. These are: (1) the internal organisation of an e-business venture, (2) its relationships with suppliers, and (3) its relationships with customers and users.

Chapter 9 deals with a firm's internal organisation. The concepts of deconstructing the value chain and unbundling the corporation stemmed an extensive debate among managers and academics as to how integrated a firm should be in the digital age. During the Internet boom years, popular management thinking suggested that firms should focus on their core competence (or core business) and outsource all other value-creating activities to external providers. However, this did not turn out to be a panacea. The main question in this chapter is therefore: 'How should we organise internally our e-business activities?'

Chapter 10 addresses the upstream issue of supply chain management. The main question here is how to set up B2B relationships with external providers. A special focus is placed on different types of electronic B2B transaction platforms and on third-party e-service providers such as IBX, which is discussed in detail in the case studies section of this book.

Over the last couple of years, user-generated content has become a critical success factor of some of the well-known e-business start-up companies such as YouTube,

MySpace, Facebook, openBC and Second Life (the last two start-ups are feature... case studies section of the book). Chapter 11 presents different conceptual frame..., such the 'long tail' and the 'tipping point', which provide insights into how best to leverage the power of user-generated content for creating and capturing value.

Chapter 12 presents some conceptual frameworks that are specific to mobile e-commerce applications. Chapter 13, which is included in the 'Lessons Learned' part of this book, discusses operational issues related to the implementation of an e-business strategy. It also suggests an e-business strategy roadmap that covers the main steps (from vision to alignment) of formulating an e-business strategy.

SUMMARY

- This chapter first stated the main goals of strategy, which focus on overarching decisions that determine the fundamental direction of a company.

- Next, it described the key challenges that companies face when formulating a business strategy. These challenges include (1) the high uncertainty of future developments and (2) contradictory decision criteria that need to be evaluated during the strategy analysis and formulation process.

- Finally, this chapter provided a brief overview of the e-business strategy framework and its main elements, which are strategic analysis, strategy formulation and strategy implementation.

REVIEW QUESTIONS

1 What are the key challenges that companies face during the strategy formulation process?

2 What are the key elements of the e-business strategy framework?

RECOMMENDED KEY READING

- For a more detailed discussion of the SWOT concept, see G. Johnson, K. Scholes and R. Whittington, *Exploring Corporate Strategy*, 7th edition, Prentice Hall, 2005.

- For a discussion of strategies in different types of organisations, see H. Mintzberg, J. Quinn and S. Ghoshal (eds), *The Strategy Process: Concepts, Context and Cases*, 4th edition, Prentice Hall, 1998.

NOTES AND REFERENCES

1 See W. Kirsch, *Wegweiser zur Konstruktion einer evolutionären Theorie der strategischen Führung*, Kirsch, 1997.

CHAPTER 3

External analysis: the impact of the Internet on the macro-environment and on the industry structure of e-business companies

Chapter at a glance

3.1 Examining trends in the macro-environment
- 3.1.1 The political and legal environment
- 3.1.2 The economic environment
- 3.1.3 The social environment
- 3.1.4 The natural environment
- 3.1.5 The technological environment

3.2 Examining industry structure with the five forces framework
- 3.2.1 Industry rivalry
- 3.2.2 Barriers to entry
- 3.2.3 Substitute products
- 3.2.4 Bargaining powers of buyers and suppliers

3.3 Complementing the five forces framework with the co-opetition framework

3.4 Defining industries, segmenting markets and targeting markets in e-business
- 3.4.1 Defining an industry
- 3.4.2 Segmenting markets in an industry
- 3.4.3 Targeting specific markets in an industry

Related case studies

Case study	Primary focus of the case study
11 e-Government	Political macro-environment
12 Online file-sharing	Industry structure
16 Sony BMG	Industry structure
13 StayFriends/openBC	Social environment
17 NTT DoCoMo	Technological environment

Learning outcomes

After completing this chapter, you should be able to:

- Analyse trends in the macro-environment and explain their implications for e-business ventures.

- Understand the value of the five forces industry framework for the analysis of industry attractiveness.

- Explain the key characteristics of the co-opetition framework and show how it expands the five forces industry framework.

- Define industries, segment and target markets for e-business applications.

INTRODUCTION

When an industry with a reputation for difficult economics meets a manager with a reputation for excellence, it is usually the industry that keeps its reputation intact.

Warren Buffet

e-Business ventures, or any ventures for that matter, do not operate in isolation from their environment. Instead, success depends not only on just what a company does by itself but also on the actions of other actors in the industry, such as competitors or suppliers, and on broader environmental developments such as changes in technology or government regulation. While individual companies can typically at least partly shape the industry environment through their competitive behaviour, the broader developments in the macro-environment can hardly be influenced.

To adjust accordingly to environmental changes, companies need to be able to have a clear understanding of important developments in their external environment. At this stage, for e-business companies, technological changes are of critical importance, since, for instance, an increase in available bandwidth for data transmission or new web development techniques (such as Ajax or RSS feeds)[1] open up new possibilities for creating new business models. At the same time, there are also societal changes such as changing demographics and changes in government regulations that potentially have an impact on the sustainability of e-business ventures.

Making sense of this very dynamic environment and acting sensibly is a highly complex task which requires us to filter the multitude of signals to keep track of the really important developments. This task becomes even more challenging due to the wealth of public information that is available through print media and online sites. As a result, there is just as much danger of information overload as of information unavailability.

One important first step is to organise information about new developments in the macro-environment and cluster them in such a way that they will not be overlooked. As a starting point for such a systematic analysis, this chapter first provides a framework for analysing the macro-environment. Second, it discusses Porter's five forces framework for analysing the attractiveness of an industry. It also analyses the impact of the Internet on each force of Porter's framework, i.e. industry rivalry, barriers to entry, threat of substitute products and the bargaining power of buyers and suppliers. Third, this chapter presents the co-opetition framework, which offers an alternative perspective for industry analysis. Finally, it addresses the issues of how to define industries within which to compete and how to segment specific customer groups that a company should target through its e-business offering.

3.1 Examining trends in the macro-environment

The macro-environment takes a broad perspective of the factors that influence a firm's strategy and performance.[2] Evolving trends in the macro-environment can present significant opportunities and threats to a firm's strategy. Therefore, at the outset of any strategy formulation, it is useful to analyse the trends that characterise the macro-environment in its different dimensions: *political, legal, economic, social* and *technological* (see Exhibit 3.1).

Exhibit 3.1 e-Business companies are impacted by their industry and macro-environment

Source: Adapted from H. Hungenberg, *Strategisches Management in Unternehmen*, Gabler, 2006, p. 90.

3.1.1 The political and legal environment

The political and legal environment relates to issues on different organisational levels. At country and industry levels, it includes issues such as taxation, monopoly legislation and environmental laws.

Because of the difficulty of agreeing on cross-border matters, taxation has been a difficult issue in electronic commerce. Yet, because of the boundary-less nature of the Internet, it presents a major issue for governments and a source of opportunity for e-business ventures. For instance, numerous online betting companies have set up their operations on the low-tax Isle of Man, which, in turn, reduces government revenues from gaming in countries such as the USA, where gamblers previously had to pay a gaming tax (see the FT article: 'E-business: The odds lengthen').

Regarding monopoly legislation, throughout the 1990s Microsoft was accused of violating its dominant position in the operating systems market by leveraging it to move into other software markets at the expense of competitors.[3] More recently, Google has been criticised for a similar dominance in the online advertising market.

When Amazon.com entered the German market, it was confronted with the price-fixing regulation, which sets a common price for all new books sold in the country. This made it impossible for Amazon.de to compete on the price dimension with rival bookstores.

Furthermore, in light of peer-to-peer file-sharing networks such as Kazaa or eMule, the Internet has always been criticised for violating copyright laws. Contrary to the interests of the music industry, however, considering the convenience and range of files available, the online file-sharing practice is still highly popular among members of the

Internet community. Similarly, so-called mash-ups provoke further discussion on copyright protection and digital rights management tools.

At the individual level, political and legal debates revolve around the extent to which companies should be allowed to intrude into the private lives of Internet users. This includes topics such as the placement of cookies[4] and aggressive marketing via spam mails.[5]

FT

E-business: The odds lengthen

The US crackdown on online gaming has been shattering for the fast-growing sector, with companies plunging in value because of fears that they could no longer do business in the lucrative market. Some fallout has settled on the Isle of Man, one of a number of jurisdictions to make an explicit effort to attract e-gaming companies and others from the world of e-business.

E-gaming holds clear appeal to promoters of business and growth on the island. It has been one of the most lucrative and fast-growing of online opportunities, with an ability to generate high-quality jobs as well as extra business for the island's financial and professional community. Hosting gaming websites was also seen as a way of significantly increasing traffic over the fiber optic links to the UK mainland, thereby generating a critical mass needed for the island to strike better-priced deals for the use of those links. The idea was that cheaper telecommunications, allied to the low-tax environment and other attractions, would generate more e-business from other sectors in a virtuous circle of development.

The US attack on online gaming, via legislation aimed at preventing companies from processing transactions, has had a chilling effect on the sector; although the final status of online gaming in the US will not be clear until regulations to accompany the recent legislation are developed over the next nine months.

It has naturally left some analyses of the Isle of Man's opportunities open to question. But Bill Mummery, head of e-gaming development at the island's department of trade and industry, insists not all bets are off. In fact, he says, the 'pro-position' of the Isle of Man has 'just got stronger'. 'If you are going to manage your way through the hiatus, and be seen as an acquirer and consolidator, the need to get yourself into a premier jurisdiction just got greater,' Mr Mummery says. 'Of course, there is going to be some realignment. There will be some major winners in the sector who see opportunities arising out of the ashes and can navigate their way through.'

The island is convinced that it ranks among the best quality jurisdictions, which are highly competitive in trying to secure the big names of the industry. The stable of resident companies includes: Playtech and Microgaming, two software developers; Neteller, one of the main payment processors; and PokerStars, a gaming site. Mr Mummery was previously a director at Betinternet.com, which is also based on the island and floated on Aim in 2000. Many of these and other companies have said they will refocus their businesses away from the US, and will seek more opportunities in Europe and Asia.

The UK is shortly to publish its 'white list' of non-EU jurisdictions whose companies will be allowed to market and promote gaming in the UK. There is a feeling within the industry that the Isle of Man will be included, along with Alderney, and that such a move will help companies from 'white list' jurisdictions to do business throughout the EU.

Mr Mummery believes companies from Asia already see the Isle of Man as a good jurisdiction from which to enter the EU market, citing interest from Singaporean and Japanese companies in establishing operations on the island. 'Clearly, the sector is at a major crossroads,' says Mr Mummery. 'But when the history of e-gaming is looked at three to five years from now, it will be seen as determining a significant change in strategic direction to the industry, away from a reliance on North America.'

This analysis of the Isle of Man's continuing opportunities does not convince everyone. One influential voice that wishes to remain anonymous says the island should rethink its e-gaming strategy rather than risk conflict with the US. 'As an island, we can't afford to be seen to be provoking the US. You do not want to be on their enforcement radar.'

Source: Adapted from J. Wilson, 'E-business: The odds lengthen', FT.com, 14 November 2006.

3.1.2 The economic environment

The economic environment refers to broader economic developments within the context of a country, a region or globally. Important factors in the economic environment are interest and exchange rates, evolution of stock markets and, more generally, economic growth rates. The favourable economic environment of the 1990s and the resulting cheap availability of capital contributed strongly to the rapid rise of Internet companies.

This rise came to an abrupt halt with the burst of the dotcom bubble in March 2000 and the subsequent demise of a large number of Internet start-ups. The launches of some Internet start-ups such as the online fashion retailer boo.com (see FT article 'Burning money at Boo: The founders of the infamous Internet company were fools rather than knaves') or mondus.com, which is discussed in the case studies section of the book, were feasible only because capital was accessible so easily at the time. However, during the ensuing consolidation phase, which was characterised by depressed stock markets and cautious venture capitalists, it became much more difficult to gain access to capital, even if the underlying business idea was sound.

In the more recent past, as e-business companies have shown their ability to operate profitably, investors have once again started to fund young and innovative start-ups. In contrast to the previous heydays of the Internet, however, investors seem nowadays to be more reasonable and driven by promising business models. In addition to venture capital companies, there are today established Internet companies that are willing to invest in or acquire start-ups and integrate them into their existing business portfolio. The $3.1 billion acquisition of DoubleClick by Google or the $4.1 billion purchase of the VoIP[6] telephone service provider Skype by eBay are prime examples of this newly found confidence.

3.1.3 The social environment

The social environment considers factors such as population demographics, income distribution between different sectors of society, social mobility of people, and differing attitudes to work and leisure. Social developments were the main driver behind the development of numerous e-commerce applications. For instance, if, due to their careers, members of a developed society increasingly become cash rich but time poor, then businesses that address this specific customer segment can create substantial benefit. The online retailer Tesco.com, for example, primarily targets customers who do not have the time or the desire to shop systematically in a physical grocery store.

Other important dimensions of the social environment that impact on the development and use of the Internet are online usage patterns. These are measured by the percentage of the population using e-mail or the web for information or transaction purposes. These types of measurements provide good indications of the evolution of the population towards forming an information society and establishing an e-habit. An additional indicator of changes in the social environment is the degree of usage of online communities, such as Second Life, where Internet users come together in a virtual world (for a more detailed description of Second Life, see the FT article 'Get a second life' and the case study in the case studies section of this book).

The advent of social networking sites such as MySpace or Facebook shows, along with their popularity, that the Internet has become a place for people to interact and share experiences. Unsolicited self-presentation and open communication through social networking sites or weblogs underline the democratisation of the web and indicate an important paradigm shift in society, especially among teenagers and youngsters (for a more detailed discussion of this issue, see Chapter 11).

FT

Get a second life

In 1841, the British journalist Charles Mackay enjoyed quite a hit with his book *Extraordinary Popular Delusions and The Madness of Crowds*, a history of popular folly that debunked everything from witch-hunts to the South Sea Bubble. More recently, in 2004, the American journalist James Surowiecki won a large audience for his book The Wisdom of Crowds, an Internet-fuelled argument about collective intelligence. Somewhere between these two opposing poles lies an almost mythical nirvana, rich in vegetation and nightlife, which calls itself Second Life.

If you haven't heard about it yet, you should be getting a little nervous. Surely someone has told you that forward-thinking people and companies of all kinds are heading there in droves. Or maybe you've read a feature article in a paper or magazine, in which a journalist grabs your attention by claiming they've been lap-dancing, flying around by waving their arms, or boogieing the night away in the company of a colourfully dressed minotaur, only to reveal – a little disappointingly – that they've been doing all this in a virtual universe only accessible on a computer.

There is no doubt that Second Life is the new, new thing. The most visually impressive of the new generation of social-networking sites that are fuelling a resurgence of commercial interest in the web, it has suddenly and brazenly tipped its way

into the popular imagination. Second Life is, according to its website, 'a 3-D virtual world entirely built and owned by its residents' and a 'vast digital continent, teeming with people, entertainment, experiences and opportunity'.

New members are invited to create an avatar, or visual persona, which can be as weird or wonderful as their imagination allows. They then guide that avatar through three-dimensional landscapes in which they can chat – via a keyboard and speech-bubbles – to other avatars, purchase virtual land and teleport themselves anywhere they want to go. The result, according to one 'travel guide' to Second Life, is 'a world of endless reinvention where you can change your shape, your sex, even your species as easily as you might slip into a pair of shoes back home.'

Since opening three years ago, Second Life has grown with ever-increasing vigour. On the day I joined, Wednesday October 18, it claimed its millionth inhabitant. Only two weeks later, it had added another 200,000. All this activity is the brainchild of Philip Rosedale, a 28-year-old Internet entrepreneur who was inspired to create a virtual universe by Neal Stephenson's sci-fi novel Snow Crash. The book depicts a future in which much of people's time is spent in a 'metaverse' – or metaphysical universe – which Stephenson sees as the highly sophisticated successor to the Internet

→

and in which people communicate via their avatars, as on Second Life.

Rosedale and his San Francisco-based company Linden Lab govern Second Life in the sense that they 'rent' land to new inhabitants (what began as only 64 acres now covers 20,000) and enforce a few simple ground rules. Other than that, their approach is laissez faire in the extreme. On a single day in Second Life, you can buy virtual clothes, fly a virtual plane, or even enjoy virtual sexual liaisons in marked areas. Some have likened it to a virtual version of the board game Monopoly, playing with millions of strangers. Don't make the mistake, however, of telling a Second Life aficionado that this is all a game. There is, they point out, no over-riding objective or goal. It is much more life-like than that.

But if Second Life is only an animated version of real life, what is it all for? The question is pertinent because, at least for those of us of a non-technical disposition, it is frustrating to work. Its interface can be intimidating for the uninitiated, and the maps that govern its virtual universe are difficult to read. It took me a full two weeks to learn how to adjust properly to Second Life, and then only with the help of a stranger I bumped into on the virtual street.

Though it is difficult to tell what Second Lifers do in their real lives – they are often cagey about personal details – the people I met seemed to be young professionals with vivid imaginations acting out their fantasies. One man I encountered, whose strapping avatar had the physique of a weightlifter, turned out to be a 27-year-old microbial ecologist from Liverpool. The value of Second Life, he told me, was that it offered a space 'in which you can utterly control every aspect of your second life'. When I wondered aloud about the difference between his Second Life character and the real him, he got a little shirty. 'What do you mean?,' he said. 'The character ... he's really me. It would take an awful lot of effort to maintain a full extra persona.' In almost the next breath, he happened to mention that he had just signed up to be a dancer at a Second Life strip club for women. 'It would take an awful lot of alcohol to wear a G-string in public in reality,' he admitted, 'but I don't mind so much when my nipples are pixels.'

Another interpretation of Second Life is that it is a virtual incubator for innovation and entrepreneurship. Second Life, its PR boasts, 'is a fully integrated economy architected to reward risk, innovation and craftsmanship'. The economy has its own currency, Linden dollars, which can be bought and sold on LindeX, the official Second Life currency exchange, for real currency. (Exchange rates fluctuate, but remain relatively stable at 250 Linden Dollars to the US Dollar.) Trade works on the usual principle of supply and demand. Inhabitants can build anything they please (a house, speedboat, nightclub) with Second Life software tools, and they can then sell these goods on to other members for an agreed price. Building something worth having takes a good deal of practice (though lessons are offered for free by volunteers and Linden Lab staff) but you retain the rights to your digital creations.

If you have neither the time nor the patience to build anything, you can simply buy what you need from other residents. According to Linden Lab, thousands of Second Life residents are making at least part of their income from their virtual businesses – selling virtual land, clothes, jewellery, weaponry, or even sex. Innovations are plentiful, if eccentric – one Second Lifer, for example, is reported to have manufactured virtual glasses that enable players who don't speak the same language to communicate. Another entrepreneur earns hundreds of thousands of dollars a year as a real-estate mogul.

Thanks to a mutiny among some of Second Life's first inhabitants (a virtual equivalent of the Boston Tea Party, by some fevered accounts), an early idea to tax residents on the objects they made was overturned. As a tax-free free-trade area with minimal regulations, Second Life has more in common with a kind of spirited frontier capitalism than it does with the collaborative, everything-for-free ethic of sites such as Wikipedia. Perhaps as a result, businesses of all kinds are falling over each other to raise their institutional flag on its terrain. For companies keen to show that they are on the futurological ball, a home on Second Life is a must. Everyone from Coca-Cola to Microsoft, Intel to Adidas, has moved in – Adidas, for example, has geared its presence around a marketing campaign to show off one of its new products.

The demographics are appealing for marketers: there are, according to Linden Lab, as many women as men on Second Life and the average age is 32. Toyota is selling virtual cars; IBM, which has plans for its own 3-D intranet, has paid one of its software engineers to hang out there and ad agency Leo Burnett is building an 'Ideas Hub' where its global staff can meet and interact. In October, Sun Microsystems even hosted a 'virtual news conference' in Second Life to flag up its new gaming strategy.

But it is not just money that people are looking for in Second Life; virtual talent is increasingly being hunted too. Greene & Heaton, the London-based agent for the likes of P.D. James and Michael Frayn, claimed at the end of October to be the first literary agency to open an office in Second Life. I tracked down that virtual office and its manager Will Francis, to ask whether business was trickling in. In a meeting in his swanky new workplace, Francis was big enough to admit that much corporate interest in Second Life is no more than a marketing gimmick. He pointed out, however, that it is very difficult to find gifted young writers simply by scanning newspapers and magazines, and that some of the writers' groups on Second Life might throw up fresh sources of talent.

Some old names are already doing the rounds – Kurt Vonnegut visited Second Life to promote his new book and in August veteran rockers Duran Duran announced their intention to create a virtual island in order to perform live concerts. Politicians, too, are getting in on the act; Mark Warner, the former governor of Virginia, who briefly thought he might be in with a chance of securing the Democratic Presidential nomination in 2008, held a question-and-answer session there. Second Life also now has its first tabloid newspaper to sate the virtual population's appetite for gossip, launched a few weeks ago by German publisher Axel Springer.

In the middle of October, the news organisation Reuters loudly announced that it had assigned a full-time beat reporter to Second Life. Adam Reuters, real name Adam Pasick, spends his day writing business and finance stories about goings-on there. In real life he is based in London's Canary Wharf; in Second Life, where I caught up with him for a chat, he is based in a swish office which Reuters purchased on his behalf. The best things to get into in Second Life, Pasick tells me, are real estate, banking and retail. Stories he has broken include one which, at the end of October, disclosed that Linden Lab tipped off a group of long-time inhabitants before it announced higher fees for private islands, leaving the company

vulnerable to the allegation that it had perpetrated a kind of insider trading. It subsequently and swiftly admitted its mistake. Pasick has also been tracking political developments; a guerrilla movement now stalks Second Life, he told me, called the Second Life Liberation Army, which is agitating in favour of greater democratic representation for SL inhabitants.

Second Life is not the only virtual universe to have emerged on the web in the past five years – other examples include Habbo Hotel and Entropia Universe. It is not even the biggest; it is dwarfed, for example, by World of Warcraft, which boasts 6.5 million members. Edward Castronova, an online gamester turned associate professor at Indiana University, calls these alternative universes synthetic worlds. In his book of the same title, he argues that these alternative universes have grown so powerful and their architecture so intricate that they are now in direct competition with our daily lives. As many of us begin to spend as much time in these make-believe worlds as the real one, Castronova sees the relationship between real and synthetic worlds becoming increasingly blurred, leading to clashes between the two.

Governments are beginning to recognise this. The fact that property is virtual, for example, has not been a bar to court cases being fought over its theft – earlier this year an American lawyer and virtual real-estate speculator on Second Life filed a lawsuit against Linden Lab for confiscating some of his virtual property. Neither does the absence of virtual taxation mean that there is no taxation to be paid in the real world. People who take cash out of virtual economies are already required to report their incomes to the Internal Revenue Service in America.

In the middle of October, a US Congressional Committee confirmed that it was looking into the possibility of how better to levy taxes on the virtual income from economies like that of Second Life. At the end of that month, the Australian Tax Office issued a stark warning to players in online games such as Second Life that if their virtual fortunes could be converted into real money, they needed to declare it in their tax returns. In a recent article, the writer Steven Johnson (author of the book Everything Bad is Good for You) argues that a gravitational pull may draw all these virtual universes together, and that common standards will emerge to enable their players to jump seamlessly from one to another. The result will be an online experience of truly global proportions and a synthetic world with vast financial clout.

But what will we do there? If digital utopias such as Second Life are supposed to tip us a few hints about how their inhabitants would like to live in everyday life, it is telling that much of it seems to be fuelled by illicit virtual sex. Cajoled by my editor to experiment with the more libidinous side of Second Life and unable to get lucky while ambling around the place, I manfully walked my avatar into a sleazy-looking club and attempted to strike up a conversation with two scantily clad women.

To my surprise, my opening gambit – 'You two ladies need any company?' – met with success. 'Looking good for a newbie,' leather-clad Laura typed, but it rapidly became apparent that she and her suspender-wearing friend Shaylah were in business too. Like the microbial ecologist I had met several days earlier, these were erotic dancers in search of tips. Claiming to be one of those punters who likes to talk, I asked both Laura and Shaylah who they were in real life. Shaylah told me that she was a Texan while Laura owned up to being a hairdresser from Shropshire.

When I asked what they liked about Second Life, Laura mentioned the shops and Shaylah told me that it was possible to 'meet someone and fall in love'. Given the camaraderie that had developed between us and my looming deadline, I decided to ask if either of them wanted to have sex with me. Laura immediately offered to 'give me the full works' in return for L$1,200 upfront – about $5 in real money. Things quickly came unstuck. For one thing, I had neglected to buy any virtual genitalia, which came as a disappointment to Laura when I took off my pants.

For all its faults, Second Life does succeed in pushing the Internet experience into three garish dimensions, and makes most previous attempts to build an alternative universe on the web look like black-and-white television. But for all the hype that surrounds it, the stampede among the media and the business worlds to kneel at its altar is a little puzzling.

Only about half of Second Life's listed inhabitants actually use it more than a few times and only 10,000 Second Lifers are online at any one time. Many have likened Second Life as a digital successor to the utopian ambitions of California's 1960s hippies, but there is precious little utopian ambition about the place. Perhaps this is only fitting. Stephenson's Snow Crash is laced with satire and black humour, and the future it imagines is one in which America's economy and government have collapsed and its citizens have retreated into a lonely alternative universe in which they do little but hang around.

The microbial ecologist turned stripper I met there, though a huge fan of the Second Life, joked that most of it was about 'sex and shopping'. As easy as it is to make a little money out of Second Life, it seems more difficult to take friends out of the place. He told me that he had made many new contacts here, but admitted that he had not spoken to any of those people outside of the Second Life environment.

If Second Life and synthetic worlds like it really are to be our lab for experimenting with the future, they have a long way to go. At its worst, I found the experience of being in Second Life – endlessly hanging out, walking around looking in vain for something worth doing, trying rather awkwardly to make conversation with total strangers and computer geeks – a little soporific.

With its illicit sex, endless boutiques and long stretches of boredom, Second Life reminded me less of any utopian or dystopian vision and more of how people used to think of life in the suburbs – full of secrets and intrigue punctuated by fitful attempts among strangers to get to know one another. Second Life is still a work in progress, and will perhaps blossom. In the meantime, and before you invest too heavily in a second life, my advice is to make sure you've exhausted the possibilities of the first.

Second life for beginners

Getting started

Second Life is a three-dimensional online world. To enter it, you first sign up on the website (www.secondlife.com) and create a username, choosing a basic look for your avatar (for example, Girl Next Door) which can be refined later. Second Life provides software tools (much like Photoshop) to tweak anything from the tip of your nose to the tint of your skin. More advanced bodily requirements, such as genitalia, have to be purchased. Basic membership is free, but you can also pay for premium levels of membership that give you a financial allowance and property rights.

Getting around

Adventures in Second Life can be conducted by either walking, flying or teleporting your avatar, using videogame-style graphics and the computer mouse and cursors. At any time there will be dozens of events in Second Life where you can party, attend fashion shows and art openings, or just play around and chat.

A Second Life map shows you different areas of activity, or you can view upcoming events on the search page. To talk to other Second Lifers, you press a 'Chat' button and communicate as you would with instant Internet messaging. It will not be clear if the person has chosen an avatar faithful to their real-life appearance and profession – unless you ask probing questions.

Money matters

Second Life has its own internal currency, Linden dollars. They can easily be bought or sold on LindeX (Second Life's official currency exchange), or other third-party sites, for real currency. The current rate is about 250 Linden dollars (L$) to the US dollar.

Getting settled

Owning a plot of land is simple and cheap – it allows you to build, display, and store your virtual creations, as well as to host events and businesses. If you want to earn your keep you could get a job – occupations already include tattooist, casino operator, private detective and pet manufacturer. Retail businesses of all kinds are thriving on Second Life, selling everything from virtual clothes to virtual weapons. Your business plan need not be limited to your Second Life; at least in theory, for example, you could prototype a fashion line there, and then – having raised some money from impressed investors – go on to make a real-world version.

Source: Adapted from J. Harkin, 'Get a second life', FT.com, 18 November 2006.

3.1.4 The natural environment

In the environmental sphere, governments in many countries, such as Spain and Britain, have zoning laws which make it difficult, if not impossible, for grocery retailers to set up new hypermarket stores. Thus, some retailers in these countries thought of the Internet and online sales as a possible alternative for business growth.

Global warming has also had an impact on the activities of e-business companies. Tesco.com, for instance, has started to react by running a fleet of battery-powered home delivery vans (see the Blog Box below).

BLOG BOX

First zero-emission home delivery vans hit the roads in Shrewsbury

The first set of Tesco.com zero-emission vans have been launched today at the brand new Tesco Extra environmental store in Shrewsbury. Tesco.com is to be the first company in the UK to run a fleet of battery powered, zero-emission home delivery vans. Each zero-emission van will save 21 tonnes of CO2 per year – the equivalent of driving 51,000 miles in a car. This saving is in addition to the 6,000 car journeys that an average dotcom van takes off the road each year.

Laura Wade-Gery, CEO of Tesco.com, comments: 'Tesco has made a commitment to significantly reduce CO_2 emission throughout the business, and we're very proud to be the first company to invest in this new van technology, helping to create a low-carbon society. The carbon neutral vans we have ordered for the dotcom business are both quiet and pollution free – a double benefit for urban environments.'

The vans, supplied by Coventry based company Modec, have the same carrying capacity as a standard Tesco.com van, cover a range of over 100 miles before they need recharging and are governed at a maximum speed of 50 mph. In addition each van is fitted with eutectic refrigeration panels which are filled with a refrigerant gas and brine, and re-charged over night to retain their low temperature throughout the day. The panels are much less likely to leak HFC gas than conventional fridges used in delivery vans.

Jamie Borwick, Chairman Modec, said: 'We're delighted to be supplying Tesco with Modec zero-emission home delivery vans. When we first set up the company, our mission was to build an exceptional commercial vehicle that happens to be environmentally friendly. By using the latest modern technology, the Modec team has developed a zero-emission vehicle that is able to store up to 5 times more energy and is suitable for mainstream users too.'

The new environmental store in Shrewsbury, which has created 100 new jobs for the local community, has been designed to reduce its energy consumption by at least 40% when compared to a store of a similar size and will feature a whole host of energy saving systems. The store frame and roof are made from renewable timber instead of steel and also boasts innovative heating and cooling systems.

Other technology in the environmental store includes a cold air retrieval system, which extracts and pumps the excess cold air generated by the refrigeration into other areas of the store and reduces the need for air conditioning by recycling the already cooled air. There are also boreholes underground so that natural heat can be used to heat water and also aid cooling in the summer.

In the roof of both the store and petrol filling station, roof lights have been used to reduce artificial lighting. The store will feature fully dimmable controls to reduce artificial lighting during daylight hours. The petrol filling station will also boast 'stage 2 vapour recovery' meaning fuel vapour will be recovered at the nozzle to reduce the amount escaping into the atmosphere.

Special light collecting cells will feature on the side of the store roof to generate electrical power. The store foyer has also been designed to help air seal and energy consumption with internal signage and shopfitting using timber from sustainable sources instead of the traditional laminates. And rainwater will be harvested and used to flush toilets and also to recycle into the car wash.

To support the commitment to significantly reduce CO_2 emissions throughout Tesco, plans have been put in place at the Shrewsbury store to encourage staff and customers to cut their car emissions. Staff showers and additional bike racks have been built to encourage more staff to cycle to work. And information on bus routes, walking and cycle routes are also displayed in the store to encourage staff and customers to use alternative environmentally-friendly forms of transport.

Source: Tesco.com website, 24 April 2007.

3.1.5 The technological environment

For e-business ventures, the technological environment is of significant importance. Technological innovations (such as the Internet or wireless devices) led to the emergence of new market opportunities and business models. During the early years of the Internet, important drivers of technological developments were standards and languages such as the TCP/IP (Transmission Control Protocol/Internet Protocol), HTTP (Hypertext Transfer Protocol), HTML (Hypertext Mark-up Language) and XML (Extended Mark-up Language).[7] More recently, new web development techniques such as Ajax or RSS feeds open up new possibilities for keeping better track of content updates and for speeding up the web experience.

The actual network infrastructure of the Internet has also changed dramatically over the last few years. The spread of broadband Internet connections led to an increasing number of people spending more time online and allowed for richer content to be created and viewed, in turn making it easier for new start-ups to create new service sites based around user-generated content.

After most of the technological standards have become more commonplace in wireline e-business applications, much attention has been paid to the evolution of new technology standards for wireless devices. This includes, for instance, the security features for mobile phones, an issue that is discussed in the paybox.net case studies (included in the case studies section of this book). The case study on NTT DoCoMo (also included in this book) illustrates how a company can establish new technological standards in the mobile e-commerce industry, as happened with the i-Mode system described in the case study.

The factors mentioned within the five dimensions above should serve only as a starting point for a careful analysis of the macro-environment. Depending on the industry and country at hand, the importance of these dimensions will obviously differ. Needless to say, a comprehensive understanding of the macro-environment is an essential prerequisite for the formulation of a sound e-business strategy.

3.2 Examining industry structure with the five forces framework

What does the profitability of any given firm depend on? First, a firm needs to be able to create higher value than its rivals. Second, it also needs to be able to capture the value that it creates in the form of prices that exceed its costs. If a firm can charge high prices for its products or services, then it captures large parts of the value it creates. If, on the other hand, prices are driven down by competition, then consumers will capture most of the value. (For a detailed discussion of value creation and value capturing, see Chapter 8.)

This highlights the fact that profitability depends not only on the internal competencies and activities of an e-business company, which we shall discuss in detail in Chapter 4, but also on its surroundings, i.e. the industry in which it competes. In this context, an industry is defined as a group of firms that produce products or provide services that are close substitutes for each other.[8]

As an example, let us consider the personal computer (PC) industry. During the past few decades, this industry has created immense value for consumers, in the form of increased capabilities of both desktops and laptops. While performance has also increased over the years, prices have not risen; instead, they have actually decreased significantly over time, thereby placing heavy constraints on the profitability of most computer manufacturers. In contrast, there are industries such as software development where a firm

Exhibit 3.2 Five forces influence the attractiveness of an industry

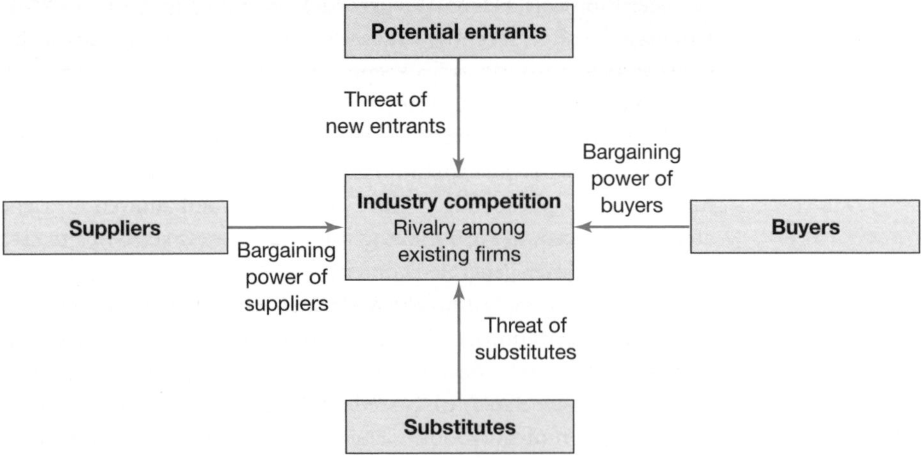

Source: Adapted with the permission of The Free Press, a Division of Simon & Schuster Adult Publishing Group, from COMPETITIVE STRATEGY: Techniques for Analyzing Industries and Competitors by Michael E. Porter. Copyright © 1980, 1998 by The Free Press. All rights reserved.

such as Microsoft was able to capture large parts of the value created (e.g. for computer operating systems), thus turning it into one of the most profitable companies in the world. This stark contrast between industries raises the question as to what determines the ability of a company to capture value.

Porter proposes a five forces framework, which outlines the main factors determining a firm's ability to capture the value it creates.[9] In essence, this ability is determined largely by the attractiveness of the industry in which a firm competes. Obviously, the advent of the Internet has profoundly affected the structure of many industries. Yet there are no general conclusions regarding how the Internet affects the structure of different industries; instead, it is necessary to analyse each industry individually.[10]

The five forces shown in Exhibits 3.2 and 3.3 provide a guiding framework for understanding the sustainability of profits against competition and bargaining power. The five structural features that determine industry attractiveness are: (1) *industry rivalry*, (2) *barriers to entry*, (3) *substitute products*, (4) *bargaining power of buyers*, and (5) *bargaining power of suppliers*.

3.2.1 Industry rivalry

Industry rivalry occurs when firms within an industry feel the pressure or the opportunity to enhance their existing market position. High intensity of rivalry within an industry results from the following structural factors:

- *Large number of competitors*. If there are numerous competitors in a given industry or business sector, then individual firms may want to make a competitive move, e.g. by lowering prices. Furthermore, the Internet has reduced the importance of geographic boundaries, which traditionally limited the number of competitors within a region. For instance, the business-to-business (B2B) e-marketplace IBX (featured in the case studies section of the book) quickly expanded outside of its home country (Sweden) into other Scandinavian and Nordic countries and eventually to Germany and France. Since competitors followed the same strategy, competition became more intense.

- *High fixed costs.* High fixed costs (such as extensive physical infrastructure) create strong pressure to fill capacity, even at the expense of having to cut prices. Consider bricks-and-mortar retail stores, which have specific capacities that must be utilised. To create the necessary turnover, retailers often find themselves in highly competitive price wars. Through the Internet, the ratio between fixed and variable costs shifts more towards fixed costs. Developing software has initially high costs, but rolling it out across different markets is comparatively cheap. Thus, industry rivalry tends to increase because e-business ventures want to optimise the use of their capacity.

- *High strategic relevance.* Rivalry increases when firms have a strategic stake to succeed in a given industry. One of the most prominent examples is Microsoft's decision in 1996 to design all its new products for Internet-based computing. This decision led to the browser competition between Netscape's Navigator, the incumbent browser software, and Microsoft's Internet Explorer, a competition that Microsoft was determined to win. In order to beat Netscape, Microsoft offered for free the web server software (which Netscape sold for $1,000) and put 800 people to work on an upgraded version of Explorer.[11] Ultimately, Explorer pushed most competing products out of the market and became the dominant Internet browser worldwide. However, with the rise of Mozilla's Firefox browser, which as of summer 2006 had a global market share of roughly 14%, Microsoft's dominant position might be challenged once again.

- *Little differentiation between products.* Rivalry also increases when there is little differentiation among products, which then become more like commodities. This is the case, for instance, in the computer-chip industry, where profits are low compared with the value created.

- *Low growth rate of the industry.* Intensity of rivalry also depends on the growth rate of a given industry. Fast-growth industries can accommodate a larger number of providers since, as the overall size of the market expands, each competitor gets its market share. In slow-growth industries, rivalry tends to be intense since growth can be achieved only at the expense of some competitors.

- *Excess capacity.* When the Internet became an online platform for commercial use, scores of start-up companies in different industries embraced it, which resulted in highly intense competition. Venture capitalists and stock markets provided cheap capital, which led to an over-investment in Internet start-ups, thereby creating overcapacity.

However, companies need not always be rivals and just that. As explained in Section 3.3, some competitors co-operate with each other, hence the term 'co-opetition'.

3.2.2 Barriers to entry

Barriers to entry determine the threat of new competitors entering the market of a specific industry. New entrants, bringing additional capacity and the desire to gain market share, have two negative effects on the attractiveness of an industry. First, new entrants take away market share from existing incumbent companies. Second, they bid down prices, which in turn reduces the profitability of incumbents. Consequently, the profitability of any given industry tends to decrease as barriers to entry are lowered, and vice versa. The impact of the Internet on barriers to entry, however, has been more ambivalent than initially assumed, when it was commonly thought that the Internet would wipe out most barriers to entry. In general, high barriers to entry result mainly from the following factors:

■ *High fixed costs* deter many potential entrants because they do not have the required capital and/or the willingness to invest large amounts of money in a risky market entry. While it was necessary in the past to set up an extensive bricks-and-mortar infrastructure to reach out to a large number of customers, the Internet has reduced this requirement. This is especially true for digital goods, which can even be distributed online while the retailing, for example, of music CDs used to take place fully through physical outlets.

The rise of the online peer-to-peer file-sharing systems, such as Napster, illustrates how a single person (Shawn Fanning in this case) with an ingenious idea can threaten a whole industry, with its elaborate and high fixed-cost physical distribution network. Through the Napster platform, individual Internet users were able to exchange music files of their favourite songs, which undermined the traditional business model of the music record industry. Subsequently, music companies attempted to raise barriers to entry again by declaring file-sharing services illegal, yet it is clear that the Internet has profoundly changed the way music gets distributed (for a more detailed account of how the Internet has caused a paradigm shift in the music industry, see the case study in this book on online file-sharing). The pressure on music companies that rely on a physical distribution infrastructure has become so strong that some of them – Bertelsmann's BMG and Sony – merged their music divisions in December 2003.[12] In contrast, the computer manufacturer Apple recognised that through online distribution, the barriers for entry had been reduced substantially and that the Internet would also be a viable channel to distribute music commercially. It successfully developed the iTunes online music store, which has become the most successful format for selling music online.

In industries that involve the distribution of physical goods or require a high level of personal interaction, the impact of the Internet on barriers to entry is more ambiguous. Amazon.com, for instance, initially thought that it could focus solely on the customer interaction aspects of its business and outsource to external providers all the logistics and distribution activities, which would have required substantial investment. However, Amazon.com soon found out that in order to guarantee a high level of reliability, it had to operate its own warehouses and distribution centres, which in turn increased the required capital investment. Set-up costs for a warehouse averaged $50 million and operating costs were also significant. In order to finance these infrastructure investments, Amazon.com was forced to issue more than $2 billion in bonds.[13]

Similarly, in banking, several direct banks initially thought that they could acquire and service customers solely through online channels. The case study of Nordea Bank, however, illustrates that an extensive branch network can be crucial for the acquisition of online customers and the selling of more complex financial products. As a result, such physical assets created effective barriers to entry for new online competitors.

■ *Trust and brand loyalty* are essential for customer acquisition and retention. Bricks-and-mortar companies were able to launch their online activities more easily than Internet 'pure-play' ventures, since they already possessed a respected brand and consumers trusted them. Pure online businesses, on the other hand, have to invest heavily in marketing activities to build up their brand. Building trust is even more difficult for a pure online business since, in case of problems, customers do not have a nearby physical branch that they can go to or a customer adviser with whom they can interact face to face. Companies such as Spreadshirt or openBC, which are featured in the case studies section of the book, leverage the trustworthiness of their existing users to acquire new customers.

■ *A steep learning curve* allows a firm to reduce its cost structure quickly or to find ways to create more customer benefits. Any competitor that wants to move into an industry needs to accept low returns while it goes through the same learning experience as incumbents. Otherwise, it has to find ways to make the incumbents' learning experience obsolete by offering a new way of running the business. (See Chapter 7 on how to create new market spaces.) Amazon.com's early start in online book retailing helped the company to stay ahead of its competitors, such as BOL, the online book retailer of Bertelsmann. The latter was never able to catch up with Amazon.com and ultimately withdrew from the online book retailing business.

■ *High switching costs and strong network effects* help an incumbent to keep its customers, even if a new entrant offers a higher value. Think about the retail banking industry. If customers want to switch from one bank to another, they have to change all their automated bill payment procedures to the new bank account, and also inform relevant companies and individuals about the change. The effort associated with doing so could be an effective deterrent for many customers to move to another bank even though the latter offers better value. In the Internet context, the so-called 'stickiness' of a website refers to the switching costs involved with moving from one Internet site to the next. High stickiness makes it unlikely that a user will move from one website to another one. Similarly, strong network effects also tend to increase barriers to entry.

eBay, for instance, has created strong barriers to entry for potential competitors through the large customer base it has created over the past few years. For individual customers, it makes sense to switch to a new provider only if they know that all or at least most other current users would make a similar switch as well. Only then would they be able to enjoy the same type of market liquidity as they did before. Similarly, through the creation of strong network effects, social networking sites such as openBC have established a leading market position. Once users have built up a significant number of contacts and are active in different interest groups on openBC, it is unlikely that they will switch to another platform unless their contacts migrate with them.

■ *Strong intellectual property protection* is essential for firms that sell products with high development costs but low reproduction costs. This is the case with digital goods such as music, video and software. When intellectual property rights are not enforced rigidly, barriers for new (albeit illegal) entrants are lowered, thus allowing them to push cheap, pirated copies onto the market. Furthermore, without strong intellectual property protection, it will be increasingly difficult in the future to entice authors or artists to write and compose, since they will not be compensated adequately.

3.2.3 Substitute products

The intensity of pressure from substitute products depends on the availability of similar products that serve essentially the same or a similar purpose as the products from within the industry. As the availability and quality of substitute products increase, so profits generated within the industry tend to decrease. This is due to the fact that substitutes place a ceiling on prices that firms within the industry can charge for their products. The Internet has helped to increase the pressure from substitute products, as it tends to increase the variety of products available to customers.

For instance, online music-sharing has evolved so quickly that it has become a formidable substitute for physical music CDs, thereby threatening the traditional music industry in its foundations. In the software arena, Microsoft, the dominant producer of software for desktop PCs, is facing new substitutes in the form of mobile devices that increasingly provide many of the same functionalities as traditional PCs. However, the software for these products is not primarily Microsoft based.[14] Similarly, Google has developed a free package of online applications, including calendar, e-mail, word processing and spreadsheet functionalities, that operate as a substitute for Microsoft's high-end Office software package. (The threat of substitution resulting from disruptive innovations is discussed in more detail in Chapter 6.)

3.2.4 Bargaining powers of buyers and suppliers

The bargaining powers of buyers and suppliers are two sides of the same coin; this is why we discuss them jointly. The bargaining power of buyers tends to be high (and that of suppliers low) if the industry displays the following characteristics:

- *High concentration of buyers*, which allows them to leverage their purchasing power through pooling. One important feature of many B2B e-marketplaces – such as IBX, discussed in the case studies section of the book – is the aggregation of buyers' orders. This helps them to achieve better terms from suppliers than they could obtain individually.

- *Strong fragmentation of suppliers*, which makes it difficult to establish a joint approach to pricing. In the PC industry, many producers are constantly trying to gain market share at the expense of other competitors by undercutting each other's prices. This, in turn, undermines the pricing power of the whole industry.

- *A high degree of market transparency*, which allows buyers easily to compare offers between different suppliers. Today, advanced search tools available on the Internet allow customers to choose from a larger pool of suppliers and to compare prices instantaneously, thus making it easier for them to find the best deal. This is particularly the case for highly standardised products that can be easily compared using search engines such as **www.kelkoo.com** or **www.pricerunner.com**.

- *Products are increasingly becoming commodities*, resulting in little or no differentiation between different providers. The pricing of commodity products that do not require extensive purchasing advice or after-sales service is especially affected by a higher degree of market transparency, since customers can then safely choose the lowest price provider.

- *Low switching costs and weak network effect*, which make it easy for buyers to change suppliers.

Conversely, the bargaining power of suppliers is high if the opposite of all or some of the above characteristics holds true. As an example here, consider the case of Google's acquisition of the online advertising company DoubleClick, which helped Google to acquire a highly dominant position in the online advertising market (see the FT article 'All eyes on Google advertising').

The impact of the Internet on the five industry forces is depicted in more detail in Exhibit 3.3.

Exhibit 3.3 **The Internet has a profound impact on the five forces that influence industry attractiveness**

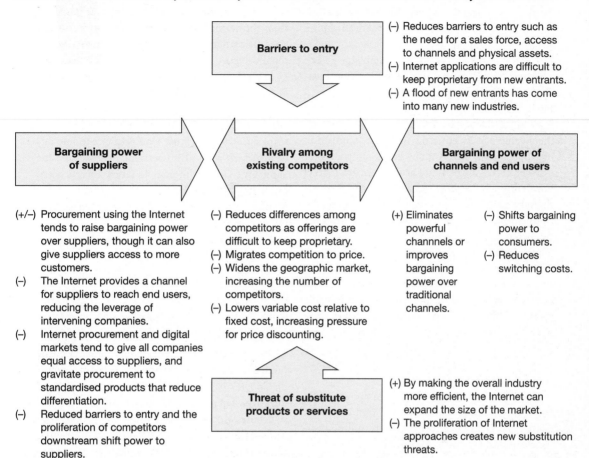

(–) Reduces barriers to entry such as the need for a sales force, access to channels and physical assets.
(–) Internet applications are difficult to keep proprietary from new entrants.
(–) A flood of new entrants has come into many new industries.

(+/–) Procurement using the Internet tends to raise bargaining power over suppliers, though it can also give suppliers access to more customers.
(–) The Internet provides a channel for suppliers to reach end users, reducing the leverage of intervening companies.
(–) Internet procurement and digital markets tend to give all companies equal access to suppliers, and gravitate procurement to standardised products that reduce differentiation.
(–) Reduced barriers to entry and the proliferation of competitors downstream shift power to suppliers.

(–) Reduces differences among competitors as offerings are difficult to keep proprietary.
(–) Migrates competition to price.
(–) Widens the geographic market, increasing the number of competitors.
(–) Lowers variable cost relative to fixed cost, increasing pressure for price discounting.

(+) Eliminates powerful channnels or improves bargaining power over traditional channels.

(–) Shifts bargaining power to consumers.
(–) Reduces switching costs.

(+) By making the overall industry more efficient, the Internet can expand the size of the market.
(–) The proliferation of Internet approaches creates new substitution threats.

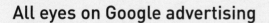

FT

All eyes on Google advertising

The irony of seeing Microsoft voice antitrust complaints against arch-rival Google over the weekend has not been lost on its adversaries. Long accustomed to being the subject of regulatory scrutiny itself – in part prompted by complaints from rivals – the software company has finally acted to try to turn the tables. Yet among at least some observers on Monday, there was a strong suspicion that

Microsoft's charges – echoed by others, including AT&T – would fail to convince regulators to block Google's proposed purchase of the online advertising company DoubleClick.

At the heart of the complaint is that Google's share of the search adverts placed on third-party websites, combined with DoubleClick's dominance of the business of serving up graphical – or display – adverts, would give the enlarged company a dominant position in the overall online advertising business.

Central to the analysis of this complaint will be whether the search and display advertising businesses, until now separate, should be treated as a single market for regulatory purposes. 'It seems there is a clear distinction between Google's business and the business it is entering with the acquisition of DoubleClick,' said Andrew Frank, an analyst at Gartner. If so, Google is not acquiring extra market power through the proposed deal. Some opponents, though, make the opposite argument. The search company has clearly stated an intention to integrate the two online markets closely together, says Brad Smith, general counsel at Microsoft.

Announcing the proposed $3.1bn deal last Friday, the company said it would let advertisers manage their search and display campaigns using the same tools, making it easier to compare the effectiveness of their overall online advertising. However, to the extent that the integration only happens at this level, the two markets could still be considered separate, with their own pricing dynamics.

Even if the two markets remain separate, though, combining a dominant position in each in a single company like this could put online publishers at risk, say critics. According to Jim Cicconi, head of external and legislative affairs at AT&T, it would make any web company that depends on online advertising dependent on a single supplier. In effect, Google would be able to influence the revenue lifeline of other internet companies, some of whom are its direct competitors.

A further consideration, however, is whether the specialised nature of DoubleClick's services in the online display market, which are far narrower than the services Google operates in the search advertising market, are central to the workings of that business to make the union anti-competitive.

While DoubleClick's technology serves up many of the display ads that are inserted into web pages, it does not run its own network to sell advertising space, as Google does. Instead, it works with advertising agencies, which use DoubleClick's technology to distribute ads. Advertisers and agencies use the company's Dart technology to target adverts based on demographic or behavioural criteria, track the number of people who see them, and manage their online campaigns.

Google may eventually be able to leverage DoubleClick's technology to gain a stronger position to sell display advertising. That opportunity helps account for what many analysts described as a very high price for a company understood to have revenues of only $300m to $400m.

Some rivals in the online display market, meanwhile, argued that advertisers and website publishers could react to any excess market power on Google's part by simply switching to another ad network. There are no barriers to prevent this switching, which reduces any anti-competitive concerns from a deal, said Dave Moore, chief executive officer of 24/7 Media, a rival online advertising services firm. 'In the advertising business, there's never been anyone who has been able to consolidate a market and hold on to it,' he says. 'Google continues to build a Roman empire. We all know what happened to that.'

Source: R. Waters, 'All eyes on Google advertising', 16 April 2007, FT.com.

3.3 Complementing the five forces framework with the co-opetition framework

While the five forces framework focuses on the negative effects that market participants might have on the industry attractiveness, the co-opetition framework enriches this perspective by highlighting that interactions with other players can also have a positive impact on profitability.[15] These interactions can include: (1) joint setting of technology and other industry standards, (2) joint developments and (3) joint lobbying:

■ *Joint setting of technology and other industry standards* is often a prerequisite for ensuring the growth of an industry. For instance, the wireless marketing company YOC (featured in the case studies section of this book) joined other wireless marketing providers to set up ethical and data privacy industry standards on how to conduct marketing campaigns over the mobile phone.

■ *Joint developments* between different firms can offer the opportunity for improving quality, increasing demand or streamlining procurement. Through its Zshops, Amazon.com has made it possible for other sellers, who are, in principal, competitors, to sell through the Amazon.com website. Similarly, competing car manufacturers (i.e. General Motors, Ford and DaimlerChrysler) teamed up to set up the common e-purchasing platform Covisint aimed at streamlining their purchasing processes. (For more details on Covisint, see the case studies section of this book.)

■ *Joint lobbying* for favourable legislation is also frequently a prerequisite for growth and for erecting barriers to entry.

The value net framework (see Exhibit 3.4), which is similar to the five forces framework, focuses on the positive aspects of interactions and seeks to identify opportunities for value creation through collaboration.[16] Therefore, it provides a complementary perspective to the one offered by the five forces framework. The 'value net' framework looks at four categories of players, which, through their interactions, characterise the market environment. These players are customers, suppliers, competitors and complementors.

■ *Customers* (who sometimes are the consumers) are the recipients of products or services that a given firm offers in the marketplace.

■ *Suppliers* are companies that supply the firm with resources, including labour and (raw) materials.

■ *Competitors* are companies whose products or services are considered to be substitutes to the firm's own offerings.

■ *Complementors* are companies whose products are complementary to a firm's own offerings. The underlying idea is that customers value a given product more if they can also buy a related complementing product from somebody else. This is the case, for example, with CD and DVD players, or game cartridges and consoles.

The role of competitors and complementors can change depending on the context. For instance, with the above-mentioned Zshops, Amazon.com has changed competitors into complementors. Instead of looking at them only from a 'negative' (or zero-sum game) perspective, Amazon.com decided that allowing these companies to offer their products on its website would improve its overall value proposition and create a win–win situation for both parties.

Similarly, when three major car manufacturers (i.e. General Motors, Ford and DaimlerChrysler) joined forces to set up the shared e-procurement platform Covisint, they aimed at pooling their purchasing needs and thereby reducing procurement and supply chain costs. (For other examples of complementary relationships, see the FT article 'Take your partners for the IT dance'.)

Take your partners for the IT dance

Seven years ago, Apple Computer introduced a line of Macintosh computers based on the Motorola G3 microprocessor. Apple aired several biting TV advertisements claiming that the G3 was twice as speedy as the Pentium II microprocessor, then the central brains of most machines in the Windows computing world.

Times changed. So did Apple, which on June 6 announced that Intel, maker of the Pentium chips, would be its new supplier. And when Steve Jobs, Apple's chief executive, embraced his counterpart at Intel, Paul Otellini at Apple's Worldwide Developers Conference in San Francisco, the world witnessed an enduring reality in the high-velocity technology business: yesterday's rivalries are today's alliances.

This is not exactly shocking. We see it all the time elsewhere, especially politics, where two people will slash and burn each other's records and reputations, and then, after the election, act as if they'd been best of friends all along. They do so for good reasons. Only the most narrow-minded ideologues fail to understand that it's possible to be bitterly opposed on most issues but find common ground on a few – because human beings can disagree in good faith.

The resemblances among top politicians and major technology figures have always been striking. Egotism, bordering on megalomania, is common. So, frequently, is the conviction that one is doing something to change the world, quite possibly for the better.

The shifting alliances in technology seem less rooted in a sense of mutual respect, however, than in the need to get a temporary advantage. In a field that moves so quickly, that can be worth an enormous amount. One can rattle off a long list of such alliances. Intel's relationship with Microsoft, for example, has been the basis for the so-called 'Wintel' desktop computing platform.

Less appreciated has been the frequent tension between the two companies, which became briefly visible when a former Intel executive testified against Microsoft in the big anti-trust trial in the late 1990s. Consider also Mark Benioff, former protégé of Oracle chief executive Larry Ellison and now head of his own web applications company, Salesforce.com. Mr Ellison was an investor in Mr Benioff's company, but Oracle is now aggressively moving into Salesforce's territory.

The most famous shifting alliance is the one that helped turn the PC into a mass-market phenomenon: IBM's partnership with Microsoft in the 1980s, when Big Blue shipped its PCs with Microsoft DOS. The partnership was better for Microsoft which proved smarter, more nimble and far less interested in playing by the old rules, while IBM squandered its position and ultimately ceded control of desktop computing.

The one-time alliance had turned seriously sour by the 1990s, when Microsoft and IBM became enemies in operating systems. Today, IBM is the principal big-company sponsor of the open-source software movement that continues to dog the Microsoft monopoly. Yet when IBM was selling PCs, it was one of the highest-volume dealers of computers pre-loaded with Windows. Meanwhile IBM and Microsoft are collaborating on some key web standards. The made-up word for this kind of relationship is co-opetition.

Making such arrangements work can be tricky. Companies have to seal off one set of workers from another. One engineer may know details about a competitor's technology but be prohibited, via a non-disclosure agreement, from telling the person inside his own company who most wants to know those details.

There's always a whiff of hypocrisy when former enemies become best friends on the very issues over which they'd fought. Apple finesses its former contempt for Intel by saying the chip maker's road map to the future is now compelling, but those years of scorn will remain in people's memories. Or maybe they will not. Politicians, at least in America, have learned that their best friend is the typical voter's short attention span. Business people count on this as well.

As someone who long ago publicly suggested that Apple move to the Intel architecture, I'm naturally in favor of this move. As someone who long ago publicly suggested that Apple move to the Intel architecture – an arena teeming with competition from not just Intel but also Advanced Micro Devices (AMD) and others – I'm in favor of this move. (As an underdog, Apple might have picked AMD as its new supplier, but Apple is being rational if cold-blooded.)

Will the alliance last? Perhaps. But recall Mr Jobs' keynote speech at the Worldwide Developers Conference just two years ago. That was the day Apple announced the G5 chip, made by its friend and partner, IBM. The road map was also clear that day.

Source: D. Gillmore, 'Take your partners for the IT dance', FT.com, 15 June 2005.

Exhibit 3.4 The value network outlines the main players in the co-opetition framework

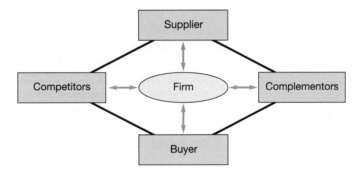

Source: Adapted from A. Brandenburger and B. Nalebuff, *Co-opetition*, 1998, Currency Doubleday, p. 17.

In the PC landscape, Microsoft's Windows operating system is more valuable, i.e. faster and more reliable, when it runs on a computer powered by an Intel microprocessor than on a computer with a lesser quality microprocessor. Yet, Microsoft would typically not be part of Intel's 'five forces industry analysis' screen, and vice versa. However, whatever Microsoft does is of great importance to Intel. In contrast to the five forces framework where a decrease in the bargaining power on the part of one of the five players leads to an increased attractiveness of the overall industry, this logic for complementors is more differentiated. In the case of Microsoft, Intel benefits if Microsoft's operating system becomes more successful over time, since this also opens up new market opportunities for Intel's microprocessors.

CRITICAL PERSPECTIVE 3.1

Benefits and drawbacks of industry analysis tools

In all likelihood, Porter's five forces industry framework is one of if not the most widely used frameworks in the field of strategic management. The framework has numerous positive qualities that have contributed to its far-reaching success. Most importantly, it is a systematic and comprehensive way to analyse industry structure. The five forces that the framework addresses are mutually exclusive and they cover the most important players in a given industry. In addition, the framework claims that there is a monotonic relationship between the power of each individual player and industry attractiveness. This means, for instance, that as the bargaining power of buyers or sellers increases, the industry becomes less attractive. Similarly, as competition increases, the industry attractiveness also goes down.

This required monotonic relationship between the power of the actors and industry attractiveness is the main reason why Michael Porter decided not to include government as a sixth force. In an interview,[17] Porter explains why, to his mind, government does not present a sixth force:

> After much further work using and teaching the framework, I have reaffirmed my original conclusion that government is not a sixth force because there is no monotonic relationship between the strength and influence of government and the profitability of an industry. You can't say that 'government is high, industry profitability is low', or that 'government is low, industry profitability is high'. It all depends on what exactly the government does. [...] And how do you assess the consequences of what government does? Well, you look at how it affects the five forces.

In essence, Porter states that government is a variable that has an impact on the five forces, which in turn impact on the profitability of the industry. Yet, there does not seem to be a direct and, most importantly, no monotonous effect of government on industry profitability. On the one hand, governments in many countries have passed laws to deregulate industries, which has led to a strong increase in competition and reduced profitability for incumbent companies. This was the case, for instance, in the German telecom industry where the entry of numerous new players in recent years is severely threatening the position of the market leader Deutsche Telecom. On the other hand, governments might also pass laws that prevent suppliers from colluding and setting overly high prices. This, in turn, reduces the bargaining power of suppliers, thereby making the industry more attractive for incumbents.

The comprehensiveness and clear structure that the five forces industry framework provides is especially valuable during the initial stages of a strategy project when the task is to gain a quick and broad understanding of the relevant players in an industry. Yet, there are also a number of drawbacks associated with the five forces industry framework, which one needs to be aware of. Most importantly, it has been said that the framework is overly static in a rapidly changing business world, where industries are in constant flux. It is, indeed, increasingly difficult to define industry boundaries, which are becoming more and more blurred due to, among others, mergers and acquisitions. However, this does not mean that the five forces industry framework has become irrelevant, since it still helps to pinpoint competitive and industry conditions that are subject to change.

Furthermore, the framework assumes that competitors' behaviour and industry structure can be explained by analysing a single industry. However, frequently there is multi-point competition where firms compete in more than one industry and, more importantly, their behaviour in one industry is sometimes determined by competition in other industries. For instance, Apple competes not just in the music industry through its iTunes online store but also in the music player industry, where it sells its iPod music player.

3.4 Defining industries, segmenting markets and targeting markets in e-business

3.4.1 Defining an industry

As discussed in Critical Perspective 3.1, one important challenge that we need to consider when conducting an industry analysis is to define appropriately the industry boundaries. On the one hand, if we define our relevant industry very narrowly, then there will be few competitors and there is a high probability that the industry will be rather attractive. Yet, there is great risk that a company from an adjacent industry might enter the industry. On the other hand, if we define the industry too broadly, it becomes overly difficult to reach any sensible conclusions.

Consider the example of the networking platform openBC, which was briefly mentioned above. A narrow definition of the market might limit the industry to online networking platforms, which would focus the competitor analysis on a very small set of companies such as linkedIn in the USA or Stayfriends.com in Germany. A broader definition, including all companies that offer one or more functionalities that openBC offers, would lead to a vast competitive landscape including companies such as Microsoft. (For a detailed illustration of this industry, refer to the openBC case study in the case studies section of the book.) This example illustrates that, depending on the industry definition, there could be different customers and competitors that need to be considered.

The key question that always needs to be taken into account when defining an industry is: Which other products do customers consider as substitutes? Depending on the task at hand, it is possible to use different types of definitions for a given industry. For instance, for a more short-term-oriented external analysis, it might be sensible to scrutinise closely the main players in the direct environment and thus conduct a rather focused industry analysis. However, if the task is to gain an understanding of longer-term competitive developments and threats, it might be more sensible to adopt a broader industry definition that includes also more remote substitutes and potential disruptive innovations that threaten industry incumbents.

3.4.2   Segmenting markets in an industry

Even narrowly defined industries are frequently too broad of a category to allow for any meaningful analysis. Consider the car industry, which consists of a broad array of different car manufacturers catering to different customer segments. To conduct an industry analysis that contains both high-end manufacturers (such as Porsche and Jaguar) and mass producers (such as Toyota and Volkswagen) would provide only very limited insights into the attractiveness of the industry. Similarly, lumping together different types of customers, such as private consumers and corporate customers, also does not provide much insight, since their needs are completely different. To remedy this, we need to segment industries and markets within a specific industry into finer units and then decide which ones to target.

Why is it sensible to divide markets into finer segments?[18] We need to do so because different people have different preferences regarding product features and, therefore, appreciate different value propositions. Let us look for example at mobile phones. A busy, young management consultant might value the possibility of checking his/her bank account balance via a mobile phone, while a senior citizen, who may be having some eyesight problems, may not be attracted by mobile e-banking services. However, the latter customer group might find valuable mobile phones that have enlarged dialling pads, allowing them to key-in phone numbers more easily. This example illustrates how differences in customer preferences are the foundation for market segmentation. According to this, a market segment is defined as a group of customers who have similar needs.

Historically, segmenting markets and catering to different needs have not always been as important as they are nowadays. For instance, in 1909, Henry Ford started offering car buyers in the USA the Model-T car 'in any color they wish, as long as it is black'! By 1926, Ford had sold over 14 million Model-T cars. Obviously, with the advent of more sophisticated production technologies and, more recently, the Internet, it has become possible and necessary to segment markets in a much finer way and to tailor different products and services to different customer segments. (See e-Business Concept 3.1.)

E-BUSINESS CONCEPT 3.1

The e-business market segmentation matrix

The e-business market segmentation matrix[19] provides an overview of the different participants in electronic business. It differentiates three types of participants – consumers, businesses and government – who can act as both suppliers/providers and buyers/recipients. This results in the nine quadrants shown in Exhibit 3.5. Below, we shall explain each one of these configurations, taking the perspective of a supplier/provider who is dealing respectively with a buyer/recipient, who can be a consumer, a peer or a citizen, as well as a business or a governmental agency. In other words, we shall proceed with the description of the proposed matrix row by row, rather than column by column.

The consumer/peer/citizen as a supplier/provider

Through the Internet, consumers can act as suppliers themselves. Consumer-to-consumer (C2C) e-commerce relationships are those where one consumer acts as a supplier and sells goods to other consumers. The most prominent examples for C2C interactions are online auction places, such as eBay, where consumers can sell new and used products to other consumers. When interactions between consumers are not of a commercial nature, we call them peer-to-peer (P2P) interactions. These are voluntary in nature and are free of charge. Examples of P2P sites include online music-sharing platforms, such as Kazaa and e-mule. Other forms of C2C interactions are social networking sites. Although these interactions are not of a commercial nature, they happen to take place on an online commercial platform brokering user-related information.

The second relationship type in this segment is the consumer-to-business (C2B) relationship, where, in general, consumers supply businesses with information about their experiences with products or services. Examples of C2B interactions are the book reviews at Amazon.com and consumer opinions at Ciao.com, a product-comparison platform. The information that consumers provide is then shared with other consumers to help them make more informed purchasing decisions. Furthermore, metadata comprising information on the actual user behaviour allows companies to cater better to individual needs. Collaborative filtering of metadata, for instance, enables Amazon.com to recommend particular books to a customer by analysing other users' buying and viewing patterns.

The third category in this segment contains consumer-to-government (C2G) interactions, such as the online submission of tax return forms and citizen-to-citizen interactions. An example of the latter is the partly Internet-based campaign that the candidate Nicolas Sarkozy ran in France for the 2007 French presidential election. During the election, Sarkozy leveraged the Internet as a platform for interacting with supporters and citizens, outlining his viewpoints on different policy issues and raising funds.

The business as a supplier/provider

The most typical form of interaction is one where businesses act as suppliers to other parties. In business-to-consumer (B2C) e-commerce interactions, firms sell products and services through online means directly to their customers. A number of case studies featured in the book, such as Tesco.com or Ducati, focus on B2C interactions.

Business-to-business (B2B) interactions are platforms for the online purchase of operating or manufacturing inputs that other businesses need for making their products and services. The e-marketplace platform Covisint, which serves car manufacturers (as buyers) and component suppliers (as sellers), is a prominent example of a B2B platform.

Business-to-government (B2G) interactions include, for instance, the online submission of corporate tax return forms.

The government as a supplier/provider

Compared with the above two categories (i.e. consumers and businesses), government activities in e-commerce have so far been relatively low. However, this is changing, and it can be expected that in the future a significant part of governmental agencies' interactions with citizens and businesses will be conducted online (for a comprehensive example of e-government applications, see the case study on e-government in Estonia).

The e-business market segmentation matrix shown in Exhibit 3.5 provides a classification of the different interaction types made possible through the Internet. This allows e-business players to position their own Internet operations within one or more quadrants of this matrix, and also to consider the option spaces into which they may want to expand.

For instance, Amazon.com started out in July 1995 as a pure B2C firm, selling books online to customers. It soon added a C2B component through the online reviews, which customers posted on the company's website. Later, Amazon.com expanded into C2C, when it allowed customers to sell used books through its website, using the Amazon.com online payment mechanism.

Exhibit 3.5 The e-business market segmentation matrix classifies different types of interaction between consumers, businesses and governmental agencies

	Buyer/recipient		
	Consumer/peer/citizen	Business	Government
Consumer/peer/citizen	**Consumer-to-consumer** (e.g. eBay) Peer-to-peer (e.g. Napster) Citizen-to-citizen (e.g. French presidential election 2007)	**Consumer-to-business** (e.g. Amazon.com)	**Citizen-to-government** (e.g. online tax return forms)
Business	**Business-to-consumer** (e.g. Ducati.com)	**Business-to-business** (e.g. Covisint.com)	**Business-to-government** (e.g. online filing of corporate tax returns)
Government	**Government-to-citizen** (e.g. information about pension statements of citizens)	**Government-to-business** (e.g. information about most recent legal regulations)	**Government-to-government** (e.g. exchange of diplomatic information)

Supplier/provider (left axis label)

67

Another example is Nordea, which, like most other banks, was primarily offering retail (B2C) and corporate (B2B) banking services. Through the Internet, Nordea now enables government-to-citizen (G2C) interactions through an online connection with the Finnish government's database that maintains the pension records of Finnish citizens. Through this online link, Nordea customers have instant access to their pension statements, an important feature when deciding, for instance, on a savings plan for retirement. Coincidentally, Nordea bank also offers savings plans for retirement.

There are two main reasons why it is useful to segment markets: (1) gaining insights into customer preferences and (2) getting information about the potential segment size. These two factors are now explained briefly:

- *Insights into customer preferences.* Segmentation enhances the understanding of the target customer group and its preferences. First, this knowledge is helpful in determining how to shape a product and what kind of features to include. Obviously, these features differ depending on the target customer segment. Second, customer preferences help in deciding which distribution channels to select. For instance, Nordea Bank found out that older customers were more likely to start using the Internet for online banking services if they were enticed to do so during a personal face-to-face conversation at a physical bank branch.

- *Information about the potential segment size.* Segmentation also helps to assess the potential market. To have an approximate idea of how many customers might be using a product or a service is crucial for estimating possible scale effects, the overall sales turnover and subsequently the possible return on investment. Webvan in the USA is an interesting case, since it illustrates the disastrous effects of faulty market segmentation and sizing. Assuming an immense market potential, Webvan built large, centralised warehouses that could serve a huge customer base. As it turned out, however, the market segment attracted to this service was much smaller than expected. As a result, the picking and packing facilities were underutilised and most of the delivery trucks drove around half-empty.

Effective market segmentation that actually helps to meet customer preferences is by no means easy. There are many different ways in which a market can be segmented. Kotler proposes a number of different requirements that any type of segmentation should fulfil.[20] A market segment should be:

- *Measurable.* It should be possible to measure the size of a defined segment in order to determine its purchasing power and its peculiar characteristics.

- *Substantial.* A segment should be large enough to justify that it is addressed separately. During the Internet boom years, many category specialists entered specific market segments with a very targeted offering. Yet, as it turned out, the targeted segments were not large enough – at least then – to be served profitably.

- *Differentiable.* The segments must be exclusive and react differently to a variety of marketing approaches.

- *Actionable.* It should be possible to develop sales and marketing approaches to serve specific segments. For instance, the case study of YOC illustrates how mobile marketing campaigns can be designed specifically to target the segment of 15–25-year-old mobile phone users.

As mentioned above, there are myriad ways of segmenting any market. However, depending on the specific product and context, some ways are obviously better than others. For instance, it might be possible to segment the market of Ducati's customers based on hair colour and come up with blond, brown, black-haired and bald customers. In all likelihood, doing so will not provide much insight regarding different preferences and will also not be actionable. In this case, a segmentation between male and female groups or between income groups would be much more valuable. The point is that segmentation is not one-size-fits-all; instead, it requires creative and innovative thinking to differentiate meaningful market segments.

Below, we outline the main possibilities for segmenting a given market. These possibilities include *geographic, demographic, psychographic,* and *behavioural* segmentations (Exhibit 3.6):

■ *Geographic segmentation* entails the selection of specific geographic areas – for example, continents, countries or specific regions within a country – and tailoring offerings according to the customer preferences within that area or territory. For instance, in Europe, certain countries (such as Finland and Sweden) have a very high Internet penetration rate while others (such as Italy and Greece) do not. Segmenting according to countries or regions can bring out these differences and help to design custom-fit strategies for each region. Websites such as Google.com recognise whether a user is logged on from Germany or the USA, for instance, and displays information accordingly in the local language, thus improving the Internet experience of each individual customer.

■ *Demographic segmentation* focuses on different personal attributes of population segments. Demographic segmentation can be done, for instance, by looking at (1) age, (2) gender, (3) income and (4) lifestyle. For instance, regarding the age dimension, YOC has positioned itself clearly to attract young mobile phone users to its mobile marketing services.

Regarding the gender dimension, the virtual community ivillage.com initially aimed at serving both men and women. However, as it turned out that women were much more interested in ivillage's offering, the company decided to focus on the female user segment.

■ *Psychographic segmentation* entails lifestyle issues such as personality type and personal interests. For instance, the 'cash-rich, time-poor' segment of customers has been a primary target for online grocery shopping services such as Tesco.com. In order to save time for their social activities and hobbies, members of this segment are more inclined to shop online (and pay the delivery fees) than spend hours in a physical supermarket.

Exhibit 3.6 **Segmentation variables are the basis for strategic customer analysis**

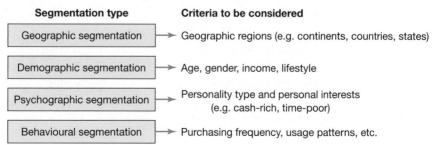

Segmentation type	Criteria to be considered
Geographic segmentation	Geographic regions (e.g. continents, countries, states)
Demographic segmentation	Age, gender, income, lifestyle
Psychographic segmentation	Personality type and personal interests (e.g. cash-rich, time-poor)
Behavioural segmentation	Purchasing frequency, usage patterns, etc.

■ *Behavioural segmentation* divides customers into segments based on their use of a product or service. This can be done, for instance, according to usage occasions or usage rates. Dell uses an occasion-based segmentation to group its customers into the following segments: home office, small business, medium to large business, government, education and healthcare.[21] Segmenting according to usage rates is often useful when different customers show vastly different shopping behaviours. For many firms, 20% of customers make up 80% of revenues. Placing frequent and less frequent customers into different segments and providing them with different levels of marketing or service can then be appropriate.

Men propel surge in online shopping

Men are driving the rapid growth of Internet retailing as they seek to avoid physical trips to shops, according to a new study of British attitudes to shopping on the web. The old truism that many men are immune to the pleasures of lengthily browsing before they buy is borne out by the survey by the British Council of Shopping Centres (BCSC). Men still have a 'hunter' approach to shopping, says the report. That is, they have a specific idea of what they want and want to secure it as painlessly as possible. And doing so is often easier and quicker from behind a computer screen than in a busy high-street store or shopping mall.

'Men find it much more convenient and cost-efficient to shop on the Internet than in shopping places and envisage that in future they will do more of their shopping on the Internet,' says the report. 'Women were at the opposite spectrum compared to men when it came to their future intentions. They were certainly not planning to do more shopping online nor did they think it was more convenient to shop online.' While many adults expect to spend 40 hours doing Christmas shopping they could do the same chores in just 10 hours online, says the report.

The news comes amid new evidence of the rapid encroachment of the Internet into the public's shopping habits. Britons are expected to spend a record £7bn online in the run-up to Christmas day; double the same period of 2004;

according to the Interactive Media in Retail Group. And Asda on Monday said it would double the number of stores with Internet services as it sought to keep pace with the change in customers' habits.

The BCSC report, carried out by Cushman & Wakefield, the property agents, used a poll of more than 1,000 consumers, as well as interviews with 65 retailers and more than 100 developers and retail property investors. The survey could ring alarm bells among investors, as it suggests that Internet sales could triple within a decade. Retailers predicted that the proportion of their sales from the web could increase from 4.5% at present to 14.7% in 10 years' time; with some expecting the Internet to account for more than half of transactions.

Some analysts have predicted that retailers may have less need for physical shops if they are selling more and more online. As a result, there could be implications for pension funds, insurance companies and property companies which are the main owners of Britain's malls. This is particularly true given that developers are planning tens of millions of square feet of new retail space in the coming years. 'Shopping is a social activity in the main, particularly for women who enjoy shopping for recreation,' it says. 'Men consider it a necessity and often feel duty-bound when accompanying partners on shopping trips.'

Source: J. Pickard, 'Men propel surge in online shopping', FT.com, 6 November 2006.

3.4.3 Targeting specific markets in an industry

After dividing markets into individual segments, it is still necessary to determine how to target a specific market segment. There are two main choices associated with market targeting. First, we need to determine which market segment(s) to target. Second, we need to determine how many different products and services to offer to the selected market segment(s). As a manager at a car manufacturer, for example, you could decide to produce just limousines for the upper-income class. Another manager might decide that it is more appropriate to produce also sports utility vehicles (SUVs) and family vans for other market segments. When deliberating the choices, managers always need to keep two main questions in mind:

- *Is the market segment or the group of market segments attractive?* The attractiveness of market segments can be analysed through the five forces framework (discussed in Section 3.2). To find out about the attractiveness of a segment, one could, for instance, analyse the overall growth of that segment, its current profitability and current competition within the segment.

- *Can we compete successfully in this market segment?* This depends on the ability to create value through the resources and skills that a firm possesses. (For a detailed discussion of value creation, see Chapter 8.)

Companies can choose from five main possibilities to target market segments (see Exhibit 3.7). These possibilities are: (1) *single-segment concentration*, (2) *selective specialisation*, (3) *product specialisation*, (4) *market specialisation* and (5) *full market coverage.*

- *Single-segment concentration.* Premium providers, such as Ducati, which specialises in the production of racing motorcycles for the higher-income motorcycle market, frequently concentrate on single segments of a market. This allows them to gain profound knowledge of customers, develop specialised production know-how, and cater exactly to the needs of their specific customer segment. The Ducati brand is positioned clearly as a premium brand, undiluted by lower-class products, which allows Ducati to charge a premium price for its motorcycles. Competitors with a broader positioning are likely to over- or under-serve this specific customer segment. The downside of single-segment concentration is that if the targeted segment fails to generate the required revenues, then the whole firm is endangered.

- *Selective specialisation.* A company that pursues selective specialisation targets different market segments with different product types. Doing so has the advantage of spreading out the business risk. However, it also poses the danger that the firm loses focus, thereby becoming vulnerable to attacks by more focused competitors. The German media group Bertelsmann, for instance, offers a wide variety of media products in the online, print, TV and radio areas, which target different customer groups.

- *Product specialisation.* A category specialist such as Spreadshirt.com, which focuses on providing printing services, concentrates on one type of service but wants to reach out to as wide a market as possible. The goal of product specialists is to generate either economies of scale or special learning effects that set them apart from their competitors. The risk of product specialists is that if their specific product loses favour with customers, then they would not be able to make up for a fall in revenues through other products.

Exhibit 3.7 Target-market selection depends on the number of markets served and the number of different products and services offered

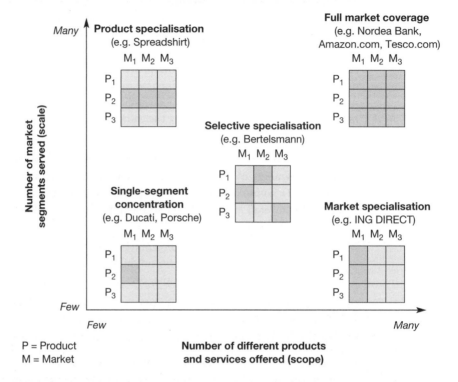

Source: Adapted from D. Abell (1977); "Strategy and Structure: Public Policy Implications" in Proceedings of Marketing and the Public Interest. Cambridge, Mass.: Marketing Science Institute.

The online mobile payment provider paybox.net failed with its mobile payment service for online and offline transactions because the uptake by customers and merchants was not large enough to cover costs. Since paybox.net had focused only on the mobile payment service, it was unable to generate enough revenues to sustain its business.

- *Market specialisation.* Firms that concentrate on a specific market segment aim at gaining a strong reputation and trust with members of the targeted segment, and then expanding by offering a range of products to the same segment. Cross-selling can be a valuable option to increase revenues, since it limits customer acquisition costs. ING DIRECT, for instance, which is featured in the case studies section of the book, offers a complete range of banking products, yet targets primarily the cost-sensitive customers.

- *Full market coverage.* Firms that attempt to achieve full market coverage want to sell a wide variety of product types to the whole spectrum of target segments. The economic logic behind full market coverage is to create economies of scope by leveraging existing production capacities, technological platforms or a strong brand name. Amazon.com is an example of a full market provider. Although the company started out selling only new books, it has subsequently added used books and a wide variety of product categories, ranging from baby toys, to pet food, to consumer electronics. OpenBC has also been moving into full market coverage in the social networking market. The company initially focused primarily on business users, as was expressed through its brand name openBC (where BC stands for business community). However, market specialisation poses the risk that the segment in question is not large enough. That is one of the reasons why openBC was recently relaunched as a global networking platform under the Xing brand name.

Sole listener is target for online radio

Martin Stiksel is not predicting that Last.fm, the fast-growing online social music site he co-founded, will sound the death knell for radio. 'It's an alternative,' says the 32-year-old after careful consideration. But, Mr Stiksel adds, the site's name derives from the 'cheeky, arrogant assumption that it is the last music station you will ever need'.

The former music journalist from Austria launched Last.fm in London in 2003 with two other university graduates and music buffs. It has attracted more than 1m users around the world. Nielsen/NetRatings counted the unique monthly users in October at about 1m in the US and 300,000 in the UK, followed by Germany, Canada, Brazil and Japan.

Last.fm's growing popularity stems from the way it combines Internet services that have already proved popular – namely online music, social networking and the tailored recommendations made popular by Amazon.com. It is a textbook example of the new breed of so-called Web 2.0 services, based on standardised interfaces so they can be combined quickly into composite services, called mash-ups.

Its core service is a customised Internet radio station that streams music tailored to each individual's taste – acts they are already fans of and unfamiliar music they are likely to appreciate. The company's software monitors a user's preferences and then cross-matches them with what like-minded users listen to. You can further personalise your station by clicking tabs to indicate whether you like or loathe a track being played – one tab is called 'Never play me this again' – or skip a track altogether.

The site has a library of more than 1m tracks it is licensed to stream compared with the 3.5m i-Tunes has available for download. In this way Last.fm helps people discover new music in a world of overwhelming choice. 'It's about reignit-

ing a passion for music', Mr Stiksel says. 'People get out of touch after they graduate from university; they often listen to the same artists until retirement age because they don't have time to search out new music ... Last.fm offers a low-involvement, easy lean-back approach to music discovery.'

However, the site offers much more than free, tailored radio. It ambitiously aims to be a one-stop shop for all a listener's music needs. One of its goals is to make listening to music as social as it can be online – a sort of MySpace for music. For example, users get their own page and can search for a musical 'neighbor' who shares their taste, view that person's music journals, send them a message or add them as a friend. The website also has 7m artist pages – the main space for targeted advertising, says Mr Stiksel. Last.fm, and a host of similar services such as the US-based Pandora.com, have captured the public's imagination.

According to Mark Mulligan, analyst at Jupiter Research, European Internet-based audio services doubled their share of internet users from 7% in 2002 to 14% in 2006. 'A new generation of services is emerging that aims to tap into music fans' more extensive but free music consumption habits online', he says.

Like many of the hottest sites of the Web 2.0 world, Last.fm has grown virally – the only money spent on advertising was '£50 on some stickers', says Mr Stiksel. An investment of less than $5m last year from Index Ventures, a Europe-based venture capital firm that was an investor in Skype, allowed the three-strong outfit operating out of an east London flat to move into a swanky new office and expand to 28 employees. The company, which expects to make a profit within 12 months, also plans to sell data to record companies and is trialling a paid-for service.

Before Last.fm can challenge the enduring appeal of conventional radio, however, it must avoid the type of licence fees that several years ago put many smaller online stations in the US out of business. Mr Stiksel says the online streaming business fears the possible introduction of royalties, which is being debated by the UK Copyright Tribunal and could involve charging a royalty fee per track each time it is listened to rather than a percentage of a site's total revenue. Unless the cost per track were extremely low, a free, advertising-supported model would not be sustainable, he says. The company would have to stop broadcasting in the UK. Mr Mulligan argues it is in the music industry's interests to support the likes of Last.fm. 'The [industry] needs to experiment with alternatives to digital downloading.'

Source: M. Guha, 'Sole listener is target for online radio', *Financial Times*, 16 January 2007.

SUMMARY

- This chapter addressed the question of where a firm should compete and offered frameworks for analysing the macro-environment, which includes political, legal, social and technological factors.

- Second, the chapter discussed Porter's five forces as a guiding framework for determining the attractiveness of an industry. It also analysed the impact of the Internet on industry rivalry, barriers to entry, threat of substitute products and the bargaining power of buyers and suppliers.

- Third, the chapter introduced the concept of 'co-opetition', which refers to companies that at the same time co-operate and compete with each other. It illustrated how the Internet enables the implementation of such a concept and how it supports the underlying interactions between the companies involved.

- Finally, the chapter addressed the issues of how to define industries within which to compete and how to segment specific customer groups that a company should target through its e-business offering.

REVIEW QUESTIONS

1 Explain the impact of the Internet on the macro-environment.

2 Review the impact of the Internet on the five forces industry framework.

3 How can the Internet enable companies to implement the co-opetition concept?

4 Outline the e-business market segmentation matrix based on its two underlying dimensions.

DISCUSSION QUESTIONS

1 Illustrate the five forces industry framework through two e-commerce examples drawn from the same industry: one of an Internet start-up and the other of an established bricks-and-mortar company.

2 Choose an e-commerce example and discuss how a company can use the Internet to implement the 'co-opetition' concept.

3 Provide a real-world example of your choice for each one of the nine quadrants that make up the e-business market segmentation matrix.

4 You want to define the industry of Amazon.com. What are the major players in the industry? What are possible substitutes?

RECOMMENDED KEY READING

- G. Johnson, K. Scholes and R. Whittington discuss the macro-environment of firms in *Exploring Corporate Strategy*, 7th edition, Prentice Hall, 2005.

- For a more in-depth analysis of the five forces, see M. Porter, *Competitive Strategy*, Free Press, 1998.

- A. Brandenburger and B. Nalebuff introduce the concept of co-opetition in their book *Co-opetition*, Currency Doubleday, 1998.

- For an extensive discussion of market segmentation and market targeting, see P. Kotler, *Marketing Management*, Prentice Hall, 2005, pp. 251–296.

USEFUL THIRD-PARTY WEBLINKS

- www.ecommercetimes.com provides a sound archive of e-business-related articles and publications.

- www.Icompli.co.uk is a portal concentrating on e-commerce laws.

- www.brint.com provides deep coverage of articles on e-business and e-commerce.

- www.davechaffey.com contains updates about digital marketing and strategy.

NOTES AND REFERENCES

1 For a detailed explanation of these terms, refer to the technology appendix on the Companion Website.

2 A good discussion of macro-environmental influences can be found in G. Johnson, K. Scholes and R. Whittington, *Exploring Corporate Strategy*, Prentice Hall, 2005. A more e-commerce-specific discussion of environmental factors is contained in D. Chaffey, *e-Business and e-Commerce Management*, FT Prentice Hall, 2002, pp. 143–156.

3 'Windows of opportunity', *The Economist*, 15 November 2003, p. 61.

4 Cookies are text files stored on a PC that allow the website operator to identify that PC.

5 Spam is unsolicited e-mail messages.

6 VoIP telephony stands for 'Voice over Internet Protocol'.

7 TCP specifies how information should be separated into individual packets and reassembled at the destination. IP specifies how individual packets should be sent over the network. HTTP is a method of jumping back between different files. HTML is a computer language for formatting hypertext files. J. Cassidy provides an informative account of the most important Internet standards and technologies in his book entitled *Dot.con*, Perennial, 2003, pp. 16–24.

8 For a detailed discussion of industry analysis, see M. Porter's book *Competitive Strategy*, Free Press, 1998, pp. 3–34.

9 The five forces industry framework is described in M. Porter's book entitled *Competitive Strategy*, Free Press, 1998, p. 5.

10 R. D'Aveni suggests that levels of competition have risen in the past decade, leading to a phenomenon that he calls 'hypercompetition' (see R. D'Aveni, 'Coping with hypercompetition: utilizing the new 7S's framework', *Academy of Management Review*, 1995, Vol. 9, No. 3, pp. 45–57). However, G. McNamara, P. Vaaler and C. Devers have empirically tested this thesis and have not found conclusive evidence for an intensification of competition (see 'Same as it ever was: the search for evidence of increasing hypercompetition', *Strategic Management Journal*, 2003, Vol. 24, No. 3, pp. 261–278).

11 J. Cassidy, *Dot.con*, Perennial, 2003, pp. 105–106.

12 T. Burt and P. Larsen, 'Sony and BMG sign music merger deal', www.FT.com, 12 December 2003.

13 F. Vogelstein, 'Mighty Amazon', *Fortune*, 26 May 2003, p. 64.

14 'Software's great survivor', *The Economist*, 22 November 2003, p. 70.

15 The concept of 'co-opetition' was developed by A. Brandenburger and B. Nalebuff, *Co-opetition*, Currency Doubleday, 1998. It entails simultaneously co-operating and competing with other companies.

16 Ibid.

17 N. Argyres and A. McGahan published an interview they conducted with Michael Porter in the *Academy of Management Executive*, 2002, Issue 2, pp. 43–53.

18 For an extensive discussion of market segmentation, see P. Kotler, *Marketing Management*, Prentice Hall, 2005, pp. 251–296.

19 See also T. Hutzschenreuter, *Electronic Competition*, Gabler, 2000, pp. 28–29.

20 P. Kotler, *Marketing Management*, Prentice Hall, 2005, pp. 251–296.

21 This segmentation becomes apparent on the opening page of www.dell.com, where visitors can choose between different segments.

CHAPTER 4

Internal analysis: e-business competencies as sources of strengths and weaknesses

Chapter at a glance

4.1 Understanding core competencies in e-business

4.2 Analysing the Internet-impacted value chain

4.3 Leveraging the virtual value chain

4.4 Selecting activities for online interaction with customers – the ICDT framework
    4.4.1 Information activities
    4.4.2 Communication activities
    4.4.3 Transaction activities
    4.4.4 Distribution activities

4.5 Moving beyond the value chain to value networks

Related case studies

Case study	Primary focus of the case study
1 Tesco	Internet-impacted value chain
14 Spreadshirt	Internet-impacted value chain
5 Otis	Value chain transformation
2 Nordea	Virtual value chain
4 Ducati vs. Harley	Value network
15 Second Life	ICDT framework

Learning outcomes

After completing this chapter, you should be able to:

■ Understand the meaning of core competence in e-business.

■ Assess the impact of the Internet on the value chain.

■ Appreciate how a company can leverage the virtual value chain.

■ Understand the four virtual spaces of the ICDT (Information, Communication, Distribution and Transaction) framework.

■ Apply the ICDT framework for selecting activities suited for e-business.

■ Recognise that companies move from managing an internal value chain to operating along a value network.

INTRODUCTION

This chapter first defines the concept of core competence and discusses it in the context of e-business. It then presents the value chain concept as a way to analyse the individual steps in the value-creation process. Afterwards, it introduces the virtual value chain concept and suggests ways for companies to leverage it for value creation. The chapter then describes the four virtual spaces of the ICDT (Information, Communication, Distribution and Transaction) framework and indicates ways of using it when selecting activities suited for e-business. Finally, the move for companies from managing an internal value chain to operating along a value network that involves external partners is highlighted.

4.1 Understanding core competencies in e-business

The goal of strategy formulation is to position an e-business venture so that it can exploit the opportunities that are afforded by its environment and so that it can avoid the risks that it is exposed to. Doing so requires managers of e-business ventures to do two things. First, they need to be able to recognise the opportunities and threats that arise from the external environment. Second, they also need to be able to assess the unique strengths and weaknesses that allow them to exploit opportunities and avoid the threats. A company that is able to align its strengths with the business opportunities and eliminate weaknesses in order to avoid threats creates a 'strategic fit' between its internal competencies and the external environment.[1] In addition, competencies are also important from a different perspective, since they can be the source of creating new market opportunities that previously did not exist. That is what Hamel and Prahalad call 'strategic stretch'.[2]

The terms 'competence' and 'core competence' have been used widely, meaning different things to different people. Let us therefore establish some basic definitions before proceeding (see Exhibit 4.1).

Most importantly, a *competence* is a combination of different resources and capabilities:

- *Resources* are all the tangible and intangible assets of a firm that can be used in the value-creation process. Tangible resources include assets such as IT infrastructure, bricks-and-mortar infrastructure and financial capital. Intangible resources include employee knowledge, licences, patents, brand name and reputation of a firm.

- *Capabilities* represent the ability of a firm to use resources efficiently and effectively. Skills manifest themselves in the design of processes, systems and organisational structures. For instance, even before the Internet became a mainstream technology, Dell had already built up significant skills in managing the process flow of its direct sales model. Adding the Internet was relatively easy, since the necessary skills were already in place.

However, not all competencies that a firm has are necessarily *core competencies*. Instead, in order for a competence to be considered as core, it needs to be:

- *Valuable.* Customers have to appreciate the value of what the competence produces. This can be achieved through either the lowering of costs or the increasing of customer benefit, as perceived by customers.

Exhibit 4.1 Distinctive e-business competencies result from the combination of unique resources and capabilities

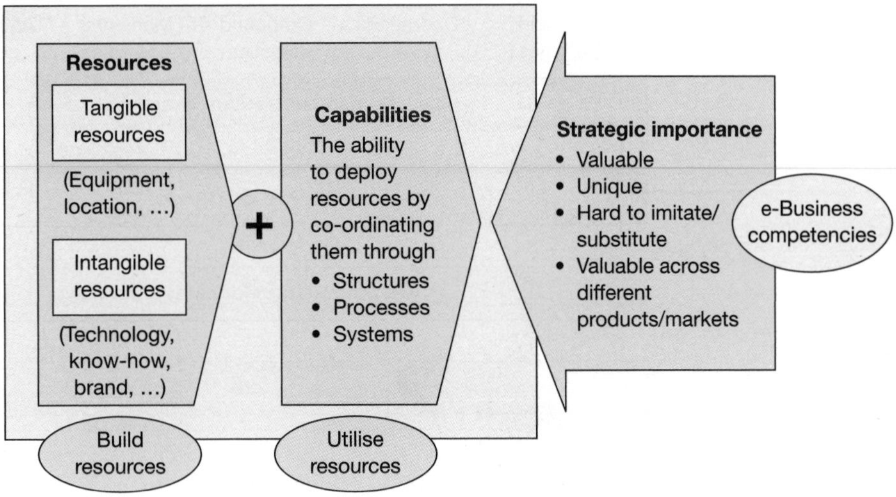

Source: Adapted from H. Hungenberg, *Strategisches Management in Unternehmen*, Gabler, 2006, p. 143.

- *Unique.* The competence needs to be unique so that it not only offers a source of value creation but also allows the firm to capture the value it creates in the form of profit. If a competence is not unique, then competition with other firms will drive down profits.

- *Hard to imitate.* The uniqueness of a core competence is sustainable only if other firms find it difficult to imitate that competence. First, competencies are hard to imitate if they require the tightly interlinked participation of many functions or divisions of the firm. Nordea's core competence in the integration of offline and online banking, for instance, is hard to imitate because it requires the alignment of activities across multiple functions and channels. Second, causal ambiguity also increases the barriers to imitation. Causal ambiguity exists when there is no clear understanding of the sources of a core competence, which makes it hard for an outsider to imitate the competence.

- *Valuable across different products or markets.* A competence is of major value to the firm only if it is not limited to one product or to one market. One of Amazon.com's core competencies is its ability to manage the flow of merchandise from receipt of a customer's online order to shipping the product to the customer. To create this core competence, it built up resources in the form of warehouses and IT infrastructure and created internal skills. As the company moves into different product categories such as toys, home electronics and clothes, it can reuse its skills and resources.

Both skills and resources are required in processes that run across the different business functions of a firm. In fact, an important building block of the competence-based approach is that strategy rests less on functional divisions and products (as is the case with the value chain concept described in more detail in Section 4.2) but rather more on processes that cut across different functions (see Exhibit 4.2).

Exhibit 4.2 **The core competence approach cuts across different functional areas within a firm**

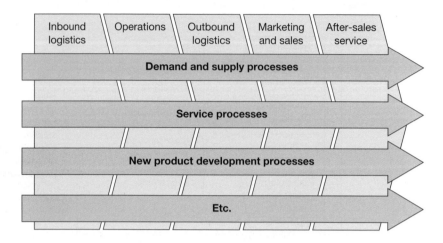

4.2 Analysing the Internet-impacted value chain

The value chain framework helps to address the question of how value is created within a company.[3] It does so by disaggregating a company into strategically relevant and inter-related activities. In essence, the internal value chain of a company revolves around value creation, where value is created through individual activities of the value chain.

Ultimately, competitive advantage rests on activities that a firm can perform better or more efficiently than its competitors. There is no general blueprint prescribing which activities should be included in analysing a company's value chain. However, the following criteria should be used when including specific activities. An activity should:

- *Display different economics.* For instance, the development activity of a new software program displays very large economies of scale since the software can be replicated at a negligible cost.

- *Provide high differentiation potential.* These are activities that can greatly increase tangible and intangible consumer benefits, such as product and service quality, convenience and reputation.

- *Present sizeable costs.* These are activities that add significantly to the overall cost structure of the firm. For instance, in the case of Ducati, these might be activities related to product development and manufacturing. In the case of Spreadshirt, major costs are incurred for product purchasing.

On an aggregate level, a company's value chain contains primary and support activities (see Exhibit 4.3).

To get a better understanding of the ways in which the Internet can change the value chain, we shall take a closer look at how Dell has transformed its value chain:

- *Inbound logistics* consist of receiving, storing and distributing incoming goods within the company. On a more detailed level, this might include activities such as checking inven-

Exhibit 4.3 A company's value chain consists of distinct value-adding activities

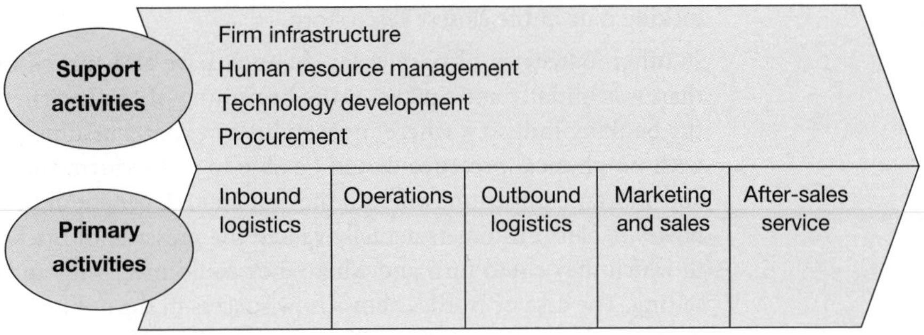

Support activities	Firm infrastructure				
	Human resource management				
	Technology development				
	Procurement				
Primary activities	Inbound logistics	Operations	Outbound logistics	Marketing and sales	After-sales service

tory levels and order placement. Through close linkage with its suppliers, Dell has managed radically to change its inbound logistics. For instance, when Dell sources monitors from Sony, the boxes are not shipped to a Dell plant from where they are distributed. Instead, Dell has made arrangements with logistics companies, such as UPS, to pick up the monitors as needed from the Sony manufacturing plant, match them with the corresponding computers, and then deliver them to customers. Doing so reduces the need for warehousing capacity and inventory, and cuts out transportation steps.[4]

■ *Operations* consist of those activities necessary for the making of a product or a service. The Internet has, in many cases, drastically changed a company's production activities. By taking orders online, companies can significantly shrink the time between order placement and production, enabling them to start production in 'real time'. For instance, through the close linkage between the ordering website and the production facilities, Dell can build products that match orders, thus increasing turnover and reducing inventory costs.[5] In the case of YouTube, it is the user who generates content such as videos, therefore becoming a crucial part of the value chain.

■ *Outbound logistics* consist of activities required for getting the product to the buyer, which can be done either physically or electronically (for digital goods). For example, the reduction of inbound logistics by leaving products with suppliers also reduces Dell's efforts and expenses for outbound logistics. Complementary components, such as PC monitors, are shipped directly from the supplier to the final customer. Furthermore, Apple's iTunes, for instance, proved to be a profitable online distribution channel for music and shows how legal music downloads can be implemented.

■ *Marketing and sales* activities aim at enticing customers to buy a product and to provide the means for doing so. This includes activities such as providing online catalogues and running online marketing campaigns. For example, the Internet has enabled Tesco to increase grocery sales significantly by adding the Tesco.com online channel. In addition, through the launch of Tesco Direct, the company has added a wide range of non-food items such as electronics and furniture to its offerings. While leveraging the online channel for creating incremental sales, Tesco also relies on its store network to market the online channel. For instance, paper catalogues containing all products that are available online are made available at the cash registers in the

Tesco physical stores, thereby promoting online sales. Customers who have purchased products online can choose between having the product delivered to their home or picking it up at the closest Tesco store.

In other industries, physical sales channels have also turned out to be more valuable than was initially anticipated at the beginning of the Internet boom years. Consider the banking industry, where most industry experts assumed then that virtual banks with no physical presence would be able to outperform their cost-intensive bricks-and-mortar competitors on both the cost and the benefit dimensions. As it turned out, however, bank customers actually valued the presence of bricks-and-mortar branches, to which they could turn and where they could meet with an adviser in a face-to-face setting. The case of Nordea shows how success in the online world depended to a large degree on integrating online activities with sales activities in the physical branches.

■ *Service* activities deal with the after-sales phase, which includes the installation of a product, supplying spare parts and exchanging faulty products. In the case of Tesco, it is possible for customers to return faulty products that they purchased online to a store.

The importance of the different activities in the value chain varies from one industry to another. For service firms, operations, marketing and sales activities are crucial. A retailer of physical goods such as Amazon.com places a major emphasis on inbound and outbound logistics as well as marketing and sales. To create high levels of consumer benefit, Amazon.com offers sophisticated sales and marketing tools, such as the personalised recommendation list, which is based on a customer's previous purchases. As part of sales, Amazon.com has patented the one-click payment mechanism, which allows customers, after having gone through a one-time registration process, to make a purchase simply by clicking on an icon and without having to provide any further information about themselves. Thus, the above-outlined value chain is not a blueprint for analysing any individual business. Instead, it should be set up based on the individual context of the firm and with the goal of providing a good understanding of how the business operates.

In addition to the primary activities that are related directly to the production and sales process, the value chain also comprises the following support activities:

■ *Procurement* deals with the primary inputs for different processes within the organisation. This includes the purchasing of, for example, machinery, PCs, servers and office equipment. Procurement is often a crucial element of the overall cost structure of a company. The IBX case study in this book deals specifically with how procurement processes can be made more efficient through the use of electronic platforms (see also Chapter 10 for a discussion of B2B e-marketplaces).

■ *Technology development* includes specific research and development (R&D) for product design. It also refers to development activities that optimise the functioning of other activities of the firm. For instance, one of the core assets of Spreadshirt is its highly developed website that allows shop owners easily to create new online shops offering customised designs. Constantly updating and adapting this website to changing customer needs requires a major investment in technology development.

■ *Human resource management* consists of recruiting, managing, training and developing people. The Internet transformed this activity through online recruiting, web-based training and intranet-based knowledge management. Human resources issues also influence the choice of an Internet-company's geographical location because employees represent the least mobile corporate asset. Amazon.com, for example, set up its headquarters in Seattle, USA, to be able to attract qualified IT specialists.

Exhibit 4.4 **The Internet impacts on all activities in the value chain**

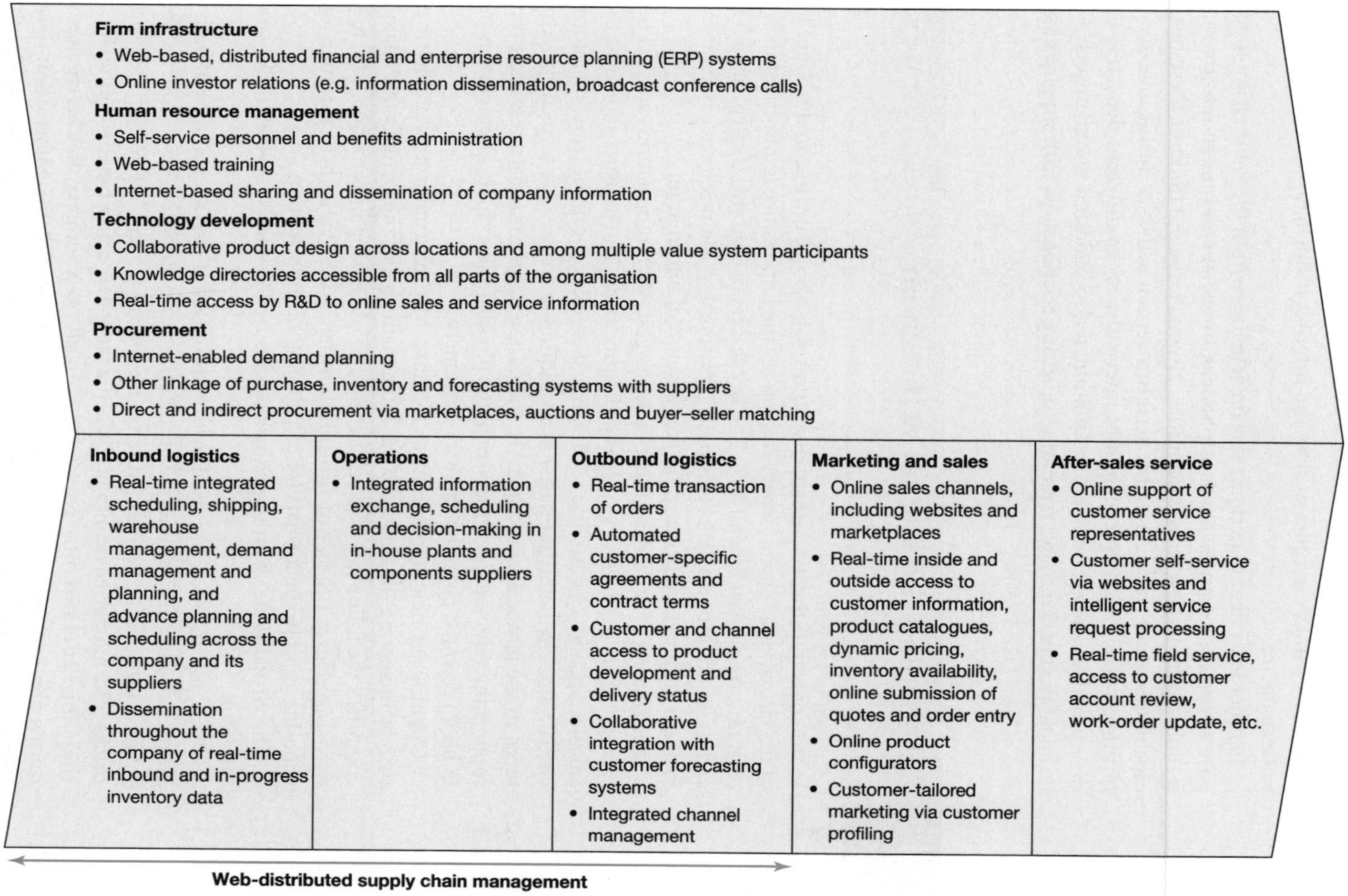

Firm infrastructure
- Web-based, distributed financial and enterprise resource planning (ERP) systems
- Online investor relations (e.g. information dissemination, broadcast conference calls)

Human resource management
- Self-service personnel and benefits administration
- Web-based training
- Internet-based sharing and dissemination of company information

Technology development
- Collaborative product design across locations and among multiple value system participants
- Knowledge directories accessible from all parts of the organisation
- Real-time access by R&D to online sales and service information

Procurement
- Internet-enabled demand planning
- Other linkage of purchase, inventory and forecasting systems with suppliers
- Direct and indirect procurement via marketplaces, auctions and buyer–seller matching

Inbound logistics
- Real-time integrated scheduling, shipping, warehouse management, demand management, and advance planning and scheduling across the company and its suppliers
- Dissemination throughout the company of real-time inbound and in-progress inventory data

Operations
- Integrated information exchange, scheduling and decision-making in in-house plants and components suppliers

Outbound logistics
- Real-time transaction of orders
- Automated customer-specific agreements and contract terms
- Customer and channel access to product development and delivery status
- Collaborative integration with customer forecasting systems
- Integrated channel management

Marketing and sales
- Online sales channels, including websites and marketplaces
- Real-time inside and outside access to customer information, product catalogues, dynamic pricing, inventory availability, online submission of quotes and order entry
- Online product configurators
- Customer-tailored marketing via customer profiling

After-sales service
- Online support of customer service representatives
- Customer self-service via websites and intelligent service request processing
- Real-time field service, access to customer account review, work-order update, etc.

Web-distributed supply chain management

■ *Infrastructure* refers to a firm's physical premises, including offices, plants, warehouses and distribution centres. In spite of being an online retailer, Amazon.com operates a network of its own warehouses in its key markets to co-ordinate the logistics of delivery.

Exhibit 4.4 shows examples of how the Internet influences the different activities of a value chain.

In order for a firm to perform certain activities within the value chain, it needs to dispose of certain resources (such as physical, financial and human resources), as well as technology and know-how capabilities. However, the portfolio of these resources and capabilities is not static. As a firm performs certain activities during an extended period of time, it also builds up capabilities internally, as the different departments improve their processes and create assets. In addition, it also builds up resources such as improved technology, superior brand reputation or strong relationships with suppliers and buyers.[6]

4.3 Leveraging the virtual value chain

In the context of the value chain discussion, it is also of interest to introduce the concept of the virtual value chain,[7] which emphasises the importance of information in the value-creation process (see Exhibit 4.5). The key drivers behind this concept are advances in IT and the evolution of CRM (Customer Relationship Management) systems, which have increasingly provided firms with a vast amount of information.

The concept of the virtual value chain suggests that information captured in the physical value chain for activities such as order processing and logistics should be used to offer enhanced quality of customer service. Based on this concept of recycling information, the virtual value chain illustrates new opportunities to create value by using information captured in the physical value chain. In the past, a lot of information was captured only to support the value-adding processes in the physical value chain, although this information in itself presented potential value for customers.

Opening up new opportunities to make this information available to customers, thereby increasing the value created, is the main goal of the virtual value chain. The latter comprises the following steps: gathering and organising information, selecting and synthesising relevant pieces of information that are of value for customers, and finally choosing appropriate formats for distributing the information.

The virtual value chain framework can be used to analyse several of the case studies in this book.

Tesco, for instance, has used information that it had access to or already owned to create value for its customers. Through the Tesco clubcard, Tesco collects detailed customer information about purchasing patterns and preferred products in the bricks-and-mortar environment. When a customer starts buying online, his/her online shopping list is instantly populated with all the products that he/she has purchased during previous visits to the physical store. By leveraging this information, Tesco makes it easier for customers who are new to Internet-based shopping to find quickly the products that they are likely to purchase.

Exhibit 4.5 **The virtual value chain illustrates how information captured in the physical value chain can be used to develop new markets**

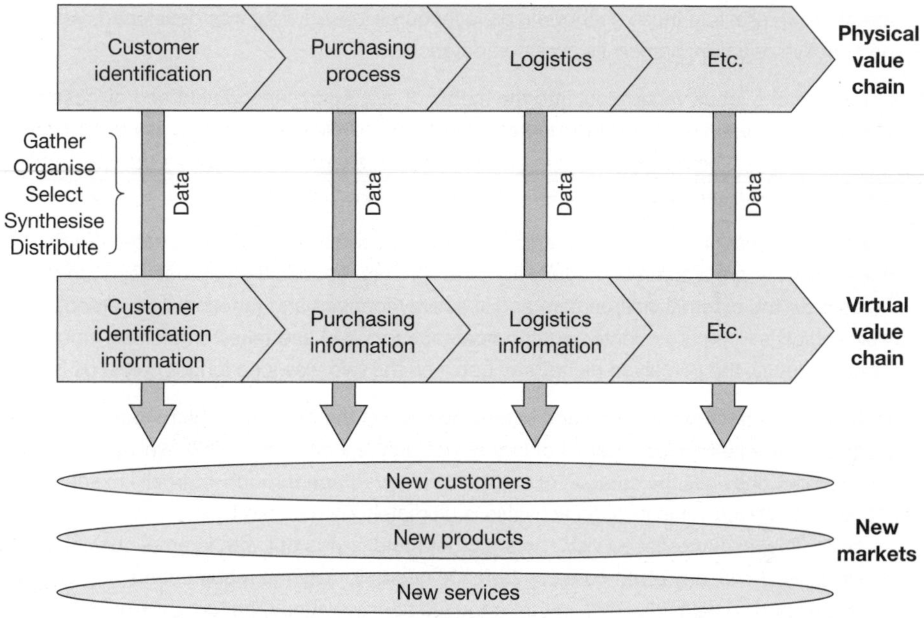

Source: Adapted from A. Enders and T. Jelassi, 'From e-Banking to e-Business at Nordea (Scandinavia) – The World's Biggest Clicks-and-Mortar Bank', *Management Information Systems Quarterly Executive*, Vol. 5, No. 1, 2006, pp. 31–44.

Nordea bank allowed its customers to access their pension statements electronically, which are maintained by a government agency. The bank also made its online customer-authentication process available to other companies that need to use Nordea's e-identification and e-signature services.

Amazon.com has also extensively used information captured throughout its physical value chain to create value. Customers have the possibility of tracking online past purchases and checking the status of delivery. The personalised book-recommendation list, where customers get recommendations based on what other people with a similar profile have bought, is another example of how Amazon.com has also tapped into the previously unused information stored in its databases. Furthermore, including reviews from other customers and providing sample pages of selected books create value for customers while requiring only marginal investment, since the required information-capturing systems are already in place.

CRITICAL PERSPECTIVE 4.1

Compatibility between the resource-based view and the market-based view of strategy

Since the beginning of the 1990s, Porter's approach to creating competitive advantage, which is also called the market-based view, has been criticised primarily because of its seemingly one-sided market orientation. The focus of the criticism is that Porter's approach might help to diagnose a specific competitive problem but it →

does not provide any means to solve it. Other factors that have an important impact on a firm's competitive positioning, such as internal structure, processes, resources and capabilities, do not receive adequate attention. To alleviate these shortcomings, a resource-based view was developed, which focuses on the internal perspective of a firm, namely its core competencies.

For a moment, let us venture out into the theory of strategic management and discuss the relationship between the resource-based view and the market-based view. While many authors assume that the approaches are fundamentally different, there is a growing strand of research that suggests that the two approaches are not in competition with one another but rather complement each other.[8]

Although the resource-based view and the market-based view approach strategy formulation from two different angles, they share a common underlying thinking. This reduces the gap between the market-based view (which focuses on the external environment and is activity focused and functionally oriented) and the resource-based view (which is internally oriented and competence focused and takes on a cross-functional perspective). Upon closer scrutiny, the perceived dichotomy between the two views no longer holds, as is shown below:

- Dichotomy between external and internal focus. On the one hand, the market-based view emphasises the competitive landscape in terms of industry structure (see Section 3.2), which is external to the firm. However, it also emphasises the creation of competitive advantage through internally executed activities, and the ability to create value through activities is ultimately determined by the quality of internal resources and skills. The resource-based view, on the other hand, starts out with internal considerations of resources and skills. However, any given core competence needs to fulfil the requirements of creating value and being unique and sustainable. This, in turn, requires considerations that are external to the firm and that provide insights into consumer preferences and the competitive landscape.

- Dichotomy between activities and competencies. The market-based view starts out with the definition of activities such as operations or marketing and sales. Yet, to perform these activities in such a way that they create a competitive advantage, a firm ultimately needs to possess superior resources and skills because they are the building blocks of superior activities. The resource-based view, on the other hand, starts out with the core competence as the main building blocks of a competitive advantage. However, competencies that consist of resources and skills create value only as part of activities. A strong brand, for instance, is not valuable in and of itself. Instead, it creates value when a firm is able to spend less money on marketing activities while still achieving the same results in consumer awareness as other firms that need to spend more heavily because they do not possess the same brand reputation. Thus, competencies ultimately also rely on activities as sources of a competitive advantage.

- Dichotomy between functional and cross-functional perspective. Through the analytical framework of the value chain, the market-based view starts out with functional divisions that perform discrete activities. Yet, building on the divisional structure, it also includes a cross-functional perspective when it emphasises the requirement of fit between different activities that can be achieved via consistency, reinforcement and optimisation. The resource-based view, on the other hand, begins with competencies that are generally cross-functional processes. Yet processes, in the end, also consist of individual activities, which are located in functional units.

4.4 Selecting activites for online interaction with customers – the ICDT framework

As companies have developed their e-business activities, they have started to offer increasingly elaborate e-business capabilities. The ICDT model describes the main features that a firm can offer to its customers.[9] Essentially, there are four options, which are depicted in Exhibit 4.6.

4.4.1 Information activities

Information activities include advertising and posting information on the company website. This includes company, products and services-related information. When the commercial use of the Internet became widespread in the mid-1990s, companies first designed their web presence to provide customers with information about their products and services. At that point, the Internet was not yet tightly integrated with other marketing channels or enterprise resource planning (ERP) systems.

Since then, information provision has changed drastically. Today, many companies closely link their Internet advertising with other channels, as is illustrated in the YOC case study featured in this book. Furthermore, information provided over the Internet is no longer of a static nature. Instead, online catalogues are linked closely to warehousing and production planning systems, enabling customers to find out instantaneously when their order will be fulfilled and delivered.

The FT article 'The message is being spread' illustrates the importance in today's online world of information activities in the form of advertising.

Exhibit 4.6 The ICDT model describes the four main usage dimensions of the Internet in the virtual market space

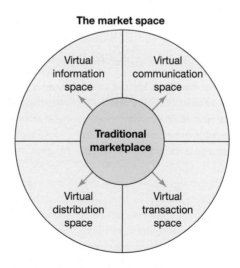

Source: Adapted from A. Angehrn, 'Designing mature internet strategies: the ICDT model', *European Management Journal*, 1997, Vol. 21, No. 1, pp. 38–47.

FT

The message is being spread

Online advertising is growing fast: research from ZenithOptimedia predicts that global spending on Internet ads will overtake radio in 2008. It says the rate of spending on Internet ads will grow six times faster than traditional media between 2006 and 2009, a trend already taking shape in the Middle East and Europe. 'You're seeing more companies, such as Unilever, creating better user experiences for people online,' says Theresa Wise, an Internet marketing specialist for Accenture. 'These companies don't do e-commerce but want to improve their brand presence.'

A few years ago, an online advertising campaign consisted of just banner and pop-up ads. No longer. 'The future of online ads is not just online – digital is digital,' says Will Lebens, managing director of Airlock, a London-based online ad agency. 'It has become seamless. For us, the remit has broadened to blogs and microsites. All these things constitute an ad now.'

Airlock ran a big campaign for clothing company Diesel in which four angels were cast down from heaven and stripped of their wings. Mr Lebens' team left clues to the location of the angels around the Internet on blogs, forums and YouTube clips to build interest in the campaign until they finally released the brand name and all became clear. 'In total, the views reached 3.5m,' he says. 'It was all quite elaborate.'

Many other big companies have started to use Web 2.0 technologies, such as blogging and video clips, to increase brand awareness. Last year in China, Pepsi invited people to write screenplays for company spokesmen and a famous pop singer. And when it launched its Qashqai car in the UK last month, Nissan offered a game website where people could try to shoot the car; it broadcast video clips of the car, which could be linked to blogs and social networking sites; and it ran banners over some Yahoo sites. 'We were coming into a market with something very different, so we wanted to drive brand recognition as well as name

recognition,' says Justin Elias, marketing director of Nissan. 'We had several thousand unique visitors to the website and the films were seen more than 1m times on other websites.'

But were they the right viewers? And what do clicks really mean?

There are several online advertising models. Pay-per click means a company pays every time their ad is clicked on. Google, Yahoo and other companies offer these platforms, but they are susceptible to abuse – companies can click on a rival's ad to drive up its costs, possibly getting them removed from the search results page if they reach their maximum ad budget. While the likes of Google and Yahoo keep figures of click fraud confidential, they refund companies that can prove abuse. Few legal cases have arisen.

Other models include paying per visitor to a website; paying per thousand people exposed to a message; and paying per action, where a company only hands over commission if an actual transaction takes place. So, what are the advantages of the bigger campaigns that run over different media? And how much do they cost? 'A company can launch a broad-reaching online campaign for anything from £20,000 to well over £2m, depending on the mix and the media plan,' explains Mr Lebens. 'In terms of tangible benefits, the most obvious is the ability to create a dialogue with consumers rather than a one-way broadcast.' Other benefits include accountability, precision targeting, and real-time feedback on campaign performance.

Google argues that online advertising is 'transparent' – even though it holds on to click-fraud figures – and that it is 'targeted and measurable'. But not everyone in the industry agrees. 'Although the number of clicks can be counted, advertisers tend not to be able to handle the analytics that can improve their performance,' says Ms Wise. 'Clients are probably not buying as effectively as they could.'

One way companies can ensure a campaign is effective is to monitor who is reached and not just the number of people reading the material. 'It's about collaborating and sharing', says Blake Chandlee, director of media sales for Yahoo. 'That's created an environment that's very different from the one we've been used to over the past 50 years. It's not about banner campaigns but starting a conversation. Any company that tries to introduce a commercial angle will get it wrong.' Mr Lebens agrees: 'It's about engagement. Whether that's through user-generated content, it's about giving the user a chance to engage with your brand. But the brand has to sit in the background. If you're interested in branding, you don't want to double up and do online the same way as offline.'

The Internet Advertising Bureau has recommendations for anyone planning to market online, such as avoiding pop-up ads. It recommends paid search advertising and to include keywords in websites for natural listings in search engines – not forgetting words relating to offline campaigns. 'Integrate your online campaign with your traditional media activity, rather than treating internet marketing as an afterthought,' the organisation recommends. 'Similarly, it is not enough to stream a TV ad online, or replicate outdoor advertising within the traditional banner format. It is essential to make the most of the medium.'

Ms Wise warns companies not to get caught up in flashy technology. 'Viral advertising is important if you're a lifestyle brand,' she says. 'A lot of business owners are forgetting about practicality – they're a bit like startled bunnies in front of the headlights. I'd say: look at the next trend and distinguish whether these thing are R&D or really adverts and stick to the demographic that reflects your trade.'

Television currently owns the largest share of global advertising but what happens when TV goes on to the Internet and the Internet moves on to TV? Some organisations are ending contracts with traditional TV channels to broadcast their own programmes over the web. College teams involved in the US March Madness basketball tournament are broadcasting their own games and taking the advertising revenues away from the TV channels.

This summer, two companies, Joost and BabelGum, will start to broadcast entire TV programmes free over the Internet. The content owners in effect have their own channels and advertising will pay the way. Mr Bishop comments: 'People will watch Friends on a website. We will see the death of the TV station and the birth of the network station.'

Source: D. Ilett, 'The message is being spread', *Financial Times*, 18 April 2007.

4.4.2 Communication activities

Communication activities include two-way communication between a company and its online visitors and customers. This can take place via Internet applications such as e-mail and real-time chat. In order to make communication more personal, the online fashion retailer Landsend.com has included a Lands' End live icon on its website. By clicking on it, customers can request to be called by a Lands' End employee or to enter an online chat to ask questions and obtain specific product information. Similarly, the online service e-Diets.com provides the possibility to interact in real time with nutrition experts to analyse personal eating habits and make appropriate recommendations (see the Blog Box below).

In addition to facilitating communication between businesses and their customers, the Internet also facilitates communication between customers who are members of a virtual online community. For some firms, such as eBay and openBC, the communication that takes place among members of their online communities is much more important than the communication between the company and its customers.

BLOG BOX

Moving back to personalised interaction – e-Diets.com

eDiets.com is an online diet, fitness and healthy living destination offering professional advice, information, products and services to those seeking to improve their health and longevity. Since 1997, and as of 30 June 2006, over 2 million consumers worldwide have become eDiets.com members. eDiets.com offers 24 personalised online programmes including eDiets.com® Weight Loss Plan, the Atkins Nutritional Approach™ and the New Mediterranean Diet.

Members choose a plan and complete a personal profile questionnaire to determine how best to tailor the programme to their unique needs. To ensure success, members have 24/7 access to eDiets.com's community through which they can garner real-time motivation and support from eDiets.com's on-staff experts and member peers.

Source: Adapted from www.ediets.com.

4.4.3 Transaction activities

Transaction activities include the acceptance over the Internet of online orders (i.e. commercial transactions) and electronic payments (i.e. financial transactions). At the outset of the commercial usage of the Internet, there were two main drawbacks associated with online transactions.

First, most Internet users, who were afraid of fraud, considered making e-payments as too dangerous, which held back the evolution of e-commerce. However, as payment mechanisms mature and trusted e-payment companies evolve – consider, for instance, the case of Nordea – online transaction activities are becoming more and more commonplace.

Second, since payments were limited to credit or debit card transactions, the offering of low-priced products or services (such as newspaper articles) was not economically feasible, since transaction costs would have been prohibitively high. The development of online micro-payment systems, such as paybox.net (featured in the case studies section of this book), address this shortcoming.

4.4.4 Distribution activities

Distribution activities include the online delivery of digital goods, such as software, music, videos, films and e-books, by letting customers download the purchased product(s). The main bottleneck that has restricted online distribution so far is the limited bandwidth of online connections. As broadband access becomes more commonplace, even in households, online distribution will be used increasingly with products and services that can be digitised.

First, the online distribution of music, games or even movies will become the norm over time, eventually replacing physical distribution through CDs and DVDs. Online shops such as iTunes have already provided a first glimpse of this revolution in distribution (see the case study in this book on the music industry's paradigm shift). Second, service providers from different realms, such as consulting and education, will use the Internet increasingly to deliver lectures, presentations and services to their customers and students.

4.5 Moving beyond the value chain to value networks[10]

e-Business ventures do not operate in isolation from other companies. Instead, their value chains are frequently closely intertwined with the value chains of suppliers and with external partners who provide other support services. The group of partners that a company works with to deliver a product or a service to its customers is called a 'value network'.

Through the increased usage of IT-based communication, value networks have gained importance as companies have outsourced numerous non-core activities to outside partners. As a consequence, the importance of managing external value networks has increased as well. In the context of e-business ventures, this raises especially the question of which activities should be maintained in-house, off-shored to different geographic locations or completely outsourced to external providers. (See Chapter 9 for a discussion of this deconstruction of the value chain.)

Exhibit 4.7 shows the main partners in a value network. These are:[11]

■ *Upstream value chain partners* include direct suppliers and business-to-business exchanges.

■ *Downstream value chain partners* include wholesalers, distributors, retailers and customers. For instance, Tesco Direct co-operates with the logistics services company CEVA and Expert Logistics to deliver to customers' households the products that are ordered through the Tesco Direct catalogue and website.

Exhibit 4.7 The value network includes numerous partners with differing functions

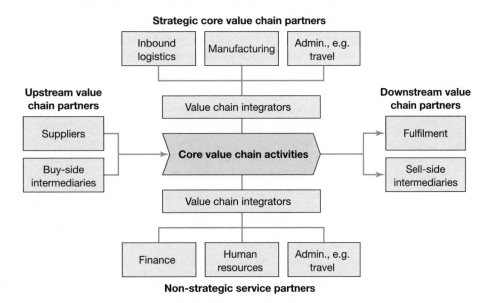

Source: Adapted from D. Chaffey, *E-Business and E-Commerce Management*, FT/Prentice Hall, 2007, p. 282.

- *Strategic core value chain partners* are those partners that fulfil core value chain activities. Before Tesco started Tesco Direct, it co-operated with the mail order company Grattan, which administered all back-end processes ranging from product selection to delivery. As it became obvious that online selling of non-food products would be a substantial market opportunity, Tesco decided to build up in-house the capabilities that were previously provided by Grattan.

- *Non-strategic service partners* fulfil functions such as finance, accounting or travel.

- *Value chain integrators* such as strategic outsourcing partners, application service providers (ASPs) and system integrators provide the electronic infrastructure for a company.

Although there are certain similarities between a company's value chain and the value network in so far as both are involved in providing a product or a service to the end customer, value networks and value chains differ in some key dimensions. Most importantly, the value network is characterised by its dynamic nature. Typically, it is much easier to introduce or remove partners from a value network than it is to add or, more importantly, remove functions and employees from a more permanent value chain. Linking external service providers with the internal value chain has become easier through advanced electronic communication as is illustrated through the case of IBX (described later in the book) that functions as a value chain integrator.

Depending on the closeness of the interaction, different types of technologies will be used. In the case of strategically relevant and frequently recurring interactions, it might be sensible to install proprietary electronic connections that interlink closely with the systems of each partner. In other cases, e-mail correspondence might suffice.

SUMMARY

- First, this chapter defined the concept of a competence as a combination of different resources and skills. It outlined the attributes that a competence must fulfil in order to qualify as a core competence; these are: being valuable, unique, hard to imitate, and valuable across different products or markets. It also highlighted the core competence concept in an e-business context.

- Second, the chapter discussed the value chain which disaggregates the firm into strategically relevant activities. It recognised two types of activities within a firm: primary activities (which include inbound logistics, operations, outbound logistics, marketing and sales, and after-sale service) and support activities (which include firm infrastructure, human resources, technology development and procurement). It then discussed the impact of the Internet on the value chain.

- Third, the chapter introduced the concept of the virtual value chain, which suggests that information captured in the physical value chain (e.g. for activities such as order processing or logistics) should be used as a new source of value creation to enhance the quality of customer service. It also provided a critical perspective of the resource-based view versus the market-based view of strategy formulation.

- Fourth, the chapter presented the ICDT (Information, Communication, Distribution and Transaction) framework and illustrated its four spaces through some specific examples.

■ Finally, the chapter described how a company can move beyond managing an internal value chain to operating along an IT-enabled value network. It also listed the different types of external partners that are typically members of such a value network.

REVIEW QUESTIONS

1 What is a competence and what criteria does it need to fulfil in order to qualify as a core competence? What makes a competence distinctive for e-business?

2 What are the primary and secondary activities of the value chain? How does the Internet impact on these activities?

3 Through what measures can a firm improve the fit between activities in the value chain? Explain how the Internet can influence these measures.

4 Define the concept of the virtual value chain. How does it relate to the traditional value chain concept?

5 Describe the ICDT framework and outline how a company can use it for selecting e-business activities.

6 What is a value network and who are its main partners? What specific issues does a company face when it moves beyond a value chain to become part of a value network?

DISCUSSION QUESTIONS

1 Discuss whether competence-based thinking is more suitable for e-business strategy formulation than the activity-based approach outlined in the value chain concept.

2 Analyse the value chain of an e-commerce venture that you are familiar with. Explain how the Internet has impacted on the primary and support activities of its value chain.

3 Think critically of possible applications of the virtual value chain concept within specific industries and business sectors. Are there some specific business sectors where this concept fits better than in other sectors?

4 Illustrate the ICDT framework through the example of an Internet venture that you are familiar with.

5 Critically assess the ICDT framework and pinpoint its shortcomings.

6 Based on the specific context of the e-commerce venture which you considered in question 2 above, how could this company move beyond managing an internal value chain to operating along a value network? How could it implement the value net concept and what benefits can it expect to gain from it?

RECOMMENDED KEY READING

- D. Besanko, D. Dranove, M. Shanley and S. Schaefer provide a detailed discussion of value creation and value capturing in *Economics of Strategy*, John Wiley, 2003, pp. 358–402.

- M. Porter's book, *Competitive Advantage*, Free Press, 1998, is a seminal work on value creation and the value chain. M. Porter expands on his thinking about competitive advantage in 'What is strategy?', *Harvard Business Review*, 1996, November–December, pp. 70–73.

- R. Amit and C. Zott specifically discuss this chapter's topic in 'Value creation in e-business', *Strategic Management Journal*, 2001, Vol. 22, No. 6, pp. 493–520.

- Within the field of strategic management, there is a broad literature on the resource-based view. While there was already previous research on the resource-based view of the firm, most notably in 1984 with the article by B. Wernerfelt, 'A resource-based view of the firm', *Strategic Management Journal*, 1984, Vol. 5, No. 2, pp. 171–180, this approach became popular in the mainstream management literature through the work of C.K. Prahalad and G. Hamel, 'The core competence of the corporation', *Harvard Business Review*, 1990, May–June, pp. 79–91, and G. Stalk, P. Evans and L. Shulman, 'Competing on capabilities', *Harvard Business Review*, 1992, March–April, pp. 57–69. M. Peteraf provides a more recent academic perspective on the resource-based view in 'The cornerstones of competitive advantage: a resource-based view', *Strategic Management Journal*, 1993, Vol. 14, No. 3, pp. 179–191.

- In the article 'Towards a dynamic theory of strategy', *Strategic Management Journal*, 1995, Vol. 12, No. 8, pp. 102–105, M. Porter attempts to reconcile the market-based and the resource-based views of strategy.

- J. Rayport and J. Sviokla present the concept of the virtual value chain in 'Exploiting the virtual value chain', *Harvard Business Review*, 1995, November–December, pp. 75–85.

USEFUL THIRD-PARTY WEBLINKS

- www.ctvr.ie is the website of the Centre for Telecommunications Value Chain Research and provides publications on related topics.

- www.ecommercetimes.com provides a sound archive of e-business-related articles and publications.

- www.brint.com contains a useful collection of articles on e-business.

NOTES AND REFERENCES

1 For the concept of strategic fit, see also N. Venkatraman and J. Camillus, 'Exploring the concept of fit in strategic management, *Academy of Management Review*, 1984, Vol. 9, pp. 513–525.

2 See G. Hamel and C.K. Prahalad, 'Strategy as Stretch and Leverage', *Harvard Business Review*, 1993, Vol. 71, No. 2, pp. 75–84.

3 For an extensive discussion of the value chain concept, see M. Porter, *Competitive Advantage*, Free Press, 1998, pp. 33–61. A detailed discussion of the impact of IT on the value can be found in M. Porter and V. Millar, 'How information gives you competitive advantage', *Harvard Business Review*, 1985, July–August, pp. 149–160.

4 Michael Dell describes the PC manufacturer's approach to supply-chain management in an interview with J. Magretta, 'The power of virtual integration: an interview with Dell Computer's Michael Dell', *Harvard Business Review*, 1998, March–April, pp. 72–84.

5 R. Waters, 'Dell aims to stretch its way of business', *Financial Times*, 13 November 2003, p. 8.

6 M. Porter, 'Towards a dynamic theory of strategy', *Strategic Management Journal*, 1991, Vol. 12, pp. 102–105.

7 J. Rayport and J. Sviokla developed this concept in 'Exploiting the virtual value chain', *Harvard Business Review*, 1995, November–December, pp. 75–85.

8 For this discussion, see also M. Porter, 'Towards a dynamic theory of strategy', *Strategic Management Journal*, 1991, Vol. 12, No. 8, pp. 102–105.

9 The ICDT model is described in A. Angehrn, 'Designing mature internet strategies: the ICDT model', *European Management Journal*, 1997, Vol. 21, No. 1, pp. 38–47.

10 D. Chaffey, *E-business and E-commerce Management*, FT/Prentice Hall, 2007, pp. 281–283.

11 M. Deise, C. Nowikow, P. King and A. Wright, *Executive's Guide to E-business. From Tactics to Strategy*, John Wiley and D. Chaffey, *E-business and E-commerce Management*, FT/Prentice Hall, 2007, p. 281.

CHAPTER 5

Strategy options in e-business markets

Chapter at a glance

Related case studies

Case study	Primary focus of the case study
2 Nordea	Differentiation strategy
16 Sony BMG	Differentiation strategy
14 Spreadshirt	Outpacing strategy
♢ ING DIRECT	Cost leadership strategy
1 Tesco	Fit between strategy and value chain

Learning outcomes

After completing this chapter, you should be able to:

■ Understand the fundamentals of competitive advantage in e-business.

■ Explain the generic approaches to strategy formulation.

■ Appreciate the meaning of an 'outpacing' strategy.

■ Assess the risk for companies of being 'stuck in the middle'.

■ Understand the levers that improve the fit between the chosen strategy and the value chain activities.

INTRODUCTION

When formulating a business strategy, managers typically choose between two basic options: cost leadership or differentiation. They aim at outperforming competitors either by having lower costs or by offering a superior product or service. A third possibility is to opt for an outpacing strategy through which they aim at achieving at the same time cost leadership and differentiation. However, by doing so, they run the risk of getting stuck in the middle. This chapter discusses the above strategy options, presents their advantages and drawbacks, and illustrates them through some e-business examples.

5.1 Understanding the fundamentals of competitive advantage in e-business

The analyses of external opportunities and threats and internal strengths and weaknesses are important steps in the strategy formulation process. Yet, ultimately they provide only the basis for deciding how a company is to compete in the marketplace. The decision about competitive positioning is at the heart of strategy development, which is the focus of this chapter.

Since the concept of competitive advantage is not trivial, it is useful to look at the requirements that need to be fulfilled in order to gain this type of advantage vis-à-vis rival firms. The strategic triangle, shown in Exhibit 5.1, addresses the main drivers of competitive advantage. In essence, a company needs to take into account customer needs, competitors' offerings and its own offering. The goal of this framework is to address the following four questions regarding the underlying drivers of competitive advantage:

1 *Is the price/benefit ratio (also called value for money) that we offer better than the price/benefit ratio of our best competitor?* Having only a low price is usually not enough to entice a customer to purchase a product (or a service). In addition, the product needs to fulfil minimum customer requirements to be considered attractive. Similarly, a product with a superior performance still needs to be priced within the range of the customer's ability to pay.

2 *Is the value that we offer to our customers perceivable and important to them?* Customers need to be able to recognise the value of the product that is offered to them and they also need to consider it to be important and worth paying for.

3 *Are our costs for making the product (or service) lower than the costs that we incur?* Even though this requirement should be quite obvious, especially during the Internet heydays until 2000 there were numerous business models that had such a high cost structure that it would have been difficult to offset these costs through revenues. For instance, at that time an online pet-food retailer was offering free shipping, which turned out to be an unprofitable business proposition, since the shipping costs (think about a 20lb dog-food bag) destroyed any margins that might have existed in that business.

4 *Is this advantageous position sustainable into the future?* Once actual and would-be competitors find out that a specific way of running a business proves successful, they

Exhibit 5.1 **The strategic triangle addresses the main drivers of competitive advantage**

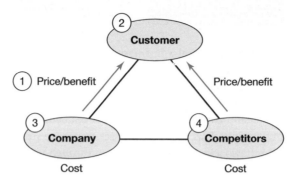

Source: Adapted from H. Hungenberg, *Strategisches Management in Unternehmen*, Gabler, 2006, p. 185.

will typically attempt to imitate this source of competitive advantage. (The process of imitation is discussed in Section 6.1.) Although e-business ventures rarely succeed in building a competitive advantage that is sustainable for an extended period of time, companies such as eBay and openBC managed to create a sustainable advantage through strong network effects.

The framework depicted above highlights the fact that the creation of benefits, as perceived by customers, presents one core element of strategic decision making. In this context, it is useful to differentiate between two kinds of benefits: (1) those that customers consider to be *threshold features,* and (2) those that they consider to be *critical success factors.*[1]

- *Threshold features* are the minimum requirements that a firm must fulfil in any product or service. If a firm cannot meet these minimum requirements, then it will get excluded from the market because customers will not even consider that firm's offering. A threshold feature might be, for example, a website with functioning links or a secure payment mechanism for online transactions. As shown in Exhibit 5.2, improving threshold features beyond a certain point has only a marginal impact on customer satisfaction, which implies that these types of features are not suitable for differentiating a product.

- *Critical success factors,* on the other hand, are those benefits that are crucial for a customer's decision to purchase a given product. At Amazon.com, these features include the large selection of books, their reviews, as well as the convenient and fast shopping experience which is made possible through the company's one-click ordering application. At Nordea Bank, critical success factors include the ease of use of the online banking site and the variety of e-business services that are offered through it.

To summarise, both threshold features and critical success factors create consumer benefit, but only the latter help a firm to differentiate itself from its competitors by creating superior consumer benefit.

Exhibit 5.2 **Impact of threshold features and critical success factors on consumer benefit**

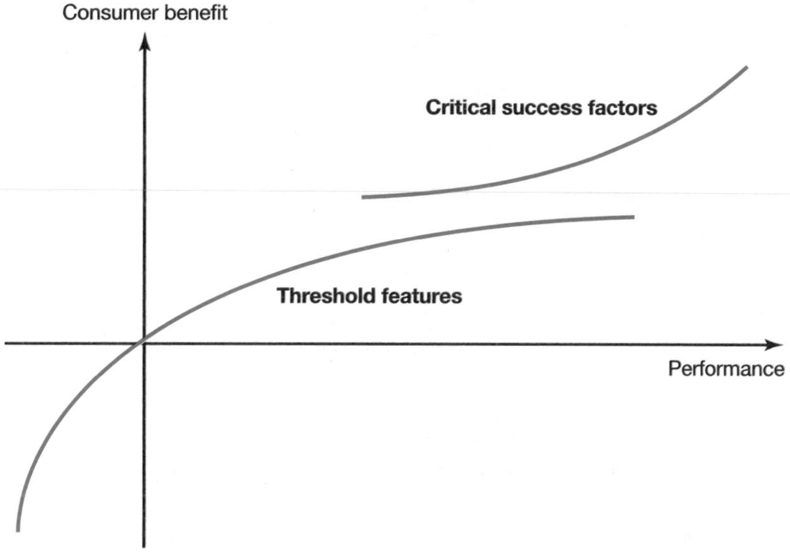

Source: Adapted from H. Hungenberg, *Strategisches Management in Unternehmen*, Gabler, 2006, p. 185.

5.2 Examining the landscape of strategy options for e-business

There are different strategy options that companies can pursue in order to achieve a favourable position in their respective e-business markets. To gain a better understanding of such strategy options, Michael Porter proposed two generic strategies that build on two distinct types of advantage: (1) a price advantage and (2) a performance advantage.

If a firm wants to be able to compete on low prices, it will adjust its cost structure and aim for a *cost leadership strategy* in its industry. If, on the other hand, it can offer comparatively higher performance than competitors, then it will aim for a *differentiated strategy* (see Exhibit 5.3).

In addition, there is a third strategy option called *outpacing strategy*, which aims at combining the advantages of a cost leadership and of a differentiation strategy. These different strategy options are discussed in more detail in the sections below.

5.2.1 Cost leadership strategies

Consider easyJet, the UK-based low-cost airline. The company's ability to compete on low airfares is primarily determined by keeping costs down throughout its value chain while not compromising its threshold requirements such as the security or punctuality of its flights. This example illustrates that a firm that wants to attain a cost leadership position in its industry needs to strive to fulfil the following two requirements:

Exhibit 5.3 **There are two generic approaches to achieve a competitive advantage**

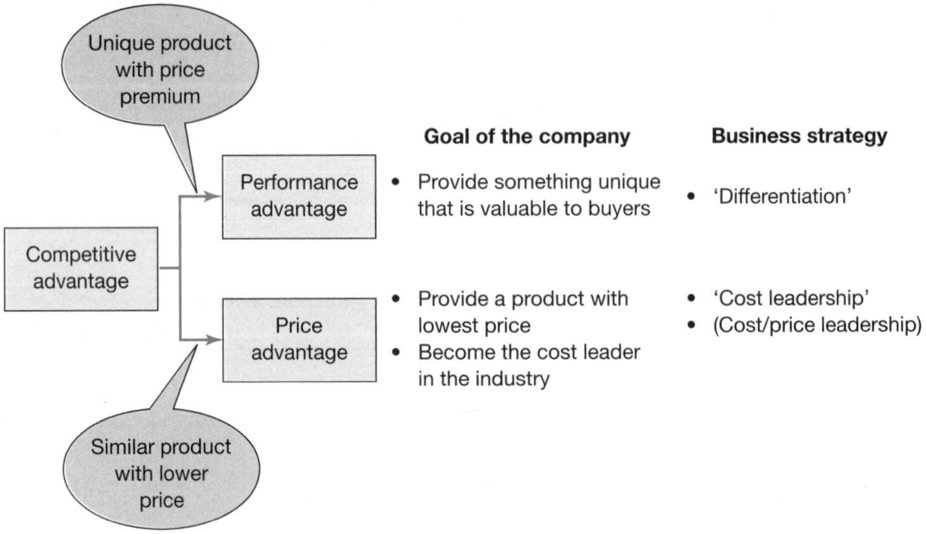

Source: Adapted from H. Hungenberg, *Strategisches Management in Unternehmen*, Gabler, 2006, p. 189.

■ *Lowest cost position.* A firm that aims for a cost leadership position has to be able to produce its product or service at substantially lower costs than its competitors. Lower costs enable the firm to earn profits even in an intensely competitive environment.

■ *Benefit proximity.* Having the lowest costs, however, is not sufficient. In addition, a firm also needs to achieve benefit proximity relative to its competitors, which means that it needs to fulfil at least all threshold criteria. If it is unable to do so, then it will eventually have to offer even lower prices, which reduces or eliminates the benefits gained through the low-cost position. For instance, through its unique direct sales model, Dell, until recently, was able to position itself as a cost leader in the PC industry while, at the same time, achieving high levels of consumer benefit.

Several levers (including *economies of scale and scope*, *factor costs* and *learning effects*) help a firm to achieve a cost leadership position:

Economies of scale

The basic concept of economies of scale is that as a firm increases its product output, it decreases its unit production cost. Why is that so? In general, any production process consists of fixed costs, which do not change as output increases, and variable costs, which go up with an increase in output. Examples of fixed costs are software development, warehouses and machinery, while examples of variable costs are raw materials and package delivery.

High economies of scale usually exist in production processes that have high fixed costs and low variable costs. As the cumulative production quantity increases, fixed costs are spread out over a larger number of products, thereby reducing the unit production costs (see Exhibit 5.4). Once existing production costs reach their constraints, fixed costs increase again as new facilities are required. Variable costs, on the other hand, increase proportionally with output. For instance, as a mail order company handles more packages, postage costs increase proportionally.

Exhibit 5.4 **Economies of scale lead to a decrease in per-unit costs as output increases, whereas dis-economies of scale lead to an increase in per-unit costs**

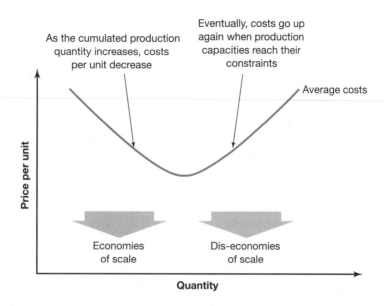

Due to extensive scale effects and efficient IT processes, Wal-Mart in the USA can sell its products at massive discounts in comparison with competitors such as Ahold, Safeway and Kroger. For example, it sells Colgate toothpaste at 63% of rivals' prices, Tropicana orange juice at 58% and Kellogg's corn flakes at 56%.[2]

The expectation of high economies of scale was an important reason why Internet ventures were so popular with business managers and entrepreneurs and highly valued in the stock market. In the traditional book-retailing and banking industries, for example, whenever a company wants to expand its offerings to new customer groups, it has to build new branches or sales outlets. Such physical infrastructure requires high capital investments, while providing only limited potential for scale economies.

Amazon.com thought that it would be able to limit its investment to IT infrastructure, website management and call centres, and then scale up these facilities depending on customer demand. By doing so, it would not need to make any substantial additional investments, while still being able to provide a highly customised service.

The evolution of Internet-based grocery retailing and the different approaches taken by Webvan and Tesco.com illustrate further the concept of economies of scale. The strategy of Webvan relied heavily on the realisation of economies of scale. It set up throughout the USA centralised and highly automated warehouses at a unit cost of $30 million. These were essentially fixed costs, since they were incurred independent of utilisation. The expectation was that variable costs for each shipment would be very low, since the picking and packaging processes were highly automated, thereby reducing the need for expensive labour.

The business rationale was that Webvan would be able to position itself as a low-cost leader while still being able to deliver high levels of consumer benefit through the automated delivery process. It was thought that as customer numbers increased, the warehouses would operate at capacity, which in turn would create substantial economies of scale. The latter were also crucial for the grocery delivery process, whereby delivery trucks were filled at the centralised warehouse and then driven from house to house, delivering the items. Costs for the delivery varied only marginally if the truck left half-empty or completely full. Thus, having enough customers to be able to fill up the truck was another source of substantial economies of scale in the delivery process. We cannot say whether the above reasoning would have worked out eventually, since Webvan filed for bankruptcy only one year after going public.

The important insight from this experience is that economies of scale are valuable only if they can be realised, which usually requires a large throughput. Tesco.com reached a different conclusion after analysing the economies of scale potential of warehouse-based delivery. The company decided, contrary to the common wisdom, that it would be sensible to organise the order fulfilment and delivery process out of its existing stores. By doing so, it was able to reduce substantially the need for additional investment, which would have created high fixed costs. Furthermore, through this model, Tesco.com was able gradually to scale up its operations by adding additional regions on a store-by-store basis.

Economies of scope

The logic behind economies of scope is similar to that of economies of scale. While economies of scale can be realised by increasing the production of one product type, economies of scope result from expanding the variety of products sold using the same R&D, production and delivery assets.

The main goal here remains the same: it is to spread fixed costs over a wider basis by adding new products or services to the existing offering. Economies of scope can be achieved by extending into different markets and sectors of an industry. Amazon.com, for instance, has achieved economies of scope through the introduction of additional categories of goods on its website, thereby potentially increasing its share of the wallet of any given customer. Although it started out with just books, Amazon.com has since added new product categories, such as CDs, videos, electronics and clothes, using the same technology platform and delivery infrastructure.

Economies of scale and scope should be considered within the context of a specific strategy and not pursued just for the sake of lowering costs. What always needs to be kept in mind is the type of value proposition that a company offers to customers. Adding scale by reaching out to new customer groups, or adding scope by offering new products, might help to reduce the cost position of a firm. In addition to costs, however, it is also important to consider the revenues that can be generated after expanding into different customer segments or adding new product categories.

Factor costs

Factor costs represent a crucial cost driver, especially for retailing companies that act as intermediaries. The ability to bargain down input prices, for instance through bulk purchasing, can be an effective lever for lowering costs. Both low factor costs and scale effects are most likely to be realised through high volumes. Thus, a large market share in comparison with that of competitors is generally a prerequisite for being a low-cost provider. The goal of e-marketplaces such as IBX, for instance, is to pool the purchasing power of different business units within an organisation, thereby reducing factor costs.

Learning effects

Learning effects can lower costs as a firm improves its efficiency over time, thereby reducing slack and wasteful activities.

5.2.2 Differentiation strategies

A differentiation strategy can be achieved by providing comparatively more consumer benefit than competitors. The main questions that a firm that is striving for a differentiated positioning needs to ask are: What creates consumer benefit? What is unique? What cannot be imitated? There are tangible sources for differentiation, such as product quality, service quality and speed of delivery, and intangible sources, such as brand and reputation.

Similar to the cost leadership approach, firms seeking a differentiated position need to ensure cost proximity to other competitors to guarantee superior value creation. This means that the cost disadvantage has to be small enough so the differentiation advantage can override it.

It is not uncommon for firms to overlook the need for cost proximity when they focus solely on providing the highest-quality product in the market. Motorola's development of the Iridium phone is a prime example of a differentiation approach that did not pay close enough attention to costs.

At this point, it is important to clarify the definition of benefit. It is inherently difficult to measure, because consumer benefit cannot be objectively quantified, regardless of place, time and person. Instead, it varies from individual to individual, depending on:

- *Personal preferences.* You might derive a high benefit from driving a sports car, whereas your nextdoor neighbour, who has three children, will get much more benefit from driving a mini-van.
- *Place.* Think of a freezer in the Arctic versus a freezer in the Sahara.
- *Time.* Think of the benefit of electric light during the day versus at night.

What elements need to be considered when determining the level(s) of consumer benefit?[3] There are a wide range of sources for consumer benefit, which can be divided into *tangible* and *intangible* sources, depending on whether they can or cannot be observed directly (see Exhibit 5.5).

Tangible sources of consumer benefit include the following:

- *Product/service quality.* This characteristic refers to the objective traits of a product, such as its functionality, durability (or reliability) and ease of installation. For instance, the quality of Ducati motorcycles can be determined accurately by metrics such as maximum speed, acceleration, fuel consumption or breakdown rate. In the service dimension, for instance, the quality of Tesco.com's online grocery business can be measured by the freshness and overall quality of the goods delivered. Furthermore, service quality entails characteristics such as the friendliness and know-how of salespeople or, in the case of a website, the degree of personalisation, ease of use, and response time and information quality of online enquiries.

Exhibit 5.5 Tangible and intangible sources of differentiation

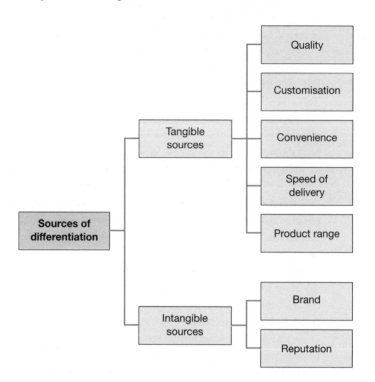

- *Degree of product or service customisation.* The more a product or service can be adapted to specific customer needs, the more benefit it creates for the individual user. Dell manufactures its PCs to customer specifications, resulting in two types of benefit. First, all the components that an individual customer values in a PC are included; second, all components that are not valued are left out, thus helping to keep down PC prices.

- *Convenience.* The mental energy, effort and time that buyers have to spend during the purchasing process need to be taken into account when comparing different providers.[4] This is why people do not drive 10 km to the discount supermarket just to buy one item, but instead go to the local corner store, even though that item might be more expensive there. Through its online grocery service, Tesco.com aims at increasing convenience for shoppers, and especially for busy people.

- *Speed of delivery.* The ability to deliver products and services quickly is an important source of consumer benefit. Speed depends on the availability of products, location of the seller and quality of the logistical process. A firm that has the ability to deliver faster than its competitors because of its management approach, superior process flow and IT systems and applications can create a significant competitive advantage. Amazon.com, for instance, installed proprietary warehouses to be able to ensure that products are available and get shipped out in a timely manner.

- *Product range.* A broad and deep selection provides an important source of differentiation since it allows convenient and quick one-stop shopping. Amazon.com is a prime example of a retailer with a deep and broad product range, since customers can find, for example, most book titles that are currently in print (and out of print).

Intangible sources of consumer benefit include the following:

- *Brand.* This characteristic refers to the perceived traits that consumers associate with the company that is selling a product or a service. A strong brand tends to result from products that meet high-quality standards, yet this may not necessarily be so. It might also come as a result of intensive and innovative marketing activities. Brands need to be built and nurtured in order to use them as a differentiating characteristic in the marketplace.

  Most online firms, which could not benefit from 'viral growth' (i.e. through word of mouth), had to invest heavily to build up their brand, as shown in the StayFriends example contained in the case studies section of the book. On the other hand, for established physical firms such as Tesco, Nordea and Ducati, it was much easier to acquire online customers, since they already benefited from a strong brand through their store outlets, branch network or physical dealerships.

- *Reputation.* The perceived past performance of a company is a major factor influencing reputation. Customers value reputation because it decreases their purchasing risk. When it comes to making online payments, a company's reputation is especially critical, since many online customers still feel uneasy providing their credit card information to an unknown vendor.

5.2.3 Outpacing strategies (and the risk of getting 'stuck in the middle')

Porter argues that in order to have a unique and defendable competitive position, it is advisable to seek out one of the above two strategies.[5] The underlying assumption is that powerful strategies require trade-offs: a high level of quality usually entails high costs, while a cost leadership strategy usually impairs the ability to provide above-average levels of consumer benefit. As a result, firms that try to be both a quality and a cost leader at the same time tend to end up getting 'stuck in the middle', a position that is characterised as neither low-cost nor differentiated.

More recently, Porter's concept of the generic strategies has been challenged by numerous empirically-based studies.[6] A main conclusion of these analyses is that, in reality, companies can also combine both types of advantage, i.e. a cost and a differentiation advantage, following an 'outpacing' or 'hybrid' strategy (see Exhibit 5.6).

For example, one possible source for an outpacing advantage is quality management. This can be demonstrated using the example of Toyota. On the one hand, the Toyota Production System increases the perceived use value of Toyota's cars, since, for the past decade, they have proven to be more reliable and functional than the products of most other car manufacturers. On the other hand, the high reliability that guarantees high levels of use value also helps to improve Toyota's cost position by reducing the number of expensive call-backs.

Similarly, during the early 1990s Tesco competed in the British grocery retailing market primarily on low price. At that time the motto of the company was 'Pile it high and sell it cheap', in reference to the shelving practice of trying to accommodate as many products in as little space as possible. Over the years, Tesco has refined its value proposition by adding differentiating elements such as the online grocery retailing channel while still remaining highly cost competitive, thereby outperforming competitors on both the price and the quality dimensions. In doing so, Tesco effectively resolved the trade-off dilemma between quality and costs.

Exhibit 5.6 **Perceived performance and relative price position determine a firm's strategy**

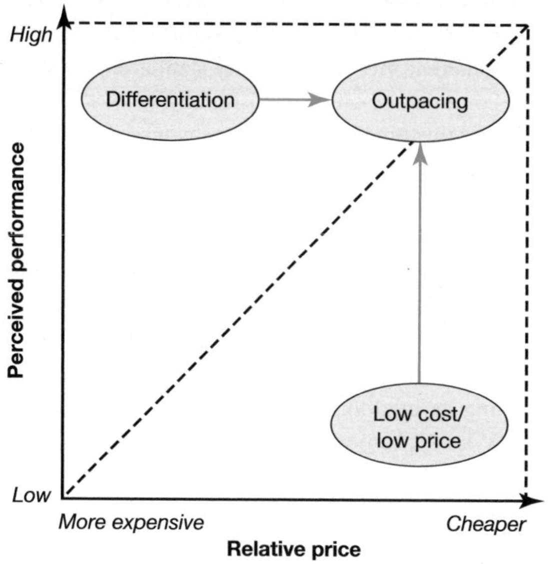

Source: Adapted from H. Hungenberg, *Strategisches Management in Unternehmen*, Gabler, 2006, p. 194.

From a theoretical perspective, the following factors can actually undermine this trade-off: (1) the development of new technologies, (2) wastefulness and (3) economies of scale and learning effects.

■ *The development of new technologies*, as is the case with the Internet, offers innovative firms the opportunity, at least initially, to make large leaps in both the cost and the differentiation dimensions. Consider again the example of Amazon.com. Compared with other online book retailers and also with most bricks-and-mortar bookstores, it offers the most differentiated product and service, yet at the same time prices are highly competitive. This is possible because Amazon.com has been continuously improving its technology to lower costs.

For instance, from 1999 to 2003, Amazon.com increased the volume-handling capacity of its warehouses threefold, which has helped to reduce warehouse operations cost from 20% of revenues in 1999 to 10% in 2003.[7] While this approach is possible as long as the technology is still evolving (and serious competition has not yet emerged), one may at least question its sustainability once the Internet and its associated back-end logistics become commonplace.

If Internet ventures can persistently have lower costs or offer higher value than their bricks-and-mortar competitors, then there will be two possible scenarios. First, if both types of businesses (i.e. the online and offline businesses) continue to co-exist and serve different markets, then competition will take place between Internet ventures. Second, if Internet-based firms turn out to be a substitute for bricks-and-mortar firms, then the latter will increasingly be driven out of business and the competition will start out all over again among Internet players. Either way, competition, and with it the need to have a clear strategic position, is likely to increase.[8] Other more mature industries, where new technology developments are of only secondary importance, indicate that it then becomes necessary to seek a more precise positioning.

■ *Many firms and industries are wasteful in their activities*, which makes it possible to optimise quality while at the same time reducing costs. When companies are highly inefficient they can make great strides without having to face the trade-off between quality and costs. Yet, at this point, we are also dealing not really with strategic decisions but with issues of operational effectiveness. During the Internet boom years, many start-up companies, such as the online fashion retailer Boo.com, were spending lavishly on marketing, PR events and travelling (see the FT article 'Burning money at Boo', p. 18). Cutting costs in such situations is easy since there are no real trade-offs to be made.

■ *Scale economies and learning effects* might allow a firm to generate significant cost advantages while still pursuing a differentiated strategy. They enable a firm to achieve both low costs (through scale effects) and a superior product offering. Tesco, for instance, can offer both its online and offline customers low prices because, due to its sheer size, it can source products at lower purchasing costs than most competitors.

In spite of the above factors, the trade-off between differentiation and cost is an important issue to consider in strategy formulation, because, more often than not, a firm cannot excel in everything it does.

5.3 Developing strategy alternatives

In the above sections, we described different generic types of strategy alternatives such as cost leadership strategies, differentiation strategies and outpacing strategies. In contrast to these generic strategy types, real-world strategies are characterised by numerous individual aspects that in sum constitute the overall strategy. The strategic gameboard framework provides a structural approach to determine systematically the different dimensions of a strategy (see Exhibit 5.7).

The strategic gameboard framework raises three key questions that help managers to formulate consistent business strategies. The first question relates to the type of competitive advantage that the company wants to strive for. Is the focus on being a low-cost provider, on having a differentiated product offering, or pursuing an outpacing strategy? These options were discussed in detail in the previous sections.

In addition to the decision regarding the type of competitive advantage, it is also essential to think where the company wants to compete, i.e. which market(s) or market segment(s) it wants to target (for a more detailed discussion of market targeting, see Section 3.4.3). On the one hand, it is possible to pursue a niche strategy by only offering highly specialised products for special customer segments or for limited regions. This type of a niche strategy can lead to a competitive advantage because it opens up the opportunity for building up specific know-how (in the case of highly specialised products) or specific customer knowledge (in the case of regional target markets). However, the problems of niche strategies are that they can lead to a dependence on single customer segments, which increases the overall business risk, and that they cause a lack of scale, which in turn increases the per-unit costs. This is the main reason why low-cost strategies typically cannot be pursued in niche markets. On the other hand, it is possible to address the whole market with a given strategy type.

Exhibit 5.7 **The strategic gameboard helps to formulate consistent business strategies**

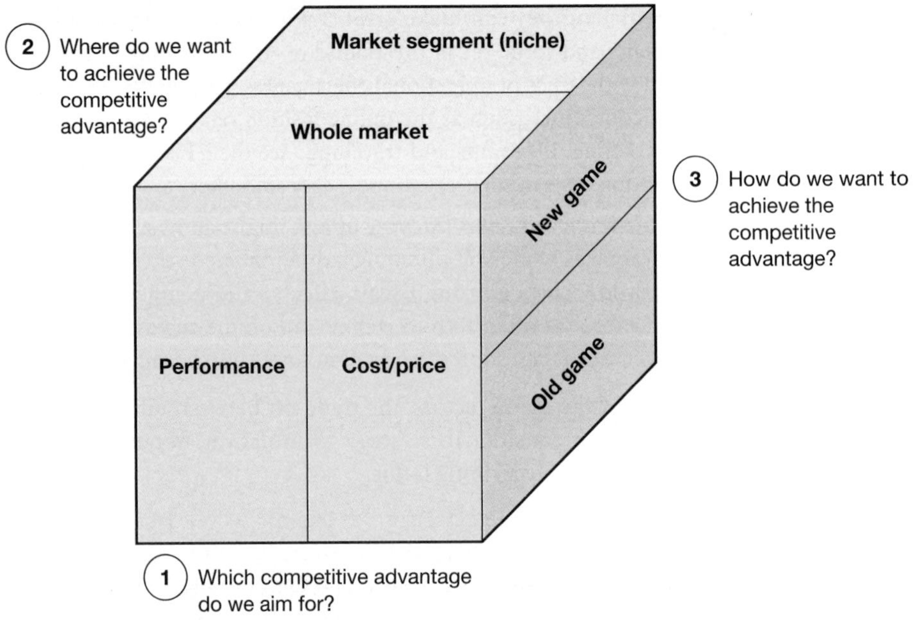

Source: Adapted from H. Hungenberg, *Strategisches Management in Unternehmen*, Gabler, 2006, p. 251.

Finally, it is also important to determine the type of business model to implement the strategy. The strategic gameboard differentiates between pursuing (1) an old game and (2) a new game. The old game stands for business models that historically have been used by other companies in the industry. For instance, an entrepreneur who was thinking about setting up a traditional bricks-and-mortar bookstore in the mid-1990s was pursuing the old game of book retailing. When playing an old game, a competitive advantage can be achieved primarily through better execution such as higher quality, higher productivity or faster time-to-market. An old game business model carries a lower risk because it has been done before, but at the same time it also offers lower potential for differentiation vis-à-vis competitors because everybody else is playing the same type of game.

In contrast, playing a new game implies using a business model that is fundamentally different from what has been done before by other players in the industry. At the time when it was first implemented, Dell's business model of selling PCs through direct sales channels presented a new game in the industry. In doing so, Dell was able to leapfrog the competition. Similarly, through its innovative use of the Internet, Amazon.com was able to become one of the largest booksellers worldwide, even though the book-retailing market had been crowded and highly competitive before. However, it also needs to be pointed out that the advantages derived from playing a new game do not necessarily last indefinitely. Instead, they whither away as other companies imitate the game. (See in Section 6.1 for the different ways through which a company can build up barriers to imitation.) Nowadays, for instance, Internet retailing by itself can no longer be considered a new game. Instead, companies aiming at playing a new game again need to look for new ways to redefine markets. Chapter 7 presents the framework of value innovation that helps to develop systematically new-game business models.

5.4 Creating a fit between the chosen strategy and the value chain

Activities in the value chain are not performed in isolation; instead, they are linked to each other throughout the value chain.[9] A firm's ability to create a better and unique fit between activities is ultimately responsible for its competitive advantage. Thus, the whole of the value chain is more important than the sum of its individual activities. Sustainability also results from a unique fit, since it is much more difficult for competitors effectively to imitate a set of interrelated activities than just to replicate one activity.

There are three main levers that determine the fit of activities within a firm: (1) *consistency between activities*, (2) *reinforcement of activities* and (3) *optimisation of efforts*.

5.4.1 Consistency between activities

Consistency ensures that individual activities with their respective advantages build on each other instead of cancelling themselves out. For instance, if a company's goal is to differentiate itself from its competitors through a premium product or service, it needs to design activities such that each activity adds to the differentiation advantage, i.e. increase benefits for customers and create uniqueness. On the other hand, if the goal is to be a low-cost provider, then the costs of each activity should be kept to a minimum, while still maintaining the threshold features that are required to stay in the market. Lack of consistency dilutes the positioning of a company.

Why is that so? Porter argues that strategic positions are not sustainable if there are no trade-offs with other positions.[10] If a firm wants to provide the highest-quality standards, then this usually entails higher costs, while the desire for lower costs usually results in a decrease of quality. This trade-off arises from the following sources:

- *Activities.* The trade-off results in part directly from the activities involved. Different positions require different processes, resources, skills and value chain set-ups. A firm that wants to achieve a differentiated position needs to invest heavily to ensure the highest-quality standards (and, hopefully, to be able to command a price premium). Cost leaders, on the other hand, need activities that provide the lowest possible cost structure because they want to compete through low prices. Customers of these firms want to receive the basic service at the lowest possible price. Thus, a firm that wants to be a cost leader and unnecessarily bloats its costs by over-engineering its activities is actually destroying value.

- *Image and reputation.* Trying to be both a low-cost and a differentiated provider can easily cause inconsistencies in a firm's image and reputation. It is much easier for a firm to communicate its strategy credibly to its different stakeholders (such as customers and shareholders) when it has a clear position. Think of the car manufacturer Porsche. To build up and maintain the reputation of premier sports car manufacturer, Porsche needs to position itself clearly with its products and services. Similarly, a low-cost provider such as the US retailer Wal-Mart focuses its efforts on providing its products at the lowest possible costs.

■ *Strategy implementation.* It is much easier to implement a strategy within a firm if employees have a clear guiding vision of the strategy and if they do not have to ask themselves with every decision: 'Are we competing on low cost, or are we trying to be a differentiated provider?'

The need for consistency emphasises the requirement that strategy is not just about deciding which activities a company should perform but also, and equally importantly, which activities not to perform. If a company wants to be everything to everyone, it runs the risk of not being able to do anything better than the competition and will end up being 'stuck in the middle', where it has neither a cost nor a differentiation advantage vis-à-vis the competition. Porter argues that strategic positions are not sustainable if there are no trade-offs with other positions. If a company wants to provide benefits, this usually entails higher costs, while the desire for lower costs usually results in a decrease of use value for customers.

The low-cost airline easyJet is a good example of a company that is continuously striving for consistency across different activities of its value chain (see the Blog Box below). To minimise costs, easyJet forgoes many of the features, frills and perks that are offered by traditional airlines. While the latter rely heavily on expensive ticketing offices and sales agencies, easyJet sells almost solely through the Internet. Furthermore, customers do not receive printed tickets. Instead, upon arrival at the airport's check-in counter, they receive their boarding pass following passport identification. On board, passengers are not offered free meals and drinks; instead they have to pay for each drink or snack. Finally, after landing, aircraft are turned around much faster than the industry average, which helps to reduce standing fees and increase capacity utilisation.

5.4.2 Reinforcement of activities

Reinforcement is the second important characteristic of a good fit between the different activities of a company. Its underlying thinking is that competitive advantage comes as a result of how some activities influence the quality of other activities to create higher quality in products or services, thereby increasing the use value for customers. As emphasised above, in terms of the value framework, this implies that the total value created throughout the value chain is larger than the sum of the values created in the individual steps of the value chain.

For instance, if a company has a highly motivated and skilled sales force, it is much more effective if the company also has excellent R&D and production facilities to produce a high-quality product. Similarly, a sophisticated website, such as the one of Amazon.com, becomes more valuable when it is combined with a warehouse system that allows for fast, reliable and efficient deliveries. The case of Nordea illustrates the importance of reinforcement. Among other reasons, Nordea is successful because it managed to create a tight fit between all its online and offline banking activities, which allowed the bank to move quickly online a large number of its branch customers. Pure online banks cannot imitate this effective customer-acquisition approach, since they do not have a physical branch network. Other bricks-and-mortar banks that tried to follow suit did not realise the importance of closely connecting the online and offline businesses. They opted instead for distinct profit-centre structures, thereby creating competition between their online and offline activities. A firm's ability to cross-sell and/or sell through complementary distribution channels is critical, since, especially in the service industry, the cost of acquiring a new customer can be two to three times the cost of selling to an existing customer.

5.4.3 Optimisation of efforts

The third characteristic of a good fit is the optimisation of efforts. While reinforcement primarily focuses on improving the customer experience by linking up separate activities, optimisation emphasises the importance of cost reduction through the elimination of redundancy and wasted activity. For instance, Internet companies that have optimised their order-taking process can reduce their costs for truck fleet and personnel. Dell currently presents the best practice in optimisation of efforts. Activities such as sourcing, production, sales and service are connected in such a way as to minimise costs while still providing superior customer benefits. Within the value framework, optimisation of efforts implies that the cost reduction in one area of the value chain leads to cost reductions in other parts of the value chain as well.

Creating fit between activities through consistency, reinforcement and optimisation of efforts connects the conceptual act of strategy formulation to operational implementation issues, which determine how to choose and structure a company's activities. The value-process framework helps to conceptualise this leap from broad strategy formulation, e.g. the low-cost positioning of easyJet, to the actual implementation throughout the different steps of the value chain.

It is necessary to analyse closely the vertical and horizontal boundaries of a firm and to set up the internal organisation accordingly, in order to create fit among activities. This requires substantial resources and managerial skills, which also explains why strategy has long-term implications. Changing strategies randomly makes it hard to obtain a competitive advantage, because creating fit takes time and effort. This does not mean that new tools and concepts such as total quality management (TQM), which might help to increase operational effectiveness, should generally be discarded, yet it is important to realise that it is sensible to implement these tools only as long as they do not alter the fundamental basis of the strategic position and its trade-offs.

BLOG BOX

EasyJet – setting up an organisation for a low-cost strategy

easyJet keeps costs low by eliminating the unnecessary costs and frills' which characterise 'traditional' airlines. This is done in a number of ways:

- *Use of the Internet to reduce distribution costs*. easyJet was one of the first airlines to embrace the opportunity of the Internet when it sold its first seat online in April 1998. Now approximately 95% of all seats are sold over the Internet, making easyJet one of Europe's biggest Internet retailers.

- *Maximise the utilisation of the substantial assets*. Maximising utilisation of each aircraft significantly reduces the unit cost.

- *Ticketless travel*. Passengers instead receive an email containing their travel details and booking reference when they book online. This helps to reduce significantly the cost of issuing, distributing, processing and reconciling millions of tickets each year.

→

■ *No free lunch*. Everybody always jokes about airline food – so why provide it if people don't want it? Eliminating free catering on board reduces cost and unnecessary bureaucracy and management. It is also an important differentiator between easyJet and other airlines and a potent reflection of its low-cost approach. Passengers can purchase food on board and, ironically, easyJet has won awards for its catering service! The concept of a 'simple service model' also reflects a more general point about eliminating other unnecessary, complex-to-manage and costly services, such as preassigned seats, interline connections with other airlines and cargo/freight carriage.

■ *Efficient use of airports*. easyJet flies to main destination airports throughout Europe, but gains efficiencies through rapid turnaround times and progressive landing charges agreements with the airports. By reducing turnarounds to 30 minutes and below, easyJet can achieve extra rotations on the high-frequency routes, thereby maximising utilisation rates of its aircraft.

■ *Paperless operations*. Since its launch easyJet has simplified its working practices by embracing the concept of the paperless office. The management and administration of the company is undertaken entirely on IT systems which can be accessed through secure servers from anywhere in the world, enabling huge flexibility in the running of the airline.

Source: Adapted from www.easyjet.com.

SUMMARY

■ This chapter focused on strategy options in e-business markets. First, it reviewed generic strategy options for value creation in e-business. These options revolved around cost leadership and differentiation strategies.

■ Second, this chapter discussed the concept of being stuck in the middle, which refers to companies that focus on neither a cost leadership nor a differentiation strategy. These companies face the risk of not possessing any competitive advantage vis-à-vis more specialised rivals. However, there are also factors that can allow a firm to outpace its rivals by offering both lower costs and differentiation. These include the development of new technologies, wastefulness of companies, scale economies and learning effects.

■ Third, in order to develop strategy alternatives to the above generic strategies, the chapter suggested using the strategic gameboard framework. The latter provides a structural approach to determine systematically the different dimensions of a strategy.

■ Finally, this chapter discussed how to create a better fit between the chosen strategy and the value chain activities in order to achieve a sustainable competitive advantage. It described the three main levers that determine the fit of activities within a firm; these are: consistency between activities, reinforcement of activities and optimisation of efforts.

REVIEW QUESTIONS

1 What generic strategies can a company use to create value for its customers?

2 What levers can a company use in e-business to create a cost or a differentiation strategy?

3 Why do some companies end up being 'stuck in the middle'?

4 What are the factors that allow a company to pursue an outpacing strategy?

5 How can a company look for new market spaces outside its own industry?

6 What are the three main levers that determine the fit of activities within a firm?

DISCUSSION QUESTIONS

1 Illustrate each quadrant of the generic strategy options matrix through an e-business example.

2 Explain how the Internet can help a company to achieve a competitive advantage in the marketplace through (1) cost leadership and (2) differentiation. Illustrate each case through an actual example, other than those mentioned in this chapter.

3 Pick out one e-business company of your choice. Which type of competitive advantage does it pursue? What factors help this company create superior customer value? Is the strategy sustainable?

4 Analyse how the Internet can help companies not to get 'stuck in the middle'. Illustrate your answer through an actual example.

5 Discuss how an Internet venture can outperform its competitors on both the price and quality dimensions. Provide some examples to support your arguments.

6 Consider an Internet venture that you are familiar with and think of ways in which it could further improve the fit among its activities through consistency, reinforcement and optimisation.

RECOMMENDED KEY READING

■ M. Porter's book *Competitive Strategy*, Free Press, 1998, provides detailed accounts of different generic strategy types.

■ B. Henderson emphasises the importance of differentiation as a key element in strategy formulation when he compares strategy to biological evolution in 'The origins of strategy', *Harvard Business Review*, 1989, November–December, pp. 139–143.

USEFUL THIRD-PARTY WEBLINKS

- www.brint.com provides a useful archive containing articles on e-business.
- www.davechaffey.com contains updates about diverse aspects of strategy.
- www.ecommercetimes.com is an online newspaper specific to e-commerce developments.

NOTES AND REFERENCES

1 For a detailed discussion of threshold features and success, see G. Johnson, K. Scholes and R. Whittington, *Exploring Corporate Strategy*, 7th edition, Prentice Hall, 2005.
2 'Make it cheaper, and cheaper', *The Economist*, 13 December 2003, pp. 6–7.
3 There are numerous approaches available to estimate consumer benefit. They include (1) the reservation price method, (2) the attribute-rating method, (3) hedonic pricing and (4) conjoint analysis. For a more detailed discussion of these approaches, refer to D. Besanko, D. Dranove, M. Shanley and S. Schaefer, *Economics of Strategy*, John Wiley, 2003, pp. 416–419.
4 See also P. Kotler, *Marketing Management*, Prentice Hall, 2002, pp. 60–61.
5 Ibid., pp. 41–44.
6 A. Fleck discusses the concept of outpacing strategies in his book *Hybride Wettbewerbsstrategien*, Gabler, 1995.
7 F. Vogelstein, 'Mighty Amazon', *Fortune*, 26 May 2003, pp. 64–66.
8 For a discussion of the economic fundamentals, see S. Liebowitz, *Rethinking the Network Economy*, Amacom, 2002, pp. 115–117.
9 For different types of strategic fit among activities, see M. Porter, 'What is strategy?', *Harvard Business Review*, 1996, November–December, pp. 70–73.
10 Ibid.

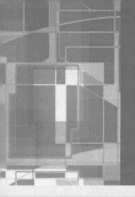

CHAPTER 6

Sustaining a competitive advantage over time

Chapter at a glance

Related case studies

Learning outcomes

After completing this chapter, you should be able to:

■ Understand the requirements for a successful imitation and the barriers to imitation.

■ Appreciate how companies can assess the threat of a disruptive innovation.

■ Identify the ways that companies can follow in order to deal with a disruptive innovation.

■ Recognise the cognitive frames that companies can adopt when facing a disruptive innovation and understand the reasons underlying their contradicting nature.

INTRODUCTION

This chapter first discusses how a company can build up barriers to imitation. It then focuses on how to deal with the threats of a disruptive innovation in e-business. More specifically, it stresses the importance of understanding the fundamental process of disruptive innovations and determining the underlying reasons for the incumbent's failure. Next, the chapter suggests some questions that companies need to raise in order to assess the threat of a disruptive innovation. Possible ways for dealing with a disruptive innovation are then suggested. The chapter concludes by providing some ways for selecting the appropriate mental frame for an efficient response to a disruptive innovation.

6.1 Building up barriers to imitation

Maintaining a competitive advantage, be it through cost leadership or through a differentiated position, is a difficult challenge for most companies, especially in the realm of e-business where there are few sources of competitive advantage that remain stable over time. Consider for example the rise of Netscape Navigator, the most prominent web browser in the mid-1990s. At that time, Netscape Navigator had a global market share of over 80%. When Microsoft started to include online capabilities in all of its software products, it also developed Internet Explorer, essentially an imitation of Netscape Navigator, albeit with more advanced functionalities. Ultimately, Netscape lost its dominant position to Microsoft.

However, successful imitation is not trivial and there are measures that companies can take to reduce the risk of being imitated. Below, we discuss the requirements that need to be fulfilled for a competitor to imitate successfully, and we also discuss the barriers to entry that incumbent companies can build up to prevent others from invading their market (see Exhibit 6.1).[1]

First, in order to become aware of a successful business model, potential imitators *must be able to identify* its competitive superiority. In the case of non-public companies, finding out about successful business models is not trivial since there are frequently no hard data available regarding profitability or even sales. During the writing phase of this book, we had an interesting exchange with the leading German auction platform www.My-Hammer.de where private homeowners place requests for painting or repair jobs and carpenters and other craftworkers offer their services to them. The business model has proven to be highly successful in Germany and would have provided an excellent source for writing a case study. Even though, in principle, the management of My-Hammer was interested in collaborating in the development of a case study, they finally decided against it, because they did not want to divulge information about their company to potential would-be competitors.

Second, potential entrants in a market *must be willing to imitate* the successful business model. Incumbents can take measures to prevent them from entering the market. One way to do so is through deterrence. For instance, if a low-cost competitor wants to enter a market, existing companies might signal to the new entrant that they will retaliate by also

Exhibit 6.1 A company can build up numerous barriers against imitation

Imitator	Incumbent
Requirements for successful imitation	**Barriers against successful imitation**
(1) Must be able to identify competitive superiority	• Withhold information about profitability • Forgo short-term profits for long-term success
(2) Must be willing to imitate	• Deterrence: signal promise of retaliation • Make commitments to make threat credible • Pre-emption: exploit all available investment opportunities/secure access to resources
(3) Must be able to understand sources of competitive advantage	• Tacit knowledge: rely on skills, processes or culture/resources that are implicit • Causal ambiguity: rely on a complex, multidimensional mix of sources
(4) Must be able to build/acquire necessary resources	• Base differentiation on resources that are rare/immobile/contracted • Exploit time lags

Source: Adapted from H. Hungenberg, *Strategisches Management in Unternehmen*, Gabler, 2006, p. 251.

lowering their own prices, which would render the market entry unattractive. Furthermore, to make threats via potential imitators credible, it is often helpful to 'burn the bridges', i.e. make irreversible commitments by investing substantially. Finally, it is also possible to pre-empt potential competitors by exploiting all available investment opportunities and by securing access to scarce resources (such as patents or crucial personnel). For instance, pre-emption might entail buying up a small competitor with the sole purpose of ensuring that other, potentially more threatening, would-be competitors do not acquire the company and its know-how.

Third, potential entrants *must also be able to understand the sources of competitive advantage*. Most frequently, the competitive advantage does not just result from one resource or capability but instead from the complex interplay between multiple different factors that might not even be clearly understood by the incumbent company itself. Obviously, acquiring this type of tacit knowledge is even more difficult for outsiders who do not have direct access to the company. Also, it is not always clear what the causal linkages between different factors are that lead to a competitive advantage. For instance, it is not entirely clear whether it is the free time that developers at Google have to work on their pet projects that contributes to the success of the company, or whether it is Google's success that allows management to give this time to developers.

Fourth, a would-be imitator *must also be able to build or acquire the necessary resources and capabilities* successfully to copy the incumbent's business model. The most promising way to provide protection from this is to base the competitive advantage on resources that are rare, immobile or contracted. For instance, in the case of openBC, a core element of the company's competitive advantage lies in its broad membership base. Replicating this membership would be very difficult for a potential imitator.

Protecting against imitators is only one of two key levers for the preservation of competitive advantage. The other possibility is to upgrade constantly one's own capabilities through continuous innovation, thereby making imitation attempts irrelevant. We discuss this possibility in more detail in Chapter 7, which deals with 'value innovation'.

6.2 Dealing with the threats of disruptive innovations in e-business[2]

Let us think back to the mid-1970s. During those years, Apple introduced the first PC in the private consumer market. The Apple II, developed by Steve Wozniak, was technologically inferior to the then dominant mini-computers which were first developed in the 1960s. They were the size of a large refrigerator, cost $20,000 or more, and were meant for accounting departments and other corporate users that required advanced computing capabilities. When confronted with PCs, highly successful mini-computer manufacturers such as Digital Equipment Corporation considered them to be 'toys' that were of no interest to their demanding main customers. As a result, they did not invest in this new technology.

Due to its technological simplicity, however, the Apple was also much cheaper (an Apple II was about $2,000 while a mini-computer cost at least $20,000), it was much smaller (an Apple II had the size of today's PCs while the mini-computer was as big as a closet) and much easier to use than a mini-computer. As the technological performance of PCs improved over time, they attracted new users who hitherto had not been using computers and also caused customers, who had previously bought mini-computers, to switch over to PCs. Interestingly enough, by then, incumbent manufacturers of mini-computers were unable to integrate PCs into their existing business models, which, ultimately, led to the demise of the mini-computer industry.

6.2.1 Understanding the fundamental process of disruptive innovations

This failure of once highly successful incumbents and the parallel rise of successful start-up companies is not uncommon. The disruptive innovation theory attempts to explain the reasons for this seemingly inexplicable demise of established incumbents. The fundamental assumption of the theory of disruptive innovation is that there are two distinct types of circumstances that companies can find themselves in: (1) *sustaining circumstances* and (2) *disruptive circumstances.*

In sustaining circumstances, established companies develop innovative products that help them to generate higher margins by selling better products to the most demanding customers. Sustaining innovations can be year-by-year gradual improvements, such as increased processing power and larger storage capacity of PCs or added features on the current Windows Vista operating system. Somewhat counter-intuitively, sustaining innovations can also be of a ground-breaking, radical nature that helps companies to leapfrog their competitors. For instance, the transition from electromechanical to electronic cash registers was a radical but sustaining innovation. NCR (National Cash Register) dominated the market for electromechanical cash registers but missed the new technology in the 1970s, which led to a drastic decrease in sales. Yet, NCR decided quickly to introduce its own electronic cash register and, through its extensive sales organisation, was able quickly to regain its old market share.

Whether incremental or radical, what all sustaining innovations have in common is that they entail a better product that can be sold for higher profit margins to the best customers. As the example of NCR shows, while incumbents are not always first to develop a sustaining innovation, they generally succeed in their large-scale commercialisation. This is due to the fact that, compared with their start-up competitors, incumbents tend to have more financial resources, dispose of a larger customer base and have the processes in place to push the innovation onto the market.

In contrast to sustaining innovations, disruptive innovations are not focused on bringing better products to existing high-end customers. Instead, they usually tend to be significantly worse in the performance dimensions that traditionally were important in the industry. The Apple PC, for instance, had far less computing power than mini-computers. Yet, disruptive innovations offer other benefits such as simplicity, convenience and, most importantly, a lower price. As a result, they initially appeal primarily to less demanding customers with lower willingness to pay. Since, at that time, typical PC buyers had not previously owned a computer at all, they would probably have not purchased a clumsy and expensive mini-computer.

The two trajectories of sustaining and disruptive innovations development are illustrated in Exhibit 6.2. The upper trajectory shows the performance evolution of the mini-computer industry, which was moving along the path of sustaining innovations developing evermore powerful, yet also more expensive and more complicated, mini-computers to meet the demands of their large corporate customers. The lower trajectory shows the performance evolution of the PC industry, which started out at a much lower absolute performance level than the mini-computer industry. Yet, PCs also became increasingly powerful as they continued to evolve along their path of innovation.

In addition to the two trajectories of sustaining and disruptive innovations, the third important trajectory in this framework depicts the evolution of customer needs shown by the dashed line. Over time, customers demand increasingly higher performance from the products they purchase. However, technological progress typically evolves faster than customers' demand for better performance. This implies that technologies that, during their

Exhibit 6.2 Disruptive innovations enter the market from below and improve over time until they meet the demands of mainstream customers

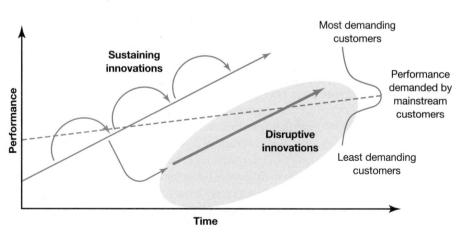

early development stages, do not fulfil customer's performance requirements continue to evolve and, at one point in time, outstrip the ability of customers to absorb it. That is the point where the two trajectories intersect. Consider the functionalities of Microsoft Office and how they have evolved over time. Early versions were characterised by frequent crashes, incompatibilities with other programs and lack of important functionalities. During that time (bottom left of the graph) customers were under-served, i.e. they did not get as much performance as they asked for to do the jobs they wanted to do. Over time, the Office package continued to improve, reliability and compatibility increased and new functionalities were added. By now, Excel and Word have become so powerful and all-encompassing in their functionalities that most users only use a fraction of what these software tools offer. Undoubtedly, the few high-end users who require cutting-edge functionalities for their work are pushing software packages to their limits, but this group is probably fairly small.

The different user groups are visualised through the bell curve on the right side of the framework. It presents the distribution of users according to their performance requirements. The dashed line presents the average, mainstream customers who constitute the broad base of a user group. At the upper end of the distribution there are few customers who have much higher performance requirements than the average user. Similarly at the lower end of the distribution, there are also some customers who have much lower requirements than the average user.

As more and more customers are over-served by the expanding functionalities of Microsoft Office, opportunities open up for disruptive innovations that address this segment with less powerful, yet cheaper and more convenient offerings. Consider Google's spreadsheet, word processing and calendar software that can be accessed online free of charge. Although these packages are certainly not as good as the Office software, they are in all likelihood good enough to meet the needs of less demanding users. Incidentally, these users also happen to be the customers who provide the lowest profit margins to established incumbents anyway. As a result, the latter are typically not upset to see them leave. However, the theory would suggest that as Google's software improves over time, it will eventually reach the point where its performance is good enough to meet the demands of mainstream customers. At that point, the mass market switches over to the new technology.

6.2.2 Discovering the underlying reasons for incumbents' failure

The pattern that is described above raises the question of why these types of disruptive innovations take place over and over again in different industries and countries. Frequently it is argued that it is the inability of companies to develop the appropriate innovations that later turn out to be successful. Yet, established companies, as for instance Kodak with digital imaging, do constantly innovate, and oftentimes even develop the technologies that later turn out to be the disruptive innovation.

Instead, the driving force behind the inability of incumbent companies to commercialise these innovations successfully is not located in R&D departments, but instead in how companies allocate their resources (i.e. management time and financial resources). Here, the theory of resource dependence provides interesting insights that explain more fully why incumbents fail in the face of disruptive innovations. The theory states that it is actually customers and investors – not managers – who control the allocation of resources in an organisation. This is so because companies that invest in projects that do not satisfy the needs of their best customers and do not suit the risk structure of their investors will not receive the necessary funding over the long run. Furthermore, companies generally generate most of their profits from their most demanding customers who are willing to pay premium prices for more sophisticated products. At the same time, profit margins from customers in lower segments are generally much lower. Consequently, innovation efforts tend to revolve around the improvement of products at the high end.

Similarly, when deciding whether to maintain or even increase their stake in a company, investors look for innovations and other growth initiatives that promise a substantial increase in revenues, which then translates into a share price increase. Since the market potential of disruptive innovations is typically small during the early years and cannot be measured precisely, developing a solid business plan is largely guesswork, which makes it hard to sell to investors.

The problem for incumbent firms would be less critical if new competitors entering the market with disruptive innovations remained in the low-margin market segments. Yet, once disruptors have entered a market, they are motivated to move upmarket into more demanding customer segments in order to increase their profit margins. On their part, incumbents are motivated to flee upmarket into their most demanding customer segments since that is where their most profitable customers are located. This asymmetric motivation is at the core of the innovator's dilemma.

FT

Why disruption can be good for business

The problem with most management theory, says Clayton Christensen, leaning forward in his chair, is that it breaks fundamental rules about how good theory should be created. 'Too many academics and business researchers make the leap from observation to theory without paying attention to the intermediate step categorisation,' he says. 'They don't think about their recommendations in a circumstance-contingent way.'

I am perched on a sofa in Prof. Christensen's spacious basement office, deep in the bowels of Harvard Business School, struggling to keep pace. I am here ostensibly to talk about *The Innovator's Solution*, his new book, but the conversation has taken an epistemological turn. What he is saying – or at least what I think he is saying – is that a good deal of what passes for management theory is, well, bunk. Study 10 successful companies, work out what they have in common and recommend that everyone does the

same. The genre was popularised by *In Search of Excellence*, Tom Peters' and Bob Waterman's 1984 management blockbuster. A more recent example was *Good to Great* by former Stanford University academic Jim Collins, the biggest-selling business book of the post-dotcom bubble era.

If Prof. Christensen is slating his peers, he is doing so with great grace. 'I have enormous respect for Jim Collins,' he says in his slow, sincere voice. 'He's got a good head and very high principles. But take his finding that the people who run these *Good To Great* companies are solid, grounded, humble people. The next question should be: is there a circumstance when you really need a Rudi Giuliani [the famously truculent former mayor of New York]? We need circumstance-based categories for all these things. Part of the reason why that kind of research plays so well is that many managers are just looking for an easy answer, a silver bullet. There is a lot of pressure on writers to cater to that need.'

Prof. Christensen has done very well by catering to something quite different: the hunger of a certain type of manager for books more grounded in theory than *Good to Great*-style bestsellers, but less taxing than textbooks. His first book, *The Innovator's Dilemma*, sold by the truckload and made him one of the biggest names in management theory. He remains arguably the brightest star on Harvard Business School's star-studded faculty. His contribution to the lexicon of management is great – 'disruptive innovation' is used and abused the world over.

That said, Prof. Christensen's stellar trajectory has engendered a certain amount of professional jealously. Rivals have claimed that the best ideas in *The Innovator's Dilemma* were already present in *Innovation: the Attacker's Advantage*, a book written a decade earlier by McKinsey luminary Richard Foster. Others cock a snook at the way disruptive innovation has become a kind of pseudo-intellectual fashion item.

A more substantive charge is that the world view laid out in *The Innovator's Dilemma* – in which innovations are classified as 'disruptive' or 'sustaining' – is in itself too simplistic. Surely, I suggest, the world is a more complicated place than suggested by this two-part taxonomy.

Prof. Christensen's response is that the distinction between disruptive and sustaining innovations has been widely misunderstood. 'If I had to do it again, I would have found another word. Disruption had so many prior connotations,' he says.

There is some truth in this. Like 'core competences' and 'business process reengineering', the other big business concepts of the 1990s, disruptive innovation has been stretched in common usage. The true Christensen meaning is precise. Disruptive innovations are technologies or business models that allow companies to offer simpler, less expensive products or services than have been offered before. Often these are not breakthrough innovations but clever repackaging of old technology. A classic example is Linux, the open-source computer operating system that is a repackaging of technology found in Unix, the dominant enterprise computer platform.

As spelled out in *The Innovator's Dilemma* and recapped in the sequel, market leaders find it difficult to respond to a disruptive innovation because it tends to appeal first to non-customers, people who don't use that category of product, or to low-end customers, who are prepared to accept a less-than-brilliant product if it saves money. Neither segment is particularly appealing to companies that lead their industries. They prefer to invest in serving existing customers with proven technology and predictable returns.

Prof. Christensen is clearly bothered by lazy application, or rather misapplication, of his ideas. The distinction between disruptive and sustaining innovations is no panacea. In answer to the charge of over-simplification, he also points out that getting to grips with the subtleties of disruptive/sustaining innovation is the easy part. The real work begins when you try to place new technologies and business models into one or another category.

'An innovation that is disrupting to one firm is sustaining to another firm. So the Internet was sustaining technology to Dell Computer, which already sold personal computers by telephone. But it was a disruptive technology to Compaq Computer [which sold mainly through stores].'

What really lights Prof. Christensen's fire is applying his framework to companies, industry sectors and economies. Like a scientist with a new microscope, he cannot resist turning it on whatever comes to hand. Semiconductors, education, healthcare – each is examined, disected and diagnosed in the course of our 90-minute conversation.

The Innovator's Solution, Prof. Christensen's sequel, adds at least one important element to the oeuvre: a model for trying to understand why the ability to make profits seems to migrate between parts of what strategy wonks like to call the 'value chain'. Why, for example, did profits in the personal computer industry migrate from the designers and builder of machines (Apple, Compaq, and IBM) to the makers of sub-systems (Microsoft and Intel)? Why does the balance of power appear to be shifting away from large car companies and towards the makers of value-added components and sub-systems?

His answer is that the basis of competition changes when products 'overshoot' the needs of the majority of customers. As this happens, raw performance becomes less important than the ability of manufacturers to get products to market quickly and in wider variety. The companies that concentrate on designing and assembling finished products (Apple or General Motors) thrive in the first era. They use proprietary technology and vertical integration to achieve maximum performance. Once performance is 'good enough' for the average consumer, however, product architectures tend to become modular. This enables shorter development times and products that are easier to customise.

In this environment, it is the sub-system and component suppliers whose products are no longer good enough. They come under greater pressure from manufacturers to improve performance but reap attractive profits for their trouble. Prof. Christensen summarises all this in one pithy sentence: 'The power to capture attractive profits always shifts to the activities in the value chain where the immediate customer is not yet satisfied with the performance of available products.'

Simple, right?

Like the disruptive/sustaining innovation framework, this is a lot easier to grasp in the abstract than it is to apply in practice. In the hands of the master, however, it all looks so easy. Thus the semi-conductor industry is on the verge of a huge upheaval, Prof. Christensen believes, as the basis of competition changes from trying to cram more and more transistors on a chip to offering customised products to the makers of the new breed of wireless and similar devices.

He switches the discussion to the US healthcare system, explaining that he sits on the strategy board of one of Boston's big teaching hospitals. 'We commissioned a study that showed that 70% of the people in the hospital would have been in intensive care 30 years ago, and 70% of the people in intensive care would have been dead 30 years ago. In other words, hospitals are moving to the high-end, focusing on intractable, multi-dimensional diseases.'

The disruptive innovation in this case is coming from technology that enables procedures that used to be handled in hospitals to be dealt with in specialist outpatient centres, and procedures that would have been handled in outpatient centres to be dealt with in doctors' offices. Then there is a whole category of things, including complex procedures such as dialysis, that people can now handle at home.

'The focus now in America is how do we get these very expensive hospitals to become cheaper, when we should be thinking about how we can help the inexpensive venues to do more. We should be facilitating the disruption rather than trying to make the status-quo less expensive. Yet public policy, like corporate policy, works against disruption.'

Think of The Innovator's Solution, Clayton Christensen's much anticipated new book, as 'the nine habits of highly disruptive companies'. While The Innovator's Dilemma (1997) spelt out why well-run companies find it so difficult to respond to what Christensen termed 'disruptive innovations', the sequel is nothing less than a handbook for managers who would rather disrupt than be disrupted.

The promise is rich: 'The Innovator's Solution summarises a set of theories that can guide managers who need to grow new businesses with predictable success and ultimately kill their well-run, established competitors.'

Source: S. London, 'Why disruption can be good for business', 2 October 2003, FT.com.

6.2.3 Raising the right questions to recognise the threats of disruptive innovations

The main contribution of the theory of disruptive innovation is that it challenges conventional management thinking that is perfectly logical and rational in most situations yet leads to failure in the face of a disruptive innovation. Before discussing the key questions that need to be asked to recognise threats of disruptive innovations, we want to take a closer look at the key fallacies of conventional thinking that lead to failure in the face of disruptive innovations.

First, conventional thinking would suggest that most advanced customers who are using products that are of cutting-edge quality will be key to recognising imminent changes in industry structure. In contrast, disruptive innovations have their roots with those customers who are over-served by existing products or with those users who had previously not been using the product.

Second, conventional thinking would also suggest that managers need to pay most attention to the largest competitors in an industry. In contrast, companies that disrupt industries frequently are not even on the competitive radar of those companies which are competing in that industry.

Third, conventional thinking suggests that those companies with the most resources that can be spent on activities such as R&D or marketing are likely to be successful. In contrast, those companies that succeed with disruptive innovations leverage asymmetric motivation and serve those customers that their competitors are unable to or do not want to serve.

To counter these traps of conventional thinking and to determine whether there exists a threat of a disruptive innovation in their industry, managers of established incumbents need to ask the following set of questions dealing with (1) non-served customers, (2) over-served customers and (3) the disruptiveness of the innovation relative to competitors:

- *Non-served customers:* Is there a large group of people who previously did not have the money or the skills to purchase the product themselves? Did customers have to go to a central, inconvenient location to purchase the product? For instance, families with grown-up children who wanted to sell the clothes and toys they no longer needed belonged to the group of non-served customers because they had the desire to get a job done but did not have the appropriate means to do so, with the exception of a garage sale or the local second-hand store, both of which have a very limited market potential. eBay provided a simple and relatively cheap format to extend this market to a much broader audience thereby substantially increasing the revenue potential.

- *Over-served customers.* Are there customers at the bottom end of the market who would buy the same product with fewer features for a lower price? Is it possible to build a profitable business model while keeping down prices? One important indicator of over-served customers is that they do not use many of the features that are offered in the most up-to-date version of a product. As we showed above, the market for spreadsheet and word processing software contains numerous customers at the bottom end of the market who would be willing to work with fewer features, as offered by Google's online version. For over-served customers, price or other performance features that had not been of dominant importance previously become the primary drivers for purchasing and usage decisions. In contrast, under-served customers are eagerly awaiting the next upgrade or new product version.

- *Disruptiveness to competitors.* Is the innovation disruptive relative to all relevant rival companies that are currently competing in that market? This question emphasises the crucial point that a technology or business model is never disruptive in absolute terms but only in relation to an existing technology or business model that is already used by established companies. For instance, the Internet as a technology is neither disruptive nor sustaining. Instead, it is an infrastructural technology that can be used in either a sustaining or disruptive way. Thinking of the Internet as only a means to disrupt established firms and failing to look at the whole market was actually a critical failure factor for many dotcom start-ups during the early years of the Internet. For instance, the online retailing of PCs was certainly highly disruptive relative to manufacturers who were selling their PCs through physical stores. Consequently, companies such as HP or Compaq were threatened by the rise of Internet-based retailing. Yet, for other companies such as Dell the Internet was a sustaining innovation. Previously, Dell had used the telephone and fax as primary sales channels, and the Internet was a natural extension to serve better its existing customer base and to attract new customers. As a result, Dell had the incentives and resources to compete in the online world and it did so very successfully, becoming by the end of the 1990s the world's largest PC retailer. The disruptive innovation theory would have predicted that new start-up companies attempting to sell PCs over the Internet would have been successful if they only had to disrupt competitors such as Compaq.

The banking industry is another example where the Internet had a sustaining impact. The case of Nordea illustrates how an established company successfully integrated the Internet into its value proposition because it was a way to serve existing customers better by offering online access to bank account statements, bill payment, etc. In contrast, pure Internet banks that sprung up in droves during the late 1990s have been struggling to make significant inroads into the banking industry or to sustain a significant growth.

The questions that we raised in the above three areas aimed at increasing the awareness for disruptive threats and providing the basis for appropriate reactions, which we shall discuss in the following section.

6.2.4 Finding ways to deal with disruptive innovations

A large part of the literature on disruptive innovations discusses the question of how incumbents can react successfully once they realise that a specific innovation has a disruptive potential.[3] In principle, there exists a broad spectrum of possibilities ranging from not responding at all to leapfrogging the disruptor. The different possibilities with their respective advantages and disadvantages are discussed in more detail below:

- *Not responding at all.* That is what many traditional firms did when e-business ventures started to enter the market on a large scale in the late 1990s. At that time, typical justifications of such no-response strategy were voiced through statements such as: 'Internet ventures are not my business'; 'e-Commerce will only make up a small niche of the overall market and is therefore not attractive for our company'; 'We don't want to set up an online channel that could cannibalise our physical operations'; and 'We don't have the IT skills or the necessary IT systems to compete online.' Obviously, managers were (and still are) bombarded with a myriad of new technologies and business threats and opportunities on a daily basis; the challenge for them is determining which of these threats and opportunities could materialise in the future. Yet, in the face of substantial threats, paying too little attention to a changing environment is often more hazardous than paying too much attention.

- *Migrating/harvesting* entails a less passive form than not responding at all. While the above strategy of not responding is quite often based on ignoring or not properly assessing the underlying facts, the migration strategy is based on a conscious decision to 'milk existing resources'. This means, for instance, that if the book retailer Barnes & Noble had come to the conclusion that Internet-based book retailing would overtake physical book retailing, it would have stopped investing in its network of physical bookstores.

■ *Defending* entails an active response to the new threatening business model. When defending their existing markets, incumbents need to improve their business model in such a way that they are able either to lower their prices or disproportionately to increase the benefits they provide to their customers. However, this option is usually difficult to implement successfully because the new business model or technology tends to have faster improvement dynamics than those created through a defensive strategy.

■ *Straddling* means to rely on the old business model while simultaneously introducing the new model. This can either be done as a transitional hedge to determine the potential of the new technology or be set up right from the start as a long-term strategy where both models will co-exist. This strategy attempts to combine the best of both worlds, i.e. to continue profiting from the old business model while simultaneously gaining traction in the new business model. While this option might seem to be the more promising at first sight, it also entails major risks. First, continuing to invest in something that may no longer work might mask a company's unwillingness to make tough choices. As we pointed out in Section 1.1, the willingness of top management to make tough trade-off decisions is one of the cornerstones of strategy formulation.

Second, when companies try to integrate the disruptive innovation into their own existing business model, this frequently leads to 'cramming'. Cramming means that the new technology is primarily used to improve the existing business model. For instance, the newspaper industry provides an interesting example of how publishers initially attempted to cram Internet-based news publishing into their existing business model. In the late 1990s, the *LA Times*, like many other newspapers around the world, recognised the importance of the Internet and decided to enter this market with an online version of its print edition. In essence, it opted for a straddling strategy. Yet, as in most cases, it was primarily the journalists and editors of the traditional print version who became involved with the creation of the online format. This has resulted in an online edition that mirrored largely the print edition with the same content and similar layout. Yet, such newspapers did not leverage the distinct advantages of electronic publishing such as discussion boards, site-searching tools and breaking news from third-party sources. The following quote by a newspaper executive sums up this inability to operate two distinct businesses simultaneously:

> Where I think we missed the boat is that we saw it [the Internet] as an extension of the newspaper. […] Our Internet operations were really run by people who came out of the newsroom, so they were editors who tended to look at this [online channel] more as a newspaper.[4]

■ *Switching completely* is a more radical response than straddling, since it entails a complete switch to the new business model. The obvious attraction of this option is that it focuses all managerial and financial resources on the strategy, which helps to avoid distractions (as was the case in the straddling examples mentioned above), create a sense of urgency and build implementation speed. Yet, it is also the riskiest of all options since there is always a high degree of uncertainty associated with these types of innovations. Furthermore, it is at least questionable whether the resources and capabilities (see Section 4.1) that were valuable in the old bricks-and-mortar environment, such as physical assets, know-how in store management, etc., will be valuable for managing an online venture.

■ *Leapfrogging* the disruptive competition means that a company tries to out-substitute the substitution. From a long-term strategic perspective, this option is highly attractive, yet it requires a very deep understanding of how technology and market demand will evolve. It is not enough to have just a clear understanding of which future technology could be successful. In addition, it is also essential to get the entry timing right, because entering a market too early can be just as detrimental as entering it too late (the issue of entry timing is discussed in more detail in Section 7.4). If, for instance, Barnes & Nobles had attempted to compete against Amazon.com by selling books in a digital format (as e-books), it would have leapfrogged the competition by skipping one technology generation. Obviously, doing so would not have been an easy task, especially considering the fact that Amazon.com was in all likelihood better equipped to make the move to digital goods than Barnes & Noble.

6.2.5 Selecting the appropriate mental frame for efficient reactions

In recent years, management researchers have further developed the theory of disruptive innovations, mainly driven by anomalies that the existing theory could not explain. In this section, we want to delve more deeply into these extensions of the theory.

One of the most important claims of the disruptive innovation theory is that incumbent firms do not invest in disruptive innovations because they focus on the needs of their best customers, which leads to resource dependence. This lack of resource, the theory goes, explains why they are unable to commercialise disruptive innovations successfully.

Yet, more recent research has shown that there are, in fact, numerous companies that have invested substantially in disruptive innovations, but still failed. Consider, for instance, Kodak's move into digital photography in 1996.[5] George Fischer, then CEO of Kodak, knew that digital photography would eventually threaten Kodak's core business. He and other senior executives at the company were tempted to ignore it because the profit margins were much lower than on the core business and digital photography also did not address Kodak's traditional customers. Nonetheless, Fisher rallied support from his top management and invested more than $2 billion in R&D for digital imaging. Yet, because Kodak was so worried about the threat, most of the money was spent before it became obvious how the market would develop. Instead of basing the new digital products on home storage and home printing capabilities, which later turned out to be the successful business model, Kodak invested hastily in 10,000 digital kiosks in its partner stores and committed itself to price points and product specifications that were difficult to change later on. Industry outsiders, such as Hewlett Packard, Canon or Sony, in contrast, invested in the home storage capabilities, thereby driving the development of digital photography.

A similar development can be observed in the newspaper industry. Initially, most newspapers underestimated the potential of the Internet. In the mid-1990s, only a small number of Internet users were getting their news from online sources. At that time, most readers of physical newspapers did not even have access to the Internet.

Thus, managers who tried to secure funding for Internet initiatives in the early 1990s, before the threat of the Internet to the existing business model became obvious, had a hard time convincing management of the potential of the Internet. As a result, newspaper companies did not enthusiastically embrace the opportunities of online publishing. The report of an online publisher of an established newspaper company sums up this sentiment:

I had trumpeted the new business to everyone and asked for their cooperation with the online group. One day, I asked a staff member of the online business how things were going and if the newspaper staff was helping out. He told me that he had recently asked for some help and the response was, 'Get the hell out of here; I've got a real newspaper to get out'![6]

Only when it became obvious in the late 1990s that Internet portals, such as Yahoo!, or job search sites, such as Monster.com, were threatening the traditional profit pools of classified advertisements and job posts did the newspaper industry wake up to the potential impact of the Internet on their business. This sentiment is exemplified through this publisher's statement:

I live in terror that some big thing is going to happen and I don't see it coming.

This sense of threat and urgency was then also translated in substantial investments in the new technology. For instance, at one newspaper company that was studied, staff for online operations increased from 15 to 40 people within a matter of months.

Interestingly enough, however, the framing of the threat also had a strong influence on the reaction patterns of top management. In the face of a threat, the typical reaction pattern of top management is to centralise decision making at the top and to reduce experimentation. For instance, line managers of the online sites received sample budgets, marketing plans and checklists that they had to adhere to. One top manager remembers:

It was very centralized in the beginning, which was very uncharacteristic, because the culture is very much to let each newspaper run its own business. We had a basic business model for every [online] site. We gave them money. We told them they could hire people, but we told them exactly how to run the site.[7]

The resulting websites were simply longer versions of the printed newspaper – with more than 75% of the content directly imported from the print edition. The features that other Internet start-ups in e-publishing had long integrated, such as customisation and community building, were not included. In the advertising realm, the company also did not experiment with new revenue sources such as demographic advertising, e-mail marketing and classified services.

The important insight of this example about the newspaper industry's reaction to the Internet is that the mental frame with which top management approach a disruptive innovation strongly influences both how many financial and management resources are allocated and how the innovation is implemented within the organisation. In essence, management face a framing paradox that is difficult to resolve.

If, on the one hand, a mental frame is used that focuses primarily on the opportunities that are opened up by the disruptive technology, then, so the theory goes, there will be plenty of freedom for line managers to experiment with novel ways of employing the technology. Yet, it will be difficult to get the required resources approved. If, on the other hand, a mental frame focusing on the threat is used, the willingness to invest in the new technology will be much higher. But because of the importance of the new technology and the associated fear, centralisation of decision making and lack of experimentation will result in a lacklustre implementation of the new technology within the corporation.

This paradox is illustrated in Exhibit 6.3, which differentiates between different frames during the resource commitment stage and the implementation stage. As is shown in the upper left quadrant, threat framing during both stages leads to an intense, yet rigid reaction. The opposite bottom right quadrant is equally problematic, because not enough resources are made available. The theory proposes that only by combining threat framing during the early investment stage with opportunity framing during the implementation stage is an incumbent organisation able to commercialise a disruptive innovation successfully. This combination leads to high financial commitment and a flexible plan, which is shown in the top right quadrant of the matrix.

This raised the question of how companies can possibly manage simultaneously these two opposing mindsets. The example of the newspaper industry revealed that newspaper companies that managed the integration of the new Internet-based news publishing more successfully shared two common characteristics.

First, they received advice from people outside of the newspaper industry. For instance, in one case, the opinion of a CEO had been shaped by the recommendations of a friend who had been based in Silicon Valley where he was observing the changes created by the Internet. In addition, they also hired industry outsiders who had gained previous online experience in other unrelated industries.

Second, they decided to separate the online organisation structurally from the print organisation. During the early years of e-business, most newspaper companies had decided to integrate the online organisation with the print organisation motivated by the desire to leverage the assets of the print business. This is summarised by the following CEO quote:

> Our basic goal is an integrated strategy. [...] In the local information market, the newspaper has an advantage. To separate the online unit from the newspaper is to give away a lot of that advantage.

However, the influence of outsiders also led the newspaper companies to reconsider this initial strategy. The structural separation combined with the hiring of industry outsiders allowed the separated online unit to frame the Internet as an opportunity instead of a threat as had been perceived by the parent organisation. One online manager of a separated website reported:

> When we simply changed our name from the newspaper name to 'the city.com' [...] it changed people's expectations of what would be on the [web]site. This, in turn, changed how people in our online organization viewed who they were and what they were producing.[8]

Exhibit 6.3 To overcome organisational rigidities, incumbents who are faced with disruptive innovations need to adopt two contradicting cognitive frames

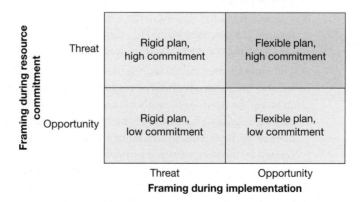

Source: Adapted from C. Gilbert, 'Change in the presence of residual fit', *Organizational Science*, 2006, Vol. 17, No. 1, p. 152.

Another manager of a separate online division reported:

> Now that we are separate, we own the opportunity in a way we never did when we were still with the [physical] newspaper.

This thinking in terms of opportunity allowed the online organisations to think creatively about developing new revenue streams without having to worry about cannibalising the existing print business. One website editor who came from the print business commented about the online director who was brought in from outside:

> He is constantly seeing digital media in different ways than I am used to or appreciate. At first, this bothered me, but now that I see it working, I increasingly endorse the input.

These new revenue sources, which hitherto had not been used by the online editions of newspapers, included fee-based archival access, e-mail marketing, e-mail list rental, fee-based data analysis, and behavioural and demographic targeting.

SUMMARY

- This chapter first discussed how a company can build up barriers to imitation. These include (1) withholding information about profitability, (2) forgoing short-term profit for long-term success, (3) signalling the promise of retaliation, (4) exploiting all available investment opportunities or securing access to resources, (5) relying on resources that are implicit (such as skills, processes and culture), (6) basing differentiation on rare or contracted resources and (7) exploiting the time lag with the imitator.

- The chapter then focused on how to deal with the threats of a disruptive innovation in e-business. More specifically, it stressed the importance of understanding the fundamental process of disruptive innovations and determining the underlying reasons for the incumbent's failure.

- Next, the chapter suggested some questions that companies need to raise in order to assess the threat of a disruptive innovation. These questions deal with (1) non-served customers, (2) over-served customers and (3) the disruptiveness of the innovation relative to competitors.

- Possible ways for dealing with a disruptive innovation are then suggested. These include (1) not responding, (2) migrating/harvesting, (3) defending, (4) straddling, (5) switching completely and (6) leapfrogging.

- The chapter then discussed the issues underlying the selection of the appropriate mental frame for an efficient response to a disruptive innovation. It concluded by stressing the need for incumbents facing a disruptive innovation to adopt two contradicting cognitive frames: one that primarily focuses on the opportunities that are opened up by the disruptive innovation, and one that focuses on the threats that are created by the same disruptive innovation.

REVIEW QUESTIONS

1 What are the requirements for successful imitation and the barriers to imitation?

2 What questions do companies need to raise in order to assess the threat of a disruptive innovation?

3 What possible ways can companies consider taking to deal effectively with a disruptive innovation?

4 What are the main cognitive frames that companies can adopt when facing a disruptive innovation? Why are these cognitive frames contradictory in nature?

DISCUSSION QUESTIONS

1 Can you find examples of how companies built up barriers to imitation? Pick out specific examples from different industries and explain what these companies did. Were they successful in their attempts?

2 Consider different industries of you choice (e.g. music, book retailing, etc.) and analyse whether they are faced with the threats of disruptive innovations. If so, discuss how the new entrants are attempting to compete. Also, discuss the reactions of the incumbents.

3 Why did Intel develop the Celeron chip? Can you explain this decision using the disruptive innovation logic?

RECOMMENDED KEY READING

■ C. Christensen and M. Raynor provide an excellent account of the theory of disruptive innovations in their book *The Innovator's Solution*, Harvard Business School Press, 2003.

■ C. Gilbert discusses the influence of framing on an incumbent's ability to react to discontinuous change in 'Unbundling the structure of inertia: resource versus routine rigidity', *Academy of Management Journal*, 2005, Vol. 48, No. 5, pp. 741–763, and in 'Change in the presence of residual fit', *Organizational Science*, 2006, Vol. 17, No. 1, pp. 150–167.

USEFUL THIRD-PARTY WEBLINKS

■ Consult www.innosight.com for up-to-date research findings and practical implications of the disruptive innovation theory.

■ www.innochallenges.com provides ways for putting the insights of the disruption innovation into practice.

■ www.innovationzen.com provides a detailed overview of different management theories dealing with innovation.

NOTES AND REFERENCES

1 For a detailed description of barriers to imitation, see P. Ghemawat, *Strategy and the Business Landscape*, Prentice Hall, 2005.

2 For a detailed and comprehensive description of the theory of disruptive innovations, see C. Christensen and M. Raynor, *The Innovator's Solution*, Harvard Business School Press, 2003.

3 See P. Ghemawat, *Strategy and the Business Landscape*, Prentice Hall, 2005, p. 106.

4 See C. Gilbert, 'Unbundling the structure of inertia: resource rigidity versus routine rigidity', *Academy of Management Journal*, 2005, Vol. 48, No. 5, pp. 741–763.

5 For a detailed account of Kodak's foray into digital photography, see C. Gilbert and J. Bower, 'Disruptive change: when trying harder is part of the problem', *Harvard Business Review*, 2002, May, pp. 95–101.

6 Quoted in C. Gilbert, 'Change in the presence of residual fit', *Organizational Science*, 2006, Vol. 17, No. 1, pp. 150–167.

7 Ibid.

8 Quoted in C. Gilbert, 'Unbundling the structure of inertia: resource versus routine rigidity', *Academy of Management Journal*, 2005, Vol. 48, No. 5, pp. 741–763.

CHAPTER 7

Exploiting opportunities of new market spaces in e-business

Chapter at a glance

7.1 Gaining insights into new market spaces through the value curve

7.2 Looking outside one's own box

7.3 Pinpointing possibilities for new value creation

7.4 Finding the right time to enter a market

       7.4.1 Early-mover advantages

       7.4.2 Early-mover disadvantages

Related case studies

Case study		Primary focus of the case study
2	Nordea	Early-mover advantage
1	Tesco	Early-mover advantage
3	ING DIRECT	Value innovation
5	Otis	Value innovation
17	NTT DoCoMo	Value innovation

Learning outcomes

After completing this chapter, you should be able to:

■ Explain how firms can open up new market spaces and thereby create completely new types of value.

■ Understand how to draw a value curve and gain insights through it.

■ Explain the six paths framework and be able to use it for value creation in e-business.

■ Appreciate the importance of finding the right time to enter a market.

■ Recognise the advantages and disadvantages of being an early mover in e-business.

INTRODUCTION

The strategy options presented in Chapter 5 mainly focus on the traditional form of competition, which assumes a clearly defined set of competitors within an industry. The key performance measure is relative performance vis-à-vis competitors. As a result of this competitor-focused competition, improvements tend to be incremental through an increase of benefits or a decrease of costs. An alternative way to approach strategy development is to move beyond the sole industry focus and look for new market spaces across different industries.[1]

Doing so allows a firm, at least temporarily, to break out of the cycle of ever-increasing competition within an industry, either by redefining the industry competition or by creating a new industry. The goal of this approach is drastically to increase consumer benefit while at the same time reducing price.

The first three sections of this chapter deal with the value innovation logic. Section 7.4 discusses the advantages and disadvantages of being an early mover in a new market.

7.1 Gaining insights into new market spaces through the value curve

The concept of the value curve depicted in Exhibit 7.1 is used to illustrate how to redefine competition along different dimensions of benefit. In the book-retailing example, these dimensions include price, convenience, selection range, speed and face-to-face interaction. Obviously, on these dimensions, traditional and online bookstores offer varying levels of benefit. This is shown in Exhibit 7.1 where, on the vertical axis, a value of '1' refers to the highest level of benefit and a value of '0' refers to the lowest level of benefit.

Sketching the value curves of different companies in a specific industry that have diverging value curves is a valuable exercise to gain an understanding of what drives value creation and how companies are positioned along the key dimensions that determine customer benefit. Drawing the value curves in the book-retailing industry (as shown below) requires us, first, to think about what the key dimensions of customer benefit are. During this first step, it is important to ensure that all key dimensions are listed, i.e. nothing important such as selection range or price is forgotten, and that the dimensions listed are mutually exclusive, i.e. that they do not overlap logically. Second, we need to determine how different competitors rank on each dimension. Connecting the different dots then allows us to draw the value curve for each company.

The visualised profile of the value curves provides the basis for thinking about new types of value curves that might break the existing trade-offs of the existing business models.

Exhibit 7.1 The value curve provides insights into new market spaces

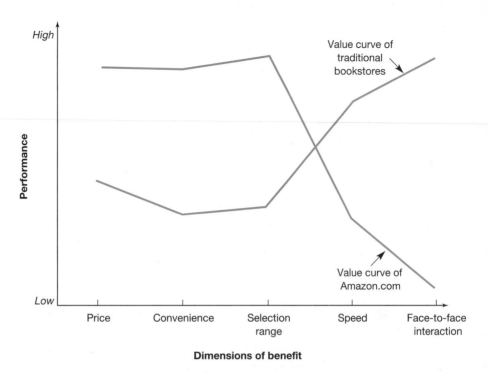

Source: Reprinted by permission of *Harvard Business Review* [Exhibit 99105]. From 'Creating new market space' by C. Kim and R. Mauborgne, January–February 1999. Copyright © 1999 by the Harvard Business School Publishing Corporation, all rights reserved.

7.2 Looking outside one's own box

How can this type of value creation be attained? A firm needs to analyse the way it wants to create value by 'looking outside the box', i.e. outside the standard business practices of its own industry. Doing so can lead to the discovery of uncovered market spaces between separate industries.[2]

The six paths framework developed by Kim and Mauborgne suggests numerous ways of doing so (see Exhibit 7.2):

- *Looking across substitute industries.* The main question that needs to be asked here is how customers make trade-offs between different products (or services) that serve as substitutes. The goal is to determine why customers choose one product and not the other, and what criteria they use in making their decision. In the traditional business environment, the most severe competition does not necessarily come from within the industry. Customers make trade-offs, for example, between using cash or a credit card, travelling by car or train, and using a pen or word processing software. In the online world, customers make trade-offs between shopping online or going to the store, and between banking online or going to the bank branch. When Nordea Bank considered this trade-off, it found out that customers who go to the branch value the ease of use

Exhibit 7.2 The six paths framework suggests different starting points for creating value innovations in e-business

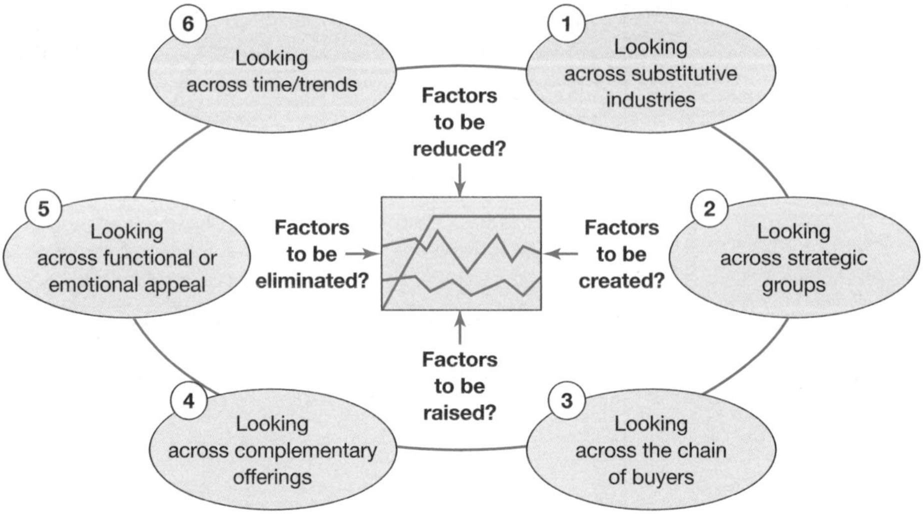

Source: Based on C. Kim and R. Mauborgne, 'Creating new market space', *Harvard Business Review*, 1999, January–February, pp. 83–93.

of over-the-counter banking. Thus, Nordea set out to develop a highly user-friendly online interface to offer the ease of use of a branch office with the benefits (and the lower costs) of an online channel.

- *Looking across strategic groups.* A strategic group consists of firms that produce the same type of products, for instance cars, for a certain customer segment. Firms usually compare themselves with competitors positioned in the same strategic group as themselves. Doing so usually does not lead to radically new insights since firms in the same strategic group tend to be similar in their product offerings. Looking across strategic groups means looking at what companies do that produce the same basic product for different customer segments, thereby finding out potential new ways of creating value. In car manufacturing, for instance, Mercedes, after analysing lower-ranked strategic groups, developed the Smart Car, which is offered at prices that compete with low-cost cars while still containing the Mercedes technology inside. Similarly, car manufacturers from lower-ranked strategic groups, such as Toyota, developed cars that possess many features of higher-ranked competitors while still maintaining a low price position.

- *Looking across chains of buyers.* The underlying logic of this perspective is that the person in charge of purchasing is not necessarily the one using the purchased product or service. For instance, the procurement department and the corporate user usually have different definitions of value. While price and the purchasing procedure are important for the former, the latter focuses on ease of use. If a firm has previously considered only one of the two groups, taking on the other group's perspective might lead to new value creation. For example, the Spreadshirt case study featured in the case studies section of this book illustrates how the firm moved up the chain of buyers. While printing shops typically targeted the end consumer with their offerings, Spreadshirt entered the market by mainly addressing potential online shop operators who were provided with the means to customise a shop easily to meet their needs.

■ *Looking across complementary products and services.* Most products and services are not used in isolation, but instead need others to complement them. Computers, for instance, require software in order to operate. Amazon.com recognised the power of complementary products when it launched its personalised book recommendation service, which suggests to customers a list of books that might be of interest to them based on their previous purchases. Nordea Bank wants to push the concept of offering complementary services even further through the use of a triggered database, which works as follows. When there is a change in a customer account – for instance, a large incoming money transfer, a change of address or a change in marital status – a trigger in the database is set off and informs the bank about this change, which then raises a number of questions regarding complementary products: what does this change mean for the customer in terms of financing, long-term payments, insurance and e-services? (See also the FT article 'Dell's move from PCs into complementary products'.)

FT

Dell's move from PCs into complementary products

If things go according to plan, Michael Dell could eventually become the Henry Ford of the information age. For a maker of desktop personal computers who founded his company, famously, in a University of Texas dormitory 20 years ago, this may sound unlikely. But the ambitions of Dell Inc. are boundless – and thanks to a simple business idea that has proved highly adaptable, and a fearsome relentlessness, things at Dell have a way of going according to plan. Consumer electronics are about to provide what could well be the biggest test of the Dell way of doing business. Until now, the company has sold mainly to corporate customers: only a fifth of its sales in the US are to consumers, and much less than that elsewhere.

Yet executives at the Texas headquarters are now busy laying plans to take on some of the giants of the consumer electronics world. According to Kevin Rollins, the president and chief operating officer who has had much to do with its remorseless rise, there is no reason why Dell should not aim for 30–40% of the global market for all the products it makes. Applied to the $800bn (£480bn) computing and consumer electronics markets that Dell now targets, that suggests it believes it could one day easily exceed the $160bn sales of General Motors. Mr Rollins says this is not a specific target

that has been 'written down and pinned to the wall', but he does not shrink from the ambition.

Dell's simple but effective idea has been to sell standardised electronic products direct to customers, usually over the Internet. That removes most of the research and development that is normally required, while also cutting out retailers and other middlemen.

Armed with the information it gets from taking orders directly from customers, Dell has gained two other powerful advantages. One is the ability to build products to match orders as they come in, slashing its inventory costs. The second is a highly efficient marketing machine that can adapt its message based on real-time results as orders arrive.

With its lower costs, Dell sets out to undermine profits in the markets it enters and destroy the margins that sustain its more entrenched competitors. 'Our goal is to shrink the profit pool and take the biggest slice,' says Mr Rollins. Consumer electronics companies, often with gross profit margins of more than 30%, make an obvious target for this ruthless approach. 'Our gross margins are in the 18–19% range: we don't need 40%,' he says. A former partner from Bain, the Dell president applies the cool analytics and familiar jargon of the strategy consultant to this relentless expansion: search out the ➔

markets with the biggest 'profit pools' to be plundered; pick ones with close 'adjacencies' to those Dell already serves to reduce the risk of wandering into unknown territory; and apply its 'core competences' to conquering new ground.

As a textbook case of applying a proven and repeatable formula, Dell takes some beating. It used the formula to move from selling PCs to businesses to selling them to consumers. Next it followed its business customers into servers, then into storage hardware. Now it wants to follow consumers into other areas of electronics as well. It has started with products closely linked to the PC, such as MP3 digital music players and 17-inch flat-panel television sets that resemble computer monitors. According to Dell's rivals, success in the PC business in the US has disguised the fact that the company has found it harder to break into other products and new geographic regions. 'Dell's success is backward-looking,' claims Jeff Clarke, head of global operations at Hewlett-Packard.

According to Steve Milunovich, technology strategist at Merrill Lynch, not all markets are as susceptible to all aspects of the Dell approach as the PC business. Yet he adds that the company has shown great discipline in attacking only those areas where its strengths still give it a clear economic and operational advantage. Even most of the company's competitors concede that the shift in consumer electronics from analogue to digital technology plays to Dell's strengths. It is already the biggest purchaser of liquid crystal display (LCD) screens and computer hard-drives, for instance, putting it in a strong position as these components come to play a bigger role in television sets and other household items. 'When you combine monitors and LCD televisions, we will blow away the consumer electronics guys,' says Mike George, chief marketing officer.

More importantly, Dell also benefits from the standardization that brings down the cost of components and removes the advantage once enjoyed by companies that invest in their own technology. As more of a product's functions come to reside in standardized components such as micro-processors and hard drives, the differentiation that comes from making new versions declines. The contrast with others is stark. Sony chief Nobuyuki Idei, for

instance, told the FT two weeks ago that the Japanese company was putting a growing emphasis on proprietary components to differentiate its products. In the past four years, 70% of Sony's investment has been in silicon chips.

While the digitization of consumer electronics may have played to Dell's core strengths, though, there are at least three things about the market that are likely to test its business model. One is the fact that it will rely, at least for now, on manufacturing by other companies, reducing its ability to drive down costs. Also, the consumer electronics business is based on common products that are not configured individually for different customers: according to Mr Clarke, that removes one main advantage of Dell's build-to-order model, the ability to customize products for each buyer. Using outside manufacturers is also likely to mean the company 'will not be able to operate on inventory that is as thin as it is in PCs,' says Charlie Kim, a consultant at Bain. Company executives suggest that once manufacturing volumes reach a high enough level, Dell is likely to start production itself. Also, while the cost advantages may be less in 'back-end' activities such as production and sourcing, the real opportunity for Dell in consumer electronics lies in the 'front-end' marketing and sales area, says Mr Milunovich. 'There's a big chunk of money to be taken out of distribution,' he says.

Whether Dell can take advantage of this opportunity with its direct sales system will be the second big challenge. Retail stores suit consumer products best because they bring an instant mass-market and let users test the look and feel of products, says Mr Clarke. That is particularly important for products such as television sets, which buyers want to see, or hand-held devices, which they want to pick up, say rivals. Dell executives retort that similar doubts were once expressed about its efforts to sell PCs online, and that its early sales of personal digital assistants suggest that consumers familiar with the quality and style of the company's PCs are willing to buy other items online too.

The third test will be whether the Dell brand and marketing approach can be adapted to suit the new market. High name-recognition helps, but will get Dell only part of the way. 'Everyone knows who Dell is; it's still a PC-focused brand,' says Mr

Kim at Bain. For a company that still relies heavily on selling to corporate customers, this will pose a big challenge. 'We're very humbled by the fact that there are virtually no other companies that are both consumer and enterprise brands,' says Mr George. He adds, though, that the basic attributes of the Dell brand – with its connotations of a certain level of value, quality and service – should extend across both types of market.

Overcoming obstacles such as these will stretch the Dell model in ways that it has never been stretched before. '[In the past] they've been able to push new products through their system without having to change it much,' says Mr Kim. 'Now, they're going to have to adapt.' Henry Ford, famous for designing the first system capable of mass-producing a standardised product, would have approved of what Dell has already done to the PC business. To do the same in the consumer electronics world, though, it will have to prove that it can constantly re-tune its business model without losing the power that has set it apart.

Talk to senior Dell executives and before long the phrase crops up: 'maniacal focus'. A ferocious attention to detail, applied to a tried and tested business model, accounts for the company's continuing edge, despite efforts by rivals to copy its methods. 'We don't let the paint dry on any process,' says Ray Archer, formerly a rear-admiral responsible for logistics in the US Navy and now in charge of Dell's supply chain. That is evident at the company's Texas assembly plant, where up to 25,000 machines are produced each day – more than double the plant's capacity when it was opened three years ago. Dell executives say they see no end to the continual adjustments that can be made, to speed the company's processes and bring down costs. Dell's way of doing business is no secret but the years of maniacal focus on fine-tuning the system make it difficult for others to catch up, says Mr Rollins. 'Why doesn't Kmart do what Wal-Mart does? It's built up over many years; it's in our DNA.'

Source: R. Waters, 'Dell aims to stretch its way of business', *Financial Times*, 13 November 2003.

- *Looking across functional or emotional appeal to buyers.* Products or services often focus either on functional or tangible characteristics (such as durability and breadth of choice) or on their emotional appeal, which is captured by the strength of the brand. Looking across boundaries by, for instance, turning functional products into emotionally appealing products can lead to a vast increment in the perceived consumer benefit. Take the example of the coffee house Starbucks, which has turned a functional mass product (i.e. coffee) into an emotional experience for its customers, thus being able to charge a premium price for it.

- *Looking across time.* By assessing early on the impact of future changes in the macro- or competitive environment, a firm can adapt its value-creation strategies based on the expected changes. For instance, Nordea realised in the 1980s the importance of electronic channels and swiftly introduced PC-banking services. This helped Nordea to create substantial cost savings while at the same time significantly increasing customer benefit.

- *Looking across unrelated industries.* It is also possible to venture out and look across completely different industries to see how value is created there. This is one of the key messages that the case studies in this book convey. Looking across different industries requires creative leaps on your side, but it has the potential to create surprising insights. An insurance salesperson might ask, for instance, what lessons can be taken away from Ducati's exclusive Internet sales of new motorcycle models directly to consumers, and to what extent the learning can be adapted to the insurance business.

7.3 Pinpointing possibilities for new value creation

After looking across the above dimensions, different questions arise in the four areas listed below (see Exhibit 7.2). Answering them opens up the opportunity for new value-creation potential:[3]

■ *Eliminate.* Does what we do really create consumer benefit? If not, which components or features of our product or service should we eliminate? Even if a company has made a proper assessment of these issues at some point in time, it should then raise these questions again since buyers' preferences are dynamic by nature.

■ *Reduce.* Where can we reduce our range of offerings? What costs us a lot of money but does not create benefit?

■ *Raise.* Where should we raise the standard of products or services? Where can we increase benefit by expanding our existing offering?

■ *Create.* What can we do that has not been done so far?

Tapping into hitherto uncovered market spaces provides firms with the opportunity not only to capture large parts of the market by taking away market share from competitors, but also to expand the overall market size. Amazon.com, for example, did not just take buyers away from traditional bricks-and-mortar bookstores. It also turned people who previously had not purchased many books into avid buyers through the depth of its offerings and value-adding services such as the book reviews and personalised recommendations.

However, the move into new market spaces is not a one-time affair, since superior profit will last only as long as competitors do not move into this newly discovered market space. Just as it is with generic strategies, competitors will try to catch up if they believe that the new model promises attractive returns, thereby eroding profitability. The sustainability depends again on the uniqueness of the positioning and on how difficult it is to imitate this positioning.

Summarizing the value innovation thinking, there are five characteristics that differentiate this type of thinking from conventional competitive thinking:

■ *Different assumptions.* Conventional thinking tells us that an industry's value curves follow one basic shape. Value innovation logic assumes that new value curves can be shaped by creatively resolving historic trade-offs.

■ *Strategic focus.* Conventional thinking tells us that the primary goal is to pursue a competitive advantage and to beat the competition. Value innovation logic pursues a quantum leap in customer value where competition is no benchmark.

■ *Customers.* Conventional thinking tells us that the primary goal is to retain and expand the existing customer base through segmentation and customisation. Value innovation logic focuses on the mass of buyers. The focus is on finding the key communalities that customers value.

■ *Resources.* Conventional thinking tells us to exploit existing assets and capabilities. In contrast, value innovation thinking poses the question: What would we do if we were starting anew?

■ *Offerings.* Conventional thinking tells us to offer the products and services of the industry we are competing in. Value innovation thinking refocuses the thinking on offering total customer solutions exceeding industry boundaries.

7.4 Finding the right time to enter a market

Early- or first-mover advantages were a major driver for the Internet boom during the late 1990s. No potential entrepreneur or investor wanted to miss out on the profit potential that was promised to early movers. Thus, they all rushed into setting up or financing Internet start-ups, accepting large initial losses but expecting high returns over time due to first-mover advantages.

Undoubtedly for some Internet start-ups, such as eBay, Yahoo! and Amazon.com, early-mover advantages helped to pave the way for a dominant market position. In most cases, however, companies that started out early during the Internet boom have either gone out of business or been acquired by other firms that embraced the Internet much later.

Before moving into a more detailed discussion of early-mover advantages, we want to emphasise that a major difference between the Amazon.com-like ventures and the bankrupt Internet companies is that Amazon.com was not only early but also best in class. Since its launch in Seattle (USA) in July 1995, Amazon.com has strived continuously to improve customer experience while simultaneously increasing operational efficiency, thereby reducing costs. In other industries, early movers were unable to compete with late entrants and eventually went out of business.

Similarly, Yahoo.com, eBay and other successful Internet start-ups managed to get the timing right and also deliver superior value on a continuous basis. Thus, while early-mover advantages are important, it is equally important that a firm maintains its quality or cost lead over competitors to keep its dominant position.[4]

In the following sections, we first analyse the different types of early-mover advantages and discuss how they affect Internet-based industries. Early-mover advantages can result from (1) *learning effects*, (2) *brand and reputation*, (3) *switching costs* and (4) *network effects*. We then analyse early-mover disadvantages, which are (1) *market uncertainty*, (2) *technological uncertainty* and (3) *free-rider effects*.[5]

7.4.1 Early-mover advantages

Learning effects

The idea of learning effects is that as output increases, a firm gains experience.[6] This allows it to conduct its business more efficiently, thereby reducing costs and increasing quality. When Amazon.com entered the German online book market in 1998, it was able to capitalise on its three years of experience in the USA where it had learned how to do online and offline marketing, make its website user-friendly and streamline its logistics and delivery processes.

Germany's Bertelsmann Online (BOL), on the other hand, entered the online book-retailing business later and still had to go through the learning process, while Amazon.com kept improving at the same time. Ultimately, BOL was never able to provide a shopping experience that could compete with Amazon.com's, a shortcoming that contributed to the Bertelsmann Group's eventual decision to abandon BOL.

Brand and reputation

Companies that come to market first with a new product or way of conducting business impress consumers quite strongly, thus gaining reputation and brand awareness. Furthermore, media coverage creates free and strong publicity, which can enhance the brand and reputation. The business press is always interested in new business developments, successful or not, and covers them extensively. When Amazon.com went public in the middle of the 1990s, major business newspapers and journals wrote about it, thereby creating free and credible publicity. For instance, in 1996, *The Wall Street Journal* published a front-cover story on Amazon.com; on the following day, book sales on the company's website doubled.[7] Other early movers such as Yahoo.com and eBay have received similar levels of media coverage.

Being an early entrant in a market can also help to build up a strong reputation with customers, provided that the company can meet customer expectations during the first few contacts. This may seem obvious, but many Internet start-ups were unable to do so due to their badly designed websites and the lack of timely and reliable product delivery. More successful Internet start-ups such as Amazon.com managed early on to provide customers with a superior shopping experience. Customers who had a good experience with one provider are unlikely to switch to another. Therefore, any new competitor must provide a higher value than that offered by the early entrant in order to offset the uncertainty of being new and to induce the customer to switch over.

However, an established brand and reputation are no guarantee of lasting success. The case of the search engine Google is an excellent example of how a newcomer managed to overcome the brand recognition and reputation of older and more established rivals such as Overture and AltaVista. Google was able to do so because it offered radically higher user benefits through higher speed and better search accuracy than all other companies. Without doing any massive advertising, Google quickly became the preferred search engine for millions of Internet users. In fact, Google has been so powerful that critics have launched a website (**www.google-watch.org**) to scrutinise the intrusive search techniques that Google uses.

Switching costs

Switching costs, also called self-compatibility costs, result from moving from one product to another. Even if a new product is superior to the one you already possess, you might still decide to keep the old product because of switching costs, which, in effect, create a weak form of lock-in. The expectation that switching costs on the Internet would be high was one of the main drivers behind the race for 'eyeballs' and 'clicks', whose levels determined the stock market valuation of many companies (more traditional metrics such as price/earnings ratios were not considered to be suitable for Internet start-ups).

The common belief was that once customers got used to the set-up of a website, and once they had provided their customer information, they would no longer want to switch because of switching costs. This belief turned out to be fatal for many companies that spent heavily on marketing and customer acquisition, only to find that their customers were happily switching to other websites when a competitor offered better value.

Four sources of switching costs can be identified: (1) switching costs from relearning, (2) switching costs because of customised offerings, (3) switching costs because of incompatible complementary products and (4) switching costs resulting from customer incentive programmes. These are defined below:

- *Switching costs from relearning* are a result of getting used to a new product. Users of software programs who are thinking about switching from one provider to another often stick with the old product for as long as they can in order avoid relearning costs. Consider the case of IBX, which developed a proprietary B2B e-purchasing software platform. Once customers get used to this software and train their personnel to use it, switching to a competitor would entail considerable relearning. Similarly, Internet users get used to the functionalities of a specific website and might not want to switch to another website. The more website-specific the knowledge is, the less likely it is that a person will switch to another website. In other cases, such as with search engines where the usage is easy and intuitive, switching costs are minimal. This was another reason that helped Google to become, within a matter of months, the most popular Internet search engine. (At the same time, this lack of lock-in is also the greatest danger that Google faces today as competitors, such as Microsoft, start investing heavily in search engine development.) As the Internet continues to mature and users become more accustomed to using it, relearning-induced switching costs are likely to decrease.

- *Switching costs because of customised offerings* result from a firm's ability to adapt a website to the specific needs and preferences of individual customers. For instance, as customers make purchases and search for books, Amazon.com learns about their preferences and is then able to make customised recommendations based on previous purchase patterns. If customers want to switch to a competitor, they first need to 'teach' their system through a number of purchases before the latter can provide them with the same level of customised offerings. Similarly, when Tesco.com customers first enter the online retailing site, their shopping list is instantly populated with all the items that they had previously purchased in physical Tesco stores with their Tesco clubcard. This customisation eliminates the initial effort for Internet shoppers to set up their shopping list online.

- *Switching costs because of incompatible complementary products* result from the inability to use the new product in combination with old products. An illustrative example of this was the introduction of the CD player, which rendered the existing vinyl record collections of music lovers worthless if they decided to switch to the new technology. Through the symbiotic relationship between the iPod player and the iTunes music downloading service, Apple also created high switching costs for customers. When iTunes users contemplated the idea of purchasing a digital music player other than an iPod, they would have faced the switching costs of not being able to play the songs that they purchased through the iTunes platform, since their format was only compatible with the iPod product (see also the FT article 'Apple's sound strategy for the i-Pod').

- *Switching costs resulting from customer incentive programmes* occur when firms offer customers benefits in return for their loyalty. A prominent example here is the frequent-flyer bonus programmes offered by airlines, where passengers earn free upgrades or free tickets after having flown a certain number of miles with the specific airline. Also, Tesco has created switching costs for customers through its Tesco clubcard. Owners of a Tesco clubcard, who have been using it for shopping in physical stores, have strong incentives to prefer Tesco.com over other online grocery and non-food shopping sites because they can continue collecting incentive points by shopping online.

For consumers, it is sensible to consider overall costs, including switching costs, when deciding on a new purchase. With hindsight, it is surprising that switching costs received so much attention during the Internet boom years, since the above-mentioned types of switching had been around before then. Therefore, for many online businesses there was really no need to gain market share as rapidly as possible and to invest heavily in new technology. History has shown that in most cases, if a new entrant offers a substantially better product, then it will most likely drive the weaker product out of the market, even if there are substantial switching costs.[8]

Network effects

Network effects are present when a product becomes more useful to consumers in proportion to the number of people using it.[9] There are two types of network effects, *direct* and *indirect*:

- *Direct network effects.* The strength of these effects depends directly on the number of users of a given device or technology that exhibits a network effect. An example of a product with strong direct network effects is the mobile phone. While a single mobile phone by itself is essentially worthless, it becomes very valuable when large parts of the population own a mobile phone and can use it to communicate with each other. Similarly, the Internet increases in value for the individual user as the number of users increases. Bob Metcalf found that the value of a network increases proportionally to the square of the number of people using it. Thus, if you double the number of participants in a given network, the value for each individual participant doubles, which leads to a fourfold increase in the overall value of the network.[10] This coherence becomes especially relevant in the context of social networking sites such as openBC, where the number of users determines directly the value of the overall network due to the likely interaction between community members.

- *Indirect network effects.* Similar effects also apply with products that require complementary goods, such as video recorders and video games. Their value increases as the size of the installed user base increases, because more companies offer complementary products such as video tapes and games cartridges.

Whether a firm can benefit from network effects depends largely on the nature of the network. If network effects exist in a publicly owned platform that is open to all firms, then network effects benefit the whole community but do not accrue special benefits to any individual party. The mobile phone and the Internet, for instance, are open networks where the benefits of network effects accrue largely to customers. If, on the other hand, network benefits are specific to a particular website or community, then the operator of this website can reap benefits from these network effects.

In e-commerce, a vivid example of network effects is eBay. On a stand-alone basis, this online auction platform is not valuable at all; its value comes from the millions of users who post products for sale and search for products to buy. This results in a highly liquid market, where it is easy to match sellers and buyers.

Furthermore, the strength of network effects is increased through the information that is posted about sellers and buyers, who both get rated by their peers on criteria such as timeliness of delivery, payment and quality of the products sold. eBay users who have received strong peer ratings are likely to continue using eBay because of their reputation, which makes it easier for them to sell items. eBay, as the operator of the community, can capture parts of the value, e.g. through fees for posting on its website information about the product on offer, and sales commission once the product is sold.

Through its book reviews, Amazon.com has also created network effects. As more customers use its website and post their comments about books and other products, Amazon.com becomes more valuable to other customers, who can now retrieve information from many different reviewers about any given book. Other companies, such as ciao.com, have turned customer reviews into a complete business model, where they create a website that consists primarily of consumer ratings of different kinds of products.

From the individual customer perspective, switching from a network that is built around a large installed user base is sensible only if everybody else switches as well. It is possible, at least in theory, that a company with strong network effects can induce customers to stay in spite of the advent of new competitors with superior products. Users decide not to switch because they do not want to lose the compatibility with other users. If all users could agree to switch to the new product, however, then they would be better off to do so as well.

The logic of the Internet boom years was that if companies wanted to generate strong network effects, then they needed quickly to generate large market share, even if the costs for doing so were high. Part of this thinking was also that quality in comparison with competitors was not of central importance, because it was assumed that barriers to entry would increase as a result of network effects, making it difficult for newcomers to steer away customers. However, network effects, when they existed, often did not turn out to be strong enough to keep customers at one website. In fact, there were only very few instances, such as online auctioning, where network effects were sufficiently strong to have a substantial impact on user value. Today, however, as online social networking sites continue to gain importance, the lock-in due to network effects is more relevant than ever.

Additionally, even if network effects are strong, this does not necessarily mean that consumers will not switch to a new, superior product. When choosing between an existing and a new product, customers do not look just at the existing situation; they also anticipate its future evolution – otherwise, CD players, for example, because of their need for CDs, would never have become popular. Thus, as has always been the case, in order to succeed new entrants need to demonstrate the superiority of their product and to give the impression among the general public that their product presents the most attractive features for the future.

Apple's sound strategy for the i-Pod

More than three years after the music companies handed Steve Jobs the keys to the kingdom by releasing their catalogues to him in digital form, Apple's dominant position in the digital music business looks secure.

Bad strategy and execution on the part of rivals have made its position seem more impregnable than it is. But even with better planning, there is probably little they could have done to change this picture. That is worth remembering this week after news of yet another apparently radical attack on Apple's stronghold, in the shape of an advertising-supported music download business.

First, consider the source of Apple's strength. Its execution of its digital music strategy has been a textbook example of how to consolidate an early market advantage. It has extended its product range and segmented the market, moving into lower-priced devices and up into video. It has poured money into advertising, turning the i-Pod into one of the fetishistic objects of the age.

It has also been able to rely on two things that often characterise technology leaders: network effects and technology lock-in. Buy an i-Pod, and there is a good chance a friend will let you download all his or her i-Tunes music to your machine – not a bad network effect, even if of dubious legality. The lock-in comes from the digital rights management (DRM) software that lets the i-Tunes music store and i-Pod feed off each other.

History shows that technology leaders, once established, are seldom dethroned by direct competition. It usually takes a shift in business model, or in a technology paradigm, before that happens.

When changes like that do occur, the news for the challengers is surprisingly good. Very few companies that dominate one era of technology go on to dominate the next. Just think of Sony's Walkman. A company that thrived on its engineering prowess – based on its skill in miniaturising analogue technologies – was left high and dry when the digital era arrived.

Not surprisingly, attempts to change the business model and the technology paradigm in portable digital media are now coming thick and fast. This week brought news of one of the most drastic: Universal Music plans to make its entire music catalogue of music available for download free of charge through an advertising-supported service called SpiralFrog.

An advertising-supported music market, though, seems a stretch. As Mike McGuire, an analyst at Gartner, points out, other music companies may well feel that giving away their songs would risk devaluing their product, even if the advertising revenues are big enough. Users who want free music still turn illegally to peer-to-peer networks.

Also, apparently radical attempts like this to beat Apple by changing the rules of the game are likely to fail because they are only a partial answer. Universal's plan would be hobbled by restrictive DRM – users would have to return once a month to refresh their music and it would not play on i-Pods.

This gets to the heart of the problem. Taking aim at parts of the i-Tunes-plus i-Pod system, now that it has become a de facto standard, is unlikely to work. At one end of the spectrum are the Internet services that want to outflank i-Tunes by finding different ways to introduce people to new music. Changing this process of discovery – usually by adopting the sort of social networking tools employed by MySpace – is at the heart of services such as MTV's Urge.

At the other end of the spectrum are devices that try to outclass the i-Pod. Sony's PSP may have been invented for games but it has a screen that is far better suited for watching videos than the i-Pod. In between are new distribution mechanisms that change the way music is downloaded to portable devices. In Asia, where the mobile phone rules, accessing music over a cellular network is already a big business.

Innovations such as these will find a market and Apple's position will undoubtedly be eroded somewhat, to the relief of an entertainment industry that does not want to see it become the gatekeeper to all digital media. Its 85% market share of digital music in the US is twice Wal-Mart's share of the DVD retail business, and even that is far too large for Hollywood's comfort.

Yet Apple is still the only company that can tie it all together. Others have set out to copy it but are far behind. Microsoft, after a false start, wants to build a rival ecosystem of its own, called Zunes, while Sony has been cleaning up its Connect service after a weak beginning. Watching these companies chase Apple, though, is like watching rival Internet search engines take on Google.

For now, Apple looks well placed to absorb all these innovations into its digital media ecosystem, either through its own inventions or becoming a copyist in its own right. Recent hints by a senior executive seemed to point to an i-Pod phone as the next product to hit the market and no doubt social networking through i-Tunes will be coming soon. As long as those white headphone cords maintain their allure and Mr. Jobs does not put a foot wrong, Apple should be able to stay at the head of the pack.

Source: R. Waters, 'Apple's sound strategy for the i-Pod', 4 September 2006, FT.com.

7.4.2 Early-mover disadvantages

Firms entering the market early with a new technology do not necessarily achieve a competitive advantage over their rivals.[11] In fact, there are a number of reasons why a late entrant might actually accrue some benefits. These reasons are (1) *market uncertainty*, (2) *technological uncertainty* and (3) *free-rider effects*.

Market uncertainty

During the early stages of an innovation cycle, it is very difficult to establish clearly what customers' needs are. During the 1990s, Internet start-ups were trying out various business models and value propositions, many of which misjudged the actual consumer needs.

In banking, for instance, there was a much higher desire for security, trust and face-to-face interaction than was anticipated initially when many online financial institutions entered the market. In the end, banks with established brand names and branch networks were in a better position than their online competitors to fulfil customer needs through a multi-channel banking approach.

Market uncertainty is aggravated if the market is not ready for a new product or service. Consumers need to get used to a new product or service before it becomes valuable to them. However, they will not do so unless there are already a sufficient number of providers in the market. On the other hand, providers will not invest unless they believe that there will be enough consumers to make their investment worthwhile. Thus, both sides face a 'chicken-and-egg' situation, which results in uncertainty regarding future developments.

Furthermore, the market also needs to be ready from a technological perspective. Many of the online services that turn out to be successful today rely on the widespread availability of always-on, broadband Internet connections. For instance, social networking sites such MySpace, the videosite YouTube or the Internet telephony provider Skype depend on broadband access of their users to be able to provide their services.

Technological uncertainty

Betting on wrong technologies can be as problematic as overestimating market demand. In mobile e-commerce, for instance, early adopters of the Wireless Application Protocol (WAP) found that this highly praised technology did not deliver on its promises to create superior customer value. Instead, it proved to be very cumbersome to use, with a complicated 35-step procedure to configure a mobile phone for WAP access, long connection time (over 60 seconds) and the tiny screen space of a handset. As a result, market pick-up was much lower than expected.

Third-generation (3G) mobile phones are now facing the same type of uncertainty. European telecommunication firms bid billions of euros for the acquisition of 3G licences to be able to enter the market early. Yet it is still uncertain whether the investment in this specific technology will pay off.

Free-rider effects

Learning effects can constitute a first-mover advantage. However, if they cannot be kept proprietary, then competitors will benefit from them without having to make the same mistakes as the first mover(s). In general, developing a market as a first mover is more expensive than just imitating it.

Many traditional bricks-and-mortar retailers who were initially hesitant to enter the online business and then embraced the Internet profited greatly from the failed experiences of the early movers. They leveraged their well-known brand and installed customer bases to overtake quickly their pure online competitors. Thus, for example, Wal-Mart in the USA has become one of the largest Internet retailers by leveraging its strong brand name and synergies with its physical store network.

SUMMARY

- This chapter analysed how firms can break away from traditional forms of competition and redefine their value proposition by opening up new market spaces. This can be done first by gaining insights into new market spaces through the value curve. It can also be done through the six paths value creation framework by looking across (1) substitutive industries, (2) strategic groups, (3) the chain of buyers, (4) complementary products and service offerings, (5) functional or emotional appeal to buyers and (6) time and trends.

- This chapter also discussed timing issues for market entry in e-business. More specifically, it analysed the different types of early-mover advantages and disadvantages that an Internet venture can exploit (or should avoid). Early-mover advantages include (1) learning effects, (2) brand and reputation, (3) switching costs and (4) network effects. Early-mover disadvantages include (1) market uncertainty, (2) technological uncertainty and (3) free-rider effects.

REVIEW QUESTIONS

1 How can a company look for new market spaces outside its own industry?

2 Explain the six paths framework. How can it be used to create value in e-business?

3 Outline the timing issues for market entry in e-business.

4 What are the advantages and disadvantages that early movers in e-business should exploit or avoid?

DISCUSSION QUESTIONS

1 Working in a group, pick out an e-business company of your choice. Write down what you consider to be the key product/service elements. As a group, discuss and reach consensus on these key elements. Using a chart similar to the one shown in Exhibit 7.1, rate the offering's level on each key element against the main competitors. Do you see competitors with radically different value curves?

2 Adopt the perspective of a new industry entrant and consider the existing value curves. Use one or two of the paths to experiment with the creation of a new value curve.

   ■ Industry: Which elements of substitute industries are un/important to target buyers?

   ■ Strategic groups: Which key elements of the offer compel buyers to buy up or buy down?

   ■ Buyers: Who are the decision makers and how would changing buyer focus affect the key elements?

3 As discussed in the FT articles in this chapter, both Dell and Apple have moved into new product categories in recent years. Which company was more successful and why? Back up your position with arguments.

RECOMMENDED KEY READING

■ C. Kim and R. Mauborgne developed the concept of creating new market spaces by looking outside one's own industry in 'Creating new market space', *Harvard Business Review*, 1999, January–February, pp. 83–93. See also 'Value innovation – the strategic logic of high growth', *Harvard Business Review*, 1997, January–February, pp. 103–112.

■ Building on their insights from the value innovation studies, C. Kim and R. Mauborgne published the book *Blue Ocean Strategy: How to Create Uncontested Market Space and Make Competition Irrelevant*, Harvard Business School Press, 1995.

USEFUL THIRD-PARTY WEBLINKS

- www.blueoceanstrategy.com revolves completely around value innovations and provides up-to-date examples of successful innovations and their underlying drivers.

- www.innovationzen.com provides information on innovation management, business strategy, technology and more.

- www.brint.com contains numerous articles on innovation and e-commerce.

NOTES AND REFERENCES

1 See C. Kim and R. Mauborgne, 'Creating new market space', *Harvard Business Review*, 1999, January–February, pp. 83–93, and also G. Johnson, K. Scholes and R. Whittington, *Exploring Corporate Strategy*, 7th edition, Prentice Hall, 2002, pp. 132–133.

2 See C. Kim and R. Mauborgne, 'Creating new market space', *Harvard Business Review*, 1999, January-February, pp. 83–93.

3 A detailed discussion of this approach to value creation can be found in W.C. Kim and R. Mauborgne, 'Value innovation: the strategic logic of high growth', *Harvard Business Review*, 1997, January–February, pp. 103–112, and 'Creating new market space', *Harvard Business Review*, 1999, January–February, pp. 83–93.

4 S. Rangan and R. Adner discuss the pitfalls of early-mover advantages in the Internet world in the article 'Profits and the Internet: seven misconceptions', *Sloan Management Review*, 2001, Summer, pp. 44–46.

5 For different types of early-mover advantages, see D. Besanko, D. Dranove, M. Shanley and S. Schaefer, *Economics of Strategy*, John Wiley, 2003, pp. 438–446. W. Boulding and M. Christen point out that there are also important early-mover disadvantages in 'First-mover disadvantage', *Harvard Business Review*, 2001, October, pp. 20–21.

6 The importance of learning and experience first received attention through the development of the experience curve: B. Henderson, 'The experience curve reviewed', in C. Stern and G. Stalk (eds), *Perspectives on Strategy*, John Wiley, 1998, pp. 12–15.

7 J. Cassidy discusses the story of Amazon in *Dot.con*, Perennial, 2003, pp. 135–150.

8 S. Liebowitz refutes the frequently cited QWERTY keyboard and VHS/Betamax examples in *Re-thinking the Network Economy*, Amacom, 2002, pp. 47–48.

9 A good discussion and critique of the impact of network effects on e-commerce companies can be found in S. Liebowitz, *Re-thinking the Network Economy*, Amacom, 2002, pp. 13–48. S. Rangan and R. Adner also discuss network effects in e-commerce in 'Profits and the Internet: seven misconceptions', *Sloan Management Review*, 2001, Summer, pp. 44–46.

10 George Gilder coined the term 'Metcalf's Law' in 1993. The article can be found at www.discovery.org.

11 For a detailed discussion of first-mover disadvantages, see M. Liebermann and D.B. Montgomery, 'First-mover (dis-)advantages', *Strategic Management Journal*, 1998, Vol. 19, No. 12, pp. 47–49.

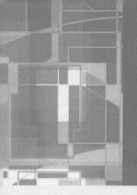

CHAPTER 8

Creating and capturing value through e-business strategies: the value-process framework[1]

Chapter at a glance

Related case studies

Case study	Primary focus of the case study
16 Sony BMG	Value creation and value capturing

Learning outcomes

After completing this chapter, you should be able to:

- Identify the main drivers for value creation and capturing.

- Understand how the value-process framework integrates the value chain and the five forces analyses.

- Apply the value-process framework to conduct an overarching strategy analysis.

INTRODUCTION

> Unless at some point the company can see the design, see how the pieces fit, and make the interdependent choices consistent, the company is not going to be successful.

Michael Porter[2]

In essence, strategy formulation revolves around the concepts of value creation and value capturing. During the Internet boom years, online ventures often did not pay enough attention to these fundamental economic concepts. Nowadays, though, economic viability of any e-business venture is of paramount importance to managers and investors alike. This is why we devote a full chapter to the concepts of value creation and capturing. The goal of this chapter is to bring together, into one framework, the value-process framework (VPF), the two strategy analyses which we discussed earlier in the book: the five forces analysis which focuses on the external environment of the firm (see Chapter 3) and the value chain analysis which provides an internal perspective of the firm (see Chapter 4). By using the VPF, you should be able to:

- Integrate the findings of the above-mentioned strategy analyses in order to assess the different levers of competitive advantage.

- Develop an integrated business strategy that takes into account both the internal and external environments of the firm.

- Communicate this integrated business strategy to a management audience in a comprehensive way.

8.1 The value-process framework for e-business strategies

The concept of value creation and value capturing is at the core of any (e-)business strategy since creating superior value than rivals and the ability to capture parts of this value in the form of profit are prerequisites for building a competitive advantage. The latter is the basis for reaching the fundamental goal of any company: that is, achieving sustainable success.[3] Building on the two concepts of value creation and value capturing, the following sections outline the main elements of the VPF.[4]

8.1.1 Creating value

In order to create value, a company must provide customers with a product's perceived use value that is greater than the costs incurred for providing that product. Accordingly, the value created is the difference between a customer's *perceived use value* from a given product[5] and the firm's costs for providing that product. Exhibit 8.1 illustrates the relationship between these two terms.

Exhibit 8.1 Value is created if the perceived use value exceeds costs

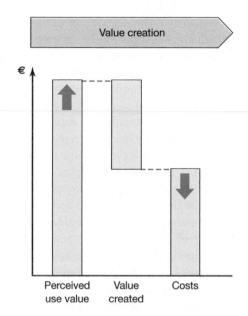

When discussing the concept of value creation, it is essential to clarify the definition of value within the VPF context, since previous definitions of the term were sometimes unclear. For instance, when Porter states that 'value is what buyers are willing to pay, and superior value stems from offering lower prices than competitors for equivalent benefits',[6] he subsumes in one term the similar yet conceptually distinct concepts of perceived use value and consumer surplus. However, if we do so, it then becomes conceptually impossible to differentiate between value creation, which results largely from activities within a company, and value capturing, which is largely driven by the competitive environment.

In this chapter, we use the term *perceived use value*, which is defined as 'the price that a customer is prepared to pay for the product if there is a single source of supply'.[7] Important categories for the creation of use value are quality, speed and brand. Quality includes product characteristics such as functionality, durability and reliability. Speed refers to how fast a company can deliver a given product. Brand entails the perceived traits that consumers associate with the product or its producer, including trust and the emotional benefit derived from a product. Here, it is important to notice that the perceived use value depends entirely on the customer's subjective perception. Each customer will perceive the use value of a given product differently depending on factors such as gender, age or cultural background.

The second dimension that drives value creation entails *costs*. These include (1) the costs for the purchase of resources (labour, materials, information and capital), (2) the costs of combining resources in production, marketing and delivery, and (3) the costs of selling the product.

Creating value that is positive is a first necessary condition for building a competitive advantage. As we shall describe below, in order to capture parts of the value created, a company's value created must be larger than that of its competitors, and must be imperfectly imitable and substitutable.

8.1.2 Capturing value

Value creation by itself does not provide any information about how the value is distributed from producers to consumers. Porter emphasises this point when he stated that 'satisfying buyer needs may be a prerequisite for industry profitability, but in itself it is not sufficient'.[8]

Instead, in order to succeed, a firm must not only be able to create superior value over a sustained period of time, but also be able to capture the value created in the form of an economic profit (producer surplus). Porter states that 'if profitability is the firm's foremost goal, [strategic] positioning must start with price and cost'.[9]

In VPF terminology, the value captured, or producer surplus, is the difference between the price charged for a product and the costs incurred for producing that product. In general terms, the consumer surplus is the difference between perceived use value and price (see Exhibit 8.2). Thus, the overall goal of strategic management is to help managers (1) maximise the value created by increasing the perceived use value and by minimising the cost of providing this use value, (2) capture as much of the value created as possible in the form of producer surplus, and (3) do so in a sustainable way over an extended period of time by defending the company's position against imitators and substitutes.

At this point of the analysis, it also becomes clear that the frequently used term 'superior value' should more concisely be called superior consumer surplus, since it refers to the difference between the use value and the price paid. This conceptual clarification is of fundamental importance when distinguishing between value creation and value capturing.

When determining the levels of value creation and value capturing, it is helpful to differentiate between a monopolistic and a competitive environment. In a monopolistic environment, the VPF is rather simplistic. Here, the use value, as perceived by the customer, represents the maximum amount he/she is willing to pay for a product. Hence, in

Exhibit 8.2 The price indicates how the value created is distributed between the producer and the consumer

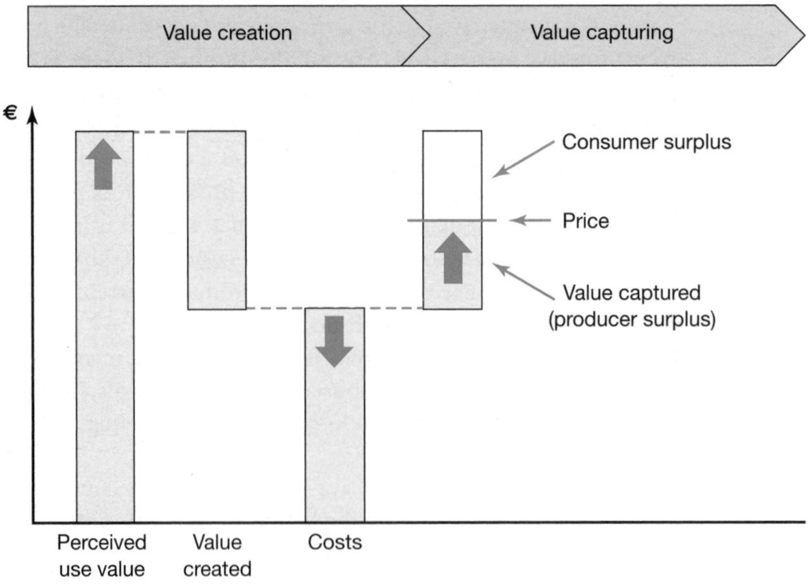

Exhibit 8.3 Producers completely capture the value created in a (quasi-)monopolistic environment

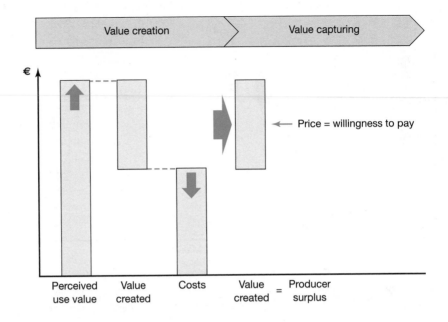

a perfectly monopolistic environment, producers are able to capture (almost) completely the value created, provided that (1) there is no other source of supply and (2) they are able to discriminate on price (see Exhibit 8.3).[10]

In reality, however, companies usually operate in a competitive environment where the consumer surplus provided by rival companies determines the customer's choice. This has important implications for the company's ability to capture the value it creates. Conceptually, the willingness to pay is reduced by the amount of consumer surplus offered by the strongest competitor or the best substitute product.

To illustrate this point, we use the hypothetical example of two companies A and B, which are competing in the same industry (see Exhibit 8.4). Let us suppose that Company B, which is the strongest competitor of Company A, offers a product with a high perceived use value at a low price, thereby generating high potential consumer surplus. A given customer will only consider purchasing Company A's product if the consumer surplus provided by Company A is either equal to or higher than the one offered by Company B. We call this reduction in the consumer's willingness to pay *competitive discount*.

In our example, Company A provides a use value of €20 for a given consumer. Production costs and other costs, including marketing and overheads, amount to €12. The value created is thus €8 (as shown in step 1 of Exhibit 8.4). The competitive discount is then determined by the value creation and capturing of the strongest competitor. As shown in step 2 of Exhibit 8.4, Company B creates a value of €5 by producing a perceived use value of €20 at costs of €15. As shown in step 3 of Exhibit 8.4, Company B sells its product for €19, thereby creating a consumer surplus of €1.

Exhibit 8.4 The competitive discount is equal to the consumer surplus provided by the strongest competitor

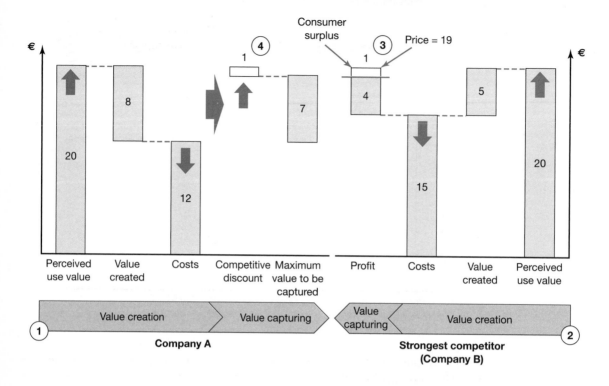

The crucial point of this analysis is that as a result of the competitor's offering, Company A will no longer be able to raise its price to the level of perceived use value. Instead, the maximum value that can be captured needs to be reduced by the amount of consumer surplus offered by Company B. As shown in step 4 of Exhibit 8.4, Company A now needs to charge a price that is at least marginally lower than €19. If it charged more, the consumer surplus would drop below €1 thereby enticing the customer to switch to the competitor's offering that provides a higher consumer surplus.

In industries with highly intense competition such as the PC industry, the competitive discount might even increase to the point where it is equal to the entire value created by the strongest competitor. In our example, Company B would decrease the price in order to compete with Company A until it reaches a level of €15. Company B would not be able to lower this price further since at any price below this level, it would not be able to cover the costs it incurred. This is the reason why companies can only compete successfully if their value created is larger than that of competitors.

After having discussed the concepts of value creation and capturing it is now possible to summarise the key steps of the VPF as in Exhibit 8.5.

Although only the main VPF dimensions were outlined above, this overview provides an overarching understanding of the three main levers that influence a company's value creation and value capturing. These three levers are (1) use value as perceived by the customer, (2) costs for creating this value and (3) competitive discount, which reduces the customer's willingness to pay and, in turn, reduces profit (see Exhibit 8.5).

Exhibit 8.5 **The VPF – to achieve profitability, companies must be able to create and capture value**

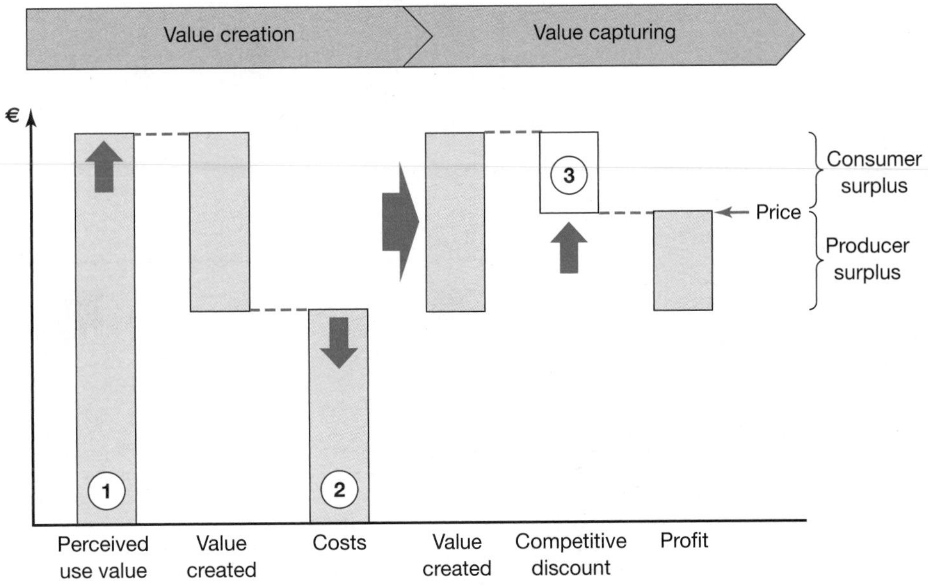

In order to achieve a sustainable competitive advantage, a company needs to fulfil the following requirements with respect to value creation and value capturing:

■ *Value creation.* First, a company must create value by providing customers with a perceived use value that exceeds the company's production costs (levers 1 and 2). However, only if this value created is greater than the value created by the strongest competitor does the company have the opportunity to provide a higher consumer surplus to customers while still being able to capture value itself in the form of an economic profit (or producer surplus).

■ *Value capturing.* Furthermore, in order to limit the amount of the competitive discount, the consumer surplus (i.e. the 'value for money' a company offers) needs to be unique (lever 3). This uniqueness can be achieved, for instance, through exceptional quality, a strong brand image or a fast time-to-market. Only uniqueness leads to a reduction in the number of competitors, which, in turn, also limits the maximum consumer surplus offered elsewhere. In order to sustain the achieved competitive advantage over time, it is also important that this consumer surplus is imperfectly imitable or substitutable.

8.2 Integrating strategic management analyses through the VPF

In this section, we show how insights from the two main strategy analyses (i.e. Porter's value chain analysis and the five forces model) can be integrated through the VPF by analysing their various interdependencies (see Exhibit 8.6).

Exhibit 8.6 **The VPF integrates different strategy analyses**

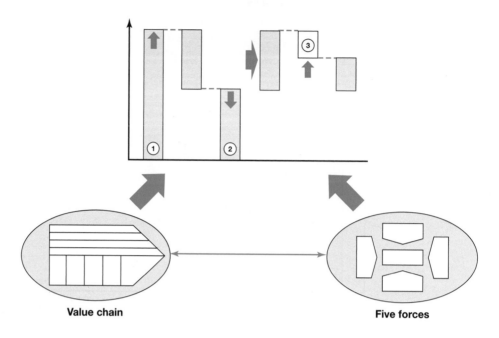

Value chain   **Five forces**

8.2.1 The value chain analysis and the VPF

Porter's value chain analysis helps to address the question of how value is created within a company. It does so by disaggregating a company into strategically relevant and inter-related activities. Within the VPF, the value chain primarily helps to analyse the left-hand side of the framework, i.e. the interaction between perceived use value and costs. In essence, the value chain model revolves around value creation, where value is created by the individual business activities of the value chain (see Exhibit 8.7).

On the one hand, each (primary) activity contributes to the aggregate use value as perceived by the customer. On the other hand, each activity also creates costs. Thus, based on a mapping between the value chain and the VPF, the aggregate 'perceived use value' is equal to the sum of 'perceived use values' resulting from the different business activities, and the aggregate costs correspond to the total costs incurred by these activities.[11] Therefore, firms should (1) invest in value-enhancing activities and (2) reduce costs, especially for non-value-enhancing activities. For example, a fancy product brand that drastically increases the perceived use value from shoes in the lifestyle segment is likely to justify increased marketing expenses to establish the brand image. If, on the other hand, the manufacturing process of these shoes does not create a high perceived use value for the customer, then this business activity could be outsourced in order to reduce costs.

Exhibit 8.7 Value is created by the individual business activities of the value chain

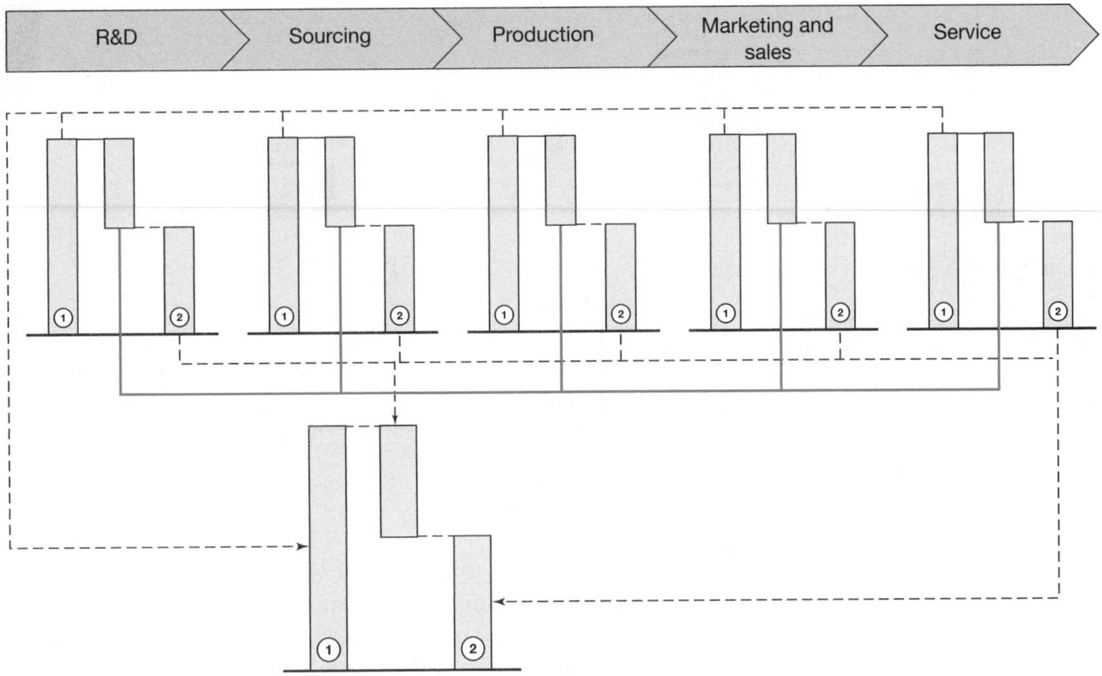

8.2.2 The five forces analysis and the VPF

After discussing value creation, which is primarily based on the value chain model, we now focus on the value-capturing dimension of the VPF using Porter's five forces analysis. Conceptually, if, on the one hand, a company can charge high prices for its products or services, it captures large parts of the value it creates. If, on the other hand, prices are driven down by competition, consumers will capture most of the value.

The purpose of Porter's five forces model is to determine the attractiveness of an industry by analysing the power of the different actors. The five forces include (1) the competition within the industry, (2) the threat of new entrants, (3) the bargaining power of customers, (4) the threat of substitute products and (5) the bargaining power of suppliers. The first four factors determine the competitive discount as is illustrated by the upper arrow in Exhibit 8.8. As the power of the different actors increases, so does the competitive discount, thereby lowering the customer's willingness to pay. The bargaining power of suppliers mainly influences the cost position and thereby the value creation of a company; this is illustrated by the lower arrow in Exhibit 8.8.[12]

Porter's five forces highlight the fact that profitability depends not only on the internal activities of a company but also on its business environment, i.e. the industry in which it competes. One of the primary goals of the VPF is to integrate the industry attractiveness perspective with the internal company perspective. Industries with a highly intense competition, low entry barriers and readily available substitutes are likely to have higher competitive discounts. Thus, even though companies in these industries might create high levels of value, through either low costs or high perceived use value, they can capture only a fraction of this value in the form of profits.

Exhibit 8.8 Porter's five forces influence the cost lever and competitive discount

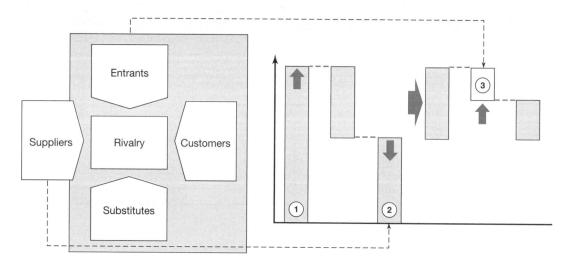

We briefly illustrate this logic using the example of the German fixed-line telecommunications industry. Due to deregulation and the advent of substitutes (such as VoIP telephony),[13] barriers to entry were significantly lowered and rivalry increased dramatically. As a consequence, customer power rose, too. Fixed-line telecommunication operators started reducing their charge rates and ended up in a price war that eroded their profitability. In VPF terminology, the above industry developments reduced the customers' willingness to pay, thus increasing the competitive discount and thereby decreasing the value captured by the telcos.

Exhibit 8.9 Porter's strategy models can be used to analyse the levers of the VPF

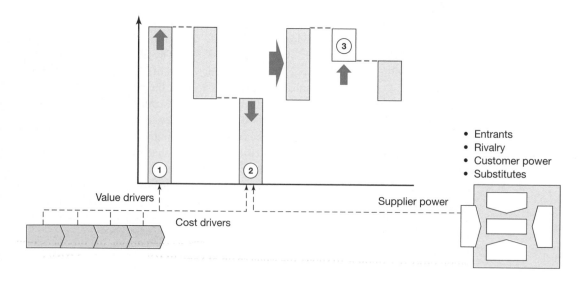

In introducing this chapter, we stated that one of the main goals of the VPF is to integrate the internal company perspective with the external industry perspective. In this section, we used the VPF to show conceptually how to integrate the results of Porter's value chain and five forces analyses. The resulting overarching framework (shown in Exhibit 8.9) helps us to understand better the interdependencies and analyse the different levers of competitive advantage as well as their effects on value creation and value capturing.

8.3 Sony BMG (Germany): an actual application of the VPF

In this section, we provide an illustrative example of how to apply the VPF to an actual business situation. The context for this real-world application is Sony BMG (Germany), which is also featured in detail in the case studies section of this book.

8.3.1 The business context

Between 1995 and 2005, the German music major Sony BMG grappled with a ubiquitous crisis that threatened the entire music industry. This crisis, which was mainly caused by increased piracy through illegal online music downloading and burning of compact discs, led to declining physical CD sales and dwindling industry revenues. The latter dropped at an almost double-digit rate for 10 consecutive years. In order to secure its future, Sony BMG looked for ways to exploit the growth opportunities in the nascent digital music market. In particular, mobile music, driven by increased UMTS[14] and multimedia handset penetration, was gaining a strong foothold and presented a lot of potential. eMedia, the department in charge in Germany of Sony BMG's digital music business, pondered the launch of its own mobile service, equipped with Sony BMG digital music content. This MVNO[15] concept, targeting the 12- to 25-year-old mobile phone users, was designed as a prepaid mobile offer comprising a UMTS-enabled multimedia handset and downloadable premium content scattered around in virtual music worlds (rock, pop, Latin-American, etc.).[16] This business expansion entailed a very high risk but had a strong potential to impact on the future bottom-line performance of Sony BMG (Germany). In the following sections, we use the VPF to analyse the extent to which Sony BMG would have been able to create and capture value through the implementation of the above-mentioned MVNO project.

8.3.2 Value creation

We start with an examination of the value and cost levers and their influence on Sony BMG's value creation. We do so by integrating the results of a value chain analysis into the VPF to identify (1) what value drivers could have created perceived use value for Sony BMG's customers, and (2) what major costs would have accrued during the product's realisation process. Exhibit 8.10 shows the value chain of Sony BMG's prospective MVNO.

Exhibit 8.10 **A value chain analysis of the MVNO project reveals numerous value and cost drivers**

	Handset purchasing	MNO services	Content, product design	Marketing, branding	Sales, distribution	MVNE services
Value drivers	UMTS multimedia handset	UMTS technology	Concept, design, artist roster, applications, features	Concept, image, concept brand	Content distribution over the air	/
Cost drivers	Wholesale costs	MNO service fees	Royalties	Advertising	Retail margins	MVNE service fees

To achieve a differentiated positioning for its MVNO, Sony BMG considered including multiple value drivers along the business activities of its value chain. It expected that the purchase of UMTS-enabled multimedia handsets would drastically increase the attractiveness of its prepaid starter packages. In contrast to competitive prepaid offerings, Sony BMG also wanted to offer wireless telecommunication services (i.e. MNO[17] services) based on cutting-edge UMTS technology. Furthermore, the content component of its mobile offering, i.e. the concept design of the virtual music worlds, was unique and the first on the market. It was supposed to create additional value through unique music-based applications and features. Sony BMG's artist roster and digitised music catalogue were thought to serve as the backbone of the virtual music worlds. Furthermore, Sony BMG wanted to enhance the perceived use value through large-scale marketing and branding activities that were expected to create a strong concept brand enticing customers to become Sony BMG mobile subscribers. The underlying UMTS technology was seen as an enabler for Sony BMG to sell and distribute its premium content directly over the air to its customers' handsets.

At this point in the analysis, it is crucial to discuss how each one of the above-listed value drivers could have been converted into actual use value as perceived by prospective Sony BMG mobile customers. Based on our experience, both managers and students often omit this important step of specifically working out how particular product features or a company's technology actually translate into perceived use value. For example, in the case of Sony BMG, customers would not have appreciated the underlying UMTS technology of a mobile offering but would have enjoyed the fast 'anytime and anywhere' access to entertainment content. In the same way, customers would not have derived value from a Caribbean beach itself but from the enjoyment they would have experienced when spending time at that beach. In the Sony BMG example, multiple value drivers were supposed to create use value mainly for the following three dimensions: quality, brand and speed (see Exhibit 8.11).

Exhibit 8.11 Multiple value drivers create perceived use value mainly in three dimensions

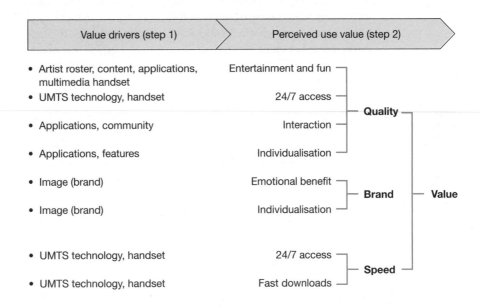

We now describe in more detail how Sony BMG considered translating the different value drivers into perceived use value.

■ *Quality (of the product)*. Potential customers who would have downloaded and consumed Sony BMG content would have valued its entertainment and fun dimension. Furthermore, they would have appreciated the 'anytime and anywhere' access to the virtual entertainment worlds. Through applications and community features, customers could have satisfied their interaction needs too. Furthermore, the diverse content applications would have allowed customers, through customised mobile phone configurations, to differentiate themselves. All these features were designed to increase product quality.

■ *Brand*. Customers would have derived emotional benefits from possessing the starter package of a specifically branded virtual world. For example, a Latin-American music fan would have perceived the emotional benefit of owning a specific 'Latino-branded' handset that would have the corresponding genre-related content. The branding would have enabled Sony BMG subscribers to differentiate themselves from common mobile phone users and perceive a strong sense of customisation.

■ *Speed*. Compared with common General Packet Radio Service (GPRS) data transfer, UMTS technology creates use value in the form of fast downloads and short waiting periods. By providing UMTS services, Sony BMG would have enabled customers to take advantage of 'anytime and anywhere' access to entertainment content. In particular, customers who needed to kill some 'idle time' (e.g. when waiting for a bus or a train) would have been expected to appreciate these product features especially.

After having analysed the drivers of perceived use value, we now identify the corresponding cost drivers (see step 2 in Exhibit 8.11). Due to its differentiated positioning, the Sony BMG MVNO concept was thought to lead to substantial costs. First, the wholesale costs of top-end handsets would have been very high, which would have forced Sony BMG to subsidise its handsets strongly. Second, the provision of cutting-edge UMTS technology would have resulted in high service fees charged by prospective MNO partners. Third, Sony BMG would have to pay royalties to its artists for the sale of music-related content. Fourth, since no concept brand was established, advertising costs for TV, print and online promotion would have been another major cost pool. Additional cost drivers that were identified through the value chain analysis included retail margins for distributors and service fees to MVNEs[18] for their technical support.

Moreover, the moderate to high bargaining power of suppliers (i.e. the handset manufacturers and wireless operators) would have further increased Sony BMG's purchasing costs. Handset manufacturers like Nokia or SonyEricsson produce prepaid phones with similar basic functionalities. However, their handsets differ in terms of brand and image, features that are very important to customers. In sum, the bargaining power of handset manufacturers was moderate and would have slightly increased the wholesale costs of Sony BMG's handsets. Wireless operators, in turn, provide telecommunication infrastructure and sell air traffic to MVNOs. Since E-Plus was the only wireless telecom operator willing to sell air traffic to potential MVNO partners, its bargaining power was substantial. Thus, Sony BMG's MNO service fees to E-Plus would have risen considerably and therefore decreased the value created. This last step again highlights the fact that the process of value creation would have depended not only on the internal activities of a company, but also on its external environment, i.e. the industry it competed in.

Exhibit 8.12 **Perceived use value and costs for the Sony BMG MVNO would both have been high**

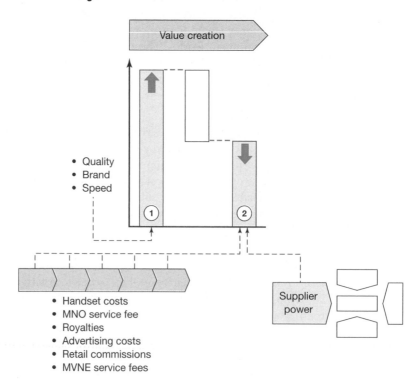

In this section, we have shown how the value creation dimension can be analysed by integrating findings from Porter's strategy models into the VPF and assessing their impact on the value and cost levers, and thus on the value created (see Exhibit 8.12).

8.3.3 Value capturing

In the previous section, we found that Sony BMG could have created value as the prospectively high perceived use value could have exceeded the high costs of the MVNO project. We now focus on the value-capturing dimension to determine to what extent Sony BMG would have been able to capture parts of the value created in the form of profit. To do so, we analyse Sony BMG's ability to influence the level of competitive discount.

As stated in Section 8.1.2, the level of competitive discount depends on the uniqueness of a product. The probability that a product is unique is high if (1) the internal resources and capabilities enable the firm to create a unique product, and (2) the industry structure is such that it remains unattractive for new entrants. First, we analyse the resource base of Sony BMG and its internal power to create a unique product. We then apply Porter's five forces model to assess industry attractiveness and its impact on the competitive discount.

Sony BMG's internal key resources must be valuable, rare and imperfectly imitable to enable the company to create a potentially unique product that appeals to customers. From the VPF perspective, if a company is able to offer a unique product based on resources that are valuable, rare and imperfectly imitable, it can then limit the number of competitors and keep the competitive discount small. In our case, Sony BMG's major valuable resources were (1) concept design, (2) artist roster and (3) marketing expertise.

- *Concept design.* This comprised value-added services, special applications and additional features that were likely to satisfy customers' entertainment, customisation and interaction needs. As the first on the market, the SonyBMG concept design was not only valuable but also rare. Thus, it could have created a unique product with a limited competitive discount. However, since followers did not face major barriers in duplicating the concept design, the competitive discount would have increased over time.

- *Artist roster.* Since all three major competitors (Universal, EMI and Warner) controlled more or less similar artist rosters, Sony BMG's artist roster represented a valuable but not rare resource. Furthermore, it was not imperfectly imitable since content aggregators such as Napster or iTunes faced no major hurdles for acquiring the rights to sell digital music themselves. This implied that the artist roster was not a source of a unique product and therefore would not have decreased the competitive discount.

- *Marketing expertise.* Launching a new premium product would have forced Sony BMG to carry out large-scale marketing campaigns. Strong marketing expertise would have guided Sony BMG efforts to introduce successfully on the market a new product brand and image. However, the competing music majors also claimed to have strong marketing competencies. As a result, marketing expertise did not constitute a resource that would have created a unique product vis-à-vis competitors and thus would not have reduced the competitive discount.

In conclusion, the concept design was in the short term the only source of product uniqueness. However, Sony BMG did not control valuable resources that were rare and imperfectly imitable. Therefore, in the long run, it would not have been able to achieve a sustainable product uniqueness or a competitive advantage. As a result, the competitive discount would have been relatively small in the beginning but, in all likelihood, would have increased substantially over time.

We now use Porter's five forces model to assess the industry's attractiveness from a new entrant's perspective and analyse its effect on the competitive discount. Exhibit 8.13 summarises the competitive environment in which Sony BMG considered the set-up of its own MVNO.

By the end of 2005, the German wireless telecommunications industry was close to saturation. Rivalry in the industry was steadily rising; voice traffic had become a commodity; and differentiation via premium content was essential for future growth. However, in contrast to other incumbents, one major wireless telecom operator (namely E-Plus) pursued a different strategy and started to gain market share by selling air traffic to emerging virtual telecom operators. Due to the low technical entry barriers, easy access to distribution channels and low exit barriers, these virtual telecom operators started to flood the market. As a consequence, prepaid mobile customers especially who had almost no switching costs were able to choose from a large pool of mobile telecom offerings with low differentiation.

Exhibit 8.13 **The German wireless telecommunications industry is of relatively low attractiveness**

Threat of new entrants
(*moderate to high*)

- Low technical barriers, high barriers for brand and access to attractive content
- Low switching costs for prepaid customers
- Low exit barriers, only sunk costs for advertisement
- Easy access to distribution channels

Bargaining power of suppliers
(*moderate to high*)

- No input differentiation in terms of air traffic (this argument applies only to resellers and MVNOs)
- Moderate input differentiation in terms of handsets
- Strong supplier concentration (only E-Plus in Germany)

Industry rivalry
(*moderate to high*)

- Telco market is close to saturation
- Player concentration depending on market definition
- Low exit barriers for non-MNOs
- Product differentiation only via premium content

Bargaining power of customers
(*relatively high*)

- No considerable switching costs
- Huge amount of prepaid offerings ➝ low differentiation parameters
- Willingness to pay important for premium content providers
- High market transparency

Threat of substitutes
(*relatively low*)

- No devices in sight that could adequately fulfil the product's major functions

Now, we draw on the main insights gained from the five forces analysis of the German wireless telecommunications industry and integrate our findings into the VPF. In our example, three forces had a major impact on the degree of product uniqueness and thus explicitly influenced the competitive discount. As uniqueness is hard to achieve in the face of rising competition, the moderate to high threat of new entrants and the moderate to high industry rivalry both drove the competitive discount up, thereby reducing the value captured. Only the low threat of substitutes had an increasing effect on the value captured as industries with a low threat of substitutes usually have lower competitive discounts.

In this section, we focused on the competitive discount as the third lever of competitive advantage to find out whether the value created by Sony BMG could also have been captured. We have shown how insights from strategic analysis increased the competitive discount and demonstrated its impact on value capturing. We visually integrate the results of this section in Exhibit 8.14. For Sony BMG, the competitive discount would have been substantial over time, especially due to the imitability of its key resources, the moderate to high industry rivalry and the moderate to high threat of new entrants.

8.3.4 Findings

Ultimately, Sony BMG had major doubts as to whether the MVNO project would have been profitable taking into account the high risk due to the high cost structure, the moderate to low industry attractiveness and the imitability of its key resources. Therefore, Sony BMG decided to put on hold the project's implementation plan. However, in order to enter the digital music market, Sony BMG started leveraging its resources and capabilities through co-operation with other service providers.

Exhibit 8.14 The five forces analysis indicates a high competitive discount

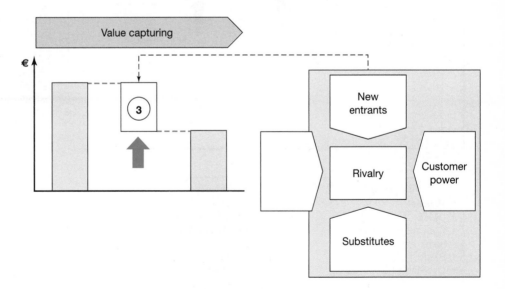

The VPF helped us to understand and explain Sony BMG's decision and its underlying rationale. Exhibit 8.15 shows the findings of the analysis which can be summarised as follows:

- *Perceived use value (1)*. Perceived use value was expected to be substantial, mainly driven by features such as UMTS handsets, concept design, artist roster, strong concept brand and over-the-air distribution of music content.

- *Costs (2)*. As a consequence of the differentiated positioning, the costs of the project would have been very high. MNO service fees, resulting from the high bargaining power of mobile operators, were likely to result in high costs to Sony BMG.

- *Competitive discount (3)*. Even if the perceived use value had exceeded the costs, the relatively low entry barriers and the high industry rivalry would both have led to an increasing effect on the competitive discount, thereby reducing the value captured (i.e. the profitability). Moreover, the uniqueness of the concept design would have only temporarily limited the number of competitors. In the long run, the concept and its underlying resources would have been imitated and not be a source of sustained competitive advantage. As a result, the competitive discount would have risen over time and substantially eroded the value captured by Sony BMG.

Exhibit 8.15 Perceived use value has to be extremely high to achieve profitability

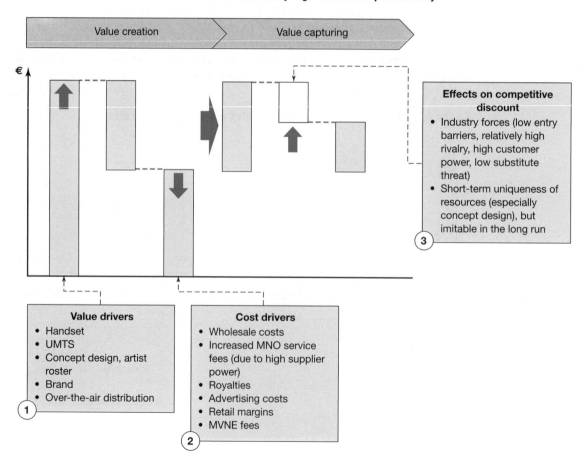

Overall, our analysis shows that implementation of the MVNO project would have been very risky for Sony BMG. Since costs and the competitive discount would have been relatively high, only a blockbuster product would have had the potential to create sufficiently high perceived use value. In addition, Sony BMG would have been forced to aim at a very fast cost amortisation and a short payback period due to the high imitability of the project.

SUMMARY

In this chapter, we presented the value-process framework (VPF), which is a conceptually unifying analysis tool that addresses the main levers of sustainable competitive advantage. This framework stipulates that, in order to succeed, companies need to create and capture value. In particular, when formulating a business strategy, managers need to bear in mind the following key points:

- Value creation and capturing are ultimately the only two levers of strategic management. All other concepts in the field serve to address one or both of these two core dimensions.
- When creating value, a company needs to focus on the use value as perceived by customers. Only value that is considered as such by customers will eventually translate into value created.
- In order to maximise the value created, a company needs to optimise the trade-off between perceived use value and costs.
- In order to be competitive, a company needs to ensure that the value it creates is at least as good as (or better than) the value created by its rivals. Otherwise, competitors offering a higher level of value created will be in a position either to undercut prices while still maintaining a good profitability margin, or to provide a higher level of consumer surplus at a similar price. Both scenarios will severely undermine the company's profitability.
- In order to limit the size of the competitive discount, the value created has to be somehow unique.
- In order to sustain a competitive advantage over time, a company needs to ensure that its value created is difficult to substitute or imitate, since only value created that can be shielded against current and future competitors will ultimately lead to sustainable profitability.

It is important to emphasise that the value-process framework is not just intended to help make decisions at the product level. It also helps address, at the business unit or corporate level, strategic issues such as outsourcing, diversification or mergers and acquisitions. Whenever managers contemplate, for instance, the introduction of a new product line or the outsourcing of a business process to an external provider, it will be insightful to analyse how these decisions impact on the value that is being created and the ability of the company to capture this value.

REVIEW QUESTIONS

1 What is meant by 'perceived use value and what are its main drivers?

2 What is meant by 'competitive discount' and what determines its level?

3 Which requirements does a company need to fulfil in order to achieve a sustainable competitive discount?

DISCUSSION QUESTIONS

1 How would you personally define value creation? Does your definition differ from the one suggested in this chapter? If so, how?

2 Discuss through the value-process framework how companies in an industry (of your choice) create and capture value. Visualise your findings through the diagrams of the framework.

RECOMMENDED KEY READING

■ The concept of perceived use value is described in more detail in C. Bowman and V. Ambrosini, 'Value creation versus value capture: towards a coherent definition of value in strategy', *British Journal of Management*, 2002, No. 1, pp. 1-15.

■ For a more detailed discussion of these approaches, refer to D. Besanko, D. Dranove, M. Shanley and S. Schaefer, *Economics of Strategy*, John Wiley, 2003, pp. 416–419.

■ The five force industry framework is described in M. Porter's book *Competitive Strategy*, Free Press, 1998, p. 5.

■ N. Argyres and A. McGahan, 'An interview with Michael Porter', *Academy of Management Executive*, 2002, No. 2, pp. 43–52.

NOTES AND REFERENCES

1 This chapter was written by Albrecht Enders, Andreas Koenig, Thomas Engelbertz and Tawfik Jelassi.
2 Quoted in N. Argyres and A. McGahan, 'An interview with Michael Porter', *Academy of Management Executive*, No. 2, 2002, pp. 43–52.
3 See M. Porter, *Competitive Advantage*, Free Press, 1998.
4 In order to simplify the model, we use the example of a single consumer with an unlimited spending budget.
5 In the context of this chapter, we use the term product to include both goods and services.
6 See M. Porter, *Competitive Advantage*, Free Press, 1998.

7   The concept of use value is equivalent to the idea of consumer benefit, which we introduced in Section 5.2. Since, in this chapter, we attempt to delve more deeply into the theory of strategic management, we decided to use the specific, albeit somewhat clumsy terminology of perceived use value suggested by C. Bowman and V. Ambrosini, 'Value creation versus value capture: towards a coherent definition of value in strategy'. *British Journal of Management*, 2002, No. 1, pp. 1–15.

8   M. Porter emphasises this point in 'Towards a dynamic theory of strategy', *Strategic Management Journal*, 1991, Vol. 12, No. 8, pp. 102–105.

9   Quoted in N. Argyres and A. McGahan, 'An interview with Michael Porter', *Academy of Management Executive*, 2002, No. 2, pp. 43–52.

10 This means that a company knows the maximum amount a customer is willing to pay, which entails that it can set a price which is only marginally lower than the customer's perceived use value and the customer would still be willing to purchase. Since perfect price discrimination is not possible, even in a perfectly monopolistic environment, consumers will always capture at least a marginal proportion of the value created in the form of consumer surplus. This reduction of the value created is of conceptual importance. However, we chiefly designed this framework for pedagogical purposes and practical application. Thus, in the following, we neglect the effect of a marginal reduction of producer surplus due to the lack of price discrimination.

11 M. Porter in 'What is strategy', *Harvard Business Review*, 1996, Vol. 74, No. 6, pp. 61–79, argues that by creating a fit between the individual business activities through consistency, reinforcement and optimisation, a firm can even create value that increases the sum of the parts. For example, reinforcement of activities has a positive influence on the overall perceived use value, whereas optimisation efforts can potentially reduce total costs.

12 In fact, the behaviour of suppliers also affects the competitive discount. For example, the better the relation of a supplier is with a competitor, the lower will be the competitor's cost position. Accordingly, the value created by the competitor and, as a consequence, the competitive discount will be larger.

13 Voice over Internet Protocol (VoIP).

14 UMTS is the third-generation cell phone technology that provides data rates of up to 2 megabits per second.

15 A mobile virtual network operator (MVNO) is a mobile operator that does not have its own network infrastructure. Instead, MVNOs buy minutes of use (MOU) from traditional operators for sale to their own customers. In Germany see Lidl, Tchibo, etc. On a global scale check out Virgin Mobile/USA, UK, Universal Scoop/France, Mobile ESPN/USA, etc.

16 A preliminary version of the virtual music worlds included a Rock&Pop, R'n'b&Hip-Hop and Latin-American music world. Each world made genre-related content available for over-the-air download. The download offer comprised at least content in the form of ringtones, news, games, videos and full tracks.

17 Mobile network operator (MNO).

18 Mobile virtual network enablers (MVNEs) are intermediaries and position themselves between MVNOs and MNOs. In terms of services, MVNEs offer a one-stop shopping solution for MVNOs by providing and selling infrastructure and a full range of services necessary for MVNOs to launch and run their operations.

CHAPTER 9

Choosing the appropriate strategy for the internal organisation of e-business activities

Chapter at a glance

9.1 Reasons determining 'make-or-buy' decisions in e-business
      9.1.1 Reasons favouring 'make' decisions
      9.1.2 Reasons favouring 'buy' decisions
9.2 Choosing the organisational structure for e-business activities
      9.2.1 Separate e-business organisation
      9.2.2 Integrated e-business organisation
9.3 Value chain deconstruction over the Internet
9.4 Unbundling the corporation over the Internet
9.5 Managing conflicts between online and offline distribution channels

Related case studies

Case study	Primary focus of the case study
9 eBay	Outsourcing
4 Ducati vs. Harley	Deconstruction of the value chain
5 Otis	Business process re-engineering
1 Tesco	Managing online and offline channel conflict
2 Nordea	Managing online and offline channel conflict

Learning outcomes

After completing this chapter, you should be able to:

- Describe the spectrum of 'make-or-buy' options.

- Identify the main reasons that favour 'make' decisions.

- Identify the main reasons that favour 'buy' decisions.

- Describe the concept of value chain deconstruction and the role of the Internet within this concept.

- Understand the concept of unbundling the corporation.

INTRODUCTION

Following the discussion in the previous chapters of the strategic positioning of e-business ventures, Chapter 9 deals with internal organisational issues that need to be addressed in order to implement effectively an e-business strategy. We focus on two main questions that are crucial in the context of e-business strategy formulation. The first question is: Which activities within the value chain should we perform in-house and which ones should we outsource to external providers? The second question is: How should we align our e-activities with our physical activities in order to avoid possible conflicts between our online and offline channel offerings? This question, which is addressed in Section 9.4, is only relevant to companies that have both online and offline operations, as is the case, for instance, with Tesco, Ducati and Nordea (which are featured in the case studies section of this book).

9.1 Reasons determining 'make-or-buy' decisions in e-business

Consider the merger of AOL and Time Warner in 2000. The two firms merged because they wanted to create an integrated value chain in the media industry that spanned from content production to content delivery and leveraged both the physical and online channels. Substantial synergies were expected from this merger. As it turned out, these synergies proved difficult to achieve and many critics argue that it would have been better to have kept the two firms separate.

From a more historic perspective, let us consider the evolution of the PC industry. In 1985, IBM, which then dominated this industry, conducted in-house all the value chain activities, from the development of microprocessors to production, marketing, sales and distribution. As a result of open standards and the increased use of mass production, this integrated value chain became more fragmented over time. Today, as shown in Exhibit 9.1, companies focus on (and dominate) only some individual activities of the PC industry value chain.

The above-mentioned examples illustrate how companies can choose from a variety of options available to them for making a product or service. They can decide to perform some activities internally ('make') or 'purchase' them on the open market ('buy'). The different options that companies can choose from are as follows:

- *Market transactions* entail the purchase from an external provider on an individual contractual basis.

- *Long-term contracts* entail the purchase from an external provider on a contractual basis, spanning an extended period of time.

- *Alliances* entail the close co-operation of two separate firms that join up in the production of a certain product or service.

- *Parent/subsidiary constellations* entail the setting up of a distinct firm that operates separately from, yet under the auspices of, the parent company.

- *Internal production* entails a process that is managed completely internally, without any outsourcing to external providers.

Exhibit 9.1 During the 1990s, the PC industry became increasingly fragmented

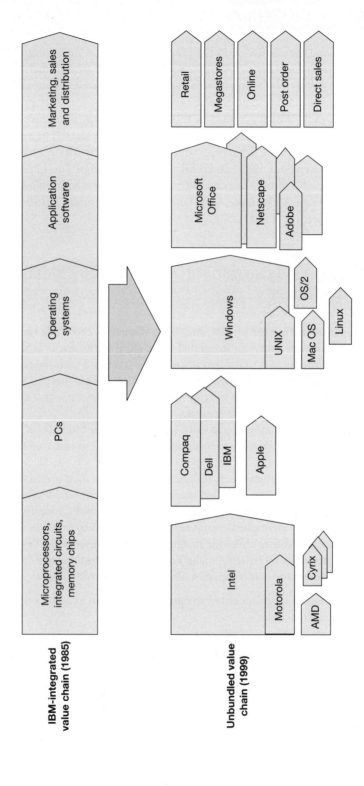

Source: Adapted from D. Heuskel, *Wettbewerb jenseits von Industriegrenzen*, Campus, 1999, p. 53.

At one end of the spectrum, firms that rely heavily on input from external providers include car manufacturers, such as DaimlerChrysler and BMW, and sports goods manufacturers, such as Nike and Adidas. Another example is Dell, which concentrates on tightly integrating different suppliers to deliver the components for the PCs that it assembles and sells. At the other end of the spectrum, highly integrated firms, such as Procter & Gamble and Nestlé, perform most functions internally, ranging from R&D and production to marketing and distribution.

Tesco.com is situated somewhere in the middle of this continuum. On the one hand, Tesco sources itself many activities that were previously fulfilled by outside providers. Consider for instance the arrangement that Tesco had reached with the online vendor Grattan. Through this agreement, all the back-end activities of the value chain were outsourced to Grattan, while Tesco only managed the front-end activities. When Tesco recognised the potential business impact of selling non-food products, Tesco Direct was set up in-house to provide the services that were previously performed by Grattan. Tesco Direct even decided to set up an internal publishing studio with a staff of 40 employees to produce high-quality photos for the 8000-item print catalogue and the Tesco Direct website. On the other hand, Tesco Direct has outsourced the goods delivery activity to external partners.

Many e-business analysts have argued that the increased use of the Internet makes it more attractive to rely more heavily on external providers and perform fewer activities internally. In order to assess this claim, we need to analyse the different factors that favour 'make' and 'buy' decisions and determine how the Internet affects them.

9.1.1 Reasons favouring 'make' decisions

There are three main reasons that favour performing activities in-house (i.e. the 'make' option). These are: (1) *a strong linkage between activities*, (2) *confidentiality of information* and, most importantly, (3) *high transaction costs*.

Strong linkage between activities

We discussed extensively in Section 5.4 the importance of linkage between activities. If it is crucial for a company to integrate tightly different activities of its value chain, then these activities should be performed internally if that is the only way to achieve such integration. Creating close linkages throughout the value chain can help a firm either to provide superior customer benefit through reinforcement of activities or to lower costs through an optimisation of efforts.

Confidentiality of information

Confidentiality of information is another reason that can lead a firm to perform activities internally. The sharing with external providers of critical information about R&D processes, customers and production methods may undermine the firm's competitive advantage. Microsoft, for instance, refuses to provide other software development firms with the source code of its software because it fears that doing so would eventually result in a leak into the public domain.

High transaction costs

The costs relating to the actual transaction process, also called transaction costs, represent an important factor in the 'make' versus 'buy' decision.[1] These consist of costs that a firm incurs when it relies on the market to make a product or service. Transaction costs arise because buyers and sellers usually have diverging interests, which make them act opportunistically. The seller wants to maximise profits by charging as high a price as possible, while the buyer wants to keep costs down by paying as little as possible. To avoid *opportunistic behaviour*, a company needs to invest time and effort in searching for an appropriate business partner, negotiating conditions, and monitoring and enforcing the contract.

Which factors determine whether a firm acts opportunistically and how does the Internet influence these factors? We will now look at two main factors that drive opportunistic action and, therefore, strongly influence transaction costs, *asset specificity* and *information asymmetry*:

■ *Asset specificity* refers to the investment that needs to be made in order to set up a transaction between two or more parties. Before the advent of the Internet, companies that wanted to engage in electronic transactions with one another had to invest in proprietary electronic data interchange (EDI) systems, which were quite costly to install and rather complex to manage technically, especially if multiple partners spanning different industries were involved. Once such a system was in place, the parties were locked into the agreement because of the high investment made and the limited choice of partners.

Imagine the case of the tyre manufacturer Tire Inc., which sources rubber from the rubber producer Rubber Corp. In order to optimise the production flow, Tire Inc. has agreed to install an EDI system that connects it to the IT system of Rubber Corp. The two companies draw up a contract and delivery takes place as planned. Subsequently, Rubber Corp. informs Tire Inc. that it needs to raise prices by 20%, knowing that Tire Inc. needs to keep the business relationship going to recover the investment in the EDI system. Tire Inc. might decide to accept the price increase, or to take Rubber Corp. to court, or to terminate the relationship altogether. In any case, there will be substantial costs involved for Tire Inc. Knowing what might await it next time, Tire Inc. decides to produce the rubber internally, thereby avoiding transaction costs.

Now, let us think about what this scenario might look like today. Over the Internet, Tire Inc. could connect to the system of Rubber Corp., thereby substantially reducing the costs for specific IT investments. Rubber Corp. at the same time would not be inclined to try to raise prices because it knows that Tire Inc. could easily switch suppliers. Therefore, transaction costs are now much lower due to lower asset specificity, which makes it more likely that Tire Inc. will outsource activities to external providers.

■ The second important factor that influences transaction costs is the degree of *information asymmetry* between the involved parties. Often, a buyer lacks vital information about a seller because it does not know the track record of the seller and vice versa. If a buyer can hide past cases of fraud, then it is much more inclined to act opportunistically in the future and try to commit fraud again.

This type of information asymmetry is also easier to remedy over the Internet. Through virtual communities, such as those at eBay, buyers can rate the quality of sellers, and sellers can rate the reliability of buyers. This has a twofold effect. First, any buyer who is considering a purchase can base his/her decision on the track record of the seller. If a seller has hundreds of positive ratings, then it is very likely that he/she will also fulfil his/her promises during the next transaction. Second, as the number of positive ratings increases, sellers are more likely to maintain their high standards in order to protect their reputation. Thus, a self-reinforcing virtuous cycle is set in motion through the rating system, which deters opportunistic behaviour, thereby also reducing transaction costs.

Because of the lower asset-specific investment and the improved information, it is sensible to assume that the Internet reduces transaction costs. This should, in turn, make it more attractive to outsource parts of the value chain to external providers.

9.1.2 Reasons favouring 'buy' decisions

Today, many companies rely heavily on sourcing parts and services from external suppliers. There are four main reasons for doing so: (1) *high economies of scale*, (2) *high capital requirements*, (3) *specialised know-how* and (4) *higher efficiency of the open market*.

High economies of scale

A firm that produces only for its own use usually requires a much smaller quantity than a supplier that produces for many different firms. Therefore, the external supplier has the possibility to reap much larger economies of scale than the individual firm that decides to make the part by itself. Dell, for instance, could decide to build its own factories for producing the microchips that it uses in the PCs it sells. However, the investment required for doing so internally is too large, relative to the expected output, and would make every chip produced prohibitively expensive. Therefore, Dell sources the chips from specialised manufacturers, such as Intel and AMD, which also supply many other computer manufacturers with chips. In fact, Dell has chosen this approach for almost all its inputs. Since it is a large customer for most of its suppliers, it is in a position to capture large parts of the economies of scale in the form of low prices.

High capital requirements

If the production of a specific part requires a major investment upfront, such as the construction of a specialised plant, then it may be sensible to find an external supplier that already has the required facilities in place. Doing so might be more expensive on a per-unit basis, yet it reduces the overall risk. For instance, Webvan, the US online grocery retailer, might have fared better if it had relied more on external suppliers when it set up its online grocery business. Instead, Webvan organised by itself all parts of the value chain and invested heavily in a custom-built IT platform, highly automated warehouses and a large fleet of delivery trucks, only to find out that the business model did not work the way it was anticipated. The expensive IT platform, the warehouses and the trucks were later sold during the bankruptcy proceedings for a fraction of their original prices.

Specialised know-how

Specialisation effects are likely to be related to economies of scale. A firm that produces large quantities of goods also tends to build up over time substantial know-how regarding R&D processes and production methods. This specialised know-how should then lead to lower-cost production and higher quality standards, or both. Consider Tesco Direct's delivery system. The company owns large warehouses to organise the logistics of incoming and outgoing shipments. Yet, for the actual shipment process, Tesco Direct relies on specialised logistics firms, which possess strong experience in logistics and delivery and have over time optimised their processes.

The open source movement, which is described in the FT boxes below, presents another illustrative example of highly specialised know-how that is brought together by numerous external providers.

Higher efficiency of the open market

Finally, external suppliers are often more efficient because they are facing permanent competitive pressure from other companies within their specific industry. If performed internally, the production of a sub-product or the provision of a service can become highly inefficient over time because of a lack of control, thereby causing unnecessary costs. External firms producing that same product, on the other hand, do not enjoy the same type of 'protection' and are therefore forced constantly to maintain high levels of efficiency, thus keeping down costs.

FT

The open source movement has great promise

The potential importance of open-source models is beginning to dawn on mainstream business and government. How companies and nations respond could help to determine who thrives in the growing knowledge economy. Yet a high proportion of decision-makers is only dimly aware of what open-source is and why it matters.

It is only 14 years since Linus Torvalds, then a computer student at the University of Helsinki, tentatively solicited collaborators to help build a free operating system. By 2002, the system that resulted, Linux, had a quarter of the global market for server operating systems.

The operating system was founded on a simple idea: the source code should be publicly available, but anyone using it had to provide their own modifications on the same basis. Much to the surprise of many in the industry – and contrary to the conventional economic wisdom – Linux proved both cheaper and more reliable than the alternatives.

Wikipedia, the online encyclopedia, has become an equally visible example of the open-source idea. After barely four years, it has grown to be larger than the Encyclopaedia Britannica and Encarta combined and, like Linux, has been built almost entirely by volunteers. It now features more than 1m articles in more than 100 languages.

Information technology was the first industry to wake up to the potentially huge ramifications of these new methods. Some, such as IBM and Sun Microsystems, have chosen to side with the open-source movement against Microsoft.

The European Parliament and Council of Ministers have come out on different sides over a directive to impose intellectual property rights on software. Some nations, notably Brazil, see open-source methods as critical in helping them break free from a dependence on Microsoft and other big US and European media companies.

Other sectors remain largely oblivious to the potential impact of open-source models. A few businesses have learnt how to involve consumers in designing new products, and Amazon.com has benefited from opening up product reviews to its customers. But most businesses would be aghast at the risks of involving a wider range of people from outside the organisation in shaping their key decisions. Although governments have become more open about information and performance data, the use of open-source methods to improve legislation and policy making remains in its infancy.

A new agenda could greatly help those cities and nations that want to be at the forefront of the new knowledge economy. That agenda would include: a presumption in favour of open-source software rather than proprietary systems in public purchasing of IT; promotion of new ownership rules for new knowledge to encourage the maximum use and adaptation of ideas; strict requirements that publicly-funded research should be openly and freely available to the public; and the promotion of open methods in everything from urban planning to bylaws.

Open-source ideas are far from a panacea, and 'open-source' as a term is both over-used and misused. A plan for an open-source political party, to which the public can contribute their own policies, is unlikely to succeed. But there can be little doubt of the potential of open methods in diverse fields. In law, open methods could provide much easier access to information about the law and the likely results of court cases. In the media, open source could offer an effective alternative to the current regulation and self-regulation.

Recent experience has shown that markets involving knowledge are radically different from markets for physical commodities. Over the past decade, businesses and public organisations have learnt, painfully, about the potential and the challenge of the web. Over the next decade, open-source methods could have just as much impact, leaving behind just as stark a pattern of winners and losers.

Source: G. Mulgan, 'The open source movement has great promise', FT.com, 1 June 2005.

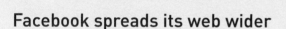

FT

Facebook spreads its web wider

Facebook's move last month to open the inner workings of its web site to outside programmers has sent ripples through the Web 2.0 world, as entrepreneurs rush to build services that take advantage of the connections between the site's millions of users. By allowing outside companies to integrate their features with Facebook's messaging infrastructure and other services, Mark Zuckerberg, the company's 23-year-old founder, is attempting to transform Facebook from a social networking site into a springboard for launching internet applications.

It is a move that may amount to a step-change in the development of the internet, according to some Silicon Valley entrepreneurs and venture capitalists. 'This is basically a move by Facebook to become the next major operating system,' says Max Levchin, a co-founder of PayPal and chief executive of Slide, one of hundreds of companies that have rolled out features designed specifically for Facebook. 'Instead of building your own website, Facebook are saying you can build applications on top of their own popular web site,' Mr Levchin says.

Just as software developers rushed to write applications for Windows after it emerged as the dominant operating system for the PC, the past several weeks have seen a surge in interest in Facebook. 'There is a giant sucking sound you are hearing in Web 2.0 start-ups, and it's all going towards Facebook,' says Andreas Stavropoulous, managing director at Draper Fisher Jurvetson, a venture capital firm whose investments have included Skype, the voice over IP company, and Baidu, the Chinese search engine. One such Web 2.0 company is iLike, a popular music-sharing service. 'We have reappropriated 80 per cent of our staff to work on Facebook,' says Avi Partovi, iLike's chief executive. 'Our own website is still growing by 1m users a month, but on Facebook we're growing by 1m users a week.'

Entrepreneurs say Facebook's open approach offers several advantages over the more restrictive approaches employed by MySpace and other rivals. By granting outside programmers access to the site's inner workings, Facebook is not just offering access to its millions of users. It is also offering access to the connections between those users by allowing outside companies to tap into the site's messaging and file-sharing infrastructure. 'Facebook applications can initiate a message between two users,' Mr Levchin explains. 'It's really powerful. Anything that's useful or interesting will get spread very quickly, because there are a lot of touch-points where Facebook users get together and see what each other are using.'

Even though MySpace users are free to embed features built by outside companies into their profile pages – a video clip from YouTube, for example – MySpace's closed approach means companies cannot integrate their features with the site's messaging service. That makes it more difficult for users to share interesting videos with friends. Facebook has also granted its outside developers unprecedented flexi-

bility when it comes to making money from the applications they launch on the Facebook platform.

Whereas MySpace strictly controls advertising by third parties and limits outgoing links from its site, Facebook has granted outside companies broad leeway to embed outgoing links and to advertise inside their applications. 'Facebook is the one site where it's easiest to make money,' Mr Levchin says.

Facebook may have stolen the momentum from MySpace and its other rivals, but it remains a distant second to MySpace in terms of overall user traffic. As rival sites open up, Mr Zuckerberg is likely to face stiff competition. 'You can expect the whole industry to follow suit,' said Joanna Shields, head of international operations for Bebo. Her company hoped to attract many of the same developers and would announce its own plans to open its platform soon, she added. MySpace and LinkedIn are also weighing moves to open up to developers.

Source: K. Allison, 'Facebook spreads its web wider', FT.com, 28 June 2007.

9.2 Choosing the organisational structure for e-business activities

In 1998, when Bertelsmann was about to launch its online bookstore BOL, the company faced a difficult issue. Should BOL operate as an independent business, or should it be integrated within the company?

Many traditional bricks-and-mortar companies that launched their e-business ventures during the Internet boom years faced the above question. They had several organisational options to choose from. The clicks-and-mortar spectrum shown in Exhibit 9.2 helps to analyse these different options.[2]

Exhibit 9.2 The clicks-and-mortar spectrum spans from integration to separation of a company's e-business activities

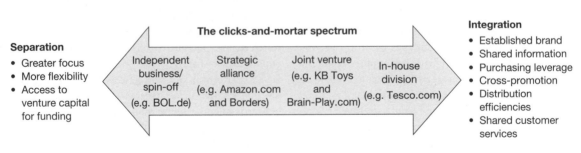

At one end of the spectrum, companies fully integrate their e-business activities within the firm. At the other end, the e-business operation is completely separated from the company and spun off. Both approaches have distinct advantages and drawbacks.

9.2.1 Separate e-business organisation

Let us first consider separating the e-business activities from the parent company, an option that was particularly popular during the Internet boom years. Bertelsmann, for instance, decided to launch BOL as a separate business to enter the online market for book retailing. At the time, many other bricks-and-mortar companies chose this separation approach of their online activities because they believed that it gave them the following advantages:[3]

- *Greater focus.* Due to the fast-moving business environment and the increasing Internet-based competition, companies wanted to set up entities that focused solely on e-business activities and did not have to take into consideration the overall strategy of the firm (Section 6.2 also deals with the benefits of creating separate organisational structures, which is especially important when companies are faced with disruptive innovations).

- *More flexibility and faster decisions.* A separate e-business organisation also allowed for a more flexible and faster decision-making process.

- *Entrepreneurial culture.* Established management approaches and business procedures were considered to be inadequate for the Internet world, where 'everything' had been turned upside down. To accommodate this change, e-business ventures were often staffed with young individuals, having an entrepreneurial drive, strong IT know-how and analytical capabilities, yet often little knowledge of the industry.

- *Access to venture capital.* The soaring stock markets of the late 1990s were another reason for separating an online business from its parent company. The outrageously high valuations of companies were focused primarily on pure dotcom businesses without any physical bricks-and-mortar structures that may hold them back or dilute their business strategy.

With the burst of the Internet bubble in March 2000, many companies that had spun off their e-business activities could not exploit the synergies between their online and offline channels and operations and, therefore, were not able to pursue a clicks-and-mortar strategy. After wasting large sums of money on doomed dotcom businesses, shareholders wanted to see fewer fast decisions and more sustainable strategies and profitable business models.

As a result of the above developments, many of the companies that initially spun off their e-business operations have reintegrated them into the parent company. A prime example of this development is the case of the Internet bookseller BOL, which started out as a completely separate business with its own management structure and business model. However, as the Internet boom subsided, the online book-retailing operation was reintegrated into the Direct Group of Bertelsmann (see the FT article 'Chapter closes for online books venture').

Chapter closes for online books venture

The sound of dotcoms hitting the rocks across Europe has become so familiar since Boo.com started the trend last year that most problems now barely cause a tremor. But Tuesday's decision by Bertelsmann to roll BOL, its books and CDs e-tailer, into its more mature book clubs is still significant. It signals the end of the home-grown challenge to Amazon.com's European dominance. Heidi Fitzpatrick, an analyst at Lehman Brothers, says: 'It is another indication that the economics of pan-European e-tailing are just not there.'

Bertelsmann set up BOL as a stand-alone business in 1999 with the hope of spinning it off as a separate public company. Despite being the second largest pan-European online bookstore – with 16 countries giving it the biggest geographical footprint – BOL has found it hard to achieve widespread brand recognition and has failed to catch up with Amazon's head start.

Tuesday's move illustrates that Bertelsmann believes it has to take advantage of all the available synergies such as sharing purchasing, warehousing and marketing costs with its book clubs. Klaus Eierhoff, head of Bertelsmann Direct Group, said on Tuesday: 'By merging BOL with the book clubs we will have a combined entity that will generate a significant profit by 2003.' The international book clubs were set to become profitable next year by themselves and BOL was expected to break even in 2004.

Mr Eierhoff told Financial Times Deutschland that his company was talking to its US partners about folding Barnesandnoble.com, the US online bookseller, into its book clubs. Talks are continuing over the future of BOL's French, Spanish and Japanese operations. The German, UK, Dutch, Italian, Swedish and Finnish branches will be merged with local book clubs while branches in Denmark and Norway will be closed.

Source: T. Barker and B. Benoit, 'Amazon sees off Bertelsmann', FT.com, 16 May 2001.

9.2.2 Integrated e-business organisation

Some companies chose right away to integrate their e-business activities tightly with their bricks-and-mortar operations. Office Depot seamlessly integrated its website with its physical retailing network. Thus, it was able to leverage its existing infrastructure with a call centre and a vast fleet of delivery trucks. Similarly, when deliberating whether to fulfil orders using its existing store network or warehouses, Tesco.com opted for the integrated in-store-based fulfilment approach.

Today, it seems that in most cases the benefits of an organisational structure that combines online and offline channels outweigh those of a separated organisation. These benefits include:[4]

- *Established and trusted brand*. Companies moving from the physical world into the online world can leverage the brand they have established with their customers. Trust is a critical issue in e-business, and it increases when customers can resort to face-to-face interaction in case of problems.

- *Shared information*. Information about customers can be shared across different channels. For instance, Tesco.com uses purchasing information from its online channel to adapt offerings in its physical grocery outlets.

- *Cross-promotion.* Online and offline channels can benefit from one another through cross-promotion. Nordea uses its bank branch staff to convince customers to use the online channel. At the clothing company Gap, signs throughout the physical stores point to the online presence of Gap.com.

- *Purchasing leverage.* Purchasing can be pooled for offline and online channels. This increases a company's bargaining power vis-à-vis its suppliers, thereby reducing purchasing costs.

- *Distribution efficiencies.* Different channels within a company can use the same infrastructure facilities, thereby increasing utilisation and scale effects. Consider Tesco and its store-based picking approach. There, most of the picking is done during the store's off-peak hours, when there are fewer customers. At barnesandnoble.com, customers can browse and order their books online and pick them up at the physical store.

- *Shared customer service.* The offline channel is very useful for providing customer services for the online channel. It is much easier for customers to return defective or unwanted purchases to a physical store than to repackage them and return them by postal mail or courier service. Similarly, employees at physical stores can also help by providing maintenance and inspection work.

There are also some hybrid options spanning the two extreme choices of full separation and full integration. These include setting up joint ventures and strategic partnerships. These approaches seek to combine the technological know-how, nimbleness and entrepreneurial culture of an online venture with the strong brand name and existing customer base of a bricks-and-mortar company.

Consider, for instance, the partnership between the Borders Group, one of the largest US book retailers, and Amazon.com. As part of this agreement, Amazon.com provided the Borders Group with its e-business solution, technology services, site content, product selection and customer service for the co-branded 'Borders teamed with Amazon.com' site. Amazon.com records all orders that take place through the site and passes on a fixed sales percentage to the Borders Group. Through this agreement, the two companies leverage Amazon.com's strong technological know-how and the Borders group's extensive physical store presence. Depending on availability, customers who order through the website have the possibility to pick up their purchase on the same day at the nearest Borders store. Customers then receive an e-mail confirmation from Borders, informing them that the purchased item has been picked and reserved under their name for express in-store pick-up.[5]

9.3 Value chain deconstruction over the Internet

The concept of *deconstruction* builds on the foundations of transaction cost theory.[6] The fundamental idea of this concept is that traditionally integrated value chains within industries get unbundled and are reconfigured as a result of two main developments. These are: (1) the separation of the *economics of things (physical goods)* and the *economics of information (digital goods)*; and (2) the *blow-up of the trade-off between richness and reach*. (The limitations of the concept of deconstruction are discussed in Critical Perspective 9.1.)

Let us take a closer look at the first point. How do the economics of things and of information differ? When physical goods, such as a chair or a table, are sold, ownership is transferred from the seller to the buyer. Informational goods, on the other hand, can be used many times, with low (if any) incremental costs. Take a newspaper article that is published online. It does not affect costs much if it is read by 10 or 10,000 people. Furthermore, physical goods are location dependent. They cannot be moved easily, and they often take up substantial space. Information, on the other hand, can be sent across the globe quickly and requires only disk storage space on a computer server.

In the past, the two different types of economics were combined within a unified business model, which led to compromises. Consider the example of used-car dealerships. What are the reasons for customers to go to a used-car dealership? They want to find out about different choices, go for a test drive, get an attractive financing scheme, and receive a warranty and maintenance services.

In order to provide the customer with as much product information as possible, it makes sense to put many cars on display, so that customers can easily compare between different models and make a more informed purchasing decision. On the other hand, since the information about cars is held in the physical car, maximising the number of cars in the showroom conflicts with the desire to keep down costs by limiting showroom space and inventory. A further compromise is that, for sales purposes, it is sensible to build large car dealerships in central locations to maximise the number of cars on display. For servicing purposes, however, it would be much better to have small repair shops located near the car owners' homes.

The online auction company, eBay, has effectively deconstructed the used-car business, thus becoming the largest used-car dealership in the USA. Like a traditional car dealer, eBay offers a wide choice of cars, but unlike physical dealers it is not constrained by physical space on a car lot. eBay acts as an integrated market maker for sellers, thereby offering unsurpassed choice. Through the deconstruction and reconfiguration of the value chain with external partners, eBay can offer higher benefits to consumers at reduced costs.

How does it work? Sellers wanting to sell their car on eBay face the problem of not being able to convince potential customers of the quality of their car. To remedy this, eBay works in partnership with the certified vehicle inspection chain PepBoys, which inspects the car and then issues an authorised inspection certificate which the seller can post on the eBay website. The information about the state of the car is even better than in the traditional marketplace, where the buyer, who typically does not know much about cars, has to inspect the car him/herself. eBay also has partnerships with financing companies and with neutral third-party payment operators, which, to prevent fraud, act as proxies and send the payment from buyer to seller.

Overall, this deconstruction leads to a development called *de-averaging of competitive advantage*. Here, a firm picks out individual parts of the value chain and decides to compete on only one dimension through larger-scale, higher degrees of specialisation, or other factors that contribute to competitive advantage, while outsourcing other activities to external providers or even to customers themselves as in the case of *Spreadshirt*, which provides website owners with a shop system allowing for mass customisation.

CRITICAL PERSPECTIVE 9.1

The limitations of deconstruction and unbundling

How should we evaluate the applicability of the 'unbundling' concept? Its proposition is similar to that outlined in the concept of deconstruction.[7] Both state that different parts of the value chain, here called businesses, should be reconfigured so that the trade-offs and compromises inherent in integrated firms can be resolved. The examples of eBay and Dell, where deconstruction has worked out very well, thereby rewarding the two companies with high profitability, need to be contrasted with other companies engaged in e-business where this type of deconstruction has been more limited. There are different reasons why deconstruction might not be appropriate for a firm:[8]

- *Lack of linkage between externally and internally performed activities.* Amazon.com, for instance, initially set out with a highly deconstructed business model in which the focus rested on the front end of interacting with the customer. Back-end warehousing and logistics were to be left to external suppliers. However, integrating the front end with external logistics providers turned out to be more cumbersome than anticipated, and thus it became impossible to deliver the promised customer benefit in terms of speed of shipment, quality and reliability. Amazon.com therefore decided to reintegrate parts of the value chain by setting up a proprietary warehousing system.

- *Increased convergence and ease of imitation.* When key steps of the value chain that previously constituted substantial sources for competitive advantage are outsourced to external providers, this creates the risk that competitors turn to the same vendor, thereby making purchased inputs more homogeneous. Doing so decreases possibilities for differentiation and increases price competition. Furthermore, it also lowers barriers to entry because new entrants only need to assemble purchased inputs rather than build their own capabilities.

9.4 Unbundling the corporation over the Internet

The concept of 'unbundling the corporation' is very similar to the deconstruction approach.[9] It also argues that companies need to rethink the traditional organisation and unbundle their core businesses (or core activities) as a result of falling transaction costs made possible by the Internet. (The limitations of this concept are discussed in Critical Perspective 9.1.)

The 'unbundling' concept recognises that a corporation consists of the following three core businesses (see Exhibit 9.3):

- *Product innovation*, which focuses on R&D but also includes activities further down the value chain such as market research to find out about consumers' preferences. The globally operating firm IDEO, which designs products and services for large corporate customers, is a prominent example of a company focusing primarily on the product innovation business.

- *Infrastructure management*, which focuses on logistics and support functions. This business includes the building and management of physical facilities, such as manufacturing or assembly plants, retail outlets and truck fleets, for high-volume production and transportation processes. Through its extensive physical retail network, Tesco.com is strongly involved in managing the infrastructure business.

Exhibit 9.3 The traditional corporation can be unbundled into three distinct businesses

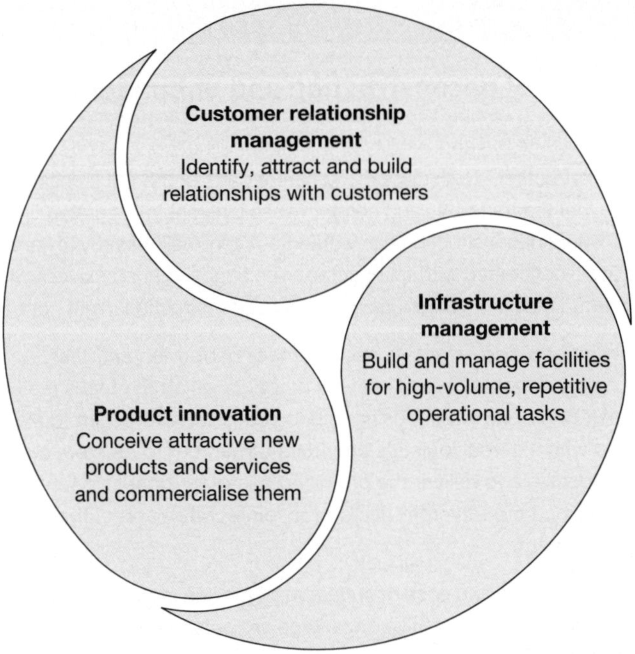

Source: Reprinted by permission of *Harvard Business Review* [Exhibit 99205]. From 'Unbundling the Corporation' by J. Hagel and M. Singer, March–April 1999. Copyright © 1999 by the Harvard Business School Publishing Corporation, all rights reserved.

- *Customer relationship management*, which focuses on the interfaces between the firm and its customers. These interfaces include activities such as marketing, sales and service. Their common goal is to attract and retain customers. For example, ING DIRECT (an online bank which is featured in the case studies section of the book) focuses on the customer relationship management business while outsourcing its product innovation to external financial providers and minimising its infrastructure requirements through its direct banking approach.

The reason why the different businesses conflict with one another is that they have the following differing economic, cultural and competitive imperatives (see Exhibit 9.4):

- *Economics.* In product innovation, speed, which allows a firm to introduce to the market new products sooner than the competition, is the most valued asset. However, in the customer relationship and infrastructure management business, what matters most are, respectively, economies of scope (getting a large share of the consumer wallet) and economies of scale.
- *Culture.* Product innovation focuses on creative employees who are responsible for developing new ideas. This is mirrored in flexible pay schemes and work schedules that are designed to make employees content. The customer relationship business, on the other hand, focuses on the external customers, while the focus of the infrastructure business is on costs. To operate large-scale operations efficiently, it is necessary to create a culture of standardisation, predictability and efficiency.

Exhibit 9.4 **Different businesses within a corporation have different imperatives regarding economics, culture and competition**

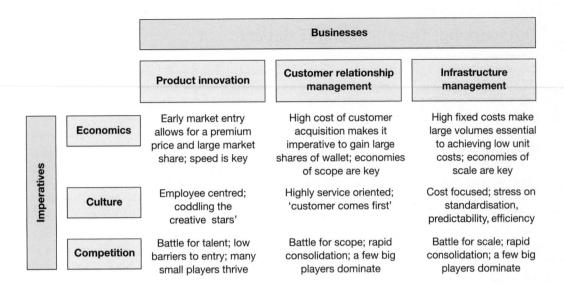

	Product innovation	Customer relationship management	Infrastructure management
Economics	Early market entry allows for a premium price and large market share; speed is key	High cost of customer acquisition makes it imperative to gain large shares of wallet; economies of scope are key	High fixed costs make large volumes essential to achieving low unit costs; economies of scale are key
Culture	Employee centred; coddling the creative stars'	Highly service oriented; 'customer comes first'	Cost focused; stress on standardisation, predictability, efficiency
Competition	Battle for talent; low barriers to entry; many small players thrive	Battle for scope; rapid consolidation; a few big players dominate	Battle for scale; rapid consolidation; a few big players dominate

■ *Competition.* For a successful product innovation, it is essential to gain access to skilful and talented employees. Developing innovations often does not require large start-up costs, as is illustrated by the founders of some of the e-commerce success stories (such as Amazon.com, eBay and Google). Therefore, in product innovation, there are usually many small players, of which few will succeed. In both of the other businesses, however, competition tends to be driven by economies of scope and/or scale, which leads to a consolidation where a few big players dominate the competition.

The problem for integrated firms is the difficulty of simultaneously optimising scope, speed and scale; therefore, firms need to make trade-offs. For instance, in order to maximise scope, a retailer should provide a vast variety of products, possibly also from external stores.

This is what Amazon.com has been doing with its Zshop system, which allows other used-book retailers to sell their products through the Amazon.com website. Doing so makes the site more attractive for customers because they find not only the new Amazon.com offerings but also used books, which are generally cheaper. From a scope perspective, this makes a lot of sense. However, if doing so leads to fewer orders originating from Amazon.com, this would then result in a lower utilisation of physical infrastructure, such as warehouses, thereby compromising the company's economies of scale.

Outsourcing: The shrinking IT department

Business leaders are learning a few lessons about IT. After spending small fortunes on equipment and technical specialists over the last decade or so, many have started to realise that a lack of cost savings and profit avenues from these investments means a shake-up is required.

In a bid to reset the IT profit model, larger businesses are now starting to mimic smaller ones by contracting specialist IT companies to service their technology while they focus on selling their product. 'You've now got the virtualised server environment where you can host things remotely,' says Mark Kobayashi-Hilary, author of Global services – moving to a level playing field. 'With that, all the grunt work is then taken away from the office. It'd be better to stick to what you're best at, write down your technical requirements and ask someone else to do it.'

Several services are now on offer that remove the burden of administration from the IT department. For example, some companies opt for software as a service, such as Google's spreadsheet and word-processing applications that can be used over an Internet browser. More commonly in larger companies, this type of hosted service involves customer relationship management (CRM) programs from providers such as Salesforce.com. 'You can also outsource IT maintenance by paying a retainer or an hourly rate to another company,' adds Mr Hilary. 'Smaller companies do that because it's cheaper than the salary of an engineer. All this means you have a virtualised IT department.'

Such actions to shrink the IT department's staff and equipment have been coined as moving to an 'IT lite' environment – a trend that has been noticed in some of Europe's largest companies. The Corporate IT Forum (CIF), a CIO-end-user organisation for big companies, said its members are now employing more business-minded people to negotiate outsourcing contracts. '[Our members] were all experiencing the same thing,' says David Roberts, CEO of the CIF. 'We found there'll be fewer people in the IT depart-

ment but they'll spend higher amounts of money and will be much more commercially aware. The corporation really has to have these skills to compete with the Accentures of this world.'

Mr Roberts explains that CEOs are also pressuring the IT department to find ways of profiting the business, which requires a radical shift in thought from simply saving the company money and time – a move which could see the IT department slim down considerably. 'These models are threatening the old establishments,' he says. 'This has been a long time coming, where technology alone can build a profitable business. You're therefore going to need business people for IT who can procure and you can now procure almost anything from the other side of the globe.'

Yet some outsourcing companies have been waiting for this moment for years. For example, companies based in China and India, which recruit tens of thousands of highly-qualified technical people every year, have based their entire business models on this very shift. Now jobs such as programming, support and administration could soon be offshored to these firms while project managers and architects will remain safely employed internally. 'The need for programming is reducing as this is not an essential skill to have in house,' says Ian Campbell, group CIO of British Energy. 'If you look at new companies, they're being more virtual in IT, but British Energy is coming from a traditional position – if it was new, I would go for that new model.'

'The role of the CIO is to understand the business and provide added value. But to do that you need commercial IT managers who can sort contracts. IT people don't come with these skills and I'm spending a reasonable amount of my time working on relationship management. I've seen one or two organisations that have gone from hundreds of people in the IT department to 50. They are really going for it while others are waiting for it to become standardised.'

Of course outsourcing IT jobs could also spell turbulent times for people with technical skills. While many can design databases, build back-end offices and speak programming languages to each other, businesses are starting to require commercial knowledge and better communicative skills. On the other hand, IT recruitment agencies are having difficulty in finding the next generation of IT workers. 'The salaries can be anything up to £200,000 because of these trends,' says Albert Ellis, CEO of recruitment firm Harvey Nash. 'These people are a mixture of project managers and business analysts. One of the interesting things about this is they not only need understanding of technology and offshoring but sales, cultural issues and how to manage expectations for the board and the customers. This is all new territory.'

Research from US employment IT analyst Foote Partners backs this up. It claims employers are 'desperate for employees who have more than just technical skills'. Capgemini's Global CIO report also urges CIOs to move away from IT-centric management. The IT director of European catering firm Elior Alastair Fuller changed the staff on his IT team in a bid to improve the business: 'The sector we work in is changing so the IT needed to change,' he says. 'What was apparent was that the 20 people in the IT department were clearly not fit for purpose. Now we have almost a new team and only have four of the original. The new people have brought a much broader set of skills on board. For the IT departments in some organisations it's about doing the minimum. In the same organisations you can see the self-sustaining interest in IT.'

Source: Dan Ilett, 'The shrinking IT department', FT.com, 9 May 2007.

9.5 Managing conflicts between online and offline distribution channels

Manufacturers and retailers that have, in the past, sold their products through physical outlets using a sales force fear that moving into online sales will cannibalise their offline sales.[10] Their argument is that the new online channel is not creating a new market or extra sales but merely siphoning off existing sales.

To understand whether manufacturers should fear distribution channel conflicts, they need to analyse how new online channels affect their offline channels, and whether the various channels actually serve the same customer segments. For instance, companies may believe mistakenly that different channels are competing with one another when in fact they are benefiting from each other's actions. They may also believe that the loss of sales is ascribed to a new channel when, in reality, it results from the intrusion of a new competitor.

The channel conflict matrix (see Exhibit 9.5) analyses how traditional bricks-and-mortar retailers should react towards possible conflicts between their offline and online channels. There are two main dimensions that determine how to deal with possible channel conflict: (1) the prospect of destructive conflict between different channels and (2) the importance of the existing channel that is threatened by the new online channel.

The resulting matrix provides insights into how to deal with possible channel conflicts. The four quadrants of the matrix are now described:

■ *Quadrant 1.* If the prospect of destructive conflict between channels is high and the importance of the threatened channel is also high, then it is sensible to address the problem and find ways to reconcile the two channels. For instance, when Nordea Bank started its online banking operations, it was positioned clearly in quadrant 1. Branch-based banking was threatened severely by the rise of the online channel, yet it was of great importance

189

Exhibit 9.5 **The channel conflict matrix analyses how different types of channel conflicts should be resolved**

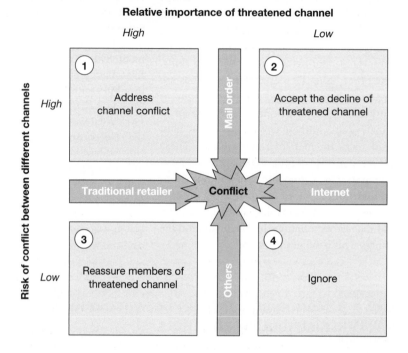

Source: Adapted from C. Bucklin, P. Thomas-Graham and E. Webster, 'Channel conflict: when is it dangerous?', *McKinsey Quarterly*, 1997, No. 3, pp. 36–43.

to the overall functioning of the bank. Contrary to many other banks, Nordea decided to integrate fully its online banking within its physical banking operations, thereby eliminating possible competition between the two channels. In fact, branch employees were enticed to move branch customers over to the Internet. Ultimately, the ability to leverage the branches to move customers to the Internet, thereby eliminating the need for expensive marketing campaigns, was one of the main reasons why Nordea managed to acquire a dominant position in the online banking world.

■ *Quadrant 2.* If the prospect of destructive conflict between channels is high and the importance of the threatened channel is low, then it is usually sensible simply to allow the threatened channel to decline.

■ *Quadrant 3.* If the prospect of destructive conflict is low but the importance of the threatened channel is high, then the latter's employees need to be reassured that they will not be affected. This is the case, for instance, with Tesco's bricks-and-mortar retail store network. In spite of the drastic increase of online sales through the Tesco.com channel, retail stores continue to play a major role. Thus, it is important to let employees know that the new channel does not present a threat to them. To alleviate fears of cannibalisation, Tesco physical stores are credited with all sales that they fulfil. Similarly, when Ducati started selling motorcycles directly to consumers exclusively over the Internet, it was necessary to comfort the network of dealers and reassure them of their continuing importance. To back up this claim, Ducati identified the closest dealer to an online customer and then informed that dealer about the online transaction. The dealer could subsequently accept or reject to hand the motorcycle over to the online customer. In the case of acceptance, the dealer would receive a 10% commission of the total price, which was less than the average commission received on a normal Ducati motorcycle sale. However, with online sales, dealers had no inventory management cost, no inventory risk and no advertising or marketing costs. The goal of Ducati's online sales was not to cannibalise sales made through the offline channel, but instead to expand into hitherto untapped market segments.[11]

■ *Quadrant 4*. If the prospect of conflict between the online and offline channels is low and the importance of the threatened channel is also low, then the channel conflict is not important and therefore, it can be ignored.

SUMMARY

■ First, this chapter analysed the degree of integration of individual activities of the value chain. More specifically, it discussed which activities a firm should perform (or 'make') by itself and which activities it should source (or 'buy') from external providers. Reasons that favour 'make' decisions include strong linkage between activities, confidentiality of information and high transaction costs. Reasons that favour 'buy' decisions include high economies of scale, high capital requirements, specialised know-how and higher efficiency of the open markets.

■ Second, the chapter analysed how to choose the organisational structure for e-business activities and presented the following four options: (1) in-house integration, (2) joint venture, (3) strategic partnership and (4) independent business (i.e. spin-off). It then discussed the benefits and drawbacks of each organisational option.

■ Third, the chapter analysed the unbundling of the traditional organisation as a result of falling transaction costs made possible by the Internet. The unbundling concept distinguishes three core businesses in a corporation: (1) product innovation, (2) infrastructure management and (3) customer relationship management. These three businesses have different imperatives regarding economics, culture and competition.

■ Finally, the chapter analysed how a company can choose between online and offline channels to conduct its activities. It also offered a framework to assess the impact of a possible channel conflict and ways to resolve it (or even pre-empt it).

REVIEW QUESTIONS

1 Describe the different organisational options along the 'make-or-buy' spectrum.

2 In general, which factors determine whether a firm should make or buy a product or a service?

3 Why should a company consider deconstructing its value chain over the Internet?

4 Outline the concept of unbundling the corporation and explain its underlying rationale.

5 Explain the online/offline channel conflict matrix and illustrate it through specific examples.

6 What are the different options that a company has when choosing the organisational structure for its Internet venture?

7 What criteria should a company use when deciding on whether to integrate its Internet activities in-house or whether to spin them off?

DISCUSSION QUESTIONS

1 Illustrate through different examples how the Internet enables companies to integrate activities across their value chain.

2 Provide examples of Internet ventures that favour (or have favoured) either 'make' or 'buy' decisions.

3 Explain how a company deconstructs its value chain over the Internet and illustrate your answer through an actual example.

4 Provide two examples from two different industries (one dealing with physical products and one dealing with digital goods) that demonstrate the concept of unbundling the corporation.

5 Critically assess the deconstruction and unbundling concepts, and show their limitations using actual e-business examples.

6 Should a company refrain from launching an Internet venture if it judges the prospect of a destructive conflict with the offline channel to be high? Defend your arguments.

RECOMMENDED KEY READING

■ R. Coase wrote the first influential article on transaction cost theory in 'The nature of the firm', *Economica*, 1937, Vol. 4, pp. 386–405. O. E. Williamson provided an additional foundational perspective on this topic in *Markets and Hierarchies: Analysis and Antitrust Implications*, Free Press, 1975.

■ P. Evans and T. Wurster developed the concept of deconstructing the value chain in *Blown to Bits*, Harvard Business School Press, 1999. For a condensed version of this concept, see, by the same authors, 'Strategy and the new economics of information', *Harvard Business Review*, 1997, September–October, pp. 71–81.

■ J. Hagel and M. Singer wrote the article 'Unbundling the corporation', *Harvard Business Review*, 1999, March–April, pp. 133–141.

■ M. Porter criticises the deconstruction and unbundling concepts in 'Strategy and the Internet', *Harvard Business Review*, 2001, March, pp. 72–74.

USEFUL THIRD-PARTY WEBLINKS

■ web.mit.edu/ctpid/www/Whitney/morepapers/make_ab.html provides an article, which addresses the challenge of making 'make-or-buy' decisions.

NOTES AND REFERENCES

1 Transaction costs are an important concept for explaining firm structures. For a detailed discussion of the impact of the Internet on transaction costs, see A. Afuah, 'Redefining firm boundaries in the face of the Internet: are firms really shrinking?', *Academy of Management Review*, 2003, Vol. 28, No. 1, pp. 34–53.

2 R. Gulati and J. Garino, 'Get the right mix of bricks and clicks', *Harvard Business Review*, 2000, May–June, pp. 107–114.

3 Ibid.

4 Ibid.

5 'Borders and Amazon.com announce in-store pick up', www.writenews.com/2002/042602_borders_amazon.htm.

6 For more detailed discussions of the concept of deconstruction, see P. Evans and T. Wurster, *Blown to Bits*, Harvard Business School Press, 1999, pp. 39–67, and D. Heuskel, W*ettbewerb jenseits von Industriegrenzen*, Campus, 1999, pp. 57–72.

7 J. Rayport and J. Sviokla developed a similar concept to the two concepts mentioned here. It proposes an unbundling along the dimensions of content, context and infrastructure. Since the findings are essentially the same as in the deconstruction and unbundling concepts, we do not elaborate further on this concept. However, for a detailed discussion of this concept, see J. Rayport and J. Sviokla, 'Managing in the market space', *Harvard Business Review*, 1995, November–December, pp. 141–150.

8 M. Porter, 'Strategy and the Internet', *Harvard Business Review*, 2001, March, pp. 72–74.

9 For a detailed discussion of this concept, see J. Hagel and M. Singer, 'Unbundling the corporation', *Harvard Business Review*, 1999, March–April, pp. 133–141.

10 For a more extensive discussion of channel conflicts, see C. Bucklin, P. Thomas-Graham and E. Webster, 'Channel conflict: when is it dangerous?', *McKinsey Quarterly*, 1997, No. 3, pp. 36–43.

11 T. Jelassi and S. Leenen, 'An e-commerce sales model for manufacturing companies: a conceptual framework and a European example', *European Management Journal*, 2003, Vol. 21, No. 1, pp. 45–46.

CHAPTER 10

Choosing the appropriate strategy for interaction with suppliers

Chapter at a glance

10.1 Advantages and drawbacks of online purchasing

10.2 Classification of B2B e-marketplaces based on the purchasing process and the purchased products

10.3 Classification of B2B e-marketplaces based on their degree of openness

10.4 Integrating e-procurement systems

Related case studies

Case study	Primary focus of the case study
6 Mondus	Public horizontal e-marketplace
7 Covisint	Consortium-based vertical e-marketplace
8 IBX	Adding a vertical e-marketplace to a horizontal marketplace

Learning outcomes

After completing this chapter, you should be able to:

■ Understand the basic concepts and issues in business-to-business e-commerce.

■ Assess the advantages and drawbacks of B2B electronic purchasing.

■ Differentiate B2B e-marketplaces based on the 'what' and the 'how' of purchasing.

■ Distinguish the different levels of openness in B2B e-marketplaces.

■ Appreciate the functionalities offered by different e-procurement solutions and the trade-offs that companies need to make when choosing one of these solutions.

■ Recognise the increasingly competitive dimension of e-supply chain management.

INTRODUCTION

In order to produce their own products and services, companies rely heavily on purchasing raw materials and other manufacturing inputs as well as maintenance, repair and operating (MRO) goods, from external providers. There are different types of business-to-business (B2B) electronic marketplaces where companies or other organisations make their purchasing.[1] First, *industrial markets,* where buyers purchase raw materials to turn them into tangible goods, are primarily used by companies from industries such as agriculture, manufacturing, electricity or construction. Second, reseller markets, where buyers purchase products or services with the sole purpose of reselling them later on, have mainly the wholesale and retail industries operating in them. Finally, there are also *government markets* where government agencies buy goods and services. Transactions in government markets take place, for instance, when government agencies make purchases for running the public administration or equipping the armed forces.

This chapter provides a comprehensive understanding of the basic concepts and issues in B2B e-commerce. First, it presents the advantages and drawbacks of electronic purchasing. Second, it suggests a classification of B2B e-marketplaces based on the purchasing process (i.e. the 'how' of e-procurement) and the types of goods that are purchased online (i.e. the 'what' of e-procurement). Third, the chapter identifies different levels of openness among B2B e-marketplaces and discusses issues that are specific to each level. Fourth, it recognises the functionalities offered by different e-procurement solutions and highlights the trade-offs that companies need to make when choosing among these e-procurement solutions.

10.1 Advantages and drawbacks of online purchasing

When organisations in any one of the above B2B markets make buying decisions, these decisions are influenced by different factors:[2]

- *Who is buying?* Typically, different members in an organisation are involved in the buying process, which include the actual users, influencers, buyers and decision makers. Depending on a company's requirements regarding financial control and authorisation procedures, the constellation of this group varies. As more parties get involved, purchasing processes tend to get more complicated and protracted.

- *What is the type and size of purchase?* Purchases can be categorised according to volume and value. Low-frequency, high-value transactions such as the selling of large passenger aircraft tend to be purchased where the Internet does not have a high impact. This is because these transactions typically require substantial negotiations, special contracts and financing arrangements. In contrast, for high-volume, low-value transactions, such as the purchasing of office supplies or travel services, that are repetitive and of relatively low strategic importance, placing orders over the Internet is much more widespread because of the faster speed and the possibility to access more detailed information.

■ *How much information is required to make the purchasing decision?* Typically, the information requirements of commercial purchasers are higher than those of individual consumers, since they need to match product specifications more closely with buying requirements. Therefore, the buying processes also tend to be longer and more complicated. The B2B e-purchasing service provider IBX, which is featured in the case studies section of the book, offers a platform that provides purchasing departments with detailed information and product specifications from potential suppliers.

The most frequently cited advantages of online procurement are the following:[3]

■ *Higher transparency.* Online procurement ensures access to comparable information for all parties who are involved in the purchasing process, including buyers, decision makers and users. In contrast, paper-based purchasing systems can cause confusion in human-based systems as parties may not have access to the same information. In addition, online systems allow buyers to track and trace the purchase process and to control different aspects such as delivery and internal distribution. (See the FT article 'Competing supply chains are the future').

■ *Reduced risk of maverick spend.* The above-mentioned point of higher transparency is closely coupled with the reduced risk of maverick spend that can be achieved through online procurement systems. 'Maverick' purchasing takes place when employees buy items or services that are outside the preferred process or system. Instead of buying from a preferred supplier with which the company has negotiated a contract with discount pricing, an individual goes outside the normal process and purchases that same item at retail prices. Setting up a dedicated system through which purchases need to be made, and having the means to monitor whether buyers adhere to the rules, lowers the risk of maverick spend.

■ *Price reduction through online negotiations.* For instance, the e-Sourcing solution of IBX, which is explained in more detail in the IBX case study, allows buyers to obtain lower prices through reverse online auctions, where suppliers compete to capture the purchase volume by offering lower prices and better conditions. The auction events occur online, reducing the sourcing cycle duration by almost 30%, when compared with the offline method.

■ *Process optimisation.* Fully integrated online procurement systems eliminate the need to rekey ordering information, thereby getting rid of data entry errors, cutting back on manual labour, and speeding up the procurement process.

Yet, there are also a number of disadvantages and risks that are associated with the introduction of e-procurement systems:[4]

■ *Organisational risk.* Depending on the level of integration, which is discussed in more detail below, there is a crtitical need to adjust the organisational structure to make e-procurement work. As individual employees are allowed to make e-purchases from their desktop computers, the procurement department loses importance.

■ *Technology risk.* Implementing an e-procurement system usually entails a substantial commitment to a given technology with the risk of getting involved with a marketplace that could go out of business over time.

■ *Supplier resistance.* Frequently, suppliers are not eager to enter online purchasing systems since doing so may force price cuts and disrupt stocking and labour agreements.

Competing supply chains are the future

More than 500 years ago, an Italian explorer called Christopher Columbus pleaded with Spain's King Ferdinand and Queen Isabella to finance an expedition that would speed access to Indian markets. Columbus's vision for quick access to key markets went against the prevailing scientific view that the world was flat. Columbus thought it was round.

Now, an American author named Thomas Friedman has written a best-selling book concluding that the world is flat after all. And I very much agree with Friedman, who says in his book The World is Flat, that technology and fast access to Asian markets are levelling the global playing field – creating, in effect, a 'flat' world. I view technology as the key enabler of the global economy.

In a 'flat world', nations – like companies – are becoming more specialised and assuming certain areas of expertise. For example, China is known as a manufacturing base, while India is considered the low-cost information technology and financial services hub. This has led companies to take advantage of this specialisation to outsource parts of their operations to appropriate countries. This increased collaboration – with technology as the catalyst – means that instead of companies competing against companies, by 2010 supply chains will be competing against supply chains.

Historically, the competitive advantages of a company's supply chain were under-rated. Companies competed on products and services, not processes. But those days are over. The intensity of global competition is forcing companies to compete on the strength of their supply chains.

Growth-oriented leaders understand what is at stake. They know that supply chain strategy is really business strategy, and vice-versa. In the past decade, process and technology improvements in supply chain management have lowered total US business inventories by billions of dollars and helped reduce order-to-cash cycle times by 10%. Dell, for example, engineers systems in design centres in five countries. It operates seven factories – three in the US,

one in Europe, two in Asia and one in South America. It has a supplier network involving a few hundred companies across the globe.

Internet-enabled links between Dell's supply chain partners have allowed better co-ordination and collaboration among the various supply chain segments; and providers. The company is famously efficient because of its direct-to-customer, build-to-order business model; just-in-time manufacturing at its best. What is less known, however, is how Dell partners with other companies for its service parts logistics process. This allows technicians to call a number staffed by its supply chain solutions provider and request a part or parts needed to service a machine. In the market for computer repair services, a four-hour commitment on parts delivery is often essential.

In another example, Dell set out to improve visibility of its shipments as they moved through the supply chain. Dell and its logistics provider worked on a system that would achieve this as the parts packages were loaded into the trailers at their distribution centres all the way through the freight and small package networks to the destination. The system eliminated an 18-hour manual process and increased service reliability and outbound visibility.

Supply chains now also run up against customs requirements and other complexities and processes that accompany shipping around the world between a company's locations and with outsourcing partners. Security and compliance initiatives, trade agreements, customs regulations, duty rates, and import and export processes can make it more difficult than ever to conduct trade internationally. And non-compliance with government regulations can bring potential fines, penalties, and even legal action.

According to a 2005 Aberdeen research report, nearly two-thirds of companies still rely heavily on spreadsheets or paper-based systems to manage global trade. But companies can no longer afford to treat global logistics, trade compliance, and trade finance activities as separate functions. They →

need to outsource solutions that will tie these functions together across their companies and synchronise the process with regulatory agencies, logistics service providers, and trading partners.

For example, US-based companies now need to comply with the US Customs-Trade Partnership Against Terrorism (C-TPAT) initiative, a government-business initiative designed to build relationships that strengthen overall supply chain and border security. Through this initiative, US Customs and Border Protection (CBP) can provide tight security in co-operation with the ultimate owners of the supply chain: importers, carriers, brokers, warehouse operators, and manufacturers. The challenge for a company is first knowing how its global supply chain measures up against the requirements set forth by C-TPAT, then measuring timeline

achievement and establishing follow-up reminders with the customer's supply chain partners to ensure the company meets the requirements. This sharpens the need for new technology-based controls and record-keeping tools to reduce the added complexity.

Ultimately, no company can compete in a global economy alone and the increasing reliance on outsourcing and partnerships has reduced room for error. These relationships require trust, collaboration, visibility, and a focus on results to make them successful. Technology is the tie that binds, allowing companies fully to synchronise their supply chains and grow in a flattening global economy. Just like the Nina, the Pinta and the Santa Maria, technology is sailing into a brave new world.

Source: D. Barnes, 'Competing supply chains are the future', FT.com, 8 November 2006.

10.2 Classification of B2B e-marketplaces based on the purchasing process and the purchased products

To systematise the landscape of rapidly changing B2B markets, Kaplan and Sawhney propose a classification of B2B electronic marketplaces based on *what* businesses purchase and *how* they purchase it.[5] 'Regarding the *what*, there are essentially two different types of goods:

- *Operating inputs*. These goods are also often called MRO (Maintenance, Repair and Operations) goods or indirect goods, because they do not form part of the final products a company produces. MRO goods, which are typically not industry specific, include items such as office supplies, airline tickets and travel services. For instance, companies such as Spreadshirt and Ducati, which are in very different industries, both need computers and office supplies for their employees. MRO goods are usually purchased from horizontal platforms and shipped through third-party logistics providers. These items are typically not strategically relevant to a company's production process and therefore not crucial for developing a competitive advantage.

- *Manufacturing inputs (raw materials and components)*. These industry-specific goods are also called direct goods because they are used for the final product that is delivered to the customer. These goods, which include raw materials (such as steel or cement) and goods that are used for final products (such as electronic components) are usually purchased from vertical suppliers/distributors. To handle and deliver these manufacturing inputs, it is typically necessary to use specific fulfilment mechanisms. For instance, a motorcycle manufacturer, such as Ducati, that sources engine parts on a continuous basis from an external supplier is unlikely to use courier services, such as Federal Express, DHL or UPS, for delivery.

The second determining dimension is *how* these goods are purchased from suppliers. There are two main types of sourcing:

■ *Systematic sourcing.* This type of sourcing involves negotiated contracts with qualified suppliers. Contracts are usually long term and built on mutual trust, hence leading to lasting relationships between buyer and seller. The goal of systematic sourcing is to create value for both buyer and seller, by sharing, for instance, sales forecasts, customer data and production statistics. Thus, systematic sourcing relationships are usually about more than optimising just price. To corporate customers, it is more important to get the right product at the right time with the right service than to save an additional 1–2% of the price. Usually, it is advisable to set up systematic sourcing contracts when (1) complicated products are involved that need specific adjustment and service, and (2) it is necessary to make investments that are specific to the relationship. The relationship that Dell maintains with external suppliers of PC components is an example of systematic sourcing.

■ *Spot sourcing.* Firms typically use this type of sourcing to fulfil an immediate need at the lowest possible price. Commodities (such as oil, gas and iron) are typically purchased via spot sourcing. Thus, it rarely involves a long-term relationship between buyer and seller. In contrast to systematic sourcing, spot sourcing focuses primarily on price, so that both buyer and seller try to maximise their own benefit at the other party's expense.

Based on the above dimensions, it is possible to construct a B2B Internet matrix depicting the following four different types of B2B e-marketplaces (see also Exhibit 10.1):

■ *MRO hubs* are horizontal e-marketplaces with long-term supply relationships for operating inputs. For instance, Grainger in the USA (see the Blog Box below) sells goods that companies need to keep their plants and facilities running. IBX, a case study featured in this book, is another example of an MRO hub that sells, among other things, non-strategic, low-value items.

■ *Catalogue hubs* sell manufacturing inputs through a systematic sourcing system. Goods sold through catalogue hubs are tailored specifically to meet the individual needs of the purchasing company. An example here is Covisint, which is a vertical e-hub for the automotive industry, linking car manufacturers with their suppliers. (For more details, see the Covisint case study in the latter part of this book.)

Exhibit 10.1 **The B2B e-commerce matrix classifies different types of B2B e-marketplaces**

	Operating inputs	**Manufacturing inputs**
Systematic sourcing	**MRO hubs** Horizontal markets that enable systematic sourcing of operating inputs	**Catalogue hubs** Vertical markets that enable systematic sourcing for manufacturing inputs
Spot sourcing	**Yield managers** Horizontal markets that enable spot sourcing of operating inputs	**Exchanges** Vertical markets that enable spot sourcing for manufacturing inputs

How do firms buy?

What do firms buy?

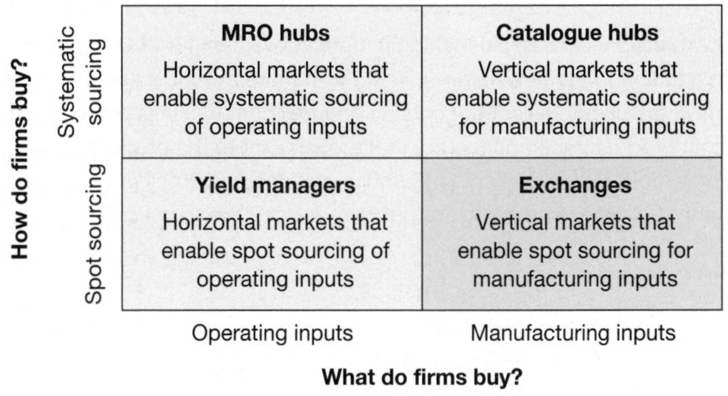

Source: Reprinted by permission of *Harvard Business Review* [Exhibit ROO 306]. From 'E Hubs: The New B2B Marketplaces' by S. Kaplan and M. Sawhney, May–June 2000. Copyright © 2000 by the Harvard Business School Publishing Corporation, all rights reserved.

- *Yield managers* are horizontal e-marketplaces for spot sourcing of operating inputs. They are most valuable for operating inputs that display high fluctuations in price and/or demand. An example here is mondus.com, a horizontal e-marketplace for small and medium-sized enterprises (for more details, see the mondus.com case study in the latter part of this book).

- *Exchanges* are closely related to more traditional commodity exchanges. They are used primarily for the selling of commodities (such as steel and copper) that are used in the production process. An example of such an Internet-based exchange is e-steel.com.

BLOG BOX

Grainger's MRO hub on the Internet

W.W. Grainger, with 2006 sales of $5.9 billion, is a broad line supplier of facilities maintenance products serving businesses and institutions in Canada, China, Mexico and the United States, offering more than 138,000 facilities maintenance products, including 7,000 plumbing products such as high-grade pipes, valves and fittings; 4,000 material handling supplies such as conveyors, hoists and casters; 5,000 fasteners such as nuts, bolts and screws; as well as 1,600 security products such as locks and hinges.

'Our customers count on us to be a one-stop shop for a broad selection of maintenance, repair and operating (MRO) supplies so they can efficiently manage their facilities,' said Kevin Peters, Grainger's senior vice president of supply chain management.' Grainger aims to match customer product requirements with a broad product offering, enabling customers to consolidate their MRO purchases and drive efficiency in their businesses.

In order to drive down the high costs associated with procuring unplanned items, customers including facilities managers, contractors and purchasing professionals need quick access to a broad array of facilities maintenance supplies across multiple product categories. This provides businesses and institutions the opportunity to consolidate their spending and achieve volume discounts, saving them time and money.

'Our customers told us they turn to our [printed] catalog as a reference tool for sourcing facilities maintenance products, even when making a purchase over the phone or online,' said Peters. 'As Grainger broadens its product line, we're also enhancing our catalog to help customers find the right products as quickly and conveniently as possible.'

With its expansion, Grainger is making it more convenient for customers to source the products they need. In addition to the new, larger catalog with more products and information, the company has added new search and selection tools on grainger.com to assist customers in narrowing their selection to the right product based on factors that are relevant to the product or application. Advanced cross-referencing tools, a new dedicated plumbing catalog and employee product training will also help customers save time in sourcing the right product for their applications.

Source: www.grainger.com.

10.3 Classification of B2B e-marketplaces based on their degree of openness

This classification focuses on the degree of openness of B2B e-marketplaces.[6] At one end of the spectrum, e-marketplaces with a high degree of openness are those that are publicly accessible to any company. At the other end of the spectrum, e-marketplaces with a low degree of openness are accessible only upon invitation. Based on this distinction, we recognise three main types of e-marketplaces: public e-markets, consortia and private exchanges (see Exhibit 10.2):

■ *Public e-markets* are generally owned and operated by a third-party provider. They are open to any company that wants to purchase or sell through the e-marketplace. Because it is easy to enter and leave public e-markets, businesses processes are primarily standardised

Exhibit 10.2 Different B2B e-marketplaces display varying degrees of openness

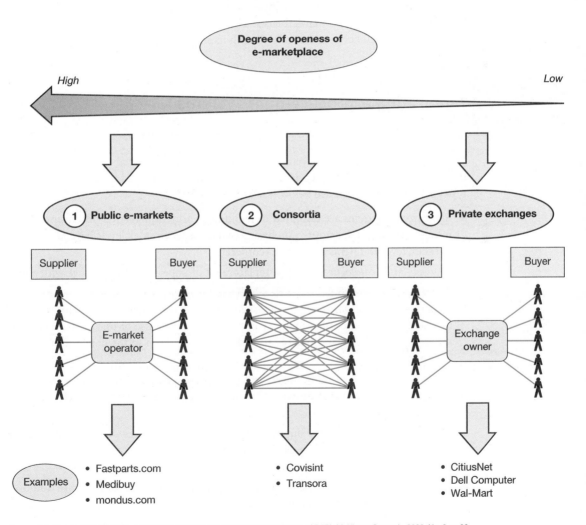

Source: Adapted from W. Hoffman, J. Keedy and K. Roberts, 'The unexpected return of B2B', *McKinsey Quarterly*, 2002, No. 3, p. 99.

and non-proprietary. Products that are most likely to be sold through public e-market-places are commodities that need little or no customisation. An example of a public e-market is mondus.com.

■ *Consortia* are typically jointly owned and operated by companies that participate in the online B2B exchanges. Access is much more limited than in public e-markets, since only equity holders and selected trading partners are admitted. Covisint, founded by General Motors, Ford and DaimlerChrysler, is an example of a B2B consortium.

■ *Private exchanges* are the most restrictive e-marketplaces in providing access to external parties. They are typically operated by a single company that wants to optimise its sourcing activities by tying its suppliers closely into its business processes. The operator of the private exchange invites selected suppliers to participate in the private exchange and provides them with detailed information about, for instance, sales forecasts or production statistics. In turn, this helps the supplier to optimise its supply chain. In order to achieve this type of close integration, it is generally necessary to build a customised system that tightly integrates the information systems of both buyer and seller. As a result, business relationships in private exchanges tend to last longer than in public e-marketplaces. The most prominent example of a highly successful private exchange is that of Dell with its suppliers.

10.4 Integrating e-procurement systems

When thinking about e-procurement solutions, it is also essential to determine if only part of the procurement cycle or the whole supply chain should be covered. Different types of systems are discussed below (see Exhibit 10.3):[7]

■ *Stock control systems* are designed to facilitate production-related procurement. For instance, these systems notify purchasing managers when stock levels have fallen below a certain level and items need to be reordered.

■ *CD/web-based catalogue* presents a replacement of paper-based catalogues with search functions to make it easier to locate specific items.

■ *E-mail or database-based workflow systems* integrate the order of originator, approval by manager and order placement by buyer. Through the use of one of these systems, orders can be quickly and reliably passed from one person to the next without losing information.

■ *Order entry on website* allows users to buy items directly on the seller's website. Yet, since there is no integration with the internal accounting system, purchasing data needs to be rekeyed.

■ *Accounting systems* allow the buying department to place orders and simultaneously to pass the information on to be used for internal accounting processes e.g. to make payment upon receipt of the invoice.

■ *Integrated e-procurement systems* integrate all of the above functionalities. In addition, they are also integrated with the suppliers' systems.

Exhibit 10.3 e-Procurement solutions cover different parts of the supply chain

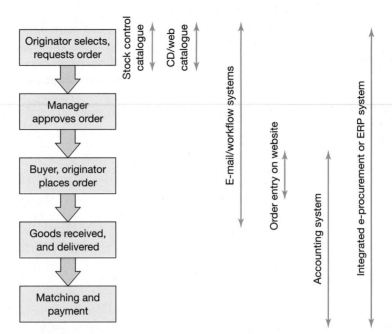

Source: D. Chaffey, *E-business and E-Commerce Management*, FT/Prentice Hall, 2006, pp. 320–321.

When choosing between different types of e-procurement solutions, difficult trade-offs need to be made. At one end of the spectrum, it is possible to link existing legacy systems with new technologies or to purchase a completely new system that completely integrates all functionalities. Buying a new system might be the simplest option, but upfront investment is usually higher than adjusting existing systems. In addition, switching completely to a new system requires staff training.

With the advent of new technologies, supply chains are becoming increasingly integrated. One example of the integrative power of advanced technologies is the RFID (Radio-Frequency Identification) chip, which can be used for monitoring anything it is attached to in a store location or a warehouse (see FT article 'RFID – the price must be right').

RFID – the price must be right

A shopper takes a bottle of shampoo from the supermarket shelf, and a signal from a state-of-the-art smart tag is sent to staff, updating them on stock levels. RFID (radio frequency identification) is working and ready to replace conventional bar codes. But not for at least 15 years, according to German retail giant Metro AG, the world's fifth largest retailer, which since March 2004 has been introducing RFID in stages along its supply chain.

So far, it has 25 distribution centres using the technology, mostly on the wooden pallets which carry the goods; more than 40 suppliers now attach RFID tags to their pallets. In the coming weeks, the company will start using tags on individual cases of products. The ultimate aim is to deploy RFID at all levels, including the individual item, at all of its 2,300 locations; but that day is years away, concedes Gerd Wolfram, managing director of MGI Metro Group Information Technology. 'We will see RFID increasingly replace bar codes for certain products but the technology won't be used to identify all products for a good 15 years,' he says, citing high unit prices for the tags as one of the main reasons. Unit prices, Wolfram notes, will need to drop to 0.01 per tag or less to make RFID a viable alternative to a bar code.

Metro views RFID technology as a way to manage the huge flow of merchandise in and out of stores more effectively, while at the same time reducing inventory losses and labour costs. Wolfram says: 'We firmly believe that we'll be able to lower our operating costs with this technology and also provide our customers with a richer shopping experience.' Since 2003 Metro has been testing RFID in a live retail setting at the Extra supermarket in Rheinberg, near Düsseldorf, as part of its Future Store Initiative.

Among the innovative smart tag implementations being tested at the store is the 'smart-shelf,' which automatically informs staff to replenish merchandise. RFID tags are attached to packages of Gillette razor blades, Philadelphia cream cheese containers and plastic bottles of shampoo from Procter & Gamble. As customers pick up the tagged products, signals are transmitted via a wireless network to the merchandise management system, which tracks the number in stock and issues alerts to clerks carrying PDAs.[8]

Metro is also carrying out development work on RFID at its RFID Innovation Centre in nearby Neuss, where it is testing more than 40 applications, most of which are focused on logistics, warehousing and retail operations but a few also involve consumers. For instance, the 'smart fridge' identifies products and informs household members when expiry dates are approaching.

In Neuss, around 20 technology partners, including IT industry heavyweights IBM, Intel and SAP are collaborating with Metro. EPC global, which has been leading the drive to establish a global RFID standard, has established its European performance test centre within the German centre.

Source: J. Blau, 'RFID – the price must be right', FT.com, 30 May 2006.

SUMMARY

- The chapter proposed a classification of B2B e-marketplaces based on *what* and *how* companies purchase goods from suppliers. It also discussed varying degrees of openness in B2B e-marketplaces.

- First, this chapter discussed some issues in B2B e-commerce and presented the main advantages and drawbacks of electronic purchasing. The advantages include (1) higher transparency, (2) reduced risk of maverick spend, (3) price reduction through online negotiations and (4) process optimisation. Drawbacks consist of (1) organisational risk, (2) technology risk and (3) supplier resistance.

- Second, the chapter suggested a classification of B2B e-marketplaces based on the purchasing process (i.e. the 'how' of e-procurement: is it spot or systematic sourcing?) and the types of goods that are purchased online (i.e. the 'what' of e-procurement: are they operating or manufacturing inputs?). Based on these two dimensions, four distinct quadrants are recognised; these are 'MRO hubs' and 'Yield managers' for horizontal e-marketplaces, and 'Catalogue hubs' and 'Exchanges' for vertical e-marketplaces.

■ Third, the chapter identified different levels of openness among B2B e-marketplaces and discussed issues that are specific to each level. At one end of the spectrum, 'Public e-marketplaces' have a high degree of openness and are accessible to any company. At the other end, 'Private exchanges' are e-marketplaces with a low degree of openness and are accessible only upon invitation. In between, 'Consortia e-marketplaces' have a medium level of openness and are jointly owned and operated by a few companies.

■ Fourth, this chapter recognised the functionalities offered by different e-procurement solutions including stock control systems, database-based workflow systems, accounting systems, and integrated e-procurement systems. It also highlighted the trade-offs that companies need to make when choosing among these e-procurement solutions.

REVIEW QUESTIONS

1 What are the advantages and drawbacks of e-purchasing systems?

2 Outline the business-to-business (B2B) e-commerce matrix based on its two underlying dimensions.

3 What B2B purchasing models do companies use? What criteria determine what specific B2B model to use?

4 Explain the concept of openness in B2B e-marketplaces. What different types of e-marketplace can you differentiate based on their degree of openness?

5 What are the different types of e-procurement systems? What part of the supply chain does each e-procurement type cover?

DISCUSSION QUESTIONS

1 Illustrate each quadrant of the B2B e-commerce matrix through a real-world example.

2 Provide an example of a B2B e-marketplace for each one of the B2B purchasing models outlined in this chapter.

3 Discuss the advantages and disadvantages of the varying degrees of openness in B2B marketplaces, i.e. public e-markets, consortia and private exchanges.

4 Discuss the trade-offs that companies need to make when choosing between different types of e-procurement solutions.

RECOMMENDED KEY READING

■ S. Kaplan and M. Sawhney developed the concept of e-hubs in 'e-Hubs: the new B2B marketplaces', *Harvard Business Review*, 2000, May–June, pp. 97–103.

■ W. Hoffman, J. Keedy and K. Roberts differentiate e-marketplaces according to their degree of openness in 'The unexpected return of B2B', *McKinsey Quarterly*, 2002, No. 3, pp. 97–106.

USEFUL THIRD-PARTY WEBLINKS

- www.efficientpurchasing.com is the website of an industry magazine for sourcing and procurement professionals.
- www.brint.com provides numerous articles and other resources on managing supplier relationships in e-business.

NOTES AND REFERENCES

1 See D. Chaffey *et al.*, *Internet Marketing*, FT/Prentice Hall, 2006, p. 494.
2 Ibid., p. 502.
3 Ibid., p. 501.
4 See D. Chaffey, *E-business and E-Commerce Management*, FT/Prentice Hall, 2006, pp. 318–320.
5 S. Kaplan and M. Sawhney, 'e-Hubs: the new B2B marketplaces', *Harvard Business Review*, 2000, May–June, pp. 97–103.
6 W. Hoffman, J. Keedy and K. Roberts, 'The unexpected return of B2B', *McKinsey Quarterly*, 2002, No. 3, pp. 97–106.
7 See D. Chaffey, *E-business and E-Commerce Management*, FT/Prentice Hall, 2006, pp. 320–321.
8 PDAs stand for personal digital assistants.

CHAPTER 11

Choosing the appropriate e-business strategy for interacting with users[1]

Chapter at a glance

Related case studies

Learning outcomes

After completing this chapter, you should be able to:

- Understand the technological developments leading to the advent of Web 2.0.

- Recognise how these technological developments brought about user generated content and change of behaviour.

- Use the insights gained from the 'mass customisation' and 'long tail' concepts to increase the richness of interactions with customers.

- Use the insights gained from the 'tipping point', network externality effects and 'viral growth' concepts to increase the reach of interactions with customers.

INTRODUCTION

Since the grassroots of e-business, which we discussed in Chapter 1, the Internet has changed dramatically. While years ago it was closer to a read-only web with a static and unidirectional information flow, users today have the opportunity to become editors and active content generators on the Internet. In this chapter, we take a closer look at how companies leverage the new technological capabilities of the Internet to involve their customers and website users more deeply in the information-sharing and content creation process.

The chapter starts out by giving an overview of Web 2.0,[2] including the technological advances which led to its emergence, the service concepts offered through it, and users' behaviour on the so-called social web. In Section 11.2, we analyse the trade-off between richness and reach. Building on this trade-off, we then discuss the concepts of mass customisation, 'viral growth', 'tipping point' and 'long tail'.

11.1 The Internet and social commerce

Compared with its early years, the Internet has become an increasingly interactive platform, thanks to its huge number of users and a large variety of new service sites catering to their users' communication wants and transaction needs. In the following, we examine the Internet's main technological developments and their induced applications.

11.1.1 The advent of Web 2.0

The advent of Web 2.0, which has opened up new ways to communicate, share content and collaborate, symbolises a paradigm shift from website provider or supplier-generated content to user-generated content. Tim O'Reilly calls Web 2.0 'the business revolution in the computer industry caused by the move to the Internet as a platform, and an attempt to understand the rules for success on that new platform.' The applications should 'harness network effects to get better the more people use them'.[3]

The two key areas of these technological developments are *network infrastructure* and *software capabilities.*

Network infrastructure

In recent years, households' access to *broadband Internet* has increased rapidly. One important driver for this development was the overinvestment during the Internet boom years in fibre-optic cable companies, which then laid out massive amounts of fibre-optic cable thereby driving down data transmission costs. For Internet users, this increased bandwidth has resulted in higher connection speed, which, in turn, translates directly into an improved Internet experience. This, in turn, attracted more users and made them spend more time online.

The rapid decline in *storage costs* in recent years has also had a major impact on companies whose business models rely heavily on storage capacity. Today, it is not unusual to have more than a gigabyte of storage space on an e-mail account such as Gmail, or an unlimited uploading of photos on a social networking site (such as Facebook) free of charge. Depending on the amount of data that needs to be stored, there are different business models in use. For example, online back-up solutions (such as Mozy.com or Box.net), which handle a large volume of data, use a subscription model to recover their high storage costs. On the other hand, social networking sites (SNS) try to cover these costs through online advertising revenues.

Software capabilities

Capitalising on technological advances in network infrastructure and using the web as a platform, new software standards have emerged that allow for user participation in creating content. The deployment of web application development techniques (such as AJAX) started to make the Internet experience faster and more convenient as it enables websites to reload separately different parts of a page. As a result, it became possible to surf web pages like navigating traditional desktop programs. Google Docs, for instance, offers text processing, spreadsheet modelling and calendar functions that can be accessed directly online from any PC with an Internet connection.

Software has also made it easier for users actually to publish content on the Internet. It was just a few years ago that writing on a website was the privilege of programmers or those having the necessary HTML technical skills. To do so today, users no longer need to install some tools or programs; instead, they log on to their account on the service website that hosts a blog and allows its users to manage their profiles and content. Active communities of developers were actually created around websites and specific programs that either use an 'open source' approach for collaborative software development (as is the case with the Linux operating system), or grant access to an application program interface. (See in Section 9.1 the FT article: 'Facebook spreads its web wider'.)

Furthermore, the creation and adoption of new syndication formats (such as RSS) enable users easily to track content updates on other websites. Also, by allowing users to subscribe to other people's content, communication, sharing and collaboration have significantly improved. Furthermore, blog software installation and administration made it easier for individuals to manage their own web space. Wordpress, for instance, is a state-of-the-art blog publishing tool which offers powerful, yet easy to handle customisation and administrative features.

11.1.2 Web 2.0 services

Different business models for Web 2.0 applications (which are sometimes referred to as Enterprise 2.0) currently try to seize new business opportunities. Media-sharing portals (such as Flickr and YouTube), free voice-over-IP applications[4] (such as Skype), major online collaborative applications (such as the encyclopedia Wikipedia) and the broad 'blogosphere'[5] realm rely on new technologies to promote the collective spirit of the Internet. In general, the flock of new services and applications can be divided into the following categories:

- *Blogs and blog aggregators.* User-generated websites containing continuously updated entries in periodic order. Blogs can be generated through different blog providers such as blogger or Wordpress. Several services such as Technorati provide tools to browse through the sheer number of blogs (often referred to as the 'blogosphere').

- *Wikis.* Derived from the Hawaiian word 'fast', these websites display content that users can incorporate as is or modify at will. In order to assure the quality of its content, Wikipedia, for instance, relies on users' mutual content control, article rating and indexing.

- *Social networking sites (SNS).* These online communities enable users to communicate and connect with each other, build up a personal network, as well as share personal content. On these sites, members create their personal profile to present themselves to others, while community providers primarily act as enablers, offering support capabilities as well as search and communication tools. The €482 million acquisition in 2005 of MySpace by Rupert Murdoch's media conglomerate News Corp. made it the poster child for these new SNS services. More recently, in December 2006, the business networking site XING, previously called openBC, staged its initial public offering (IPO), thus becoming the first Web 2.0 company in the world to go public.

- *Social bookmarking.* Users of these services, provided by companies such as Delicious.com, can collect their favourite websites as bookmarks, using 'tags', i.e. short descriptive key words instead of the traditional browser-based folder taxonomy. They can also share their favourites with other users who can browse for certain 'tags' when looking for interesting weblinks.

- *Media and information-sharing platforms.* The 2008 presidential campaign in the USA has already discovered the huge reach of sites such as YouTube, where users can upload, index, share and rate all kinds of videos. Another media and information-sharing platform, Flickr, which was acquired by Yahoo! in March 2005 for $35 million, is similar to YouTube but uses photos instead of videos.

- *Web-based tools.* A variety of services can be accessed directly from the web but offer a degree of customisation and functionality that rather resembles conventional programs and desktop applications. There are services providing map and navigation data, such as Googlemaps, or websites such as netvibes that offer a fully customisable desktop surface where users can receive RSS feeds, weather forecasts, e-mail notifications and other features.

- *Web-based desktop applications.* Even though these applications use the web as a platform, they can be downloaded and installed on a local computer, not just accessed through an Internet browser. Skype was one of the first applications successfully to offer a working service, enabling people to talk to one another over the Internet for free. Telecommunication operators, realising the disruptive nature of Internet-based telephony, soon jumped on the bandwagon, offering their own VoIP products. Online file-sharing networks such as Napster, Kazaa, Gnutella or BitTorrent have shown how peer-to-peer (P2P) networks can impact on traditional businesses by eliminating (or decreasing) the friction between producers and consumers, thereby changing users' behaviour and causing a paradigm shift in some industries.

11.1.3 Understanding user behaviour on the social web

Two key developments that led to changing user behaviour are: (1) the ease with which people can share information through conveniently accessible service sites and (2) the improvements in network infrastructure. The Internet has always been about exchanging information; however, we are just starting to tap into the vast potential of the web as a communication platform. Exhibit 11.1 highlights the interaction processes that underpin social networking sites.

Since the most recent applications usually contain a social component that lets users generate and share content and thereby engage in social interactions, it is important to look at what motivates people to interact with each other on the web. There are essentially three main motives: (1) finding valuable peers (discovery); (2) associating with valuable peers (homogeneity); and (3) imparting information (sharing):

■ *Finding valuable peers (discovery)*. One of the basic motives for getting to know people is curiosity and an interest in discovering new things (learning). People like to explore and have an innate interest in communication, either in order to solve problems or for the sake of conversation. In return they expect *entertainment* in the form of casual or random conversations or *problem solving* through target-oriented discussions. SNS such as Xing, previously called openBC, provide sophisticated search tools that allow users to find other peers who have the information required to solve a specific problem. Users' satisfaction with a platform is directly linked to (1) the ease with which they can browse through a social network of friends and (2) the accuracy of the search results when they look for individuals with certain characteristics. The case study on openBC vs. StayFriends (contained in the second part of this book) vividly illustrates the different search functions that support users' desire for discovery.

■ *Associating with valuable peers (homogeneity)*. The motivation to have like-minded people around oneself is as natural as exploring one's personal environment. Just like gregarious animals in nature, people like to surround themselves with peers with whom they share personal beliefs, values or attitudes. Furthermore, for most people, conformity increases *security* and *identity*. One fundamental aspect of SNS is therefore the possibility to connect with like-minded individuals, since users provide information about their preferences, tastes and interests in their personal profile that can be viewed by others. In addition, communication tools such as instant messaging functions, online chats or private e-mail, provided by some web services, facilitate users' information exchanges according to their individual preferences.

Exhibit 11.1 Social networking sites help users to pursue their motives of discovery, homogeneity and sharing by providing various communication tools

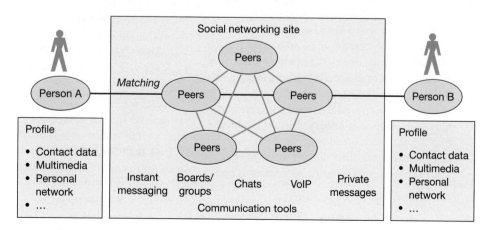

■ *Imparting information (sharing).* People enjoy communicating and sharing what they have learned from their peers. Peers can be relatives, friends, colleagues, mere acquaintances, experts or social contacts of any other kind. While every individual has a certain personality recognised by others, some like to try to control the impression(s) other people form of them. This *impression management* is closely related to *self-presentation*, where a person tries to influence the perception of his/her image. Self-portrayal and, in more extreme cases, craving for recognition are some of the underlying motives for people to make themselves stand out from the masses and personally express themselves. SNS let people articulate their personality. Depending on the context and focus of the SNS platform, individual profiles contain various data and diverse information and let the individual build a reputation. Furthermore, this leads to *opportunities* to signal one's competence or interests to others who are in the stage of discovering people. For instance, on media-sharing platforms (such as YouTube), where users can upload and promote their videos, users can present themselves with the content they have created.

FT

Advertisers discover the merits of networking

The dramatic growth of social networking websites such as MySpace and Facebook is encouraging advertisers to step up their experiments with consumer-created Internet content. Small-scale, early efforts have highlighted some of the benefits of allying with such content, as well as the dangers.

The rise in particular of YouTube.com, which allows people to upload, watch and share home-made and often bizarre video clips, has caught the eye of brands keen to reach consumers spurning mass media. Brian Monahan, of the emerging media lab at IPG, the US marketing services group, says: 'I have been doing online advertising for years and have never seen a jump like that (at YouTube).'

The general expansion of web advertising – Zenith-Optimedia, the media buyer, predicts it will account for 7% of all global advertising by 2008 – has persuaded the likes of YouTube that there will be enough revenue to fund the increasing costs of running such bandwidth-hungry websites. And moves by MTV, the music broadcaster, CNET, the technology publisher, and other media owners to embrace more user-generated content have convinced agency

strategists that the trend will survive any start-up failures. Last week WPP, the marketing services group, announced a joint venture to tap social networking websites, which typically allow users to create and share content on a shared interest.

Currently, most advertiser activity could be described as digital dabbling. Some brands are releasing commercials to websites, hoping people will pass on the clips 'virally'. GoViral.com, a specialist company which offers TV spots to carefully selected web users, points to work for brands such as Goodyear, the tyre maker. Software tracks how many people open the clips or forward them. This month, three spots for Goodyear notched up an estimated 5.7m views. But Thomas Weikop, chief executive of GoViral.com, says the experience also illustrates that 'we are not in control'.

Unlike traditional press or TV campaigns, which last only as long as advertisers are willing to buy media, virals endure as long as Internet users want to pass them on. As such, virals are sometimes quoted in support of the fashionable 'Long Tail' theory. Broadly, this argues that the web is able to sell a wider range of products to a larger number of potential customers than conventional retailers and therefore can support myriad niche markets comprising one 'long tail'. Many of these niches involve products, such as books out of print, that are past their sell-by dates in conventional sales channels, with their need to maximise returns on floor space by selling 'hit' mass-market products. The 'sting' in the long tail for advertisers is that virals can be seen on the web when any marketing messages they contain are no longer appropriate or even accurate.

Amy Fuller, group executive, marketing, Americas, for MasterCard, says: 'This is a different era. When you ran a spot on television, you could control its distribution. It lives for ever online. That requires a lot of discipline.' And other initiatives to open up advertising to consumers also carry risks. When Chevy Tahoe, the General Motors car brand, invited consumers to construct a TV spot online, some created films blaming the vehicle for global warming. Opinions are divided over whether it suffered long-term damage.

Mr Monahan of IPG adds: 'It is a little bit scary right now for brands. They get targeted when they air on relatively tame parts of television. Imagine the letters they will get if their ad is playing next to a YouTube video of a kid repeatedly crashing his bike.'

Source: C. Grande, 'Advertisers discover the merits of networking', *Financial Times*, 16 July 2006.

11.2 The trade-off between richness and reach

As mentioned above, SNS operators can help fuel an individual's communication needs and goals by providing the user with access to diverse information (discovery), like-minded people (homogeneity) and the possibility to provide information themselves (sharing).

Below, we discuss how companies can address a large number of users and provide them with rich means of communication at the same time, a trade-off that has been considerably weakened by the changes of the Internet leading to Web 2.0. The trade-off between richness and reach focuses on the constraints that companies traditionally have faced when interacting with existing or prospective customers.[6] In this context, *reach* refers to the number of people exchanging information. *Richness* is defined by the following three dimensions:

- *Bandwidth.* This dimension refers to the amount of information that can be moved from sender to receiver in a given time: e-mail requires only narrow bandwidth, while music and video require broad bandwidth. On a different level, face-to-face interaction provides a broad bandwidth. This offers an information exchange that goes beyond the content level by also including facial expressions, gestures and tone of voice. The telephone, on the other hand, is much more limited in its bandwidth since it cuts out the visual aspects of interaction; e-mail is even more limited since it also excludes the voice component of the interaction.

- *Customisation.* This dimension refers to the ability to address the needs and preferences of individual customers. For instance, a bank employee at a branch office can provide a much higher degree of customised service than a mass mail advertisement.

- *Interactivity.* This dimension refers to the possibility of having bidirectional communication. Traditional one-way TV broadcasting has a very low level of interactivity. The Internet on the other hand is very interactive, since it allows for an almost instantaneous bidirectional exchange of information (see Exhibit 11.2).

Exhibit 11.2 **The advanced capabilities of the Internet help to dissolve the trade-off between richness and reach**

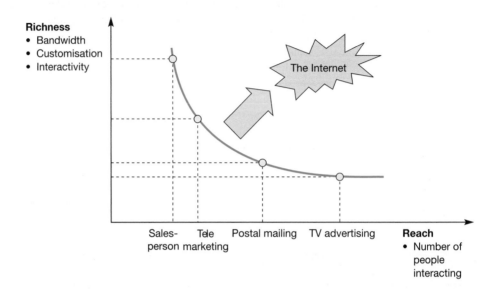

Let us now turn to the historic trade-off between richness and reach. Traditionally, the communication of rich information required proximity to customers and also channels suited for transmitting such information. For instance, rich information exchange takes place in a bank's branch office, where customers talk in person to the bank agent.

However, reaching a large number of customers used to come at the expense of richness, which was due to the limited bandwidth of most mass media devices. This resulted in little customisation and a lack of interactivity, as is the case, for example, with a TV advertisement. To achieve reach and richness at the same time used to require substantial investments in physical infrastructure and sales force. In other words, scale economies were very limited when a firm wanted to expand its customer base – that is expand reach – while still maintaining a high level of richness. Proof of this is the extensive branch network of universal banks through which banks can reach a large number of customers while serving each one of them individually. As the number of customers goes up, so do the costs.

The main argument of the richness and reach framework is that two important drivers have blown up this trade-off between richness and reach. These drivers are: (1) *the increase in connectivity* made possible by the Internet and (2) *the development of common standards* such as TCP/IP, HTML and XML. Connectivity and open standards have allowed firms to reach out to a larger number of customers, while at the same time ensuring a high degree of richness.

Does this concept stand up to reality? In many cases it does. A global auction place such as eBay would not have been possible in the pre-Internet days. Then, people could sell their used lawnmowers and stamp collections at a local garage sale. There, they had very high levels of richness, where buyers could actually touch and try out the product, yet reach was very limited since, typically, it did not extend beyond the immediate neighbourhood of the seller.

eBay has created a much more liquid market by connecting buyers and sellers across cities and countries, enabling them to share rich information about products as well as the reputation of buyers and sellers. Similarly, the Zshops at Amazon.com, where customers and other booksellers can sell their used books, also provide a high level of reach and richness. For setting up these business models, traditional assets such as a large sales force or an extensive physical branch network, which allowed for richness in the traditional bricks-and-mortar world, would have been more of a liability than an asset. In the case of digital products or services, the concept of reach and richness becomes especially viable.

SNS allow their members to manage more contacts more efficiently than is possible offline, therefore they increase their personal contact reach. In addition, users have more information about their contacts or potential contacts due to visible virtual profiles, therefore they also increase personal information richness.

CRITICAL PERSPECTIVE 11.1

The limitations to blowing up the trade-off between richness and reach

Due to several reasons, the blow-up of the trade-off between richness and reach has not happened to the expected extent. On the bandwidth dimension, the Internet cannot replicate the richness of face-to-face contacts, which can only be achieved in the physical world.

Dell, the struggling computer maker, recently outlined plans to reverse two decades of reliance on direct sales by broadening its business model to include third-party vendors and retailers. The move to embrace computer resellers, the vendors who design and install computer systems for clients ranging from hedge funds to hospitals, represents a change in strategy for a company that built its business on direct sales of computers to customers over the telephone and through its website.

Dell had previously hinted that it was examining ways to broaden its retail presence, which so far consists of a single experimental store and more than 100 smaller kiosks. Michael Dell, chief executive, said in an interview, published in CRN, a trade magazine focused on resellers: 'There are certainly folks out there who don't want to buy direct. So now those customers will have a chance to have Dell product as well.' He said the company intended to build on its relationships with resellers and retail partners 'not only here in the US, but around the world'.

While other computer makers – including IBM and Hewlett-Packard – have long relied on resellers and retailers for a substantial chunk of their annual sales, Dell has shunned such indirect relationships, arguing that direct contact with the customer is the best way to streamline costs and respond to changing demand. Although the company has links with some third-party vendors, it said it had never before viewed the channel as a significant business. Mr Dell indicated that would change. 'There is great interest here,' he told CRN. 'We're going to ramp it up quickly.'

Dell declined to comment on any other retail plans. It has traditionally avoided selling computers through retailers, because it allows the company to avoid carrying costly inventory. Shares of Dell rose 3.3% on Wednesday to $25.49. They had fallen from a high of $41.29 in August 2005, before the company's stumbles began. The rise came in spite of news that Andrew Cuomo, New York's attorney general, had sued the computer maker, alleging that its sales practices had deceived customers. Dell said it intended to fight the suit.

Last year, a series of stumbles led Dell, which was founded by Mr Dell in his University of Texas dorm room more than 20 years ago, to lose its place at the top of the PC market to HP. This year, Mr Dell returned to the chief executive role, replacing Kevin Rollins, in an effort to put the company back on track.

Source: K. Allison, 'Dell to broaden sales model', FT.com, 16 May 2007.

11.3 Increasing the richness of interactions with customers

In Section 11.2, we identified bandwidth, customisability and interaction as the main drivers for richness of interaction with users. We now focus on how a company can leverage these drivers in order to foster the richness of interactions with customers. In the following sections, we look at two possible ways of enhancing such richness: (1) electronic customer relationship management (e-CRM) and (2) mass customisation, which entails the tailoring of products and services to specific customer requirements.

11.3.1 Electronic customer relationship management (e-CRM)

e-CRM refers to the use of the Internet and IT applications to manage customer relationships. As the Internet has permeated all the activities of a company's value chain, e-CRM has also become more important. Specifically, it aims at:

- Creating a long-term relationship with customers to offset their acquisition costs.
- Reducing the rate of customer defections.
- Increasing the 'share of wallet' through cross-selling and up-selling.
- Increasing the profitability of low-profit customers.
- Focusing on high-value customers.

e-CRM comprises the following four main elements (see Exhibit 11.3): (1) customer selection, (2) customer acquisition, (3) customer retention and (4) customer extension:

Exhibit 11.3 **Customer relationship management consists of four elements**

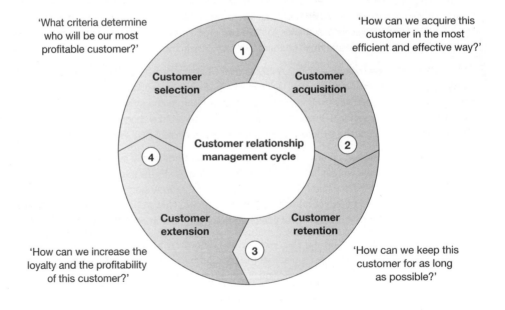

■ *Customer selection* refers to customer segment targeting, which was discussed in detail in Section 3.4.

■ *Customer acquisition* includes promotions and other incentives to (1) acquire new customers and (2) entice existing customers to use the company's Internet-based offering. In order to engage a customer in a relationship through the online channel, a firm needs to have at least the customer's e-mail address. More detailed customer profiles include information such as a customer's personal interests, age, financial status and role in the purchasing process. To acquire this more detailed information, it is usually necessary to offer customers an incentive, e.g. a gift certificate or a free product sample. e-Commerce companies use a number of different tools to get the attention of potential customers. Initially, this was done primarily through banner advertising. More recently, marketers have added more sophisticated tools such as 'viral marketing', where customers forward a website address or other types of company information to each other via e-mail or SMS. Another effective way of acquiring customers is link building, which Amazon.com does in partnership with affiliate sites that refer to the Amazon.com site. For instance, the alumni club of the Leipzig Graduate School of Management in Germany maintains an affiliate relationship with Amazon.de. As part of this agreement, the alumni club's homepage hosts a link to the Amazon.de website and receives a 5% commission on all sales that take place through this link.

■ *Customer retention* aims at (1) turning one-time customers into repeat-purchase customers and (2) keeping customers for as long as possible in the online channel. Customer retention is achieved primarily through two features: personalisation and communities. The personalisation of a website designed to meet specific customer needs helps to create 'stickiness'. If customers want to change their online provider, then they will incur switching costs. Strong online communities with many different users help to create network effects. Both personalisation and online communities entice users to stay with a specific website.

■ *Customer extension* focuses on maximising the lifetime value of a customer. Companies achieve this primarily by expanding the scope of an existing customer relationship through cross-selling. Nordea, for instance, is turning towards triggered data mining to cross-sell additional financial products to existing customers. Triggered data mining works as follows: when there is a change in a customer account – for instance, a large incoming money transfer, an address change or a marital status change – a trigger in the database is set off and informs the bank about this change. This, in turn, raises the following question: What does this change mean for financing, for long-term payments, for insurance and e-services?

11.3.2 The concept of mass customisation

The concept of mass customisation acts counter-intuitively to the large wave of standardisation and exploitation of economies of scale, which originated from industry economics. The amount of customisation in a given product or service is an important determinant driving the richness of interaction between a company and its customers. However, in the past, customisation was rather expensive and customers had to pay a significant price premium, for instance for the customised interior of their apartment or car. Exhibit 11.4 illustrates how mass customisation includes almost all primary activities of the value chain.

Exhibit 11.4 **The mass customisation value chain puts the user in charge of many steps traditionally performed by the company**

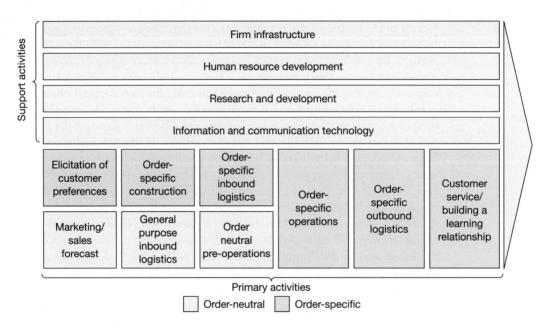

Source: Adapted from F. Piller, *Mass-Customization*, Gabler, 2006, p. 175.

If a company wants to pursue a mass customisation approach, it first needs to elicit the customer's preferences, which form the basis for the individual construction of the product. Frequently, the procurement of customisation-relevant parts only takes place once the preferences' elicitation has been completed. The most prominent example of a mass customisation company is Dell, which lets customers specify exactly which parts should be included in their PC. Tesco.com also leverages customer data to tailor the product list to a customer's needs, e.g. by recommending special offers on a one-to-one basis.

From a strategic perspective, mass customisation opens up the opportunity to pursue an *outpacing strategy* (see Section 5.2.3) that combines low prices with superior performance. A mass customisation company does not have to opt for one of the two directions of competitive advantage, but can simultaneously pursue the two generic strategies using IT and the vast possibilities of user-generated content. On the one hand, mass-customised products are, by definition, highly differentiated, since they are based on each buyer's specifications. For instance, 'The Mongolian Shoe BBQ'[7] by Puma can deliver highly differentiated products to fashion followers by letting them choose and combine different materials, textures and colours for a sneaker or trainer, which is then manufactured and delivered to them. On the other hand, due to efficiency advantages of customer-pulled production, which results in lower business risk and smaller stock levels, mass customised products are also competitive on the price dimension.

Mass customisation options can generally be divided into two different approaches. First, the *soft customisation* approach involves only activities that take place after manufacturing. One example of soft customisation is to provide customers with the possibility to customise products themselves after their purchase. For instance, when users configure the set-up of their Microsoft Office software, they essentially customise it to meet their specific needs. The main drawback of this approach is that, in order to allow multiple customisation options, the product must have a certain built-in flexibility, which typically results in a relatively high product complexity as well as high development and production costs. Yet, the limited overall variety opens up opportunities for standardisation, which in turn leads to economies of scale. From the customer's viewpoint, this mass customisation concept is suitable if customisation needs change often during product use, which, for instance, is the case with many software applications.

In addition to soft customisation, we also recognise the *hard customisation* approach, which entails a customised manufacturing process. The starting point of this approach is the splitting of the production process into a customer-specific part, which is performed in direct interaction with the buyer, and an order-neutral part. For efficiency reasons, the latter should outweigh the former so that economies of scale can be achieved. Puma's 'Mongolian Shoe BBQ' is an example of a hard customisation approach which takes place at the beginning of the manufacturing process. Another example is IKEA's web-based PAX planning that enables users to combine and customise online modules of a popular wardrobe design to create individual furniture that can then be delivered to them.

11.4 Increasing the reach of interactions with customers

SNS can greatly increase the richness of users' interactions. As the openBC case study illustrates, one crucial prerequisite for creating richness is the ability of an Internet service to attract a critical mass of users. SNS can only work if there are enough people registered on them so that users can actually build up a personal contacts' network of a sufficient scale.

More generally, any e-commerce venture that wants to leverage the power of user-generated content needs to devise a growth strategy that allows it to reach a critical mass of buyers (or members, as is the case for SNS). In the following section, we first explore how growth can be fostered by tapping into the power of network effects which could lead to a 'viral growth', then explain the concept of the 'tipping point', and finally investigate the applicability of the 'long tail' concept to SNS.

11.4.1 Viral growth

Any business trying to benefit from viral growth needs to offer incentives for users to invite others to join the service. Incentives can be intrinsic when users know that inviting other users to the platform will enrich their own experience because they can add them as contacts. When these intrinsic motivations fail, as in the case for StayFriends.com (featured in the case studies section of this book), a company has to think about providing appropriate incentives for users.

Information (in its broadest sense, including everything from a simple fact to new products) sometimes spreads epidemically. Like a virus that spreads by infection, information spreads through word of mouth. (This is actually where the term *viral growth* is derived from.) The mechanism of viral information spread is simple and can be compared with the tradition of fairy tales or legends, which spread all over the world only through word of mouth, being retold uncountable times and passed on from generation to generation. Transferred to a broader basis, this means that if only 10 people are addressed in the first generation (at the top of the pyramid), 10,000 people can be reached by the fourth generation. This huge potential has attracted the interest of marketing researchers: if viral news spread could be systematically implemented as a marketing vehicle, this would have major advantages. First, in comparison with traditional marketing campaigns whose effect gets diluted over time, the effect of viral news spread is self-reinforced with an increasing degree of distribution, resulting in a sustainable anchoring of information. The reason for this effect is simple: when moving down the pyramid, the absolute number of people further spreading the news gets continuously larger. Second, the expected costs of viral news spread are low, as no additional costs occur after a certain start-up investment to initiate the news spread (seeding). This is possible because consumers act as a medium to spread the news, once it is seeded.

Viral marketing thus aims to find a way of using epidemical news spread as a marketing tool, making it measurable and repeatable. The goal is to create a viral marketing campaign as a planned initiative where advertisers develop and spread online marketing messages (viral agents) that motivate the receiver to become a sender. However, there are some barriers to implementing viral news spread as a marketing tool. These barriers are:

- *Lack of control over people.* Viral marketing is consumer driven as opposed to traditional interruption marketing, which is driven and controlled by the marketer. It is therefore unpredictable what kind of content people will recommend, when and why. Furthermore, even if people forward the message, it is uncontrollable what they will add to it or say about it when doing so.

- *Lack of control over content.* The content of a viral marketing campaign cannot be protected from being tampered with or modified by the people passing it on. Once the news is seeded, there is no way of stopping it from spreading. Thus the danger of a viral marketing campaign backfiring at the advertising company must not be underestimated. *Hotmail*, for example, included an e-mail footer with a Hotmail advertisement in each e-mail that was sent over a hotmail account. Recipients forwarding such an e-mail could easily modify this footer or add some other content such that the viral campaign would backfire for the initiating company.

11.4.2 The 'tipping point' concept

Malcolm Gladwell's concept of the 'tipping point'[8] builds on the idea of viral growth. Based on his observations in different industries and areas of life, Gladwell suggests that news or products sometimes spread at quite moderate rates and then at some point in time – the tipping point – start to spread epidemically. In one of the original examples used by Gladwell, he analysed the increase in sales of fax machines in the 1980s. Around 1986, there was a massive surge of sales that can be regarded as the tipping point. Tipping points in new technologies can often be attributed to *network (externality) effects* (see also Section 7.4.1).[9] These effects also exist in Web 2.0 applications as users benefit from other users joining the platform, for instance on business networking sites that can provide a vast network of skilled and specialised individuals. Gladwell identified three factors influencing viral spread: (1) the *law of the few*, (2) the *stickiness factor* and (3) the *power of context*.

The law of the few focuses on the *people* involved in spreading a message. It suggests that when seeding a message, one has to concentrate on three types of people: connectors, mavens and salesmen:

■ *Connectors* are people with an extraordinary high number of contacts, friends and acquaintances, who ideally belong to 'different worlds', i.e. different areas of life. Gladwell argued that almost everyone knows people who seem to be connected across social, geographic or organisational boundaries, and who have a very diverse circle of friends and acquaintances. Lars Hinrichs, for instance, started his social networking site openBC with only the help of his direct network of entrepreneurs and business professionals.

■ *Mavens* are people who have expertise in various products, prices or places. Furthermore, they enjoy sharing their knowledge with their friends and acquaintances and other users on Internet platforms. Due to their knowledge and their ability to connect, they also have the ability to start word-of-mouth epidemics. Numerous online platforms such as ciao.com, an online product evaluation forum, or trivago.com, a site where users exchange recommendations about travel destinations, restaurants, etc., leverage mavens to generate content and create traffic on their website.

■ *Salesmen* are people who have the skills to persuade others when they are unconvinced. Gladwell provided a typical example for this group of people using an extremely dedicated car dealer. On the Internet, 'salesmen' could be a dedicated corporate blogger such as the openBlog of openBC.

The stickiness factor deals with the *content* of the message that is to be spread. Gladwell postulated that in order to spread epidemically, the content has to be memorable enough to create change and move people to the action stage. Gladwell used the compelling example of the famous television show *Sesame Street*. By testing the single episodes uncountable times, while monitoring the children's attention, *Sesame Street* managed to increase its stickiness to almost hypnotic levels among its young target group. Viral marketing seems to have a great potential for stickiness, as content spread by peers is more memorable than content distributed by traditional marketing channels.

The power of context focuses on the conditions and circumstances under which epidemics can occur. It has two implications:

■ *Outer circumstances* have a significant impact on people's inner states. The immediate context of behaviour influences people's convictions and thoughts. Even very small changes in certain outer circumstances can cause a situation to tip, for example a small temperature change triggering a flu epidemic.

■ *Small sub-movements.* In order to create one contagious movement, many small movements have to be created first. In order to magnify the epidemic potential of a message or idea, groups must be close-knit, as in bigger groups people become strangers to each other and the group loses its tightness. An analogy could be a fire started by a number of small fires, maybe a bonfire that got out of control or a cigarette that was thrown away carelessly. If the small fires make their way through a wood, they can create a huge forest fire once they come together. This was the case in one of the biggest online viral spreads in the last years, the 'Coke/Menthos experiments'.[10]

11.4.3 The 'long tail' of Internet-based social networks

To illustrate the concept of the 'long tail', Anderson[11] initially compared online music retailers (such as Rhapsody) with traditional bricks-and-mortar retailers (such as Wal-Mart), just as we compare Internet-based networking (such as StayFriends.com or openBC) to traditional 'flesh-and-blood' networking.

Wal-Mart distributes through a large chain of physical stores the variety of physical goods it sells. However, it can only offer a predefined selection of products due to limitations in shelf space as well as the costs of producing (or sourcing), storing and delivering the goods. Therefore, Wal-Mart and other physical retailers are likely to offer only the 'hits' (i.e. in the case of music, the songs and albums which sell best and are most worthwhile providing), just as people in the case of networking will only keep in touch with others whom they consider to be the most 'valuable' contacts in one way or another.

In contrast to the above, digital content can be stored, replicated and distributed at much lower costs. Goods here include media-based products (such as music, photos and videos), or personal content (such as profiles, online group discussions and personal networks). At Rhapsody, an online music downloading service, 98% of all products sell, and the fact that they sell is reason enough for carrying them, especially since shelf space is not as restricted as it is in the real world. Since digital products can be offered at virtually no additional cost, it is a viable strategy for online retailers to 'sell less of more', i.e. to offer a large array of products including those that sell only in small quantities. Due to the fact that digital products bring no additional costs or complexity, they are worthwhile carrying. These niche products make up the 'long tail', as opposed to the hits that reflect the 'short head' offered by bricks-and-mortar retailers (see Exhibit 11.5).

Transferring the 'long tail' concept to the realm of Internet-based social networks helps us to understand more fully the above-mentioned benefits of networking sites. First, via traditional means of networking, individuals almost exclusively contact people they have

Exhibit 11.5 **The 'long tail' represents a large addition to the product range of traditional retailers**

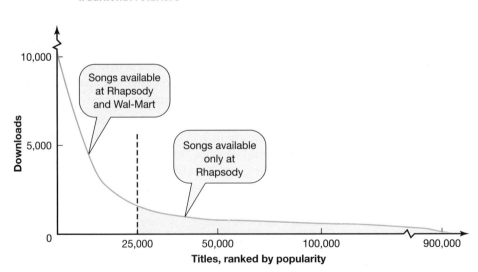

Source: Adapted from C. Anderson, *The Long Tail. How Endless Choice is Creating Unlimited Demand*, Random House, 2006.

personally known in the past. For the most part, this is the inner social circle of people that an individual has a strong relationship with, either in business or socially. However, via traditional networking, people usually do not have easy access to the contacts of their contacts. Yet, in many situations, such as advice seeking or job searches, we do not benefit so much from the people with whom we have strong social bonds, but we quite often benefit from people we do not know directly or only very superficially – our so-called *weak ties*.[12] By granting access to these weak ties, SNS offer a much larger pool of potentially interesting contacts than the traditional means of physical networking can typically provide.

Second, traditional networking allows individuals to stay in touch only with a limited number of people due to time restrictions. It requires simply too much effort to update permanently all contact data in a traditional address book or an Excel sheet, since contacts do not regularly inform the individual about changes in their contact data such as address, telephone number, job position or e-mail address. Hence, contact data is not always up to date and the individual might lose track of these people, even if he/she would, in theory, be willing to retain the contact. Relationships thus expire over time due to a lack of interaction. On SNS, however, terminating a relationship requires the user's active intervention; otherwise, a contact will be retained in a user's contact list. Thus, it becomes possible to manage a constantly growing number of contacts without any additional effort. Actively used SNS grant users access to valid contact data at all times, with the profiles acting as a *de facto* self-actualising address book.

The combination of the above two factors, i.e. the impact of weak ties and the improved contact management, creates a vast potential for online networking. We call this potential the '*long tail*' *of social networking* (see Exhibit 11.6).

The X-axis depicts the number of a user's contacts, ranked by networking intensity, while the networking intensity, depicted on the Y-axis, is a function of the contact frequency and the amount and type of information that is exchanged between individuals and their contacts. The 'long tail' curve reflects the fact that we tend to have a few people with whom we have very close relationships (the very top left of the graph), whereas there are a lot of people we know only superficially and contact only infrequently (on the lower right of the curve).

Exhibit 11.6 **The 'long tail' of social networking can give users access to previously inaccessible market niches**

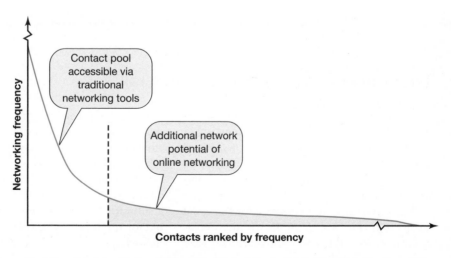

Source: Adapted from C. Anderson, *The Long Tail. How Endless Choice is Creating Unlimited Demand*, Random House, 2006.

In addition to facilitating communication between businesses and their customers, the Internet also facilitates communication between customers who are members of a virtual online community. For some firms, such as eBay and openBC, the communication that takes place among members of their online communities is much more important than the communication between the company and its customers.

The 'short head' on the left contains those contacts that are easily accessible via traditional networking. It consists of a limited number of contacts with which we have frequent contacts. After the 'short head', there is a cut-off point beyond which contacts either are inaccessible via traditional networking or have such a low contact intensity that the connection is not worthwhile maintaining and will therefore get diluted over time. Social networking sites offer the possibility to get to know more people and stay in touch with them, even if they are contacted only once a year or even less. SNS grant their users access to these contacts in the 'long tail'. Therefore, a cut-off point after the 'short head' as with traditional networking does not exist.

The 'long tail' concept has three main implications for companies that want to access and leverage the 'long tail' for their customers:

- *Lengthen the tail.* By giving people access to a large pool of individuals, SNS lengthen the tail of potential social contacts. In the same way, other services revolving around user-generated content provide their users with access to unique and individual content. In Second Life (see the case study in the second part of this book), users even generate virtual content that is actually traded and sold – for real money.

- *Fatten the tail.* SNS use a variety of mechanisms to enrich communication between users and thereby fatten the tail by increasing the frequency of interaction. Personal messages, guest books, 'poking' people virtually on Facebook or 'Twittering'[13] about the latest news are ways that increase the overall level of communication between users.

- *Drive demand down the tail.* This can be achieved by shifting users' attention to content that normally is not as easy to find. Amazon.com has done this for quite a while with its unique recommendation mechanism, but, today, services like YouTube do the same thing by constantly providing a given user with similar videos or more favourite videos that match his/her interest.

FT

Lulu aims to wag the Internet 'long tail'

The Curta calculator, a mechanical adding machine shaped like a coffee grinder, was made redundant in the 1970s when its electronic successor was popularised by Texas Instruments. Bob Young, who collects the antiquated devices, wants to wreak similar havoc in the book publishing industry today. Such chutzpah might be dismissed if Mr Young did not have form for successful, disruptive ideas. As co-founder of Red Hat, the open-source software company, Mr Young has built a formidable challenger to the dominance of Microsoft by helping rethink the industry's business model, making himself a billionaire in the process.

Back in the mid-1990s, Red Hat broke with the industry tradition – in which a tightly knit group of software developers produced tools that were sold for royalties – by allowing anybody to contribute to programming code. With Red Hat, now →

the biggest distributor of the landmark open-source operating system known as Linux, Mr Young has proved that money can be made from providing installation and support.

For his next business opportunity, Mr Young decided to 'solve a social problem' while also building a new company – rather than using the money earned at Red Hat to make a large purchase. 'I'm not Rupert Murdoch, so I'm not going to throw half a billion dollars at MySpace or whatever the next MySpace is. I'm an entrepreneur – so if I can find the next engineer building the next MySpace, I'd be happy to help.'

There is no guarantee, of course, that his latest venture, Lulu – a self-publishing outfit for books and films – will have the impact on dead trees and celluloid that Red Hat had on software. 'I have no idea what I'm doing,' says Mr Young. 'The guys running Google have no idea what they're going to do. We're making it up as we go along.'

Lulu.com, a self-publishing site, and Lulu.tv, a novel way of distributing revenues to film-makers, are the twin weapons in this. Both rely on the Internet's 'long tail' – the term describing its capacity to help niche products find an audience and make a profit. Authors write a description of their book, upload it, choose a binding, find a cover image and set the price. 'We make you the publisher so you don't have to go through Random House and get lots of rejection slips,' says Mr Young.

The revolution is not only Internet-driven; it relies on advances in printing technology too. New professional digital printers can cost as much as their traditional offset rivals, but there is little or no additional cost for printing different books. Until recently, volume has been essential to profitability; but on a digital printer 1,000 copies of 30 different books costs the same as 30,000 copies of a single book.

The Lulu top 10 bestseller list is an extraordinary collection ranging from Pay-Per-Click Search Engine Marketing Handbook at number one, through The Didymus Contingency, a super-natural thriller, to How to Become an Alpha Male, described as 'the lazy man's way to easy sex and romance with 20 or more women a month'.

Although Lulu was founded on the possibility of exploiting the 'long tail', Mr Young still had to learn that traditional marketing could sometimes be futile. Near the beginning of the project, which was launched three years ago, Mr Young saw that a serious-looking scientific title had been uploaded to Lulu. He contacted the author to ask if he wanted a big promotional slot on the site. 'The author said: "I should warn you that there's a worldwide market for my book of about 162 people and I know 148 of them",' says Mr Young. In traditional publishing, he contends, an academic imprint would have turned down the project or sought a high price from buyers for covering the costs of a short print run. 'At Reed Elsevier, they would have a price of $1,500 and you would have sold three,' says Mr Young.

With the self-publishing Internet model, this part of the 'long tail' can find its select band of readers, who pay a modest price – of which 20% goes to Lulu and 80% to the author. The motive for self-publishing is often to pass on specialist skills rather than make a quick buck. Mr Young says 'that a scientist-author, for example, makes money on the project – admittedly not a lot of money but he makes the world a better place'.

About 50 people are making a 'decent wage' from publishing through Lulu, according to the company; and Lulu itself is seeing moderate but fast-growing sales as it takes a slice from each book. It made revenues of $1m in 2004, $5m in 2005 and is forecasting $15m (£7.9m) for 2006. The model has been 'highly profitable' but most of the spare cash is ploughed back into Lulu and its associated projects. 'We'd be even more profitable if we stopped doing wild and crazy things,' says Mr Young.

Mr Young is in London to spread the message about one of these: Lulu.tv, the next step in his self-publishing vehicle's evolution and the latest attempt to profit from the Internet's 'long tail'. Constantly smiling, wiry and nervously energetic, the 52-year-old entrepreneur is evangelical about this latest assault on the media world.

Video-makers pay $14.95 a month. Eighty per cent of the fees are put into a pot and this money is divided according to which videos attract the most viewers. Mr Young says the competition here is coming not just from the traditional media companies – although they are hungrily acquiring new media assets as their audience fragments – but from the new breed of online video companies →

225

such as YouTube and Google Video. 'They're doing a good job as channels but a less good job in funnelling back money to the creators,' says Mr Young.

In contrast to Lulu the publishing vehicle, Lulu.tv is 'embryonic', Mr Young admits. Its business model is not as developed as the 'dead-tree' side and, while publishers have been shaken by the digitisation of their medium, video has quickly attracted the biggest Internet companies, including Google and traditional giants such as Viacom. Mr Young is not alone in seeking profits from the 'long tail'. But given his record, he stands more chance of finding the right business model than being left with the latter-day equivalent of the Curta calculator.

The world of open-source software was once anathema to US software giants such as Microsoft and Oracle. Its emphasis on sharing intellectual property went against the grain of established companies that spent time and money safeguarding their products' secrets. But Bob Young, who co-founded Red Hat, the open-source software company, is no anarchist. His hero is Adam Smith. 'If the citizen and the consumer are the same thing in a free-market economy, the bigger the social problem you can solve, the bigger the business opportunity must be,' he says.

Coming out of Red Hat in 2002 and searching for the 'social problem' on which to base his next venture, he was struck by the controversy shaking the music industry over file-sharing on websites such as Napster. 'We were watching the music industry suing their customers because they didn't understand [the phenomenon],' he says. 'It wasn't about price. The music industry wanted you to get into your car, drive across town to the music store, pay $20 for a CD with 19 songs you didn't really want, drive back home and somehow get the music on to your computer to listen to it. It took Steve Jobs, a computer geek [and CEO of Apple Computer], to see this problem and come up with the solution [the iTunes online music store and iPod music player].'

He has a personal motivation, too, for setting up Lulu, his self-publishing venture. In 1999 he published Under the Radar, his account of the rise of Red Hat. Mr Young was upset about the quality of printing in the book, the meagre royalty payment he collected and the fact that several thousand unsold copies of the book were due to be pulped. He demanded they be sent to him and had them converted into furniture.

Source: T. Braithwaite, 'Lulu aims to wag the Internet "long tail"', FT.com, 24 August 2006.

CRITICAL PERSPECTIVE 11.2

Is there unlimited choice and does it create unlimited demand?

While Chris Anderson finds good examples in electronic retailing, empirical evidence has yet to be produced. Even before publishing his book, Anderson was criticised for his blunt and straightforward statements in several articles in *WIRED* magazine that seemed to turn retailing upside down. However, this is maybe not the case.

Wall Street Journal's Steve Gomes straight-out contradicts Anderson's findings: he claims figures published by Rhapsody contradict the statement that '98% of all products sell'; the no-play rate, meaning songs offered on the website that are not downloaded at all, is more like 22%. Closely related to that is Anderson's statement of 'misses outselling hits', meaning the traditional 80/20 rule of making 80% of revenues from 20% of the products offered, the 'hits'. Gomes again contradicts using Rhapsody data showing that the top 10% of all songs roughly get more than 80% of all streams.

Shortly after the first wave of comments on his findings, Anderson had to step back from his initial claims and rephrased some of them for the book published in 2006. And still a lively discussion is spreading throughout the blogosphere about the validity of his claims.

While the potential of the web, especially considering new developments towards 'Web 2.0', to offer far more choice, e.g. by letting users generate content, certainly exists, the actual question is how this potential can be monetised. It seems that hits still do account for the largest amount of retailers' revenues, and it is doubtful whether that will change any time soon.

SUMMARY

- This chapter provided an overview of Web 2.0. It explained how advances in network infrastructure and software development led to an increased number of web users and a richer user experience. Furthermore, the chapter depicted the Web 2.0 service variety and showed how it enables better networking and sharing of information and content among peers.

- Social networking sites (SNS) allow their members to manage more contacts more efficiently than is possible offline; therefore, they increase personal contact reach. In addition, users have more information about their contacts or potential contacts due to visible virtual profiles; therefore, SNS increase personal information richness.

- Through the mass customisation approach, manufacturers or service providers try to elicit customer preferences and then tailor the product or service to their client's liking.

- Businesses that want to benefit from 'viral growth' need to provide incentives for users to invite others to join the service. These incentives can be intrinsic when users know that inviting others to join the platform will ultimately enrich their own experience.

- Viral marketing is a tool that has a strong potential for building brand awareness. Therefore, finding a way (e.g. Gladwell's 'tipping point') of controlling viral growth is essential for companies.

- By giving members access to a large pool of other individuals, SNS lengthen the 'long tail' of potential social contacts. They further use a variety of mechanisms to enrich users' communications, thereby fattening the tail by increasing the frequency of inter-actions. Driving demand down the tail can be achieved by shifting users' attention to content that normally is not as easy to find.

REVIEW QUESTIONS

1 Several new business models have been suggested for 'Web 2.0'. Try to position them within the reach versus richness framework (shown in Exhibit 11.2).

2 Review users' motivations for joining Internet-based social networks and for each one of these motivations provide an example of real-world social interactions.

3 Explain how Anderson's 'long tail' concept can be applied to Internet-based social networks. What are the main similarities and differences between the application of this concept to SNS and to traditional networking?

4 Suggest at least two examples of people you know for each one of the categories proposed in the law of the few by Gladwell's 'tipping point'.

DISCUSSION QUESTIONS

1 Assess the following statement: 'Unlimited choice creates unlimited demand.'

2 Chart the value chain of an Internet-based mass customisation service. (To answer this question, you may want to refer to the value chain model shown in Exhibit 11.4.)

3 Can you think of products that do not have the potential of spreading virally through the Internet? For services that have such a potential, is it worth giving up control of the spread of the message about them?

4 Make a critical assessment of the following statement: 'The application of Anderson's "long tail" concept leads to an unlimited choice and creates an unlimited demand.' Try to illustrate your answer with some actual examples.

RECOMMENDED KEY READING

■ See M. M. Tseng and F. T. Piller, *The Customer-Centric Enterprise: Advances in Mass-Customization and Personalization*, Springer, 2005, for an in-depth look at mass customisation.

■ More practical examples of the 'long tail' concept can be found in C. Anderson, *The Long Tail – How Endless Choice Is Creating Unlimited Demand*, Random House Business Books, 2006.

■ M. Gladwell's *Tipping Point*, Abacus, 2001, provides further vivid examples of how information can spread virally.

USEFUL THIRD-PARTY WEBLINKS

■ http://radar.oreilly.com is a widely recognised blog from the US media company O'Reilly Media who started the first conferences under the label Web 2.0.

■ http://www.web20workgroup.com is a network of premium blogs on new-generation web services.

■ http://mashable.com is a blog dedicated to social networking sites.

■ http://venturebeat.com presents news about new Web 2.0 ventures and their funding.

■ http://www.virales-marketing.net is a blog on viral marketing campaigns, videos, etc.

NOTES AND REFERENCES

1 We greatly appreciate the assistance of Sebastian Mauch and Matthias Promny (former Masters students at the University of Nuremberg) in preparing this chapter.

2 The term Web 2.0 originated from a series of conferences about new web technologies of the same title. These conferences were initiated by Tim O'Reilly, an internationally renowned expert on the Internet and open source technologies.

3　Tim O'Reilly, 'Web 2.0 compact definition: trying again', O'Reilly Radar, http://radar.oreilly. com/archives/2006/12/web_20_compact.html.

4　Voice over Internet Protocol (VoIP) is the routing of voice conversations over the Internet or through any other IP-based network.

5　Blogosphere is the collective term encompassing all blogs as a community or social network. Many weblogs are densely interconnected, and have grown their own culture. Technorati: http://www.technorati.com.

6　P. Evans and T. Wurster developed the richness and reach concept in their book *Blown to Bits*, Harvard Business School Press, 1999, pp. 23–38.

7　http://mongolianshoebbq.puma.com/.

8　M. Gladwell, *The Tipping Point*, Abacus, 2000.

9　Network effects exist whenever a service has a value to a potential customer which depends on the number of other customers who are already using the same service.

10　A YouTube video showing a drastic explosion-like reaction when dropping a Menthos, a type of candy, into a bottle of Coke fuelled a huge chain reaction of imitators.

11　C. Anderson, *The Long Tail. How Endless Choice is Creating Unlimited Demand*, Random House Business Books, 2006.

12　M. Granovetter, 'The strength of weak ties', *American Journal of Sociology*, 1973, Vol. 6, pp.1360–1380.

13　See http://www.twitter.com. The service provides users with the possibility of reaching out to a large number of people by sending frequent updates about themselves free of charge. The hype around twitter has resulted in a whole variety of mash-ups and applications for the service.

CHAPTER 12

Moving from wired e-commerce to mobile e-commerce

Chapter at a glance

Related case studies

Case study	Primary focus of the case study
18 YOCAG	Mobile marketing
19 paybox.net	Mobile payment solutions
17 NTT DoCoMo	Mobile technologies and services
16 Sony BMG	Mobile music

Learning outcomes

After completing the chapter, you should be able to:

- Define mobile e-commerce and outline the key components of the mobile value network.

- Recognise mobile e-commerce applications and be able to categorise them.

- Depict the advantages of mobile e-commerce over wired e-commerce.

- Understand how wireless technologies affect the value chain and influence the industry's five forces.

INTRODUCTION

The first part of this chapter provides an overview of mobile e-commerce. It highlights (1) wireless technology providers, (2) mobile e-commerce applications and services, and (3) their most salient benefits compared with wired e-commerce. The second part of the chapter discusses how wireless technologies influence Porter's value chain and the industry's five forces. It also provides some illustrative examples drawn from different industries.

12.1 Mobility and unwired e-commerce

Mobile e-commerce, or m-commerce, is a subset of electronic commerce. While traditional e-commerce refers to transactions conducted via fixed or wired Internet terminals, m-commerce refers to e-commerce transactions via mobile or wireless terminals.[1] The Internet, for instance, was at the beginning fixed to a wired location. Mobile access to the Internet, however, allows users to become time and location independent and, therefore, broadens traditional e-commerce characteristics. Furthermore, Internet-enabled mobile devices enable users not only to make voice calls and use messaging functions, but also to make it possible to access databases, retrieve information, download content and carry out transactions.

12.1.1 Understanding the value network of mobile e-commerce

The mobile e-commerce value network[2] comprises different players which interact and collaborate within the industry. These players are mobile technology providers such as mobile vendors for infrastructure and devices, wireless network operators, IT enablers, application and content providers, as well as portal providers. The m-commerce value network (see Exhibit 12.1) outlines the multi-faceted role of these players. Based on their business focus, the latter offer different kinds of mobile e-commerce services and can be assigned to the application, technology or service area:

■ *Mobile network operators (MNOs)* are the industries' linchpin. Their close contact with customers positions them at the centre of the network and gives them a dominant service role. Since MNOs carry out payment and billing activities they enjoy a loyal and trustworthy relationship with their customers. Furthermore, since MNOs have access to their clients' data (such as geographical location or Internet behaviour), they enjoy a unique and privileged position within the network.

MNOs differ in their service offerings. While offering a wireless network with an Internet gateway implies a low degree of involvement in the mobile value network, providing an additional mobile portal or further access to applications and services increases an operator's involvement. T-Mobile, for instance, not only offers customers voice calls, but also promotes its mobile portal T-Zones through which it sells content ranging from ringtones and videos to games.

Exhibit 12.1 The mobile e-commerce value network outlines the key players

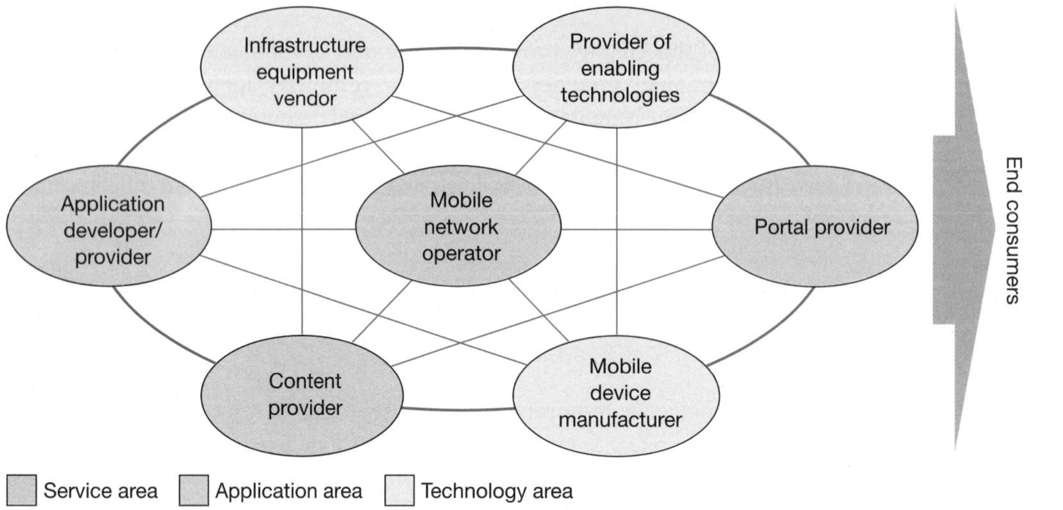

Source: Adapted from F. Müller-Veerse *et al.*, *UMTS report – An investment perspective*, Durlacher Research, 2001, p. 23. Reprinted by permission of Panmure Gordon & Co.

Mobile virtual network operators (MVNOs), such as Virgin Mobile, are a variation of traditional MNOs. They become part of the value network by buying bandwidth from traditional operators for resale to their own customers. MVNOs have their own market presence and a billing relationship with end users and, therefore, share similar characteristics to traditional MNOs. Furthermore, MVNOs sometimes bundle their services with other offerings, such as mobile music (as featured in the Sony BMG case study included in this book), in order to establish a deeper relationship with their end consumers.

■ *Mobile device manufacturers* play another crucial role within the industry. They not only determine the design and functionality of mobile phones, but also set the communication standards and take care of the pre-installation of browser, operating system and other applications. Furthermore, device manufacturers have a close relationship with end consumers and therefore play a key role in influencing m-commerce developments.

The competition in the hand-held industry is fierce, since product cycles have become shorter and profitability margins thinner. Mobile device manufacturers have seen their market share erode, thus having to extend their business by developing additional activities. Motorola, for instance, also acts as an infrastructure equipment vendor, while Nokia offers a variety of applications to mobile portals. Data-ready mobile phones, personal digital assistants (PDAs), music players and similar wireless handsets are converging, thus increasing the functionality of the hand-held device and therefore affecting consumer electronic providers and other industries.

■ *IT enablers* provide operating systems, micro-browsers, databases and other middleware technologies. These enabling technologies determine a user's mobile experience in terms of usability. Companies such as Microsoft, Symbian, Nokia or Sun Microsystems generate revenues from licensing, leasing, consulting and/or maintenance fees. YOC, a mobile marketing service provider from Berlin (Germany), featured in the case studies section of this book, covers activities ranging from the design of mobile marketing campaigns to the provision of content and applications, and also acts as an enabler in the mobile marketing space. YOC can thus guarantee a fit between single activities and make users' mobile experience as seamless as possible.

■ *Infrastructure equipment vendors* provide the technical backbone of mobile communication networks comprising access points and broadcasting towers. The design and implementation of mobile networks is simpler and more cost efficient than that of fixed-line networks. Developing countries rely heavily on wireless technology, especially in regions with poor fixed-line telecommunication infrastructure. Furthermore, since mobile networks can reach out to users with limited resources, they cover a broader consumer base than fixed mobile networks.

■ *Portal providers* bundle on the starting page customer's preferred services and applications. Horizontal portal providers cover a broad spectrum of topics, while vertical portals focus on a single subject area and provide in-depth information. Portal providers generate revenues through monthly subscription fees, traffic-based revenue-sharing arrangements with mobile telecom operators, commissions on transactions, advertising, and so forth.[3] Mobile network operators (such as T-Mobile), mobile device manufacturers (such as Nokia) and portals from the wired web (such as Yahoo!) are trying to play an important role in this segment.

■ *Application and content providers* often co-operate with portal providers in order to gain access to customers and make their products (such as news, shopping and games) available to their target audience. Widsets.com, for instance, provides users with a wireless application that allows customised access to a variety of content items through RSS feeds.

12.1.2 Segmenting mobile e-commerce consumers and business services

Hand-held devices allow for a wide range of wireless applications and services to be deployed in either consumer or business markets. Depending on the context, these applications and services can help to improve lifestyle on a personal level or productivity on a business level. Basic uses of the mobile phone include the following voice, Internet and messaging functions:

■ *Voice*. In addition to basic telephony functions, data-ready mobile phones allow for richer voice applications. Rich voice services use the data connection of a device to offer advanced call capabilities. Compared with traditional mobile voice calls, VoIP (Voice over Internet Protocol) calls are cheaper and can enrich a user's call experience through video support. In a business context, VoIP allows for substantial cost savings and enables a company to maintain voice, image and text contact with its field staff, thus boosting productivity.

■ *Internet*. Connectivity to the Internet allows users to access e-mail accounts and is expected to become a major driver of the 'fixed-mobile convergence'. It is anticipated that voice as well as Internet traffic will soon shift from wired to mobile networks and will not only provide wireless Internet access to users in consumer markets, but also offer Internet, intranet and extranet access to business clients. In communication-intensive industries (such as finance, transportation, insurance, public safety or health care), mobile access to desktop applications such as e-mail, contact lists or spreadsheets will be increasingly crucial. Furthermore, there is a variety of Java applications, for instance, which allow users to download, view, edit or send a variety of content through a hand-held device.

■ *Messaging.* Mobile messaging services are dominated by SMS and MMS, and are widely used among young people for asynchronous conversation through text or multimedia messages. Since blogging has gained importance on the Internet, the interest in other people's lives and the wish to share one's own life is addressed by services like MySpace.com or Facebook. Twitter takes this phenomenon mobile and implements it through group SMS. Twitterers define their friends online (through the twitter.com website) and provide their mobile phone number. Then users send a text message to Twitter answering the question: What are you doing? Twitter then resends this text message to all defined friends and posts the update on a user's web profile page.

Similar to the idea behind Twitter, mobile messaging can also be used for *notification-based solutions.* That way, real-time sports results or real-time information for decision making can be delivered to users independent of time and location. Location-based services (LBS) include location-sensitive information in their service. In the business context, this can be of tremendous importance for emergency services. It has also implications for fleet management and the tracking of vehicles or remote mobile workforce management. In consumer markets, localised content such as weather, news, hotels, restaurants, traffic and travel information and navigation prevail.

m-Commerce consumer services

The following segmentation focuses on m-commerce consumer services. Consumer services can be categorised into (1) information, (2) communication, (3) transaction and (4) entertainment services (see Exhibit 12.2):

■ *Mobile information* comprises news, weather or other information. Many newspapers have embraced the Internet and started developing applications that make content available through mobile phones. Bild.de, the biggest German tabloid newspaper, for instance, is accessible through a WAP portal developed by YOC.

Exhibit 12.2 **m-Commerce consumer services and applications**

Information	Communication
• News	• m-Advertising
• Weather	• m-Health
• Catalogues	• SMS/MMS
• ...	• ...
Transaction	**Entertainment**
• m-Banking	• m-Games
• m-Tailing	• m-Gambling
• m-Payment	• m-Music
• ...	• ...

Source: Adapted from F. Müller-Veerse *et al.*, *UMTS report – An investment perspective*, Durlacher Research, 2001, p. 80. Reprinted by permission of Panmure Gordon & Co.

■ *Mobile communication* includes services that allow users to communicate with each other or with remote systems. Mobile marketing, for instance, is still highly dominated by SMS and used as a means of prompting consumers to a point of sale or to some desired action. In push campaigns, marketing services are delivered directly to the user on the mobile device through a text message. In response-oriented mobile marketing campaigns or pull campaigns, it is the user who initiates the communication by sending in a promotional code that is, for example, found on a bottle or seen on TV.

■ *Mobile entertainment* refers to downloading ringtones, games, music or videos and trivia through wireless technologies. Companies such as Jamba sell all kinds of content to mostly younger users, generating massive revenues. In Japan, mobile entertainment has even become a cultural phenomenon for the millions of commuters who daily spend a lot of time on trains.

■ *Mobile transactions* allow users to conduct various transactions over the mobile phone. Mobile e-banking applications give users access to their bank statements or account balance and allow them to pay bills or transfer funds. Users also receive alerts, for example, in case a payment is due or the account balance has fallen below a specified amount. There are also mobile e-shopping and mobile e-payment services such as paybox.net (which is featured in the case studies section of this book), which allow users to make ticket reservations, for instance, or take part in auctions (as in the case of eBay). NTT DoCoMo even developed specific mobile phones that let users store credit card information for mobile payments at convenience stores.

m-Commerce business services

Business services can be categorised into mobile supply chain management (M-SCM), mobile customer relationship management (M-CRM) and mobile workforce services and applications (see Exhibit 12.3):

■ *Mobile supply chain management services and applications* aim at enhancing the performance of activities along the supply chain and facilitate collaboration with partners, since information sharing can be conducted in real time. Mobile inventory applications alert suppliers, for instance, if a given stock of products or materials has

Exhibit 12.3 m-Commerce business services and applications

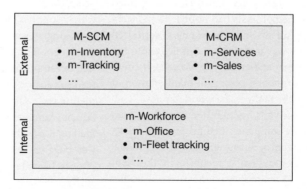

Source: Adapted from F. Müller-Veerse *et al.*, *UMTS report – An investment perspective*, Durlacher Research, 2001, p. 80. Reprinted by permission of Panmure Gordon & Co.

fallen below a predetermined level (push approach), but also allow for remotely checking the availability of items in warehouses and reordering in case of unavailability (pull approach).

■ *Mobile customer relationship management services and applications* enhance interactions with customers before, during or after sale by gathering data about customer preferences, purchased products and required maintenance. Access to this data enhances a sales agent's productivity and allows for an effective response to customer demands. Therefore, these services help to increase customer satisfaction and company's revenues.

■ *Mobile workforce services and applications* support field staff and other employees working on client sites. Hand-held devices give sales teams or managers on the move secure wireless access to corporate LANs and VPNs and to their offices, or help track vehicles and dispatch them to new locations.

FT

Barcode hope for mobile advertising

Readers of some French magazines were greeted late last year with an unusual invitation in an advertisement for the Audi Q7. They were asked to point the cameras in their mobile phones at a special code in the advertisements. That would connect them automatically to a website that streamed video of the vehicle in action. It only worked, though, if they first downloaded an extra piece of software to their handsets.

That is a big 'if'. The potential for turning mobile phones into devices capable of 'reading' information in the physical world and connecting it back to the Internet has been a dream of the mobile communications industry for years. Like many of the other visions of how the 'mobile Internet' would take shape, however, it has yielded far less than the optimists had hoped. To judge by the Audi experiments and others, a more concerted effort is under way to get this technology into the hands of a bigger audience. If it succeeds, it could turn out to be the first successful manifestation of advertising in the mobile data world.

For now, such ads have limited appeal, as even the technology companies behind them concede. Christian Steinborn, European head of NeoMedia, the US technology group involved in the Audi experiment, says few mobile phone users will bother to download the software needed to read so-called

'2D barcodes', which are versions of the more familiar Universal Product Codes capable of being 'read' more easily by a camera phone. That has not stopped other advertisers, consumer product companies and publishers rushing to experiment with the technology. Prompting this latest burst of interest have been the first signs from Japan and South Korea of widespread consumer interest in the technology, according to technology and marketing professionals. For instance, News of the World, a UK Sunday newspaper owned by News Corp, is considering printing 2D barcodes with its sports reports so that readers can link to highlights of football games.

The codes could also soon appear on consumer products after a decision last month by DuPont, which supplies bottles, cans and other types of packaging, to start offering to print the codes for its customers. The potential of 2D barcodes extends well beyond their uses in marketing and the offline media industry. 'Navigating the web on a phone is a nightmare,' says Jonathan Bulkeley, head of Scanbuy, another specialist technology company. By making it possible for mobile users to connect to a web page with a simple 'point and click' of their phones, barcodes could take the pain out of mobile surfing, he says. That, in turn, could create a new layer of linkages between the physical and electronic worlds, says Chas Fritz, head of NeoMedia. Imagine if a unique barcode were printed on every physical object: you could point your camera phone and find out everything you wanted to know about it. Such uses might eventually turn 2D barcodes into the hyperlinks of the physical world, as common and easy to navigate as the links that let users follow links easily around the Internet.

That hope was the impetus behind the Mobile Codes Consortium, an initiative just launched by Hewlett-Packard, Publicis, the marketing services company, and NeoMedia to push for greater technology standardisation in this area. While publishers and marketers are starting their own experiments with the use of 2D barcodes, widespread adoption is likely to depend on organisations that have the power to put the technology into millions of consumers' hands: mobile network operators and handset makers. DoCoMo's support of the idea was central to its adoption in Japan, according to technology executives. And Nokia has started to pre-load software capable of reading 2D barcodes in some handsets.

Eventually, mobile operators could come to see barcode-driven advertising as a significant source of revenue, Mr Bulkeley says. A former head of AOL in the UK, he compares the mobile companies to the early Internet service providers, with their total reliance on monthly subscription income. Eventually, with the emergence of advertising, the subscription business died away. If that comparison holds, the mobile industry will have incentives to promote mobile barcodes, potentially putting the technology into the hands of anyone with a camera phone. Tomorrow just arrived and it is about time.

Source: R. Waters, 'Barcode hope for mobile advertising', *Financial Times*, 5 March 2007.

12.1.3 Comparison of mobile e-commerce and wired e-commerce

Compared with wired e-commerce, mobile e-commerce has unique value-adding attributes. When formulating a new business strategy, managers need to be aware of these attributes and leverage them service-wise. These unique value-adding attributes are (1) ubiquity, (2) convenience, (3) localisation and (4) personalisation. They are now discussed in more detail:

■ *Ubiquity* is the most decisive characteristic of mobile e-commerce applications. It means that users are able to use their device at any time and in any location whether to obtain information or perform a transaction. Ubiquity increases the immediacy of communication and is equally valued in consumer and business markets.

■ *Convenience* is high, since the functionality and usability of wireless devices have increased. Mobile content is inferior to other media in terms of screen size and downloading speed. However, it is superior to other media in terms of convenience and ease of use. Mobile e-commerce is comparable with a convenience store where customers buy daily but in small quantity, whereas wired e-commerce can be compared with a hypermarket where customers spend a lot of money but only occasionally.[4]

■ *Localisation* of devices and their users is based on the portability of wireless devices and knowledge about a person's location. It enables location-based services which provide their users with location-specific information.

■ The degree of *personalisation* in mobile e-commerce is higher than in wired e-commerce. When calling a mobile phone, users call the number of a person and not the number of a location as in the case of a fixed-line phone. Furthermore, as demonstrated by Apple's iPhone, the mobile phone is increasingly integrating different multimedia functions and reflecting the user's lifestyle dimension. However, although it is more challenging to optimise content for the handset's small screen size than for the wired PC, the iPhone is a glimpse into the future of converging consumer electronics.

Mobility in general allows for more flexible and efficient communication; it also enables users to socialise with their peers and friends. Informative and/or entertaining content can be targeted much more to the user's needs and made more personal by tracking the user's wireless transactions and by drawing implications from these. User-related information can be used to tailor specific products for consumers in ways that were not feasible with traditional e-commerce. However, there are also disadvantages including (1) privacy and security and (2) device and network limitations, such as screen and keyboard size as well as connectivity and transmission speed:

- *Privacy and security* are decisive prerequisites for all wireless transactions. Users are likely to insist on having privacy and security safeguards. They also need to be in control of their data, especially if it contains information about their geographical location.

- *Device and network limitations.* Due to slow transfer rates and limited connectivity, a user's wireless Internet experience can be very restricted. When this is added to the small screen and tiny keyboard of the handset, users are still often reluctant to try out the emerging wireless services. However, as technology advances, these problems are likely to be overcome in the near future.

12.2 Strategy and mobility

Although the wired Internet enables users to access information from any computer around the globe, it is tied to a physical location. Wireless technologies, however, make users independent of place and time. They may be used strategically in most industries, especially those that are information and communication intensive. Being able to incorporate wireless technologies into business operations could result in a first-mover advantage. What makes companies successful, however, is the translation of a first-mover advantage into a sustainable competitive edge. It is important not only to align IT with strategy, but also to align mobility with strategy in order to make a company more efficient, attract new customers with a differentiated product or service, and ultimately outperform competitors. In the sequel, we shall (1) discuss how to achieve a competitive advantage through wireless technologies, (2) examine how these technologies affect a company's value chain, and (3) analyse how they influence the five forces of the industry.

12.2.1 Leveraging wireless technologies to create a competitive advantage

Mobility benefits mainly those organisations that manage to integrate wireless technologies seamlessly into their business processes. By improving the linkages between their human resources and business processes, companies can substantially improve their overall performance. Wireless technologies strengthen these linkages by making information available where and when users need it.

As seen in Chapter 8, the creation of economic value depends on the gap between perceived use value and costs. Wireless technologies can increase use value and decrease costs and, therefore, increase a firm's operational effectiveness. Each (primary) activity of the value chain contributes to the aggregate use value as perceived by customers. A more effective mobile workforce, for instance, increases productivity and allows a company to decrease its overhead costs or increase the perceived use value. In the next section, the concept of the value chain will be analysed in the context of mobility.

The goal of every firm is to outperform its competitors and eventually achieve above-average returns. Long-term strategic positioning means that a company is able to outperform competitors by offering customers a better price/performance ratio than competitors. While economic value depends on a customer's willingness to pay a price for a product that is higher than its production costs, strategic positioning depends on industry forces and the profitability of the average competitor within the industry. The five forces model presented in Section 12.2.3 shows how mobility can affect industries.

12.2.2 Impact of wireless technologies on a company's value chain

Companies perform value-creating activities, which are interdependent with activities of suppliers or customers. *Porter's value chain* provides a framework for identifying all these activities and analysing how they affect a company's relative cost position and the value delivered to customers. IT is relevant to all the primary and support activities of the value chain, since every activity involves the creation, processing and communication of information. (For a detailed discussion of how the wired Internet impacts on a company's value chain, see Chapter 4.)

Wireless technologies help to create new kinds of activities or enable streamlining of existing activities. They influence the design, production, marketing, sales and support of products, services and processes (see Exhibit 12.4).

Support activities can be generically categorised into a firm's infrastructure, human resources management, technology development and procurement:

- *The firm's infrastructure* supports all the company's activities. Moving from physical (paper-based) activities to digital applications that can be remotely accessed through wireless devices allows a company to reduce its data collection time and operational costs while improving its responsiveness to customers and its overall service level. Salespeople in the field, for instance, can access through hand-held devices corporate databases (such as phone directories), and marketers can receive customer feedback in real time or supervise a delivery status.

- Mobile technologies can also affect *human resources'* activities such as recruiting, training, developing and rewarding staff members. Wireless access in the field to a company's knowledge base, for instance, enables employees to keep in touch with their colleagues (whether in the office or on the move) and also to foster their productivity.

- Through wireless devices, a company's *technology development* can improve products, services and processes. It is important to note here that mobile business professionals often seek better on-the-move work tools and practices, while IT managers want to have reliable and secure IT systems and applications. In order to reconcile both dimensions, issues of interoperability, usability, security and privacy need to be addressed early enough in the technology development process.

- *The procurement* of raw materials and other inputs can be improved through wireless technologies. For example, the use of radio-frequency identification (RFID) enables

Exhibit 12.4 Impact of wireless technologies on the value chain

Firm infrastructure
- Mobile financial and ERP systems, incl. legal and government information
- Mobile investor relations (e.g. information dissemination, broadcast conference calls, alerts)
- Voice-to-data conversions: mobile forms-based applications, multimedia cellular and wireless broadcast
- Mobile services: rich vioce (image, video), Internet (intra-extranet), messaging (SMS, MMS, LBS) and content
- Mobile access to e-mails, personal information management

Human resource management
- Mobile activities in recruiting, hiring, training, development and compensation
- Mobile self-service personnel and benefits administration, incl. mobile time and expense reporting
- Mobile sharing and dissemination of company information
- Mobile services via HRM: voice guidance, messaging (SMS, MMS, LBS push or pull), internet and infotainment

Technology development
- Mobile teams, distributed collaborative product design across locations and among multiple value-system participants
- Knowledge directories accessible from any location
- Real-time access by R&D to mobile sales and service information

Procurement
- Mobile demand planning and fulfilment
- Other mobile linkage of purchase, inventory and forecasting systems with suppliers and/or buyers
- Mobile direct and indirect procurement via marketplaces, exchanges, auctions and buyer/seller matching

Inbound logistics	Operations	Outbound logistics	Marketing and sales	After-sales service
Mobile activities in receiving, storing and disseminating inputs to products/services	Mobile activities associated with transforming inputs into final products/services	Mobile activities associated with collecting, storing and distributing products/services to buyers	Mobile activities with means for buyers to purchase products/services and inducing them to do so, incl. advertising, promotion, sales force, channels, pricing	Mobile activities associated with providing service to enhance or maintain the value of products/services
• Mobile scheduling, shipping, warehouse/ demand management and planning and scheduling across the company and its suppliers • Mobile distribution across the company of real-time inbound and in-progress inventory data	• Mobile information exchange, scheduling and decision making in in-house plants, contract assemblers and components suppliers • Mobile available-to-promise information to sales force and channels	• Mobile order processing and scheduling • Mobile delivery vehicle operation • Mobile forms of customer-tailored agreements and contracts • Mobile customer/channel access to product development and distribution status • Mobile channel management, incl. information exchange, warranty claims, contract management (versioning, process control)	• Mobile sales channels, e.g. websites, marketplaces • Mobile access to customer information, product catalogues, dynamic pricing, inventory, quotes, order entry • Mobile product/service configurators • Mobile push/pull advertising • Mobile customer feedback, incl. mobile surveys, opt-in/ opt-out marketing and promotion response tracking	• Mobile support of customer service reps (incl. voice guidance, SMS, MMS, LBS, e-mail, billing, co-browse, chat, VoIP, video streaming) • Mobile customer self-service via portals and mobile service request processing, incl. updates, alerts and notifications to billing, shipping, etc. • Mobile field service access to customer account review, availability and ordering, work-order updates, service parts

← Mobile supply chain management →   ← Mobile customer relationship management →

Source: The mobile revolution: The making of mobile services worldwide, D. Steinbock, Kogan Page. 2005, p. 260.

better real-time tracking of goods and inventory items. RFID tags can be automatically read from remote locations and therefore do not need to be held near a reader (or a scanner) as is the case with barcode-based tags.

Wireless technologies can also affect a company's primary value chain activities such as inbound logistics, operations, marketing and sales, as well as after-sales service:

■ Through wireless technologies, a company can foster its *inbound logistics* by receiving, storing and disseminating inputs to products and services. For example, in the context of user-generated content whereby users are an active part of the value chain, mobile technologies can become a valuable input medium. For instance, the German tabloid newspaper *Bild* encourages readers to send in pictures of events or celebrities through MMS. Thus the reader is turned into a newspaper affiliate, encouraged to contribute content to the latest edition.

■ *Operations.* Especially in industries where information is a crucial part of the product, wireless technologies can add to a customer's perceived use value. For example, directory services (such as the German '11833') provide callers with phone numbers and address information. In addition to announcing over the phone the result of the customer query, '11833' offers callers the option of receiving an SMS containing the requested information. By doing so, '11833' better supports the caller (who may or may not have readily available writing materials) and improves its overall customer service.

■ *Outbound logistics* refer to wireless activities which are associated with collecting, storing and distributing products or services to customers. Mobile music providers (such as Jamba) enable users to access content instantly while on the move. Also wireless portals (such as Yahoo! mobile) deliver to consumers, through mobile applications, various types of information.

■ *Marketing and sales.* Mobile marketing approaches (described in the YOC case study included in the latter part of this book) enable companies to enhance brand or product awareness, lead consumers to the point of sale, generate dialogue with marketing contacts, increase sales or support customer loyalty programmes. Coca-Cola, for instance, uses on-pack promotions in order to entice consumers at the point of sale to buy a Coke. Handsets and other hand-held devices also allow companies to offer a high level of personalisation and the possibility of treating each customer as a segment of one (see the FT article: 'Mobile marketing: The most personal way to reach out').

■ *Service.* As customers become increasingly mobile, companies need to extend their reach to these customers by offering support services through wireless channels. By doing so, they can respond to customer needs faster than ever before. For example, airlines (such as Lufthansa) allow passengers to make or confirm a seat reservation through an SMS, thus helping customers to save time.

Mobile marketing: The most personal way to reach out

It is so intimate that it is dangerous; but exciting. Mobile marketing offers an unmatched channel for one-to-one relationship building, though poor campaigns can burn a brand in seconds. Mobile marketers use text messages (SMS) and multi-media messages (MMS) to reach consumers on one of the most personal devices people possess, their mobile phones. Some foolish marketers are attracted by the low-cost opportunity to spam millions in seconds. But more rational minds use targeted campaigns that encourage consumers to initiate a relationship, building trust and tying them into a community.

The main attraction of mobile marketing is that, unlike direct mail or e-mail, people tend to read the message. Ben King, marketing manager of WIN, a mobile messaging service provider, claims that 94% of text messages get read, usually within an hour of receipt. Response rates for well-designed mobile marketing campaigns can easily reach 25%, says Tim Dunn, who heads marketing services at Mobile Interactive Group. Even more common results of between 7 and 10% are well above direct mail rates that often hover just above zero per cent.

'The key to successful SMS marketing is relevance,' says Ariya Priyasantha, managing director of ActiveMedia Technology, a mobile content aggregator. He points to a program by Hutch India that allows customers to download coupons to their mobiles for two-for-one offers at nearly 400 retail outlets in India: 'Customers get a sense of personalized communication delivered direct to their pocket, since they initiate the dialogue. Only a one-to-one phone call can beat that level of personalization.'

Most mobile campaigns today are inbound, usually prompting consumers to send a text message to a short number code. In return, they receive product information, free content or the chance to win prizes. When Peugeot introduced its 1007 compact car in the UK, television and billboard advertisements carried a short code that allowed people to reserve a test drive at the nearest dealership. In Israel, Coca-Cola sends coupons via an MMS with a bar code that can be swiped directly from the mobile phone. Some applications are more subtle. One UK insurance company sends customers an SMS five days before a policy expires, warning that they will soon find themselves without cover. The result has been a 20% reduction in churn.

Nonetheless, mobile marketing can be seen as intrusive. E-mail spam and ring-tone frauds have made consumers wary of granting access to their mobile numbers. 'Brands are still nervous about what they can do with mobile,' says Mark Jones, UK sales director of Mobile 365, a messaging service provider. Gartner analyst Daren Siddall agrees: 'There has to be a value exchange with consumers, and that is what companies have a hard time with. But future marketers will have to learn to deal with this.'

So far, mobile marketing has not grabbed the attention of traditional advertising agencies. 'SMS hasn't offered an opportunity to big agencies because of the low fees. They are looking for six or seven figure deals,' says Mr Siddall. Rather, the industry is being pushed by a vast number of specialist agencies and SMS aggregators. The result is a cluttered sector that seems to be gradually orienting itself. Often, the lines between the creative role, the agency managing the campaign, the messaging platform provider and even the mobile operator are confusingly blurred. 'We've expected consolidation but the fact this hasn't occurred says the money is still coming in,' says Mobile 365's Mr Jones. The lack of heavyweight above-the-line agencies has probably kept mobile marketing from integrating more fully with the broader marketing mix.

Many mobile campaigns appear as one-off tests that fail to deliver long-term relationships. 'Most brands are doing bolt-on mobile campaigns. Only a few are building it in from the ground up,' says Mr Dunn of MIG. 'For every innovative campaign we develop, we get half a dozen "text to win" offers. These fall well short of realising the full potential of mobile as a marketing tool,' says Steve Procter, chief executive of iTAGG, a mobile marketing agency.

Another obstacle for brands seems to be the difficulty of measuring the effectiveness of mobile campaigns. A survey of 50 leading companies, commissioned by software company Airwide Solutions, showed that 58% of respondents were unsure about how to implement and measure an SMS campaign. But this is not keeping big brands away from sophisticated mobile marketing. Coca-Cola in the UK is running an interactive World Cup campaign in which customers send in photos via MMS to win match tickets and other prizes. 'People love peer-to-peer content. And these campaigns allow them to be part of the brand,' explains Mr King.

Source: I. Limbach, 'Mobile marketing: The most personal way to reach out', *Financial Times*, 21 June 2006.

12.2.3 Influence of wireless technologies on the industry's five forces

A company's position within an industry determines its ability to create value for the marketplace. Industries with a high information intensity, a large mobile workforce and activities can leverage wireless technologies in a significant way.

As stated in Chapter 3, the five forces model helps determine the attractiveness of an industry in general. In particular, the wired Internet influences each one of the industry's five forces (see Exhibit 3.3), as do wireless technologies (see Exhibit 12.5):

■ *Industry rivalry.* Since wireless technologies widen the physical marketplace by reducing the importance of geographical boundaries, it increases the number of competitors within an industry and, therefore, tends to lower the attractiveness of an industry. However, for wireless technologies and mobile applications, charges for international roaming continue to be very high and represent an important uptake factor for consumers.

■ *Bargaining power of suppliers.* Companies that embrace wireless technologies can capitalise on a quite unique online channel to reach out to customers and, thus, to reduce the leverage that other suppliers may have in the market. However, these technologies also offer a direct channel for dis-intermediating traditional players in an industry. For instance, Sony BMG (which is featured in the case studies section of this book) investigated the possibility of creating its own MVNO in order to position itself in the growing mobile music market. It, however, eventually refrained from launching its MVNO due to the high cost structure that is required and the high risk of such a venture. (See also the FT article: 'Little harmony in mobile music').

■ *Bargaining power of buyers.* Wireless technologies can shift the bargaining power to end consumers; they can also complement existing channels and improve the bargaining power over traditional channels. For example, newspapers are becoming accessible not only through stationary PCs, but also through hand-held devices. These devices allow readers to circumvent traditional newspaper stands and at the same time to increase the number of accessible newspapers.

■ *Barriers to entry.* On the one hand, wireless technologies can increase barriers to entry by helping companies to streamline some of their business processes and thus contribute to efficient operations. On the other hand, since mobile applications are difficult to keep proprietary, barriers to entry could therefore be rather low and consolidation in the industry favours incumbents. For example, YOC is facing new entrants from multimedia agencies which are trying to transfer to mobile marketing their competence in digital marketing. However, the technical complexity involved in creating and managing mobile marketing campaigns favours specialised companies (such as YOC) over multimedia agencies. Furthermore, technical competence in wireless technologies and mobile applications is viewed as a key factor for the sustainability of specialised companies such as YOC.

■ *Threat of substitutes.* Companies should view wireless technologies as an enabler for creating complementary opportunities and not just a threat of substitute products or services. Mobile phones and wireless communication networks are substitutes for fixed-line phones and wired networks and, therefore, are becoming a threat to some industries. For instance, O2, the UK-based mobile communication network, is offering customers a 'home zone' option, which allows subscribers to make local calls from their handset for cheaper rates.

Exhibit 12.5 Impact of wireless technologies on the industry's five forces

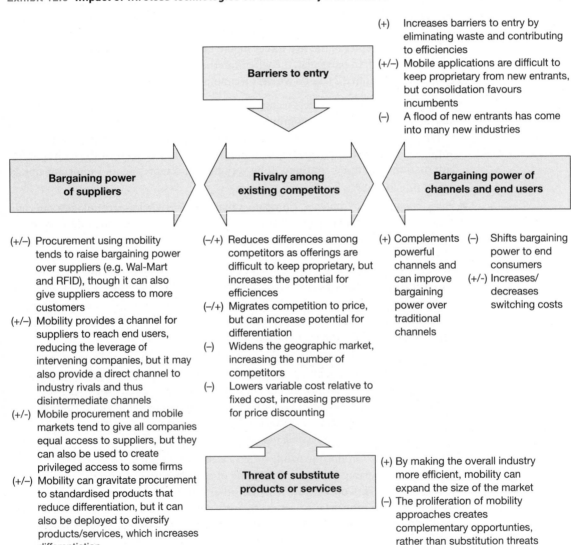

Source: The mobile revolution: The making of mobile services worldwide, D. Steinbock, Kogan Page, 2005, p. 266.

244

Little harmony in mobile music

The arrival of Apple's i-Phone poses a dilemma for mobile phone operators. The device is expected to push more people to access music on their handsets, and operators may gain kudos by having the much-hyped device in their portfolio. But mobile operators have invested heavily in their own music services, and may be reluctant to promote Apple's rival i-Tunes service.

Some operators, like Vodafone, feel strongly they want to retain a key role in selling music to handsets. 'We would absolutely hope to give i-Tunes a run for its money,' said Paul Kenny, content and product executive for Vodafone Music. 'We think it is important to keep the Vodafone label on our music services. We think it is something we can compete on.' Such sentiments could make signing a deal with Apple difficult. Orange takes a similar stance. 'We are mobile specialists and we know what works on mobile better than many other companies coming into the business. We are keen to build up our position as a content provider,' said Gavin Forth, head of entertainment at Orange. While T-Mobile is willing to let its customers access rival music services over its mobile Internet, it is still keen to promote its own Jukebox offering, which was revamped this week.

However, mobile phone operators have so far struggled to get their music download services to take off, despite a head start of several years. High prices, confusing payment structures and a lack of music-enabled handsets have all been blamed for slow take-up. A study by M Metrics in January indicated that in the UK, although 40% of consumers had a music-enabled phone, only 12% had used their phone for that purpose, and only 2.7% had downloaded a track over the air. Mobile phone operators had hoped to make money from sales of tracks this way, but executives at T-Mobile and Vodafone admit that so called 'side-loading' – transferring music from a PC or personal CD collection direct to the handset through a wire – is the most common way for customers to access music.

Of the UK operators only 3 and Orange provide figures on the number of tracks downloaded over the air each month by their customers: over 1m for 3 – one of the few operators doing well with music downloads – and around 100,000 for Orange.

Thanks to this patchy track record, many in the music industry are welcoming new entrants. 'New devices like the i-Phone and new innovative services like MusicStation will help us drive the digital music business forward at a faster rate,' said Rob Wells, senior vice-president at Universal's international digital music business. Smaller operators, or those who do not see music as a priority, may abandon their own music sales and join up with new entrants, said Phil Makinson, telecoms analyst at Greenwich consulting. 'There is a huge investment of technology, commercial and operational time to support a music service, especially in multiple territories,' he said. 'Smaller operators will either make music a key part of their strategy and invest in it heavily, like 3 in the UK, or Helio and Amp'd in the US. If it is not critical to them, they may partner with well known music specialists.' AT&T in the US, while not small, has taken this approach, working with a variety of music specialists from Apple to Napster and Yahoo's music download services, rather than develop an offering. And O2 has chosen to work with Napster in Ireland, as has Swisscom in Switzerland.

But many of the other operators are adamant that improvements to their own services will help them compete with the likes of i-Tunes. Vodafone has launched aggressive pricing – 99p per downloaded track in the UK – and is offering customers 'dual downloading' where songs can be sent to both the customer's mobile and a PC at the same time. T-Mobile unveiled a similar dual downloading service – at £1 a track – this week, and Orange is planning to launch such a service at the end of the year.

By offering downloads to both PCs and phones, the mobile operators believe they can meet the challenge of i-Tunes going mobile, and even take a share of Apple's fixed-line download market. 'The market for digital music is still very fragmented. iTunes dominates but others like Napster, Yahoo Unlimited and Rhapsody have penetrated less than 1% of the US population together,' Mr Kenny said. 'There is still a big opportunity to establish a position in the market.'

Cacophony of services on offer

Consumers seeking to put some music on their mobile handsets face a bewildering array of options, reports Maija Palmer.

As well as the operators' own services, such as Verizon's VCast or T-Mobile's Jukebox, there are a number of music services run by hardware manufacturers, such as Apple. It is understood that Nokia, the Finnish mobile manufacturer, is also planning to launch its own music service later this year, building on its $60m acquisition of Loudeye, the US online music company, last year. SonyEricsson, meanwhile, last year launched a music service called M-Buzz, together with its parent company Sony, which features new artists from the SonyBMG label. Then there are music services run by independent music specialists, such as MusicStation, run by UK start-up Omnifone, which is planning to launch a flat-rate service with operators such as Telenor of Norway, and Vodacom in South Africa. Jamba, the company behind the Crazy Frog ringtone, also launched a flat-rate €14.95-a-month ($20) music service in Germany last September, and is planning to extend this to other countries.

Source: M. Palmer, 'Mobile marketing: The most personal way to reach out', *Financial Times*, 5 July 2007.

SUMMARY

- This chapter started out by giving a definition of mobile e-commerce and depicting the players of the mobile value network. These include mobile equipment vendors for wireless infrastructure and hand-held devices, mobile network operators, IT enablers, application and content providers, as well as portal providers.

- By segmenting mobile e-commerce consumer and business services, this chapter illustrated the many uses of wireless applications. While consumer services can be categorised into information, communication, transaction and entertainment services, business services can be categorised into mobile supply chain management, mobile customer relationship management and mobile workforce services.

- Next, this chapter explained the main advantages of mobile e-commerce over wired e-commerce. Ubiquity, convenience, localisation and personalisation represent some of the key capabilities of wireless technologies that can be leveraged for value creation.

- While the value chain framework exemplified how wireless technologies impact on the primary and support activities of the firm, the five forces framework illustrated how these technologies can affect the strategic positioning of a firm within its industry.

REVIEW QUESTIONS

1   Outline the value network of mobile e-commerce and briefly explain its players.

2   Which categories can be used to segment mobile e-commerce applications?

3   What are the advantages of mobile e-commerce over wired e-commerce?

4   Pick two support and two primary activities of the value chain and describe how wireless technologies can affect them.

5   Explain to what extent wireless technologies increase or decrease an industry's rivalry.

DISCUSSION QUESTIONS

1   Critically assess to what extent mobile network operators play a key role in mobile e-commerce.

2   Illustrate the advantages of mobile e-commerce through a real-world example.

3   Provide an example of a company that uses wireless technologies for customer relationship management and discuss how it adds value.

4   Pick an industry of your choice and show how wireless technologies affect its incumbents.

RECOMMENDED KEY READING

■   For an in-depth portrayal of mobile services, see D. Steinbock, *The mobile revolution: The making of mobile services worldwide*, Kogan Page, 2005.

■   For more information on the categorisation of mobile content, also see F. Müller-Veerse *et al.*, *UMTS report – An investment perspective*, Durlacher Research, 2001.

USEFUL THIRD-PARTY WEBLINKS

■   www.mmaglobal.com is the website of the Mobile Marketing Association, which strives to stimulate the growth of mobile marketing and its associated technologies.

■   www.ecommercetimes.com is an online magazine, which also provides in-depth coverage of mobile commerce topics.

■   www.fiercemobilecontent.com is a website that provides frequent updates from the mobile content and mobile marketing sector.

■   www.mobileinfo.com provides mobile computing information.

NOTES AND REFERENCES

1   R. Dholakia and N. Dholakia, 'Mobility and markets: emerging outlines of m-commerce', *Journal of Business Research*, 2004, Vol. 57, pp. 1391–1396.
2   F. Müller-Veerse *et al.*, *UMTS report – An investment perspective*, Durlacher Research, 2001, p. 23.
3   N. Sadeh, *M-Commerce: Technologies, Services and Business Models*, John Wiley, 2002, p. 52.
4   D. Steinbock, *The mobile revolution: The making of mobile services worldwide*, Kogan Page, 2005.

PART III

A roadmap for e-business strategy implementation

PART OVERVIEW

This part proposes a roadmap for e-business strategy implementation; it addresses the following issues:

- Vision
- Objectives
- Value creation
- Target segment(s)
- Privacy, ethical and legal issues
- External partners
- Organisational model
- Revenues and costs model
- Strategy alignment.

CHAPTER 13

A roadmap for e-business strategy implementation

Learning outcomes

After completing this chapter, you should be able to:

- Explain the nine steps of the e-business strategy formulation roadmap.
- Link the individual steps of the roadmap to the different parts of the e-business strategy framework.
- Understand the main business and management issues involved in each stage of the e-business strategy formulation roadmap.

INTRODUCTION

To help you, as an executive, manager or manager-to-be, to develop and implement an e-business strategy for your company, this chapter proposes a roadmap consisting of the following elements: (1) vision, (2) business objectives, (3) customer-value creation, (4) market segmentation and targeting, (5) privacy, ethical and legal issues, (6) vertical boundaries, (7) organisational model, (8) revenue and cost model, and (9) strategy alignment (see Exhibit 13.1).

Exhibit 13.1 **The roadmap for e-business strategy implementation addresses nine interrelated issues**

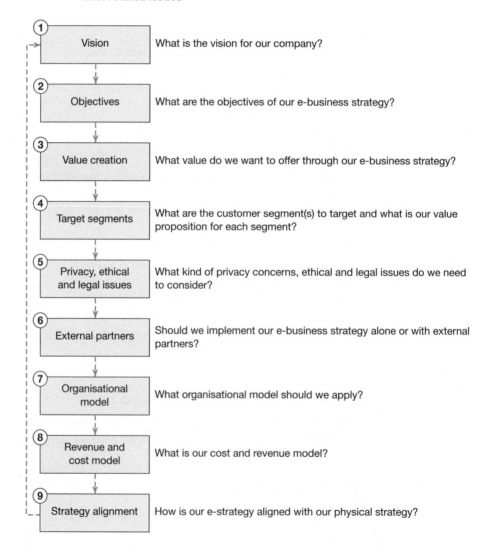

1. Vision — What is the vision for our company?

2. Objectives — What are the objectives of our e-business strategy?

3. Value creation — What value do we want to offer through our e-business strategy?

4. Target segments — What are the customer segment(s) to target and what is our value proposition for each segment?

5. Privacy, ethical and legal issues — What kind of privacy concerns, ethical and legal issues do we need to consider?

6. External partners — Should we implement our e-business strategy alone or with external partners?

7. Organisational model — What organisational model should we apply?

8. Revenue and cost model — What is our cost and revenue model?

9. Strategy alignment — How is our e-strategy aligned with our physical strategy?

After having presented the e-business strategy framework in the course of the previous chapters, what is the purpose of this implementation roadmap? While the e-business strategy framework outlines from a structural perspective the key elements of strategy formulation, the goal of this roadmap is to propose from a process-oriented perspective the different steps involved in setting up and implementing an e-business strategy.[1]

In spite of their different perspectives, the roadmap and the strategy framework are closely interrelated. On the one hand, this roadmap aims at providing you with a practical way to develop an e-business strategy. On the other hand, the cross-references to the more extensive e-business strategy framework allow you to reference back depending on your previous knowledge and the specific organisational situation at hand. As we discuss in Chapter 15, the depth of the analysis depends on the issue at hand. If you do not choose carefully where to drill deep and where to stay at the surface, you increase the risk of over-analysing issues of relatively low importance while overlooking other issues of critical importance.

13.1 What is the mission of our company?

As mentioned above, the mission presents the starting point of strategy formulation. It reflects the strategic intent of the firm and points to its desired future state.[2] As examples, consider the following mission statements by some of the companies featured in the case studies section of the book:

> We will be valued as the leading financial services group in the Nordic and Baltic financial market with a substantial growth potential. We will be in the top of the league or show superior profitable growth in every market and product area in which we choose to compete. We will have the leading multi-channel distribution with a top world ranking in e-based financial services and solutions.[3]   **Nordea Bank**

> We seek to offer the Earth's biggest selection and be Earth's most customer-centric company, where customers can find and discover anything they might want to buy online.[4]
>
> **Amazon.com**

> Google's mission is to organize the world's information and make it universally accessible and useful.   **Google.com**

> We want to be the world's creative apparel platform, inspiring people to create, buy or sell individualized apparel with the best tools, assortment, content and fulfillment. We want to be admired by designers, consumers, shop partners, our stakeholders and our industry. We want to build the best possible online creation experience for everyone from Homer Simpson to Salvador Dalí. We communicate openly and engage our community in accomplishing this mission. We want to be a fun and inspiring place to work, where integrity, delivery, and innovation reigns.   **Spreadshirt.com**

> OpenBC is committed to powering relationships based on trust for all professional people. Based on the theory that 'No two people are more than six degrees apart', openBC enables members to grow their trusted network by making their contacts' contacts visible to them.

As an active and productive community, we constantly strive to create real value for the world's professionals, as an everyday online and live resource – across all countries, languages and industries. OpenBC crosses barriers – for a sustainable world.   **openBC.com**

We want to be the recognized leader in service excellence among all companies – not just elevator companies – worldwide. We will inspire our customers' total confidence through exceptional service that earns us 100% of their business, 100% of the time.[5]   **Otis Elevator**

By expanding the applications of mobile phones beyond communication, we are promoting the creation of a lifestyle infrastructure.

Our goal is to serve our clients as a lifestyle service provider.[6]   **NTT DoCoMo**

The goals of formulating a company's mission are threefold. As is shown below, mission statements typically address one to three key questions of 'where' and 'how' a business wants to compete, as well as 'why' it wants to do so (see Exhibit 13.2):

- *Definition of business scope (Where?)*. On a very broad level, this question addresses the areas, both on a regional and product basis, in which a firm wants to compete. This decision is of essential importance because it serves as a guideline to prioritise the resource allocation. For instance, openBC explicitly states in its mission statement that the company wants to be 'an everyday online and live resource – across all countries, languages and industries', which is, admittedly, a very broad definition of its business scope.

- *Definition of unique competencies (How?)*. This questions addresses, also on a highly aggregate level, which competencies a firm wants to develop and exploit. Regarding the issue of competencies, Spreadshirt emphasises in its mission statement that it 'wants to be the world's creative apparel platform, inspiring people to create, buy or sell individualized apparel with the best tools, assortment, content and fulfillment'. In doing so, Spreadshirt explicates the different types of capabilities that need to be developed in order to fulfil the mission.

Exhibit 13.2 A mission statement serves multiple different purposes

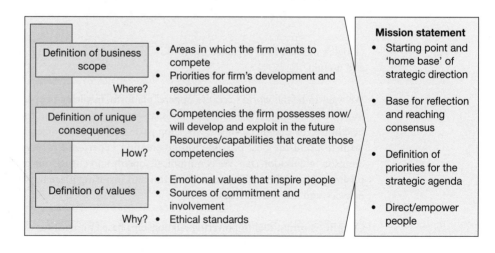

■ *Definition of values (Why?)*. Laying out the emotional values that the firm should guide has the goal of inspiring people, thereby securing their commitment and involvement in their work. In addition, the definition of values helps to establish ethical standards of which behaviour is acceptable and unacceptable. The Spreadshirt mission statement also addresses this dimension when it states that 'we want to be a fun and inspiring place to work, where integrity, delivery, and innovation reigns.'

By addressing these three dimensions and providing broad guidelines, mission statements serve as a starting point during strategy discussions, since the ideas laid out in these statements serve as a common basis for reflection and reaching consensus and since they help to define priorities for the strategic agenda. In addition, ethical standards that are made explicit in the mission statement direct and empower employees.

However, developing a powerful mission statement that will be supported by all members of an organisation over many years presents a challenging task. On the one hand, it needs to consider the specific characteristics of the company and its employees. On the other hand, it also needs to incorporate the broader context within which the company operates. Doing so can include asking questions such as: What are the major recent technological developments that we can leverage in the future? How are demographics changing in our society and what does this mean for our company in the long term? For a structured approach to formulating these types of questions, it is helpful to analyse the different dimensions of the macro-environment, which were outlined in Chapter 3.

13.2 What are the objectives for our e-business strategy?

While a mission statement is important to establish the direction of your company, it is equally important that you select parameters to measure the success of your efforts towards achieving the vision. These parameters are the quantifiable objectives, which can include measures such as revenues, market share, profits and customer satisfaction level.

Depending on the type of mission statement, the objectives will differ. Yet all of them should have in common the fact that they can be measured and quantified. Only then can they provide goals for the employees to strive for, and only then is it possible to track progress and make adjustments along the way in order to achieve the objectives.

Consider the example of the vertical e-marketplace Covisint. The founding car makers, General Motors, Ford and DaimlerChrysler, stated their objective to achieve $6 billion of savings per year through online collaboration, e-procurement and e-supply chain management.

13.3 What value do we want to offer through our e-business strategy?

13.3.1 What type of competitive advantage do we aim for?

When answering this question, you need to determine why customers would want to buy your products or services. They could do so because of low prices or high quality, or both.

255

If your company decides to compete primarily on price, you need to strive to become a cost leader within your industry. The low-cost airline easyJet is a prime example of a low-cost leader. The Internet is an integrated part of the company's strategy since it allows easyJet to cut out expensive ticketing offices and sales agents.

The other option is to strive for a differentiation advantage vis-à-vis rivals (see Section 5.2). You can achieve this, for instance, by offering high levels of convenience, broad product selection, high service quality or a superior brand name. Additionally, you can leverage information that is already available in your organisation to create benefits for your customers (see Section 4.3 on the concept of the virtual value chain).

Regardless of which of the two options you choose, it is important to create a strong fit between different activities by (1) aiming for consistency among them, (2) ensuring reinforcement between activities to increase customer benefits, and (3) optimising overall efforts so as to reduce costs (see Section 5.4).

Finally, you can also aim at achieving both cost leadership and differentiation advantages at the same time, similar to what Amazon.com and Tesco.com have achieved in their respective markets. However, doing so entails the risk of getting 'stuck in the middle', where you possess neither a cost nor a differentiation advantage vis-à-vis rivals (see Section 5.2.3).

The likelihood of outpacing your competitors along both the price and differentiation dimensions improves if you find ways to open up new and attractive market spaces (see Chapter 7). For instance, you can break out of traditional ways of conducting business by looking across substitute industries, strategic groups, complementary products or unrelated industries.

13.3.2 How much breadth do we want to have in our product and service offerings?

In addition to the type of competitive advantage that you want to provide to customers, the second key dimension of the value you offer to your customers relates to the breadth of products and services that you want to offer. This breadth depends to a large degree on the target market segment(s) that you want to serve (see Section 4.2). If your company wants to achieve broad coverage, you will, in all likelihood, need to offer a broad variety of products to meet the needs of different customer segments. This is the case, for instance, with the car manufacturer Volkswagen, which offers different models covering all target segments. If, on the other hand, your target segment is very narrow with well-defined preferences, as is the case with, for example, Ducati, then it is advisable also to limit the number of products offered. When thinking about an extension of scope, you need to consider the trade-offs involved. The opportunities are increased market reach and sales, while the risks include a possible loss of internal focus and a dilution of the brand name from a customer perspective.

In addition to a company extending product scope by itself, it can also leverage the Internet to establish partnerships with complementors. Here, the critical question is: What else would your customers want to buy in addition to the products and services which are currently offered? The online travel agency ebookers.com, for instance, has links on its website that point to weather reports, currency exchange information, car rental services and travel insurance. Amazon.com went even beyond the Amazon.com vision statement mentioned above. It invited all types of retailers to sell their products on its online platform (including new and used books) which might be in direct competition with its own product offerings.

13.4 What are the customer segments to target and what is our value proposition for each segment?

Closely linked to value creation is the decision about who your customers should be. Deciding on a target market entails two steps. First, you need to select criteria for dividing your potential market into segments. The chosen criteria will have a significant impact on the segmentation outcome (see Section 3.4). For instance, you can segment markets according to customer types (i.e. consumers, corporate and governmental/public-sector customers) or according to age or income.

Based on the market segmentation, you need to decide which segments to target (see Section 3.4) with what products and services that are tailored specifically to a segment's needs. Consider how some of the companies featured in the case studies section of this book have chosen their target segments. Tesco.com, for example, focused initially on targeting upper-income shoppers with its online grocery service. Subsequently, it expanded into mass market segments. Spreadshirt primarily targets entrepreneurs who want to set up their own online shop to sell customised T-shirts and other merchandise.

13.5 What kind of ethical issues, privacy concerns and security risks do we need to consider?

13.5.1 Dealing with ethical issues and privacy concerns

Ethics refers to the principles of right and wrong that individuals use to make choices to guide their behaviour.[7] The pervasive nature of the Internet raises a host of new ethical issues that managers need to address in their daily work. Most important in this context is the issue of privacy, which stands for the right of individuals, be it in the online or offline world, to be left alone from surveillance or interference from other individuals or organisations.

As an e-business manager you need to deal with privacy issues primarily on two important levels. First, and most importantly, you need to manage the trade-off between the desire to profit from information gathered about customers and the need to safeguard privacy. The Internet provides unprecedented opportunity to collect data about customers and to adjust market targeting accordingly. Regarding different types of customer information, it would be interesting to collect some or all of the following data:

- *Conctact information.* Includes name, postal address, e-mail address. This information is typically collected through online forms.
- *Profile information.* Includes information about a customer's personal characteristics including age, sex, occupation, etc. To obtain this type of information, companies usually have to provide some kind of incentive to users. Tesco, for instance, asks customers who register for the clubcard to provide information about dietary preferences and who they live with. In return, clubcard owners receive promotional offers when shopping both online and offline.
- *Behavioural information (on a single site).* Includes click-through patterns or purchase history on a single website, such as Amazon.com.
- *Behavioural information (across multiple sites).* Includes information on how Internet users navigate through different websites.

Obviously, the data only becomes relevant when it is used in one way or another to understand customers better, by scrutinising and analysing customer information using data-mining techniques, and to target these customers directly. As we discussed in Section 3.4 on customer segmentation, the more you know, the more it becomes possible to target customers with specific product advertisements (see also the FT article 'Google's algorithm of life: rejoice and be wary').

Google's algorithm of life: rejoice and be wary

Tomorrow just arrived and it is about time. How many George Orwell novels or Ray Bradbury stories has it taken us? At long last, we may soon be able to click on the electronic screen to find out what is in our heads.

Thank you, Google. You are aiming to organise what so many of us have confused – namely, our lives. Flummoxed by the choices and complications of multi-dimensional reality, you are reducing it all to a simple computational problem. And you remember to do what the rest of us have been forgetting: save the receipts.

Also e-mails, web surfing destinations and e-searches. Keep a list of those, run a few algorithms the size of Portugal, and presto: optimisation problems solved. Careers, mates, consumption, investment, leisure and spiritual replenishment all laid out trim and tidy. Uncluttered, just like the Google Search page. This is well beyond our wildest.

To think that people are complaining. They are unnerved that, after all these millennia, it took a couple of geeks from California to get the rest of us straightened out. They point to the massive intrusion into our private lives that would be entailed when a corporate behemoth, now valued at $150bn (£76bn), stored so much information about our choices, lifestyles and thoughts that it ended up knowing quite a bit more about where we should be headed than we do.

There is a point to the fear. New information flows require some hard choices about whom we trust. Intention-based advertising has led Google to untold riches in financial markets, supplying a 21st century death knell to the old advertising model. Those banner ads of the internet, not to mention the ubiquitous e-mail spams made lucrative by virtue of the demand for male potency and hair restoration products, are almost wholly eclipsed by the sensational efficiency of pinpoint advertising, with news of what one might actually want to purchase, as pioneered by Google Search.

But that very progressive business model is an invasion of privacy, if you are going to get picky. Google knows that when you search 'Orlando hotels' you are a sitting duck for a rich raft of commercial offers, just as if it was reading your mind. Or your e-mails. Hence, when Gmail was introduced to make that reading a bit easier for Google, the squawking was intense. 'Google is scanning your private e-mail to locate the keywords that generate the ads,' wrote Walter Mossberg, the influential technology columnist, in The Wall Street Journal. 'Google is risking its reputation for honesty.'

A bill to ban the service passed the California state senate, receiving only one dissenting vote. Respected internet activists expressed outrage. Google's executives were dumbfounded – particularly when they saw that Gmail accounts, then tightly controlled and hard to acquire, were trading on Ebay for $100. The company grasped the irony instantly. While its reputation truly was at stake, it was offering innovative services that consumers really wanted. Intention-based advertising is revolutionary in its efficiency. People flock to this environment. Gmail is today a runaway hit.

At the same time, they will continue flocking only so long as the price is right. If Google fails to protect personal data from abuse, the company's single most

→

important asset goes up in smoke. Without the reputational capital to do seamless business with hundreds of millions of internet users, Google's profits would go the way of the dotcom bubble.

Google Search, Gmail and myriad other services are today intrusive data mining enterprises – and extremely popular with customers. The company's enormous capital resources, driven by Wall Street's excitement over a media model that actually works, help solve the consumers' conundrum. The share values of the search giant can only tip-toe in the troposphere so long as those hard disks remain protected. When Google scans them to find what job listing we might like to see or what spa we need to visit, we tend to be pretty happy. Where standards slip and private information leaks to unwanted purposes, or is sold to low-ball retailers, we are all going to get crazy. We will take Google's equity with us.

Google's marketing under the 'Don't be evil' theme is one of the last old-style types of advertising slogan that still works. For customers and shareholders alike. The rude awakening for many is that they supposed that this was a different kind of company and that the markets it opened were upside down from others. They are finding that privacy, like other goods, has trade-offs, and that even the purest of souls must make hard choices.

Source: T. Hazlett, Google's algorithm of life: rejoice and be wary', *Financial Times*, 24 May 2007.

Both the act of data collection and data mining entail the risk of undermining the privacy of customers, especially so when computers are leveraged to combine data from multiple sources to create electronic dossiers of detailed information on individuals – a procedure which is called profiling.

On another level, e-business managers also need to determine to what extent they want to monitor their employees' online activities such as websurfing or e-mail correspondence. Technological advances have made it possible to monitor all incoming and outgoing traffic on a permanent basis. The underlying goal of these monitoring activities is to increase productivity and to prevent employees from wasting time on non-business activities. However, employees have the competing goal of having their privacy protected.

The conflicting goals described in these two realms point to a more fundamental basis of making ethical choices, which is to manage trade-off between different goals. Below, we summarise some of the key issues that you need to consider in order to make some ethical choices.[8]

Typically, ethical conflicts refer to higher values such as freedom, privacy or protection of property. Having a clear understanding of what these higher-value orders specifically mean is a first step to making an ethically responsible choice. Only after an understanding of the higher-order values has been generated does it become possible to outline clearly the dilemma between two opposing goals, e.g. the goal of gathering as much as data as possible about customers and their goal of maintaining a certain minimal level of privacy. Furthermore, you also need to understand clearly who is involved and affected by the choices that you make. For instance, these stakeholders might be customers and consumer rights groups, on the one hand, and companies such as Tesco, on the other hand. Finally, when it comes to making a choice there are a number of questions you can ask yourself to determine whether the choice is ethical:

- Would you want to be treated the same way if someone else made this type of decision that affected you personally? If not, the choice you made is unlikely to be ethical.
- Would it be appropriate if everyone in the organisation behaved this way? Would the organisation or the larger society you live in be able to survive and prosper?

■ Could this action be taken repeatedly over time? An action that is carried out only once might not seem problematic. However, if you imagine extending this decision into the future, then it might become obvious that the long-term effects would not be acceptable.

13.5.2 Addressing security risks

The greatest asset of the Internet, which is its openness, also presents at the same time the biggest risk to security for both companies and customers. Since information about commercial or financial transactions passes through many computers, where it is captured, monitored and stored and processed, e-business ventures are particularly susceptible to outside penetration. Numerous problems include stolen credit card details. These threats in the online environment are similar to those in the offline world; they include burglary, breaking and entering, embezzlement, trespass, malicious destruction and vandalism.[9]

Below, we briefly discuss the most prominent security threats that e-business companies and their customers face today:[10]

■ *Malicious code* refers to security threats such as viruses, worms or Trojan horses.

■ *Phishing* refers to deceptive attempts by third parties to obtain financial information for financial gain. It does not involve malicious code but instead relies on misrepresentation and fraud. One well-known example of a phishing attack is an e-mail from a rich uncle in Nigeria who is seeking a bank account to store millions of dollars for a short time. In return, he is willing to give you a few hundred thousand dollars. Some people are fooled and provide their bank account information.

■ *Hacking and cyber-vandalism* refer to acts committed by individuals who attempt to gain unauthorised access to a computer system. They do so by finding weaknesses in the security procedures of websites and computer systems.

■ *Credit card fraud* is one of the most feared occurrences on the Internet. This fear prevents many users from providing their credit card information online. In reality, however, this type of fraud is much lower than what users think, since it represents less than 2% of all online card transactions.[11]

■ *Spoofing (pharming)* takes place when hackers misrepresent their true identity or misrepresent themselves by using fake e-mail addresses. When a hacker spoofs a website, it is called pharming, which involves redirecting a weblink different from the intended one. Once an unknowing user has been redirected to the fake website, hackers then collect and process orders, effectively stealing business from the real site.

■ *Denial of service (DOS)* refers to large-scale e-mail attacks on websites with useless traffic. The goal of these e-mail floods is to shut down websites. When they succeed, the costs for the affected website operator are substantial, since, while the site is shut down, customers cannot inform themselves through the site and, more importantly, they also cannot make purchases. For instance, in April 2007 a series of DOS attacks disrupted Estonia's most vital websites, including the websites of the president, the parliament, almost all of the governments ministries, two of the biggest banks and firms specialising in communication. The government had to take emergency measures and block access to the websites from the outside world, which resulted in substantial economic losses.

There are a number of different ways to protect against security threats. These include, on the one hand, technological measures such as encryption, firewalls or virtual private networks (VPNs). On the other hand, companies can also implement procedures and policies to limit the danger of outside attacks on their systems. These measures include clear online authentication and authorisation for users of the system, and conducting routine reviews of access that identify how outsiders are using the website.[12]

13.6 Should we implement our e-business strategy alone or with external partners?

When deciding on the degree of integration of the e-business activities, you need to analyse the value chain again and decide which e-business activities to perform in-house and which ones to outsource to external providers (see Chapter 9). The main reasons that favour 'make' decisions are strong linkages between individual activities within the firm and high transaction costs. Reasons that favour 'buy' decisions include high economies of scale, high capital requirements, specialised know-how and higher efficiency of the open market.

As the Tesco.com example illustrates, making the right 'make-or-buy' decision can be a major source of competitive advantage. Tesco's success in the past resulted partly from its ability to find the right balance between activities that are sourced from external providers, thereby reducing costs, and activities that the company performs in-house to ensure differentiation from other competitors.[13] Consider, for instance, Tesco Direct's internal build-up of a media centre for a team of 40 experts including designers, photographers and publishers.

13.7 What organisational structure should our e-business activities have?

As part of the internal set-up of your company, you need to choose the appropriate organisational structure for the e-business activities. At one end of the spectrum, this would mean completely integrating the e-business activities into your existing organisation. At the other end of the spectrum, it would mean setting them up as a independent entity or spin-off (see Section 9.2).

The benefits of setting up a spin-off include factors such as greater focus, a faster decision-making process and a higher degree of entrepreneurial culture. As valuations of online companies are soaring again and IPO activities are picking up, access to venture capital might also once more become a relevant reason for spinning off online operations.

However, overall, favour has tilted towards integrating e-business activities into the existing operations of the firm. By doing so, companies can leverage their established brands to attract customers to the online channel, as is illustrated through the examples of Ducati and Tesco. Additionally, it becomes possible to provide multi-channel offerings, where customers can choose between the online and offline interaction, depending on their individual preferences and needs. This opens up the opportunity for cross-promotions, shared information systems and integrated customer services, where customers can, for instance, return products purchased over the Internet to a physical store.

13.8 What is our cost and revenue model?

The final and most critical issue to address concerns the financial matters involved in the e-business activity. To find these out, you need to analyse the business model of your firm in terms of both the cost structure and the revenue structure.[14]

13.8.1 What is the cost structure of our e-business activities?

To determine the cost structure, you need to consider the individual parts of the value chain – such as production, IT, marketing, sales and after-sales service – and analyse their underlying cost drivers (see Section 5.2). This entails asking questions such as 'How will costs evolve as the scale of operations increases?' (see Section 7.1) and 'How can we use the Internet to lower costs across the value chain?'

As the focus of investors has shifted towards the profitability of e-business ventures, it has become much more important to control costs. Ultimately, the cost structure of your e-business venture determines the gross profit margin that your company must earn in order to cover overheads and generate profits. However, if you start out from the beginning with high costs due to, for example, high fixed costs or marketing expenses, then this limits your spectrum of business opportunities. Obviously, your cost structure dictates the types of revenues you need to generate in order to achieve the desired profitability. For instance, with a cost-intensive infrastructure in place, you will generally find it difficult to justify targeting small markets (although these may be very promising), since they are unlikely to generate enough revenues to cover costs. In addition, you will also find it more difficult to adjust your e-business strategy if market realities do not meet your expectations.[15]

To determine the required scale, you need to analyse the (expected) cost structure of your e-business activities. This entails an analysis of each activity of the value chain and its underlying cost drivers. If costs are primarily fixed, as is the case with warehouses or website development, it is likely that they display high economies of scale. This, in turn, requires that your operations need to be sufficiently large in order to benefit from the cost reduction brought about by scale effects.

Beware, however, that scale effects are achieved only if your company is also able to generate the required sales volume. As the example of Webvan shows (see the FT article 'Webvan's billion dollar mistake' in Section 1.2.3), many companies during the early Internet boom years ramped up operations very quickly in order to achieve economies of scale. However, they did so without first having understood the underlying economics and customer demand. After having developed expensive proprietary technology platforms and putting into place vast physical warehouse infrastructure, it became impossible for Webvan to adapt the chosen strategy to meet the different market conditions.

13.8.2 What is the revenue structure of our e-business activities?

In order to determine the revenue structure of your e-business activities, you need to analyse the different options for generating revenues. The latter depend on the type of business you are operating and can include the following sources:

- Advertising revenues and usage fees, as is the case in P2P e-commerce.

- Information posting and transaction fees, as is the case in C2C e-commerce.

- Hosting service fees, membership fees, transaction fees and/or (monthly) subscription fees, as is the case in B2B e-commerce.

- Transaction fees, advertising revenues and subscription fees, as is the case in B2C e-commerce.

In addition to analysing revenue sources, you also need to assess the sustainability of your business model, which depends to a large degree on the customer's ability to bargain down prices, intensity of competition, substitute products and barriers to entry (see Section 3.2).

In order to sustain revenues, you should consider the following two options, which are not mutually exclusive. The first option is to 'reinvent' continuously your e-business activities to stay abreast of changes and avoid being pushed out of the market. As the Internet matures, it becomes less likely that fundamental changes will overthrow established business models (see Section 1.2). Nowadays, the rise of Internet-based start-up companies, such as Google, Amazon.com and eBay, which revolutionised ways of doing business by using the Internet, is still possible, yet they become more unlikely as the technology matures and e-business applications become established.

The second option is to aim at creating customer lock-in (see Section 7.2), which you can achieve through the following means:

- By setting up *customisable websites* where customers can adapt the company's website to their own needs. For instance, in Second Life, customers can construct their personal virtual world including building infrastructure and creating inhabitants. At Tesco.com, online shoppers can store their shopping list for future purchases.

- By leveraging *data-mining techniques* to analyse customer information (age, gender, income, etc.), click-stream patterns, past purchases and comparisons with other like-minded customers. The information gathered by means of data mining can then be used to make specific targeted service and product offerings based on individual preferences. Numerous companies, including Nordea, Tesco, eBay and YOC, all of which are featured in the case studies section of this book, have used data-mining techniques extensively to build up loyalty among their customers.

- By leveraging *network effects*. To do this, you need to find ways in which your product or service becomes more valuable for customers as the overall number of customers increases (see Section 7.4 on network effects). The most popular way of achieving this is to set up social networking communities in which online users have the opportunity to interact with one another on topics that are of special interest to them (see Chapter 11).

13.9 How should we align our physical-world strategy with our e-strategy?

Reaching a decision on how to align the online activities with the offline ones is only relevant for those companies that are already running physical operations and now want to branch out into the online world. The alignment of a company's physical-world strategy and its e-strategy requires strategic decisions to be made on issues such as branding, product/service offering, pricing, IT and multi-channel management. The guiding question here is as follows: For each one of these issues, what should we do regarding our physical operations and our Internet operations? For example, regarding branding, should we name our Internet activity after our physical world brand (e.g. Ducati.com at Ducati, Tesco.com at Tesco), or should we use a different brand name (e.g. ooshop.fr at Carrefour)?

Regarding the channel management issue, when adding the online channel, you need to determine how to align it with the existing physical channel (see Section 9.2). This includes addressing the following three issues: What products/services to offer online compared with what has been offered offline? What should be the pricing strategy for goods sold online? How to pre-empt (or proactively address) any conflicts between the online and offline channels?

Regarding the online offering, although it can consist of the same product/service range that is offered offline, most often it is either (1) a totally different portfolio of goods (as is the case on Ducati.com where the company sells new, limited edition motorcycles, apparel and accessories that cannot be found at physical dealerships), or (2) a combination of new products/services and some of the existing offline offering (as is the case on Tesco.com where online customers can find grocery items which are also available in stores and at the same time financial, travel and legal services that are only offered online).

Regarding the issue of what pricing strategy to use for products/services sold across the online and offline channels, there are three main options (as illustrated below in the context of, for example, Internet-based grocery retailing):

■ Apply online the *same product prices* as in stores (the way Tesco.com does in Britain) to convey the message that the value is elsewhere than in price savings.

■ Charge *lower prices* online (as Alcampo.es did in Spain) to attract, through this financial incentive, a large number of online shoppers and quickly build a critical mass of customers.

■ Charge *higher prices* (the way Ahold does) to reflect the extra costs involved in order fulfilment, and packing and delivery of the goods.

In financial services, Nordea has used a differentiated pricing strategy. Customers pay a significantly lower fee for a given banking transaction if it is carried out online rather than in a physical branch office of the bank. This approach has helped Nordea to attract customers to its Internet-based banking services.

If the offline and online channels compete for the same customer group, then this is likely to result in a conflict because of cannibalisation effects. If the offline channel is expected to remain important and the likelihood of a channel conflict is high, then it is essential to address this conflict early on and to find ways to reconcile the interests of the two channels. This can be achieved, for instance, by creating one unified profit centre or, as in the case of Ducati, by providing dealers with a financial incentive if they support the online direct sales channel.

SUMMARY

- First, the chapter suggested in broad terms a roadmap for e-business strategy formulation.
- It then described in detail each of the nine steps involved in this roadmap and illustrated them through some examples and some of the case studies contained in this book. These steps consist of:

1 Defining a vision.

2 Setting up quantifiable business objectives.

3 Deciding on the specific customer value to create.

4 Selecting the target market(s) and customer segment(s).

5 Addressing the privacy, ethical and legal issues of the e-business activity.

6 Deciding on the vertical boundaries for the e-business activity (should it be carried out internally or in partnership with external organisations?).

7 Defining the organisational structure of the e-business activity (including scale and scope).

8 Establishing a business model that outlines the expected cost and revenue structure of the e-business venture.

9 For companies that are adding clicks to bricks, aligning their e-business strategy with their physical-world strategy.

REVIEW QUESTIONS

1 What are the nine steps involved in the e-business strategy formulation roadmap?

2 What strategic issues does a company need to address when adding clicks to bricks?

3 What possible decisions can a company make regarding branding and goods' pricing across channels?

4 What options does a company have for solving the online/offline channel conflict?

5 What possible revenue streams can a company consider for its e-commerce activities?

DISCUSSION QUESTIONS

1 Illustrate the nine steps of the e-business strategy formulation roadmap through a real-world example that you are familiar with.

2 What challenges do traditional companies face when moving from bricks to clicks?

3 Critically assess the three broad pricing strategies for goods sold online, which are outlined in Section 13.9.

4 Choose an e-business activity of your own and formulate it through the nine steps of the e-business strategy roadmap.

RECOMMENDED KEY READING

- N. Venkatraman suggests a five-step approach for developing e-business strategies: 'Five steps to a dot-com strategy: how to find your footing on the Web', *Sloan Management Review*, Spring 2000, pp. 15–28.

- D. Chaffey presents different types of e-business strategy processes in *e-Business and e-Commerce Management*, FT/Prentice Hall, 2002, pp. 164-169.

- C. Christensen and M. Raynor provide a detailed account of how to choose different strategy development processes depending on the type of innovation at hand: *The Innovator's Solution*, Harvard Business School Press, 2003, pp. 214-231.

NOTES AND REFERENCES

1 For an excellent discussion of different forms of strategy formulation processes, see C. Christensen and M. Raynor, *The Innovator's Solution*, Harvard Business School Press, 2003, pp. 217–234.

2 See also R. Grant, *Contemporary Strategy Analysis*, Blackwell, 2003, pp. 29-30, and G. Johnson, K. Scholes and R. Whittington, *Exploring Corporate Strategy*, 7th edition, Prentice Hall, 2005.

3 Taken from Nordea company website.

4 Amazon.com, Annual Report 2002, Part I, p. 1.

5 Ari Bousbib, CEO of Otis Elevator, quoted in the Otis case study contained in the latter part of this book.

6 Quotes from respectively Masao Nakamura, President & CEO of NTT DoCoMo, and Yuichi Kato, President & CEO, NTT DoCoMo Europe, both cited in the NTT DoCoMo case study contained in the latter part of this book.

7 K. Laudon and J. Laudon, *Essentials of Management Information Systems*, Pearson, 2005, p. 153.

8 Ibid., pp. 157–158.

9 See K. Laudon and G. Traver, *E-commerce*, Prentice Hall, 2007, p. 252.

10 Ibid., pp. 257–268.

11 See CyberSource Corporation, *7th Annual Online Fraud Report*, 2006 edition.

12 See K. Laudon and G. Traver, *E-commerce*, Prentice Hall, 2007, pp. 257–268.

13 C. Christensen and M. Raynor, *The Innovator's Solution*, Harvard Business School Press, 2003, pp. 170–171.

14 The term 'business model' has been widely used, entailing many different elements. To keep things simple, we decided to include only costs and revenues in it. For a more extensive definition of the business model concept, see D. Straub, *Foundations of Net-Enhanced Organizations*, John Wiley, 2004, pp. 237–239.

15 For an insightful discussion of how companies should manage their cost structures during different stages of growing a new business, see C. Christensen and M. Raynor, *The Innovator's Solution*, Harvard Business School Press, 2003, pp. 216–231.

PART IV

Case studies

PART OVERVIEW

This part consists of the following three main sections:

- A conceptual chapter that outlines how to learn through case studies
- A case study synopses section
- The case section consisting of 19 field-based case studies.

The introductory chapter of this part provides a linkage between the conceptual chapters covered earlier in the book and the subsequent case studies. More specifically, it shows how the e-business strategy framework and the case studies contained in this book can help students and managers involved with e-business strategy development to expand their skills and knowledge along the dimensions of creativity and analytical ability.

The case study synopses section provides an overview of all the case studies included in the book and offers an abstract of each one of these cases. Following this overview, this part contains the individual case studies.

CHAPTER 14

Building e-business competence through concepts and cases

Chapter at a glance

14.1 Defining creativity and analytical ability
      14.1.1 Creativity
      14.1.2 Analytical ability

14.2 Becoming a 'catalyst for change'

14.3 Learning about e-business through case studies
      14.3.1 Case studies as a context for the analysis of e-business issues
      14.3.2 Case studies as a context for the application of e-business concepts
      14.3.3 Case studies as a stimulus for creative e-business strategies

14.4 Learning about e-business through concepts and frameworks
      14.4.1 Extending the breadth of the analysis
      14.4.2 Extending the depth of the analysis

Learning outcomes

After completing this chapter, you should be able to:

■ Understand how creativity and analytical abilities contribute to the strategy development process.

■ Recognise the value of case studies for learning about e-business.

■ Explain the value of concepts and frameworks for learning about e-business.

INTRODUCTION

Let us venture out from the e-business world for a moment and compare managers in charge of strategy development with architects who are designing new buildings.[1] We will consider first what kind of qualities good architects need to have and determine in a following step to what extent this analogy is relevant for managers.

Good architects are those who bring new, creative and surprising elements into their work. While planning buildings, they do not just copy what has always been around within their cultural area. Instead, they develop a unique style that combines well-proven, generally accepted solutions with new, individual and creative ideas. It is this way of solving technical and artistic problems that sets their work positively apart from others. They design buildings where bypassers appreciate the work done and sometimes recognise who the architect was.

How do good architects develop their ideas? Architects need to become inspired and find 'food' for their minds to work and play around with. They derive their inspiration from many different sources. They can turn to the leading architects within their own country and culture and learn from their styles. To expand their horizons further, they might travel around the world to see other settings and cultures to find out more about other architectural styles. On a more abstract level, they might also turn to nature to see how plants and trees have solved their own 'architectural' challenges.

Yet good architects not only are creative; they also have the analytical ability to assess critically the feasibility of their ideas. This includes finding answers to questions such as 'Will the building be structurally sound?', 'What will the construction costs be?', 'Will people enjoy living in this building?' and 'Will my client be able and willing to pay for it?' To answer these questions, good architects need to be able to conduct their analysis both on a broad level to cover all relevant issues (such as structural soundness of the building design, legal restrictions and financial considerations) and on a detailed level to address the specific problems of the project at hand. The critical ability is that they are able to switch back and forth between broad overall considerations and important detailed issues that require in-depth analysis.[2]

The essence of this analogy is to point out that, just like good architects, successful managers are likely to be those who come up with innovative strategic ideas. Additionally, they are able to determine whether their ideas hold when scrutinised from an analytic business perspective.

We start this chapter by briefly outlining the dimensions of creativity and analytical ability.[3] Following that, we discuss how the conceptual e-business strategy framework and the case studies contained in this book can help students and managers involved with e-business strategy development to expand their skills and knowledge along the dimensions of creativity and analytical ability.

14.1 Defining creativity and analytical ability

14.1.1 Creativity

In its broadest sense, creativity can be defined as the ability to develop new ideas. Just as it is inherently difficult to determine what makes some people more intelligent than others, it is also difficult to determine why some people are more creative than others. However, in spite of this uncertainty, one predominant characteristic among creative people is that they have been exposed to different experiences, thinking styles and disciplines from which they draw in their search for new ideas.

Consider, for example, the great German baroque composer, Johann Sebastian Bach, who lived in the eighteenth century. Even though he led a rather provincial life, never travelling outside Germany, his music was inspired by other great European composers of the baroque period. Most importantly, Bach transcribed the orchestral work of Italian composers such as Antonio Vivaldi, which later had a profound influence on Bach's composition style, as can be witnessed, for example, in his *Italian Concerto* for harpsichord.

The American inventor Thomas Edison, who invented the electric light bulb and the telegraph, also immersed himself in a broad variety of knowledge from an early age. Edison's parents taught him, when he was 11, how to use the resources of the local library. He started with the last book on the bottom shelf and planned to read every book in the building. At age 12, he had read Gibbon's *Rise and Fall of the Roman Empire*, Sears' *History of the World* and Burton's *Anatomy of Melancholy*, in addition to *The World Dictionary of Science* and books on practical chemistry.[4]

These two examples are meant to illustrate that a broad knowledge or pool of experience – a characteristic that Csikszentmihalyi, a creativity researcher, calls 'differentiated mind' – seems to be a prerequisite for creativity.[5] Based on this knowledge, creative individuals are able to produce many new ideas, mostly by taking existing ideas that are seemingly unrelated and then connecting them in new ways.

The inevitable question is then: How can we improve our creativity in order to be able to develop innovative ideas? There exists a vast literature on creativity that suggests detailed methods on how to think creatively, individually or in team settings.[6] In the context of this book, we consider the following steps to be of special importance:

■ *Create a vast and diverse pool of knowledge and experiences.* Search outside your domain of expertise to provide your mind with enough 'food' for developing creative ideas. A good starting point is to capture interesting ideas from different settings (industrial, organisational, geographical, cultural, etc.). In most cases, it will probably not be clear what this information will be good for, or even whether it will ever be good for anything. The problem with creativity is that you just do not know beforehand which ideas will turn out to be valuable and which ones will not. The collection of case studies in this book provides some examples of good (and bad) ideas and successful (and failed) implementations. You might also want to look across disciplines by studying, for instance, history or biology.

■ *Produce as many different ideas as possible.* Play around with the existing ideas of others, get a feeling for why they work, or do not work, and try to connect ideas that are seemingly unconnected (see the FT article 'Breaking the barriers to creativity').

Creativity is not a plug-and-play affair; rather, it requires time and patience. However, looking for new applications of old ideas is a good way to jump-start a creative thinking process. Consider, for instance, the deployment of the steam engine in the nineteenth century. At first it was used only in mines, and it took 75 years for someone to work out that it could also be used to power steamboats. For a more recent example, consider Jeff Bezos, the founder of Amazon.com. He saw the potential of the Internet and connected that with book retailing to create the idea of Amazon.com, which, in a matter of a few years, has turned into the largest bookstore in the world. To connect existing ideas in new ways requires one to break out of the known reality by making a mental leap into new and uncharted territory.

■ *Produce unlikely ideas.* At this early stage, there is no need to think about implementation; instead, all that matters is creation. Just ensure that the ideas you produce are unlikely ideas, i.e. ideas that are very different from what other people come up with and that diverge from traditional thinking. That is what constitutes their novelty and uniqueness. At the same time, these ideas are not bizarre. Once others see them, they say: 'Oh, that's so obvious, I could have thought of that myself.' Maybe they could have, but they did not; they were unable to make this seemingly obvious connection between A and B. That is the big difference between creative and not-so-creative people – it is the almost-but-not-quite dimension that sets them apart. For instance, with hindsight it is easy to see that an online auction house such as eBay would be highly successful. Yet someone had to have the creative insight to come up with this idea and, later, the courage to implement it.

Breaking the barriers to creativity

Creativity, a philosopher once remarked, is whatever you choose to make of it. Creativity begins with recognizing opportunities as they present themselves in everyday life. Once these 'triggers' for creativity have been spotted, the manager then needs to assess the problem, often overcoming barriers to new solutions.

Creativity is achieved through breaking down existing relationships and analyzing the elements of the problem, then moving these into new patterns until a solution is found. Creativity requires a desire to experiment, an ability to understand problems and ask questions, and a refusal to be afraid of failure. Developing these traits is not easy, but it can be done. Every person in an organization has the potential to make new and better things happen, to bring into being new ideas regardless of their job or background. Whether they do so is a matter of their ability to see the world around them and whether they can recognize the opportunities or 'triggers' for creativity that can be found in everyday life.

Triggers for creativity

Intermittent windshield wipers for automobiles were not invented by an auto engineer, but by someone who tinkered with cars in his spare time. Collectively, the major automakers had thousands of engineers on their payrolls, most of whom would at some time have had the experience of driving in the rain. Yet none of these 'experts' saw this situation as an opportunity to do something new.

We are exposed to these moments every day; if we fail to notice them, they pass us by. If we pause to reflect and question, the situation might become a trigger, an impulse to creative action.

→

History has recorded other triggers. While on vacation, Edwin Land took pictures of his daughter. When she showed her disappointment that she couldn't see the results right then and there, he set his mind to the task of developing instant photography. Art Fry sang in a church choir for years. As many choir members did, he put slips of paper in his hymn book to mark each selection. His technique was not foolproof, however; the slips of paper often fell out. Taking his dissatisfaction back to his job, he developed what became 3M's Post-it note pads.

The non-stick coating Teflon was an accident. However, its subsequent application to a myriad of products happened because a curious chemist didn't throw away the accident; he played with it to learn more about its properties. He found that the new product could have many uses, such as non-stick frying pans.

These events probably happened to hundreds of other fathers, choir members, and chemists. The only difference is they were triggers to these people, and events to be forgotten by the others.

Defining the problem

It has been said that 'a problem correctly stated is half solved'. Edward de Bono talks about an office building where people complained about the time they had to wait for the elevators. Seeing the problem as one of 'How can we speed up the elevators?' the building's owners felt they were up against a brick wall of prohibitive costs. In a triumph of lateral thinking, it was suggested that mirrors be placed on the walls around the elevators. Thus people would spend the time looking at themselves, combing their hair, and would be oblivious to the wait.

However, suppose the problem had originally been stated in terms of the true choice: 'How can we eliminate the complaints about the elevators?' Speeding them up would have been an idea; mirrors might have been recognized as an idea, as well as mounting television sets on the wall or piping in news broadcasts. The problem was first looked at in terms of changing the performance of the product (the elevators). It was solved by creating change in how the product was perceived, by changing the product's environment.

Barriers to creativity

An important first step in developing creative abilities is to recognize what stands in the way of creating ideas.

■ The foremost of these barriers is your *own experience*. The advertising guru David Ogilvy once commented that 'The majority of businessmen are incapable of original thought because they are unable to escape from the tyranny of reason.' As an example, Kenneth Olsen, the president of Digital Equipment Corporation, relied on his extensive experience in computers when he told attendees at the World Future Society's 1977 Convention: 'There is no reason for any individual to have a computer in their home.' Relying on what he himself knew about the industry meant that Olsen lost out in the race to enter the home computer market, as his company was overtaken by rivals such as Apple.

■ The *assumptions* you make are another barrier to creativity. For years, the greeting card companies assumed that their competition was other greeting card companies. However, research showed that companies in other sectors, such as telecommunications company Florists Telegraph Delivery (FTD), were also significant competitors.

■ The *judgements* we make are a third barrier to creativity. When was the last time you reacted to an idea with: 'It will never work', or 'We tried that before', or 'They'll never buy it'? Think about judgments you've laughed at like, 'He'll fall off the end of the earth' (said about Christopher Columbus) or 'They'll never replace horses' (said about automobiles). Often judgements are passed on a situation before all the information is known, and thus opportunities are lost.

■ Your *thinking patterns* can be another barrier to creativity. However, while these can inhibit creativity, you could not survive without them. Like experience, thinking patterns can be both an asset and a liability. The key lies in knowing when to depend on them and when to lock them away. If you are driving down a highway and you hear a siren, a stored thinking pattern immediately takes over. You locate the source and, if it is in your line of travel, you pull over to get out of

→

273

the way of an emergency vehicle – or to receive your speeding ticket. At other times, though, thinking patterns tend to lead us to routine behaviour and thought, so that we fail to recognize the new as a source of opportunity.

- A fifth barrier is the *right answer syndrome*. So much of current education emphasizes the need to 'get the right answer'. Answers are just arrangements of information. For example, the game of tic-tac-toe has nine boxes. If each box contains a piece of information, how many combinations are there of these nine pieces of information? There are 362,880 possible combinations of these nine pieces of information. (The answer is 9 factorial, which means it is determined by multiplying $9 \times 8 \times 7 \times 6 \times 5 \times 4 \times 3 \times 2 \times 1 = 362,880$.) However, knowing this answer does not help us to win at tic-tac-toe. In the same way, knowing how many units of product we are selling does not help us to sell more. Creativity involves looking beyond the simple facts.

- The last barrier is *fear of failure*. Failure is actually a great learning tool. Unfortunately, too many managers are graduates of the right-answer school and are oblivious to the value of failure. The best answer to the fear of failure syndrome was expressed by Thomas Edison. When a friend suggested that Edison's attempts to develop an electric storage battery were a failure since he had tried thousands of materials without success, Edison replied: 'Why, I've got a lot of results. I know several thousand things that won't work.'

An approach to creativity

The path to creative ideas has three stages, which involve breaking down the previously perceived relationships between parts of the problem; then re-examining the pieces individually; then re-arranging the pieces to form new relationships until we find a pattern that works and solves the problem. The first step in creating ideas is to destroy the familiarity, the relationships of everything you know about the problem. Before Edwin Land invented instant photography, every consumer knew that seeing the results of a picture-taking session was related to developing the film, which was related to a place called a darkroom, which was related to the local drugstore as its contact point.

Everybody was a prisoner of that familiarity, including Edwin Land himself, until he let his mind destroy those relationships. Once this act of destruction has happened, you have a rich reservoir of bits and pieces of information, of unconnected facts and fantasies. However, just like the words in a dictionary, they do nothing until they are selected and assembled to become a coherent sum. The value of these pieces was neatly summed up by Albert Szent-Gyorgyi: 'Discovery consists of seeing what everybody has seen – and thinking what nobody thought.'

The final step is to look for new ways of assembling the pieces. The value and simplicity of this step was succinctly described by the painter Sir Joshua Reynolds in the eighteenth century: 'Invention is little more than new combinations of those images which have been previously gathered and deposited in the memory.' It is this development of new patterns and pictures which is the final act of creativity.

In summary

The fundamental steps to developing your own creative-thinking capabilities can be summarized as follows:

1. Recognize the triggers you are exposed to every day and see the opportunities presented.

2. Define the problem in terms of the 'true choice', and make sure the right questions are being asked.

3. Recognize your barriers to creativity and overcome them.

4. Forget everything you know in terms of relationships between the elements of the problem.

5. Remember everything you know and assess all the pieces of the problem.

6. Rearrange everything you know by moving the same pieces into new relationships with each other.

Source: W. Altier, 'Breaking the barriers to creativity', FT.com, 5 September 2002.

14.1.2 Analytical ability

Analytical ability refers to the skills that are necessary to integrate the knowledge that one possesses into a coherent whole. Thus, while creativity is concerned with *divergent thinking*, i.e. coming up with ideas that are out of the ordinary, analytical ability is concerned with *convergent thinking*, i.e. relating multiple parts of one's thinking and integrating them into a coherent whole.[7] Managers with an integrated mindset are able to break down a complex business problem into its manageable parts and identify crucial variables and questions. They do so by first looking at the 'big picture' that encompasses a broad overview of all issues involved and then focusing on those issues that are of special relevance to the problem at hand.

14.2 Becoming a 'catalyst for change'

By nature, not all managers are endowed with the genius of creativity and profound analytical ability. Instead, they differ along these two dimensions, leading to the classification of manager types explained below, which include (1) the *novice*, (2) the *visionary*, (3) the *efficient performer* and (4) the *catalyst for change* (see Exhibit 14.1).

- *Novices* have a low level of both creativity and analytical ability. In order to develop innovative yet sound strategies, they need to expand their abilities along the creativity and analytical ability dimensions. Note that novices as referred to in this context must not be confused with novices who are new to a company. The latter type of novice might well have had varied experiences and honed their analytical skills before joining the company. Thus, they already possess the skills and knowledge to become a catalyst for change. In the proposed classification, however, the novice does not possess these skills and knowledge.

- *Visionaries* are characterised by an immense level of creative energy yet little analytical ability. Throughout their lives and careers, they have collected many different ideas and they continually develop new ideas. They have a very differentiated mindset. Yet, because they are unable to integrate the many different ideas and evaluate them by means of structured, logical reasoning, their endeavours often tend to end up in chaos and are frequently abandoned prematurely.

- *Efficient performers* possess the opposite characteristics of the visionary. While they do not have the ability to develop creative new ideas, they dispose of strong analytical abilities. This is reflected in the way they perform qualitative and quantitative analyses with rigour and depth.

- *Catalysts for change* combine the positive traits of both the visionary and the efficient performer. Thus, they have high levels of creativity and of analytical ability. They know that strategy formulation is more than just crunching numbers and hoping that something will come out that ensures value creation and competitive advantage. They also know that ideas by themselves are not enough to build a sustainable, profitable business. Instead, to them, strategy formulation is a mix between creativity and analysis.

Exhibit 14.1 **Fostering creativity and analytical ability helps a manager to become a catalyst for change**

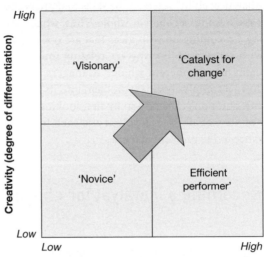

These manager types are characterised by a number of opposing attributes, which are effectively united in one person. Catalysts for change have the ability to (1) alternate between *imagination and fantasy* and a *rooted sense of reality*, (2) be very *playful* at certain times yet return to a very *disciplined* working style within a matter of minutes, and (3) shift quickly from *openness*, where they work closely together with others, to *closure*, where they seclude themselves to work out the details of their thinking.[8]

The proposed classification of different types of manager is helpful in two ways. First, at an individual level you can think where you would place yourself within this matrix. You can also discuss with your colleagues or classmates where they would place you within the matrix. Doing so also allows you to determine which abilities you need to develop further in order to become a catalyst for change.

Furthermore, when working in a team, you can also think about the different people needed to ensure a high level of both creativity and analytical ability. Selecting individuals with complementary abilities can then help your team, as a whole, to become a catalyst for change.

14.3 Learning about e-business through case studies

This book is an integrated, case-study-based learning package, as is demonstrated by the large number of cases included in it. When writing this book, we had three primary aims in mind that the case studies should provide: (1) a *context for the analysis of e-business issues*, (2) a *context for the application of e-business concepts* and (3) a *stimulus for creative e-business strategies*.

14.3.1   Case studies as a context for the analysis of e-business issues

The first aim of the case studies in the book is to provide a broad overview of the critical issues and challenges that organisations face when developing their e-business strategies and, subsequently, conducting their online activities. The diversity of settings and contexts of the cases provides insights on different issues, including e-procurement, online/offline channel conflicts, e-logistics, e-payment, one-to-one marketing and the move from mass production in the physical world to mass customisation over the Internet.

We hope that, after working through these case studies, you will have a richer pool of experiences. However, instead of providing ready-made answers to the questions they raise, these cases studies aim at giving you a deeper understanding of the issues involved and the choices and trade-offs that need to be made when you are faced with making similar decisions of your own.

14.3.2   Case studies as a context for the application of e-business concepts

The second aim of the cases is to provide real-world situations for applying the conceptual frameworks described in the e-business strategy framework part of the book. Compared with typical strategy textbooks, this 'laboratory' setting offers a number of advantages. Just like the real world, information is not neatly packaged and presented. Instead, you have to sift through the rather large amounts of information provided in the cases and distil from it the most important facts. You need then to determine which framework is most applicable to a given situation. In order to arrive at a conclusion and make recommendations, you will have to collect more data and build supporting arguments to defend your stance in front of colleagues.

However, be cautious: there is no single right answer to the questions raised in the cases. As alluded to above, strategy formulation is not maths, where you plug in the numbers and get just one clear answer. There are, however, answers that are better supported by factual evidence than others, and there are answers that use logical reasoning more stringently than others. Thus, the case setting with its inherent ambiguity provides an excellent environment for practising the development and exchange of arguments and the sharpening of analytical skills.[9]

3   Case studies as a stimulus for creative e-business strategies

In addition to providing factual information and a basis for applying the proposed frameworks, the cases in this book are also meant to serve as a source for developing creative ideas. As discussed above, it is important to collect ideas from many different sources to provide 'food' for the creative thought development process.

Just like the architect who studies different building styles from different countries, the cases from different industries and organisations aim at providing you with the opportunity to gain insights into different ways of conducting e-business. For example, consider a group of managers in the strategy division of a large German bank. How do they get inspired to develop innovative strategies? Essentially, the case studies enable the following three possibilities (see also Exhibit 14.2):

■ *Intra-industry benchmarking (within own culture).* The above-mentioned bank managers can first benchmark other banks in Germany. This might provide them with either the comforting feeling that the competition is lagging behind or the feeling that there are some relatively minor adjustments that need to be made. In any case, the closed-in perspective of looking within an industry in one's own culture is often unlikely to provide the creative ideas that would give the bank a lasting source of competitive advantage.

■ *Intra-industry benchmarking (across cultures).* The potential for relevant new insights increases as the bank managers start looking outside their own business culture. For example, they may focus on countries with an established 'e-habit', i.e. having a large portion of the population frequently using the Internet for a wider variety of activities than in Germany. Finland, where e-banking has been customary over the past two decades and where customers are now heavily into using mobile banking, represents an interesting case. The German managers could focus on this country to scout out the recent developments, which will most likely also take place in Germany in the not-so-distant future. Studying Finnish banks, such as Nordea, which is at the cutting edge of electronic and mobile banking, would thus offer an interesting benchmark to analyse in more detail.

■ *Cross-industry inspiration.* A far more innovative and ground-breaking, albeit more challenging, source of new ideas is to look across different industries and think about how their way of conducting e-business could be transferred to one's own industry. A bank might ask: What can we learn from the way Ducati sells some of its motorcycle products exclusively online, or from how YOC manages its one-to-one mobile marketing operations? Building bridges requires creative leaps; that is ultimately the source of competitive advantage, since there are only a few companies willing and able to make such leaps.

Exhibit 14.2 **New ideas can be found by analysing state-of-the-art companies within one's own industry and also across industries**

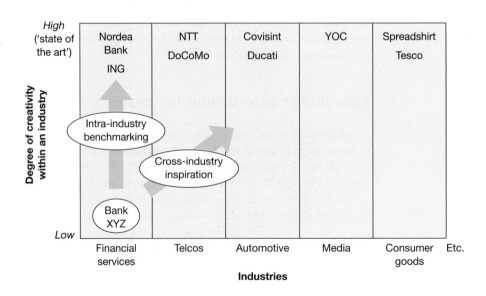

The case studies in the book are meant to be a source of inspiration for cross-industry fertilisation. For example, during our teaching we found that managers from a global insurance company were able to derive interesting and valuable insights from analysing the Ducati case study. Obviously, these cross-industry comparisons should not be adopted 'as is' in one's own industry but rather used to stimulate new and unconventional thinking and to raise the simple, yet powerful question: Would it not be possible for our company to do something similar if …?

14.4 Learning about e-business through concepts and frameworks

After discussing the creative element of strategy formulation, we also need to find ways to evaluate creative ideas and strategies and determine whether it is sensible to implement them. What are the possibilities to test the usefulness of strategy ideas? What makes one strategy more likely to succeed than another? Essentially, there are two different routes that managers can choose.

At one end of the spectrum, managers rely solely on their intuition, which is based mainly on their past experiences. At the other end, they rely on analysing the problem at hand in a structured fashion to come up with a solution. In contrast to intuitive decisions, where judgement is based on implicit criteria that are not spelled out, analytical decision making relies on a clearly defined set of explicit criteria that are used to evaluate the merits and drawbacks of different options. In most cases, managers, unknowingly or knowingly, use a combination of these approaches, as discussed in Strategy in Action 14.1.

STRATEGY IN ACTION 14.1

Business thinking: on finding the right balance between analysis and intuition

Business thinking starts with an intuitive choice of assumptions. Its progress as analysis is intertwined with intuition. The final choice is always intuitive. If that were not true, all problems of almost any kind would be solved by mathematicians with non-quantitative data.

The final choice in all business decisions is, of course, intuitive. It must be. Otherwise it is not a decision, just a conclusion, a printout.

The trade-off of subjective non-quantifiable values is by definition a subjective and intuitive choice. Intuition can be awesome in its value at times. It is known as good judgment in everyday affairs. Intuition is in fact the sub-conscious integration of all the experiences, conditioning and knowledge of a lifetime, including the emotional and cultural biases of that lifetime.

But intuition alone is never enough. Alone it can be disastrously wrong. Analysis too can be disastrously wrong. Analysis depends upon keeping the required data to manageable proportions. It also means keeping the non-quantifiable data to a minimum. Thus, analysis by its very nature requires initial oversimplification and intuitive choice of starting assumptions with exclusion of certain data. All of these choices are intuitive. A mistake in any one can be fatal to the analysis. Any complex problem has a near infinite combination of facts and relationships.

$\rightarrow$

Business in particular is affected by everything, including the past, the non-logical and the unknowable. This complexity is compounded by multiple objectives to serve multiple constituencies, many of whose objectives must be traded off. Problem solving with such complexity requires an orderly, systematic approach in order to even hope to optimize the final decision.

When the results of analysis and intuition coincide, there is little gained except confidence. When the analysis reaches conclusions that are counter-intuitive, then more rigorous analysis and reexamination of underlying assumptions are always called for. The expansion of the frame of reference and the increased rigor of analysis may be fruitful.

But in nearly all problem solving there is a universe of alternative choices, most of which must be discarded without more than cursory attention. To do otherwise is to incur costs beyond the value of any solution and defer decision to beyond the time horizon. A frame of reference is needed to screen the intuitive selection of assumptions, relevance of data, methodology and implicit value judgments. That frame of reference is the concept.

Conceptual thinking is the skeleton or the framework on which all the other choices are sorted out. A concept is by its nature an oversimplification. Yet its fundamental relationships are so powerful and important that they will tend to override all except the most extreme exceptions. Such exceptions are usually obvious in their importance. A concept defines a system of interactions in terms of the relative values that produce stable equilibrium of the system. Consequently, a concept defines the initial assumptions, the data required and the relationships between the data inputs. In this way it permits analysis of the consequences of change in input data.

Concepts are simple in statement but complex in practice. Outputs are almost always part of the input by means of feedback. The feedback itself is consequently a subsystem interconnected with other subsystems.

Theoretically, such conceptual business systems can be solved by a series of simultaneous equations. In practice, computer simulation is the only practical way to deal with the characteristic multiple inputs, feedback loops and higher order effects in a reasonable time at reasonable cost with all the underlying assumptions made explicit. Pure mathematics becomes far too ponderous.

Concepts are developed in hard science and business alike from an approximation of the scientific method. They start with a generalization of an observed pattern of experience. They are stated first as a hypothesis, then postulated as a theory, then defined as a decision rule. They are validated by their ability to predict. Such decision rules are often crystallized as policies. Rarely does a business concept permit definitive proof enough to be called a 'law' except facetiously.

Intuition disguised as status, seniority and rank is the underlying normative mode of all business decisions. It could not be otherwise. Too many choices must be made too often. Data is expensive to collect, often of uncertain quality or relevance. Analysis is laborious and often far too expensive even though imprecise or superficial.

Yet two kinds of decisions justify rigorous and painstaking analysis guided by intuition derived from accumulated experience. The irrevocable commitment of major reserves of resources deserves such treatment. So do the major policies which guide and control the implementation of such commitments.

All rigorous analysis is inherently an iterative process. It starts with an intuitive choice and ends with an intuitive decision. The first definition of a problem is inescapably intuitive. It must be in order to be recognized as a problem at all. The final decision is intuitive. It must be or there is no choice and therefore no need for decision.

Between those two points of beginning and ending, the rigorous process must take place. The sequence is analysis, problem redefinition, reanalysis and then even more rigorous problem redefinition, etc. until the law of diminishing returns dictates a halt – intuitively.

The methodology and sequence of business thinking can be stated or at least approximated.

■ State the problem as clearly and fully as possible.

■ Search for and identify the basic concepts that relate to the perceived critical elements.

■ Define the data inputs this conceptual reference will require. Check off and identify any major factors, which are not implicitly included in the conceptual base.

■ Redefine the problem and broaden the concept as necessary to include any such required inputs.

■ Gather the data and analyze the problem.

■ Find out to which data inputs the analysis is sensitive. Reexamine the range of options with respect to those factors and the resulting range of outputs.

■ Based on the insights developed by the analysis, redefine the problem and repeat the process.

■ Reiterate until there is a consensus that the possible incremental improvement in insight is no longer worth the incremental cost. That consensus will be intuitive. It must be. There is no way to know the value of the unknown.

It is a matter of observation that much of the value of a rigorous and objective examination of a problem will be found in one of three areas:

■ First, the previously accepted underlying assumptions may prove to be invalid, in fact, or inadequate as the problem definition is changed.

■ Second, the interaction between component functions may have been neglected, resulting in suboptimization by function.

■ Third, a previously unknown or unaccepted or misunderstood conceptual framework may be postulated which both permits prediction of the consequence of change and partially explains these consequences.

It is also a matter of common observation that the wisest of intuitive judgments come after full exploration and consensus on the nature of the problem by peers of near equal but diverse experience.

Finally, it is also a matter of general experience that implementation of the optimum decision will prove difficult if that discussion and consensus have not been continued long enough to make the relationship between the overall objective and the specific action seem clear to all who must interpret and implement the required policies. Otherwise, the intuition of those who do the implementation will be used to redefine the policies that emerged from analysis. This is one reason planned organization change is so difficult, and random drift is so common.

Here are some fundamental procedural suggestions. Define the problem and hypothesize the approach to a solution intuitively before wasting time on data collection and analysis. Do the first analysis lightly. Then and only then redefine the problem more rigorously and reanalyze in depth. (Don't go to the library and read all the books before you know what you want to learn.) Use mixed project research teams composed of some people with finely honed intuitions from experience and others with highly developed analytical skills and too little experience to know what cannot be done. Perhaps in this way you can achieve the best of both analysis and intuition in combination and offset the weaknesses of either.

Source: Business thinking, B. Henderson in *Perspectives on Strategy*, C. Stern & G. Stalk (eds); Copyright © (1998 John Wiley & Sons, Inc.); Reprinted with permission of John Wiley & Sons, Inc.

Intuition is valuable because it provides a quick solution to a problem. However, its value is somewhat limited when the environment changes quickly and drastically, as is the case with e-business. Then, managers risk overlooking or misjudging important factors, which results in misguided strategies.

An analytical approach to strategy formulation, on the other hand, allows for a broader and more profound analysis of the issues at hand. However, it is time consuming and difficult, since it is not immediately obvious which factors need to be analysed when evaluating strategies in a systematic way. Questions such as 'Should we start selling our products online?' and 'How should we position ourselves vis-à-vis our competitors and how should we organise our firm?' cannot be answered by just looking at individual and isolated factors. Instead, it is necessary to acquire a thorough and comprehensive perspective.

How can this be done? One possible approach is to use conceptual frameworks that break down the problem at hand into manageable subunits, which can be analysed individually. The goal of a framework is to facilitate thinking through a problem by providing a structured approach that is independent of industry or starting position. A good framework has the following qualities:[10]

■ *It captures the most important dimensions of the problem.* This means that all the important elements that constitute an integral part of the real world are included in the framework. One of the reasons why, for instance, Porter's industry analysis framework, which is defined in Section 3.2, has been used widely in the business and academic communities is that it has captured the essential factors that determine the attractiveness of an industry. At the same time, a good framework captures the essential variables with the least number of dimensions, which in turn helps manage complexity. A framework with hundreds of variables might cover all dimensions, yet it is not practical in everyday problem solving. Thus, finding the right balance between being exhaustive on the one hand and keeping the framework as simple as possible on the other hand is a crucial challenge in framework building.

■ *All the elements that the framework contains are mutually exclusive.* This means that the elements or dimensions in the framework differ systematically from each other and do not overlap. To a large extent, this criterion determines the clarity of frameworks. Consider, for example, the value chain concept, which is discussed in more detail in Section 4.2. This concept helps a manager to separate distinctive, albeit interrelated, activities within a firm such as inbound logistics, production, outbound logistics, marketing and sales, and after-sales service. The separation into discrete activities opens up the way to a more rigorous analysis and to raising questions such as 'Which of our activities should we perform internally and which should we outsource?' and 'Through which activities can we differentiate ourselves from our competitors?'

Frameworks such as Porter's five forces and the value chain are frequently criticised for being too rigid and leaving too little room for creativity.[11] There are essentially two alternatives to a framework-based approach. First, to rely solely on intuition, which presents its own set of problems as was discussed above. Second, to use an analytical approach without a structured framework and to start from scratch every time. Doing so entails two main risks.

First, you might forget an important dimension that, in the end, may turn out to be crucial for the problem-solving process. Second, it requires substantially more effort because you need to determine the most important variables that drive the analytical process. Doing so might force you to consider every variable involved but never to achieve any real depth in your analysis.

Instead of the above-mentioned approaches, it is more sensible to familiarise yourself with key frameworks and concepts and then adapt them to the needs of the specific situation at hand. The goal of the e-business strategy framework, which we presented in Part II of the book, is to make you more familiar with the most important strategy frameworks and to show, through examples, how they can be used in an e-business context. However, the proposed framework is not meant to provide any ready-made answers. Instead, it aims to raise questions and provide a structured approach to asking 'Why?' and 'Why not?'

In particular, it aims to expand the analysis along two directions: first breadth and then depth (see Exhibit 14.3).

14.4.1 Extending the breadth of the analysis

As mentioned above, it is difficult to achieve an overarching perspective of the issues involved in strategy formulation. Therefore, it is advisable first to gain a broad understanding of the relevant issues and then to embark on a more detailed analysis. The proposed sequencing of these steps is important, especially knowing managers' time limitations.

To illustrate the above issue, let us consider two companies – DeepFirst Inc. and BroadFirst Inc. – involved in oil exploration. The exploration engineers of DeepFirst Inc. start drilling in front of the company's headquarters to find out whether there is any oil. Then they move on and keep drilling randomly, in different places, until they eventually encounter oil. However, this process is very time consuming and expensive. The exploration engineers of BroadFirst Inc., on the other hand, have developed elaborate systems based on geological research and advanced ultrasound devices. Using this technology,

Exhibit 14.3 Effective strategy formulation requires the ability to cover a broad analysis horizon and to perform selective, in-depth analyses of crucial issues

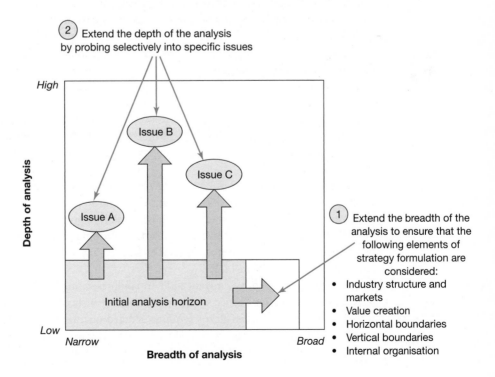

they quickly scan vast areas of land and can then predict precisely where it is worthwhile drilling. In effect, they look at the bigger picture first before investing substantial efforts in drilling, thereby reducing cost and increasing the likelihood of success.

Often, however, managers behave more like the engineers from DeepFirst Inc., overlooking the 'bigger picture' and instead focusing first on isolated issues, which often turn out to be of only marginal importance. In doing so, they collect vast amounts of data and build elaborate quantitative models only to find out later that the issue they were working on so diligently did not really matter in the broader context. However, while getting immersed in a side issue, they forgot to move on to other areas of analysis that were significantly more important.

In order to reduce the danger of missing key variables in the strategy formulation process, it is important to have a clear understanding of the overall dimensions that are likely to be relevant. In the e-business strategy framework, there are three main dimensions, which are all closely interrelated. These are: (1) external environment and markets, (2) value-creation and strategy options, and (3) firm structure and organisation. Depending on the strategic context at hand, certain dimensions are more relevant than others. In any case, however, it is important to have the broad picture in mind at the outset and only then to drill deeper into more specific issues.

14.4.2 Extending the depth of the analysis

In addition to expanding the breadth of the analysis, a second goal of the concepts discussed in the e-business strategy framework is to expand the depth of the analysis. To illustrate this point, let us consider the case of a firm that wants to enter the online auction market. At first glance, this market might seem attractive because existing players, such as eBay, are highly profitable. Digging deeper, we would then ask 'Why is this so?', a question to which there are several answers. First, there are high economies of scale, which limits costs. Second, there are also high barriers to entry, which allows incumbent firms to charge healthy margins.

Moving down to the next level of analysis, we can determine the reasons for the high barriers to entry. They result largely from network effects. Once an e-auction place has managed to attract a critical number of users, it is unlikely that customers will switch to a new competitor. This is due to the fact that much of the value of an e-auction place depends on how many other customers use it, which creates a liquid market where it is easy to sell and buy things.

Moving down one more level, we could ask how the firm was able to create strong network effects and whether these effects could be replicated. This probing can continue by always asking 'Why?' Eventually, however, there will be a point where it is no longer sensible to keep raising questions because the effort of doing so will outweigh the expected benefit. Yet, more often than not, we tend to stop asking 'Why?' too soon rather than too late (see Strategy in Action 14.2).

Furthermore, with today's advanced IT capabilities, companies can more easily collect relevant data to answer deeper-seated questions. For instance, when analysing customer service at Amazon.com, Jeff Bezos requires detailed quantitative run-downs of numbers regarding the average customer contacts per order, average contact length, breakdown of e-mail and telephone contacts, and total cost of each contact.

The move along the chain of causality by asking 'Why?' helps you to understand the root causes of successes and failures. You can then use these insights to evaluate your own ideas and make more informed strategy decisions. To foster the analysis, the concepts discussed in this book represent the following three levels of thinking:

- *e-Business specific concepts.* On the first level, concepts such as a company's virtual value chain (see Section 4.3), the unbundling of the traditional organisation (see Section 9.4) and the ICDT (Information, Communication, Distribution and Transaction) model (see Section 4.4) are specific to e-business. Frequently, these concepts implicitly or explicitly build on concepts from the strategic management literature (such as the value chain concept) and also on fundamental economic thinking (such as the concept of transaction costs).

  The strength of these concepts is that they are tailored to the e-business context; therefore, their applicability is rather straightforward. However, this specific tailoring presents, at the same time, their main weakness, since, as the experiences of the last few years have shown, these concepts often fall short of explaining more complex cause–effect relationships, thereby possibly misguiding managers into seemingly obvious yet faulty strategies.

  Consider, for instance, the concepts of deconstruction and unbundling that became popular during the Internet boom years (see Chapter 9). Managers were supposed to take apart their company's value chains and focus on individual activities or businesses where they possessed a competitive advantage. The initial logic was, in many cases, compelling. In other cases, however, it did not turn out to be fitting because crucial linkages between different activities within the firm were overlooked. Probing beyond the initial level of analysis might have provided a more profound explanation and, in turn, would have led to more sensible conclusions and better strategies.

- *Generic strategic concepts.* In order to move beyond the initial level of analysis and find deeper cause–effect relationships, it is useful to have a good understanding of the key strategic concepts, such as the five forces industry model, the concept of co-opetition, the generic strategy options and the value chain. These concepts can be applied irrespective of the industry or firm at hand. The common characteristic of these concepts is that they do not provide any ready-made answers. Instead, they define the relevant variables and thus help managers to raise the right questions. We discuss these concepts at length in the e-business strategy framework and link them to some real-world examples to illustrate how they can be applied in the specific e-business context.

- *Fundamental economic concepts.* Underlying the strategy concepts there is another level of thinking based on fundamental economic concepts. These include economies of scale and scope, transaction costs and value creation. They are also relevant in the e-business context and provide a strong basis for more in-depth analysis.

Summing up this section on conceptual thinking, we would like to stress again that concepts and frameworks are not meant as a substitute for the development of creative ideas. Creative ideas are a prerequisite for any innovative strategy. Conceptual thinking is the next step to help select those creative ideas that are likely to succeed.[12]

STRATEGY IN ACTION 14.2

'Why?' – the importance of questions in strategy formulation

The single most important word in strategy formulation is why.

Asking why is the basic act of probing. Searching for root causes takes strategy formulation away from the unconscious repetition of past patterns and mimicry of competitors. Asking why leads to new insights and innovations that sometimes yield important competitive advantages.

Asking why repeatedly is a source of continuous self-renewal, but the act of inquiry itself is an art. It can evoke strong reactions from the questioned. It is only rarely welcomed. It is sometimes met with defensiveness and hostility, on the one hand, or, on the other, the patronizing patience reserved by the knowledgeable for the uninformed.

To ask why – and why not – about basics is to violate the social convention that expertise is to be respected, not challenged. Functional organizations in mature industries have a particular problem in this regard. One risks a lot to challenge the lord in his fiefdom.

Questioning the basics – the assumptions that 'knowledgeable' people don't question – is disruptive. Probing slows things down, but often to good effect. It can yield revolutionary new thoughts in quite unexpected places.

To probe to the limits is to simplify the problem to its essentials and solve one problem rather than many. To pursue such probing takes a special, strongly motivated person, unless one makes it the norm for the organization. Asking why five times is easy to say, but hard to do. It challenges people's knowledge and even self-respect. It can call into question their diligence and the basis of their expertise. It requires fresh thinking on all sides. Yet it's so basic to learning, to seeing new things from the familiar. In the early 19th century, doctors routinely went, without washing, from autopsies to the treatment of patients – with disastrous results. Ignaz Semmelweis is the man who first hypothesized the basic relationship and proposed and tested a change to clean hands – yet in his own time he had to struggle with his peers because he questioned the accepted practice.

Probing takes us beyond data analysis

Good strategy depends critically on knowing the root causes. Finding them is often a task beyond quantitative analysis. One must look to broader frames of reference and bring basic judgment and common sense to bear. Probing – asking why – is the often intuitive search for the logic that heavy data analysis can miss or bury.

Asking why is a qualitative act. It is different from quantitative analysis, but the one gains power from the other. It propels analysis forward by raising new questions to be subjected to rigorous analysis. It takes us beyond the numbers to new answers, new solutions, and new opportunities. Quantitative analysis should not become both the means and the end.

Asking why can raise the questions that are fundamental, but not necessarily answerable through rigorous analysis itself. These are the basic questions of leadership and common sense. They are the search for 'the point.' For example:

- Why do we continue in this business?
- Why should anyone buy this product?
- What will prevent competitors from matching us? What will we do then?
- Why are we making so much money?
- Why won't it eventually come to an end?
- What must we do now to prepare for or moderate that change?

→

These sorts of probes search for the bedrock reasons for value and advantages to test how enduring they may be. They ask whether the shape and character of the business and its strategy make sense.

Asking why is easy in concept, but harder in practice. It can be very rewarding. Why not do it?

Source: Probing, J. Isaacs in *Perspectives on Strategy*, C. Stern & G. Stalk (eds); Copyright © (1998 John Wiley & Sons, Inc.); Reprinted with permission of John Wiley & Sons, Inc.

SUMMARY

- First, this chapter outlined the dimensions of creativity and analytical ability and pointed out the importance of these two qualities in the strategy development process.

- Second, this chapter suggested a categorisation of different manager types along the dimensions of creativity and analytical ability. The resulting four manager types are (1) the novice, (2) the efficient performer, (3) the visionary and (4) the catalyst for change. The goal of the concepts and case studies presented in this book is to help you move closer towards becoming a catalyst for change.

- Third, this chapter showed how case studies can serve as an inspiration for creative strategy development. Readers can use them to conduct intra-industry benchmarking (within one's own culture and across cultures) and as a source for cross-industry inspiration.

- The chapter then discussed the value of frameworks in the strategy formulation process and outlined the key requirements that a good framework needs to fulfil. First, it must capture the most important dimensions of the problem at hand. Second, all the elements contained in a framework must be mutually exclusive.

- The last section of this chapter outlined two analytical techniques to evaluate strategies. First, this includes expanding the breadth of the analysis to ensure that each important element is considered thoroughly. Second, it includes expanding the depth of the analysis to ensure that the most important issues for the problem at hand are assessed rigorously.

REVIEW QUESTIONS

1 What are the three possibilities mentioned in this chapter that can help you to improve your creativity?

2 How do the four types of managers mentioned in this chapter differ? What are the specific qualities of the 'catalyst for change'?

3 What are the three ways in which case studies can help you to learn about e-business?

4 What are the key characteristics of a good framework?

5 What are the three levels of conceptual thinking presented in this chapter?

DISCUSSION QUESTIONS

1 Where do you position yourself within the 'catalyst-for-change' matrix?

2 Discuss your above assessment with colleagues. In light of their feedback, in which area would you especially like to improve your abilities?

3 Discuss how case studies can help you to develop creative strategies. Provide some examples.

4 Is it always sensible to try to get a broad understanding of a problem before addressing more detailed issues? What problems do you foresee with this approach?

5 How can you increase the depth of analysis through the concepts and frameworks presented in this book?

RECOMMENDED KEY READING

■ B. Nalebuff and I. Ayres outline an approach to creative problem solving in *Why Not? How to Use Everyday Ingenuity to Solve Problems Big and Small*, Harvard Business School Press, 2003.

■ M. Csikszentmihalyi analyses different dimensions of creativity in *Creativity*, Harper Perennial, 1997.

■ E. de Bono, one of the leading thinkers in the field of creative thinking, proposes 'lateral thinking' as a way for creative idea development in his book *Lateral Thinking – A Textbook of Creativity*, Penguin, 1990.

■ G. Gavetti and J. Rivkin provide excellent insights into how analogies from different industries can be used to jump-start creative idea development in 'How strategists really think – tapping the power of analogy', *Harvard Business Review*, April 2005, pp. 54–63.

■ For a practical and very insightful discussion of structuring and problem solving, see B. Minto, *The Pyramid Principle*, FT/Prentice Hall, 2002.

■ M. Porter discusses the importance and value of frameworks in the article 'Towards a dynamic theory of strategy', *Strategic Management Journal*, 1991, Vol. 12, No. 8, pp. 95–117. For further reading on M. Porter's thinking about frameworks, see also N. Argyres and A. McGahan, 'An interview with Michael Porter', *Academy of Management Executive*, 2002, Vol. 16, No. 2, pp. 43–52.

■ R. Rumelt, D. Schendel and D. Teece discuss the tension between case-based approaches and theoretical constructions for the strategy formulation process in 'Strategic management and economics', *Strategic Management Journal*, 1991, Vol. 12, No. 8, pp. 5–30.

■ S. Huff, T. Jelassi and J. Cash discuss how to teach information systems courses through the case-study-based approach in 'Teaching information systems management with cases', *Information Systems (IS) World*, 1995.

USEFUL THIRD-PARTY WEBLINKS

- www.creativitypool.com is a database with creative and original ideas.

- www.pyramidprinciple.com is the website of Barbara Minto. She invented the Pyramid Principle, which provides a structured approach to problem solving.

- www.thomasedison.com is a website containing biographical information about the inventor Thomas Edison.

- www.trendwatching.com is a website that spots emerging consumer trends and related new business ideas on a global basis.

- www.whynot.net is the online forum for people to share and talk about their ideas.

NOTES AND REFERENCES

1 T. V. Ghyczy describes the usefulness of metaphors for strategy development in the article 'The fruitful flaws of strategy metaphors', *Harvard Business Review*, 2003, September, pp. 86–94. One of his key messages is that, contrary to popular thinking, the true value of a metaphor for generating new strategic perspectives becomes apparent when the metaphors themselves stop working, which is the case when a metaphor is not entirely transferable to the problem depicted. Attracted by the familiar and repelled by the unfamiliar connections, one is, at the same time, left in a state of understanding and incomprehension. In this state of mind, the likeliness of looking at things in new and creative ways increases.

2 Obviously, strategy development is not the same as designing a building. Most importantly, architects face nowhere near as much uncertainty regarding environmental changes as managers do in the still rapidly evolving e-business environment. If we were to include this business-like level of uncertainty, this would mean that the architects would not know whether the buildings they are designing will be built on quicksand or on rock, in the tropical rainforest or in the Arctic Circle.

3 Due to the length limitation of this book, this chapter might not cover many of the aspects that pedagogues or psychologists would want to see discussed in this context. Nonetheless, for students who have previously had only little exposure to the case method and conceptual approaches to problem solving, we believe that this chapter can provide a valuable context for their learning experience.

4 For more information on Thomas Edison's life, visit www.thomasedison.com.

5 See M. Csikszentmihalyi, *Creativity*, HarperPerennial, 1997, pp. 368–370.

6 For a good discussion on idea development and creativity, see A. Hargadon and R. I. Sutton, 'Building an innovation factory', *Harvard Business Review*, 2000, May–June, pp. 157–166, and B. Nalebuff and I. Ayres, *Why Not?*, Harvard Business School Press, 2003. For more recommended reading on this topic, refer to the list above.

7 M. Csikszentmihalyi, *Creativity*, HarperPerennial, 1997, pp. 362–363.

8 Ibid., pp. 360–363.

9 See R. Bruner, B. Gup, B. Nunnally, *et al.*, 'Teaching with cases to graduate and undergraduate students', *Financial Practice and Education*, 1999, Vol. 9, No. 2, pp. 138–147.

10 For an excellent discussion of the value of frameworks in strategy research, see M. E. Porter, 'Towards a dynamic theory of strategy', *Strategic Management Journal*, 1991, Vol. 12, No. 8, pp. 95–117. For a practical discussion of structuring and problem solving, see B. Minto, *The Pyramid Principle*, FT/Prentice Hall, 2002.

11 R. Grant criticises Porter's frameworks in *Contemporary Strategy Analysis*, Blackwell, 2002, p. 89.

12 R. Grant offers an excellent explanation of the value of analysis in the strategy development process in his book *Contemporary Strategy Analysis*, Blackwell, 2002, pp. 31–32.

A guide to the main focus of the case studies

Category	#	Case study name	Page	3 External analysis	4 Internal analysis	5 Strategy options	6 Sustaining a competitive advantage	7 New market spaces	8 Value process framework	9 Internal organisation	10 Relationship with suppliers	11 Relationship with users/customers	12 Mobile business
B2C in retailing	1	Tesco	299	●	●●	●●	●	●●		●●	●	●	
B2C in financial services	2	Nordea	314	●	●●	●●	●●	●●		●●		●	●
	3	ING DIRECT	330	●	●●		●	●●	●	●●		●	
B2C in manufacturing	4	Ducati vs. Harley	343	●	●●		●				●●		
	5	Otis	356		●●		●	●●		●●	●●	●●	
B2B e-commerce	6	Mondus	370		●		●					●●	
	7	Covisint	388		●					●	●●		
	8	IBX	407								●●		
	9	eBay	423		●						●●		
Corporate portals	10	Shell	437	●●	●●		●●			●●			
e-Government	11	e-Government	451	●●	●		●●						
P2P model	12	P2P file-sharing	468	●●			●●	●		●●			
Online communities and user-generated content	13	openBC	482	●●			●●				●	●●	
	14	Spreadshirt	505	●	●●	●●	●●	●	●			●●	
	15	Second Life	525	●●	●			●●	●●			●●	
Mobile e-commerce	16	Sony BMG	548	●●		●●	●●	●●					●●
	17	NTT DoCoMo	570	●	●			●●		●	●●	●●	●●
	18	YOC	585	●				●				●	●●
	19	Paybox	601										●●

Chapter

●● Primary focus of the case study ● Secondary focus of the case study

SYNOPSES OF CASE STUDIES

Business-to-consumer (B2C) e-commerce in retailing

1 From A(pples) to Z(oom lenses): extending the boundaries of multichannel retailing at Tesco.com

Ten years have passed since Tesco, one of the world's largest grocery retailers, introduced its online grocery shopping business 'Tesco.com'. The time is therefore right to look back at this online venture and assess its past performance and current business model, especially that, for the first time, company officials were willing to co-operate with the case study authors. Tesco.com CEO Laura Wade-Gery and other executives were interviewed and provided valuable information and insights on 'The Tesco way' of doing Internet business, which served as a basis for writing this case study.

The objectives of this case study are twofold: first, to look back at the past 10 years and appraise how Tesco's online service and its underlying business model have evolved, especially with respect to the in-store order fulfilment approach. The second objective is to understand and assess Tesco's recent expansion of its multi-channel retailing activities with the start of a new online portal called 'Tesco Direct'.

The case study concludes with an outlook of possible future extensions of the Tesco.com business model. In this context, it briefly presents 'Tesco Diets' as an example of how the company pushes out the boundaries of online retailing. The question that the case study ends with is whether there are any limits to this extension into new business areas.

B2C e-commerce in financial services

2 From e-banking to e-business at Nordea (Scandinavia): the world's biggest clicks-and-mortar bank

This case study focuses on the move of Nordea, a leading Scandinavian bank, from e-banking to e-business. It starts out by presenting Nordea's vision for e-banking and shows how the e-habit and e-trust among the Finnish population have contributed to fulfilling the company's vision.

The case study then describes the main e-business services that Nordea offers to its retail and corporate banking customers. These include e-identification, e-signature, e-billing, e-salary and e-payment. The case study also discusses how Nordea integrates and manages its different banking channels, which include branch-based banking, ATMs and pay terminals, PC-banking, TV-based banking and mobile electronic banking. As part of its channel management strategy, Nordea also uses pricing schemes to entice customers to move online. The case raises possible future competitive threats, from other physical banks and Internet pure players, to Nordea's multi-channel banking approach.

The case study concludes by outlining Nordea's future growth opportunities in existing markets and through new services. The latter include using triggered data-mining techniques to improve customer service and also offering risk management services for e-business.

3 ING DIRECT: rebel in the banking industry

ING DIRECT is one of the six business lines of an integrated financial services provider, the ING Group, and is active in nine different countries. This case study describes how ING DIRECT has become the largest Internet-based bank in the USA, and one of the 30 largest banks of any sort in the country. It focuses on the strategic positioning of ING DIRECT in the US retail banking industry and the strategic actions that the bank has undertaken to achieve and maintain its unique position. The case study describes how ING DIRECT started its business and evolved it over time, and sheds some light on the future challenges which the company currently faces.

B2C e-commerce in manufacturing

4 Ducati (Italy) vs. Harley-Davidson (USA): innovating business processes and managing value networks

This case study compares the e-business strategy of two leading motorcycle manufacturers and demonstrates how Ducati, unlike Harley-Davidson, has made the Internet an integral part of its business strategy. More specifically, the case study describes how Ducati has successfully repositioned itself and adopted a new focus on R&D, marketing and sales, moving away from its initial manufacturing focus. It also analyses how Ducati has fundamentally changed its business model, from traditionally operating through a narrow value chain to setting up a value network that integrated online and offline processes and business partners. The case study contrasts this approach with that of Harley-Davidson, which uses the Internet mainly as a communication channel with its dealers and customers, including the creation of a virtual online community. It also highlights the way each company manages its business processes and the roles that IT and the Internet play in R&D and design, purchasing, manufacturing and assembly, logistics, marketing and sales, and after-sales service.

5 Otis Elevator: accelerating business transformation with IT

This case study focuses on a major business transformation that recently took place at Otis Elevator. Led by the CEO, this transformation represents a remarkable long-term re-engineering of all the business processes of the firm to drive operating costs down and service performance up. Otis's business transformation is the continuation of a change process that has been going on for more than 20 years. The learning objective of the case study is to demonstrate the implementation and impact of a major IT-enabled business and organisational change in a manufacturing context.

Business-to-business (B2B) e-commerce

6 Business-to-business electronic commerce: mondus.com – an e-marketplace for small and medium-sized enterprises

This case study describes the development and use of mondus.com, a third-party B2B marketplace set up for small and medium-sized enterprises. It analyses how mondus matches buyers and sellers through the request-for-proposals model. The case study also describes the international expansion of mondus and the entrepreneurial leadership of its founders, and highlights the benefits and drawbacks for the e-marketplace players.

This case study aims at (1) demonstrating how the Internet helps streamline the purchasing process and creates value for all parties involved; (2) analysing the information flows between the buyer, seller and e-marketplace operator during an online purchasing transaction; and (3) assessing the business opportunities and risks that an e-marketplace operator faces.

7 Covisint (A): the evolution of a B2B marketplace

Ford Motor Co., General Motors and DaimlerChrysler – the three original equipment manufacturers (OEMs) that dominated the automotive industry throughout the twentieth century – launched Covisint in February 2000 as an industry supply chain exchange that would drive out cost and help manage the complex communications within the rigidly hierarchical industry. The Big 3 sourced entire components of cars from large Tier 1 suppliers. By limiting the number of partners and using online technologies to support collaboration and performance tracking, as well as drive out costs from the supply chain, the OEMs hoped that cycle times could be shortened and they could finally achieve a build-to-order model for the car industry. A successful exchange that united the industry was vital to this vision. Covisint was founded with 'borrowed' Big 3 employees and over $250 million in funding from the OEMs. Its business model morphed several times as it raced to bring products to market and to meet the demands of its founders. The start-up burned through six CEOs in three years and now Bob Paul is considering whether to take on the CEO hot seat.

8 IBX (Northern Europe): expanding B2B e-purchasing from indirect to direct goods and services

This case study discusses the key success factors that helped IBX survive the dotcom crash and position itself as one of the most successful B2B platforms in Europe. It starts with a brief description of B2B e-commerce, its evolution over time, and the business outlook in this sector. It then describes the history of IBX and the importance of forging business and technological alliances. The company's business model is reviewed, emphasising (1) its on-demand solutions portfolio (for sourcing, procurement, payment and supplier network modules) and (2) the subscription-based revenue model in terms of its advantages, customers' acceptance and impact on IBX financial viability.

The case study also illustrates the 'anchoring' marketing strategy that IBX used to build its brand and discusses how contract compliance reduced maverick buying. It then

293

assesses some success factors, such as contract compliance, process transparency and system interoperability, that helped IBX achieve a leading position in the B2B market. The case study concludes by presenting the challenges that IBX faces following its move into the (direct) vertical platform market. It highlights the governance problem raised by such a move and the IBX strategy to meet the new challenges.

9 eBay customer support outsourcing

Offshore outsourcing is hotly debated today in business and political circles, driven by the unrelenting growth of technology and the global economy. The case study provides insights into eBay's unique online business model, explores the critical role of customer service in rapidly growing online enterprises, and stimulates in-depth discussion of the issues managers working in customer service face when making outsourcing decisions. The case is set in late 2004 when the operations director is scheduled to present a new 'three-tiered' outsourcing strategy to the senior management team led by CEO Meg Whitman. In addition, at the last minute an unanticipated and largely untried approach to outsourcing is introduced in response to a question posed by eBay's vice president of global customer support: 'If we are to continue outsourcing, and even consider expanding it, why should we keep paying someone else to do what we can do for ourselves'? This question, and related issues, provides the stimulus for students to reflect on and analyse the details of the strategy involving: (1) a 100% increase in volume; (2) outsourcing potentially sensitive risk-related enquiries; (3) the addition of a second vendor; and (4) the viability of a back-out plan, as well as the growing concerns among senior executives about outsourcing altogether. Finally, students are challenged to evaluate a hybrid strategy for eBay to work with a third-party vendor to 'Build, Operate, and ultimately Transfer', or 'BOT', facilities to eBay.

Corporate Internet portals

10 The exploration and production enterprise portal of the Royal Dutch/ Shell Group

Within the Royal Dutch/Shell Group organisation, the exploration and production (EP) business is increasingly a knowledge-driven activity and information/knowledge management is becoming a core element of the corporate strategy. Several portal initiatives were being implemented and one of these, coined EP-One, aimed at improving collaboration across the whole organisation. The case study investigates the design and implementation in 2004 of the EP-One portal. It describes the pilot portal project and its results within the R&D activity of Shell EP. The pilot project revealed the critical importance of clearly and thoroughly defining users' functional requirements on the Internet, and showed how different metrics were used to measure a portal's success. The case study also highlights areas where EP-One use can be extended, and concludes with a future outlook of the applicability of portal technology at Shell.

e-Government

11 e-Government in Estonia: establishing the world's leading information society

This case study focuses on the development of e-government in Estonia in the context of building an information society in this Baltic Sea country. It highlights the recent political and economic changes that took place in Estonia and emphasises the role of political foresight and leadership in promoting the use of ICT in the country. It then discusses the history of public-sector transformation and development of e-government.

The case study provides an overview of Estonia's state-level information systems and describes in detail the e-government IT infrastructure and its three pillars: (1) the data exchange layer X-Road, (2) the PKI infrastructure (the national ID card and digital signature) and (3) the 'virtual office', a unified service space which offers citizens a 'one-stop approach' to access all public services.

The case study provides some illustrative examples of e-government services in Estonia: e-Cabinet, e-Democracy, e-Voting and e-Tax Board. It discusses security and privacy issues and highlights the challenges that the Estonian government faces to create an efficient e-government and the measures taken to overcome these challenges. The case study concludes with an outlook of Estonia's future e-government plans.

The case study aims at: (1) demonstrating how the use of ICT in public administration helps create value for citizens; (2) analysing Estonia's approach to e-government and the reasons for its success; and (3) serving as a platform for discussing the applicability of Estonia's e-government approach to other countries and, more generally, issues related to e-government and e-democracy.

The peer-to-peer (P2P) model

12 Online file-sharing: the music industry's paradigm shift

Ever since they succeeded in closing down the original Napster in 1999, the major music companies have struggled to deal with its successors, the peer-to-peer (P2P) networks. Yet, is this really the paradigm shift that many claim it to be? Is P2P directly responsible for the tumbling sales of music between 1999 and 2003? Putting together the emotional response that many people have for music with the hard-nosed world of business is always likely to be a balancing act. This case study helps us to look at how established industries respond to threats and to consider the complexity of the value chain between the original producer of a product (the writer or performer) and the end user (the consumer who buys the CDs and merchandise).

Virtual online communities and user-generated content

13 openBC vs. StayFriends: Germany's biggest Internet-based social networking sites

This case study illustrates the emergence of social networking sites as an example of Web 2.0 applications. It compares the two leading German social networking sites, openBC and StayFriends, which have different target groups, business strategies and revenue models. openBC is a business networking site connecting professionals from different industries, and serving as a tool for managing contacts and enabling business. StayFriends is a service for reconnecting former classmates with each other.

The case study objectives include: (1) understanding the market for Internet-based social networks; (2) assessing openBC and StayFriends' business model and its impact on viral growth; and (3) appraising the value that social networking sites create and users' capture of this value.

14 Spreadshirt: mass customization on the Internet

This case study describes the evolution of Spreadshirt since its foundation in 2001 and highlights the key role that Lukasz Gadowski, the company's founder and CEO, has played in the process. It stresses the major milestones of Spreadshirt's evolution from being a small German start-up to becoming one of the world's leading micro-merchandising firms. Within five years, the number of Spreadshop operators has increased from 100 in 2002 to approximately 200,000 in 2006, highly benefiting from viral effects among its existing customers and shop partners. Likewise, the company's turnover has increased exponentially to approximately €20 million in 2006, with 260 employees in Europe and the USA.

The case study focuses on Spreadshirt's business model which relies on providing free of charge its online platform (called Spreadshop) to individuals interested in selling their own customised merchandise. While the shop owner is responsible for product design and self-marketing, Spreadshirt takes care of the fulfilment process.

The case describes the five additional business areas which Spreadshirt added to its initial business, through either organic growth or acquisitions, and the company's international expansion. It also describes Spreadshirt's competitive strategy which relies on quality- and time-based differentiation and is backed by strong human resources and sophisticated processes and IT systems. The case also looks at the competition, which is mainly US based, and highlights Spreadshirt's future growth opportunities such as strengthening its product range, exploiting network effects, creating or acquiring new businesses and further expanding internationally. Spreadshirt aims at further gaining business value through Web 2.0 by creating a sophisticated Internet-based social network.

15 Second Life: Mercedes-Benz enters the Metaverse

This case study describes the world of Second Life, which is neither an online game, nor a social networking site, but rather a virtual context for presenting and trading user-generated content. While some companies use Second Life today as a new Web 2.0 marketing tool, others have developed advanced concepts in order to create through this emerging technology corporate and customer value. The case study provides several illustrative examples of corporate use of Second Life, including an in-depth description of the objectives and approach that Mercedes-Benz has used.

Key objectives of the case study include: (1) assessing whether Second Life is just a passing technological fad; (2) analysing Second Life´s business model and its sustainability over time; (3) understanding the market of virtual worlds as a step beyond the Internet; and (4) identifying potential opportunities for value creation in and by virtual worlds for 'real-world' companies.

Mobile e-commerce

16 Mobile phone meets digital music at Sony BMG

Between 1995 and 2005, the German music major Sony BMG faced a ubiquitous crisis that led to dwindling industry revenues and declining physical CD sales. Striving to find new ways for securing its future, the company wanted to exploit the growth opportunities in the thriving digital music market. In particular, it thought to leverage the increasing UMTS and multimedia handset penetration by launching a mobile music service offering equipped with Sony BMG's digital music content. This business expansion would entail tremendous risk but could also positively affect the struggling bottom-line performance of Sony BMG in Germany.

The case study first looks at the German music industry as well as developments in the digital music market. It then focuses on the mobile music value chain and discusses Sony BMG's planned mobile music offering, including the competitive threats posed by other wireless telecom operators.

The overall objective of the case study is to provide the basis for students to assess Sony BMG's new digital music project from both a qualitative perspective (through a value-chain-based analysis) as well as a quantitative viewpoint (through business modelling scenarios). The case study raises the overriding key of whether Sony BMG should proceed or not with the implementation or its digital music project.

17 NTT DoCoMo (Japan): moving from a mobile phone operator to a lifestyle service provider

With the launch in 1999 of its wireless Internet service 'i-mode', NTT DoCoMo, the world's second largest mobile communications company, evolved from a 'wireless infrastructure' to an 'IT infrastructure' operator. With the 2004 introduction of its 'Osaifu-Keitai' service, which transforms the handset into a mobile digital wallet, the company fostered its shift towards becoming a wireless 'lifestyle service provider'.

The case study traces the evolution of DoCoMo's business strategy and the impact of its Vision 2010 on transforming the company into a highly differentiated, value-adding wireless service provider in an increasingly competitive market. Its key objectives include: (1) analysing the Japanese mobile telecommunications industry; (2) assessing DoCoMo's strategy for value creation; (3) determining the revenue streams of the 'lifestyle infrastructure' business model; and (4) appraising the company's international network.

18 YOC AG: integrating the mobile phone into the marketing mix

YOC, which stands for 'your opinion counts', is one of the leading mobile marketing service providers in Europe. The case study illustrates how mobile marketing helps to increase brand awareness and product sales. It also depicts how mobile marketing campaigns lead consumers to the point of sale, generate dialogue with marketing contacts, or foster customer loyalty programmes.

The case study relates how YOC became a successful mobile marketing service provider and describes, in particular, the campaigns which 'jump-started' the YOC.de community and established YOC as a leading brand. It also highlights YOC's competitive environment and strategic positioning, as well as its business model and unique selling proposition. Regarding the latter, the case study describes the company's service portfolio and the technologies (SMS, WAP and Java-based) which it uses for its mobile marketing campaigns. The case concludes with an outlook of YOC's international expansion plan and the future of mobile marketing.

19 Paybox.net (Germany): a mobile payment service

Paybox.net, founded in 1999, is a front-runner in providing mobile payment services in Germany and other European countries. The case discusses the development and roll-out of the m-payment services, the business model and marketing approach used, the technological and organisational challenges that the company faced, and the sustainability of the paybox competitive position. The case objectives are: (1) to analyse the disruptive innovation dimension of mobile payment services compared with existing online and offline payment modes; (2) to demonstrate how an entrepreneurial firm adapts to a competitive business environment with a slow market uptake, risk-averse investors and a fast-changing technology; and (3) to understand the development, marketing and pricing of mobile payment services as an example of digital, network-based goods.

CASE STUDY 1

From A(pples) to Z(oom lenses)
Extending the boundaries of multichannel retailing at Tesco.com

Having an extremely strong existing brand, the power of the Internet, and our ability to use it – these are the key factors to our success. There is virtually no limit to what we can sell, be it physical goods or services, and where we can sell it.[1]

Laura Wade-Gery, CEO, Tesco.com

Laura Wade-Gery jumped out of the white delivery truck and looked at her watch. Delivery was right on time. So was the launch of the spring catalogue for the new online non-food operation 'Tesco Direct' that had been added to the existing dot.com operation. Integrating different order and fulfillment options was a constant challenge, and Laura had at least one more on her mind: the company had almost reached the limit of its in-store picking model in some areas in the UK and had to think about alternative fulfillment models.

As the driver started to unload bottled water, vegetables, frozen food, wine and a flyer advertising a buy-one-get-one-free offer on Californian Chardonnay, Laura took a moment to look around. It was a typical suburban neighborhood north of London, neither posh nor poor. In many ways her service had become a perfect mirror of the UK population, just as the main bricks-and-mortar business had been since the turn-around led by Lord MacLaurin in the 1980s.

Tesco – History of a grocery giant

In 1956 the first Tesco self-service supermarket was opened in a converted cinema. During the 1950s and 1960s Tesco grew primarily through acquisitions. These included 70 Williamson's stores in 1957, 200 Harrow stores in 1959, 212 Irwin's outlets in 1960, and 97 Charles Phillips stores in 1964. By the 1960s Tesco had become a chain of 600 stores. The Tesco that opened in Leicester in 1961 with 16,500 square feet of selling space entered the *Guinness Book of Records* as the largest store in Europe.

As customers began looking for quality and choice in the 1970s and 1980s, Tesco's 'pile-it-high-and-sell-it-cheap' strategy was less successful and results slipped dramatically. The primary reason for the dismal performance was that customers had a negative image of the company and the products it sold. With its exclusive focus on low prices, stores were poorly maintained and the selection of items offered was perceived as inadequate and of mediocre quality.

But by the time MacLaurin retired in early 1997, Tesco had become the largest, most profitable supermarket chain in the UK. His first move had been to pour large amounts of money into the construction of new

---

1 Unless otherwise indicated, all quotations from Laura Wade-Gery, Steve Robinson and Daniel Roberts were recorded during an on-site interview at Tesco.com on 4 May 2007 in Welwyn Garden City, UK.

This case study was written by Sebastian Mauch, Research Associate at INSEAD, under the supervision of Albrecht Enders, Assistant Professor at the School of Management at Friedrich Alexander University, Nuremberg, Tawfik Jelassi, Professor of e-Business and IT at the School of International Management at the Ecole Nationale des Ponts et Chaussées, Paris, and Charles Waldman, Senior Affiliate Professor of Marketing at INSEAD. It is intended to be used as the basis for class discussion rather than to illustrate effective or ineffective handling of a management situation.

superstores in order to attract upper market segments. Simultaneously, new systems and technology were introduced in sales and distribution to position Tesco across a range of store formats and market segments.

Another development was about to change the rules of the retailing industry: the advent of the Internet. Although Tesco had been trying to meet new customer demands and develop business models to cater to them, until the Internet provided new ways of communicating with customers, that had not been an easy task, as Laura Wade-Gery recalled:

> We started out with the basic customer demands. Since the early 1990s customers came up to us and said 'It would be great if you could deliver my groceries to my home', so we started experimenting with catalogue and phone ordering. It was an operational mess and very inefficient. So for us, the Internet came to the rescue in terms of providing the technology which enabled cost efficient and operationally effective home delivery.

Tesco's bricks-and-mortar business

The current CEO, Terry Leahy, has worked for the company for more than 20 years. Much of Tesco's recent success is credited to his leadership ability. In order to respond to increased competition and declining prices in the food segment, Tesco significantly expanded its range of products. Its largest stores now devote 40–50% of their shelf space to non-grocery items such as clothes and products for the home. In 2000 Tesco opened up a new front in retailing, selling consumer electronics, televisions, DVD players and mobile phones.

For the year 2006, overall group sales increased by 10.9% to £46.6 billion [€65.2 billion], and group profit before tax increased by 20.3% to £2,653 million. UK sales grew by 9% to £35.6 billion, of which 5.6% came from existing stores and 3.4% from new stores. UK profits climbed to £1,914 million, international sales grew by 17.9% to £11 billion and contributed £564 million to profits, which presented an 18% increase over the previous year. Tesco employs more than 450,000 people worldwide across all of its businesses.

Four key strategy elements

Tesco has a long-term strategy for growth that has been in place since 2000, based on four key elements: to grow the core UK business, to expand by growing internationally, to be as strong in non-food as in food, and

to follow customers into new retailing services. The strategy is being pursued via a number of initiatives and decisions:

- **Core UK:** The UK business consists of a dense network of more than 1,800 stores with a combined sales area of 55 million square feet [5.1 million square metres], and accounts for 75% of group sales. Around 250,000 people work in the group's UK business. Tesco plans to grow through new shopping space with a multi-format approach and from extensions of existing shops. It has a strong customer base of more than 26 million people in the UK, with more than 11 million households having a Tesco Clubcard.

- **International:** The group operates in 12 European and Asian markets outside the UK and owns more than 800 stores. Over 100,000 employees work in international operations, serving over 15 million customers. More than half of the group's space is now outside the UK. A market entry into the US took place in 2007.

- **Non-food:** Sales of non-food products account for more than £6.8 billion in the UK alone. Tesco has a market share of 7% in non-food in the UK, compared to 20% in the grocery sector. Still, only one quarter of the UK population is within reach of a Tesco Extra store offering a large non-food selection.

- **Retailing Services:** The group has moved into additional services such as Tesco Personal Finance (TPF), Tesco.net and Tesco Telecom. The latter currently serves more than 1.5 million customers, including 1 million in an MVNO[2] in cooperation with O2. These services offer a great revenue potential, with TPF accounting for £65 million in profits.

Five different store formats

Tesco aims to serve a broad range of customers and therefore takes a multi-format approach. After establishing the original superstore format in the 1970s, it has differentiated its presence into four more store formats since the early 1990s:

- **Homeplus:** This new store format, initially introduced in seven stores in the UK, offers a wide range of non-food items, including clothing. Further

---

2 Mobile Virtual Network Operator: a company providing mobile telephone services without actually owning the network infrastructure.

products are available through the Tesco Direct order and collection point in every store. With a sales area of more than 30,000 square feet, stores are stand-alone or in retail parks and complement the local Tesco food offer.

- **Extra:** Introduced in 1997, Extra stores represent the largest store format, ranging from 60,000 to 125,000 square feet. These hypermarkets offer a wide selection of non-food items as a complement to the regular supermarket product range.

- **Express:** These stores have a sales area of up to 3,000 square feet. The format was introduced in 1994 and now consists of over 700 stores selling a range of up to 7,000 lines including fresh produce, wines and spirits and bread and confectionery from their in-store bakery. Many of these stores have a petrol station (Tesco is one of Britain's largest independent petrol retailers).

- **Metro:** The first Metro store was opened in 1992, bringing the convenience of Tesco to town and city centre locations, meeting the needs of High Street shoppers and th e local community. Metros offer a tailored range of food lines, including ready-meals and sandwiches.

- **Superstore:** These stores have a minimum selling surface of 26,500 square feet and display 25,000-30,000 SKUs (stock keeping units). The oldest and most established store format of the group, there are now 433 superstores with a total sales area of 13.2 million square feet (53.7% of total UK shelf space) located in the UK.

Competition in grocery retailing

The UK has a highly consolidated and competitive food retail industry. Other leading players include Asda (owned by the US company, Wal-Mart), Morrisons (which acquired Safeway in 2004), Sainsbury's and Somerfield (see Exhibits 1 and 2). Discount players, such as Lidl and Aldi, have entered the bottom segment of the market, adding to the existing price pressure.

Traditional High Street businesses are also under competitive pressure from Tesco and other large retailing chains. Tesco's main business has come under criticism from various directions, prompted by the fear of large supermarkets eliminating High Street shopping with its small, specialized shops. Critics claim that retailing in the

Exhibit 1 Development of UK grocery retailing industry and Tesco

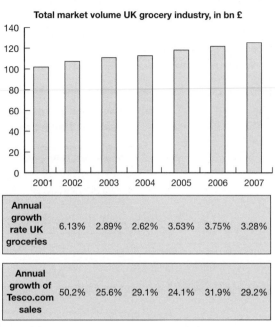

Total market volume UK grocery industry, in bn £

	2002	2003	2004	2005	2006	2007
Annual growth rate UK groceries	6.13%	2.89%	2.62%	3.53%	3.75%	3.28%
Annual growth of Tesco.com sales	50.2%	25.6%	29.1%	24.1%	31.9%	29.2%

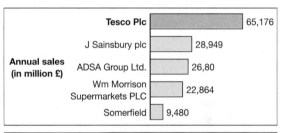

Annual sales (in million £)

Tesco Plc	65,176
J Sainsbury plc	28,949
ADSA Group Ltd.	26,80
Wm Morrison Supermarkets PLC	22,864
Somerfield	9,480

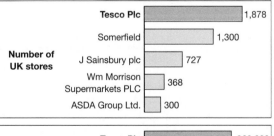

Number of UK stores

Tesco Plc	1,878
Somerfield	1,300
J Sainsbury plc	727
Wm Morrison Supermarkets PLC	368
ASDA Group Ltd.	300

Number of employees

Tesco Plc	260,000
Wm Morrison Supermarkets PLC	130,000
ADSA Group Ltd.	128,000
J Sainsbury plc	118,000
Somerfield	44,768

Source: Datamonitor 2007, company reports.

future risks being dominated by large, anonymous chains, as this comparison by Andrew Simms, Policy Director of the new economics foundation (nef),[3] indicated:

> The chains became the economic equivalent of invasive species: hungry, indiscriminate, often antisocial and destructive. [...] Britain is being sucked into a vortex of US-style, chain-store-led, clone retailing [...][4]

Local authorities have accused Tesco of using 'back-door tactics'[5] by taking over existing High Street retail sites in order to dodge the need to obtain planning permission. In response, Tesco insists that, ultimately, no retailer can

---

3 URL: http://www.neweconomics.org/gen/.
4 Quoted from the *Guardian*, 22 March 2007.
5 Quoted from *Hull Daily Mail*, 20 February 2007.

Exhibit 2 Page rank and daily reach comparison of largest UK online grocery retailing websites

Hitwise UK Online Performance Awards 2006, Category 'Shopping and Classifieds – Grocery and Alcohol'	
Rank	**Domain**
1	www.tesco.com/superstore
2	www.asda.co.uk
3	www.asda.com
4	www.sainsburys.com
5	www.sainsburystoyou.co.uk
6	www.waitrose.com
7	uk.aldi.com
8	www.tesco.com/winestore
9	www.lidl.co.uk
10	www.ocado.com

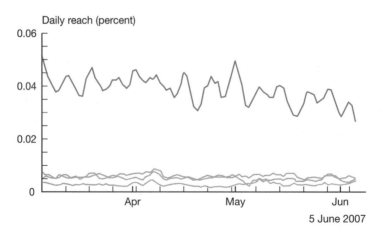

5 June 2007

Source: www.alexa.com.

move against the preferences of its customers, as the response of Lucy Neville-Rolfe, Executive Director, Corporate and Legal Affairs of Tesco plc affirmed:

> Andrew Simms' attack [...] demonstrates that he knows far more about flora and fauna than he does about modern retail. Tesco will only prosper if we meet customers' desires and demands. Simms' problem is that he doesn't like the choices people freely make![6]

Shopping for groceries at Tesco.com

> Actually, we weren't particularly bothered about the website, as long as it enabled customers to do the basics of a shopping trip: find the products they need, look at them, make their choice and pay. So we decided to keep it as straightforward as possible.
>
> **Laura Wade-Gery**, CEO Tesco.com

Registering for the website

Users who want to order groceries online via Tesco.com need to register by providing their personal data, including delivery directions. They are strongly encouraged to provide their Tesco Clubcard details when registering because this enables them instantly to review their previous purchases in physical Tesco supermarkets. In this way first-time online customers can start with their usual shopping without having to key in each item separately. If a customer does not have a Clubcard number or does not want to reveal it, the system creates a new, virtual Clubcard number to track the shopping history and award points.

Accessing the website

Customers have a number of different options to access Tesco's online services. Since 2001 shoppers at Tesco.com have been able to use mobile commerce applications to make their purchases. In partnership with Microsoft, Tesco.com launched Tesco Access, which allows users of hand-held computers and WAP-based wireless phones[7] to shop online, as John Browett, at the time CEO of Tesco.com, explained:

> Since the launch of Tesco Access, our customers can shop any time, any place, on any device, whether through the Internet, digital TV or pocket PCs.[8]

Tesco Access has since been included in the regular website Tesco.com. As of July 2007 users can choose directly from within their Tesco.com account settings how they want the site to be displayed.

Navigating the website

The website offers several types of functions to facilitate the online shopping process. They include:

- **Express Shopper:** Customers can write shopping lists on the Tesco.com website, just as they would do for a regular shopping trip. The website then searches for items from the product line that matches the customer's wishes. Customers simply choose the product they want and move on to the next item on the list.

- **Lunchbox Tool:** Aimed at busy parents and customers wanting to order complete lunch meals, this tool enables them to customize their sandwiches.

- **My Favourites:** This function displays a list of all the items that a customer has purchased recently. Customers click on any items that they want to buy again.

- **Online Recipe Book:** Customers can browse all the ingredients needed for a particular recipe and click to buy. Products are split into those that the customer probably has at home and those that are special to the recipe.

- **Organic Box:** Tesco offers pre-selected baskets of organic products in different sizes.

- **Season's Choices:** This displays items for special events such as Christmas, a barbecue or a party. Customers choose a specific list and then tick the products that they want to add to their shopping basket.

Although not every feature is used by all customers equally, there are certain occasions where Kate Cook, a regular Tesco.com shopper, makes use of some of them:

> I really like the 'favourites feature'. That way, I complete my £100 order that I do every other week in 10-15 minutes during my lunch break. When I have people come over for dinner, I check the recipe selection for some cool snacks or Season's Choice section for offers on BBQ. A colleague of mine, a mother of two, loves the Lunchbox tool for her children – if you have to make a sandwich for the little ones five times a week, all year long, you just run out of ideas.[9]

---

6 Talking Tesco, 3 April 2007, URL: http://www.tesco.com/talkingtesco/news/?page=article5.
7 WAP stands for Wireless Access Protocol.
8 'Online shopping: Tesco.com opens for WAP/PC orders', *Financial Times*, 21 July 2001.
9 Quotes from Kate Cook are taken from a telephone interview on 20 May 2007.

If customers have a preference regarding a product (e.g., they like their bananas particularly ripe), they can mention this to their shopper using a special note function that appears on the website next to each product (see Exhibit 3). If an item is out of stock, they have the option of either choosing a suitable substitute or skipping that item. If a customer does not like the substitute, they can return it to the driver upon delivery and the amount is re-credited.

The website stores the virtual shopping cart each time the customer leaves the online store, thereby making it easy for different family members to retrieve the stored shopping list next time they connect to Tesco.com. Tesco is also trying to integrate the online and offline shopping experience: Clubcard members can enter their card number through the website and view recent purchases from offline stores.

Scheduling delivery and paying for the goods

Tesco.com's prices are the same as those in Tesco stores. In-store discounts, promotions and special offers are made available to online customers, for example, a 'buy-one-get-one-free' offer. If the offer is already valid when the order is placed, it will also be displayed on the website. Payment can be made by credit card or debit card such as Visa, MasterCard, Switch, American Express and the Tesco Clubcard Plus. The account is debited when the packing is completed.

For the first couple of years Tesco charged a flat fee of £5 for home delivery, regardless of order volume and delivery time. Currently, delivery fees differ according to the day of the week, with early weekday deliveries being cheapest, and evening and/or weekend deliveries more expensive (see Exhibit 4). Customers choose a two-hour delivery slot anytime between 9.00 am and 11.00 pm. They seem to be satisfied with the model, as online shopper Kate Cook confirmed:

> They are always on time. I have been shopping at Tesco.com once a week for the last four years and delivery was late by 10 minutes once – the driver really apologized and I got £10 off my order. In fact, a lot of times they are even a little bit early. Sometimes I come home from work and the van is already parked in front of my house and the driver is waiting for me!

Items are delivered in plastic bags, with substituted items marked so that customers can inspect them upon delivery and accept or reject the substitute. In an attempt to reduce pollution and waste, Tesco is reducing plastic bags used for home delivery. A recent study revealed that for an order of 32 items Tesco.com used 11 bags[10] (other online retailers even more). The company recently announced a 'no-bag-option', whereby groceries arrive in stackable, reusable, plastic trays, which will be taken away by the driver. Consumers who shun bags are rewarded with additional Clubcard loyalty points. Around 40% of customers have already opted for no bag delivery.

---

10 'Shops fail to deliver on bags', *Scottish Daily Record*, 26 February 2007.

Exhibit 3 Choosing and specifying products on the Tesco.com website

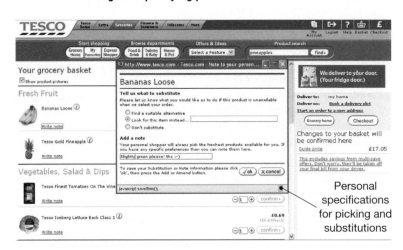

Source: Tesco.com.

Exhibit 4 Choosing a delivery slot at Tesco.com

| TESCO | Tesco home | Groceries | Finance & Insurance | Telecoms | More |

Sign in / Register ➡ **Delivery details** ➡ Review & confirm ➡ Receipt

Book delivery slot

Click on one of the available delivery slots below. You can book a slot up to three weeks from today. Once you have booked a slot it will be reserved for two hours.

See next 7 days ▸

		TUE Today	WED 23 May	THU 24 May	FRI 25 May	SAT 26 May	SUN 27 May	MON 28 May
09:00–11:00	2 hrs		£4.49	£4.99	£5.99	£5.99	£5.99	slot full
10:00–12:00	2 hrs		£4.49	£4.99	£5.99	£5.99	£5.99	slot full
11:00–13:00	2 hrs		£4.49	£4.99	£5.99	£5.99	£5.99	slot full
12:00–14:00	2 hrs		£4.49	£4.99	£5.99	£5.99	£5.99	slot full
13:00–15:00	2 hrs		£4.49	£4.99	£5.99	£5.99		slot full
14:00–16:00	2 hrs		slot full	£4.99	£5.99	£5.99		slot full
15:00–17:00	2 hrs		slot full	slot full	slot full	£5.99		slot full
16:00–18:00	2 hrs		£4.49	£4.99	£5.99	£5.99		slot full
17:00–19:00	2 hrs		£4.49	£4.99	£5.99	£5.99		slot full
18:00–20:00	2 hrs		slot full	slot full	£5.99	£5.99		slot full
19:00–21:00	2 hrs		£4.49	£4.99	£5.99			slot full
20:00–22:00	2 hrs		£4.49	£4.99	£5.99			slot full
21:00–23:00	2 hrs		£4.49	£4.99	£5.99			slot full

Source: Tesco.com.

The Tesco.com business model

When Tesco first started its delivery service, it was possible for customers to place orders through multiple devices: telephone, fax and also via the Internet. However, the ordering system turned out to be too slow and inaccurate, as each order was captured manually, leading to frequent errors and frustration for customers. Delivery costs were high since the picking system was manual and paper-based – pickers would walk around the store with order lists and take the requested items off the shelves. Laura Wade-Gery recounted the early days of grocery delivery:

> It was disastrous. You took the phone order, then typed it in manually, then sent it down to the store by fax, where it was then picked. We often had a kind of Chinese whisper effect, so when a person ordered a grapefruit, by the time he got the order, it might have become a cabbage.

To overcome these initial difficulties Tesco decided to automate its delivery service to a large degree and use the Internet as the sole ordering channel to streamline and improve the order processing. When contemplating the delivery format for its online shopping it had to choose between two different approaches: either to pursue a warehouse model or to use its British stores as

distribution centers. Both strategies carried risks: building huge warehouses would have cost millions of pounds, which Tesco was hesitant to spend on an unproven service, while packing and picking groceries from stores might clog the aisles, thereby frustrating store customers. Hence, the business model evolved slowly over time (see Exhibit 5), starting with the simplest fulfillment model of in-store picking.

In-store picking

Tesco.com CEO Laura Wade-Gery explained the rationale behind ultimately choosing the in-store picking model:

> In the beginning, a lot of people looked at our idea of in-store picking and said: 'You are mad, this can't possibly be right.' They automatically assumed that the warehouse model was the answer. But think about the costs of fulfilment: the costs are actually in delivery. That made it necessary to start near the customer – our dense network of supermarkets all over the country that were there anyway. So actually it was much less of that strategic debate than I guess it has been made to appear on the outside. It was just the obvious thing to do.

Giving customers a natural extension of the bricks-and-mortar experience also yielded advantages for the company, as Daniel Roberts, Operations Development Director at Tesco Direct, added:

Exhibit 5 Development of fulfilment models at Tesco.com

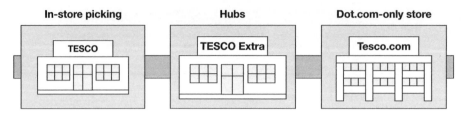

Source: Tesco.com.

If you place an order on Tesco.com, we will go and pick that order in a Tesco store. So our experience of availability, product quality, and other aspects shopping the store, is the same as that for somebody walking in from the street. In essence, Tesco.com pickers are our eyes of the regular customer on the shop floor, to the extent that the Tesco.com metric for availability has become the Tesco metric for availability.

Tesco.com picks around 250,000 orders a week from 300 British stores. By delivering from local stores no route takes longer than 25 minutes, since 94% of the population in England live within a 25-minute radius of a Tesco store. In order to ensure an undisturbed shopping experience for its customers, Tesco has refined its in-store model over the years. Picking starts at 6.00 am and continues until 2.00 pm. Over the course of the day the number of picking staff is gradually reduced as more customers do their grocery shopping. In this way the daily peaks of in-store picking and regular shopping are de-synchronized to avoid clogging the aisles. Using improved picking algorithms is another means of reducing the disturbance by spreading the trolleys more evenly across the store.

One of the biggest challenges of the daily operation is to accurately forecast the incoming orders. While on a nationwide level demand is fairly easy to forecast, exact predictions on the individual store level are almost impossible, resulting in overtime picking after 2.00 pm.

Despite all attempts at optimizing the in-store picking, eventually stores reach a limit that is hard to exceed. Other bottlenecks include the size of the backroom where orders are stored and loaded onto the delivery vans, and the parking space available for the delivery fleet, as Daniel Roberts explained:

One problem we do have is congestion, especially at Christmas. In some stores, we have literally dozens of trolleys on the shop floor and they start to cause distractions with customers and other pickers, so we can see some bottlenecks in that area. And although you might be able to work around that, you will then hit the next bottleneck – maybe because replenishment can't keep up with the rapid picking speed, causing too many items to be out of stock. So eventually, you get to a point where you run out of ideas and solutions.

Building delivery hubs

Tesco's fulfillment activities are run from about 300 shops in the UK, which vary in size from a 30,000 square foot store to a 125,000 square foot hypermarket. Constraints vary accordingly, as some stores operate only 2–3 delivery vans, while large stores with more floorspace can have a fleet of up to 20 vans. The entire delivery fleet numbers 1,800 vans. Tesco is starting to address environmental issues with its new fleet of zero-emission battery-powered 'green vans'. Fifteen of these vehicles operate in London and in an environmental model store in Shrewsbury. The vans, which have the same carrying capacity as the regular delivery vans, have a maximum speed of 50 mph [80 km/h] and a range of 100 miles [160 km] before they have to be recharged.

Occasionally Tesco has built a supermarket larger than actually needed. A couple of these Tesco Extra stores have been expanded into 'hubs' by increasing picking staff, delivery fleet and building a customized order handling area in the back of these stores. These serve a larger area, thus taking away some of the pressure from congested supermarkets.

The 'dot.com-only store'

In some parts of the UK, we have pushed the limit of the store-based model probably as far as we can. But given customer demand for the service, we tried to find a way to further our online business. So this is why, about one year ago, we built what we call our 'dot.com-only store'. From the outside it looks just like one of the huge automated warehouses built by some of our competitors.

From the inside it looks just like a Tesco store. And essentially that's what it is: a large Tesco supermarket – except without customers, cash registers and checkout staff.

Laura Wade-Gery, CEO, Tesco.com

The 'dot.com-only store', located in Croydon, south London, opened in February 2006. Its size is comparable to that of the Tesco superstores ranging from 20,000–50,000 square feet. It was pragmatically designed in a way that would enable Tesco.com to use all of its experience in the in-store picking model, including specially equipped picking trolleys (see Exhibit 6) and the logistical process know-how that had been refined over time in the stores, while dispensing with the constraints of time and space that some of the crowded Tesco stores around London were facing. The 'dot.com-only store' serves as a hybrid approach combining the benefits of in-store picking with the spaciousness of a large warehouse.

Integrating the model into the stores

Tesco had to focus on both customers and the bricks-and-mortar stores from where it would actually do the fulfillment. From the perspective of a store manager, integrating the Tesco.com operation into their daily business might at first seem like a drastic intrusion and

an extra challenge for store managers. However, it does have a significant impact on the development of sales per square foot. This being one of the key metrics for determining a store's success, store managers are quite eager to integrate the service. The online business has a similar operating margin to Tesco's physical business of approximately 5.7%; however, it has much higher sales growth rates of up to 30% online, compared to 9% sales growth at UK stores. Fulfilling online orders is seen as an opportunity rather than an additional burden, as Laura Wade-Gery confirmed:

The online business is quite a lot of extra work for the store manager, so why would he want this rather complicated time-critical operation in his store's back area? Well, the answer is, he wants it because it is providing significant sales growth. And as a retailer, the first thing that counts for him is sales – no matter where they come from. So even if the dot.com operation may only account for 4% of a store's total sales, it is a portion that is growing constantly at 25-30% per year.

Making online grocery retailing profitable – Tesco.com costs

In addition to the workload and complexity, the integration and operation of online activities incurs additional

Exhibit 6 Picking trolley interface

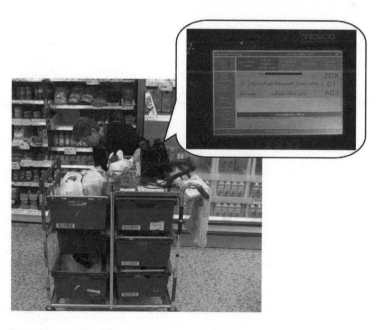

Source: Tesco.com store visit.

costs that must be split between the main business and Tesco.com in a way that fairly reflects the input involved from each side. In the past, some analysts had claimed that Tesco.com merely 'piggybacked' on the success of the main business. Tesco.com differentiates between three different types of cost that are incurred:

- **Direct costs**: Dealing with the direct costs involved in the fulfillment of the orders is quite straightforward: Tesco.com takes into account the costs of picking personnel, delivery fleet, drivers, equipment, IT system, etc.
- **Indirect costs:** Incremental costs incurred by the dot.com operation, e.g., additional cleaning costs on the shop floor, additional replenishment during picking hours, etc.
- **Pure bricks-and-mortar costs:** For instance, the operating costs of a store's restaurant will not be shared in any way by Tesco.com.

According to Laura Wade-Gery, Tesco.com follows a very pragmatic approach when it comes to splitting costs between the dot.com business and the bricks-and-mortar business:

> We clearly separate between genuine or incremental costs that are caused by us, and costs that would be there anyway. A good example is, when we started we were operating in a narrow corridor in the store's storage area, closed off by a metal bar that we put in for maybe £600. So did we charge ourselves huge amounts of the store's lighting, heating, and capital development costs? No, we didn't! By now, we have our own design standard for what we need a dot.com area to look like, which has its own freezer, its own chiller and decent amounts of space. That can cost up to a quarter of a million pounds, so we pay for that because that was genuinely caused by us, as well as for the additional heating, electricity, replenishment, and cleaning.

Growing non-food: the launch of Tesco Direct

> As long as you're doing food, it is quite clear who your competitors are. Now, with Tesco Direct, you are not only competing against multinational retailers, you are also competing against a whole range of Internet pure-plays such as e-bay, Amazon and the like. And on top of that, you are competing with Joe Bloggs from Putney who owns an electronics shop and decides to put his stuff online.
>
> **Steve Robinson**, CEO Tesco Direct

The addition of non-food products to the product range of Tesco supermarkets began on a large scale with the introduction of the first Tesco Extra stores in 1997. These hypermarkets now carry a line of 4,000 non-food products, including a small range of clothing. Some existing supermarkets were turned into Tesco Extra stores by building additional shopping areas, or, where lack of space prohibited it, with the help of mezzanine floors that basically cut shopping room height in half, which was only possible in some areas of the store. Tesco soon realized that the expansion of the bricks-and-mortar business into non-food had its limitations and that, anyway, customers wanted more ordering and delivery channels.

Tesco's entry into a non-bricks-and-mortar, non-food business was via joint venture with mail order company Grattan,[11] announced in 1998. Tesco brought its high-performance IT system into the partnership, as well as its large customer base; order fulfillment was managed by Grattan. The joint venture lasted until 2006. In essence, Tesco passed on non-food orders from its own customers to Grattan and let the fulfillment expert deal with it, and the two shared the profits. But the Grattan Joint Venture had its limitations in terms of range and flexibility in developing the customer proportion and revenue, and Tesco ultimately decided it was better positioned to grow the online non-food businesses on its own.

Using the expertise gained from a decade in the online grocery business, Tesco brought a couple of senior non-food retailing veterans into the team, including Steve Robinson, and started developing its own non-food competence under the new brand 'Tesco Direct'. Robinson had previously worked as a Financial Director at Argos,[12] one of the largest UK retailers (see Exhibit 7). In September 2006 the service went live in time for the Christmas shopping season, handling the spike in festive sales and significant increase of Grattan Joint Venture volumes with relative ease.

Setting up the organization

Unlike the launch of Tesco.com, Tesco Direct was integrated into the existing organizational structure. Steve Robinson explained:

---

11 URL: http://www.grattan.co.uk.

12 Argos is one of the UK's largest multi-channel retailers, offering goods through an extensive print catalogue, over the Internet and a network of almost 700 stores. URL: http://www.argos.com.

Exhibit 7 Daily reach comparison of largest UK online retailing websites

Rank	Feb 07	May 06	Name	Domain
IMRG/Hitwise UK 'Hot Shops List' 2007				
1	1	1	Amazon UK	www.amazon.com
2	3	4	Tesco.com	www.tesco.com
3	2	3	Argos	www.argos.com
4	4	5	Play.com	play.com
5	7	6	Amazon.com	www.amazon.com
6	6	7	Expedia.co.uk	www.expedia.co.uk
7	10	10	Apple Computer	www.apple.com
8	5	8	easyJet	www.easyjet.co.uk
9	11	9	RyanAir.com	www.ryanair.com
10	9	11	British Airways	www.britishairways.co.uk

Source: www.imrg.com, www.hitwise.com.

When I joined Tesco in July 2005, I did not step on the scene and say: 'OK, I need 400 people and a completely independent business unit to set up the business.' Instead, I saw that Tesco had already accumulated quite a lot of non-food expertise in the bricks-and-mortar business and a very successful online presence. So we basically piggybacked on this know-how and added people in the non-food and dot.com business to cope with the additional workload and get the multi-channel knowledge that we would need for the project.

The Tesco Direct team worked closely with the commercial teams in the main business. The buyers working for the bricks-and-mortar side of the business dealt with suppliers across the globe and aligned the different channels, since some of the range available at Tesco Extra stores was also included in the catalogue.

Developing a suitable value chain

Tesco believed that every part of the value chain that had significant impact on the customer experience needed to be performed by Tesco itself. One of the key insights that Robinson provided from his experience in multi-channel retailing was the fact that pure Internet-based ordering was not enough. He aimed for a customer experience that was far from cutting edge and had been used for quite a while by retailers: a catalogue.

Having experimented with a small catalogue that was printed for the launch in September 2006, the next issue of the Tesco Direct catalogue, published in March 2007, had a print run of several million copies. Scheduled to be printed twice a year in Spring and Autumn, with smaller leaflets featuring seasonal and special offers over the year, copies were distributed across the store network, where they were put on large palletes of a couple of thousand units each, as well as distributed with every Tesco.com order. Demand was high: within two weeks almost all copies of the catalogue had gone.

Producing a catalogue of more than 1,000 pages posed some serious sourcing challenges. At the time, Tesco's core competences did not include high-end photographic publishing; most people involved in developing the online non-food business were convinced that the whole design process for the catalogue had to be outsourced to a publisher. But the team was in for a surprise when Robinson arrived:

When we discussed the topic, I immediately said 'No way.' If you're going to sell something over the Internet and through a catalogue, you absolutely have to own the photography and the design. It's not like in a store where people can simply touch and look at the goods. Owning

309

the publishing facility was an absolutely crucial strategic capability we needed to develop – and that's what I did.

Robinson built up a media publishing center with a team of 40 publishing experts including designers, photographers and publishers who had previously developed catalogues for Argos and other retailers. Putting them all into one building close to the rest of the Tesco business also yielded another crucial benefit, as Robinson explained:

> It is priceless to have all these people working so closely with us. If a colleague from the web design looks at the raw shots for the catalogue, he can immediately step in and tell us that it might work in print but not on the web, or vice versa. That way, we can immediately modify the material and still benefit from only having to shoot once. That saves us a lot of time and money.

Choosing the right products and order fulfillment

Robinson's experience at Argos gave Tesco Direct a head start in selecting a product range that would appeal to consumers. Product categories of more than 12,000 SKUs include everything from garden equipment to toddler toys (see Exhibit 8). Not satisfied with merely copying the catalogue of his former employer, Robinson came up with some ideas that would soon prove to be hits:

Horse riding is an incredibly popular sport in the UK. However, none of the multi-channel retailers had got into equestrian equipment yet. We did! We even started to include swimming pools and garden sheds.

Going online also meant that Tesco could do what it had been doing in the grocery business. It extended its 'good-better-best' philosophy, offering not only the value or the standard item of each product, but also a low-cost and a luxury version of a lot of products (see Exhibit 9).

While offering products via a print catalogue or online did not pose any particular challenges, fulfillment of orders certainly did. While the Tesco Direct operation was viewed as a natural extension of non-food retailing, fulfillment could be accomplished with the proven in-store picking approach, as Robinson explained:

> In grocery, the challenge is to keep the food fresh throughout the supply chain, so everything should be available everywhere to minimize delivery time. With non-food, it's almost the opposite. I can't fulfil an order of a £5,000 television set through my store network because I will only sell one of them every 6 weeks – and I don't know where. So at the end of the year I would have a huge number of out-dated TVs that no one wants to buy. It just makes more sense to hold stuff centrally.

'One-man products' consist of smaller items, such as consumer electronics and multimedia products, that are fulfilled from a central distribution center in Daventry (see Exhibit 10). 'Two-men' products, such as

Exhibit 8 Tesco.com product range

Source: Tesco.com website.

Exhibit 9 **Tesco.com retailing brands**

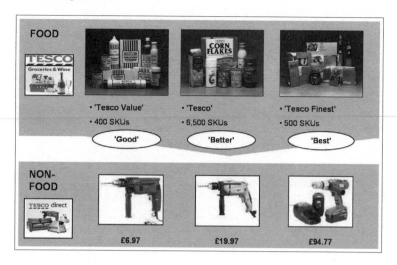

Source: Tesco.com.

furniture and white goods, are distributed through logistics specialists using dedicated warehouses. Although stocking large items incurs additional costs, Robinson is convinced that it is money well spent:

> Eighty percent of all sofas bought in the UK are black, brown or beige. We offer a selection of these models with a delivery time of 5-10 days. That's much faster than the 60-day delivery of large furniture stores. It was a gamble we took, but it has changed the landscape of retailing in the UK.

For all but the largest items, customers can choose two-hour delivery time slots, just like in the grocery business. Or they can pick up items in the stores. Besides being able to pay cash (still the preferred payment method, especially in lower-income customer segments), this gives busy customers greater freedom of choice by not having to pre-select a time window for delivery and having to stick with it. Being able to order all items over the phone and at the Tesco Direct desks installed in many larger Tesco supermarkets is yet another example of the freedom of choice Tesco strives to offer, as Robinson explained:

> Being able to offer people interaction with real human beings is something that clearly distinguishes us from Internet pure-plays such as Amazon or e-bay. It is only logical for us to use our physical store network and let the customer choose how he wants to do business with us.

Pricing at Tesco Direct

Pricing has its challenges as different order and delivery channels can incur different costs. However, customers are not willing to pay different prices according to the delivery channel. At the moment, apart from the £5 delivery fee, prices are the same for each channel, except for localized seasonal clearings in single stores or overstock items of the Internet business. These prices are merely the result of a cost-benefit trade-off, as Robinson explained:

> In general, we have the policy to provide the same price on the web as in the store. However, some stores might have an overstock of, let's say, garden furniture after the summer season. It would simply not be cost-efficient to ship these items all the way back through the supply chain. Instead, stores can clear them by offering lower prices that are not matched on the web.

Other competitors had tried differentiated pricing models. Argos, for example, originally provided free delivery for orders over £100. The order value was later increased to £135 and then £150 before finally being abandoned altogether. Clearly there are limits to this model when it comes to Tesco Direct and the option for customers to pick up their goods directly from the store: while it adds extra flexibility from customers' point of view, it can create additional complexity and costs that might result in a negative yield for smaller items.

Exhibit 10 Fulfillment options for non-food goods

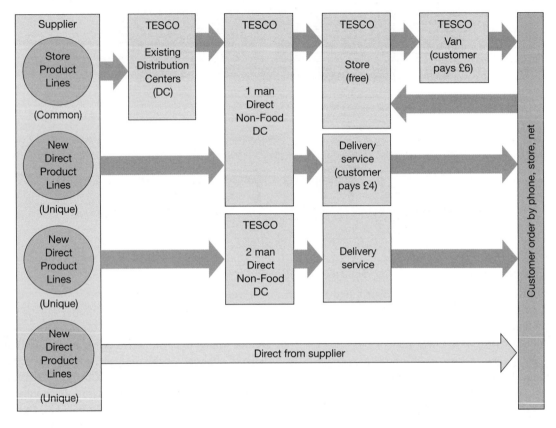

Source: Tesco.com.

The Clubcard – An ace up Tesco's sleeve?

> There's no rocket science involved with Clubcard. It's about educating, empowering and rewarding consumers.[13]
>
> **Andrew Mann**, Marketing Director, Tesco Clubcard

In 1995 Tesco introduced the first customer loyalty card, which offered benefits to regular shoppers while at the same time helping Tesco to analyze its customers' needs. Today, Tesco has 13 million Clubcard members.

Shoppers' names and addresses and the category of products purchased are recorded and used for direct-mail campaigns and other promotions. For instance, when Tesco launched its pet insurance product, it was able to pitch to customers who had recently bought dog food and cat litter at its online store. On a regular basis it distributes printed flyers along with the shopping order according to the products chosen. For example, customers ordering only vegetarian food will not receive a 'BBQ season opening' flyer. Clubcard evenings

– complimentary in-store gatherings for selected Clubcard holders – are held to promote products. Customers of the wine or cheese departments at Tesco might be invited to a wine-tasting evening; shoppers who have purchased shampoo or cosmetics might be invited to a hair-care event, as Karen Marshall, Tesco spokesperson, explained:

> It's a small 'thank-you' to customers for shopping with us. The main idea is to help serve our customers better. Besides, we get into personal contact with our shoppers and gather information about how to serve them better – something difficult to achieve in the mass-marketing age.[14]

Tesco also sends Clubcard members a monthly magazine with recipe ideas, details of new product launches and other information tailored to particular demographic groups. Each edition reflects the interests and lifestyle of

13 'Lessons in loyalty', Marketing Direct, June 2007.
14 'Getting the points at Tesco in the UK', Progressive Grocer, 19 June 1999.

a target market group such as young families, students or senior citizens. In addition, quarterly mailings are sent to all participating households, which in total make up more than 6% of the UK's annual post bag.[15]

During the first couple of years after launching Tesco.com, the Clubcard idea was of great value, as Laura Wade-Gery recalled:

> Especially in the first year of Tesco.com, we received numerous comments from new customers who couldn't find a lot of the items they regularly bought offline, the choice was simply overwhelming. So now, if a first-time online shopper already has a Clubcard, our system will recognize that and automatically populate his/her shopping list with the items they usually buy in their supermarket, making it a lot easier for new customers to find the things they want. Besides, we can track how many online shoppers are also frequent Tesco shoppers, and how many we are drawing from other chains.

Soon after Tesco.com was launched it turned out that the vast majority of Tesco.com customers shopped online *and* offline. Rather than perceiving this as evidence of cannibalization – one of the big fears when Tesco first added the online channel – Laura Wade-Gery saw it as a proof of the business model:

> Everybody who does grocery shopping for a household knows how difficult it is to buy fresh groceries for a whole week. So people buy stock items along with some fresh items and then return to a Tesco store once or twice a week to pick up fresh vegetables, fruit or meat. And that is absolutely fine for two reasons: first, because it shows how compatible the offline and online shopping experience at Tesco has become. Second, because these customers are our most valuable ones in terms of overall order volume.

The vast amount of data collected by Tesco about their customers' habits has also raised concern about privacy and data security issues (if the data stored got into the wrong hands). Tesco insists that it only uses the data for serving customers better by making tailored offers to each of its customer segments.

Future outlook

> There are four crucial things I want our customers to say about Tesco.com, regardless of what we sell:

> ■ '*I know Tesco will have it.*' So I want Tesco to be known to have pretty much anything a customer could want.
> ■ '*I trust Tesco to offer me great value*.' So we have to make sure that we offer customers the best value.

> ■ '*They make it easy for me to shop.*' We want to be able to create a different shop window for different types of customers.
> ■ '*I don't have to think about it, it simply works.*' All of our processes have to run absolutely smoothly and need to be optimized and redesigned continuously.

> **Laura Wade-Gery**, CEO Tesco.com

Laura Wade-Gery got back into the passenger seat of the white delivery truck. The journey was almost completed, with only one more stop. She took a look at the electronic delivery device: she was about to deliver a couple of low-fat products, skimmed milk, a lot of fresh vegetables and fruit and dietary information, as well as a personalized meal plan. No doubt this was a customer of Tesco's increasingly popular dieting service.

In 2004 Tesco teamed up with online dieting business 'e-diets'[16] and signed an agreement licensing the technology and using it for TescoDiets,[17] a service that is essentially the online equivalent of 'Weightwatchers'. Users get a personalized record with their previous dieting history, meal plans and the goals that they want to achieve. Then they are able to click on the appropriate shopping list for delivery to their home via Tesco.com. The subscription fee is £2.99 per week, with a minimum subscription of ten weeks.

Laura Wade-Gery describes the benefits of the model for Tesco:

> This is a very good example of using the Internet to create a new business that is actually very close to Tesco's core business. It works brilliantly in a low-cost environment, very scalable, fantastic low-cost business to deliver. You get support online; you can help one another in forums, etc. Now, people who joined the service have even started to meet – in one of the coffee shops in our store. Overall, the online dieting business is very scalable, requires almost no capital and is very low cost to deliver.

Back at her office, she reflected on the progress made in online retailing at Tesco and where the journey would go next. The issue of coming up against boundaries geographically and product-wise was getting urgent. Her objective was to come up with a plan to extend them. Adapting the order fulfillment model had been achieved slowly – hesitantly almost – after the early failures in warehouse fulfillment. But with the introduction of Tesco Direct, a pure in-store picking approach had become impossible.

---

15 'Lessons in loyalty', Marketing Direct, June 2007.
16 URL: http://www.ediets.com/.
17 URL: http://www.tescocdiets.com/.

CASE STUDY 2

From e-banking to e-business at Nordea (Scandinavia)
The world's biggest clicks-and-mortar bank

Nordea company background

> Our philosophy is both high tech and high touch, not either or.

> **Bo Harald**, Head of Electronic Banking, Nordea[1]

Customers entering Nordea's main branch in Helsinki at lunchtime on a busy weekday encounter something very different from what is typically seen at banks in other capital cities. Those long lines in front of the counter, so common at its competitors, have disappeared – even during peak hours.

During the past two decades, Bo Harald, Nordea's Head of Electronic Banking, has steadily and patiently moved the bank into the electronic age. As *Business Week* pointed out: 'Forget flash, fanfare and giant ambitions. This small Scandinavian outfit [Nordea] has quietly built the world's most successful Internet bank.'[2] Now that e-banking has become a reality at Nordea, the next big challenge for Harald is to move the bank into e-business:

> We are moving from e-banking to e-business. We are not moving into market places as such. What we are doing is taking our e-banking services and bringing them to the e-business value chain. We are an enabler for e-business.[3]

Company history

Nordea Bank is the product of several mergers between banks from four Scandinavian countries. Domestic mergers in Finland accelerated after a sustained eco-nomic crisis in the early 1990s caused by the collapse of the Soviet Union and the downturn of the global economy. The crisis strained Finland's timber-based economy and forced banks to cut costs.

The mergers took place over several years (see Exhibit 1). In 1997, the Swedish Nordbanken and the Finnish Merita merged to form MeritaNordbanken. In 1999, the Danish Unidanmark acquired TRYG and, later, Vesta. In 2000, Unidanmark and Merita Nordbanken merged to form Nordic Baltic Holding, which became Nordea after merging in 2000 with the Norwegian Christiania Bank Og Kreditkasse.

On completion of the merger process at the end of 2002, the market capitalization of Nordea reached €12.6 billion, making it the fifth largest company in the Nordic region and the fifteenth largest bank in Europe. Today, it is the largest financial group in the Nordic region with approximately €262 billion in total assets. Its market share in the Nordic banking markets ranges from 40% in Finland, 25% in Denmark, 20% in Sweden, to 15% in Norway. In the life insurance market, Nordea has a market share of 35% in Finland, 10% in Denmark, 9% in Norway and 6% in Sweden. Retail banking represents the

---

1 Nordea company presentation at Caisse d'Epargne Group, 13 June 2003.
2 'The dynamo of e-Banking', Business Week online, 16 April 2001.
3 Unless stated otherwise, quotations from Bo Harald were gathered during company interviews made in Helsinki in September 2003.

This case study was written by Albrecht Enders, Research Fellow at INSEAD (Fontainebleau), under the supervision of Tawfik Jelassi, Affiliate Professor of Technology Management at INSEAD, and Charles Waldman, Senior Affiliate Professor of Marketing at INSEAD. It is intended to be used as the basis for class discussion rather than to illustrate effective or ineffective handling of a management situation.

This case study was made possible by the co-operation of Bo Harald, Head of Electronic Banking at Nordea.

Exhibit 1 **The creation process of Nordea through mergers of Scandinavian banks**

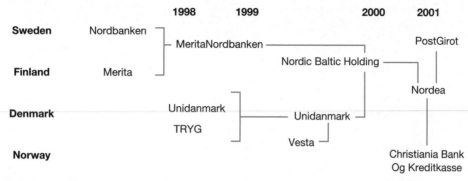

Source: Nordea Bank.

most important business area, constituting 74% of Nordea's income in 2002. Corporate and institutional banking accounted for 19%, asset management for 4%, investment banking for 2%, and group treasury for 1%.

At the end of 2002, Nordea had 10.6 million private customers, which the bank considers to be its main asset. Some 45% of the total population in the Nordic countries has either a main or secondary account with Nordea. At least 3.2 million customers are active e-banking customers (see Exhibit 2). In addition to its retail business, the bank also serves 950 000 corporate customers. Nordea employs 35 000 people and has 1260 branches throughout the Nordic and Baltic region (see Exhibit 3).

Exhibit 2 **Evolution of Nordea customers and e-banking**

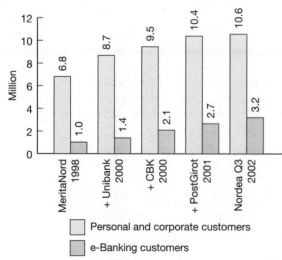

Personal and corporate customers

e-Banking customers

Source: Nordea Bank.

To outline the bank's purpose and goals, Nordea has formulated the 'Nordic Idea' and the 'Nordea Vision'. Its Nordic Idea states that:

■ We share and exchange Nordic ideas.

■ We are Nordic in operations while personal and local in delivering services. We think Nordic and act locally.

■ Our market is of a size that makes it worthwhile to develop joint concepts, products and services.[4]

Nordea's vision for the future is built upon three main pillars:

■ We will be valued as the leading financial services group in the Nordic and Baltic financial market with a substantial growth potential.

■ We will be at the top of the league or show superior profitable growth in every market and product area in which we choose to compete.

■ We will have the leading multi-channel distribution with a top world ranking in e-based financial services and solutions.[5]

Nordea's approach to e-banking

Bo Harald has been the main architect of Nordea's approach to e-banking. He joined the Union Bank of Finland in 1975 after studying law and economics, and opened the bank's first foreign office in Luxemburg in 1977 and in Asia in 1980. His job assignments pushed him to use computers to carry out banking transactions:

While away from home, I started using the computer to authorize payments. The beginning of PC banking in 1984 was a blessing for me. It became so much easier to do things from a distance.[6]

4 Taken from Nordea company website.
5 Taken from Nordea company website.
6 'Online extra: Q & A with Nordea's Bo Harald', Business Week online, 16 April 2001.

315

Exhibit 3 **Nordea's European Branch Network**

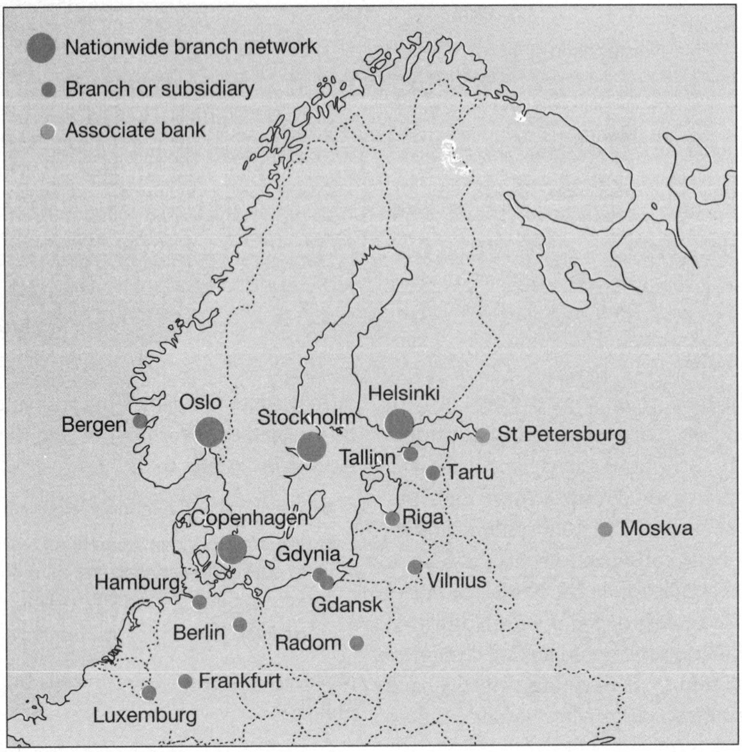

Source: Nordea Bank.

Union Bank introduced electronic payment systems and started to phase out cheques in 1982.

> I think the secret of our success was to start early. We started back in 1982 with telephone voice commands. By 1984, we added PC banking with a dial-up modem. It was like black and white compared to the color Internet, but it was a start and it gave us the experience.[7]

Starting out early also helped to keep costs down. Harald says:

> e-Banking is not expensive if you start early and you build it up gradually ... However, it can be very expensive if you wake up in the middle when things are already happening, because then you need to ask expensive consultants for advice and you end up buying all the expensive bells and whistles to outshine your competitors.

With the advent of the Internet, Bo Harald became Head of Internet Services at Merita Bank with the explicit mission to put as much business as possible on the Web in order to reduce costs and free up branch employees to focus on selling complex, higher-margin financial products.

Nordea's e-banking strategy evolved through different stages. The first was the creation of an 'e-habit' among its customers. To achieve this it was crucial to involve the 35 000 branch staff who enjoyed the trust of customers and were in frequent face-to-face contact with them. In addition, the bank strived to keep e-banking simple to understand and use in order to create a higher level of customer satisfaction. The underlying principle was that the bank's website should be designed in a way that would be easy even for 65-year-old customers to understand. Harald explains:

> I met the CEO of an important corporate customer. He had said before that he would never use a PC and that he would never retire. Now, at the age of 78, he had decided to retire. Then he came to me and said: 'Now that I am retired, I don't have my secretary doing my banking transactions anymore, so I have to do it myself. And I started using your Solo service [the Nordea online

---

7 'Online extra: Q & A with Nordea's Bo Harald', Business Week online, 16 April 2001.

banking system] and it works extremely well.' Now he is really fond of our basic e-banking service. He is even talking about it to the people of his own age group. They tested it [Solo] themselves, and they also like it. That's how it works: first, our customers become believers [in e-banking] and then they become preachers.

The goal of the second stage was to interconnect customers by integrating the different banking channels: e-banking, mobile e-banking (or m-banking), branch-based banking, contact centre and providing different types of e-services such as e-payment, e-billing, e-signature, e-ID, e-salary and e-invoicing. All the Internet services are concentrated in Nordea's Internet bank, 'Solo', which provides the following banking services: account management, transfers between own accounts, domestic and foreign invoice payments, equity (domestic and foreign), mutual funds and bond investments, electronically signed credit facilities, as well as life and general insurance.

The goal of the third stage is to personalize further the e-banking services and customize offerings by tapping into the value of data-mines. But for Bo Harald, when developing new products and services at Nordea: 'We avoid asking customers directly. We would rather use our colleagues and their experience in the branches.'[8]

Getting top-management support for e-banking has not always been easy, Harald acknowledges:

> Either you have a CEO who supports e-banking right from the beginning and has the staying power to see it through, or he lets you take care of it yourself. I can't say that our CEOs early on were particularly excited about it. If you have someone on a high enough level who pushes e-business, then the CEO does not have to do it. Actually, I am a little bit afraid if CEOs become too obsessed with something. They have such a big voice that it might be overdoing it. It must be planted somewhere in the bank, and I have been lucky to have that role at Nordea. I would love to have had more support in the past, though. We would have taken off much earlier!

While Nordea and other Scandinavian banks were developing their e-banking know-how, their e-customers simultaneously built up other assets important for the success of e-banking. These included 'e-trust' (in the security and reliability of electronic banking channels) and 'e-habit' (the routine use of the Internet for bank transactions).

Sustaining Nordea's Internet lead: from e-banking to e-business

The e-trust and e-habit have prompted Nordea to leverage the competencies built up for its e-banking services to also provide e-business solutions. In fact, Harald believes that e-banking alone is no longer a way for a bank to differentiate itself from its competitors:

> e-Banking services are kind of passé. Every bank offers them. The really important thing is launching e-banking services for e-business. It's a huge market! Banks are getting their acts together but very slowly. So I am worried that banks are losing their opportunity to earn substantial income from e-business.

Nordea started to move into e-business by leveraging the capabilities it had built up for e-banking. Bo Harald explains:

> The underlying principle is that we try to reuse technologies that we already have. For instance, we have file transfers for accounts, so why not have file transfer for bills as well?

The main e-business services that Nordea currently offers to its private and corporate customers include e-identification, e-signature, e-billing, e-salary and e-payment.

e-Identification

Through Nordea's e-identification services, Nordea customers can identify themselves on the websites of other participating companies and governmental agencies. For the latter, the Finnish Ministry of Finance has officially stated that if customers need reliable identification, they can and should use the bank's identification standards. For example, consider the case of citizens who want to access the state pension system to find out the balance of their pension in order to decide how much to save for retirement. Initially, they access the state pension system's website with links to all major banks in Finland that provide e-identification services. They then choose their bank, access the respective website and identify themselves with their one-time password. Upon registering there, they can switch to other services, including the state pension service, while staying within the identified area. 'This state pension site is accessed 2000 times a day', says Bo Harald.

---

8 'Learn from the largest Internet bank of the world', accessed at www.tietoenator.lv

Our e-identification service is so convincing that the Finnish post office has stopped its own identification service. They use banks because it's very expensive to have a reliable identification service only for the post office. Why should they do it themselves?

e-Signature

The e-signature service came about 'by accident'. When Bo Harald told executives from Sonera, the largest telecom operator in Finland, that customers could get a loan online, they said: 'Look, if you can sign up for loans through your system, you should also be able to sign a phone subscription contract.' Within a few weeks, Nordea reached an agreement with Sonera to send all interested customers an online phone contract through a link to Nordea's Solo Internet bank website where they could identify themselves and then sign the contract. This system was later extended to other businesses that wanted to provide e-signatures for their contracts.

e-Billing

Through Nordea's e-billing services, companies can send their invoices electronically to the bank, which then for-

wards them to their customers who have e-banking agreements, while those customers without e-banking accounts automatically receive a printed invoice via the mail (see Exhibit 4). Customers who get their invoice through their e-bank connection are asked: 'Do you want to pay this bill?'; they approve the payment with a mouse-click and the bill is paid. This service was first used in 1998 by Finland's main telephone companies to send invoices to customers via Internet. Bo Harald comments:

In Europe, there is a cost of $50 billion every year for paper invoices. Who pays for that? In the end, it is always the customer. We can eliminate that when we go to electronic invoicing. In Sweden, we are sending out invoice files to a Nordea switch, which are then distributed to private and large corporate customers [e.g. a telecom company that sends invoices to its customers]. In the future, you will see it with other banks as well. What's fantastic about this is that if you are an entrepreneur you can pay your bills online and you can also send out your invoices easily and quickly. The party that is sending the bills doesn't have to worry. Isn't that the obvious way? We are already sending these bills to other banks in Finland, Sweden, soon to other banks in Denmark and Norway, and later to the rest of Europe.

Exhibit 4 Nordea switchboard for invoice processing

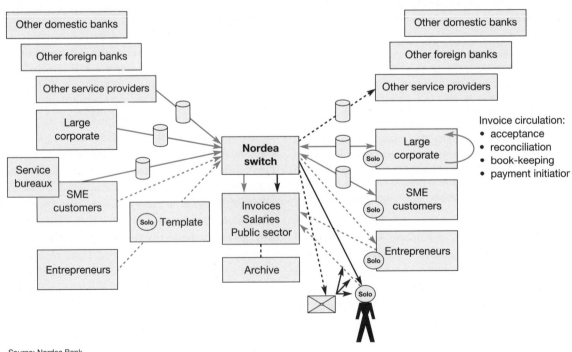

Source: Nordea Bank.

e-Salary

Through the e-salary function, companies can send income statements straight to the e-bank of their employees, thereby eliminating the need for printed salary statements sent via mail.

> If you have enough staff, say 10 000 employees, it makes sense for the employer to send out e-salaries instead of paper salaries. That's where getting to a critical size really starts to matter.

e-Payment

The e-payment function is an adaptation of the invoicing function, which online merchants on the Solo platform can use for settling payments. It allows customers to go to the website of any online store in the Solo marketplace, place an order and click on a link to Nordea's e-payment system where they request an electronic invoice. After approving the payment with a mouse click, the amount is instantly transferred to the seller's account. This method has a twofold benefit: the merchant does not need to send out paper invoices or to worry whether the buyer pays. To ensure that there is no fraud on the merchant's side, Nordea conducts a reliability check on all 2000 merchants who sell goods in the Solo e-marketplace. Says Bo Harald:

> For corporate customers, the value of the Solo e-market-place grows exponentially with the increase in the number of retail customers … We have achieved a criti-cal mass among our retail customers so we now have

people who want to buy all kinds of things – from CDs and stereo systems to kitchen appliances and bicycles. That's what we need for the e-marketplace. As part of this move into e-business, we see the evolution of value chains in which the banks are supplying essential parts. In the future, this is the most important reason for going into e-banking because each and every company and governmental agency is increasingly moving to digital value chains and the bank has a big role to play there for customer identification, direct payment in real time, invoicing, e-salary, e-pension and e-signature.

Banking channels at Nordea

After introducing online banking in 1984, Nordea con-tinued to introduce new customer interfaces such as Internet banking, TV banking, WAP-enabled[9] mobile phones and digital TV (see Exhibit 5).

According to Bo Harald:

> When adding channels, a bank's main goal should be to add value … But it is also crucial that all channels and services have the same look and feel so as to offer cus-tomers a consistent user experience. The key is to have one core to our electronic bank and then to keep adding doors to it.

---

9 Wap stands for Wireless Application Protocol, a secure specification that allows users to access information instantly via handheld wireless devices.

Exhibit 5 Evolution of banking devices at Nordea

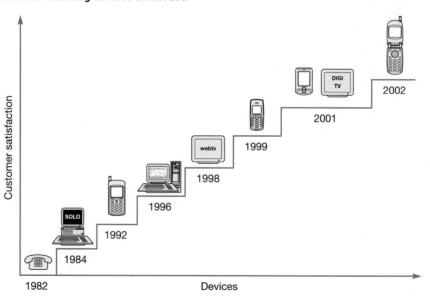

Source: Nordea Bank.

Kaisa Juhanni, a Nordea customer from Finland, considers Nordea's reliable multi-channel services to be a major asset of the bank:

> I like the quick and instant access without having to queue up at a branch. I also like the flexibility of being able to do my banking any time and any place, be it from home, the office or through the mobile phone. The Solo system is also very reliable. The system has probably been down just once during the past six and a half years. Finally, Nordea has also a very large installed base of users in Finland which allows me to transfer money to them without any delays.

ATMs and pay terminals

Automatic teller machines (ATMs) and pay terminals still play an important role in cash withdrawal and other transactions. However, as card payments and Internet transactions become more important, the role of ATMs and cash in general becomes less relevant (see Table 1). Bo Harald explains:

> In our Danish organization, we have the highest number of card payments per capita in the world; the second highest is our Finnish organization. Actually, Finland has the lowest amount of cash in relation to GNP [gross national product]. As a result, ATMs have become less important. Earlier this year, we saw a fantastic development in Finland, which we consider as a laboratory. Compared to 2002, cash withdrawals have gone down by 15–16% in our branches and 8% from our ATMs. That's excellent because ATMs are very expensive: you have to keep the money there, you need to protect them and sometimes they are destroyed. Cash is actually the most expensive way to pay for things. Transactions at pay terminals are also quickly decreasing. We have

started to charge people for using these terminals, so this year they should go down quite drastically. Just like ATMs, pay terminals are also unprofitable. Actually, I don't want to see them at all five years from now. People shouldn't be paying their bills in the street; they should do it at home. Why should people use cash at all? It's unhygienic, it's unsafe to carry around and there is a high risk of counterfeit money. It's irrational!

m-Banking

Nordea's wireless service started out with WAP phones in 1999. Through WAP-enabled phones, Nordea customers can track their account and credit card transactions, transfer funds between accounts, pay bills both domestically and abroad, trade equities and read customer mail. The WAP service extends to the mobile phone Nordea's Internet services originally available through Solo. In 2000, Nordea introduced stock trading and bank transfers via cell phone and also made it possible for customers to purchase movie tickets which are debited directly from their Nordea account. Adapting Internet services to the WAP cost Nordea less than €500,000; it mainly required adding a server for wireless services. However, Harald sees a lot of potential for wireless banking:

> I firmly believe that, with Nokia, Finland will continue to play a leading role world-wide in mobile phone technology. I was recently on a train from Arlanda airport [in Stockholm] and I saw a group of teenagers all using their mobile phones. These are our future customers.[10]

In January 2002, Nordea expanded its wireless services by providing a more elaborate m-payment version for Finnish customers who have GPRS[11] handsets and are connected with Telia's, Sonera's or Radiolinja's wireless communication networks. This service was made possible via a joint launch with Nokia of a dual-SIM[12] handset for mobile transactions. The phone has two separate slots: one for the operator's SIM card, the other for the m-payment card issued by Nordea, which is based on

Table 1 Household transactions in Finland

	Transactions (millions)				% change
	1999	2000	2001	2002	1999–2002
Manual transactions	184.9	163.9	141.0	125.3	−32.2
Pay terminals	35.5	35.6	34.3	31.7	−10.7
Card payments	234.3	263.1	306.9	363.0	+54.9
Cash-withdrawal ATMs	197.9	202.5	207.2	204.4	+3.3
Direct debit	69	75.3	78.5	81.5	+18.1
Solo payments	32.7	58.2	78.2	97.6	+198.5
Total	754.3	798.6	846.1	903.5	+20

Source: Nordea Bank.

---

10 'Online Extra: Q & A with Nordea's Bo Harald', Business Week online, 16 April 2001.
11 General Packet Radio Service (GPRS) is a technology used to send and receive data via packet delivery over a wireless network allowing the user to stay connected to the Internet.
12 A subscriber identity module (SIM) is the smart card inside a mobile phone that identifies the user account to the network, handles authentication and provides data storage for user data such as phone numbers and network information. It may contain applications that run on the phone.

wireless identification module (WIM).[13] Harald believes that customers should be free to choose the supplier of their banking services:

> You don't buy groceries from a furniture store, so why should you buy your banking services from the mobile operator? Plus, it's really not a big deal nowadays to make a handset with two chips.[14]

PC banking

> Wells Fargo, Citibank and Bank of America have, similarly, as many customers as our Internet Bank 'Solo'. But with 124 million payments over the Internet in 2002, no other bank can keep up [with us]! This number might be about twice as large as those of the previously mentioned banks combined.
>
> **Bo Harald**[15]

Online banking at Nordea started as early as the mid-1980s when Nordea allowed its customers to start doing transactions from computers at their workplace. Harald explains:

> In the mid-1980s, people didn't have computers at home, and if they did, they didn't have modems. So we asked our large corporate customers: 'Can't you allow your employees to log on to their banking account through the workplace computer? That will save you a lot of time and money because people won't have to go to the branch any more.' Ever since, workplace access has been a very important pillar for our e-banking.

e-Banking and bricks-and-mortar banking have never been in competition at Nordea. Rather, they are considered to be complementary, as Harald emphasizes:

> One of the main reasons for our success is the fact that we made e-banking already part of our branch business in 1982. We never considered it to be a competitor. e-Banking is not a separate profit center. That is important in order to quickly achieve a crucial size. Without the support of the branch employees, one is not able to reach that goal.[16]

However, direct online consultation from bank employees either in a branch or a call centre is kept to an absolute minimum:

> Nordea decided consciously to offer no consultation on the Internet and very little on the phone. You must keep your offer simple to succeed in Internet business and to gain the necessary confidence and trust of your customers. That's difficult but necessary, and if your offer is simple, you don't need to provide expensive instructions over the Internet. For complex [financial] products, customers go to the branch anyway. However, the shift of transactions to electronic channels frees up resources for improved service levels in the branch.[17]

Table 2 Evolution of online usage at Nordea

	Jan-July 00	Jan-July 01	Jan-July 02	Jan-July 03
Log-ons				
Denmark	6 091 418	8 924 759	11 721 765	14 659 759
Finland	17 495 518	20 582 125	24 671 753	28 199 328
Norway	1 595 000	3 562 704	4 528 822	6 118 581
Sweden	4 640 100	11 562 033	16 738 683	22 863 322
Nordea	29 822 036	44 631 621	57 661 023	71 840 990
Online payments				
Denmark	2 773 192	5 186 359	7 220 065	8 781 289
Finland	20 774 000	26 293 637	30 712 994	35 626 067
Norway	2 150 000	4 121 013	5 236 914	6 641 027
Sweden	6 660 147	18 845 501	25 202 502	31 401 953
Nordea	32 357 339	54 446 510	68 372 475	82 450 336

Source: Nordea Bank.

Tuukka Seppa, a Nordea customer from Finland, is fond of Nordea's banking services:

> What I really like is the simplicity of the authentication process and the website itself. It is also very helpful that it offers immediate transactions between two Nordea accounts.

Today, all Internet banking activities at Nordea take place through Solo, the company's online banking service, which has become increasingly popular (see Table 2). This is demonstrated by the following statistics (figures correspond to the highest month of usage):

- *Student loans*: 84% of all student loans are completely paperless. Students apply online by providing information about their financial status and the loan is approved within one hour through a computerized scoring system. Once approved, students sign by keying in their customer number once more and a one-time password.[18]

- *Equity orders*: 80% of all equity orders are made through Solo.

---

13 WIM allows users to identify themselves with digital signatures to confirm their banking transactions.
14 'Two slots are better than one', Silicon.com, 23 May 2002.
15 'Learn from the largest Internet bank of the world', accessed at www.tietoenator.lv
16 'Learn from the largest Internet bank of the world', accessed at www.tietoenator.lv
17 'Learn from the largest Internet bank of the world', accessed at www.tietoenator.lv
18 For more information on the one-time password, refer to the authentication section below.

- *Mutual funds*: 65% of all mutual funds are managed by Solo.

- *Foreign payments*: 59% of all private and small business foreign payments take place via Solo. Customers key the account number of the recipient into their computer (or mobile phone) and the money is received as fast as international transfers travel – within Nordea one day at most. Fees are €15 in a branch and €7 for online payments.

- *Currency deposits*: 30% of all currency deposits take place through Solo.

- *Foreign exchange*: 35% of all foreign exchange transactions occur with Solo.

- *Car finance*: 25% of all car financing takes place through Solo.

- *Home mortgages*: 24% of home mortgages come in through the Internet.

Bo Harald summarizes Nordea's challenge for 2005: 'All the numbers mentioned should be up to 80% or 90%. That's the challenge in our bank.'[19]

TV banking

TV-based banking was launched in 1996 through the use of a set-top box that connected to normal household TVs. Through this box, Nordea customers could log on to the Nordea banking system and carry out basic banking transactions. The underlying idea was that those people who disliked computers would use the TV to write e-mails and to check their account balance. However, as it turned out, TV banking has not so far fulfilled the high expectations associated with it. Says Bo Harald:

> Clearly, every family has a TV in their house, so in principle it should work well … but we believe that people just do not want to check e-mails or do their banking in front of the whole family. Those are rather private things and that's why the TV in the living room is not well suited. That's the reason why we haven't invested more in this channel. We only offer basic services for e-payments. With the continuing convergence of the TV and the PC this might change, though.

Branch-based banking

The role of branch offices at Nordea has changed in recent decades. While in the past bank clerks spent most of their time keying in transactions manually, this has drastically decreased (see Table 1). For 2003, Bo Harald expects a further reduction of 20 million manual transactions:

If every transaction takes one minute, what can you do with this time once customers start banking online? It frees up the branch staff to give customers advice. We use our branches primarily for establishing personal relationships with our customers, which is important when making a big decision (such as purchasing insurance or a pension scheme) that requires personal trust. In a sense, banking is local but it doesn't always require an expensive branch. Sometimes an office is enough. You don't have to offer transfers there but you will never be able to replace either the personal sales nor the fostering of personal relationships. To achieve this it is absolutely paramount not to create separate profit centres for Internet and branch banking because the two have to feed each other. There mustn't be competition but co-operation between the two channels. Combining and leveraging high-tech and high-touch is the key to success.

Nonetheless, the number of Nordea branches in Finland decreased significantly during the last decade – down from 1300 in 1991 to 400 in 2000. The number of employees shrunk to less than half during the same period, falling from 22 000 to 10 600 (see Exhibit 6). Getting strong and influential labour unions to agree to such staff reductions has not always been an easy task. Bo Harald recalls:

> We had to speak to the unions in great length and we had to hand out very generous packages since no employee was actually fired … But we also tried to show that Solo [the Nordea Internet bank] had led to a great increase in customer satisfaction and that this would make Nordea a more competitive and stable institution in the future. We also showed the [labour] unions that Finland is absolutely world-class when it comes to Internet banking and that it was necessary to make changes in our organizational structure in order to maintain this lead. Finally, we pointed out that it was problematic to have people do this type of manual, repetitive, low-paid work and that it would be much more valuable if we educated these people to do a more creative and interesting job.

Today, Nordea operates 1 288 branch offices throughout the Nordic region and employs 34 600 people (full-time equivalents). In addition to the Finnish branches, there are 267 branches with 8500 employees in Sweden, 151 branches with 4400 employees in Norway and 348 branch offices with 9400 employees in Denmark. Says Bo Harald:

---

19 'Learn from the largest Internet bank of the world', accessed at www.tietoenator.lv

Exhibit 6 Evolution of Nordea's staff and branches in Finland

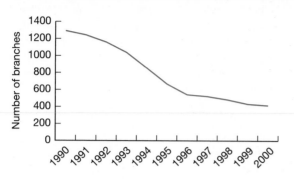 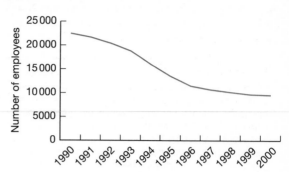

Source: Nordea Bank.

We have been cutting branches for a long time, partly thanks to mergers and now thanks to the Internet ... Finland used to be over-branched, but now it is almost under-branched. The future is to change the way branches work: we are now opening teller-less branches in places such as shopping centers. The idea is to use the branch to sell and provide services, not to make transactions. The branch staff should add value for customers. They shouldn't do routine, uninspiring work.[20]

Marketing

Due to its early start in e-banking, Nordea has spent little on marketing its Internet initiatives in comparison with other online banks. From 1996 to 2001, Nordea spent about €18 million to market its Finnish Internet initiatives. This money was not directed primarily towards attracting new customers but instead towards getting the nine million branch customers to move to the Internet.

Because of its large size, Nordea takes a mass-market approach to its banking activities. Bo Harald explains:

If you are as big a bank as we are, you can't afford not to target all customers ... There is also a misconception that there is a clear distinction between profitable and unprofitable customers. Of course, there are customers who come to the branch every day. They are unprofitable, but there is no way to get rid of them, so you might as well not even try. Another typical feature of less profitable customers is that they are young. However, soon enough they'll need a mortgage and a retirement plan. If you look at the older segments, you don't find that many unprofitable customers. Thus, when you want to talk about profitability, you really need to take a dynamic view of customers.

In its marketing activities, Nordea differentiates between two types of customer:

■ *Internet believers*. These customers have been online for years and have the know-how and trust to navigate the Internet, to shop online and to do their banking online. To them e-banking is a normal day-to-day activity; something that is not worth talking about with their friends. From a marketing perspective, these customers are therefore considered to be 'infertile'.

■ *Non-believers*. These customers are just starting to surf the Internet. They require substantial convincing to build enough trust and know-how to start doing e-banking. Friendly branch employees are best suited for removing that insecurity. Once they are online, however, these customers are amazed and proud of their accomplishments and want to pass the news on to their friends. After turning them into believers they take the next step and become preachers – a viral marketing effect where customers acquire more customers, as Harald emphasizes: 'When you get a critical mass of customers, they are the best sales force for you.'

At Nordea, the importance of a branch cannot be underestimated when it comes to turning non-believers into believers. Says Harald:

Just imagine an enthusiastic clerk serving a client, who says, 'Hey, why don't you also do e-banking? Everyone else does it' and then convincingly seals the deal ... The value of the branch network is absolutely fantastic. That's why you need to get employees to like it. Otherwise they won't move business into the online channel.

20 'Online extra: Q & A with Nordea's Bo Harald', Business Week online, 16 April 2001.

323

In spite of having achieved a high penetration rate throughout Scandinavia, Harald still sees significant potential for the bank's e-banking services, especially among senior citizens:

> Even if you are the largest e-bank in the world, of course you still have a lot to do in the 60-year-old-plus sector. We feel a social responsibility to organize evenings – especially in the countryside – where senior citizens learn how to use the Internet. For those people, we organize senior citizens' clubs. We just had one in the east of Finland that was originally set up for 100 people. In the end, 1500 people wanted to participate. When someone in that age group finds out that they can send an e-mail to their children or their grandchildren, that's a big deal. The sooner they come on board, the better it is. And then they can take part in online communities and discussion forums. Finland is a country of associations; there is an association for everything, even for Siamese cats. Whatever it is they like, they can find it on the Internet. And they need e-payment, e-invoicing and e-identification. All those services are required to manage your Siamese cat association! Then, those senior citizens will get so much more out of their lives, because there is such a huge window that opens up into the world – a new dimension. And e-banking is just one part of it.

While targeting senior citizens with its e-banking, marketing these services to the younger, Internet-savvy generation is not at the top of Nordea's agenda. Bo Harald says:

> I wouldn't spend any money on marketing to people younger than 30; there is no need for that … You can start with e-banking when you are 15; to get the message through to these people, you let them know what's possible. That's worthwhile putting some marketing money into. But from 18 to 30 or 40, there is not much you need to do. Instead, I would put all my money into the 60 years and above group.

Pricing

> e-Banking is not free because every transaction has a cost. Customers who use it should pay for it, not those who don't. If a bank comes out and says that their e-banking services are for free, they are lying. It is only a question of who pays.
>
> **Bo Harald**

Nordea's rates for retail customers contain fixed and variable elements. The monthly fee for basic services, regardless of usage, is €2 per month. Access to the credit card balance costs an additional 40 cents, and mobile WAP services an additional 30 cents; these charges are now being removed. Customers who want to do equity trading pay from €4 per month for a basic version and up to €20 for the most advanced version. Nordea's competitors tend to be cheaper. E*Trade, for instance, charges a fee of €10 per trade, a quarter of Nordea's price. However, Nordea's fees seem still to be reasonable, as Magnus Grann, a 40-year-old software engineer, points out: 'Nordea's fees just aren't high enough to make a difference.'[21]

But other customers struggle with the pricing of Nordea. Tuukka Seppa, a Nordea customer from Finland, points out:

> Nordea is definitely not cheap and charges some fees for every additional service. For instance, I really don't like it that there are additional monthly payments for accessing my investments.[22]

Tomas Bauer, a Nordea customer from Sweden, goes even further:

> I think Nordea's pricing practices are a little dubious. I actually feel that they tricked me into opening a savings account when they offered me an interest rate slightly above market level. After one year they dropped the rate to almost 1% below the comparable market level.[23]

On average, for its online services, Nordea generates revenues of slightly more than €2 per customer, which amounts to €7 million per month. These revenues cover all costs for the online banking channel and also generate a profit (which is not disclosed).

Corporate customers pay from €20 to €5000 depending on the level of service. To be a member of the e-marketplace, merchants pay a €200 connection charge up front and a monthly fee of €20. For each transaction, an additional fee of 35 cents is levied. In contrast to credit cards, the transaction fee does not depend on the volume of the purchase. This is due to the fact that with credit cards, the bank has to finance the period – up to 30 days – between when the merchant gets the money and when the customer pays the bill. Since the Solo direct payment is similar to a debit card, there is no time gap to be refinanced. Merchants benefit because they no longer have to send out invoices by mail. In addition, while previously they had to wait to be paid, they now receive payment in real-time before even shipping the goods, thereby eliminating their credit risk.

---

21 'The dynamo of e-Banking', Business Week online, 16 April 2001.
22 Personal interview, 5 October 2003.
23 Personal interview, 5 October 2003.

We pay attention to the profitability of our e-banking operations. Our basic principle when introducing new applications is that we don't give added value for free. Our customers pay a monthly fee for Internet banking. If further services are taken up such as brokerage, credit card reporting or WAP, then it costs more. Customers accept it if they benefit from it, for example, if a transfer becomes more favorable and simpler. The added value which is created here cannot be free. Many companies have just started to understand it.[24]

The pricing of banking services is also used as an effective tool for steering customer business into certain channels. Bo Harald shares his personal experience:

In 1983, we introduced a charge of 10 cents for all cheque forms, which were very popular at that time and my wife was very good at writing these cheques. But once this fee was introduced, she didn't write out one single cheque any more. In fact, chequebooks just disappeared because it wasn't worth even 10 cents to the people. Instead, they started to pay with a debit card and afterwards they used the debit card at payment terminals to pay bills. Those same people later on started using computers at their workplace to do the transactions. ... In the US, people write somewhere around 50 billion cheques a year. That amount of paper is transported by airmail to the banks and back. It costs somewhere around $75 billion a year to pay for these transactions and, on top of that, it's an environmental problem. It takes a lot of time and costs a lot of money. If you don't put an upfront price tag on costs, you still have to pay for them and you don't direct the activities of your customers. Showing the customer what it really costs allows the customer to make rational choices because they are paying for these costs.

Nordea has implemented similar pricing structures between branches and Internet banking to entice customers to move online. For instance, a foreign currency wire costs $7 online but $14 in a branch. Bill payment is free online, whereas it costs $3.50 per bill in a branch.

Customer authentication

Nordea's customer authentication procedure has been in place since the early 1980s. For all contact with the bank, whether via the Internet, mobile phone or call centre, customers use one identification number: the one-time code (OTC). These OTCs, which are printed on a card, are comparable to the transaction number which customers use for transfers. To access their bank account through any one of the above-mentioned electronic channels, customers need to have the OTC

handy. Bo Harald considers the Nordea authentication approach to be superior to most others:

To connect to Nordea, customers need to have their code, which is given after opening an account with us. The latter can be done only if the customer shows up in person at the bank branch and presents an ID document. Other banks, especially Internet banks, are not so rigorous. There, all you need to do is send in a phone bill where you can see the customer's address. That's easy to forge and then you can get into the money laundering business quickly.

He points out additional advantages of the OTC:

With the one-time-password and the identification number they [the customers] get access to a safe e-business marketplace, which they can visit from everywhere and on which they can do much more than traditional banking transactions. For example, they can sign contracts with their energy and telecom suppliers, buy credit on-line, or assign attorneys. Plus, they don't need any pedantic installations of card readers or programs. At the moment, we have a very interesting situation since the Ministry of Finance recommends that for future transactions in the public sector which require an electronic identification this should be done through e-banking platforms. Again, that's trust, which upholds our services. 'You want to know something concerning your pension? Please click here.' We – and the other banks in Finland – offer the use of OTC to everyone who has to offer identification and signature possibilities. Millions of customers already have this code, and for them it's an additional service if they can interact with other companies or governmental agencies.[25]

However, the OTC is not popular with everyone. Kaisa Juhanni, a Nordea customer from Finland, points out: 'What I really dislike about the Nordea online banking is that you always need to carry the pass-code list with you in order to access the service.'

For the future, Nordea plans to develop a public-key infrastructure (PKI)[26] that would allow customers

24 'Learn from the largest Internet bank of the world', accessed at www.tietoenator.lv.

25 'Learn from the largest Internet bank of the world', accessed at www.tietoenator.lv.

26 Public key infrastructure is an electronic framework for trusted security. Participants in a PKI each obtain a digital certificate from a trusted certificate authority (CA), which then authenticates their identity when initiating a secure transaction. Individual transactions are encrypted by each participant using their own pair of electronic keys, one of which they keep for their own private use, while the other – the 'public key' – is made available to other participants. PKI has been widely adopted as the basis for secure Internet and web services transactions.

Exhibit 7 Change of business structure to support the integration of IT and processes

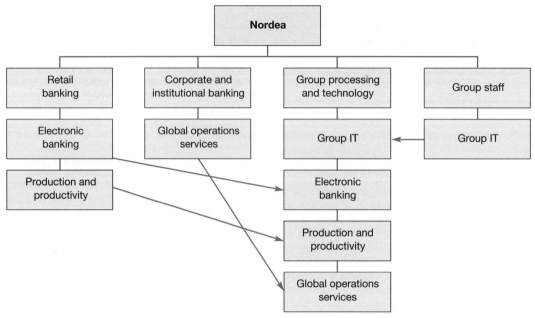

Source: Nordea Bank.

to log on to PCs or mobile phones using smart-cards equipped with chips.

Technology

The evolution of the technological platform at Nordea – the backbone of all its e-banking operations – has been strongly influenced by the original individual banks which all had different technology platforms. For instance, the Finnish Merita bank had an e-banking infrastructure that allowed customers to log on to their system with just a browser and a simple password system. At the Swedish Nordbanken, on the other hand, customers needed to install special software and get a smart-card reader before going online.

After the completion of the merger, Nordea was faced with a very complex IT infrastructure which included the following:

- *Production*: four main production centres with multiple platforms.
- *Applications*: roughly 9000 applications.
- *Networks*: four different branch networks.

Since then, Nordea has undergone efforts to integrate the various IT systems and organizational structure to streamline its activities. For example, real-time processing systems, which have been in place since 1985, needed to be aligned. On the organizational side, the changes are reflected in the increased importance of the group processing and technology unit (see Exhibit 7). The electronic banking and production and productivity units were moved over from retail banking. The corporate and institutional banking unit handed over the global operations services while group staff handed over the group IT. Several reasons led to this concentration of technology functions in one unit, including focusing on integration and cost efficiency, releasing time for business areas to focus on customers and capitalizing on change management.

Today, IT costs correspond to 20% of total expenses, averaging around €200 million per quarter. These costs are almost evenly divided between development costs (47%) and production costs (53%). Nordea has formulated a philosophy to drive its IT operations, which includes the following elements:

- *A comprehensive governance and control structure* on IT development and IT production.
- *Business-driven development*, i.e. business decides the 'what', IT decides the 'how'.

■ *Strict prioritization of development* to support integration and cost efficiency.

■ *Gradual creation of common Nordic platforms,* including consolidated production and applications.

■ *Business-case-driven approach to consolidation,* assuming that the integration of all systems will most likely not be profitable.

In relation to overall IT costs, e-banking expenses were low. From 1981 to 2000, the Finnish arm of Nordea spent a cumulative total of €19 million on its e-banking technology. However, today expenses are significantly higher because 17 different e-banking systems throughout the Nordea group need to be maintained and improved. The main cost item is the development of an integrated e-banking system, which Nordea is jointly pursuing with TietoEnator, a Finnish company specializing in consulting, developing and hosting its customers' business operations. The annual e-banking costs are in the 'two-figure millions' range.

In the late 1990s, at the peak of the dot.com years, Nordea considered selling its technology systems to other banks in Europe. Bo Harald explains:

> In the end we didn't do it because all banks are very different and it would cost a lot of effort to make them work. Banking is a complicated business and if you really want to have the best return on equity, you should have high-touch and high-tech. We ended up making money but it wasn't enough to justify the effort of selling our technology. Instead, we decided to focus all of our energy on our customers.

Competition

Even though Nordea has achieved a dominant role in the Nordic region, a number of Swedish and Finnish banks compete head-on with Nordea – also with regards to e-banking services. Swedbank, for instance, which had 1.3 million online banking customers in 2002, is planning to allow its m-banking customers to view their mobile phone account statements, update their subscription contracts and access itemized calls.

Okobank in Finland has 720000 retail customers on the Internet. Matti Korkeela, Executive Vice-President at OKO, believes in the quality of the bank's e-offerings:

> We have estimated that active users of the system make up approximately 80% of our Internet-banking clients. I believe this figure is higher than that of our competitors. With OKO Bank, Internet banking per customer is more

intensive than with most other banks. To be honest, I do not believe in pure Internet banking. We at OKO have a multi-service concept, where the banking outlet still plays an important role.[27]

In 2002, the bank saw a 48% increase in web-based transactions. In total, 40% of 110 million invoices were handled online. Other competitors with sophisticated e-banking services include Rabobank, Enskilda Banken and Svenska Handelsbanken. Says Bo Harald:

> There has been no real price competition … Cost savings have been passed on in two ways. First, if you pay your bill in a branch today, you pay a lot of money, but if you pay it online you only pay the monthly charge. Second, competition has moved to housing mortgages. All the cost savings have been pushed into mortgages with margins down from 1.6% to 0.8%. Most banks have done the same thing and have passed on the cost savings, so it's always the customer who, in the end, wins the most.

At Nordea, pure online banks are not viewed as a major threat:

> We haven't lost a significant amount of business to pure e-players … They may be cheaper than us but an e-bank has no personal selling capabilities, no customer base, and it costs them a fortune to acquire customers. I am convinced people value the safety of branches and a trusted relationship. Our vision is to be high-tech and high-touch. That will make us invulnerable to cyber-attacks. I believe traditional banks will play a central place in the e-economy. They have trust. They have established brands. Today, nobody would try to set up an Amazon.com-type bank any more. It's just too expensive and it doesn't work in our business.[28]

Customers who have been clients of Nordea for a long time are a major asset for the bank. Tuukka Seppa said:

> Initially, I was a customer of Kansallis-Osake-Pankki (KOP), which became Merita in 1976. For personal purposes, I started using the Solo online service in 1995. Through it I pay all my bills, review my account transactions as well as my credit card charges. I also use it to authenticate access to my electronic mailbox which is hosted by the Finnish Post.[29]

Where will new competition for Nordea come from? Will it be from software houses, large international

---

27 'The massive e-habit as a natural resource', Nordicum.com, No. 1, 2003.
28 'Online extra: Q & A with Nordea's Bo Harald', Business Week online, 16 April 2001.
29 Personal interview, 5 October 2003.

banks (such as Citibank or Deutsche Bank) or others? Bo Harald replies:

> These companies don't have the local branch structure and they don't have our cost-income ratios ... Telecom operators that have very broad access to their mobile phone customers might enter the competition.

However, contrary to popular belief, he does not believe that customer retention has gone down as a result of e-banking:

> The idea that the next bank is only one click away is absolutely not true. To become a customer, you need to go to the bank and open up an account. When you are used to one system, you don't want to change.

Growth opportunities

In its domestic markets, where Nordea operates its branch network, there is limited opportunity for growth. Bo Harald explains:

> We can't grow very much in Finland. In Sweden, we are the second biggest bank. In Denmark and Norway, we are still too small in private and corporate banking, which leaves plenty of room for growth. In neighbouring markets such as Estonia, we are already the third largest bank with substantial growth potential. In Poland, we bought four banks, which we now need to consolidate before we can start thinking about further growth.

Moving into other European markets as a pure e-bank without a branch network is not a real option for Nordea:

> As a pure play, you might be able to attract the tech-savvy people who are constantly checking interest rates. Those guys easily sign up for anything new but this market segment is very small. Our experience has been that if you don't have a strong brand name and a solid branch structure that allows you to get in personal contact with your customers, you will have problems addressing the mass market. I mean, if we went to southern France and said, 'Hi, we are Nordea. Come and do your banking with us on our great website!' – what would people say? That's why we have never tried to penetrate foreign markets where we don't have a physical branch network.

In addition to expanding geographically, another main growth area for Nordea is expanding its service range:

> Even in our Finnish market, we can expand quite a lot by offering new services that we didn't have before. If you look at these services, you can only offer some of them over the Internet, but not at a branch. For instance, customers won't come to the branch to check the balance on their credit card but would like to do it through their mobile phone.

For Nordea, there are two promising future e-business opportunities. First, to develop further customer relationship management, the bank is turning towards triggered data mining, which works as follows: when there is a change in a customer account – for instance, a large incoming money transfer, change of address or marital status – a trigger in the database is set off and informs the bank of the change, which then raises a number of questions: what does it mean for financing, for long-term payments, for insurance and e-services? Based on the answers to these questions, Nordea plans to make an offer either via mail or face-to-face in a branch. While Bo Harald sees substantial value in this approach, he wants to go a step further:

> Triggered data mining is not enough because it looks into the past. Instead, we should ask the customer directly: What are you going to be doing next? What's your next life event, as we call it? For instance, the most important thing that can happen to a man in Finland is the purchase of a new car. We want to invite the customer to tell us about it and then ask ourselves: What can we do? What can the private sector do? What can the public sector do? Well, he'll have to look for a car. Our Solo partners can send him car offers. He'll have to buy the car and sign a contract – this can be done through e-signature. He'll have to pay for the car – this opens up the opportunity for financing arrangements. He'll have to have his car inspected – again an opportunity for one of our partners on the Solo marketplace ... Of course, when we think about these services, a major concern is always the issue of data privacy, to which we are very sensitive. Nordea never shares any information with anyone outside the bank. Customers voluntarily decide to share information with, say, the car seller. During the initial stage it's even possible to have a protected identity which is unknown to the merchant.

The second major opportunity is risk management services for e-businesses:

> In the electronic world, business partners do not know each other well. At the same time, market volatility is very high, which has led to numerous big crashes. Therefore you shouldn't trust anybody. To accommodate this you can either use direct payment [e-payment as explained above] or get credit ratings. Today, most companies have a lot of people working in risk management. They pay tens of millions for credit information and insurance in order to reduce credit loss. In general this works well but it raises the question: How much should you pay? If you could use the bank's knowledge and its ready-made credit information and integrate it into the billing process, you could save a lot of money. That's what we plan to make available in the future. Every company in the world has a bank

and usually the bank has made a credit evaluation of that company and established a credit line. These banks have the most in-depth information and therefore it's probably the best credit evaluation anybody can get. If all banks made these evaluations available electronically by issuing trade-related bank guarantees on the Internet, companies could save a lot of money. It would be a lubricant on the e-business machinery. This is a very obvious idea but sometimes the things that are so simple and self-evident don't take off. That's the way the world works – never quite perfectly.

Future outlook

In spite of its successful e-banking and e-business initiatives, Nordea's stock performance has been below average in the last few years, falling 28% in 2002. This was due, in part, to a drop in the bank's total income which fell by 4% while expenses increased by 2%. However, Harald believes that another important factor is that investors do not value e-banking activities appropriately at the moment:

Those who know e-banking know that we are the number one in the world. During the dot.com bubble we had investment bankers and analysts here every single day – I could've spent all my time just talking to them! They told me: 'You shouldn't really be classified as a bank, you

should be an IT company and have a valuation that is ten times higher than your current valuation.' Actually, our valuation went up quite a bit. But now, how many analysts come to see us? What I am complaining about are the analysts. Now that the real thing is happening, why are they not interested in it? They were only interested in sensation. The underlying problem is that people tend to overestimate new technology in the short run but underestimate its influence in the long term.

Regarding the future, he sees the importance of e-banking and e-business in a broader perspective:

Getting people accustomed to e-banking is really a social task to make Europe more competitive. We can't afford not to do it. e-Banking services can be used to make people more productive to compete with the US and the Far East. Due to our high costs and our powerful [labour] unions, we can't afford not to increase productivity. To achieve this, the all-important thing is the national resource of e-habit that we have been building up [over the years]. That's the key to the future. Nonetheless, you can't plan or foresee the future, you can only create it – and that's exactly what we want to do at Nordea.[30]

---

30 'Learn from the largest Internet bank of the world', accessed at www.tietoenator.lv.

ING DIRECT
Rebel in the banking industry

ING DIRECT USA is built on the foundation of being unconventional. We aren't like other banks. We've not only developed a unique business model, but the way we look at the business is different than how our competitors look at it. Our purpose is to be a servant of the average person. Rather than getting people to spend more – which is what most banks do – our approach is to get the Americans save more – to return to the values of thrift, self-reliance, and building a nest egg.

ING DIRECT was born in an age of broken promises. The last thing America needed was another bank, but that didn't mean America didn't need us. ING DIRECT's mission is to make it easy to save by offering the same great values to all Americans.

Arkadi Kuhlmann, President and CEO, ING DIRECT (US & Canada)

Many organizations have tried to enter the banking industry with innovative business models. But incumbents have always been able to defend their markets successfully. Today, ING DIRECT is changing the odds. Arkadi Kuhlmann, founder of ING DIRECT, is very clear about his goals: 'There's no such thing as an industry that can't be reenergized!'

Customers welcome the company with open arms. In just five years, ING DIRECT has become the largest Internet-based bank – passing E*Trade Bank – in the United States, and one of the thirty largest banks of any sort in the country. The company adds an astonishing 100,000 customers and $1 billion in deposits every month, and in 2005 (its fifth year of operations) generated a profit of $360 million. And above all, 90 percent of the ING DIRECT customers believe it provides a much better service than the competitors.

Profile of the ING Group

ING DIRECT is one of the six business lines of ING Group, a major international financial services group. ING Group is active in over 50 countries and is often cited as the example of an integrated financial services provider, offering a wide array of insurance, banking, and asset management services to a broad customer base: individuals, families, small businesses, large corporations, and institutions and governments.

ING Group is a financial conglomerate founded in 1991 by the merger between Nationale-Nederlanden, the Netherlands' largest insurance company, and NMB Postbank Group, one of the largest banking groups in the Netherlands. NMB Postbank Group itself was the result of a merger between the very entrepreneurial NMB Banking Group and the Postbank. Postbank had been split off from the Dutch Post Office and was privatized. Many people within ING believe that Postbank has been the true inspiration for ING DIRECT.

The merger between Nationale-Nederlanden and NMB Postbank Group created the first bancassurer in the Netherlands. Since 1991, ING has developed from a Dutch financial institution with some international businesses to a multinational with Dutch roots. It acquired banks and insurance companies in the UK (Barings Bank, 1995), Belgium (Bank Brussels Lambert, 1998), Germany (BHF-Bank, 1999), United States (Equitable of Iowa, 1997; ReliaStar, 2000; Aetna Financial Services, 2000), Canada (Wellington, 1995; Canadian Group Underwriters, 1998; Allianz of Canada, 2004), and other countries. Some of these financial institutions have been sold later, such as parts of Barings and BHF-Bank. As such, ING Group has become one of the 15 largest financial institutions worldwide and top-10 in Europe (in market capitalization). Exhibit 1 provides an overview of the 20 largest financial institutions, measured by market capitalization.

This case was written by Professors K. Verweire and L. A. A. Van den Berghe of the Vlerick Leuven Gent Management School. It is intended to be used as the basis for class discussion rather than to illustrate effective or ineffective handling of a management situation.

Exhibit 1 **20 largest financial institutions worldwide**

Name		Market capitalization in € bn on May 15, 2006
1	Citigroup inc	192.2
2	Bank of America Corp	177.2
3	HSBC Holdings	157.5
4	AIG	127.2
5	Mitsubishi UFJ Financial	124.6
6	JPM Chase	120.3
7	UBS	102.3
8	Wells Fargo	87.1
9	Mizuho Financial Group	83.4
10	Royal Bank Scotland	81.8
11	Banco Santander	74.1
12	**ING**	**70.5**
13	BNP Paribas	70.3
14	Wachoma Corp	69.1
15	Unicredito	65.6
16	Sumitomo Mitsui Financial	64.9
17	Barclays	60.7
18	Credit Suisse Group	59.0
19	BBVA	58.1
20	Goldman Sachs	54.6

Source: Bloomberg.

ING also used greenfields to grow the business. Greenfields were set up in the emerging markets, where ING leveraged the bancassurance concept it continued to refine in its home markets. ING Group also set up other initiatives to fuel the group's revenue and profit growth. It created a new international retail/direct banking division, that was composed of a team of Postbank's best marketing and IT people. Hans Verkoren, CEO of Postbank, became the head of this new division. This new venture was to explore to what extent Postbank's strategy could be expanded outside its Dutch home market. Postbank operated in a 'branchless' manner for many years, offering simple checking accounts, savings, mortgages, consumer loans, and investment products.

This new division operated autonomously from the rest of the company. The parent company gave the new organization the necessary freedom to experiment. After detailed marketing research, the team introduced ING's first foreign direct banking experiment to Canada in 1996. ING chose Canada because it had no presence there, and the market was dominated by a small number of players. ING agreed it was important for this new experiment to survive or fail on its own. It created optimal conditions for success by providing it with adequate financial means and a brand new management team, lead by Arkadi Kuhlmann.

ING DIRECT: A growing success story in the banking industry

Arkadi Kuhlmann, a Harley-riding painter and poet, was a professor of International Finance and Investment Banking at the American Graduate School of International Management ('Thunderbird') in Phoenix, Arizona. He also served as President of North American Trust, CEO of Deak International Incorporated, and held various executive positions at the Royal Bank of Canada. When Hans Verkoren asked him in 1996 whether he was interested to start up a new foreign bank in Canada, he accepted the challenge.

331

Arkadi had noticed that few foreign banks had successfully entered the North-American banking industry and had built a sustainable competitive position in that market. But he realized that those incumbents were not invincible.

> Traditional banks are stuck. They have high fixed costs and use technology in an inefficient way. They have rigid distribution systems. And they charge too high prices. The customer always loses. When we came in, we said: 'How can we do something different?' We looked at other industries and copied some ideas from successful players in the retail and airline industry. It is true that we actually haven't defined something new. In the context of Southwest Airlines or Wal-Mart, there are similarities. For decades, Southwest Airlines has defied the industry's standard approaches to economics and customer service, and has achieved good results. And we are on our way to do the same in the banking industry. Most companies, especially in our industry, are truly boring. If you do things the way everybody else does, why do you think you're going to be any better?

ING DIRECT differentiates itself from traditional banks in many ways. But in essence, its differentiation lies in being direct.

> Our biggest advantage in standing out in the financial service market from all other players, is that we are Direct. Anyway we can emphasize that we are direct, thereby cutting out the middleman, is a way of saving money. So being a retail business, being simple, focused and direct adds up to good value. This is a retail trend that consumers know and one we should emphasize in everything we do.

ING DIRECT is a direct-to-the-customer operation, an Internet-based savings bank – although customers can also bank by mail or telephone. There are no branches, no ATMs, just a couple of cafés in big cities where the bank sells coffee and mountain bikes in addition to savings accounts, a few certificates of deposit, home mortgages, home equity lines, and a handful of mutual funds.[1] The bank does not offer traditional paper-based checking accounts – that costs too much. For these accounts, ING DIRECT points customer back to their local bank. ING DIRECT charges no fees and there are no minimum deposits for savings accounts and a limited number of product offerings.

What started as a small successful experiment in Canada in 1997 has become one of the success stories

---

1 ING DIRECT has opened cafés in Toronto, Vancouver, Sydney, Barcelona, Madrid, New York, Philadelphia, Los Angeles, Wilmington, and a couple of other cities.

Exhibit 2 ING DIRECT's clients and funds base

	2005 profit	Deposits	Customers
	(€, M)	(€, M)	
Canada	69.4	12,579	1,360,588
Spain	51.0	13,726	1,341,759
Australia	73.8	10,757	1,282,459
France	23.9	11,389	555,922
USA	162.9	39,031	3,785,927
Italy	29.0	13,426	699,603
Germany	242.1	57,654	5,488,865
UK	(27.7)	33,704	1,038,650
Austria	(15.6)	2,475	210,808
Total ING DIRECT	612.3	194,741	15,764,581

Source: ING DIRECT.

in today's financial services industry. ING DIRECT has launched operations in Spain and Australia in 1999. One year later, it entered France and the US. Since then, ING DIRECT has entered Italy, the UK, and Germany, and it has plans to set up operations in Japan. ING DIRECT globally ended the first quarter of 2006 with 194 bn Euro in deposits and 15.7 mln customers (see Exhibit 2). In 2005, ING DIRECT's profits constituted 7 percent of ING's total profits. Exhibit 3 shows ING DIRECT's global profit progression from its creation to 2005.

Exhibit 3 ING DIRECT's global profit progression
(€ mln)

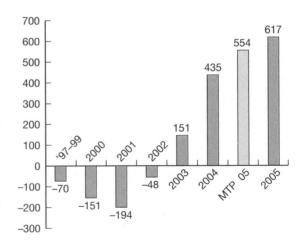

Source: ING DIRECT.

ING DIRECT: reenergizing the US retail banking industry

ING DIRECT has attracted a lot of attention in the United States for several reasons. Despite the wide acceptance of the Internet in American households, online banks have not been particularly successful. Nevertheless, ING DIRECT has experienced a meteoric growth since its launch in September 2000. What is more, the venture was break-even already after two years.

More striking is the way that ING DIRECT positions itself in the US banking industry. Arkadi Kuhlmann rejects the characterization of ING DIRECT as an Internet bank, even though the web is its primary customer channel.

> We're actually a pure savings bank, focusing on residential mortgages and savings accounts. You can't get any more old-fashioned than that.

In all of its communication, ING DIRECT points out that it is a federally chartered bank and that its savings are FDIC insured in order to guarantee credibility with its customers.[2] But that is where the comparison with typical retail banks stops. In fact, there is nothing typical about ING DIRECT.

ING DIRECT's product offering and value proposition

In a typical bank, first and foremost, it's about payment services. Once you get the payment services – such as checking, face-to-face teller services, and ATMs (Automatic Teller Machines) – you're 'owned' by the bank. But Arkadi Kuhlmann's strategy is different. The last thing he wants is to take your traditional demand deposit account (i.e. your checking account). These accounts typically have a large number of transactions per month and require a physical branch and a great deal of internal labor to process them. All this is too costly. Rather ING DIRECT wants to be 'your other bank,' offering a simple, high-return savings account, called the Orange Savings Account – ING's theme color is orange. Customers are encouraged to shift money back and forth between their ING DIRECT savings account and their checking accounts with their existing bank. The account generates one of the highest rates in the market; sometimes the rate is four times higher than the industry average (see Exhibit 4). Customers do not only get great rates, there are no fees nor service charges, and there are no minimums. ING DIRECT sells its products with the simple slogan: 'Great rates, no fees, no minimums.'

ING DIRECT also offers a limited number of mutual funds. And the bulk of the assets of the bank consists of simple residential mortgages and a small percentage of home equity lines of credit and customer loans. Nearly 90 percent of the loan portfolio consists of mortgages. All products have low fees and few requirements.

---

2 The Federal Deposit Insurance Corporation (FDIC) is a governance institution that insures deposits in thrift institutions and commercial banks.

Exhibit 4 'Great rates, no fees, no minimums'

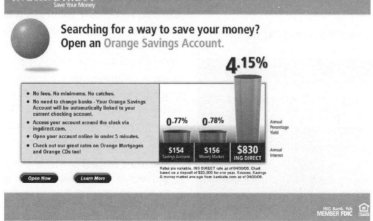

Source: ING DIRECT website (May 2006).

But what's so unique about high rates? Arkadi Kuhlmann comments:

> Nothing... What is unique is that we offer consistently great rates and at the same time a high quality service. The key to deliver high quality service is simplicity: no tricks, no catches. Customers must immediately understand ING DIRECT products. Educating people about financial products is very expensive.

Although some banking professionals consider mortgages a difficult product to standardize and to sell via the Internet, Arkadi Kuhlmann disagrees:

> You can turn mortgages into simple products too. But it requires that you reengineer the product and the processes behind it. And to some extent, you need to reengineer the customer as well.

And that strategy did not only attract many new customers, but also allowed the company to retain most of them.

Savings accounts can be set up in five minutes online. Mortgages take seven minutes to close (with all customer documentation available), as is demonstrated in Exhibit 5. The company tries to avoid that customers have to talk to anyone. The website plays a crucial role in informing customers how to deal with the bank. ING DIRECT makes opening a savings account and transferring money extremely simple and straightforward. On their website, they post: 'It's that simple to earn more!' For the people who prefer human contact, ING DIRECT's US operations have more than 500 call center associates in three call centers. Those associates are trained to provide fast response and prompt service to the customers. The company strives to get 80 percent of the calls answered in 20 seconds. As a matter of fact, employees have their bonuses tied to achieving this

Exhibit 5 Online banking: It's as easy as ...

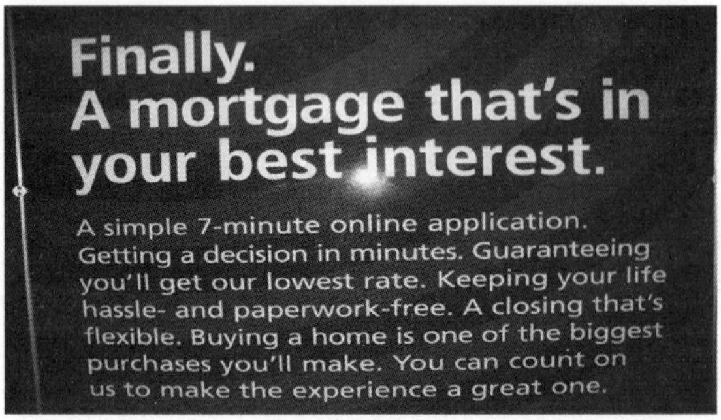

Source: Picture taken at ING DIRECT Café (New York, May 2006).

goal. In order to reach that goal, employees receive extensive training – about 20 days for five products (which is a lot compared to traditional banks). Overall, the brand strategy of ING DIRECT is best described by the acronym GRASP, 'Great deals, Responsive, Accessible, Simple and easy, and Passionate.'

The target customers

So the first order of business for ING DIRECT is to introduce products that make it easy and financially rewarding for customers to save more. But part of the strategy is choosing the products it won't offer... and the customers it won't serve. Unlike its traditional competitors, the company is not interested in the rich Americans (unless they do what it wants them to do). 'We want to *serve* the average American...' As long as he/she behaves in the way ING DIRECT wants. In 2004, the company 'fired' more than 3,500 customers who didn't play by the bank rules. Those customers relied too much on the call centers, or asked for too many exceptions from the standard operating procedures.

> People should not come and explain their financial problems. We sell products, commodities, not solutions.

Communicating the message

So far ING DIRECT USA has managed that task very well. In five years, the bank has attracted more than 3.5 million customers. This growth can partially be explained by the huge efforts the company undertook to build the ING DIRECT brand: one third of its budget is allocated to marketing programs. Many customers are attracted by the combination of rates and a hip brand. ING DIRECT's marketing campaigns project a differentiated brand and 'unbank-ness.' They have a simple, clear message, and feature the bright color orange, capturing customers' attention by communicating in a humorous, 'anti-establishment' tone. Exhibit 6 presents some outdoor advertising ING DIRECT has used in 2006. Some of those campaigns were locally adapted to the targeted markets (see Exhibit 7). (Exhibit 8 presents some marketing campaigns of ING DIRECT in other countries.) The purpose of the guerilla marketing tactics are clear, according to Arkadi Kuhlmann:

> People are sleeping. You have to shock people a little bit to get them to think differently about how they manage their money. So we wake them up with one of our marketing campaigns. They switch their money and go back to sleep.

Exhibit 6 Outdoor advertising from ING DIRECT USA

Source: ING DIRECT.

ING DIRECT does not restrict itself to the more traditional marketing campaigns. The bank continuously organizes innovative promotion campaigns to attract new customers. The company's 'Save your money at the movies' campaign attracted many spectators and publicity in the press. In Baltimore and Washington DC, ING DIRECT surprised over 8,000 people with a free movie at two participating Regal Cinemas. In a similar way, it offered free gas in Baltimore to 1,000 drivers at three selected Shell stations, and asked them to put that money into an Orange Savings Account. By the end of the three-hour promotion campaign cars lined up for more than three kilometers. And it let commuters ride the Boston 'T'

lines for free one morning, while ING representatives danced around in orange Paul Revere costumes. Those kind of events do wake people up, for sure.

Another uncommon feature of the marketing strategy are ING DIRECT's cafés. The cafés, each located in a big city of the targeted countries – such as New York, Washington, Philadelphia, Los Angeles – are no substitutes for the branches. Rather they introduce the customers to the ING DIRECT brand. When ING DIRECT started its marketing and operations in Canada, early prospects were somewhat suspicious about the new brand. So they began visiting the company's call center in Toronto to check out that new

Exhibit 7 Local marketing campaigns from ING DIRECT USA

Washington D.C.

New York

Phoenix & Philadelphia

Source: ING DIRECT.

bank to verify its physical existence. The employees from ING DIRECT Canada offered those prospectors a coffee at the coffee corner of the call center. That is how the idea emerged. It took Arkadi Kuhlmann some time to convince the managers at ING in Amsterdam to set up 'coffee shops',[3] but now the cafés are a typical element of ING DIRECT's marketing strategy. Pictures of the ING DIRECT cafés are shown in Exhibit 9.

The cafés sustain ING DIRECT's a-typical bank image, and they offer the customers a place to go to speak with an ING DIRECT café member, each a trained banker, and experience the simplicity the brand stands for. While serving you a coffee, the café staff members – called sales associates – can discuss financial products or help checking information on one of the online terminals located on the premises. Consistent with the brand, a coffee is much cheaper than a similar coffee at Starbuck's, and Internet usage at the cafés is free.

> We believe saving money should be as simple as getting a cup of coffee. So we invite you to come in and experience just how refreshing it is to sip a latte, surf the Internet for free and talk to us about how we can help Save Your Money.

---

3 Coffee shops have a different connotation in the Netherlands than in the United States.

Exhibit 8 Marketing campaigns of ING DIRECT in other countries

Source: ING DIRECT.

Exhibit 9 Pictures of ING DIRECT Café in New York, Los Angeles, Philadelphia and Wilmington

New York Café

Philapdelphia Café

Los Angeles Café

Wilmington Café

Source: ING DIRECT.

Managing a rebellious organization

Obviously, the cafés have helped to build the brand. But you need more than a handful of cafés to achieve the revenue and profit figures ING DIRECT has achieved so far. Behind that rebellious image, there is a well-oiled machine, designed to deal with high-volume, low-margin commodity products. Exhibit 10 shows the key components of the company's strategy execution. While significant attention is paid to understand demand and increase revenues, the execution challenge also involves cost control and efficiency improvement. While most retail banks in the US operate at a margin spread of 250 basis points (2.50 percentage point), ING DIRECT operates on a spread of 175 basis points. How is ING DIRECT able to operate at lower costs?

Managing the front and back office

A big part of its lower cost structure stems from the things that it doesn't offer, and where it doesn't have to invest. The company does not invest in an ATM network or in traditional branches. It encourages customers to open accounts online or by using an Interactive Voice Response (IVR) system. Online openings of accounts and applications for mortgages saves costs. The company's acquisition costs are estimated to be lower than $100. According to Jim Kelly, chief marketing officer of ING DIRECT: 'It is not unusual for a bank to have customer acquisition costs of about $300-400.'[4] Similarly, maintenance costs are kept low as well. Says Arkadi Kuhlmann:

> If you don't have any activity in a month, we're not sending you a statement. Savings account customers who insist on a paper statement should go back to Chase.

The company also communicates to its customers that more calls to the call center will lead to higher fees or lower interest rates. So customers understand why ING DIRECT discourages telephone calls to expensive live operators at the call center. To further discourage the use of these operators, customers who called frequently were put at the end of the operators' queue.

---

4 'Would you like a mortgage with your mocha?', FastCompany, Issue 68, March 2003, p. 110.

Exhibit 10 Strategy execution at ING DIRECT

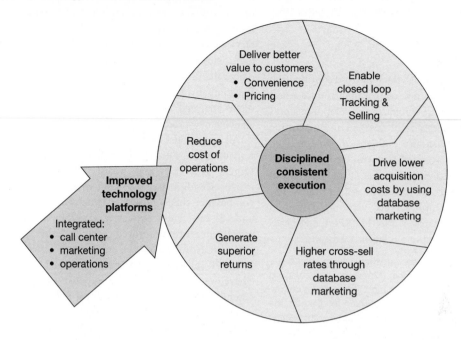

Source: ING Group.

All this requires that ING DIRECT manages its processes in a very rigorous way. Processes are documented, and a large number of guidelines and procedures exist for the core processes within the organization. The company is constantly looking to simplify financial products and financial transactions, and uses tools such as Lean Six Sigma to achieve the efficiency of the manufacturing industry. In 2004, ING DIRECT Canada won a Canadian Information Productivity Award of Excellence for its Mortgage Application Processing Solution (MAPS). This solution has enabled ING DIRECT to simplify the process of obtaining a mortgage dramatically. And this new solution is also leveraged in the other ING DIRECT entities. Sharing of best practices and sharing of materials is common within the ING DIRECT businesses. For example, ING DIRECT shares marketing campaigns across the countries, and re-uses marketing concepts and graphic designs.

Information technology
ING DIRECT can benefit from the absence of 'legacy' information technology systems. ING DIRECT could start from scratch and this helped the company signifi-

cantly to operate with a higher performing IT architecture at lower cost. The challenge was to develop a flexible IT architecture providing brand uniformity across borders, but allowing for adaptation to local banking regulations.

ING DIRECT buys the IT hardware centrally, exploiting its buying power, and then makes it available to the various country organizations. For software, the company's strategy is to 're-use (from sister companies) before buy, and buy before build.' This saves an enormous amount of money, and at the same time helps to insure a high level of service and ease in accommodating growing numbers of accounts. A Central IT Group develops and maintains the IT policies and standards across the company, and works with the various countries to update and improve the systems.

ING DIRECT also strives to have the different departments in close contact with each other. The process flow is specified for the whole organization, and considers processes from various departments simultaneously. Streamlining processes is a key element in ING DIRECT's business architecture, and business process orientation is a necessary element in that, says Arkadi Kuhlmann.

We put our marketing and IT departments in one area. If your core competencies are marketing and IT, you really have to do both of them together.

Product development

Product development is also done in close coordination with marketing and IT. To develop and introduce a new product, a country unit would first develop a business plan that includes forecasts of demand and marketing expenditures. The plan also evaluates the operational, financial, and legal risks associated with the launch of the product. And it specifies clearly what IT and operational requirements are necessary to support the product. The hurdles for a new product are very high. Brunon Bartkiewicz (former manager at ING DIRECT, now heading ING's banking operations in Poland), explains:[5]

Every new product reduces our simplicity, increases our risk and defocuses our people. A person who is working on marketing seven products cannot know all the details, all the figures, all the logic that a person focused on one product does. In the end, the whole game is efficiency: efficiency in marketing, in operations, and in systems.

Performance measurement

Another important element of ING DIRECT's business model is the obsession for measuring. Measuring how customers react to marketing campaigns and online advertising is a natural activity for an online bank. But in ING DIRECT performance measurement doesn't stop at the marketing department. The company's operations centers compete against each other for recognition and monthly bonuses based on their ability to meet sales and service goals. Everybody in ING DIRECT measures and is measured. Some performance measures are posted daily on an Intranet site, accessible to everyone within the company. The performance measures are continuously analyzed and are the input for action plans, allowing new product and process initiatives.

All operational performance measures have a direct impact on the company's five high-level targets. These targets are: (1) total profit, (2) non-marketing expenses/ending assets, (3) net-retail funds entrusted (on balance sheet) growth, (4) net mortgage growth, and (5) call-center service level. Efficiency and cost effectiveness are monitored carefully. Exhibit 11 presents the evolution of the operational costs of ING DIRECT (all countries) from 1999 to March 2006. There we can see that the expense-to-assets ratio (excluding marketing expenses) for ING DIRECT (all countries) decreased from 96 basis points in 2001 to 40 basis points in 2006. An average branch bank has an expense-to-asset ratio of about 250 basis points. In a similar way, total assets per employee are for ING DIRECT $48 million, whereas traditional branch-based banks have an average of $5-6 million per employee.

Those figures are impressive. But equally impressive is how ING DIRECT has 'structured' its measurement

---

5 'ING DIRECT: Your other bank', IMD Case, IMD-3-1343, p. 7.

Exhibit 11 Evolution of ING DIRECT's operational cost base to assets (excluding marketing)

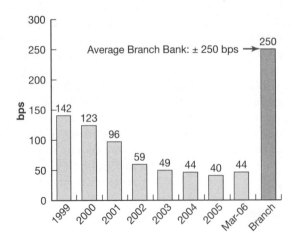

Source: ING Group.

processes. Previously, ING DIRECT had used Microsoft Excel spreadsheets to create annual reports summarizing the company's performance. But the company's fast growth necessitated a more structured approach towards measuring company performance. In 2004, the company hired a consultant who helped it to set up a performance measurement system, generating enterprise-wide, relevant management information that steers the company's future growth. The powerful reporting and analysis tools help identify further cost saving opportunities and gain in-depth visibility into the key performance metrics. In addition, the performance measurement system allows to measure the effectiveness of marketing campaigns, track market and risk exposure, and to get a better understanding of its new and existing customer base. Arkadi Kuhlmann agrees that ING DIRECT has been getting more efficient with customer acquisition and with lowering costs for acquiring new customers due to the introduction of the new performance measurement system.

Leadership, people, and culture

What really sets ING DIRECT apart from its competitors are its people. You can't be a rebel if you have all traditional bankers in your organization. That is why ING DIRECT tries to hire people that do not come from the big banks. Only for functions such as risk management, treasury, or asset-liability management, the bank hires employees with a banking background. Of course, ING DIRECT can benefit from ING's expertise in these technical matters. CEO Arkadi Kuhlmann himself is an experienced banker with a deep knowledge of all core functions within the bank. But he profiles himself as the outsider – even the bad guy – of the industry: 'When the rest of the banking industry decides to zig, I zag,' he says. And he ensures that the entire organization zags with him.

Arkadi Kuhlmann truly is a visionary and inspiring leader. You won't hear Arkadi talk a lot about financial metrics. Arkadi Kuhlmann is out for a more inspiring mission and vision.

> We are leading the Americans back to saving. One way or another, most financial companies are telling you to spend more. That's not what we want.

In all communication, the focus is on saving. And that's why credit cards, and traditional checking accounts don't fit in the product portfolio.

Above all, it is the way that Arkadi conveys the message that makes him an inspiring leader: 'You can't do meaningful things without passion and a powerful idea about what you're trying to do,' he argues. In the United States, he has about 1,300 people who help him on his crusade. What is striking is that the employees of ING DIRECT are as determined as the CEO himself.

But then ING DIRECT spends a lot of time and efforts to ensure that it hires people willing to do things differently from the industry norm, and inspires them with the same set of values that it uses to connect with their customers. The company hires people with the right attitude, who can easily be trained and introduced to a competitive selling culture. But above all, people are selected based on whether their personal values fit with the values of ING DIRECT. Rick Perles, Head of Human Resources at ING DIRECT, comments:

> Everyone, no matter what level, starts in the new hire program. The new hire program used to be three days but we have expanded it to five, which is a big investment in our people and not something most companies do. All new hires take customer calls. During those first days, they'll hear a lot about culture and what ING stands for. Some people don't subscribe to it, but they realize it even before the five days are up.
>
> The Maiden Voyage refers to the next 90 days, where we spend another week or two facilitating technical training with our sales associates. During those first 90 days, there are things the new hire has to do before coming back for the second part of new hire. Those activities include volunteering in the community, working in one of our Cafés, and reading *The Alchemist* by Paulo Coelho.[6]

Values and culture are not idle concepts within ING DIRECT. Arkadi Kuhlmann is aware that the most differentiating aspect of the whole company is situated in what is called the 'Orange Code.' The Orange Code specifies in 13 statements what ING DIRECT is all about and what it stands for. The Orange Code brings the vision to life and provides employees with common goals. For example, one of those statements is 'We will be for everyone.' In the company, this is made concrete by removing all titles and offices. Everybody is in the bonus program, and the metrics are the same for everybody.

---

6 Interview with Rick Perles by Irene Monley, *Delaware Society for Human Resource Management*, Vol. 2(4), October 2005.

The reward strategy is also particular. Employees can earn substantial bonuses, based on how they perform relative to some well-specified financial, customer and operational targets. Bonuses can be up to half of the fixed salary. Interestingly enough the employees' fixed salary is also higher than the industry average. Although a cost leader, the company prides itself on paying at the 75th percentile or higher. Maybe that's why in a recent employee survey, 99 percent of the employees were proud to tell that they are part of ING DIRECT. The survey indicated however that the employees' positive attitude is based on other facts than the reward policy. In particular, the employees consider ING DIRECT an attractive employer for the strength of its business model, and its 'non-banking' culture. ING DIRECT is a flat organization with few management layers. And employees can provide input in the many action plans that the organization sets up. Arkadi Kuhlmann describes it as follows: 'I make sure that managers tell the employees *what* to do, but not *how* to do things. This is the starting point for real empowerment.' The growth of the company and the support of the ING Group is another driving force for the employees to help fulfill ING DIRECT's ambitious goals.

Here too the Orange Code also ensures that the employees don't become too complacent. One of the statements reads as follows: 'We aren't conquerors. We are pioneers. We are not here to destroy. We are here to create!'

Challenges

The market has been created and ING DIRECT has developed an attractive position within that market. But the easy success of the online savings bank has attracted other newcomers. MetLife launched an Internet bank in late 2002 and has been heavily promoting high rates. And in 2006, HSBC's Internet Bank stepped in with higher rates than those of ING DIRECT. Other banks are soon to follow.

Arkadi Kuhlmann acknowledges that he will have to cope with more challenging competitors in the future. At the same time, the success of ING DIRECT has also created even higher expectations on the financial potential of its business model. A key question for the management team will be how the company can sustain its growth? What products should the company introduce? And which markets should it enter? Here ING DIRECT faces some challenges. Typically, the cross-selling rate within ING DIRECT was rather low. Cross-sell customers account for 18 percent of growth for ING DIRECT USA, still a small percentage but steadily increasing as customers realize the value they are getting by banking with the company. The company carefully analyzes what customers will likely accept to buy other ING DIRECT products. In line with the general philosophy of the company, such an offer will only be made with the customer's consent. But only a small number of customers have opted in to this permission marketing program. Should the company more aggressively try to cross-sell?

ING DIRECT also has to manage internal challenges. One of these challenges is how to cope with the growth the company experiences. More customers means an increasing pressure on the systems and processes. In the banking industry, size does quite often imply *dis*economies of scale. Furthermore, will the company find employees that embrace its unique culture? Managing a unique culture is easier if the company is small. But it gets very challenging when the company gets bigger and bigger.

One of the internal challenges also relates to the relationship that ING DIRECT has with its parent organization, ING Group. ING Group, known as the integrated financial services group, actively stimulates synergies between its banking, insurance, and investment entities across different countries. But Arkadi Kuhlmann has always been able to limit ING DIRECT's participation in the Mandated Synergies program to what he calls the 'low hanging fruit.' If the benefits are obvious, ING DIRECT will help to exploit the benefits of cooperation with sister companies, but not at all price. How long will ING DIRECT's management benefit from that exceptional status? And what will be the implications if ING DIRECT gets more integrated and incorporated within the traditional ING businesses?

One of those synergies is to integrate brand development. ING DIRECT positions itself as the rebel in the banking industry, but at the same time it wears the brand of one of the most respected, traditional financial institutions, ING. The more that ING DIRECT's part within ING's profits will increase, the bigger the dilemma.

Ducati (Italy) vs. Harley-Davidson (USA)
Innovating business processes and managing value networks

In 2001, as Ducati celebrated its 75th anniversary, some executives wondered whether the recent corporate restructuring had repositioned the company successfully. As part of this, the Italian motorcycle manufacturer had adopted a new focus on R&D, marketing and sales, moving away from its initial manufacturing strength. In addition, the company had embraced the Internet, deciding in January 2000 to sell its new motorcycle, apparel and accessories exclusively online. Though this had been a risky decision, it had been tremendously successful. Federico Minoli, President and CEO of Ducati.com, and Chair of the Board of Ducati Motor Holding, announced with pleasure that:

> Since 1 January 2000, we have sold over 2500 motorbikes online with the help and involvement of our official dealer network, proving the validity of our Internet strategy. With this success, we further confirm the value of our brand and our product.

Ducati: Company overview

Ducati Motor Holding SpA[1] (DMH) was a manufacturer of expensive high-performance motorcycles. Since 1926, the medium-sized company, based in Bologna, Italy, has been developing and producing racing-inspired motorcycles, winning the World Superbike Championship uninterruptedly for decades. In 1996, Ducati's parent company Caviga faced a major financial crisis which led to the sale of a 51% stake in DMH to the USA-based Texas Pacific Group (TPG) and Deutsche Morgan

Grenfell Capital (Italy). A new management team initiated a turnaround programme aiming at increased production efficiency, net sales and profit. 'Since 1996, we were really working against a backdrop that wasn't so far removed from bankruptcy', said Carlo di Biagio, Chief Executive Officer of DMH. 'Now our situation is different. Sooner or later, we think investors will see that.'

By 2001, the company had restructured its value chain activities, outsourcing 90% of its production and, in order to decrease costs, introducing a platform strategy that provided a common technical base for Ducati motorcycles. All models subsequently shared a fundamental engine configuration (L-shaped twin-cylinder engine), tubular trestle frame and many generic or commoditized parts. In addition, all models (excluding the ST2) used one of only two types of engines: two-valve – or four-valve – making assembly easier and manufacturing less costly. Furthermore, DMH restructured its distribution network by reducing the number of its dealer outlets and replacing multibrand dealers with Ducati-designed stores. Thus, after the restructuring, DMH consisted essentially of an R&D and design centre, an assembly unit and a marketing and sales department. Support and logistics were also outsourced.

One of Ducati's key strengths is its brand name and product innovation capability. The company has successfully revamped its existing product line and introduced several new motorcycle models, accessories and apparel.

---

1 SpA (Società per Azioni) is a joint stock company.

This case was written by Stefanie Leenen, doctoral student at the University of St Gallen, Switzerland, and Tawfik Jelassi, Affiliate Professor of Technology Management at INSEAD, Fontainebleau. It is intended to be used as the basis for class discussion rather than to illustrate effective or ineffective handling of an administrative situation.

The case was made possible by the co-operation of Ducati Motor SpA (Italy).

The new products were sold either through the traditional dealer network or exclusively over the Internet.

Ducati's e-commerce activities were first launched on 1 January 2000, when a new, limited-edition MH900e motorcycle, priced at €15 000 was sold exclusively over the Internet. The entire first year's production of the MH900e was sold out in just 31 minutes, despite the fact that production was not scheduled to start before June 2000. Industry-wide, it was the first event of its kind. 'Produce what is already sold' thus became a new motto for Ducati, and it subsequently set up an independent online entity, called Ducati.com on 6 March 2000.

In countries where Ducati took control of its distribution network, the company experienced a significant rise in motorcycle registrations, a key measure of retail sales. In 2001, Ducati announced the fifth consecutive year of record profits, amounting to €10.5 million (see Table 1). For the same period, the company sold 38 969 motorcycles, with revenues of €407.8 million and EBITDA[2] up by 10% to €66.1 million, i.e. 16.9% of revenues. In 2001, Ducati had a 6.4% share of the Western European market.

On 2 April 2001, DMH joined the STAR[3] segment of the Mercato Telematico Azionario of Borsa Italia SpA, a new high-standard stock segment.[4] Ducati was among the first 20 Italian companies to qualify for the STAR segment. Thereby, the company tried to obtain greater visibility in the financial markets and to enhance shareholder value through increased liquidity.

Harley-Davidson: Company overview

Another major motorcycle manufacturer was the USA-based Harley-Davidson, which was in the market niche of cruisers and touring motorcycles (see Exhibit 1). Like Ducati, Harley-Davidson offered motorcycles, spare parts, accessories, apparel and general merchandise. Harley-Davidson Inc. was active in two business segments: motorcycles and related products with Harley-Davidson Motor Company and Buell Motorcycle Company,[5] and financial services with the Harley-Davidson Financial Services (HDFS). The latter provided wholesale and retail financing and insurance programmes to Harley-Davidson/Buell dealers and customers, including credit, insurance and production options, the Harley-Davidson Extended Service Plan[6] and the Harley-Davidson Visa card.

In June 1981, 13 Harley-Davidson senior executives bought Harley-Davidson Motor Company from its former parent company AMF, through a leveraged buy-out. At the time, the company suffered from a reputation for poor quality and low reliability, and it lacked innovative product design and development. A turnaround programme was begun, comprising of a 40% reduction of the overall workforce, a 9% wage-cut, and the introduction of new products. Over 20 years later, as it celebrated its 100th anniversary, Harley-Davidson was one of the most successful motorcycle manufacturers in the world, enjoying strong brand recognition and an innovative design and development capability. In 2001, Harley-Davidson was elected Company of the Year by *Forbes Magazine*, and was described as one of the 'most admired companies' in the USA.

In 2001, Harley-Davidson announced record revenues and net earnings for the 16th consecutive year.

Table 1 Ducati financial data (million euros)

	1999	2000	2001
Total revenues (motorcycles, accessories, apparel, spare parts, etc.)	294.5	379.5	407.8
Accessories and apparel	37.1	55.9	61.4
Gross profit	118.0	150.6	166.5
Registration (units)	32 135	38 130	38 969
EBITDA	50.8	60.0	66.1
Depreciation and amortization	(24.3)	(29.6)	(34.6)
Financing expense	(14.3)	(19.4)	(12.1)
Non-recurring items	4.5	6.7	(28)
Income tax and minority interest	(7.8)	(7.2)	(8.9)
Net profit	8.9	10.5	10.5
Net debt	112.3	97.4	112.9
Total shareholders' equity	131.1	143.1	154.6
Total net capitalization	243.4	240.5	267.5
Net debt/total net capitalization (%)	46.1	40.5	42
Net debt/EBITDA	2.2×	1.6×	1.7×

Source: Adapted from Ducati documents, July 2001 and January 2002.

2 EBITDA stands for earnings before interest, taxes, depreciation and amortization.
3 STAR stands for Segmento Titoli con Alti Requisiti. This means a stock segment with high requirements.
4 The Mercato Telematico Azionario of Borsa Italia SpA is a screen-based stock exchange dedicated to small and medium-sized capitalization companies in Italy that operate successfully in traditional sectors of the economy and satisfy a series of requirements in terms of transparency, liquidity and corporate governance.
5 Buell Motorcycle Company produces sport motorcycles in addition to motorcycle parts, accessories and apparel.
6 The Harley-Davidson Extended Service Plan covers motorcycle repairs.

Exhibit 1 Expanding the niche boundaries of Ducati motorcycles: the move from performance, functional motorcycles to comfort and lifestyle-orientated motorcycles

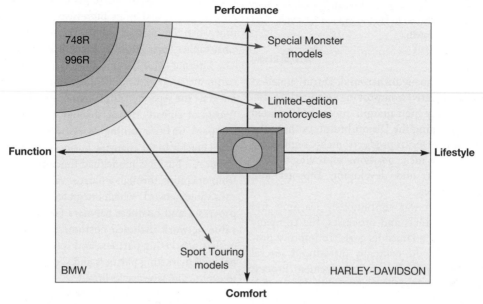

Source: Adapted from Ducati document, September 2001.

Table 2 Harley-Davidson financial data (US$ million)

	1999	2000	2001
Total revenues (motorcycles, accessories, apparel, spare parts, etc.)	2453	2906	3363
Costs of goods sold	1617	1915	2183
Gross profit	836	991	1180
Financial services income	133	140	181
Financial services interest and operating expense	105	103	120
Operating income from financial services	28	37	61
Net income	267	348	438

	2000	2001	Change (%)
Revenues			
Total motorcycles (Harley-Davidson and Buell)	2304	2692	16.8
Motorcycles parts and accessories	448	507	13.3
General merchandise	151	164	8.3
Other	2.6	0.2	(92)
Registration (units)	204 500	234 461	14.6
Harley-Davidson motorcycles	10 189	9925	(2.6)

Source: Harley-Davidson Annual Report, 2001.

The company's revenues were US$3.4 billion, an increase of 15.7% over the previous year (see Table 2). Revenues of the Harley-Davidson motorcycle division increased by 17.1% to US$2.6 billion. Net earnings of the company grew by 25.9% to US$438 million. Harley-Davidson Financial Services' net earnings amounted to US$61 million, i.e. 14% of the company's total.

For its third quarter 2002, Harley-Davidson announced record revenue and earnings, with revenues of US$1.14 billion, an increase of 31.8% over the third quarter of 2001. 'As we began our year-long 100th anniversary celebration, we achieved our biggest quarter ever, setting new records in revenue and earnings', said Jeffrey L. Bleustein, Chair and Chief Executive Officer of Harley-Davidson Inc. 'The commemorative products for our 100th anniversary celebration were a major driver for our exceptional third quarter performance and are a great springboard for growing demand for the future.' [7]

---

7 www.harley-davidson/investor relations/pressrelease, 15 October 2002.

Ducati's business strategy

Despite the challenging business environment in 2002, we are continuing to invest in innovative products and brand-building activities to lay the ground for strong and sustained future growth.

Carlo di Biagio

Since the 1996 company turnaround, Ducati aimed at the following objectives: improving production efficiency, developing high-margin motorcycle-related businesses, leveraging the Ducati brand, pushing the boundaries of the Ducati products' niche, reinforcing the company's core niche position, improving the distribution network, and developing Internet and e-commerce activities.

Although Ducati was continuously learning and enhancing its products and processes, the company believed that it had attained its goals. To improve production efficiency, the company introduced several projects, including the Ducati Improvement Process (DIP). Sales of high-margin, motorcycle-related products such as spare parts, accessories and apparel increased by 9.8% from €55.9 million in 2000 to €61.4 million in 2001. The company also leveraged its brand through the sales of apparel and accessories. Ducati expanded its niche boundaries of high-performance, functional motorcycles with the Sport Touring models, special Monster models, and limited-edition motorcycles such as the S4 Fogarty (see Exhibit 1). At the same time, it reinforced its core niche position, for example with the sale of the top-of-the-line motorcycle model 996R, and by focusing on its core competencies.

By February 2002, the company had 92 Ducati stores worldwide. These retail outlets were designed to help the company gain more control over its distribution network, develop closer contact with its customers, increase profit margins and reduce lead times. Ducati had also been selling limited-edition motorcycles, accessories, apparel and memorabilia exclusively over the Internet. Some of the products sold online, particularly motorcycles, were delivered to customers through the dealer network. Products sold online were normally not available at the dealer outlets. The dot.com line offered restyled, classic motorcycles, and collector's items. The latter included limited-edition new motorcycles not yet launched at dealers and limited editions of enhanced or redesigned current motorcycle models. With its online sales, Ducati tried to strengthen rather than undermine dealers through increased sales volume and increased cross-selling opportunities.

After announcing the successful online sale of the MH900e motorcycle, the biggest Internet-based sale ever made in Italy, DMH's share price on the Milan Stock Exchange increased by an impressive 11.7%. 'It was at the time when the Internet bubble was at its peak', reflected Christopher Spira, Head of Investor Relations at DMH. The Internet since became an inherent part of DMH's corporate strategy. By 2001, the company was trying to integrate the separate Ducati.com operation into the real 'World of Ducati'. Hence, through trial and error, the company was fine-tuning its e-strategy and trying to adapt quickly to the changing business environment.

Ducati's business model had fundamentally changed from operating through a narrow value chain to setting up a value network, which integrated online and offline processes and business partners (see Exhibit 2). The value network included customers, suppliers, dealer outlets, marketing partners and sponsors. Through its network marketing partners and sponsors, Ducati tried to expose and leverage its brand.

As a result, Ducati had closer contact online and offline with its customers and a better understanding of their needs. 'The Internet changes your relationship with customers', commented Federico Minoli. 'Your customers become your marketing department. They tell you what kind of bike they want.' Indeed, the company considered customers a valuable source of information and took into account their preferences and views when making strategic decisions. For instance, Ducati conducted a major online survey asking Ducatisti[8] whether the company should participate in the World Grand Prix Championship. The 4500 positive responses reassured Ducati executives in their decision to participate in this major event.

The role of suppliers also became more important as Ducati outsourced most of the manufacturing of parts and components. At Ducati, the decision to outsource or keep in-house a certain activity was based on a two-by-two matrix (see Exhibit 3). If the customer value generated by a given activity was low and Ducati's relative strength compared with rivals was also low, then the activity was marginal and should thus be outsourced. If the value of both criteria was high, then the activity was considered a core competence of the firm

---

8 Ducatisti are Ducati employees and Ducati fans owning Ducati motorcycles.

Exhibit 2 The Ducati value network: Ducati in-house, networked and outsourced activities

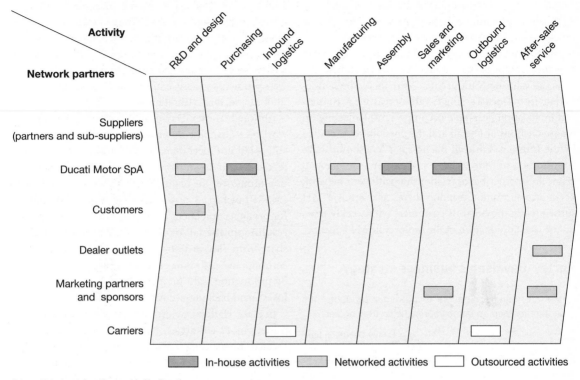

Source: Based on infomation provided by Ducati.

and kept in-house. If the value of one criterion was high and the value of the other one was low, then the decision to insource or outsource was made selectively.

Exhibit 3 The insourcing/outsourcing decision matrix

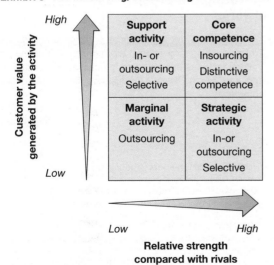

Source: Adapted from Ducati document, September 2001.

Ducati's relationship with suppliers tended towards a long-term partnership, which involved suppliers in several activities of the value chain: R&D, design, manufacturing and assembly. To improve efficiency, Ducati was intending to establish electronic linkages with its suppliers through electronic data interchange (EDI).

With its distribution network, Ducati strengthened its ties both on- and offline. First, technical training and support were intensified. Second, through the virtual Ducati store, traffic was generated to the Ducati dealer. Third, Ducati stores became virtually integrated through B2B software called Softway, which provided an electronic catalogue of spare parts and took orders and tracked processing electronically.

The value network also included marketing partners and sponsors such as Virgin Entertainment, Mattel and Maisto. Offline, Ducati partnered on the racetrack with companies such as Royal Dutch Shell, signing sponsorship and supply agreements with them. Online, Ducati.com had multiple partners such as the Italian telecommunication company Infostrada, which was a principal sponsor of the Ducati World Superbike Championship, and supported Ducati technically in establishing its communications network. Ducati.com offered dynamic partnership opportunities to drive traffic to partners' websites, enhance partners' brand exposure, and/or provide content to a wider audience.

As the value network partners were increasingly integrated into Ducati's single value-creating activities, communication became more important. Reflecting on the past actions of Ducati and the possibilities provided by the Internet, Carlo di Biagio said: 'We should have communicated more, better and earlier ... Once you create an Internet-based relationship with your network partners, you cannot abandon them.' As a result, DMH subsequently provided its customers with weekly news on the latest production of the motorcycle M4 Fogarty.

Harley-Davidson's business strategy

> It is one thing for people to buy your products. It's another for them to tattoo your name on their bodies.
>
> **Harley-Davidson Inc.**[9]

Part of Harley-Davidson's success lay in its ability to understand its products and the marketplace. Executives knew what the brand stood for and how to appeal to its customers' 'heart, soul and mind'.[10] The company also aimed at having a smooth relationship with its dealers. One initiative of Harley-Davidson's turnaround programme was to focus on its core customer base, expanding it to include CEOs, lawyers and doctors. By 2002, about 70% of the customers of the William Bartels Californian dealership were 'rubs' (rich urban bikers). Another project was the Harley Owners Group (HOG), founded in 1983 and aimed at helping Harley-Davidson dealers attract and retain customers. In 2001, there were more than 660 000 HOG members in over 115 different countries.

Despite the business climate, Harley-Davidson announced it was raising its 2002 motorcycle production to 263 000 units, up by 12% from the 234 500 in 2001. For 2003, the target was set at 289 000 units, another 10% increase over 2002. Celebrating its 100th anniversary in 2003, the company declared that its aim was to 'sustain growth...the next 100 years'.[11] More specifically, Harley-Davidson attempted to increase demand for its products and enhance its production with the goal of growing earnings faster than revenues. The company stated that its success drivers were its strong brand recognition, exciting

products and services, mutually beneficial relationships with suppliers, and experienced management team supported by an empowered workforce. With its extensive 100th anniversary celebrations, the company sought to increase its brand exposure, celebrate with family and friends, and reach out to new customers. Several events were planned, variously entitled the 'Open Road Tour', the 'Ride Home', the 'Celebration' and the 'Party'.

Although Harley-Davidson recruited 500 additional workers to increase its production capacity in 2002, it still could not meet demand. In fact, the company preferred not to do so. Some dealers even charged 20% premiums over the manufacturer's suggested retail price (MSRP) or forced customers to wait up to 18 months for products. Impatient customers often refused to wait, resulting in the fall of Harley-Davidson's US market share from 48% in 1997 to 44% in 2001. 'Harley's true earnings and cash flow generating power are held back by production', said Joe Yurman of Bear Stearns, a US investment banking, securities and brokerage firm.[12]

In 2002, Harley-Davidson had more than 1300 dealer outlets in 48 countries. Furthermore, satellite stores located in shopping malls and other high-traffic locations were convenient for customers in search of gear and collectables. Motorcycle sales rose by 19% during the first nine months in 2002. 'This, together with better than expected accessories and motor clothes sales in a difficult economy, gives us confidence in the robust demand for our products', said Bleustein.

Innovating the physical and virtual value networks

> I am like a priest for Ducati and my religion is innovation. We are pushing innovation in a broad sense. This means that we innovate our products, processes and organization, and also the way we do business through our online community.
>
> **Carlo di Biagio**

---

9 Harley-Davidson sponsors an annual rally in which the tattoo contest is a keenly anticipated event. G. Hamel, *Leading the Revolution: How to Thrive in Turbulent Times by Making Innovation a Way of Life*, Plume, 2002, p. 84.

10 'Marketing: the five best companies', www.forbes.com/2002/08/01/0801marketers.html

11 www.harley-davidson.com/investor relation/resources/events and presentations

12 http://www.forbes.com/best/2001/0910/008.html, 10 September 2001.

Our [Harley-Davidson's] success didn't happen overnight. It was built on a foundation laid by generations – past and present. And it will continue to grow well into the future.

Harley-Davidson Inc., Annual Report, 2001

R&D and design

Before the reorganization, it typically took seven years to develop a new motorcycle prototype at Ducati. R&D and design involved a long sequence of activities, with just a single activity carried out at any one time and requiring the involvement of not only the R&D and design departments but also manufacturing, external designers and suppliers. Christopher Spira explained how the process had changed:

> With this linear procedure, each time one unit of the company did a little bit they passed on the hot potato to another unit. Today, we have cross-functional experts, including those concerned with the end of the project, such as [the] marketing [department]. They work together right from the beginning, all the way through the end of the [new product development] process.

This new product development process at Ducati used a network-based design approach, enabling the company to reduce the time to develop a motorcycle prototype from seven years to four years. Starting with the R&D and design phase, several processes were carried out simultaneously, with all relevant internal and external departments and groups participating in a given process. These typically included R&D, design, manufacturing, quality control, sales and marketing as well as suppliers and sub-suppliers.

In 2000, Ducati invested almost €13 million, or 3.4% of total sales, in R&D and design activities. This sum represented an increase of 32% over the previous year. Over 150 people were dedicated to R&D and design, including 38 engineers. 'We also have a section on our website to integrate our customers in our R&D work', said Christopher Spira. The engineers used the latest CAD[13] and CNC[14] technology to design for assembly. 'We can use the parts developed for racing for our model line', commented Christopher Spira. 'Over a period of two to three years, all the innovations trickle through the model line.' R&D and design innovations were first introduced in racing and later used in the model lines, starting with the top-of-the-line models and subsequently integrated into less prestigious models.

Purchasing
Ducati

Back in 1996, the relationship between Ducati and its suppliers was tense. Suppliers were sending components in an unreliable and inconsistent manner, and Ducati's payments were often overdue. Thus, the company needed to win back supplier trust. It began by drastically overhauling its purchasing strategy: by 2002, 90% of part and component production was outsourced to suppliers and sub-suppliers, with all components delivered directly to Ducati. A hierarchical structure of four different layers of components and suppliers was developed to replace the formerly flat system. Sub-suppliers supplied to other sub-suppliers, or to Ducati partners, or directly to Ducati (see Exhibit 4); in recognition of the importance of their role, the company has developed a long-term partnership with sub-suppliers. In order to reduce costs, Ducati requested a constant supply of quality goods and services through an optimized process. Since 1998, the company has reduced the number of its suppliers by 26% to 175, while increasing purchasing costs by 59% to €196 million and increasing motorcycle production by 43% to 40 016 units.

Several criteria were used to select suppliers. First, goods and services had to be priced competitively and combined with best-practice quality. Second, the company's philosophy and values had to be shared. These requirements enabled Ducati to have consistent and reliable supply, trust in its employees, and solid financing and business continuity. Third, the supplier had to be large enough to benefit from economies of scale and to be able to invest in R&D, production technology and IT infrastructure. Fourth, the supplier had to constantly improve its processes and efficiency. Lastly, the supplier had to be able to implement innovative, personalized solutions and to react flexibly on demand as well as to deliver quickly and reduce lead time.

Several projects were under way to improve Ducati's supply network. The Ducati Evolution and Supply Management Optimization project (DESMO) examined the flow of material and information from sub-suppliers to supply partners, and from them to Ducati's production and assembly department, including outbound and inbound logistics. The objectives were to: (1) standardize the communication strategy with all companies; (2) reduce expenditure through cost analysis; and (3) enhance product and service quality.

---

13 CAD stands for computer-aided design.
14 CNC stands for computer–numerical control.

Exhibit 4 Ducati's supply management model

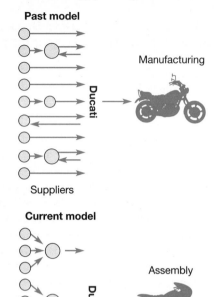

Past model

Manufacturing

Ducati

Suppliers

Current model

Assembly

Ducati

Sub-   Partners
suppliers (suppliers)

Source: Adapted from Ducati documents, September 2001.

Ducati's B2B e-commerce activities were still limited. As most of its systems were custom-designed rather than generic goods, the company was not keen on using electronic marketplaces. However, Ducati planned to launch its own e-marketplace for non-essential standard products. Other parts, including spark plugs, chains, tyres and lamps, could be purchased by joining Motoclusters, an online procurement system for the motorcycle industry set up by Giuseppe Narducci, Ducati's former Head of Purchasing.

More important to the company was its EDI connection to its major suppliers. A pilot web-based EDI project was carried out with five suppliers, aimed at electronically integrating them over the medium term with the Ducati IT system.

Harley-Davidson

At Harley-Davidson, purchases were already conducted online through traditional or Internet-based EDI. All Harley-Davidson suppliers were expected to become EDI trading partners. EDI was an effective, cost-saving way to transact business and minimize paper.

In 1996, Harley-Davidson redesigned its supply chain process. Given that over half of Harley-Davidson's products were made up of parts from outside suppliers, worth US$1 billion per annum, efficiently managing the supply chain was critical to Harley-Davidson's production and financial improvement. The company reduced the number of its suppliers by 80% from 4000 to 800. Product development time decreased by 30%, as did defective parts, from an average of 10 000 to 48 parts per million for over 75% of its suppliers. This resulted in a high reduction of waste and assembly-line downtime. Harley-Davidson's operating margins increased as a result of this redesign, going from 15% in 1997 to 18.4% in 2002.

In 2002, Harley-Davidson's online platform was still being rolled out. Even in its early phase, it offered secure access to the company's six-month billing history and to its 52-week demand forecast for parts from each of Harley-Davidson's five US plants. Suppliers could also access detailed information on purchase-order terms and conditions, e-commerce information, packing and shipping requirements, quality-assurance standards and Harley-Davidson news.

Manufacturing and assembly

> The historical achievement [of producing more than 200 motorcycles a day] is not a final goal, but an incentive to improve and satisfy the requests of our Ducati enthusiasts.
>
> **Massimo Bordi**

Part of Ducati's turnaround programme was to introduce lean production and assembly in order to improve its key production indicators. These aimed at: (1) enhancing motorcycle quality by reducing the number of defects; (2) decreasing costs by developing serial production; and (3) improving delivery service by trimming down the faulty parts at the assembly line. The company used a number of tools, such as the Kaizen[15]/Ducati Improvement Process (DIP), the zero-defects concept, the one-piece-flow principle and the total productive maintenance approach to ensure production reliability and reduce machine down-time.

___

15 The Japanese word 'Kai' means 'change', 'zen' means 'better'.

Besides its radical process innovations, Ducati also carried out incremental improvements. While radical innovations required long and costly planning and implementation processes, the Ducati Improvement Process (DIP), introduced in 1999, aimed at continuously improving the company's processes using a step-wise, bottom-up approach, as opposed to a top-down approach. To optimize the internal production procedure and synchronize processes with suppliers, DIP was carried out at three levels (see Exhibit 5): on the shop floor (operative orientation), within the company's functions (tactical orientation), and company-wide (strategic orientation).

DIP activities in manufacturing aimed at achieving a 98% availability of parts and reducing wait periods and change-over time. For assembly, the company tried to eliminate buffers, reduce the assembly stock and assembly time, and introduce production standards. Through DIP activities, the production process was redesigned to reduce operator ways (km/day) by 20%, material ways (minutes) by 34%, lead times by 50%, the default pieces by 21% and the workforce by 16% (see Exhibit 6).

To reduce stock, investment, lead time and requisite space, Ducati applied synchronized production and one-piece-flow. Hence, a maximum number of parts and components were manufactured simultaneously both in-house and by suppliers to be made ready for assembly. Since the production process redesign, daily motorcycle production increased from 25 units in 1996 to 225 in 2001, although staff numbers remained constant at 980.

In June 2002, Ducati introduced its 999 Testastretta motorcycle model. Since the previous 998 Testastretta model, the company had streamlined its assembly and decreased the component parts by 30%. Clean, renewable energy sources such as bio-gas, photovoltaic, wind, solar and biomass of agricultural and forestry derivation were all used in production.

By 2002, the dealer network provided Ducati with the company motorcycle sales forecasts, which formed the basis for production. While it typically took the company 37 days to manufacture and assemble one motorcycle, with an optimized process this would require just two days. Once produced, the motorcycle was stocked at DMH and shipped to the dealer outlet, which it typically reached four months after the order was placed. Carlo di Biagio explained the cyclical constraints on production:

> Most consumers buy their [motor]bike between March and June. The season is very short. I think it's less probable that one day we'll build to order. I know that there's a lot of pressure [from the market] in this direction. There are several constraints to deliver on order, including the quantity of supplies. If the customer now orders in March, we end up delivering in June and that is too late in the season.

Logistics

With its turnaround programme, Ducati tried to redesign its logistics process to align it with business strategy. As inbound and outbound logistics were considered non-core activities, they were outsourced to a specialized firm. Ducati still carried out its in-house logistics, which supplied the production line with parts and components, although the warehousing of spare parts and finished goods was outsourced. Giovanni Giorgini, Director of Manufacturing elaborated:

> Ducati sells 80% less in December compared to March. A service company managing stocks employs people throughout the year. It can easily even out seasonal ups and downs. But we can't change a shopfloor worker in March to [become] a warehouse operator in December.

In 2000, as part of the Ducati Improvement Process, the company launched several projects to optimize logistics. They included the reduction of expenditure and material flow within the factory as well as improving

Exhibit 5 Ducati Improvement Process (DIP): development of the DIP project

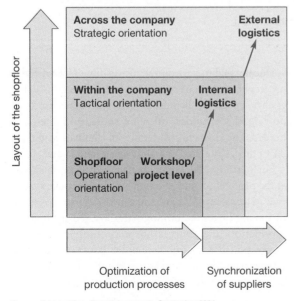

Source: Adapted from Ducati documents, September 2001.

Exhibit 6 **Impact of introducing Kaizen and one-piece flow on Ducati's efficiency: The case of the Alberi Motors workshop**

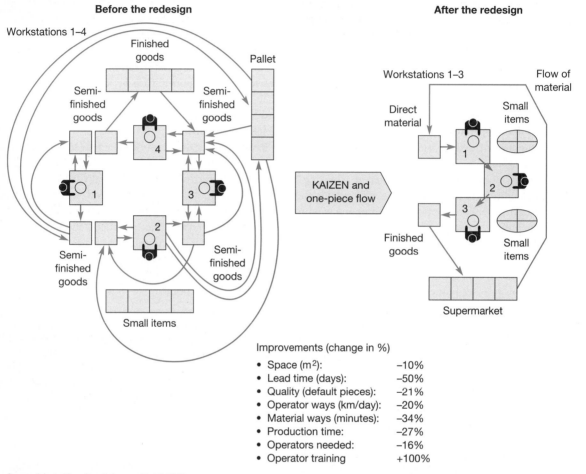

Improvements (change in %)

- Space (m²):   −10%
- Lead time (days):   −50%
- Quality (default pieces):   −21%
- Operator ways (km/day):   −20%
- Material ways (minutes):   −34%
- Production time: −27%
- Operators needed: −16%
- Operator training   +100%

Source: Adapted from Ducati documents, July 2001.

delivery punctuality. These projects were prioritized based on their duration and cost-saving potential, and were to be implemented throughout the end of 2004. The company first sought to improve its internal flow of material. For example, while in the past incoming parts remained in stock for four days before being assembled, they would henceforth be used the same day. Second, a logistics control procedure was introduced. Third, the transportation of incoming material by carriers was optimized. The punctuality of part and component delivery, for example, increased from 75% to 97%. Furthermore, inbound quality-control functions were transferred to suppliers.

Ducati tried to pass on the just-in-time (JIT) delivery process not only to its suppliers but also to its sub-suppliers. The underlying premise of JIT is that supply functions provide what is needed, when it is needed and where it is needed. The aim is to reduce or even eliminate lead time, down time, space used, as well as repairs and faults.

Furthermore, the company changed its parts supply at the production and assembly line from a push system to a pull system. This system, called Kanban, consisted of having boxes containing parts located next to the production line. Once a box was empty, shop-floor workers filled out a purchase order. Based on this, a kit was prepared in the warehouse and delivered immediately to the assembly line (see Exhibit 6).

Marketing and sales

While Ducati's target customer was an athletic male with a median age of less than 30 years, Harley-Davidson's customer median age was 45 years (see Table 3). In 2001, the average household income of Ducati customers was below that of Harley-Davidson customers (which was US$78 300). Customers of both companies are brand-loyal: repeat purchasers at Harley-Davidson represented 41% of sales, while at Ducati they were 65%. Also, there were more female riders at Harley-Davidson (9% of total customers) than at Ducati (5%).

Ducati

Ducati used two distribution channels to market its products: the dealer network and the Internet. Federico Minoli stated:

> We have the proof that we can sell products over the Internet that are expensive and complicated. And the Internet gave us the opportunity to better understand and assess the market potential of countries [in which] we were hardly represented.

Since its first successful sale on 1 January 2000 of the MH900e motorcycle, the company sold two additional limited-edition motorcycles exclusively online. Christopher Spira pointed out:

> The MH900e is a pure collector's item. It has an emotional value. The price [of €15 000 per unit] was extremely aggressive because of the experiment and the nature of the [Internet] initiative. We were offering a sort of avant-garde way of purchasing a very special item. We had no idea what the reaction was going to be and wanted to make sure that the price wouldn't be the hindrance. Actually, the MH900e online sale was not very

profitable, the main return being in terms of marketing and brand building. We could have probably sold the MH900e for more, but that's one of the issues you can never really answer.

Ducati's second exclusive online sale took place on 12 September 2000, with the new, limited-edition 996R motorcycle, which went for a unit price of €26 000. The entire annual production (350 units) was sold out in just a day. A year later, on 21 June 2001, the third online sale met with almost as much success. Within three days, the annual production (380 units) of the limited-edition S4 Fogarty, priced at €18 000, was sold out. 'With the Fogarty S4, we were taking the Monster S4 [model] as a base, adding a few more performance parts, giving it a special sort of colour scheme and promoting it', said Christopher Spira. Apart from the S4 Fogarty, all other motorcycles of the 2001 model year were sold through the Ducati dealer network.

For every motorcycle sold offline, the dealer receives a 12–15% commission. However, for every motorcycle sold online that the dealer delivers to the customer, the dealer gets 5–10% commission. Carlo di Biagio commented on this mix:

> The dealers agree that we have to use the Internet to reach out to the Ducatisti. It's right for special-edition [motor]bikes to sell them through the Internet. I firmly believe that for normal bikes, the normal distribution channel [i.e., the dealer network] adds more value because in the end you need the dirty hands of a mechanic to prepare the bike for a customer.

In September 2002, Ducati announced the online sale of a bicycle developed in co-operation with Bianchi, the 125-year-old Italian manufacturer of high-performance racing bicycles. The limited-edition series included 200 units, which were made to measure for each customer, priced at €5500 each, and sold exclusively on the Ducati.com website from 5 November to 5 December 2002.

Harley-Davidson

Harley-Davidson had a key strength in marketing and selling its products by emotionally involving its customers. Some of the appeal that a motorcycle could exert on customers was explained by one HOG member, Walter Durandetto:

> If you come along riding a Harley, people seem to notice you more. It isn't the fastest motorcycle but sounds the best. It's still a myth, a legend. Everybody I grew up with wanted to have one. Now, I have two of them and many of my friends have one. We take trips together. It's more than a bike. It's the people, the camaraderie.

Table 3 Demographic profile of Harley-Davidson customers

	1997	1998	1999	2000	2001
Gender					
Male (%)	93	93	91	91	91
Female (%)	7	7	9	9	9
Median age (years)	44.6	44.4	44.6	45.6	45.6
Median income per household (US$1000s)	74.1	73.6	73.8	77.7	78.3

Harley-Davidson purchasers, 2001:
41% had owned a Harley-Davidson motorcycle previously;
31% had come from competitive motorcycles;
28% were new to motorcycling or had not owned a motorcycle for at least five years.

Source: 'Demographics' on Harley-Davidson Investor Relation website.

In 2001, the company's motorcycles revenues reached US$2.6 billion, accounting for over 78% of total sales (see Table 2). Parts and accessories revenues also increased by 13% to over US$500 million, i.e. 15% of total sales. General merchandise grew by 8% to US$164 million, i.e. 5% of total sales. In 2001, the company had a market share of 44% in the USA and Canada, followed by Honda (21%). In Europe, Harley-Davidson had a 6.7% market share. Through its Custom Vehicles Operation (CVO), Harley-Davidson also sold limited-edition motorcycles.

Harley-Davidson Financial Services was the largest speciality motorcycle-insurance company, insuring 300 000 motorcycle owners worldwide. The company also had a motorcycle-leasing business operating in over 32 US states as well as in Canada, Costa Rica, France, Germany, New Zealand and the UK.

The Harley-Davidson website showed every motorcycle model, described its technical details and enabled the website visitor to compare various Harley-Davidson motorcycles. It offered financing and insurance options and emphasized the emotional content of Harley-Davidson products. It also illustrated the 'Harley lifestyle' with facts and figures from engine history to motorcycle rider tips. HOG members received a 15% discount when signing up for motorcycle rallies on the Harley-Davidson website. Furthermore, Harley-Davidson used the Internet to communicate with its dealers about technical tips, service bulletins and sales information. Dealers could also place orders, pass on warranties, and receive information on a motorcycle's service history.

In October 2002, Harley-Davidson increased the convenience of browsing the 4500 accessories catalogued on its consumer website, Harley-Davidson. com. The accessories section of the site was organized by model and year, so that users could view a catalogue of accessories designed for every Harley-Davidson model dating from 1984. 'Customers can view a complete selection online, from year-round riding gear and accessories to limited-edition 100th anniversary merchandise', said Jeanne Winiarski, e-Commerce Operations Manager at Harley-Davidson Motor Company. For example, a customer could enter the name of a specific vehicle, year and model and subsequently access a catalogue of accessories designed for that model, such as trousers, boots, gloves, eyewear, etc.

For Harley-Davidson customers, the online catalogue was the source of the most current information on new and updated accessories. While purchasing accessories online became possible in 2001, the company was still keen to send customers into its dealerships, stating on its website:

> For Harley-Davidson stuff, go to a Harley-Davidson dealer. Besides, it might do you some good to get away from your computer and see the real world, maybe even do a little shopping.[16]

Alternatively, customers could combine both, selecting limited-edition products online and adding them to a 'wish list' that could either be printed or e-mailed to the Harley-Davidson dealer. Riding gear, accessories and collectables could also be purchased online from the convenience of the home or office.

After-sales service

Ducati pursued its strategy of getting closer to end customers online through Ducati.com and offline though its dealer outlets. The company's high-margin after-sales sector yielded a higher percentage of total sales every year. In 2001, Ducati's online and offline sales of spare parts, accessories and apparel amounted to €62 million, i.e. 15% of total revenues, compared with 14.7% of revenues in 2000 and 12.6% in 1999. In some geographical areas, Ducati provided technical assistance through 'flying doctors', based on customer needs and location.

At its dealer outlets, Ducati had a 93% availability level for its spare parts. This was made possible by the platform strategy. Dealers could order parts using Softway, the online catalogue listing over 15 000 items. Outlets were connected electronically, and each dealer could place orders and track them online. Partnerships with carrier service companies such as DHL and SAIMA meant that products could be available at any dealer outlet worldwide within 24–48 hours.

Through Ducati.com, the company leveraged the Internet to raise levels of customer service and to develop an online community of Ducati aficionados. To increase traffic on its website, content posted on the website was constantly enriched. For example, in 2001, in co-operation with the Italian motorcycle magazine *Motociclissmo*, Ducati tried to strengthen its community through a series of five two-day courses aimed at teaching women the basics of motorcycle riding. The registration fee for this course was €100, which covered riding lessons, accommodation and meals. After the

---

16 www.harley-davidson.com

announcement was made in the magazine, 600 women applied for the 150 available slots.

Harley-Davidson's approach to creating an online community differed slightly. It opted against a chat room for HOGs, deciding that it did not fit with the company image. The company's website stated: 'Chat rooms are for people who drive cars. We prefer to chat in the middle of a national park with a few thousand of our friends.'

Future outlook

Ducati

Ducati's priority for the future is clear. We will stay focused on building our brand around the globe, revamping operations in the US, and above all, innovating our products to drive our growth.

Carlo di Biagio

Since the 1996 launch of its turnaround programme, Ducati has successfully set up a value-added network with its suppliers, customers and sponsors. Through this value network, the company aims at improving efficiency while enhancing product and service quality.

For Ducati, its 'new' core competencies were R&D and design as well as assembly, marketing and sales. Its online activities enabled it to strengthen its relationship with customers, dealers and suppliers. However, in spite of its incremental improvements through DIP, Ducati still suffered from an uneven quality of supply, out-of-stock problems and the need for bigger stocks. To alleviate these problems, Ducati planned to replace its unstable production planning system. Would this help the company to schedule production better according to the variations in seasonal demand? Could Ducati quickly implement its multiple projects with its partners? Was the decision to outsource the manufacturing process, which used to be Ducati's core activity, a wise one? How would employees perceive the changes in Ducati's corporate culture and processes? Would the human dimension in managing the new business processes become a stumbling block towards Ducati's future success? Could the company fully exploit B2B e-commerce opportunities, or would this remain a longer-term goal? Christopher Spira commented:

We would certainly like to reach a stage where customers give us an order over the Internet telling us what they would like us to have in their motorcycle. We are not there yet, and it is probably a long way from here to achieve that.

When – if ever – would Ducati be able to use a mass-customization business model?

Harley-Davidson

At Harley-Davidson, would the company succeed in its ambitions of sustaining growth for the next 100 years? Would it retain its leadership in motorcycle branding? Would it be able to effectively manage its human resources, specifically since Rich Teerlink, Harley-Davidson's former CEO and current board member, said:

We still have people who just want to bring their bodies, and not their whole selves, mind included, to work.[17]

---

17 *Harvard Business Review*, 2000, July–August, p. 52.

Otis Elevator
Accelerating business transformation with IT

At Harvard the only thing considered duller, safer, and less adventurous than working for a bank was working for some old-line can't-miss industrial firm like Otis Elevator, which only needed caretakers.

Tom Wolfe, *A Man in Full* (New York: Farrar, Straus and Giroux, 1998), p. 31

At the northeast corner of 20th Street is the turreted red-brick Victorian Apartment house . . . the first cooperative apartment house in New York City. Peek into the luxurious lobby! The foyer is adorned with stained glass and Minton tiles, and the building is equipped with Otis hydraulic elevators installed in 1883, and among the oldest of their kind still in service.

Gerard R. Wolfe, *New York*: *15 Walking Tours* (New York: McGraw-Hill, 2003), p. 261

In early 2004, Otis Elevator President Ari Bousbib (pronounced boozbe) finalized his presentation to United Technologies (UTC)—the parent company. The past 12 months had been a success for Otis, as highlighted in the 2003 Annual Report:

> Otis completed the second-largest acquisition in its history with the addition of Amtech Elevator Services. Amtech brings ... a customer base spanning universities, hotels, hospitals, airports and convention centers throughout the United States. Overall, Otis revenues grew by more than $1 billion to $7.9 billion. Operating profit increased by more than $300 million to $1.38 billion, and operating profit margin grew by more than one point to 17.4%.[1]

Otis was the largest manufacturer, installer, and servicer of elevators, escalators, and moving walkways in the world. The operating landscape was shifting. 'Today,' Bousbib said, 'we are no longer making things; we are moving things. Our differentiating focus is orders-of-magnitude improvements in logistics and service.' No longer was Otis an old-line industrial company.

Just a year earlier, when Bousbib held his annual leadership conference, he set forth a vision for Otis: 'To become the recognized leader in service excellence among all companies – not just elevator companies – worldwide.' In its quest for service excellence, Otis's future standards for comparison would be companies such as UPS that had institutionalized customer service and had developed standard work, process flows, and metrics to govern every customer interaction and every internal activity. Achieving this goal would require transforming the culture at Otis.

In Bousbib's description, the company did not simply provide elevators but total solutions to customers. This meant that every function of the business, from design to sourcing to manufacturing to new equipment installation to maintenance, needed to be run with a customer-focused mind, and all these functions further needed to be integrated into a single customer-centric business model. Otis Elevator was proving to be nothing like the company of Tom Wolfe's description.

---

1 http://www.utc.com/annual_reports/2003/review/page41.htm, accessed May 26, 2004.

Professor F. Warren McFarlan and Research Associate Brian J. DeLacey prepared this case with the assistance of the Global Research Group. HBS cases are developed solely as the basis for class discussion. Cases are not intended to serve as endorsements, sources of primary data, or illustrations of effective or ineffective management.

Company background

Otis Elevator is named for the company's founder, Elisha Graves Otis, who invented the 'safety-brake elevator' in 1853. (Exhibit 1 describes events leading up to the installation of the first passenger elevator.) Otis's core business was the design, manufacture, installation, and service of elevators and related products, including escalators and moving walkways. Otis's name had become synonymous with one of the most useful and dramatic inventions of the 1800s, the passenger elevator.

UTC's chairman and CEO, George David (who joined Otis in 1975 and became president of Otis in 1986), noted the recent accomplishments of Otis: 'Otis Elevator . . . had really good, powerful results in this last three years, even in the face of pretty tough economic conditions.'[2]

From 1997 to 1999, Bousbib was UTC vice president of strategic planning, and from 1999 to 2000 he was UTC vice president, corporate strategy and development. In 2000, at the age of 39, Bousbib became Otis's executive vice president and chief operating officer. Bousbib was elected president of Otis in 2002. Prior to coming to UTC, Bousbib had been a partner at an international management and technology consulting firm. Bousbib earned a master's degree in mechanical engineering from the Ecole Supérieure des Travaux Publics in Paris and an MBA in finance from Columbia University.

By 2004, Otis had 1.5 million elevators and 100,000 escalators operating throughout the world. Otis had elevators in 10 of the world's 20 tallest buildings and more than 1.4 million elevators and escalators under maintenance. Otis sold products in more than 200 countries and territories. Engineering headquarters was in Farmington, Connecticut with international facilities in Japan, France, Germany, Spain, Korea, and China. Of 60,000 employees, nearly 90% worked outside the United States. Otis operations were organized into seven regional businesses: North and South America, South Europe and the Middle East, North and East Europe, the United Kingdom and Central Europe, North Asia, South Asia, and Japan.

Revenues climbed from $6 billion in 2000 to $8 billion by the end of 2003 with 80% coming from outside the United States. The company's return on sales, which historically fluctuated around 10%, reached 13% in 2000 and then increased by more than 500 basis points to over 18% by first-quarter 2004. As margins expanded, productivity soared and profits grew. The company had always provided solid and steady profit contribution to UTC since its acquisition more than 25 years earlier. In the period from 2000 through 2003, Otis's contribution to UTC's profit increased from 25% to 35%. Otis's sales and profit growth helped drive the strong performance of UTC, which had projected revenue of $35 billion for 2004, 14% over 2003's. (See Exhibit 2 for the stock performance of UTC.)

Elevator industry: Competition and marketplace

Otis's main 'hardware' competitors included foreign multinationals Hitachi, Kinetek, KONE, Mitsubishi Electric, Schindler Holding, Tatung, ThyssenKrupp, and Toshiba. Industry competitors typically attained operating profit margins of 5%–10%.

For a small-building project, the elevator manufacturer was selected by the contractor, architect, or building owner. Larger projects often involved all three parties in the decision-making process. Buyers selected an elevator company on the basis of its ability to satisfy the elevator performance specifications and architectural requirements, price, reputation, and past performance on other projects.

An elevator service company was selected by the building owner or property manager on the basis of responsiveness, quality, and price. As a building aged and competition for tenants increased, the cost of service often became the major consideration, and the lowest bidder typically received the service contract. Many elevator manufacturers offered discounts for long-term service contracts. Some had begun to bundle up to a year of service for free with a new elevator sale in an effort to attract and maintain customers. New elevator sales were directly correlated with building cycles, but the elevator service market had been very stable. As the installed base grew, service historically accounted for a much higher portion of profits than new-unit sales.

The service market attracted many participants because of its steady demand, low barriers to entry, and high profitability. Thousands of elevator service companies existed, including both elevator manufacturers and many small companies devoted exclusively to elevator service. These companies serviced elevators from

---

2 CNBC: Kudlow & Cramer, Interview: United Technologies Chairman and CEO George David discusses his company's performance, May 6, 2004, ww.factiva.com, accessed May 16, 2004.

Exhibit 1 The first elevators

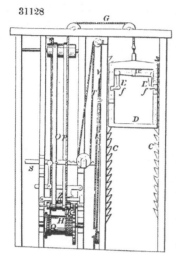

31128

The story of Elisha Graves Otis is a textbook tale of inventiveness, opportunity and enterprise. Along with other folk heroes of Victorian America, Otis took his place in books of precept and example. Imagine the scene: a small factory in Yonkers, making cheap iron bedsteads. The young Elisha Otis, master mechanic and inventor of a system for raising and lowering beds, contemplates the arid prospect of his future. Then in comes Mr. Newhouse from Hudson Street, New York, to ask if Mr. Otis could adapt his safety elevator to the problem of shifting merchandise. Could he, in fact, build him two elevators for hauling goods rather than lifting bedsteads. Two years later there were 27 Otis elevators in service in New York, and the foundations has been laid for enduring fame and fortune. Otis demonstrated his safety elevator in characteristically dramatic fashion at the New York Crystal Palace exhibition in 1853. He had himself hoisted up on the elevator platform, in full view of alarmed spectators and delighted journalists, and promptly cut the suspension cord. Nothing happened; the rack and pinion saftey lock ensured that he was *All safe, Gentlemen!* The first passenger elevator was installed in E. V. Haughwout and Co. s store on Broadway in 1857; it was the talk, and envy, of the town, attracting thousands of visitors.
Otis Collection.

BROADWAY : THE STORE OF MESSRS. E. V. HAUGHWOUT AND CO.

Source: F. Warren McFarlan and Donna B. Stoddard, 'Otisline (A),' HBS Case No. 186–304, revised 1990 (Boston: Harvard Business School Publishing, 1986).

Exhibit 2 **United Technologies stock price January 1, 2003–January 1, 2004**

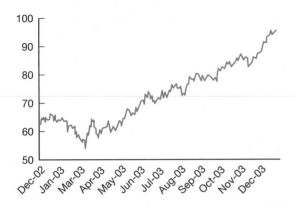

Source: Company documents.

almost any manufacturer—particularly elevators made prior to the introduction of microprocessor-based control that used similar generic technology.

The U.S. and Western European elevator markets were mature, and growth in new-elevator sales was coming primarily from emerging economies. China was a particularly hot marketplace and key area of growth: '62,000 units of elevators and/or escalators were installed in China in 2002.'[3]

From 2000 to 2004, Otis was aggressively growing with the market by acquiring elevator businesses in China. Otis's rival, Kone, was quoted as saying: 'China has become a growth engine for the world's elevator industry.'[4] Others competing with Otis and Kone for China included Schindler, Mitsubishi, and Hitachi. The market was built almost entirely on revenue and profits from new sales, compared to more mature markets where service accounted for as much as 75% of revenues and profits.

OTISLINE® Customer service center – early applications of IT

In the early 1980s, at the urging of its then executive vice president and chief operating officer, George David, Otis created a centralized customer service system to dispatch service mechanics. IT worked with many functional areas to implement this 24 × 7 concept, called OTISLINE customer service center. Previously, service personnel were dispatched from local offices, and there was no central view of service delivery, response time, or cumulative product issues in the field.

With the OTISLINE customer service center running on a newly installed mainframe, a centralized Otis service dispatch group of 160 people operating 24 hours a day could respond to a customer in less than a second. Information from multiple Otis data sources was aggregated. Rapid response was an important design element; customer service experience had shown it was unacceptable for more than 2% of transactions to take longer than a five-second response time.

OTISLINE customer service center improved visibility of the elevator service business performance to management, enabling it to provide more effective quality service to customers. Prior to this, service problems might be unknown to senior management until they had become critical situations resulting in customer complaints or in some cases service contract cancellations.

OTISLINE customer service center allowed Otis to produce 'excess' callback reports for various levels of management. For example, elevators receiving three or more callbacks in a month were reported to the district manager; those receiving eight or more in 90 days were reported to the regional vice president. Critical situations were reported to the president of the regional business. The expectation was that reducing callbacks and improving product reliability would improve customer satisfaction, thereby reducing maintenance contract cancellations. OTISLINE customer service center was first deployed in the United States and then was introduced to other Otis regions.

With OTISLINE customer service center, managers had the information they needed to truly manage service business operations. Aided by technology, Otis was able to restructure the company, eliminating several layers of management and speeding communication between field mechanics, customers, and company management.

Another important IT application of the 1980s was REM® elevator monitoring. This application enabled a microprocessor-based elevator to monitor its control system and log performance statistics directly onto a distant computer. Elevators communicated problems to a computer at headquarters. The computer analyzed problems and produced trouble reports used to dispatch service mechanics before the elevator went out of service.

3 Lu Haoting, 'GOING UP! KONE RAISES PRODUCTION,' *Business Weekly*, April 20, 2004, www.factiva.com, accessed May 16, 2004.
4 Lu Haoting, 'GOING UP! KONE RAISES PRODUCTION.'

With data from REM elevator monitoring, service mechanics adjusted running elevators to keep them operating at maximum performance levels and could handle problems before customers were even aware of them.

The OTISLINE customer service center concept fundamentally changed the expectations of customers in the elevator maintenance industry and helped stabilize the cancellation rate.

Setting the stage for the next transformation wave

Bousbib recognized that being a service company meant delivering more than flawless performance for units under maintenance. Bousbib liked the phrase, 'We maintain elevators, we service customers.' It meant that Otis needed to embrace a culture of service and to develop the processes needed to deliver world-class service. Otis had to redefine its processes beyond service support tools such as OTISLINE customer service center and REM elevator monitoring, and in fact beyond just the maintenance side of the business, to include new-equipment design, supply chain, new-equipment delivery, and field installation. Bousbib said, 'As an engineering and manufacturing company, we did not have the same focus on customer service processes . . . we needed to change the culture and better reflect that we are in fact a service company. These new processes had to be embedded in every aspect of the company's operations.'

In early 2002, Bousbib decided to focus on the new-equipment business cycle and set what he described as a BHAG[5] for achieving fivefold improvement in the order-to-hand-over cycle within five years. Historically, this complete cycle had taken anywhere from eight months to 18 months or more depending on the customer and many other variables. Bousbib's goal was to reduce the cycle time and ensure consistent delivery of quality products and services to all customers. (See Table A.)

These gains were to be achieved through the coordinated effort of multiple ongoing change programs in engineering, supply chain, and sales and field operations. In addition, a major IT initiative, the e*Logistics™ program, was established to enable and sustain the quantum leap improvement.

Engineering

Otis had acquired more than 150 companies since 1995. Each brought with it its own products and operations.

Table A Fivefold improvement in order-to-hand-over cycle

Step in overall business process	Proportion of elapsed time (current %)	Cycle time reduction (target factor)
Project proposal	3%	10×
Sales processing	8	4×
Order fulfillment	30	5×
Field installation	41	12×
Closing activities	18	2×
Total	100%	5×

Source: Otis internal documents.

These diverse products had to be rationalized in order to fit into the Otis family. At the same time, Otis needed to move from a regionally driven product strategy to a global one. Traditionally the product strategy, product development, and production were managed regionally. This led to redundancy, overall inefficiency, and complexity. Otis decided to deliver a range of global components that could be integrated into global or local systems. All engineering centers were reorganized to report centrally to a worldwide engineering function.

In 2001, Otis began a program, the SIMBA™ program, to fundamentally change the product architecture and ultimately the design process; the goal was a standard-interface, modular-based architecture defining modules and subsystems from which all Otis elevator systems could be created.

The SIMBA program reduced the number of modules in use and lowered project costs throughout the value chain. Distinct engineering programs (such as the design of new motors) fell from more than 500 to 50. Tom Saxe, who held an M.S. in engineering and an MBA, both from Stanford University, joined Otis in 1987 as an operations manager and held a variety of positions in manufacturing, branch management, and engineering before becoming vice president of engineering in 2003. Saxe recalled, 'At one time, Otis held 72 types of motors in their inventory. As a result of the SIMBA program, that had been reduced to only 10 motors needed for future designs.' (Exhibit 3 shows one of Otis's newest elevators; Exhibit 4 depicts the key subsystems used in the construction of a typical Otis elevator.)

---

5 BHAG – which stands for big, hairy, audacious goal at the intersection of what drives the economics of a firm, what the firm is passionate about, and what the firm can be world best at – was a phrase introduced by Jim Collins and Jerry Porras in their book, *Built to Last* (New York: HarperCollins, 1997).

Exhibit 3 Otis Elevator Company brings Gen2™ elevator system to North American markets

Otis revolutionised the world's elevator market when it introduced the Gen2™ elevator system three years ago, and has now brought the global product for low- and mid-rise buildings to North America. Otis Elevator Company is a subsidiary of United Technologies Corporaration (NYSE: UTX).

The Gen2 elevator has been Otis's fastest selling new product introduction in its 150-year history. A major breakthrough in lifting technology, the Gen2 elevator is the first ever to use flat, coated-steel belts to lift the elevator car. The belts are one to two inches wide (30 to 60 mm) and only one-tenth of an inch thick (3 mm), yet they are stronger, more durable and far more flexible than the heavy woven steel cables that have been in the industry since the 1800s.

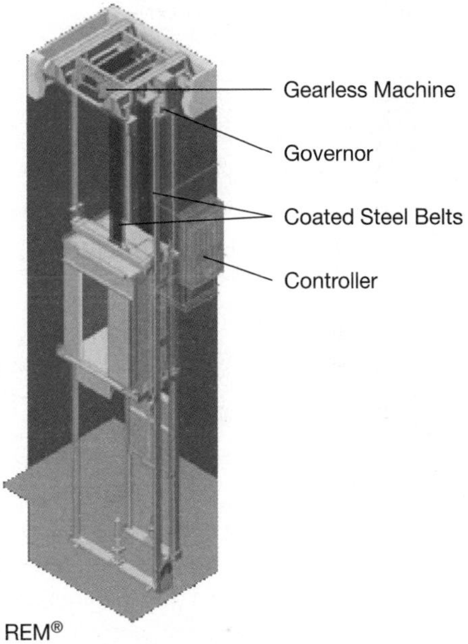

As a result of this technological innovation, the Gen2 system requires a machine that is only one-quarter the size of conventional systems, eliminating the need for a separate machine room while providing superior reliability, energy efficiency and advanced ride quality.

The Gen2™ system's flat, coated-steel belts are comprised of 12 woven high-tensile steel strands encased in a black polyurethane sleeve. They are quieter and lighter than traditional, heavy steel ropes.

The flexible belts easily bend around a sheave only 4 inches in diameter (100 mm), approximately 20 percent the size required with current steel rope technology. This compact sheave is integrated into an energy-efficient gearless machine so small that it fits easily inside the elevator shaft, or hoistway.

The Gen2 design is Otis's first application of gearless machine technology to low- and mid-rise buildings, offering customers gearless simplicity, ride quality, reliability, and energy efficiency that were previously available only in high-rise towers.

Gearless Machine

Governor

Coated Steel Belts

Controller

At the center of the Gen2 system's communications structure is the REM® remote monitoring system, which provides computer-based system diagnostics and performance measurements. REM data is tracked continuously and provides indications of elevator system performance, alerting Otis to minor equipment problems before they can cause a malfunction or shutdown. This allows Otis mechanics to make timelier elevator repairs – often before a customer or passenger is aware of a problem – and increases elevator availability.

The Gen2 system is offered in all standard passenger and serivce models up to 5,000 pounds with speeds up to 350 feet per minute, and will be immediately available for buildings up to 30 feet of rise.

Source: Otis Elevator Newsroom, May 8, 2003, www.otis.com

Part of this new process was adhering to a standard terminology that could be used with all customer settings, such as:

- Project – complete customer project (usually one contract)
- Contract – all elevators or escalators in a customer agreement
- Proposal – possible configurations of elevators or escalators
- Group – similar elevators, escalators (e.g., adjacent elevators in a high rise are a group)
- Unit – an individual elevator or escalator
- Field module – controller, machine, frame, motor, and so on (typically 20–60 depending on model)
- Subsystem – logical grouping of field modules (typically 10–15 per unit)

Exhibit 4 Elevator subsystems

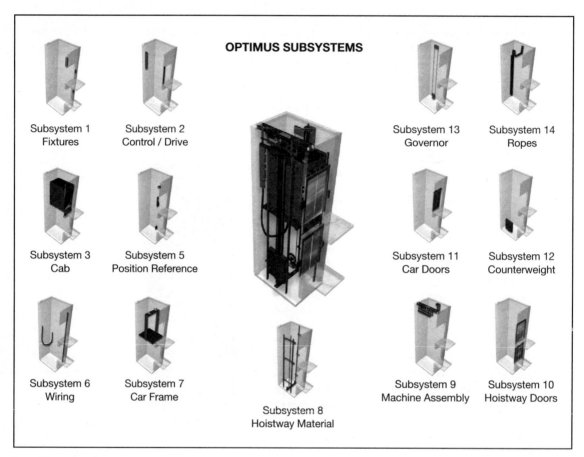

OPTIMUS SUBSYSTEMS

Subsystem 1
Fixtures

Subsystem 2
Control / Drive

Subsystem 13
Governor

Subsystem 14
Ropes

Subsystem 3
Cab

Subsystem 5
Position Reference

Subsystem 11
Car Doors

Subsystem 12
Counterweight

Subsystem 6
Wiring

Subsystem 7
Car Frame

Subsystem 9
Machine Assembly

Subsystem 10
Hoistway Doors

Subsystem 8
Hoistway Material

Source: Otis company documents.

Supply chain

Throughout the 1990s, Otis applied total quality management (TQM), lean manufacturing, root-cause analysis, and the teachings of quality guru Dr. Yuzuru Ito.[6] A UTC proprietary program, Achieving Competitive Excellence (ACE), was designed around a standard problem-solving model and standard tools that empowered employees to identify and solve problems while at the same time practicing continuous improvement.

Otis streamlined manufacturing operations from 52 factories in 1995 to 26 by 2003. Manufacturing would move to where lowest costs and highest quality levels could be achieved. Otis addressed two questions: whether or not to produce components in its value chain and, if they decided to produce, where to do the work. A number of previously manufactured items would be outsourced. In 2001, Bousbib announced a reorganization of the supply management function and of the manufacturing function into a new single global supply chain and logistics management function that would become a key driver of the strategy.

As in Tom Wolfe's description, many of the company's employees still thought of Otis as a manufacturing company. Bousbib wanted to change this mind-set and convince his organization that at a specified quality requirement, there were not any parts of the elevator that had to be made in-house for strategic reasons. 'I have concluded that we never need to make anything ourselves,' he said in a somewhat provocative statement that shocked many at Otis. 'The only reasons why we make components are cost and logistics.'[7]

---

6 See http://www.utc.com/profile/quality/ for more discussion of Dr. Ito's quality work, accessed August 4, 2004.

7 Kristin Roberts, 'UTC's new Otis CEO outlines priorities for change,' *Reuters English News Service*, May 10, 2002.

Vincent Della Valle, a director in the supply chain organization, was responsible for the elevator passenger interface modules (including doors, cabs, carpets, lighting, and other features). His team was working hard to streamline the leadtime from supply chain to manufacturing to field on a global basis. The simplest way to do this would be to produce a limited number of elevator models for sale globally. However, customer needs, code requirements, and aesthetic considerations made this impractical. Della Valle said, 'We realized we could not sell a global elevator. The challenge of the supply chain organization became the coordination of multiple global suppliers located in various parts of the world. We had to work with the suppliers to ensure that aggressive delivery times were met. E*Logistics capabilities became a key requirement.'

Sales and field operations

Tony Black, a graduate of Florida Atlantic University with a B.S. in engineering and an MBA from Darden School of Business, joined Otis in June 1991, working in field offices as an account manager and later managing field operations. Since 2001, Black was responsible for quality and field operations worldwide. He initiated an improvement program called the Sales and Installation Process (SIP). Following lessons learned in the ACE program, Black's team gathered best practices from around Otis related to sales and field operations. An important objective he had was to rationalize the 65 million hours of annual labor – at an average cost of around $40 per hour – required to install, modernize, and maintain Otis products.

Best practices were identified from the most successful sales offices, and these were made standard processes across the organization. For instance, the use of a prebid checklist became a requirement for all sales order personnel. This proved to be a key success factor in helping the customers define their needs, and it also helped bring sales and field installation teams together to discuss customer proposals early in the sales cycle.

e*Logistics—the information transformation

The critical enabler of this information transformation was a project called the *e*Logistics* information transformation project. This initiative provided IT systems to facilitate business process re-engineering that was taking place throughout the company.

The project team was made up of subject-matter experts in the areas of sales, field, and order management along with IT project managers who led process development requirements writing and system development. The team reported directly to a steering committee chaired by Bousbib that met every two weeks.

Giuliano Di Francesco joined Otis in the engineering organization. He held various positions in engineering, manufacturing, and logistics before becoming project director for the e*Logistics program in 2001. He was involved from the formal launch of the project. The first steps involved the merger of separate IT initiatives that had been under development for contract estimating, pricing, and online ordering.

Di Francesco saw the e*Logistics program as the means for connecting sales, factory, and field operations through the Web. Technology in the project relied on open standards, Internet-based communication, workflow tools, and back-end integration with established enterprise systems. Virtually all of the technology was proprietary and built by Otis software resources and based on standardized data interfaces – such as Otis's own version of RosettaNet.[8]

Bousbib's view was that Otis would become 'infinitely information enabled,' and the e*Logistics program was the key facilitator of that information transformation. Bousbib described this vision:

> Traditionally we had focused on the management of physical assets. The next step in our evolution will be the management of information flows between all the participants both in the production of our elevator and escalator systems, and in the performance and delivery of our installation and maintenance processes. This is a remaking of the entire company where information flow has mastery over product flow. It is only possible because of the technology, network, World Wide Web, and new computer and software tools available today.

Otis's 'Global State of the Business Report 2001' highlighted two overriding objectives: 'First, the continuous transformation of our business processes to improve innovation, quality, cost and speed; second, the migration of our core business competencies from product and service management to customer solution management and eventually to logistics and information management.'

---

8 RosettaNet represents industry standards for transactions between suppliers and manufacturers over the Internet. The nonprofit organization www.rosetta.org was established in 1998 to support and advance these standards.

According to Di Francesco:

> To achieve continuous transformation, the e*Logistics program makes sure the business process change sticks. At first, business executives saw process improvements from SIP, but after even just a few employees left, benefits fell off and became inconsistent. With the e*Logistics program, best practices from SIP are baked into the organization and institutionalized to achieve that continuous transformation.

Virtually everyone in the company would come in contact with the e*Logistics program, since it so thoroughly spanned the value chain. 'That's the key thing that gets me and the team up every day,' said Di Francesco, 'the extent of the impact we're having on every area of the new-equipment business.'

Each of the key processes, and the corresponding elements of the e*Logistics program, are described below.

Project proposal

At the very beginning of dealing with a new customer, SIP required a prebid checklist. Historically, these had been simple forms filled out on paper. With the introduction of the e*Logistics program, both sales supervisors and field-installation supervisors were required to review and approve the project as part of the prebid process. (Previously, field-installation supervisors might have never seen sales order information until the elevator components were delivered to a job site for installation.) The new process was completely electronic and project scope and cost seen by end users as easy to execute. The new automated process solidified commitment for the estimates, a notable improvement in an area viewed as critical for two organizations that had to work together throughout the life of a customer account.

Other elements of the project proposal included:

1 *Gathering account information.* Most Otis companies lacked sophisticated customer relationship management (CRM) systems. North America had a mainframe system; France used Siebel; many country organizations relied on simple databases running on PCs or nothing at all.
2 *Determining elevator configuration* (the act of putting together the proposed elevator specifications). Otis entities in Europe, Asia, and North America relied on configuration systems that ran on either mainframes or PCs, programmed into a simple spreadsheet. In fact, a number of branch locations still submitted requirements on paper and relied on the factory to prepare a configuration for the customer proposal.

3 *Proposal preparation.* Some countries developed front ends for creating proposals, including elevator and installation engineering drawings. Generally, there was a work template, but none of the countries had integrated to a point where they could easily push a button to prepare the proposal or readily communicate it to the factory.

Prior to the e*Logistics program, the first two steps used minimal pieces of automation, and the third was mostly manual. Data was dispersed across separate systems and in most cases had to be re-entered to be shared. With the e*Logistics program, all of this became automated and the data integrated; technology handled the basic steps and allowed easy management of changes to orders. The technology had been developed over two years by Otis, with a Web-based front end, a back-end database, and workflow technology that allowed each individual user to interact with the system based upon his or her assigned roles.

Finally, the e*Logistics program fed the proposal's information directly into Otis financial systems.

Sales processing

Once the customer accepted a proposal, the order then needed to be booked, validated, and scheduled. These steps had previously been handled manually, but the e*Logistics program automated the workflow of all these activities – electronically circulating key documents to all the appropriate supervisory personnel.

This culminated with booking the order and feeding the data directly into the various Otis financial systems using standardized interfaces. (Hyperion®[9] was used to roll the data up from around the world into corporate systems.)

Once a contract was awarded, the field-installation supervisor was required to meet with the customer and review the field-installation terms of the contract. Most crucially, before the order was released to the factory, the field-installation supervisor was required to visit and assess the quality and readiness of the job site and formally note his concurrence with the timing of delivery. This helped manage lead times, reduce inventory levels, and eliminate waste throughout the Otis value chain.

During the long sales cycle, Otis personnel routinely helped customers reengineer their orders. The e*Logistics program made the changes easy to record and visible to the entire supply chain simultaneously.

---

9 Hyperion® is a registered trademark of Hyperion Solutions Corporation.

Order fulfillment

Bousbib told his supply chain team, 'Ultimately, our long-term vision is to shift the center of gravity of our business from manufacturing to logistics and information management.'

At the heart of this shift was the creation of several regional contract logistics centers (CLCs). CLCs were responsible for accepting orders from the sales organization and delivering on-time, complete systems to job sites. CLCs did no manufacturing—they managed the supply chain including Otis factories, suppliers, field feedback, and the product improvement process. They were also responsible for market analysis, identification of customer needs, and creating product unit configurations.

Prior to CLCs, sales representatives submitted their orders by faxing or mailing documents directly to factories all around the world—the process had become unwieldy and error prone.

CLCs handled all logistics and information flows between subsystem integrators (SSIs)—which were

initially just the manufacturing facilities that existed at the time CLCs were first established. The SSI of the future would be the low-cost provider of a given subsystem (see Exhibit 3), which might be an Otis-owned entity or an outsourced provider. There was an emphasis on reducing internal lead times in the complete value chain of a CLC or SSI. In some areas progress happened quickly: Japan reduced its internal lead time to less than one week for some products. In other regions several weeks—and sometimes months—were the norm and became the subject of great management attention. Otis was edging closer to a just-in-time model for delivering product to job sites.

At the same time the e*Logistics program was being rolled out, CLCs were also being rolled out around the globe. CLCs were built with knowledgeable resources from the manufacturing arm of the business, often staffed with personnel displaced as manufacturing operations were restructured.

Exhibit 5 Contract logistics center operating responsibilities

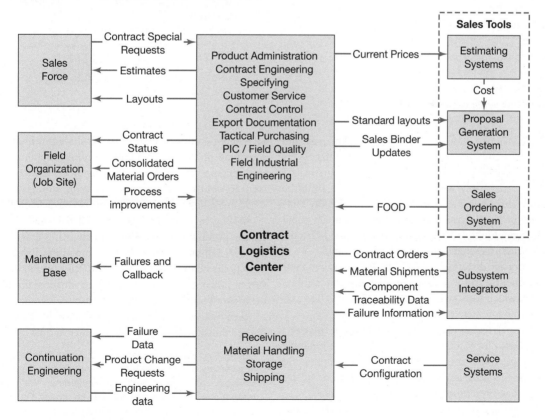

Source: Otis company documents.

Exhibit 6 Value stream and central role of CLCs

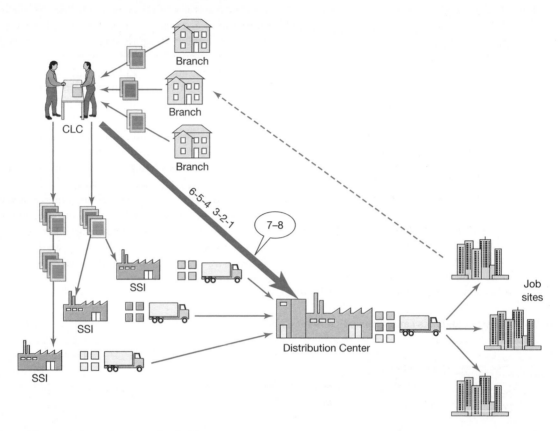

Source: Otis company documents and casewriter adaptation.

CLCs became centers of expertise around markets and their respective product models—such as Otis's Next Step™ escalator or Otis's Gen2™ elevator. At first, CLCs placed orders only with a single SSI, but in time the supply chain became more flexible and globally connected by the e*Logistics program. CLCs eventually could order from multiple SSIs—wherever they could find the lowest cost for required quality and delivery times.

Under the direction of CLCs, the SSIs shipped their components and modules to distribution centers (DCs), which were strictly cross-docking locations on the way to job sites.

Network technologies (intranets and the Internet) made it easy for CLCs to see all orders across the supply chain. Because of this, CLCs could source supplies and components from anywhere in the world. None of this would have been possible even five years earlier.

Major responsibilities of the CLCs included communications with field-installation supervisors, customers, and sales representatives. Other tasks included estimating, specifying, and processing; product administration; contract engineering and layouts; customer service and contract control; contract consolidation, storage, shipment, unloading, and placement; and overall field quality.

Staffing in CLCs and DCs varied considerably by region, product responsibility, and countries/languages served. (Exhibit 5 details the CLC functions. Exhibit 6 depicts the central role of CLCs in Otis's overall value stream.) All of these activities had been enhanced through the network connectivity of the e*Logistics program.

Cisco Systems in their online publication *IQ Magazine* noticed the transformation of Otis in these terms:

During the festivities celebrating his company's 150th anniversary in April 2003, Otis elevator's president, Ari Bousbib, made an unusual announcement. 'We're not really a manufacturing company.' Even though the company sells approximately 80,000 elevators and 8,000 escalators annually, Otis's real business, Bousbib says, is maintenance. . . . Otis is part of a vanguard of manufacturing firms that is beginning to look at the processes of how they build, sell, and service products not as individual processes but as one integrated process that is as collaborative as their enterprise software systems or computer networks.[10]

Field installation

Historically, there had been no automated globally standardized project management tools for field installation. Site conditions were impossible for Otis to control, yet materials delivery scheduling depended on predicting when the site would be ready for elevator installation. Field coordination with order processing had been poor in the past. If equipment was ordered too early, orders could sit on a job site for weeks and be damaged by weather or vandalism. If an order was placed too late, major construction delays occurred.

Otis field-installation supervisors were responsible for as many as 100 construction locations. They were responsible for communicating when sites were ready for orders to be delivered. With the e*Logistics program, they were now prompted to check site progress by workflows and could communicate job status by e-mail.

Before the e*Logistics program, a number of process improvements had been put in place to improve overall sales cycle time, but application of the process was inconsistent. Black noted, 'The e*Logistics program will take out the inconsistency—by automatically e-mailing reminders and updates it forces critical steps of SIP and makes good process part of the way you do business.'

To address cost inefficiencies and compress time to delivery, Otis moved from a *push* system (where product was sent into the field as soon as it was manufactured) to a *pull* system (where the field-installation supervisor determined when the product was needed and requested it, using electronic correspondence remotely and directly from the job site, based on its expected readiness). With the e*Logistics program, all the involved parties were asked to focus on managing to a delivery date based upon ideal site conditions – this meant holding orders until the last possible time and avoiding building slack into order and delivery schedules. This also allowed SIP to maintain lean manufacturing flows and low inventory levels.

Throughout the process, the e*Logistics program introduced timed e-mail reminders for the field-installation supervisor to visit the job site. This helped the company to maintain contact with the general contractor. The e*Logistics system required status information to come back from the job site before the company shipped any items to the field.

Orders were not allowed to go to CLCs early. While the order was still sitting in a sales queue, the account representative could sell additional product options. As a building project evolved, new elevator features could be added (e.g., mirrors, lighting fixtures, and a range of premium finishes) before the order was released to the CLC. This simplified and lowered the cost of change order management, both for customer billing and for production.

With more visibility to the order process and more control over shipping dates, the field-installation supervisor had increasing control over the financial success of each project. As one person described the shift, 'We need to change field-installation supervisors from being firefighters to being business managers. That's a huge cultural change.'

The new processes helped eliminate many hidden costs of lost, stolen, damaged, and misplaced material. As Black said, 'SIP tried to get the field-installation teams to manage the delivery date based on job-site progress, but e*Logistics helps to bake good process in.'

Closing activities

The principal activities in this phase were transitioning the unit from Otis installation to Otis service and handing the elevator over to the customer. This stage included reviewing any engineering change requests and processing final billings. The process varied greatly by geography and even by contract but generally involved meeting with the customer and presenting the final bill to review and settle all change orders.

With e*Logistics, as soon as the supervisor confirmed the job was complete, a workflow was triggered prompting a series of customer contacts and billing. This was expected to result in more accurate billing of change orders, higher conversion of new equipment to maintenance contracts, and faster collections.

Information technology at Otis

Ron Beaver, CIO, joined Otis in 1989. He initially worked in sales and marketing and became CIO in 2001. Beaver held responsibility for global IT, with seven

10 'Manufacturing: Beyond the Assembly Line,' *IQ Magazine*, July/August 2003, http://business.cisco.com/, accessed September 7, 2004.

regional IT leaders around the world reporting to him on a dotted-line basis. Each regional IT director reported directly to the president of one of these seven Otis regions: North and South America, Southern Europe and the Middle East, North and East Europe, the U.K. and Central Europe, North Asia, South Asia, and Japan.

Regional IT leaders were responsible for all local systems and operations, supported by an outsourced infrastructure agreement with CSC. They had their own local development team and technology support services.

Beaver noted, 'We're a very diverse, $8 billion company with operations in a thousand branch offices. As a company, we grew through acquisitions. We have 50 financial systems and 15 different manufacturing systems operating all around the world.' The Otis infrastructure included nearly 1,000 local-area networks with 600 wide-area networks (WANs) in the U.S. and 400 WANs internationally. There were 30 types of routers and switches supporting 3,000 applications. The Otis global network processed 60,000 orders each year—resulting from approximately 300,000 proposals.

Otis did not break out IT investment for the e*Logistics program from other process-engineering expenses such as those for ACE or SIP, nor did it account for return on investment on IT separately from returns associated with other business-process change initiatives. All these were considered together because the belief was that the benefits were tightly interrelated and could not be decoupled as easily as the costs might be.

Beaver had dotted- or direct-line responsibility for 450 Otis IT employees, in addition to 250 contractors. He had budgetary responsibility for all major IT expenditures.

About 70 people from Beaver's organization were dedicated to the e*Logistics project, reporting to Di Francesco. Beaver described the integration of e*Logistics with legacy systems: 'The goal of having a single finance and/or manufacturing system in Otis is not achievable in the short term. Therefore, building the e*Logistics system to be ERP [enterprise resource planning] system-agnostic was essential to obtaining the business benefit quickly.'

Beaver's staff was also responsible for a middleware broker used on the e*Logistics program—much of it custom coded for Otis, with some development taking place in an Otis-owned, India-based software company. Internal sales modules were built with Microsoft .NET development tools. The supply chain and field systems were built around JD Edwards ONEWORLD® software. Systems access, security, and connectivity relied on the UTC employee portal.

Remaining challenges for the e*Logistics program

There were a number of technological challenges with the e*Logistics program. According to Beaver:

> The first is the delivery of the e*Logistics program to the desktop. We have more than 20,000 PCs in the company and over 1,000 different major locations. So our ability to standardize the infrastructure and then understand how this application can perform across wide-area networks, local-area networks, etc., was very important to us.

> In the last two years we've obtained emerging technology that allows us to simulate applications across our global infrastructure. If one of the switches is wrong, or an Internet browser configuration setting is wrong, it impacts the performance of these applications. Now we can simulate this, sitting anywhere in the world but operating systems as though we are in Korea, Japan, China, or Russia.

There were also many personnel challenges. There were 1,500 sales representatives and 1,500 field-installation supervisors around the world who would use this system. Substantial technology and process training was needed for all users.

Pilot projects in the Netherlands, France, Germany, and the U.K. during 2003 had been successful. The U.K., which had a particularly long sales cycle, was able to cut its average sales cycle time for orders processed through the e*Logistics program from more than six months to less than three (corresponding to the first half of the complete cycle described in Table A). While the success was due to a number of factors – a new country manager, an involved management team, effective SIP deployment, local initiatives, and other programs – everyone recognized the critical role of the e*Logistics program in making and sustaining this reduction in cycle time possible.

From the pilots, Otis learned that it took approximately six months for benefits to become visible after an e*Logistics installation. Data entry and systems initialization would take two to three months, technology and tools training would take a month, and three to four months would be required for staff to fully adapt to the new business processes.

Full-scale rollout in Europe and China was scheduled for 2005. The system would be deployed for the rest of the company by 2006. Regions were prioritized based upon need and return on investment, with areas with the least developed systems infrastructure in their business coming first.

Adoption and success rates of the new system would be tracked by several metrics, including the number of units proposed per salesperson using the e*Logistics program and the ratio of sales support people to sales representatives. The supply chain showed improvement in factory turns and lead time as a result of the e*Logistics program. Field-installation times had been materially reduced for regions using the e*Logistics program, but scaling the system to be used by all of the field-installation supervisors remained the biggest challenge.

The next transformation

The transformation at Otis required a tremendous amount of effort on the part of management personnel and every individual employee of the company. A number of important improvement programs had been running in parallel, and they worked together to multiply the benefits. Black observed:

The rollout of the e*Logistics program is based on the maturity of SIP. If we hadn't done SIP, and just did the e*Logistics program, it would have taken much longer.

Some of the rollout is dependent on people's adaptability to change. In North America, we've put laptops into the hands of field-installation supervisors. They are salaried, nonunion personnel who have usually come from the union ranks. About 30% of them are familiar with computers, and this only works when people know how to use the technology.

Bousbib was pleased with the progress of the e*Logistics program rollout to the pilot countries in Europe. There had been approximately 300 person-years of effort invested in e*Logistics, and Bousbib realized how much work remained to gain full benefit from their global investment in IT. By early 2004, all of Otis's major products could be ordered through CLCs in certain regions. The global deployment of the e*Logistics program was proceeding according to schedule.

A simple measure marking deployment progress was the number of new orders that went full cycle through the e*Logistics program. In the U.K., for example, that amounted to 5% of all the units sold in all of 2003. But the U.K. was expected to rely solely on the e*Logistics program by the beginning of 2005 for 100% of its orders. Otis had not yet decided on a global cut-over date when all orders would flow through the e*Logistics systems.

Between 2000 and 2003, Otis revenue and operating profit had grown. But at the same time, working capital turns nearly doubled. Improvement in information flow had contributed significantly to improvement in cash flow. Bousbib took stock of his time at UTC and Otis: 'We have outstanding people with outstanding values, and we can become an ever-greater company. What we have undertaken requires a remaking of the entire company. When we launched our CLCs and SSIs and deployed the e*Logistics program it was a mini revolution, but today's results are proving the success of this approach.'

Over time, Otis realized that there was not a direct correlation between product quality (as evidenced by callback rate) and cancellation rate. Beyond a certain minimum expected level of product reliability, Otis concluded that the customer canceled maintenance agreements because of dissatisfaction with the quality of service, not the quality of the product.

Even as the e*Logistics program was still rolling out, Bousbib challenged his executive staff to launch a new initiative that would help make Otis the number one service company in the world – not just in the elevator business but compared against the greatest service companies ever: 'Our quest for service excellence will now require another mini revolution – to become number one in service – but this will also make us an ever-greater company.'

United Technologies Company (UTC), the parent company, was interested in hearing more about the progress of the e*Logistics program and also about the challenges inherent in Otis's new quest for service excellence.

Business-to-business electronic commerce
Mondus.com – an e-marketplace for small and medium-sized enterprises

Back from London, after having presented his business plan at the Catapult Competition,[1] Alexander Straub, a 26-year-old German, was wondering whether he had been able to convince the competition's expert panel of his e-marketplace business idea. When the telephone rang, the last thing he was expecting was to be told that he had just won the 1999 competition:

> From that day on, my student life changed tremendously. It was no longer a question of being a doctoral student at Oxford University, sitting in the hall with only dreams, but suddenly with US$1.7 million in my pocket ...

Alexander Straub, co-founder and
Vice-Chair, mondus.com ltd

Background: e-commerce

e-Commerce emerged in the 1980s with the use of electronic data exchange (EDI) in the retail and automotive industries. At that time, only 1% of companies used EDI for the business-to-business (B2B) exchange of electronic documents.[2] Today, widespread growth of the Internet has opened up numerous business opportunities and new sources of revenues. While in 1998, worldwide B2B revenues amounted to US$43 billion, they were expected to reach US$1.3 trillion by 2003. This figure will represent approximately 90% of the dollar value of e-commerce and 4% of the world economy, a percentage that will reach 30% by 2010.[3] Also the way of doing business will change. Today, 87% of all

deals are settled directly between companies; it was expected that by 2004 most transactions (53%) would be done through electronic marketplaces.[4]

The emergence of mondus

> In my student time, I was faced with the basics of the net economy.

When Alexander Straub started studying mechanical engineering at the University of Darmstadt, Germany, in 1991, he acquired his first e-mail address. He witnessed the advent of browsers at Cornell University in 1994. When he later joined Stanford University, he accessed disk storage space allowing him to host a web page and heard about the new evolving businesses such as Netscape and Yahoo! In 1996, he was awarded a Rhodes Scholarship[5] to study in the UK. He explained: 'I left for the sake of completing my Doctorate, but I was actually really ready to create my own company.' During the evenings, he and some friends would meet in the college halls and brainstorm over new business models and opportunities.

---

1 A competition jointly run by *The Sunday Times* and 3i, the UK venture capital firm, awarding a prize to the best Internet start-up.
2 Timmers, P. (1999), *Electronic Commerce: Strategies and Models for Business-to-Business Trading*, New York, John Wiley & Sons, p. 4.
3 Timmers, P. (1999), pp. xi and 4.
4 Forrester Research (2000), 'eMarketplaces boost B2B Trade', *Forrester Report*, February.
5 A prestigious scholarship granted to foreign students to study at Oxford University. Bill Clinton was also a Rhodes Scholar in 1968.

This case was written by Michael Müller, a participant in the Master programme of the Technical University of Aachen, Germany, and Tawfik Jelassi, Affiliate Professor of Technology Management at INSEAD. It is intended to be used as a basis for class discussion rather than to illustrate either effective or ineffective handling of an administrative situation.

The case was made possible by the co-operation of mondus.com.

In 1998, as an intern in Goldman Sachs' private investment area, Alexander Straub attended discussions on Internet start-ups:

> At that time I thought there was something tremendous about the Internet ... It was no longer just a marketing tool, nor just about information, but it was also about transactions. It was especially interesting for transactions where you have highly fragmented markets and inefficiencies. It goes beyond what B2B software solutions in ERP[6] systems can provide.

When he heard about the Catapult Competition, he wrote a business plan on his Internet start-up idea and submitted it. In February 1999, six submissions out of 1600 were invited to make a presentation in London. 'For me it was the first time I had ever presented my business plan to venture capitalists', remembered Alexander Straub. 'I didn't expect it to go well. But they liked it very much and called me the next day.'

Rouzbeh Pirouz, the co-founder of mondus, was a Canadian of Iranian origin who studied international relations and politics at Stanford University and at the Kennedy School of Government in Boston. He was also a Rhodes scholar and had met Alexander Straub at a farewell party in New York before they left the US. They both had an entrepreneurial spirit and often discussed business ideas. He was in Iran conducting research on the Iranian democratic movement when Alexander informed him about the Catapult prize. Pirouz decided to return to Oxford and help his friend launch mondus.com ltd. The name mondus.com had already been registered in 1997, when it was created by a group of students that included Straub and Pirouz. It was derived from *mundus*, the Latin word for 'world', and was supposed to be easy to pronounce and without a meaning that could lead to bias.

After setting up an office, Straub and Pirouz invited some friends, companies and consultants to reflect on their business model. While the original focus was on virtual community, commerce and content, they quickly discovered that, for a viable start-up, it was important to concentrate on transactions. They asked businesses about their procurement problems, analyzed different product categories and looked at market potential as well as the Internet adoption rate. Pirouz explains:

The opportunity for businesses to use the Internet as a tool for growth was the driving factor. The main reasons for this are cost, opportunity to compete against 'big players' and access to serious, reputable buyers and suppliers. All these factors were taken into consideration when developing mondus.[7]

On 1 April 1999, 3i transferred the Catapult prize of US$1.7 million to mondus.com. The company needed large premises to house the marketing and web design specialists who were hired, along with the database designer and the technical support team. The first website became operational in July 1999. At that time, customers were able only to register and to gain information about mondus.

By August 1999, mondus.com was valued at US$60 million, after Eden Capital, a venture capitalist firm, committed US$12 million for the company's expansion into the US and Germany. New offices were opened in New York and Hamburg. In September 1999, the UK website mondus.co.uk was officially launched. One month later, the US website mondus.com became operational and another venture capitalist, Zouk Ventures, invested US$3 million. Since the local telecommunication company could not set up the Internet connection any earlier, the German website mondus.de started in November 1999. Two months later, an office was opened in Paris and mondus' fourth national website, mondus.fr, became available just one year after the initial business plan had been submitted. The company's original name was mondus.com ltd. On 19 May 2000, it was changed to mondus ltd[8] (see Exhibit 1). Its headquarters were located in Oxford, England.

The business model

> We offer products and services in the horizontal categories. These are not goods in category A or category B, but category C. For example, not the tyres that are produced or the rubber that was used to produce the

---

6 Enterprise resource planning (ERP) systems are computer applications that allow companies to manage their business operations (e.g. finance, requirement planning, human resources and order fulfilment) using a single, integrated set of corporate data. ERP solutions are offered by software vendors such as SAP, Baan or PeopleSoft.

7 www.mondus.co.uk/mori/mori.cfm

8 Throughout the case, the term 'mondus' will be used to refer to mondus ltd.

Exhibit 1 Organizational structure of mondus.com ltd, 8 May 2000

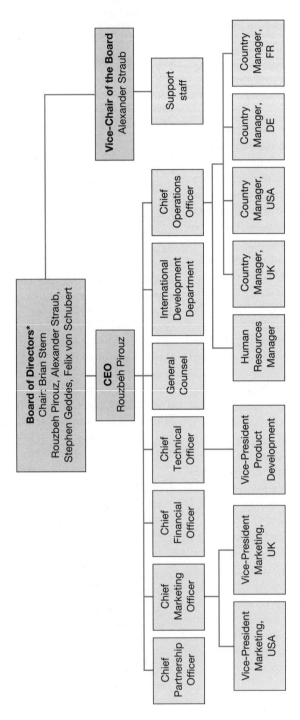

* Brian Stern was Senior Vice-President of Xerox Corporation and President of Xerox Technology Enterprises. He has served as Vice-President of Corporate Business Strategy, President of the company's Personal Documents Products Division and President of the company's Office Document Products Group. In these capacities, he oversaw the development and implementation of products for small businesses and home offices through retail distribution channels and the worldwide marketing of the industry's broadest line of office copiers. Stephen Geddes and Felix von Schubert are partners at Eden Capital and Zouk Ventures respectively.

Source: mondus.com ltd.

tyres, but in fact what I would call business needs such as office supplies, office services, human resource services, or financial services.[9]

Marcus Gerhardt, Head of Communication and UK Country Manager, mondus

Mondus was a horizontal web-based B2B marketplace.[10] It aimed at offering a one-stop procurement solution to small- and medium-sized enterprises (SMEs) by matching buyers and sellers through its website. The reason why mondus chose the horizontal approach (see Table 1) was because of branding. 'We spoke with a Goldman Sachs analyst back in the summer [1999]', explained Marcus Gerhardt:

He indicated that a horizontal brand was far easier to establish and to create [than a vertical brand]. In fact it meant that you would have leverage over the vertical markets. We have seen this with a few Scandinavian players who had very strong and successful businesses.

_____

9 Categories A, B and C are derived from the ABC analysis that attempts to classify procurement needs based on the ratio of value and volume. While there are only a few products in category A, of great importance to the company, C-type goods have a low value and account for most of the procurement needs. Category B goods are in between the two.

10 A horizontal marketplace refers to an application that is offered to a wide range of industries. In contrast, vertical markets only focus on a specific industry.

Table 1 Purchasing categories of mondus.com, 8 May 2000

Computer equipment
Desktop PCs
Laptop PCs
Apple systems
Computer software
Computer accessories
Monitors
Printers

Computer services
Software development
Network services

Corporate hospitality
Catering
Event planning

Couriers
International couriers
Messenger services
Nationwide couriers

Human resource services
Executive recruitment
Temporary staffing
Payroll services

Internet services
Internet service providers
Website design
Website hosting
Server hosting/colocation
Internet security
Transaction services
Web traffic analysis

Intellectual property services
Patents
Trademarks

Marketing services
Direct marketing
Mailing lists
Public relations
Telemarketing
CD business cards
Banner advertisements

Office services and equipment
Fax machines
Copiers
Projectors
Scanners
Printing refills

Printing and related services
Printing services
Business cards
Business stationery

Professional services
Translation services

Promotional items and services
Corporate apparel
Corporate gifts
Promotional staffing and entertainment

Telecom and communications
Paging
Video-conferencing
Telephones and accessories

Training services
Business and sales training
Computer training
Language training
Office support training

Source: mondus.com ltd.

Exhibit 2 Matching buyers and sellers through mondus.com

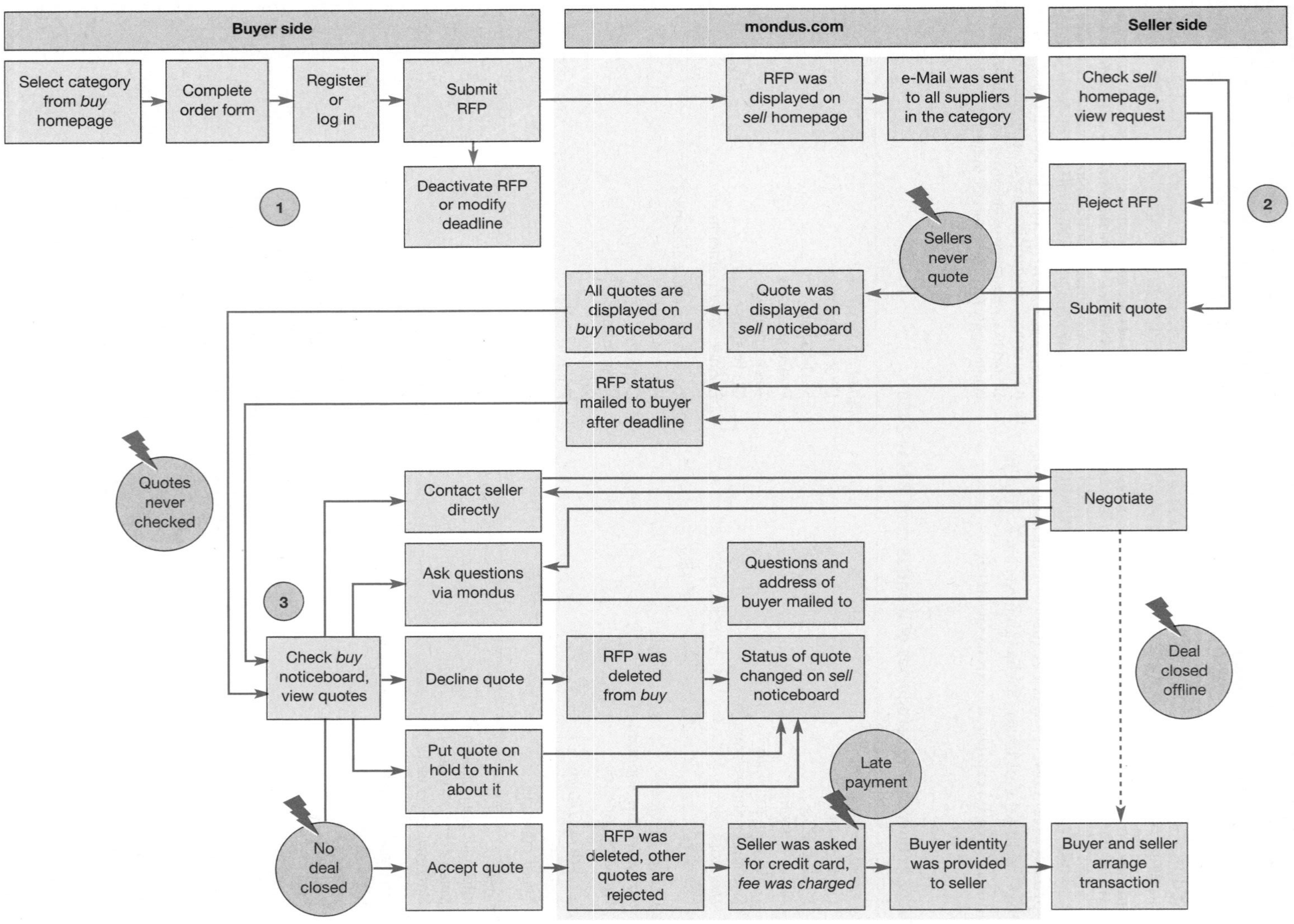

They came up with a vertical [approach and] it was very difficult for them to sustain their brand in the horizontal space and actually go beyond Scandinavia or into other markets because nobody recognizes their brand. Mondus was different; it was taking the horizontal approach. We aim at becoming the one-stop solution for the procurement needs of SMEs.

Mondus' market model was based on the use of a request-for-proposal (RFP). The matching of buyers and suppliers was a three-step procedure. First, the buyer placed a request. Second, one or more suppliers replied to the request by submitting a quote. Third, the buyer viewed all the quotes, if necessary negotiated with the sellers, and accepted or rejected the received quotes (see Exhibit 2).

The above process was facilitated through the mondus homepage, which was divided into a buy section and a sell section (see Exhibit 3). In the buy homepage, buyers requested the product or service they needed. In the sell homepage, sellers could view the requests currently submitted and place quotes. All users of the system had a personal noticeboard (my mondus) that informed buyers through the buy noticeboard about the current status of their requests, and sellers through the sell

Exhibit 3 Structure of the mondus.com homepage

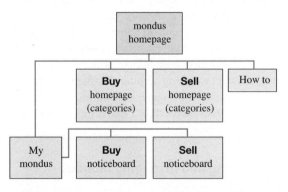

noticeboard about their quotes. There was also a 'How to' section containing information on mondus.

Placing a request for proposal

The buyer selected on the buy homepage the category of products or services they were looking for. A standardized order form popped up and the buyer was asked to specify their needs. Possible answers were provided for each question. It was also possible to use an open-format query or to attach a file with more detailed information. With every question made by the system, online help was provided (for example to explain what a hard disk is, how its size was defined and what size was necessary). Alternatively the buyer could look up the frequently asked questions (FAQs), call a toll-free number or send an e-mail to the helpdesk. Mondus set up call centres in the local markets and trained the centre agents to answer queries about any aspect of the site without having to redirect the caller. The aim was to answer all e-mail messages within an hour of their receipt, which, at the time this case was written, was true for 74% of all incoming calls. A global customer relation strategy tried to provide the same service everywhere.

After the buyer defined the service or product they needed, they were asked for the delivery date, the maximum number of quotes to be received and a deadline for the quotes. To submit the RFP they could either log on or register. When a new customer registered as a buyer, they were asked for their name and address, the name and size of their company, their position and a password; they were then assigned a username. After a request was submitted, it could be deactivated or its deadline extended.

Placing a quote

Once an RFP was submitted, it was posted on the sell homepage and an e-mail sent to all suppliers that had registered for that category. If a seller registered, they had to provide the same information as the buyer and the categories for which they could supply goods. They could decline to be notified daily about RFPs submitted in their categories. It was possible to specify the geographical area in which a seller could provide their products or services, a short description of their company (including its age) as well as the return of goods and guarantee policies.

The e-mail contained the identification number of the RFP. Sellers could go to the sell homepage, enter the RFP number and view the request. Alternatively they could check any category on the sell homepage and view all submitted quotes. The information shown to the seller did not contain the identity of the buyer nor any quotes made by other suppliers. Mondus believed that displaying competitors' prices might prevent vendors from making quotes, and that customers did not make their purchase decision based only on price but rather on the complete offer they received.

After a seller viewed an RFP, they could submit a quote or reject the request. When placing a quote the vendor had to specify the delivery date, the volume, the price and give a short description of the offer. Additionally they were asked whether their quote exactly met the buyer's request. In order to submit a quote, the seller had to log in or register. Quotes were binding and not retractable.

Selecting a quote

All quotes submitted were displayed on the buy noticeboard and could be viewed by the buyer. If the deadline expired, an e-mail was sent to the buyer to inform them of all the quotes. If no quotes were submitted, they were also notified and asked to call mondus for further help. In those cases, the customer service departments checked the requests and tried to call suppliers individually. In order to proceed, the buyer had to open the buy noticeboard. They could decline quotes, put them on hold or accept them. The buyer's choice was automatically displayed on the sell noticeboard to keep the vendor informed of the status of their quotes.

The buyer could also contact the vendor and ask them questions or negotiate with them. They could do this either directly, because each quote contained the seller's address, or via mondus. In the second case, the buyer entered the questions and their address into a query provided on the buy noticeboard. The information was then forwarded to the supplier who was asked to contact the buyer.

Once a buyer accepted a quote, all other quotes were automatically rejected. The selected vendor was asked for their credit card details and a fee was charged by mondus. The vendor then received the buyer's address and both arranged the details of the transaction. In the end, mondus asked the buyer for feedback on the seller's performance.

The revenue model

In B2B [e-commerce] the buyer has the power and was the one that decides how things work. If, in bricks-and-mortar businesses, the buyer was sitting in his chair and the salesperson was trying to impress him, in an Internet-based solution this balance of power has to be reflected as well.

Dr Florian Heupel, Director of Business Development, mondus.de, Germany

Mondus did not only want to consider buyer-centricity through its matching procedure (where sellers submitted binding quotes and buyers chose from these), but also through the revenue model set in place. Mondus only charged sellers a fee on successful transactions settled through mondus. All services provided to the buyer were free. Initially, sellers were also charged for submitting quotes, but mondus changed its policy to motivate vendors to quote and to increase the number of quotes submitted per RFP. Registration was free of charge for both sellers and buyers.

The transaction fee charged was 2% of the transaction volume. Though originally mondus planned to apply different percentages depending on the product category, it finally preferred to charge a flat fee. 'The RFP is a fairly new model and customers first have to get used to it', explained Christoph Pech, Manager of International Development at mondus. 'That's why we decided to keep the billing structure as simple as possible.' In the future, mondus could use a different fee structure that took into account the margins gained by sellers or the average transaction volume per category. Fees could also be used as a marketing tool to offer market incentives.

Developing and managing mondus

Marketing

For Dr Heupel, 'the strategy was to register through various marketing tools as many users as possible in order to make the product known to the market'. When mondus started in April 1999, it first looked at business-to-consumer (B2C) players and the way they were marketing their products and services. Having realized that a different approach would be needed for B2B e-commerce, mondus performed in November 1999, with the help of an advertising agency, a market test. Based on the test results, mondus launched an integrated marketing campaign in the UK in the first quarter of 2000, which

**Exhibit 4 Information attached to the letter sent to potential sellers –
part of the test campaign in the UK, November 1999**

mainly used direct marketing techniques. Marcus Gerhardt explained: 'Envelopes or direct mail [were] sent out to buyers and suppliers followed by an e-mail and a telephone call and another e-mail and telephone call. At the same time [we did] some radio advertising to create market awareness.' Advertising in the printed press and on TV did not seem to be effective. The information sent to customers was different for potential buyers and sellers; it contained a letter and a small brochure (see Exhibits 4 and 5). Mondus obtained the customer information from telecommunication and computer providers. 'The point is not that we used lists of computer suppliers, but in fact databases that came from companies that are active in the computer area', explained Marcus Gerhardt.

The reason is that you can assume that this kind of environment feeds into the early adopters. They will have companies [in their customer databases that] are well aware of computers and the Internet and are therefore happier than others about adopting that kind of trading platform.

The marketing campaign led to a significant increase in customer registration, though it did not have an impact until late February. In February 2000, 17 000 customers were registered worldwide; however, within one month this number had grown to 60 000. Also the number of RFPs increased twice within the same period of time (see Exhibit 6).

Exhibit 5 Letter sent to potential buyers – part of the UK marketing campaign, first quarter of 2000

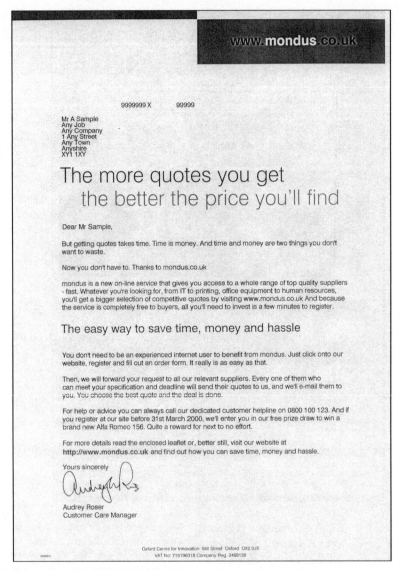

A marketing campaign was launched in Germany, its design based on experiences gained in the UK. Online banners were displayed in different websites and in newsletters of other companies starting on 22 March 2000. A one-page advertisement was placed in the major business and non-business newspapers as well as in weekly journals. Additionally radio-based advertising took place in Frankfurt and Hamburg, and direct mailing in combination with telemarketing was used. The best results with respect to customer registration were gained through telemarketing. However, these customers had not placed many RFPs. While advertising in weekly magazines seemed a cost efficient method of increasing the number of RFPs, radio advertising had no significant effect (see Table 2). It could only be used to generate brand awareness and attract customers to the website in the long run.

Another way to attract customers was via the affiliate scheme. Mondus offered companies an exchange in

Exhibit 6 Evolution of the number of customers and RFPs in Germany and worldwide

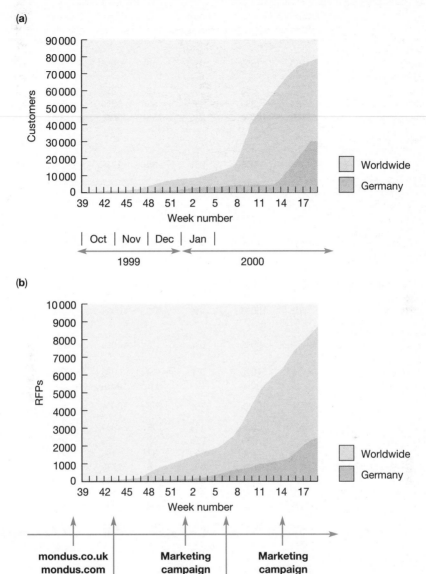

Source: mondus.com ltd.

links and logos. Affiliates displayed the mondus logo on their website and mondus placed the affiliate's logo in its so-called recourse library, a special section on the web page.

Partnerships

According to Marcus Gerhardt, there were three objectives in creating partnerships: 'To attract traffic to the mondus site, to complement our service, and to support

379

Table 2 Effects of the mondus.de marketing campaign in Germany, 5 May 2000

		Customers registered	Within category	Overall percentage	RFQs placed	Within category	Overall percentage	Contacts (1000)	Total cost (1000 DM)
Online (Ibanner)	Web sites of IT related businesses	59	16%	0%	46	29%	3%		
	Other companies' newsletter	23	6%	0%	12	8%	1%		
	Other web sites	284	78%	2%	98	63%	5%		
	Total online	*366*	*100%*	*2%*	*156*	*100%*	*9%*		
Print	Daily newspapers (FAZ, Süddeutsche Zeitung)	65	9%	0%	35	12%	2%		
	Daily business newspapers (German FT, Handelblatt)	158	23%	1%	62	21%	3%	383	192
	Weekly magazine (Focus)	338	48%	2%	133	44%	7%	972	237
	Weekly business magazine (Wirtschaftswoche)	137	20%	1%	70	23%	4%	270	96
	Other journals	4	1%	0%	2	1%	0%		
	Total print	*702*	*100%*	*4%*	*302*	*100%*	*17%*		
	Local radio station in Hamburg	9	90%	0%	3	100%	0%	750	65
	Local radio station in Frankfurt	1	10%	0%	0	0%	0%		
	Total radio	*10*	*100%*	*0%*	*3*	*100%*	*0%*		
Telemarketing		*12747*	100%	77%	106	100%	6%	25	1163
Others	Letters	247	50%	1%	108	49%	6%	100	182
	Press articles	75	1%	0%	42	1%	2%		
	Telephone	66	1%	0%	37	1%	2%		
	Promotion in exhibitions	9	30%	0%	5	27%	0%		
	TV	7	1%	0%	5	1%	0%		
	Others	429	1%	3%	201	1%	11%		
	Total others	*833*	*100%*	*5%*	*398*	*100%*	*22%*		
No information		*1911*	*100%*	*12%*	*859*	*100%*	*47%*		
Total		*16569*		*100%*	*1824*		*100%*		

it with technical services.' Partnerships in Internet business were 'crucially important, because you do not just open the market up for yourself, but you close it down to the competition as you create these partnerships'.

Accessing new customers

Mondus tried to co-operate with Internet companies that had strong brands in their markets. Partnerships signed by mondus included those with Internet.com,[11] Smart Online.com,[12] Yahoo.co.uk, Compaq, British Telecom and vertical marketplaces. Marcus Gerhardt explained:

> We don't want to become a vertical market but we could partner with vertical players. For example, we have a partnership in the UK with doctors.net. We don't offer bandages or pharmaceutical equipment, but doctors also

11 Internet.com was a provider of real-time news for the Internet industry and experienced Internet users.
12 SmartOnline.com was an application service provider (ASP), offering productivity applications and information resources to SMEs.

need desks, computers and telecommunications. So we provide the C category of goods to doctors. In Germany we just closed a deal with farmpartner.com, which was a very active vertical Internet site for the farmers.

There were also agreements signed with non-profit organizations, such as the German Federal Association for Procurement and Logistics (BME).[13] Through this agreement, mondus offered its marketplace to all BME members and supported the association through information campaigns on electronic markets.

Extending the business model along the value chain

In addition to setting up partnerships, mondus tried to extend its business model through co-operations. The service provided by mondus only extended to the point at which the deal was closed. A co-operative agreement set up with Dun & Bradstreet helped to check customers' credit ratings. Dun & Bradstreet provided a large database of information on companies, ranging from trading styles to financial statements. When a customer registered, whether as a seller or a buyer, their company was searched through the Dun & Bradstreet database. If found and the feedback was positive, a Dun & Bradstreet logo was displayed next to the customer's name on the sell or buy noticeboard.

For Alexander Straub:

In the long run you must help the buyers along the whole value chain. The next step was payment and logistics. We are [also] looking into financing. Another area which will be a challenge to the marketplace in general is to get the ERP systems on both the buyer and seller side [integrated].

Banks and logistics companies could profit from partnerships with marketplaces such as mondus because new business opportunities could be created. Mondus aimed to extend its business into payment and logistics by the third quarter of 2000 and into financing by the end of the year 2000. Of special interest, mondus and a certain bank were developing a trust account to help increase the number of SMEs that trusted the mondus marketplace. Furthermore, mondus planned to offer integration into the ERP by summer 2000.

Market models

As stated above, a key assumption underlying mondus' business model was that B2B markets were mainly buyer-driven. However, in addition to the RFP, other buyer-centric models existed, which included multi-catalogues and reverse auctions. Multi-catalogue models

worked like mail order companies. Different products were offered with fixed conditions to customers who could choose from a list. The selected goods were then shipped to the buyer. In reverse auctions, a buyer specified their need and sellers were asked to submit the lowest price. In some models, the buyer could also define the price and sellers could either accept or reject it. The RFP model was the most flexible solution since it allowed vendors to compete on price and any value-added feature. Dr Heupel said:

The RFP was a fairly new model and we are now asking ourselves: Does this model work? … From what we have seen so far, people are extremely interested in this model, which was more suitable for some categories than for others. For low volume transactions, it was probably not a good model. However, to find services, it seems to be an excellent model. In the future there will probably be more than one product offering in terms of what model you are using. We are currently extending into multi-catalogues and reverse auctions.

Multi-catalogues

Mondus believed that multi-catalogues were most suitable for urgent needs and small transaction volumes. Alexander Straub explained that a major problem for catalogue businesses was that customers could act as buyers only.

It is very difficult for catalogue businesses to attract buyers and it is often not cost efficient. We haven't seen the same problem at mondus since, in our marketplace environment, the buyer can also act as a seller and the seller as a buyer. People basically foster themselves.

Mondus did not want to own the catalogues, but to leverage its customer base when using multi-catalogues on its website.

Reverse auctions

Reverse auctions were usually applied in high value purchases, for instance, of A and B category products. The process itself was quite complicated because vendors had to be qualified and goods thoroughly specified. Mondus believed that for high-volume orders (e.g. purchasing 1000 laptops), this model was the best choice. When integrating reverse auctions into its website, mondus relied on standard auction engines that could be bought 'off the shelf'. The multi-

---

13 BME stands for Bundesverband Materialwirtschaft, Einkauf und Logistik e.V.

catalogue and reverse auction models were to be operational by the third quarter of 2000.

Seller-centric models

For some product categories, seller-centric models could be more suitable, especially in categories with few suppliers, such as electricity, gas or telecommunications. To offer such a service, mondus intended to select some power-suppliers[14] and co-operate with them. Leveraging the purchase power of its customers, mondus hoped to gain better prices. Negotiations were under way with Royal Dutch Shell. British Petroleum had also contacted mondus.

In the long run, Alexander Straub believed that extending into consumer-to-consumer models would be possible. 'Some people have maybe used equipment that they now want to sell for half of the original price, or put into an auction.'

International activities

International expansion

From the very beginning mondus focused on its international expansion. Subsidiaries were soon to be launched in Canada and Scandinavia, with others to follow in Spain, Poland, Austria and South Korea. Also market entry studies were to be conducted for Italy and Ireland. Because of Switzerland's multinational character and small market size, a future website would only provide links to the German, French and Italian sites. Christoph Pech explained how the international organization would look:

> A local office will be set up in each of the countries and run as a subsidiary of mondus.com ltd. The IT back office for all European activities will be located in the UK. For North America it will be in the US. When expanding to Asia a local back office will probably also be needed there. While a team based in Oxford will develop categories that work equally all over the world, the local offices will only be in charge of products and services related to their specific region.

Mondus also tried to have partnerships with multinational companies that offered their services in any country where mondus was present.

International sales

Although most SMEs did not sell their products and services nor fulfil their procurement needs globally, mondus believed that this situation would soon change. Straub explained: 'What I think is most attractive for international categories is everything that has to do with intellectual property and which can be delivered in a digital format and shipped across borders.' For example, software and translation services could be the first global categories.

Competition

The e-commerce market targeting SMEs was underdeveloped and fragmented. Market entry barriers were minimal since new competitors could launch, at relatively low cost, websites offering services and products to SMEs. In the Canadian and US markets, there were then two competitors providing an RFP model to the same customer segment (BizBuyer.com and Onvia.com). While Bizbuyer.com's business model was equivalent to that of mondus, Onvia.com initially started with a multi-catalogue model designed for small-sized enterprises.[15] From November 1999, it also provided an RFP model for business-related services as well as content (e.g. news, notices and downloads such as business plan checklists). Onvia.com had its initial public offering (IPO) in March 2000. In Germany, it had just begun working in co-operation with Mercateo.de, which could be accessed at Onvia.de. Mercateo.de also offered a multi-catalogue system and an RFP for services. In addition it tried to establish so-called pool buying, through which, based on the number of buyers willing to buy a product, the price of the product varies. That year, Mercateo.de planned to expand its operations into different European countries. The main competitor in the UK was buy.co.uk, which tried to sell not only to private businesses, but also to public agencies.

Furthermore, other Internet sites offered multi-catalogue models to SMEs, including Digitalwork.com and Works.com. Some sites originally targeting the consumer market also sold to small-sized enterprises (e.g. Beyond.com, Buy.com and Onsale.com). Large Internet players like Yahoo!, America Online and Microsoft also offered B2B e-commerce services or planned to do so in the near future. In addition, e-marketplaces set up by traditional multinational companies (such as the one in the automotive industry set up by General Motors, Ford and

---

14 Power-suppliers refer to suppliers with which mondus built a special relationship.

15 The company was founded as MegaDepot in 1997; in May 1999 it changed its name to Onvia.com.

DaimlerChrysler, or the one in retailing owned by Sears, Roebuck and Carrefour) could attract SMEs due to lower prices resulting from their bargaining power. However, Dr Heupel believed that mondus had a first-mover advantage: 'It must be our strategy to have a pool of users set up very quickly, so that we don't have to get customers off other websites but that others have to get them off ours.'

Customer perspective

The number of worldwide customers had increased significantly since mondus launched its first website in October 1999. As of 8 May 2000, there were 86,892 customers registered worldwide, 76% of whom were buyers (see Table 3). The average number of orders per active buyer was 1.9 (this percentage should be taken qualitatively only since some sellers had also placed RFPs). Active sellers had placed, on average, 9.7 bids. The most popular categories for RFPs were desktop and laptop PCs, computer accessories, printing services and web design; these were also the top five categories for quotes. A third of all quotes were submitted for web design and 13% for desktop PCs.

The average volume of quotes was about US$3000 worldwide; however, there was much data variation from week to week (see Exhibit 7). This was largely due to the different transaction volumes in the various product and service categories (e.g. transaction volumes for web design were significantly higher than for printing refills).

Buyer benefits

SMEs' demand for category C goods varied and trading volumes were usually small. Unlike large companies, SMEs could not effectively leverage their liquidity and bargaining power to streamline the procurement process and cut costs.

Streamlining the procurement process

Through mondus, the procurement process could be simplified, thus resulting in time and cost savings. Instead of selecting and negotiating with customers individually, procurement needs could be specified only once and quotes would be automatically requested and forwarded to the buyer. The buyer could then compare the offers and choose the one that best suited their requirements. Through its database of suppliers and the variety of services and products offered, mondus aimed to provide a one-stop procurement solution and increasing market and price transparency.

> Using mondus, I didn't have to call all my suppliers. The system will list the quotes in a way that makes it easy for me to decide. It also helps me to get a better feeling for the market and possible prices.
>
> **Marco Keilholz**, Managing Director, Office Forum, Germany

Table 3 Customer statistics per country for the period from the launch of the website until 8 May 2000

	UK	Germany	France	USA	Total
Website fully operational since	October 1999	November 1999	January 2000	October 1999	
Customers	51660	19227	354	15651	86892
Buyers	46488	15755	107	4065	66415
Who have placed RFPs	2304	1235	33	174	4846
Sellers	5172	3472	247	11586	9013
Who have placed quotes	1432	738	32	1124	3326
Who have placed RFPs	642	409	28	393	1472
Total number of PRFs	4086	2464	76	2387	9013
Total number of quotes	17904	6334	61	8188	32487
Quotes rejected	4015	1113	13	915	4056
Quotes accepted	129	82	0	33	244
Mean value of accepted quotes	£826	DM1904	–	US$2468	

On 8 May 2000, the exchange rates were: £1=US$1.5279; 1 DM=US$0.4586.

Source: mondus.com ltd.

Exhibit 7 Development of the average volume and the ratio of quotes per RFP in Germany (mondus.de)

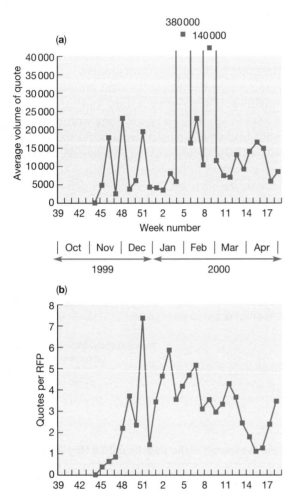

Source: mondus.com ltd.

Convenient and easy procedure

Customers found the mondus homepage and the matching process well structured, and both on and offline help was provided. The implementation of standardized request forms offered a quick and easy specification of products and services. Through the buy noticeboard, the buyer was kept informed of the current status of their requests. They could also view previous RFPs and quotes. Furthermore the website was available 24 hours a day, seven days a week.

Low investment and cost

Requirements to run the electronic mondus marketplace were minimal. Only a PC with a standard web browser, an e-mail programme and access to the Internet were required.

Customization

Although most of the RFP process was standardized and automated, individual specifications could be added to the request form using the open-format query or attached files. Quotes did not contain information only on the product and the price, but also on the guarantee and the goods' return policies. If needed, buyers could contact vendors and negotiate with them individually. It was also possible to extend deadlines and cancel an RFP at any time.

Confidentiality and safety

The buyer's identity was kept confidential until they accepted a quote or they contacted the seller. Through customer feedback, mondus was kept informed of supplier performance. Since mondus did not act as a seller itself, bias was avoided. For security reasons, encryption was used when credit card details were transmitted and customers were logged out automatically if they did not use the system for 20 minutes.

Seller benefits

Access to online trading and new market opportunities

As a study by MORI, a UK-based research institute, revealed: 'Most companies selling to SMEs see the Internet as a unique opportunity to gain and retain customers, with time and cost savings playing a major role in the drive to trade online.' However, for most SMEs trading online meant a massive commercial upheaval. They could lose online sales if they did not have the resources needed to launch professionally designed websites.[16] Mondus therefore proposed that, through its system, vendors could sell online without having to set up and maintain their own website as well as undertaking marketing activities. Access was provided to potential new customers with less lead-time and with reduced financial outlay. New distribution channels and sources of revenue could be created and possibilities for national and international expansion offered. According to Rouzbeh Pirouz:

---

16 'SMEs are flocking to buy and sell via the Internet', MORI, April 2000.

By trading through mondus, companies have the ability to exploit new markets without the expense of a bricks-and-mortar presence, or even a website. It presents the opportunity for small businesses to compete in new markets, against more established organizations.[17]

Mondus offers a huge spectrum of potential customers to me. Through its system I can get in contact with potential buyers that I would never have reached otherwise. Using mondus for four weeks, 30% of my revenues were already generated through it.

Andreas Schacky, owner of Schacky's Computer Laden, Germany explained:

According to Marco Keilholz, his company had not yet generated substantial business through mondus, but he believed there was a huge potential. 'You don't have to access customers individually and ask for their needs. Instead, the buyer specifies the product or service needed himself. This allows a seller to make individual offers without any acquisition costs.' He added:

From my perspective another benefit was that customers using mondus are generally open-minded about the Internet and new technologies. These are the customers that I'm interested in and that I like to do business with.

Using the mondus brand

It was often very difficult for SMEs to establish a brand. By aggregating the expertise of various suppliers, mondus eventually created a brand for specific services or products and drove customers to its website.

My company offers training. But there was always a trade-off because you can't make acquisitions and give courses at the same time. Through mondus, I hope to leverage their brand and get customers even when I'm teaching.

Alex Reyss, owner, Step4word, Germany

Gaining a competitive advantage

With SMEs gaining access to a larger market, they could leverage their smaller overheads against bigger competitors. Through customer-oriented offers, such as individual distribution arrangements or product-related services, SMEs could establish a niche in the market and possibly gain a competitive edge.

How customers used mondus

People have been using the site for purposes other than for what we intended.

Audrey Roser, Global Head of Customer Relations, mondus

Most buyers used the site to check prices, the number of quotes they could receive and the time it took. A survey revealed that 66% of all buyers just used mondus to see how it worked. Also a lot of suppliers used the website pretending that they were buyers to check the prices offered by their competitors.

Dropping out

Because of the revenue model adopted, it was important for mondus that customers followed through the process to the end and performed the transaction through mondus. Investigation showed customers dropping out of the process at different stages. First, not all vendors submitted quotes and RFPs could be left unanswered. In addition, most buyers did not get back to their buy notice-board to check the quotes. Because buyers had the option to contact sellers, the parties could go offline and close the deal without notifying mondus. Audrey Roser explained: '[If customers] go offline we have no way to track that effectively.' In other cases, buyers could decide to stick by their traditional suppliers or never close the deal. Because most SMEs, at least in the UK, did not have credit cards, invoices had to be sent, resulting in delayed payment.

Customers' complaints
Buyers' complaints

According to Audrey Roser, there was a lot of interest in the mondus concept but some quotes were not price-competitive and sometimes customers did not get enough quotes. Some buyers complained that they got quotes that did not match their RFP and thus were not relevant. Furthermore, others were unwilling to accept quotes from companies they did not know. However, according to mondus' research, customers would overlook brand if prices were good enough. In addition, response time was an important issue for buyers.

Sellers' complaints

Most vendors complained that they never got feedback on their quotes. One reason was that the majority of buyers never viewed the quotes they got nor followed them up. Other suppliers stated that they did not have the time to go through all the RFPs and send quotes for each of them. Many vendors felt unable to compete because they thought other suppliers offered better prices. This situation improved slightly once mondus

---

17 www.mondus.co.uk/mori/mori.cfm

no longer displayed the lowest quote. Others were frustrated with the model because the buyer was kept anonymous until the end unless the buyer contacted the vendor directly. This prevented the seller from doing their sales job. Some vendors stated that they could not give a price without actually talking to the buyer. 'If you were a supplier of a website, there was no way that you can give a price for a website based on the answers to ten questions.' Other customers suggested that mondus should ask buyers to shortlist some suppliers, which could then contact the buyer directly. Mondus in this case might charge the vendor for the service. At first there were also many complaints regarding technical problems as well as incorrect registrations that either prevented suppliers from accessing the right information or resulted in the receipt of RFP numbers for goods they were not selling.

Challenges for mondus

As a one-year-old company, mondus faced several challenges. How could it increase the number of deals closed? Could mondus recruit sufficiently qualified people to implement its expansion strategy? How was it going effectively to manage all of its activities in so many countries?

Increasing the number of deals closed
It was important for mondus to ensure that sufficient quotes were submitted on RFPs. Audrey Roser explained: '[The idea] was to have a lot of power suppliers, which are suppliers that agree to quote on a competitive level and with which we develop relationships. Currently we have power suppliers only for some categories but not [in] all of them.' Dr Heupel believed that there would be more quotes as the number of sellers grew and customers used the system more frequently. 'At first, there was only one offer per request. The number of offers was growing at a higher rate than that of registered users and RFPs. On average today you receive four offers per bid.'

Mondus also called buyers to validate orders and to ask for details that could prevent sellers from quoting. Once quotes were submitted, the customer service department called the buyer four days before the offer deadline expired to motivate them to look at their quotes and decide. Mondus hoped that this would also help filter out customers that were just testing the system (in this case mondus rejected all quotes and gave sellers instant feedback). If buyers rejected quotes, the system asked them

for feedback and offered different answers to choose from. By these means mondus hoped to get more information on customers' needs and decision criteria.

A major problem was that buyers and sellers only used mondus to get in contact with each other. Then they went offline and never returned to the system. Alexander Straub explained: 'We open the system up to the end, so negotiations can happen. We believe that this was very important to get the value to our business, especially in highly complex service categories.' He argued that mondus could prevent customers from staying offline if it offered additional services such as logistics, financing and insurance. 'At that time we know the whole process and we know the whole volume and we know about the charges.' Dr Heupel was not very worried about the small number of deals currently closed through mondus: 'Getting into the arithmetic was very difficult since often people register, look at our system and become active users later on. Plus we are growing very rapidly. So on what do you base your percentage?'

Recruitment
For Marcus Gerhardt, recruitment was one of the critical management issues at mondus. 'We are growing at a rate where it is very difficult to find qualified and relevant people who fit into our organization and still bring along the experience.' At first, mondus recruits were former university friends. Straub explained: 'At that time we had no other choice. People [in Europe] didn't know much about stock options.' In particular, professionals from the technical side preferred fixed salaries rather than share options. For Marcus Gerhardt recruiting through networking also had the advantage that 'at least you know the spirit was going to be right and you foster a certain company culture'.

Since those networks were by their nature limited, mondus had to use other means. Headhunter agencies were employed to find executives such as chief financial officer, chief operations officer and country managers. In terms of finding directors and assistant managers, these agencies were 'not helpful since they really didn't understand our needs and couldn't meet them very well', remembered Gerhardt. Instead mondus found the Internet to be a useful tool.[18] 'Our Director for Marketing and our Director for Business Development have come to

---

18 Most people applied through Internet sites like hotjobs.com, topjobs.com or monster.co.uk.

us through the Internet. They were early adopters of the Internet and brought along eight or ten years of experience in their field', he added.

Management challenges

Effectively managing all its activities was yet another major challenge for a rapidly growing company such as mondus. Dr Heupel noted:

> Focusing on the financial side to get enough money in, on the marketing side to get customers in, on the product development side in tailoring the product into a suitable form and balancing all these needs, that's a very difficult task.

The co-ordination of the four national markets and their office activities especially was a logistical challenge that needed a good communication structure in place.

Furthermore, the company was in a state of transition. While its vision was still founder-led, in terms of its processes mondus had already found its own way. Alexander Straub said: 'I have realized that very experienced managers with 10–15 years' work are much more effective than me because they know the processes.' In January 2000 Straub stepped down as the head of the US office and became Vice-Chairman of the Board of Directors. Whether Rouzbeh Pirouz stayed in the long-term as the CEO of mondus was still an open question.

Future outlook

Mondus was planning an initial public offering at the end of 2000. 'The timing of the IPO will depend primarily on whether it suits the company's development and on market conditions', explained Marcus Gerhardt.

> As for evaluation, it won't make any sense to engage now in any projections, especially in light of the current market volatility … In the future, it will be important for mondus to consolidate the four markets [where we currently operate] without becoming an overburdened organization. The high level of productivity was our big plus over established players that have the SME relations that we are seeking, the money that we could never hope to get and the resources that we would never have.

Whether mondus could sustain its business model in the medium- to long-term was still an open question. According to AMR Research, 'bankruptcy, mergers, and acquisitions could swallow up as much as 90% of the current crop of online B2B marketplaces.'[19] George Reilly, Research Director at the GardnerGroup, shared this view: 'There will be a consolidation of [electronic] marketplaces. And the winners will be those that can execute transactions with value added.'[20]

---

19 Enos, L., 'Report: most online marketplaces will vanish', *e-Commerce Times*, 26 April 2000.
20 Dembeck, C., 'B2B ventures losing their allure', *e-Commerce Times*, 11 April 2000.

CASE STUDY 7

Covisint (A)
The evolution of a B2B marketplace

The key to the success of any company is articulating a business problem that it will solve for a target market and then aligning its resources to solve that problem. Covisint was founded to address a massive business problem inside the automotive supply chain amounting to billions of dollars in inefficiencies and waste. I came to Covisint because I believed its vision of seamless data flow across the supply chain could solve this problem.

Bob Paul, Senior Vice President, Sales and Marketing, Covisint at the time of the case[1]

Throughout much of the twentieth century, the automotive industry was dominated by three original equipment manufacturers (OEMs): Ford Motor Company, General Motors, and Chrysler, the latter of which merged with Daimler Benz in 1998 to become DaimlerChrysler. Within the industry, these three large OEMs became known as 'the Big 3.' Throughout its history, the industry had been rigidly hierarchical, with the OEMs at the top primarily ordering from large Tier 1 suppliers such as Johnson Controls and Delphi, which, in turn, bought parts and supplies from smaller Tier 2 suppliers, which bought from yet-smaller Tier 3 and smaller suppliers. This hierarchical industry structure resulted in cumbersome processes, inefficiencies, and a strong culture of distrust among industry players (see Exhibit 1).

During the 1970s, the American OEMs began steadily losing market share to foreign competitors (see Exhibit 2) – especially Japanese OEMs. Lean, flexible manufacturing and kieretsu-style supply chains enabled Japanese OEMs to build and deliver cars more quickly and at much less cost, which put increasing pressure on American OEMs. The Big 3 launched Covisint in February 2000 as an industry supply chain exchange that would drive out cost and help manage the complexity. At the time, one company executive explained the vision as follows:

> At the same time that OEMs were striving to get leaner and more flexible, automobiles were becoming more highly engineered and complex. This put increasing pressure on inefficient supply chains that were already struggling to keep pace with the relentless pace of competition and changing consumer demands. Covisint was envisioned as a hub that would sit within the network of industry relationships to simplify and decrease the cost of coordinating and managing the increasing pace and complexity. There's tremendous value in making it easier to do business and share information within this network.

> For decades, this industry has been chasing the holy grail – the build-to-order or five-day car. What kept the industry from achieving this goal was that it was never wired together. If Covisint could become the 'industry operating system,' we could make it easier for everyone to do business in the industry. We are uniquely positioned to accomplish that vision.[2]

At the time it was launched, dot-com fever was at its peak, and the Big 3 expected Covisint to go public within a year or two with a market cap of $30 billion to $40 billion and annual revenues of $3 billion. But the dot-com crash, less than one month after the company

---

1 Author interview, June 2004. Bob Paul joined Covisint in 2001 as SVP, sales and marketing.
2 Author interview, January 2002.

Professor Lynda M. Applegate and Research Associate Elizabeth L. Collins prepared this case. HBS cases are developed solely as the basis for class discussion. Cases are not intended to serve as endorsements, sources of primary data, or illustrations of effective or ineffective management.

Exhibit 1 Traditional automotive industry supply chain

Leadership and governance	OEMs defined strategic direction and set policies and standards for the industry. Except for highly engineered and niche products/services, OEMs contracted directly with Tier 1 suppliers that, in turn, subcontracted with lower-tier players.
Information flow, coordination, and control	Information flows were hierarchical, and operations and performance were managed using a top-down command-and-control structure. In most cases, structured contracts defined work to be completed, information to be shared, and measures of performance. Information on any changes to the agreed-upon requirements often took place in an *ad hoc* manner with multiple channels conveying conflicting information and often reaching suppliers days or weeks after changes were made. Incompatible data formats and proprietary systems and processes made it difficult to streamline and integrate operations within and across boundaries inside industry participants and across the industry. Industry participants found it difficult to monitor progress and decisions made at each step in the chain.
Operations	Processes were structured to conform to contractual production and quality requirements. Work was typically performed in a sequential fashion with each work team passing a finished product to the next team in the sequence.
Infrastructure	Proprietary infrastructure, including operating, computing, and communications technologies, created ëwallš' between industry participants and between development teams. Duplication of effort and resources increased the cost and decreased productivity.

Source: Authors.

was announced, delayed the dream of instant return on investment. In addition, the distrust in the industry delayed the dream of immediate cost savings and improved agility. Suppliers viewed the exchange as a tool for OEMs to exert more power, and Covisint's OEM founders continued to pour money into duplicate and even competitive supply chain solutions.

It was now early 2003. While Covisint had been successful in growing revenue to $40 million to $50 million, it had yet to turn a profit. There had been six CEOs[3] since the company was founded and three in the last two years. Analysts and trade press reports were predicting Covisint's imminent demise.

Bob Paul had a decision to make. The next day he was having breakfast with Gary Valade, executive vice president at DaimlerChrysler, and Ralph Szygenda, GM's CIO. 'Each of these men controls $100 billion in purchasing power; their decisions influence the U.S. economy. It's amazing that they are troubling themselves with this nit of a company,' he mused. Paul knew the purpose of the breakfast meeting: Valade and Szygenda would ask him to become the next CEO of Covisint. 'What should I say?' he wondered. 'That I hope I keep the job longer than the last CEO, who left after 31 days? I believe strongly in the vision for Covisint and can't help but worry that I could end up being the one running the company when it failed.

Should I accept the position and try to save the company? If so, under what conditions?'[4]

Launching Covisint

> We're going to create the world's biggest, fastest, largest exchange for transacting business on the Internet.
>
> **Harold Kutner**, former VP, Purchasing, GM, and one of the founding visionaries of Covisint[5]

By the late 1990s, the Big 3's market share had been eroding for two decades (see Exhibit 2). One reason for the erosion was that the American OEMs did not have the processes in place to sense fast-moving customer trends (see Exhibit 3). Historical sales data, once a reliable indicator, was no longer an adequate guide to future demand. Nor did the Big 3 have the processes in place to respond to customer trends had they been sensed. Even more important, there was a 'glaring gap'

---

3 When Covisint was founded, these executives from the three OEMs shared the CEO responsibilities: Peter Weiss from DaimlerChrysler, Alice Miles from Ford, and Enrico Digirolamo from General Motors.

4 Author interview, June 2004.

5 Jamie Butters and Jeff Bennett, 'Covisint hits rough patch as business falling flat,' *Detroit Free Press*, December 9, 2002.

Exhibit 2 Loss of market share by American automotive OEMs

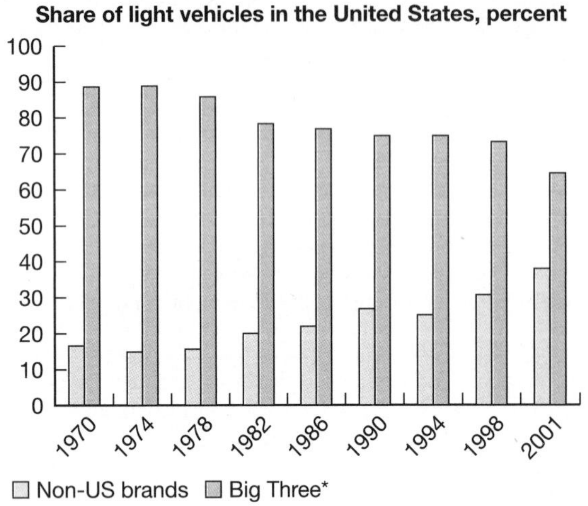

Share of light vehicles in the United States, percent

☐ Non-US brands ■ Big Three*

* Chrysler (DaimlerChrysler since 1998 merger), Ford, General Motors.

Source: Adapted by authors, using Niladri Ganguli, T.V. Kumaresh, Aurobind Satpathy, 'Detroit's new quality gap', *The McKinsey Quarterly*, Number 1, 2003, p.149. Original source of the data: *Words Automotive Yearbook*, McKinsey analysis.

between American and Japanese competitors. The Japanese were able to bring high-quality 'on-demand' vehicles to market years before the Americans could offer competing products in the same class.[6]

Furthermore, the Japanese OEMs were able to fulfill customer orders for their new models much faster than the American Big 3. They supported a relatively small number of options packages on their different models and maintained a large inventory of cars at their U.S. dealers. Then, using a 'ship-in-five-days' model, the Japanese OEMs allowed dealers to ship cars on their lots to any other dealer in response to a customer request. Given the small number of options packages, it was highly likely that the car a customer requested would be immediately available on some dealer's lot.

Global competition also imposed downward pressure on consumer costs in the U.S., tightening the vise on the American OEMs. Real car prices fell 2.6% between January 1997 and October 2001. DaimlerChrysler, for example, was forced to sell its 1999 Jeep Grand Cherokee at $250 less than the 1998 model, despite the later model's redesign and improved equipment[7] (see Exhibit 4 for the consumer price index for new vehicles, 1997 to 2004). Union contracts in the

U.S. made it even more difficult to compete on price with foreign competition. GM, for example, was forced to tack on $1,800 per vehicle produced to cover health and pension benefits for its workers.[8]

To reverse the erosion in their market share, the American Big 3 sought to leapfrog the Japanese and implement an ambitious 'build-in-five-days' model. The vision was to deliver the exact set of options each customer wanted (rather than a preset package of options that approximated the customer's wishes, as the Japanese did) and to do so at lightning speed. Dell had pioneered a similar business model in the computer industry and in the process slashed cycle time for a customer order from 92 to 13 days. At the same time, Dell was able to deliver the exact configuration of options selected by each customer (see Exhibit 3 for the build-to-order model from the information technology industry). In the boardrooms of the Big 3, Dell's model was continually referenced as the key to the solution.

To implement this vision, Detroit decided to source large components of a car – for example, the entire interior – from large Tier 1 suppliers, which would in turn source the parts they needed from smaller suppliers. Cars would be built from a small number of modules designed for reuse across product lines. By limiting the number of partners to Tier 1 and by using online technologies to support collaboration and performance tracking, the OEMs hoped that cycle times could be shortened and costs could be driven out (see Exhibit 5 for a comparison of modular and nonmodular automotive design). Forrester analysts predicted that the shift to a component manufacturing approach would slash 21% of development costs (see Exhibit 6 for the calculations supporting this prediction), and one automaker quoted in the report estimated that streamlining the supply chain, with a shift to collaborative design and development and simultaneous improvements in information flow, would shorten the firm's product development life cycle from six years to three.[9]

6 W. Daniel Garretson, 'Building tier zero auto collaboration,' Forrester, January 2002.

7 'U.S. industry & trade outlook,' U.S. Department of Commerce, McGraw-Hill, 2000, as quoted in W. Daniel Garretson, 'Building tier zero auto collaboration,' Forrester, January 2002.

8 Danny Hakim, 'How long can G.M. tread water?' *The New York Times*, March 11, 2005.

9 W. Daniel Garretson, 'Building tier zero auto collaboration,' Forrester, January 2002.

Exhibit 3 **Build-to-order models from IT industry**

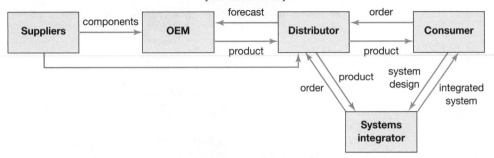

IT industry (1997)

Build-to-forecast (Traditional)
cycle time = 92 days

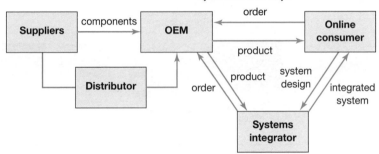

Dell Build-to-Order (1997)
cycle time = 13 days

Source: Authors.

Exhibit 4 **Five-year consumer price index for new vehicles, 1997–2004**

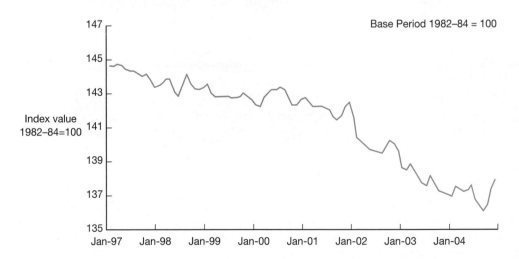

Source: Authors created from U.S. Bureau of Labor Statistics data (http://www.bls.gov/).

Exhibit 5 Modular and nonmodular design

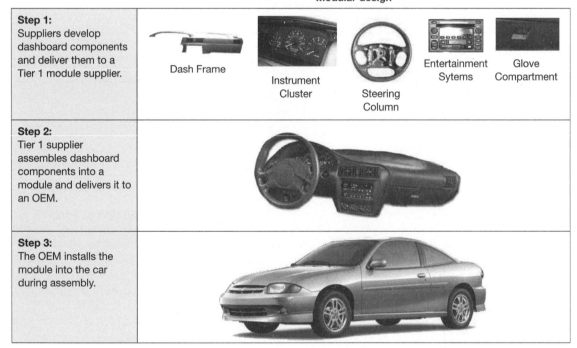

Nonmodular design

| Step 1:
Suppliers develop dashboard components and deliver them to OEMs. | Dash Frame | Instrument Cluster | Steering Column | Entertainment Sytems | Glove Compartment |
| Step 2:
OEMs install components into a car during assembly. | | | | | |

Modular design

Step 1: Suppliers develop dashboard components and deliver them to a Tier 1 module supplier.	Dash Frame	Instrument Cluster	Steering Column	Entertainment Sytems	Glove Compartment
Step 2: Tier 1 supplier assembles dashboard components into a module and delivers it to an OEM.					
Step 3: The OEM installs the module into the car during assembly.					

Source: Authors from company documents.

A successful online exchange that united the industry was vital to move the industry to what many were calling an 'on-demand' supply chain model. Information about orders – what suppliers needed to ship and when – could flow through the exchange, creating an environment, as Kutner explained, in which the OEMs could 'sense our requirements versus ordering and stockpiling supplies.'[10] Quality concerns could also be handled in real time, with the source identified quickly before members of the

10 Lauren Gibbons Paul, 'B2B e-commerce: the biggest gamble yet,' *CIO Magazine*, April 15, 2000.

Exhibit 6 Forrester predictions on cost savings from vehicle modularization

Savings per Project

Traditional U.S. new car development cost	$700 million
Savings due to expanded data access	–16 million
Savings due to streamlined information flow	–70 million
Savings due to improved project coordination	–58 million
Modular development with Internet-based tools cost	$556 million
Total savings per project	$145 million (21% of total project costs)

Savings per Vehicle

U.S. vehicle cost in 2001	$18,950
Projected savings	–$241
Savings due to module reuse during production and future development	–$134
Modular development with Internet-based supply chain cost	$18,575
Total savings per vehicle	$375 (2% of total vehicle costs)

Source: Adapted from W.D. Garretson et al., 'Building tier zero auto collaboration', Forrester Research, January 2002.

supply chain created millions of dollars of defective products using a component. In the late 1990s, each of the Big 3 announced plans to launch a proprietary online exchange even as heavily funded dot-com start-ups attempted to enter with neutral third-party exchanges.

But the February 25, 2000 announcement of Covisint, followed closely by the bursting of the dot-com bubble, ended the jockeying for power. Given the size of its founders, the potential volume of orders that could flow through Covisint was huge. At the time of the announcement, Ford spent $80 billion annually on procurement of parts, GM $85 billion, and Daimler Chrysler $73 billion, and the Big 3 accounted for 18% of the world's steel production. Handling even a small percentage of these volumes would instantly make Covisint the dominant business-to-business (B2B) industry exchange, bypassing approximately 2,000 other exchanges in operation at the time, including the 150 already used by automakers and suppliers. One of the early Covisint employees described Covisint as the 'Lewis and Clark' of industry consortia exchanges, blazing the way for similar exchanges in industries

characterized by 'an enormous amount of inventory trapped in the supply chain, large numbers of buyers and sellers, and many layers of involvement and communication.'[11]

Opinions differed concerning why the Big 3 changed course and joined in this 'unnatural marriage,' as GM's Kutner called the agreement.[12] Certainly the suppliers had painted a vivid picture of the technological nightmare they would have faced interacting with three different exchanges, each using different standards. Others saw the impetus as purely monetary: 'Such turnabouts are natural when so much money is at stake.'[13] 'Everyone at the table understood that this [was] the largest deal in e-commerce history by a factor of about 100,' said John Sviokla, vice chairman of Diamond Technology Partners, a consulting firm assigned the task of helping Oracle and CommerceOne

---

11 Eiler Communications, 'Q&A with Covisint's Shankar Kiru: creating a successful electronic exchange,' March 19, 2002.
12 Lauren Gibbons Paul, 'B2B e-commerce: the biggest gamble yet,' *CIO Magazine*, April 15, 2000.
13 Ibid.

Exhibit 7 Covisint timeline

February 2000	On February 25, 2000, Ford Motor Company, General Motors, DaimlerChrysler, Oracle, and CommerceOne announced their intention to combine efforts and form an automotive industry global platform for doing business, initially with suppliers, and later with all industry players.
April 2000	Renault of France and Nissan of Japan announced their intention to take a 5% equity stake (4% from Renault and 1% from Nissan) in Covisint and take a leadership role in developing European and Asian headquarters.
September 2000	Covisint received clearance from the FTC on September 11, 2000 and from the German Bundeskartellamt 12 days later on September 23. The European Union approved Covisint in July 2001.
October 2000	Covisint launched its first live auction on October 3, 2000. Its initial product suite included software and services for conducting auctions, managing online catalogs, and managing quotes.
December 2000	Covisint became a legal entity on December 8, 2000. The organization was structured as a multi-member joint venture limited liability corporation. In August 2001, Covisint Inc., a C corporation, was formed to act as a holding company and support long-term growth initiatives, including an initial public offering (IPO).
January 2001	On January 24, 2001, Covisint announced the names of 12 members of the board of directors. The board was eventually expanded to 17.
April 2001	Kevin English was named CEO and chairman on April 18, 2001.
May 2001	Covisint Europe was formed in May 2001, and European headquarters were opened in Amsterdam. Covisint Japan (a K.K. corporation) was formed in July 2001, and Asian headquarters were opened in Tokyo.
May 2001	PSA Peugeot Citroën announced their commitment to take an equity stake in Covisint. They joined to make use of Covisint's collaborative e-commerce, procurement, and supply chain management capabilities. PSA Peugeot Citroën eventually joined the Covisint European Advisory Council.
September 2001	On September 11, 2001, Covisint announced its commitment to begin development of its portal solution product. Pilots were implemented at Delphi, Ford, and General Motors.
Early 2002	By early 2002, Covisint had announced five solution suites: collaboration, procurement, portal, supply chain, and quality.
February 2002	The newly formed Global Customer Council, which included suppliers and automakers from around the world, replaced an earlier customer council and announced its intention to meet quarterly to help plan strategy and its execution.
April 2002	Covisint reorganized into two strategic business units: strategic sourcing (supply, pricing, auctions) and portal and connectivity (communications between manufacturers and suppliers). Senior vice president Mark Duhaime became acting general manager of strategic sourcing and Kevin Vasconi, Covisint's chief technology officer, became general manager of portal and connectivity.
June 2002	English resigns.
July 2002	Harold Kutner, former GM group vice president, worldwide purchasing, becomes CEO, and Bruce Swift, former vice president of purchasing for Ford in Europe, becomes president and COO. Almost one-third of the Covisint staff (approximately 100 people) are laid off.
November 2002	Lease is signed for smaller, cheaper office space.
December 2002	Covisint has best sales quarter ever.
January 2003	Covisint membership surpasses 76,000.
February 2003	Bruce Swift becomes CEO and quits 31 days later to become a president of Metaldyne.
March 2003	Covisint establishes Lain American sales and service office.

Source: Authors (based on Covisint Web site, http://www.covisint.com/about/history/, accessed on July 26, 2004).

come to terms for the launch.[14] By the end of 2000, two more OEMs (Renault of France and Nissan of Japan) had joined as investors, and 25 auto suppliers joined as members (see Exhibit 7 for a timeline).

The announcement drew immediate regulatory attention, given the size and clout of the three founding companies, which represented 44% of the total goods

---

14 Ibid.

sold in the global automobile industry ($379 billion) and 91% of the $20 billion annual net profits. Both the U.S. Federal Trade Commission (FTC) and the European Union (EU) conducted reviews during the early days of Covisint. During the reviews, no employees could be hired. Instead, a small number of employees were 'borrowed' from each of the Big 3, and a large number of consultants (over 400 by 2001) were brought in to develop the 'go-to-market' strategy and products. During this time, the company was run by three co-CEOs – one from each of the three founding companies.

While it was initially envisioned that Covisint would operate as an application service provider (ASP) – developing and hosting supply chain applications for industry participants – the FTC approval was contingent on Covisint limiting its sphere of control to activities and processes outside the firewalls, or company boundaries, of industry participants (see Exhibit 8 for the evolution of Covisint's strategy).

Having secured approval from the FTC and EU and with over $250 million in funding from its three founders, Covisint geared up for launch of its go-to-market offering. 'It was a speed-to-market thing. Forget expenses, just go,' said Rick Stephenson, Covisint's VP, operations and planning.[15] First on the agenda for the

OEM founders was a system to enable online auctions, which was expected to streamline the procurement process and significantly reduce OEM costs (see Exhibit 9 for a description of the auction process). Covisint licensed its auction software from a software vendor, sacrificing intellectual property for speed to market. This same process was used for many of the other applications launched during the company's first two years of existence (see Exhibit 10 for a list of applications and development partners).

The auction software was an immediate success for both Covisint and its OEM founders; in the last few months of 2000, for example, DaimlerChrysler conducted 27 auctions through Covisint, saving 17% on procurement costs for the OEM founders.[16] Volumes traded in a single auction could be huge. For example, in one four-day auction in 2001, DaimlerChrysler bought approximately $2.6 billion in auto parts (more than a quarter's gross sales at eBay, the premier consumer auction Web site).[17]

15 Author interview, June 2004.
16 'DaimlerChrysler reduces costs through online purchasing,' DaimlerChrysler news, December 22, 2000.
17 Peter Loftus, 'Making it work,' *The Wall Street Journal Online*, February 11, 2002.

Exhibit 8 Evolution of Covisint strategy

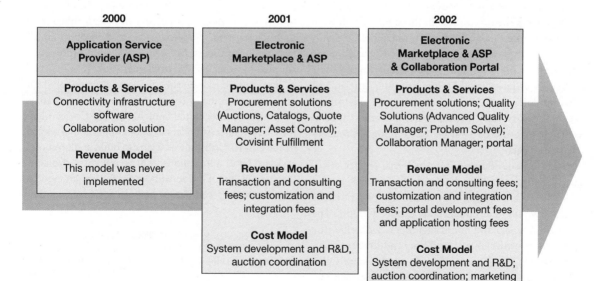

2000	2001	2002
Application Service Provider (ASP)	**Electronic Marketplace & ASP**	**Electronic Marketplace & ASP & Collaboration Portal**
Products & Services Connectivity infrastructure software Collaboration solution	**Products & Services** Procurement solutions (Auctions, Catalogs, Quote Manager; Asset Control); Covisint Fulfillment	**Products & Services** Procurement solutions; Quality Solutions (Advanced Quality Manager; Problem Solver); Collaboration Manager; portal
Revenue Model This model was never implemented	**Revenue Model** Transaction and consulting fees; customization and integration fees	**Revenue Model** Transaction and consulting fees; customization and integration fees; portal development fees and application hosting fees
	Cost Model System development and R&D, auction coordination	**Cost Model** System development and R&D; auction coordination; marketing and sales

Source: Authors.

Exhibit 9 Covisint online auction process

Step	Action
1	Big 3 purchasing manager contacts Covisint with a parts order.
2	Covinist auction engineer sets up the auction. The engineer asks for details such as data and time of the auction, parts numbers, descriptions, volumes, opening price of the maximum amount the buyer is willing to pay.
3	Auction engineer receives list of suppliers to invite, typically ranging from 3 to 20 and ranging in size from $50 million annual revenue to $1 billion.
4	Auction engineer gives buyer and invited suppliers a password for the online auction. Suppliers are given the details of what the automaker wants to buy (this information is also available on the covisint Web site).
5	Auction engineer runs a trial auction with the suppliers to ensure they know what to do. The engineer might enter an auto part, for example, with an opening bid, and would then ensure suppliers knew how to respond.
6	Over 10 to 45 minutes, supplers place bids, which they can adjust by viewing other bids in real time (invited suppliers can see the top bids but not who made them). The auction engineer is available through instant messaging to answer questions or provide updates. A covisint auction engineer also is present with the Big 3 buyer during the auction.
7	If a bid is placed within the last minute of the auction, the auction is automatically extended for another three minutes.

Prior to moving online, auto supply auctions could require days if not weeks while suppliers faxed or mailed in bids blind (with no opportunity to know the bids others were making). Big 3 purchasing managers might then ask for a new round of bidding or call a specific supplier and ask for a lower quote.

Source: Adapted from Peter Loftus, 'Making it work,' *The Wall Street Journal Online*, February 11, 2002.

Suppliers were less enthusiastic. From the suppliers' point of view, the excess costs in the supply chain were being squeezed out of their profit margins. Covisint, they argued, was allowing the OEMs to turn all parts and supplies into commodity items, destroying their ability to differentiate. As one supplier put it, 'All Covisint does is look for low bids. It's just a bid-trolling process.'[18] Covisint's protests that it was a neutral exchange that offered a variety of sourcing approaches fell on deaf ears.[19]

With revenues flowing from its initial service offerings, Covisint began development of new services that would be built on proprietary software applications for which it would retain intellectual property rights. The OEMs, as owners and board members, controlled the selection of projects that would be undertaken; however, the OEMs all had different needs. 'One OEM might need a good quote management system,' explained Paul, 'others could care less because they already had built their own quote management systems

that were working fine.' As a result, Covisint became a 'skunkworks' development organization that served multiple masters. 'We were forced to develop multimillion-dollar projects for one OEM that were never adopted by other OEMs,' explained Paul.[20]

Even getting widespread adoption within an OEM was difficult, with some of the early systems still being rolled out five years after initial launch. Nor did Covisint have the clout to force suppliers to adopt applications selected by the OEMs. 'Covisint was trying to build and promote a standard set of applications to drive out costs,' explained Stephenson, 'but it did so without paying any attention to the investments companies had already made on their

---

18 David Sedgwick, Ralph Kisiel, Robert Sherefkin, 'Kutner has tough task at Covisint,' *Automotive News*, June 30, 2002.

19 Though the culture of distrust was particularly strong in the automotive industry, other industry exchanges also found that auctions alienated suppliers. Bruce Temkin, 'The industry consortia lifeline,' Forrester, August 2001.

20 Author interview, June 2004.

Exhibit 10 Covisint product lines in Spring 2002

Application	Category	Development Partners	Users
Advanced Quality Planner (AQP)	Support APQP process by easily allowing the exchange of key quality information	Powerway (Covisint had a revenue share)	DCX, Ford, GM, other suppliers
Asset Marketplace	Enables sale and purchase of used/excess assets; integrated with ARS	Covisint developed; revenue share with services partners (Dovebid, Asset Trade, etc.)	Partners
Asset Recovery System (ARS)	Tracking, categorization, and management of a company's physical assets	None (Covisint developed)	GM
Auctions	Event-based sourcing for direct material	CommerceOne (Covisint had a revenue share)	DCX, Ford, GM, Mitsubishi, Nissan, PSA, Renault, Fiat, and each event's required supplier participants
Catalog	Online catalog purchasing and fulfillment of MRO material and select services	CommerceOne (Covisint had a revenue share)	DCX, GM, PSA, Reynolds & Reynolds (dealers), hundreds of MRO suppliers
Collaboration Manager	Virtual project workspace for project teams	Matrix One replaced Nexprise (Covisint had a revenue share)	Renault, PSA, GM, BMW, and other smaller users
Fulfillment	Vendor-managed inventory and visibility	Supply Solutions (now Tradebeam) (Covisint had a revenue share)	DCX and Magna were in pilot.
Portal	Secure, scalable, single point of connectivity for trading partner user access to applications and content	Covisint developed	DCX, Ford, Delphi, Lear Freightliner, Mitsubishi, and Visteon added in 2003
Problem solver	Tool for coordinating and managing the estimated 3.2 million cases of assembly plant problems generated per year in the automotive industry	Covisint developed with Delphi support	Delphi and other OEMs
Quote manager	Document management, analysis, and collaboration tool supporting the automotive sourcing process (eRFX)	Matrix One (Covisint had a revenue share)	Renault, PSA GM drove development and piloted but never deployed across organization
WebEx	Web conferencing	Covinist was a reseller	GM

Source: Developed by authors based on Covisint company records and interviews.

own unique applications for their own unique needs.'[21] Every attempt at such standardization, remembered Paul, raised anxiety and ran into roadblocks. Laurie Orlov, Forrester research director, e-business applications, expressed her concerns:

Being a buying service sounds good, but who's responsible if the transaction goes wrong? What if the suppliers' suppliers aren't online? Something this intergalactic will

_____
21 Ibid.

be very hard to make succeed. . . . There is a very real danger that the suppliers' purchasing process will remain largely paper based. I could see them saying they're trading online but then [the suppliers are] faxing, calling, and printing behind the scenes.[22]

An even larger hurdle was organizational: the new technologies could not fix cumbersome and convoluted processes or allay distrust in the supply chain. Value would remain 'locked away' until organizational and interorganizational changes could be made.[23] OEMs had difficulty trusting supply chain partners with proprietary design information, communication pathways were still slowed by a tangle of Tier 2 and 3 suppliers, and the lack of industry design standards made it difficult to reuse components across product lines.[24] Indeed, many industry-sponsored exchanges cited organizational and business process incompatibilities and lack of trust as the primary obstacles to success.[25]

Kevin English takes the helm

When I first came to Covisint in April 2001, the spending was out of control. There were approximately 400 consultants working in the company at a cost of approximately $300,000 per day. At times, consultant expenses approached $20 million per month. A venture capital friend of mine said that, in the 25 years he had worked in the industry, he had never seen anything like it. On my third day on the job, we had our first board meeting, and I laid out my concerns about the spending. Within one week, we had cut the number of consultants to about 50 or 60 and, by the end of the year, our total expenses were running about $8.5 million per month.

Kevin English, former CEO, Covisint[26]

Having secured approval from the FTC and EU, Covisint's OEM co-CEOs formed a new board (see Exhibit 11 for a history of the board's membership) and began the search for a non-OEM CEO. On May 1, 2001, Kevin English was hired as CEO. English had led TheStreet.com to a $100 million initial public offering (IPO) in 1999, and the board hoped that he would be able to prepare Covisint for an IPO once the economy improved. The year 2000 had seen a record high in auto demand in the U.S., with 1.4 million vehicles sold.[27] However, as early as the second quarter of 2001, revenues plunged as a global recession dampened demand.[28] By year-end 2001, profits at Chrysler and Ford dropped $4.7 billion and $5.5 billion, respectively[29] and, as the saying went, 'when the OEMs got a cold, the

suppliers developed pneumonia.' In 2001 alone, five Tier 1 suppliers filed for Chapter 11 bankruptcy.[30] The top 10 Tier 1 suppliers experienced decreases in sales equal to $9.7 billion, or 11.2%, in that year (compared with an increase of $2.4 billion in 2000).[31] Forrester analysts predicted that the 8,000 Tier 1 players would be thinned to 400 before the end of the decade.[32]

As the industry struggled, English instituted a range of measures to rein in Covisint's costs without harming its growth. He recognized that, as access to capital declined, many of the B2B industry consortia would 'run out of money long before they achieve their grandiose visions.'[33] In summer 2001, English laid out a path to profitability by Q4 2002:

By July [2001] we started to hit our stride, and the revenues started picking up. At a board meeting in July, I drew a line in the sand and said that my revenue projection for 2001 was $51 million. I also said that by late 2001, the cash spend would be $8 million to $10 million per month or less. We hit our numbers, achieving $50.8 million in 2001 revenues and reducing our total cash spending to $8.5 million. We feel good about what we accomplished, but we aren't going to take our foot off the gas. Our plan for 2002 is to reach over $60 million in revenues and to be profitable by Q4. This means we will need to cut our costs to between $5 million to $6 million per month and grow our revenue to $93 million. We also need to change the product/market mix. In 2001, 93% of our revenues came from OEMs and only 7% came from suppliers. Our 2002 budget is based on increasing the percentage of revenues from suppliers to 42%. In 2001, 90% of our revenues came from our auction/

22 Lauren Gibbons Paul, 'B2B e-commerce: the biggest gamble yet,' *CIO Magazine*, April 15, 2000.
23 Mark Dixon Bunger, 'Intercompany change fuels post-recession growth,' Forrester TechStrategy Research, May 6, 2002.
24 W. Daniel Garretson, 'Building tier zero auto collaboration,' Forrester, January 2002.
25 Bruce Temkin, 'The industry consortia lifeline,' Forrester, August 2001.
26 Author interview, January 2002.
27 Stefan Menzel, 'The Europe 500: Automotive,' *The Wall Street Journal Online*, at www.wsj.com.
28 NikkoSalomonSmithBarney, 'Autos 2002 Outlook,' February 12, 2002.
29 Glenn Rifkin, 'GM's Internet overhaul,' *Technology Review*, October 2002.
30 Mark Dixon Bunger, 'Intercompany change fuels post-recession growth,' Forrester TechStrategy Research, May 6, 2002.
31 Robert Sherefkin, 'Top 150 suppliers: industry downturn roils supplier rankings,' *Automotive News*, March 25, 2002.
32 W. Daniel Garretson, 'Auto suppliers strike back,' Forrester, September 2001.
33 Bruce Temkin, 'The industry consortia lifeline,' Forrester, August 2001.

Exhibit 11 Covisint board, 2001–early 2003

2001	2002	Early 2003
J.T. Battenberg III An industry veteran and chairman, chief executive, and president of Delphi Automotive Systems, one of the World's largest suppliers	**J.T. Battenberg III**	**J.T. Battenberg III**
Laurent Bourrelier A well-known executive in the European auto industry and vice president of business-to-business e-commerce for Renault	**Laurent Bourrelier**	**Laurent Bourrelier**
Brian P. Kelley Vice president of Ford Motor [Company], head of the automaker's e-commerce ventures, and one of the founding strategic executives of Covisint	**Karen C. Francis** (joined board January 28, 2002) Vice president, Ford Motor Company, and president and CEO of ConsumerConnect, a Ford enterprise; replaced Brian Kelly, who left to become president of Ford Motor Company's Lincoln Mercury division	**Mark Malcolm** Director, global purchasing, Ford; served in several positions at Ford since joining in 1977.
James H. Keyes Chairman and chief executive of Johnson Controls, one of the first suppliers to have agreed to participate in Covisint	**John M. Barth** (joined board January 29, 2002) President and chief operating officer, Johnson Controls. Replaced James Keyes, who left to focus on the issues directly affecting JCI.	**John M. Barth**
Olaf Koch Vice president for corporate e-commerce for DaimlerChrysler, one of the original three founding partners of Covisint	**Olaf Koch**	**Olaf Koch**
Edward G. Krubasik A professor and member of the corporate executive committee for German electronics giant Siemens	**Edward G. Krubasik**	**Edward G. Krubasik**
Harold R. Kutner Group vice president in charge of worldwide purchasing and North American logistics for General Motors	**Harold R. Kutner**	**Bo Andersson** Vice president, GM worldwise purchasing, production control & logistics (Andersson took on Kutner's role at GM when Kutner retired in 2003)
Carlos E. Mazzorin Group vice president for global purchasing at Ford and a well-known executive in Detroit	**Carlos E. Mazzorin**	**Tony Brown** Vice president, global purchasing, Ford
Ralph J. Szygenda Group vice president and chief information officer of GM, widely credited for streamlining the information technology processes at the world's largest manufacturing company	**Ralph J. Szygenda**	**Ralph J. Szygenda**
Gary C. Valade Executive vice president for global procurement and supply at DaimlerChrysler and one of the few senior American executives to have survived a massive shakeout at the merged automaker	**Gary C. Valade**	**Peter Weiss** At the time of Covisint's founding, Weiss was DaimlerChrysler's project director, e-extended enterprise, and a key member of the Big 3 executive team at the exchange.
James H. Vandenberghe Vice chairman of Lear, another large supplier that became an early and enthusiastic advocate of Covisint	**James H. Vandenberghe**	**James H. Vandenberghe**
Don Walker President and chief executive of Canadian supplier Magna International	**Don Walker**	**Don Walker**
Kevin English (joined board as the 13th member when announced as CEO, April 2001) Former managing director and chief executive officer, e-commerce, for Credit Suisse First Boston; former chairman and CEO for TheStreet.com	*Resigned June 28, 2002* Harold Kutner and then Bruce Swift took the seat.	**Bob Paul** (May 2003) CEO of Covisint; previously the SVP sales and marketing, Covisint; before coming to Covisint, Paul served as president and COO of Synapz, a developer of Web-based supply chain management applications.
Garth Saloner (joined board as the 14th member, November 2001; first nonautomotive industry member) Stanford University professor; the Jeffery S. Skoll Professor of Electronic Commerce, Strategic Management and Economics, and co-director of the Center for Electronic Business and Commerce at Stanford University's Graduate School of Business	**Garth Saloner**	**Garth Saloner**
	Dennis W. Archer (joined board as 15th member January 8, 2002); former mayor of the City of Detroit and chairman and member of the law firm of Dickinson Wright PLLC	**Dennis W. Archer**
	Marissa Peterson (joined board as 16th member February 14, 2002); executive vice president, worldwide operations, Sun Microsystems	**Marissa Peterson**

Source: Developed by authors from biographies of the first 12 members of the 2001 board quoted from Rachel Konrad, 'Cream of the crop make up Covisint board,' *CNET News*, January 24, 2001, and Covisint documents.

catalog product and only 10% from other products and services.[34] Our 2002 budget calls for growing the percentage of nonauction product revenues to 49%. Two thousand and two is a make-or-break year.[35]

Ending Covisint's reliance on consultants helped English reduce its monthly 'burn rate' to $8.5 million.[36] But, achieving further cost reductions while also meeting aggressive revenue growth goals would require that all Covisint employees work together to transform the company's strategy and how it was executed. English believed that this was one of his toughest challenges:

> When all the consultants went home, what was left were *former* Ford employees, *former* GM employees, and *former* DaimlerChrysler employees [350 strong in March 2001] – all of whom were used to being cutthroat competitors. There was no 'Covisint Culture,' and we had to change that. Throughout the summer and fall of 2001, I met with people one-on-one, and we had multiple organizational off-site and management meetings. We ended up creating a 'repatriation process' through which people borrowed from our OEM investors were free to choose whether to commit to being a Covisint employee or go back to their OEM employers. The simple act of choosing to stay at Covisint helped everyone bond to Covisint and its vision.[37]

Redefining the product/market strategy

Early in his tenure, English also recognized that Covisint suffered from a common problem of industry consortia: 'a broad set of unconnected offerings led to a value proposition that was a mile wide and one inch deep, as equity holders . . . jealously controlled strategy.'[38] To solve this problem, one of his early initiatives was to redefine Covisint's product strategy:

> In the June 2001 time frame, I convened the top 44 people in the company in a room to talk about our product strategy. I told them that a start-up company, which is what Covisint really was, typically develops one, two, or maybe three products at most. We had 17 products, and we were trying to introduce them in markets around the world. In fact, our products at the time were actually more like projects for one of our OEM investors.
>
> We listed all the products under development on the board and went around the room person by person. I asked each one: 'Which three or four products do you think are most important for Covisint to offer?' At the end of the process, four products were head and shoulders above the rest. I said: 'Fine. We will cancel the other 13.' All hell broke loose. By the end of the meeting, we had worked through a new product strategy and a value proposition for all of our stakeholders, not just the

OEMs. This served as a starting point for driving execution during the second half of 2001.[39]

One of the products English and his team kept was an industry portal[40] – a product that began to find traction after a larger percentage of the company's resources was channeled to it:

> The portal product became the core of our product strategy for 2001. The idea was to get maximum connectivity within the industry and to create the standards for how business would be conducted and information would flow. Once we had achieved connectivity and our infrastructure was connected to the supply chain systems of all industry participants, we would be in a position to layer in all kinds of value-added applications. Delphi – one of the largest automotive suppliers – was the first to put their trust in us. The CEO and chairman of Delphi said: 'You want to build the next-generation supplier portal, and we want to connect our 5,500 suppliers. This is a win-win for both of us.'[41]

With Delphi on board, OEMs soon followed. In September 2001, English received a call from a Ford Motor Company board member asking Covisint to develop and host a supplier portal for his company. A few months later DaimlerChrysler also signed on. By early 2002, Covisint had about 16 portal proposals in development. Ford alone expected to have 100,000 users on its portal by the end of 2002.

With each portal Covisint received an up-front fee for customizing the Web site and connecting the portal

---

34 By August 2001, 'Covisint had managed more than $129 billion in [auction] transactions – nearly 53% of the estimated $240 billion spent last year by founders DaimlerChrysler, Ford Motor, and General Motors.' Steve Konicki, 'Great sites: Covisint,' *InformationWeek*, August 27, 2001.

35 Author interview, January 2002.

36 Joseph B. White, 'Covisint creates holding company, sees increase in online auction value,' *The Wall Street Journal*, August 13, 2001.

37 Author interview, January 2002.

38 David Metcalfe, 'eMarketplaces: rebound and deliver,' Forrester TechStrategy Report, March 2002.

39 Author interview, January 2002.

40 The American Heritage Dictionary defines a portal as a doorway or gate, especially one that is large and imposing. This seems a fitting definition of the portal business model that is emerging on the Web. In this context, a portal refers to the entry-point Web page that serves as a gateway to information and services within a specific context, for example, an industry (automotive, chemicals, financial services), an occasion (wedding purchases), or across multiple contexts.

41 Author interview, January 2002. Oracle, one of the original Covisint investors, was Covisint's chief competitor for this project. At the time Delphi made its choice, Oracle still owned 2% of Covisint.

to key information systems for the host and its trading partners. Once launched, Covisint received a hosting fee from the portal owner and a subscription fee from each user. The up-front subscription and hosting fees provided improved visibility into future revenues and helped stabilize cash flow. 'More important,' said English, 'is the ability to connect the industry and provide both an industry-wide platform and the standards for sharing information and doing business.'[42] The portal offering also enabled the company to shift from developing software products for OEMs to providing value-added services to all participants in the industry. English explained:

> When Covisint was first launched, it was thought of as a software developer for its OEM investors. Our first product – auctions – reflected this perspective. We are now evolving to a services organization. This is an important distinction. We are not a software firm, and we are not an outsourcing firm. I don't want to pattern this firm after Oracle, CommerceOne, or FreeMarkets [a competitor in the auction space]. I want to be compared with firms like Automatic Data Processing, Inc. ADP started by providing the infrastructure and services for doing payroll. They then built many additional value-added services on this platform. These services connected into the IT systems and processes of its customers. They have had 112 straight quarters of profitability and have a P/E [price-to-earnings ratio] of more than 30. It's a remarkable business model.[43]

Another Covisint executive elaborated further on how Covisint patterned its new services strategy on the ADP business model:

> We need to evolve our products based on what we learn about customer needs from our constant interactions with them. It was this talent that made ADP so successful. They started by administering payroll and, once the relationship was in place, they said: 'You could use help with your benefits administration. Would you like us to do that for you, too? Want us to handle your 401K?' Because paying people is a fundamental activity of all companies, it provided an excellent platform for evolving into a wide range of related services. We have an opportunity with our portal strategy to create a similar platform around a fundamental activity for an entire industry. Once we run procurement for the industry, we can offer collaborative design services and many more.[44]

English deemed support for collaborative product design to be core to an industry exchange. In March 2002, Covisint signed an agreement to offer Powerway's Advanced Product Quality Planning (APQP) service through the Covisint portal.[45] Powerway was lauded on

Forbes's Best of the Web list of 2002 and identified as one of the 80 most promising B2B companies across 22 industries.[46] Powerway's collaborative planning service shortened concept-to-production cycles and cut costs 'through management of exceptions in the quality process that are not now detected until near a vehicle's launch. At that point making changes can be ten times more expensive than earlier in the production cycle.'[47]

To focus resources around the new product/market strategy, English reorganized Covisint into two strategic business units (SBUs): strategic sourcing, in charge of the company's supply, pricing, and auction capabilities; and portal and connectivity, in charge of developing the infrastructure to support communications and transactions between OEMs and suppliers (see Exhibit 12 for the evolution of Covisint's organizational structure). Analysts hailed the move, claiming that the 'wall' between the two SBUs would 'help allay fears regarding pricing transparency and information confidentiality' while still enabling 'upselling opportunities between the two SBUs.'[48]

English agreed. 'These new organizations signify a change in the way Covisint approaches the marketplace,' he said. 'They are the foundation for our global sales efforts, as we move aggressively to deploy our products and services in the automotive industry around the world.'[49] As part of the restructuring, 25 employees and 25 contractors were laid off, and 14 employees were added to the sales organization.

Throughout his tenure as CEO, English sought to involve suppliers in Covisint's governance, thus providing a channel for them to represent this important stakeholder group in key decisions while also serving as a channel for Covisint to reach out and attract and engage suppliers as full members of the Covisint community. Initially, he convinced the OEM board members

---

42 Author interview, January 2002.
43 Ibid.
44 Ibid.
45 Covisint would earn 15% of all revenues generated by Powerway through Covisint portals. While Covisint would retain ownership of customer information, Powerway would maintain rights to all intellectual property.
46 About a third of Powerway's 3,500 customers were in the automotive industry.
47 Kevin Prouty, AMR Research, quoted in Philip Burgert, 'Controlling automotive quality online,' *ecomworld*, March 27, 2002.
48 Thilo Koslowski, 'Covisint's new two-unit structure reflects what automakers want,' Gartner News Analysis, April 5, 2002.
49 Author interview, January 2002.

Exhibit 12 **Covisint organization**

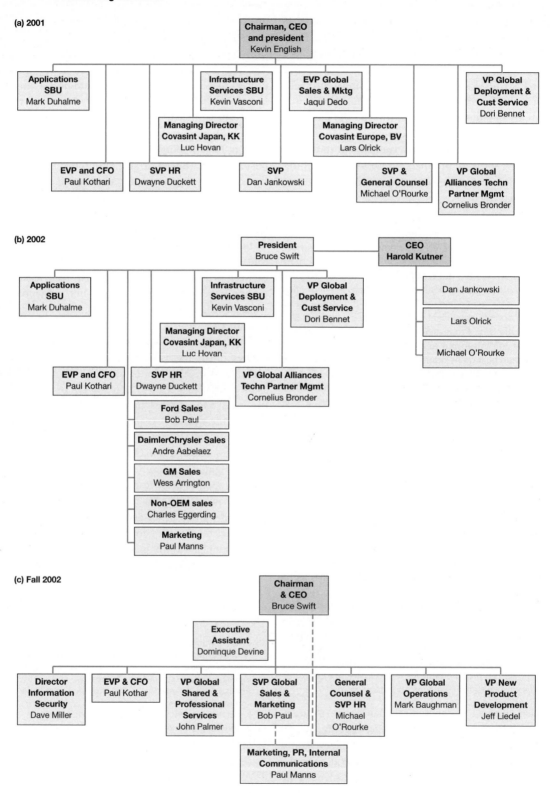

(a) 2001

Chairman, CEO and president
Kevin English

Applications SBU
Mark Duhalme

Infrastructure Services SBU
Kevin Vasconi

EVP Global Sales & Mktg
Jaqui Dedo

VP Global Deployment & Cust Service
Dori Bennet

Managing Director Covasint Japan, KK
Luc Hovan

Managing Director Covasint Europe, BV
Lars Olrick

EVP and CFO
Paul Kothari

SVP HR
Dwayne Duckett

SVP
Dan Jankowski

SVP & General Counsel
Michael O'Rourke

VP Global Alliances Techn Partner Mgmt
Cornelius Bronder

(b) 2002

President
Bruce Swift

CEO
Harold Kutner

Applications SBU
Mark Duhalme

Infrastructure Services SBU
Kevin Vasconi

VP Global Deployment & Cust Service
Dori Bennet

Dan Jankowski

Lars Olrick

Michael O'Rourke

Managing Director Covasint Japan, KK
Luc Hovan

EVP and CFO
Paul Kothari

SVP HR
Dwayne Duckett

VP Global Alliances Techn Partner Mgmt
Cornelius Bronder

Ford Sales
Bob Paul

DaimlerChrysler Sales
Andre Aabelaez

GM Sales
Wess Arrington

Non-OEM sales
Charles Eggerding

Marketing
Paul Manns

(c) Fall 2002

Chairman & CEO
Bruce Swift

Executive Assistant
Dominque Devine

Director Information Security
Dave Miller

EVP & CFO
Paul Kothar

VP Global Shared & Professional Services
John Palmer

SVP Global Sales & Marketing
Bob Paul

General Counsel & SVP HR
Michael O'Rourke

VP Global Operations
Mark Baughman

VP New Product Development
Jeff Liedel

Marketing, PR, Internal Communications
Paul Manns

to add representatives from two of the most important automotive suppliers – Johnson Controls and Delphi – to the company's board of directors. But his attempts to allow key suppliers to invest in the company failed. As a result, English formed a Global Customer Council, which included suppliers and OEMs from around the world. But the struggles of developing a truly open governance model soon took their toll, and English announced his resignation in June 2002.

The CEO shuffle: 2002–2003

I'm here until the board says otherwise or they just don't need me. I was one of the early visionaries, and I still believe in Covisint's viability. Kevin, to his credit, took the mess we left him and did something with it.

Harold Kutner, July 1, 2002[50]

Upon English's resignation, Kutner, former GM group vice president of worldwide purchasing and a founding member of the Covisint Board, stepped into the leadership void and became CEO on June 28, 2002. Bruce Swift, former vice president of purchasing for Ford Motor Company in Europe, became president and COO. At the same time, close to one-third of Covisint employees (around 100 people) were laid off. At GM Kutner was perceived as a razor-sharp negotiator who was well-known in the supplier community. Many observers agreed that suppliers would view Kutner's appointment as the OEMs' attempt to increase their power over the supply chain. 'Kutner has an immense amount of credibility. But he's not going to take any crap from anyone . . .' one analyst remarked. 'He has the clout and the power to convince both OEMs and suppliers to use Covisint.'[51]

Many believed that the vision for Covisint's growth may have been too ambitious. Said one analyst, 'The expectation that a 100-year-old industry that represents 18% of the total economic output within a country would simply change its means of purchasing and interacting with suppliers in a short period of time based on the availability of the Internet was incredibly high.'[52] But all agreed that B2B in the automotive supply chain was definitely not dead. 'Anybody who thinks there isn't a new business model is still in the cave – sleeping,'[53] said Kutner.

Kutner claimed that even if revenue targets were not reached, profitability in Q4 2002 was still possible, given the cost-cutting measures that had been put in place:

We had a hockey stick revenue model, where we would go along and then jump to a $150 million company. But we are just a $65 million or a $70 million company, and we had the costs associated with a much bigger company. So we've reduced head count, from 370 to 250, and we've cut back travel by 50% and cut back expenses. We've taken 70% of our spending out. We were fat, dumb, and happy. People here thought they had a Linus blanket with the Big 3 paying for it. That blanket is gone.[54]

To achieve the business growth necessary for profitability, Kutner said that he would continue on the path blazed by English: 'We're not anticipating drastic changes in what we're doing.'[55]

Kutner remained as CEO for 10 months, grooming Swift, who was appointed CEO in February 2003. Swift lasted just 31 days before he left to become a president of Metaldyne Corp. Paul explained his view of the shuffle:

The CEO job must have seemed Herculean to Swift. Most product lines were losing money, and our core revenue generator, auctions, was quickly becoming commoditized. Covisint was never going to be best in class in auctions. FreeMarkets already owned that space, and Covisint didn't even own the intellectual property for its auctions. Furthermore, the suppliers didn't trust the OEM power and control of the company. Bruce was doing a fine job, but the role of president at Metaldyne must have looked pretty good to him.[56]

Bob Paul's decision

I think the founding vision of Covisint was correct. Every member of the automotive industry would benefit greatly by having a separate organization that used technology to streamline processes and create a single platform upon which the industry could share information and transact business. The problem was that Covisint was pulled this way and that by its OEM owners to solve

50 Jeffrey McCracken, 'Retired GM exec Kutner to replace departing English,' *Detroit Free Press*, July 1, 2002.
51 David Sedgwick, Ralph Kisiel, Robert Sherefkin, 'Kutner has tough task at Covisint,' *Automotive News*, June 30, 2002.
52 Jon Derome, Yankee Group, quoted in Marsha Stopa, 'Was Covisint overhyped?' *The Oakland Press*, June 29, 2002.
53 As quoted in Steve Hamm, 'B2B isn't dead. It's learning,' *BusinessWeek Online*, December 24, 2002.
54 Jeffrey McCracken, 'CEO says firm, suppliers "are on the same team,"' *Detroit Free Press*, July 25, 2002.
55 Ralph Kisiel and Andrew Kietderich, 'English resigns, former Ford exec named Covisint president, COO,' *Automotive News*, June 28, 2002.
56 Author interview, June 2004.

their problems and it lost touch with the original vision. Unless you have laser-like focus on the customer and the problem you're trying to solve for them, technology is irrelevant. No amount of money or power can make people active and engaged members if they don't trust you and don't see the value for them.

Bob Paul[57]

Covisint was one of the most scrutinized small companies in the world, given its heritage. Back in 2000, the OEMs had recognized B2B e-commerce as a revolutionary force and had leapt at the opportunity to create a money-making machine in the form of an industry consortium exchange. Since then, dreams of an IPO worth billions of dollars had evaporated as suppliers balked, the industry hunkered down through the recession, and revenues continued to trickle. Three CEOs had been at the exchange's helm in the previous two years, each for a shorter period of time (see Exhibit 13 for a summary of Covisint's evolving organization and capabilities).

Paul glanced at his watch. His breakfast meeting with Gary Valade and Ralph Szygenda was only a few short hours away. He knew English had had an insurmountable task: 'The board hired Kevin to build the supply chain applications needed by the OEM founders and to formulate a strategy for an IPO. But he just couldn't get to the key metrics he needed. For sustainable value, you have to have competitive positioning, highly valuable and referenceable customers, annuity streams, and so on. The business plan when Kevin came on board was to go from a $30 million to a $112 million company. That plan didn't have a prayer.'[58]

From his senior-level position in the company, Paul had been conducting his own assessment of Covisint's business model. He focused his analysis on the 'pain' in the industry and found that the pressing problem for all players centered on problems with what the industry called 'messaging' – the passage of information back and forth in the form of documents, reports, files, and so on. Every player in the industry used multiple versions of documents, such as purchase orders, requests for proposal, and invoices. For example, a document called the fabrication authorization order (830) was used by OEMs to tell a supplier, each week, what products it needed to ship, what it was authorized to build, and what it was authorized to buy. Ford alone had eight different versions of the 830 for its different divisions. Hundreds of thousands of business documents such as the 830 were exchanged via electronic data interchange (EDI) every day. In 2003, these documents were trans-

mitted through e-mail, dedicated networks between large suppliers and OEMs, third-party networks, and a variety of other methods.

The more trading partners an OEM or supplier had, the more connections it had to establish and manage and the greater the variety of documents it had to process. 'Multiply the complexity of the 830,' said Paul, 'by the 22 documents that the average suppliers receive electronically from an OEM by the number of different formats for different data fields on the document. Then you get some understanding of the level of investment that the suppliers and OEMs face in terms of procurement.'[59]

Paul argued that Covisint's top priority should be to supply a computer-to-computer messaging hub as a core component of its portal. The messaging hub would process and translate different versions of EDI documents, allowing OEMs and suppliers to transmit data directly into and out of their core supply chain applications and databases. Over time, the industry could converge on a common messaging format for common transactions. Until then, the messaging hub would manage the complexity. Once standards were in place, the messaging hub could be used to support standardized information and transaction flow. Obtaining support for this important project would be critical to Paul if he were to become CEO.

In addition, Paul believed that further rationalization of the product strategy would be needed. While he viewed the portal project as critical, other applications, among them Powerway's APQP application and the auction product, would need to be divested. The arrangement with Powerway, however pivotal it may have seemed, had created strong negative reactions among the automotive supplier community toward Covisint. 'While collaborative design is critical, the OEMs are pressuring suppliers to buy a minimum of five Powerway IDs, which many of them can't afford,' explained Paul. 'In addition, they are being forced to install a special quality system to link with Powerway and share information across the supply chain. Many suppliers already have a quality system, and costly integration would be needed to connect it to Powerway.'[60]

---

57 Author interview, June 2004, discussing his comments quoted in Ryan Underwood, 'Fast talk: lessons from the new economy,' *Fast Company*, issue 80, March 1, 2004.
58 Author interview, June 2004.
59 Ibid.
60 Author interview, June 2004.

Exhibit 13 Evolving organization and capabilities

Organization/ Capabilities	Develop the Concept Covisint 2000	Launch Initial Products/ Services Covisint 2001	Establish Two SBUs: Covisint 2002	Continue English's Drive Toward Liquidity: Covisint early 2003
Activities	Defined the initial business model; developed founding team; secured initial funding and developed equity structure; launched the company; developed initial products and services	Completed initial products and services and began development of follow-on products and services; identified early adopters; began marketing and selling to early adopters; began providing after-sales services	Began focusing on the portal and development of products for which Covisint would hold the IP; struggled to offset the increasing commoditization of auctions by increasing revenues from vendors	Due to Paul's support, work began on messaging hub, which by its nature would increase Covisint income from vendors; portal service scaled up as more customers came on board
People/ Expertise	Teams of product experts from founding companies; all continued to be paid for and reported to founding organization	Marketing, sales, customer service, HR, finance expertise; hired functional experts who also had some expertise in managing the function; these people hired a team of operating experts	Covisint provided its ability to deliver high-quality portal software on time and on budget (it had better success in this arena than with end-user applications); continued to build internal expertise after English released over 350 consultants	Continued growth in expertise in delivering portal and messaging hub solutions; continued personnel losses through layoffs and attrition
Leadership	Three 'co-CEOs' – one from DaimlerChrysler, one from Ford Motor Company, one from GM	Kevin English was hired; English had experience building an organization and taking it through to IPO	English focused attention on portal and connectivity solutions	Harold Kutner took over until Bruce Swift was prepared to take on the CEO role.
Organization	Team-based organization; teams formed around product development projects for each founding company; 17 products under development	Simple functional hierarchy and regional headquarters; number of products cut from 17 to 3 to simplify organization, cut expenses, and achieve focus	Set up two SBUs in mid-2002: strategic sourcing (supply, pricing, auctions) and portal and connectivity (communications between manufacturers and suppliers); new structure to grow and diversify business	SBU structure dismantled; return to functional hierarchy; close to a third of workforce laid off when English left
Operations	Independent product development processes within each team	Product development, marketing, sales, service processes	Product development, marketing, sales, service processes	Product development, marketing, sales, service processes
Management	*Ad hoc* within teams	Annual budgets with performance reviews on a weekly and monthly basis	SBUs established as profit centers	More traditional structure re-established
Culture	No strong 'Covisint culture'; employees continued to relate to home organizations	Employees from founding organization were given the option of going back to their company or remaining with Covisint; development of a 'Covisint culture' was stressed; all employees worked together to develop an integrated mission and a set of core values	High energy level; 2002 was perceived as the 'make-or-break' year for Covisint	Morale fell due to the rapid turnover of CEOs and negative trade press; disagreement among the company executives

Source: Author analysis

Would the new messaging hub make it easier for OEMs to use an application such as Powerway while suppliers used their own quality systems? Maybe applications such as Powerway's APQP and auctions – another sore point for suppliers – could be returned to the OEMs and Covisint could remain as a neutral third party, passing information and documents and supporting transactions across its portal and messaging system?

Finally, Paul knew he would have to address the thorny governance issues that had proved to be the downfall of many industry consortia. No matter how he viewed the situation, he kept returning to the fact that for Covisint to be perceived as a neutral, independent information and transaction hub, it would have to truly be independent. English had fought to have suppliers become full partners and investors – and had failed. Paul wondered whether the OEMs would consider exiting Covisint by selling the company to a neutral party. He knew that all of the investors were tired of pouring money into the company, and it was unclear whether Covisint would be cash flow positive any time soon. Would the OEMs be willing to give up control of the platform? If so, could Paul find a buyer that would allow him to keep the company intact and independent? Or alternatively, would he be presiding over the company as the grand vision faded away to oblivion?

IBX (Northern Europe)
Expanding B2B ePurchasing from indirect to direct goods and services

Peter Lageson, Senior Vice President at IBX and Managing Director of IBX Germany in Frankfurt is amazed by the rapid growth in such a short period. Five years after its launch, IBX has achieved a leading position in the purchasing services provider market, or sometimes referred to as SRM on demand, working with global companies including IKEA, LEGO and Volvo. After having established a leading position as a provider of solutions in the area of indirect material and services – in the past referred to as a horizontal platform – IBX's next significant challenge is to move into purchasing of strategic and direct materials. Lageson is confident that IBX's business model meets the requirements also in direct materials in different industries and vertical segments. He states:

> Our industry experience and our collaboration with Ericsson and other large European corporations helped us succeed in the horizontal market. The success gave us the credibility needed to enter into direct materials. Now, for instance our work with Skanska, the third largest construction company in the world, gives us lots of experiences helping us to enter the vertical segment with a well-developed set of solutions and a proven business model.[1]

Background: B2B e-platforms

Long before the advent of the Internet, several attempts were made at establishing electronic communication among companies. Systems like Prestel[2] (1979) in Great Britain and BTX[3] (1983) in Germany had moderate success, with the latter having as many as 1.2 million users at the end of 1996. Nevertheless, it was the Teletel/Minitel system (1982) from France Telecom that achieved great acceptance with almost 9 million terminals and around 25 million users at the end of 1999. This system allowed access to various categories of services like databases, airplane or train ticket purchases, and mail-orders to retail companies.

However, there was another system that had survived the emergence of the Internet: Electronic Data Interchange (EDI), which was developed in the late 1960s in the shipping and transportation industries. It was established as a standard for the business-to-business exchange of electronic documents. Despite users' strong acceptance of EDI (there are currently around 125,000 organizations using EDI[4]), it was not as successful as initially anticipated. The reliance on VANs[5] to encode EDI's data, as these networks were not com-

---

1 Unless stated otherwise, quotations from Peter Lageson were gathered during an interview on March 1st 2006 in the IBX German office in Frankfurt am Main.
2 Launched by the British General Post Office, Prestel was a system which transmitted data via the telephone lines to a set-top box terminal, enabling interactive services and a crude form of e-mail. However, the costs of the required hardware constituted an obstacle for Prestel's success.
3 Bildschirmtext is a system launched by the Deutsche Bundespost.
4 This rate corresponds to 5% of all companies around the world and 2% of all American enterprises.
5 Value Added Network is a specialized application service provider (ASP) that acts as an intermediary between trading partners sharing data or business processes.

This case study was written by Fernando Endara, Master of International Business student, under the supervision of Albrecht Enders, Assistant Professor of Strategic Management, Harald Hungenberg, Chaired Professor of Strategic Management (all three from University of Nuremberg), and Tawfik Jelassi, Dean and Professor of e-Business and IT at ENPC (Paris). It is intended to be used as the basis for class discussion rather than to illustrate effective or ineffective handling of a management situation.

This case study was made possible by the cooperation of Peter Lageson, Senior Vice President, IBX.

patible with each other, increased the complexity of the system. Each industry has its own EDI standard and vertical integration was encouraged only in the form of Private B2B platforms or exchanges.

Starting in 1996, with an increasing number of companies launching web-pages, it became clear to procurement agents that they could use the Internet as a search tool for new vendors and products. When the Extensible Markup Language (XML) emerged as a replacement to the HyperText Markup Language (HTML) standard, new possibilities of combining text and other information types about a product became feasible, including eCatalogues. These kinds of tools were promptly adopted by large corporations as a way of optimizing and automating the purchasing process of indirect materials, also known as MRO[6] goods, thereby reducing their purchasing cost. With this goal in mind, Desktop Purchase Systems (DPS) were installed, allowing requesters to order materials directly from their desk through web-based catalogues, which

were linked to pre-qualified suppliers. Such platforms enhanced horizontal integration between buyers and MRO vendors.

Meanwhile, EDI evolved into web-based EDI, making web-browser transactions possible and connecting users with EDI infrastructure to those who did not have it. Soon, hybrids of Web-EDI and XML, which supported automatic data processing, were introduced in the market, thereby fostering the evolution of B2B platforms. These technologies opened up the possibility for new transaction mechanisms such as online bidding as well as forward and reverse auctions, thus enabling the procurement automation of direct goods such as machines or product parts (see Exhibit 1). The transaction structures also experienced a change, shifting from bilateral (n:m) to multilateral (n:1:m) relationships, thereby generating network effects. This permitted third-party agents such as ASP's to integrate complementary eServices like logistics,

---

6   MRO stands for Maintenance, Repair and Operation.

Exhibit 1   Strategic relevance vs. automation potential of procurement goods

A-Goods

	Investment Purchase		Direct Material Purchase	
Features	Core business requirement Tender Individual requirements Higher Value/ Small Quantity	Features	Production requirement Regular purchase Forefront product assortment Bigger Quantities
Examples	Machines Building	Examples	Tires Gearbox
System	Bidding systems eRFI/eRFP/eRFQ	System	B2B Solutions for direct materials e.g. Reverse Auctions
	Variety Purchase		MRO Purchase	
Features	Miscellaneous requirements Irregular demand Value and Quantity vary	Features	Individual requirements Regular purchase Forefront product assortment Low value
Examples	Single company car Single office furniture	Examples	MRO Goods/C-Goods Product related small parts
System	Difficult to automate	System	Desktop Purchasing/eCatalog

High ← Strategic relevance → Low

B-Goods   C-Goods

Low ← Automation potential → High

Source: Nenninger, Michael and Lawrenz, Oliver (2001), *B2B-Erfolg durch eMarkets*, 1st Edition, Vieweg Verlag, Braunschweig/Wiesbaden, p. 4.

insurance and payment services, especially in the so-called open platforms[7]. With improved user interface, many of these platforms became integrated with the ERP[8] systems of buyers and sellers, thus acting as an extended supply chain management system.

B2B platforms have been categorized into horizontal and vertical platforms based on the types of goods that are traded through them (see Exhibit 2):

- **Horizontal platforms** deal with indirect goods or MRO items across industries. Such items include office supplies and maintenance goods (e.g., electric bulbs) which are not strategically relevant to a company's production process and therefore not crucial for developing a competitive advantage.

- **Vertical platforms** are industry-specific platforms that operate in an individual industry such as the chemical industry or the automotive industry. Vertical platforms typically focus on the exchange of direct goods that are used for the final product that is delivered to the customer. These *direct* goods include raw materials such as steel or cement and goods that are used for final products such as electronic components. An example of such a platform is E2Open that provides a supply chain solution for IT providers such as Vodafone. Furthermore, there are also vertical platforms that focus on indirect goods yet within one industry.

Buyers and sellers choose to operate a B2B platform, especially if it is industry specific, to increase their leverage vis-à-vis their suppliers or buyers. In addition, there are also third-party platforms which offer a more neutral basis for transaction processing. As a consequence of the dot.com bubble burst in 2000, many B2B platforms (such as mondus.com) and exchanges had to stop their operations, reinvent their business model or, in some cases, were acquired by other companies.

However, with technological advances that enabled fast and secure multi-purpose communication between enterprises as well as increasing savings through procurement and sourcing process optimization, ePurchasing solutions and B2B platforms became more attractive. The term ePurchasing refers to the overall purchasing process which is equivalent to supply chain management. This process can be subdivided into sourcing (including spend management, supplier recognition and auctioning), procurement and payment.

According to e-business w@tch, a market research initiative launched in 2005 by the European Commission, about 25% of European[9] companies,

---

7 Open platforms, in contrast to private platforms or exchanges, allow the involvement of an unrestricted number of participants at the buyer side as well as at the seller side and are mostly operated by ASPs.

8 Enterprise resource planning systems (ERP) are integrated software applications that automate an organization's business processes using industry best practices.

9 The survey conducted by e-business w@tch included the following countries: Czech Republic, France, Germany, Italy, Poland, Spain and the UK, which represent altogether 75% of the EU-25 population and GDP.

Exhibit 2 **Characteristics of horizontal and vertical e-business platforms**

	Types of Goods Purchased on e-Platforms	**Shipping of goods**
Horizontal platforms	• Office supplies (stationary paper, writing material, office furniture, etc.) • Airline tickets, hotel bookings • Other non-industry specific products and services	• Usually shipped through courier service companies (e.g., UPS, FedEx, DHL, etc.)
Vertical platforms	• Raw materials (e.g., wood, steel, cement, fuel, liquefied gas, etc.) • Goods for final products (e.g., parts, components, electronic systems, etc.)	• Requires specific logistics, transportation and fulfillment mechanisms

across all size segments[10], bought online over 5% of their total purchase volume. IT services, tourism, automotive, publishing and machinery industries were the most active online buyers.

Exhibit 3 Procurement processes supported by special software solutions

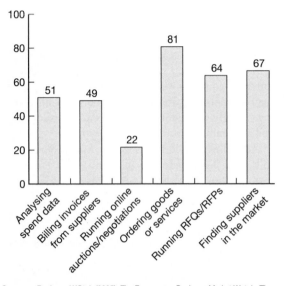

Source: e-Business W@tch (2005), *The European e-Business Market Watch: The European e-Buiness Report*, European Commission, November 2005, p. 30.

The same survey[11] also revealed that on average 26% of companies in all ten industries[12] were using some kind of eSourcing solution with the aeronautics and automotive industries having the highest participation rates with 63% and 39% respectively. The most frequently used sourcing processes were goods and services ordering (81%), finding suppliers (67%), running requests for quotations and proposals —RFQs/RFPs— (64%), and analyzing expenditure data analysis (51%). (See Exhibit 3.)[13]

There are no reliable forecasts regarding the growth rate of B2B platforms, but by observing the gap between the implementation rate of ERP systems and the acceptance of eSourcing solutions across all four European enterprise segments, especially in medium and large sized enterprises (see Exhibit 4), the demand for these solutions is likely to increase in the future.

---

10 The enterprises have been segmented according to their number of employees in four different categories; micro (1 to 9 empl.), small (10-49 empl.), medium (50-249 empl.) and large (250+ empl.).

11 The European e-Business report 2005 by e-business w@tch and the European Commission.

12 The sectors are: Food, Textile, Publishing, Pharma, Machinery, Automotive, Aeronautics, Construction, Tourism and IT Services.

13 RFI stands for request for information, RFP for request for proposal, and RFQ for request for quotation.

Exhibit 4 Companies using ERP systems and eProcurement solutions by branch and company size

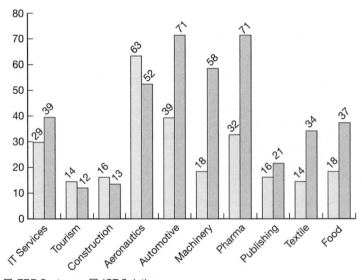

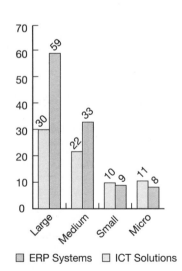

Source: e-Business W@tch (2005), *The European e-Business Market Watch: The European e-Buiness Report*, European Commission, November 2005, Annex, p. 6.

The history of IBX

The initial idea

In 1999, Christer Hallqvist, Björn Böhme and Peter Lageson left Ericsson with the idea of creating their own company and developing an innovative eProcurement platform. With Ericsson's eProcurement system 'Click-to-buy' (which operated successfully with over 15,000 users and close to 70 suppliers) as a benchmark, the newly formed team wanted to develop a similar stand-alone platform outside of Ericsson. The goal was to integrate buyer and supplier platforms into one solution – an initiative was born and was initially called 'Bizface'.

In December 1999, Bizface approached Ericsson and presented a proposal to reduce the cost of managing the 70 suppliers. The 'Click-to-buy' vendors were indirect materials and service suppliers, most of them generic also supplying other large corporations in the region. For Ericsson, outsourcing the entire Supplier Center to Bizface and sharing this with other large Swedish corporations seemed like a good solution to try to 'share' the cost with other large corporations.

Ericsson embraced the idea and expressed its interest in investing in the solution, and asked Bizface in January 2000 to develop a business plan. The Bizface initiators saw the need for senior management experience and convinced Hans Ahlinder to join the founding team. Ahlinder was in 2000 Chief Operating Officer of Gambro[14] and former Senior Vice-President of Sourcing at Ericsson. At the end of February, Ericsson and Bizface signed a Letter of Intent in which Ericsson agreed to invest in Bizface with the agreement that Bizface takes over and continues to operate and develop the supplier center of 'Click to buy' with its current and future suppliers.

At this time, lots of other B2B platform initiatives tried to convince Ericsson to join their respective business ideas. Peter Lageson recalls the importance of having Ericsson on board for the eventual success of IBX:

> We had a golden egg with Ericsson as one of the earliest adopters of eProcurement in the world.

CommerceOne, a marketplace software provider, had also been trying to find a 'franchise partner' in the Nordic region. It was essentially looking for interested companies to outbid each other in acquiring the exclusive CommerceOne license. Three consortia came into play: Bizface/Ericsson, SEB[15] in partnership with the venture capital company b-business partners and a

third initiative. Bizface started to assess possible technology providers, including CommerceOne. Realizing the magnitude of the agreement between Bizface and Ericsson, CommerceOne proposed to introduce these two companies to SEB and b-business partners.

SEB tried to convince Ericsson to join their initiative which led to intense negotiations between Ericsson, SEB and b-business partners. At last, however, the small Bizface team was brought back to the negotiation table. Two facts had kept Bizface in the deal: the agreement with Ericsson and their experience in eProcurement and B2B platforms. In July 2000, Ericsson, SEB, b-business partners and Bizface agreed to jointly launch an eMarketplace[16] called Integrated Business Exchange (IBX).

IBX started to assess all of the technology platforms available on the market. This move took CommerceOne by surprise, because it brought all the platform members together. After assessing solutions from Ariba, SAP, Oracle and others, IBX decided to go for the MarketSite platform technology of CommerceOne, primarily because of their new strategic partnership with SAP. IBX executed the first transaction on December 18, 2000.

Pan-Nordic consolidation

By May 2001, IBX had 33 suppliers connected to the platform, and in June 2001, Volvo decided to join the platform as a buyer and signed a three-year agreement, thus becoming the first customer outside of the IBX owner group. The objective was clear for IBX: in order to succeed, it had to become the leading provider in the Nordic region.

To achieve this objective, IBX started to focus on finding the right partners to use as 'anchors' prior to building a local organization in each Nordic country. Novo Nordisk, a Danish healthcare company, thus became a shareholder customer and an 'anchor' in Denmark, placing its first transaction through IBX on September 27th, 2001. In 2000, IBX held talks with a large Norwegian corporation to convince them to join in as the 'anchor' for Norway, but these talks failed. Nevertheless, on December 5, 2001, the Norwegian state awarded IBX a five-year contract to build and operate a marketplace for the entire Norwegian public

---

14 Gambro is a leading European healthcare technology corporation with headquarters in Sweden.
15 Skandinaviska Enskilda Banken (SEB) is a Swedish financial services corporation.
16 Ericsson, SEB and b-business partners each held 30% of the stock.

sector. IBX closed 2001 with 6 buying organizations and 135 suppliers on its network.

IBX continued its growth in 2002 by signing a contract with Nycomed, the Danish pharmaceuticals company, and with Fortum[17] a Finnish energy supplier, which joined in as a buyer in Finland. Through this deal, IBX reached its first goal of establishing operations in Sweden, Denmark, Norway and Finland.

Subsequently, IBX identified a good opportunity to expand across Europe by buying Emaro, an eMarket owned by SAP and Deutsche Bank. Negotiations started in mid-2002 but ultimately failed mainly due to internal changes at SAP. Deutsche Bank, though, asked IBX to carry out several e-procurement studies and an analysis of its purchasing functions in Italy and Spain. However, the long-term relationship that IBX had hoped for never materialized.

SAP and IBX decided to deepen their relationship by bringing a value proposition to large Nordic corporations. This consisted of IBX selling its IBX eProcurement solution based on MySAP SRM[18] eProcurement technology instead of CommerceOne Procurement. IBX closed the year 2002 with 23 buying organizations and 250 suppliers. In early 2003, after a few months of internal restructuring, IBX won a contract with the municipality of Oslo and later with Arla Foods and with Bang & Olufsen. The latter two got attracted by the IBX-SAP joint solution. At the end of 2003, IBX reached a turnover of 10.2 million Euros, which amounted to a 38% growth over the previous year.

In 2004, IBX closed a significant agreement with Skanska, a Swedish construction company, thus opening the doors for IBX to move into the construction industry. This deal represented a major challenge for IBX since, unlike previous agreements, the deal included all of the critical flows of construction materials and Skanska's subcontractors that were actually needed for the production process. This new contract led to an expansion of the IBX business model from the horizontal 'MRO goods and services' to the vertical 'direct materials flow' dimension.

Expansion across Europe

Together with Deutsche Post, Lufthansa and other German customers we will now prove that we can deliver to companies outside of the Nordic region.[19]

Lars Thunell, Chairman of IBX and CEO of SEB

In 2004, IBX tried hard to acquire a French marketplace but failed mainly due to a lack of commitment from

their owners to continue as major customers of the new entity. The failure was a big disappointment, although at the same time, it became obvious in the due diligence process that it would have required substantial efforts to turn the marketplace into a sound operation in France[20].

With an expected 30% growth rate, IBX went public in the spring of 2004 and secured 4.9 million Euros in additional funding. This funding was intended to support the European expansion and the extension of the value proposition by developing new products and capabilities, especially in the vertical segment. IBX started an intensive selection process to find the best possible software solution for coping with the business challenge that Skanska represented.

In mid-2004, IBX significantly enhanced its European coverage after partnering with trimondo, a German eProcurement service provider founded by Lufthansa and Deutsche Post. IBX and trimondo signed a contract with Deutsche Post that allowed IBX to take the global responsibility for 5,000 suppliers of Deutsche Post in more than 20 countries, while trimondo supported Deutsche Post in Germany. As Torsten Breuer, CEO of trimondo, explained:

> With the expansion of the product and service portfolio as well as the increased geographical coverage, we will enhance the offer to our customers in many aspects [...] The actual co-operation with IBX for the Deutsche Post global roll-out is very successful and our staff is looking forward to building a joint international team to maximize customer value.[21]

At the same time, Volvo expanded its collaboration with IBX to include global purchasing solutions, including Volvo's business in France, Belgium and the US. Volvo's subsidiaries, Renault and Mack Trucks, were also included in the agreement. Ola Hansson, e-Procurement Manager at Volvo, mentioned the reasons for this:

> In Sweden, we have had affirmative, satisfying results and therefore we chose IBX's solutions globally. During 2005 and 2006, after the expansion in these three markets, we are planning to introduce the system in several other countries.[22]

---

17 Suppliers and transporters of petroleum products, electricity, and district heat in the Nordic countries and worldwide.
18 Supplier Relationship Management: an information system that automates sourcing, purchasing and the management of daily supplier relations.
19 Taken from www.ibxeurope.com.
20 Ibid.
21 Ibid.
22 Ibid.

Other deals closed in 2005 with Saab in Sweden, Finnair in Finland, Helse Ost in Norway and Lundbeck in Denmark strengthened the position of IBX in the Nordic region.

In April 2005, IBX acquired trimondo, thereby adding 35 employees in Frankfurt and 4.8 million Euros in revenues while strengthening its position in Germany. Later in 2005, the LEGO Group signed a three-year long agreement with IBX for the provision of eCommerce solutions and consulting services for developing the LEGO Group's electronic purchase system.

In November 2005, IBX signed an important agreement with IKEA, the global furniture retailer. The deal included the complete on-demand solutions for eSourcing, eProcurement, ePayment, and access to the IBX Supplier Network for global implementation. Pontus Björnsson, country manager of IBX Sweden, points out the importance of this contract:

> The agreement is particularly important to IBX since it confirms the trend that large corporations are increasingly choosing on-demand solutions for their sourcing and procurement.[23]

IBX ended 2005 with a turnover of 20.3 million Euros and with an order stock for 2006 of 22.6 million Euros, ensuring already a growth of 14% for 2006.

The business model

Company vision

The IBX vision is built around the following four main pillars:[24]

- IBX aims to be the leading provider of services and solutions for efficient purchasing in Europe by becoming *the* source of knowledge on sourcing and procurement.

- IBX seeks to support their customers in transforming their current purchasing functions into highly efficient ones.

- IBX also expects, through their 'best of breed' eSourcing and eProcurement solutions and services portfolio, to help its customers to create savings through better compliance to corporate contracts, better prices and lower costs of operations.

- IBX started strictly in the purchasing field and will preserve that line, maintaining a skilled organization and management team with extensive experience in purchase processes, being trustworthy and professional towards its customers.

Exhibit 5 IBX modules

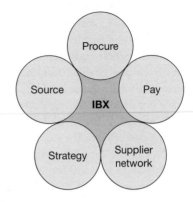

Source: IBX.

One of the key questions that IBX faced was which business model to adopt so that the company would meet the investors' financial return expectations. Peter Lageson emphasizes:

> The discussion we try to have with customers is that it comes down to how you design the project. It's not a technology question; that's not why you choose IBX. Instead, you choose IBX because of our business model that will take you through the transformation much faster than any alternative [sourcing and procurement] solution.

In order to reach this goal of quickly and cost-efficiently transforming the purchasing processes of its customer, IBX has developed a solutions' portfolio (see Exhibit 5). Peter Lageson comments on the importance of providing such an integrated solution:

> A buying organization faces a Make or Buy decision. It can buy the software, set it up, operate it and connect suppliers to the platform by itself. Alternatively, it can buy the service as part of an integrated solution. IBX's intention is to be 30% to 40% cheaper than the alternative to make it, where the buying organization doesn't need an implementation team over 12 to 18 months to ramp up, because typically, that is not part of the core business of the buying organization.

This portfolio started with a content and connectivity core. Later, on-demand solutions (also referred to as ASP tools such as eProcurement and eSourcing) and transformation capabilities and services (such as supplier activation, implementation, sourcing and consulting services) were added. This resulted in the following on-demand solutions portfolio:

---

23 Quoted in 'IKEA Turns to On-demand Supply Chain Solutions', *Supply & Demand Chain Executive*, 13 January, 2006.
24 Taken from www.ibxeurope.com.

■ **IBX Procure:** This module includes the IBX eProcurement solution based on MySAP SRM technology and the IBX search engine. The IBX eProcurement solution enables the end user to select and purchase any article registered on its suppliers' catalogues from any enabled terminal. Purchase orders were generated automatically informing the selected supplier which product to deliver while following all approval levels and affecting the corresponding cost centers. The search engine serves as an interface to the supplier community, where buying organizations searched for the desired items by vendor name, region, and commodity classification among other search options. It was also designed to provide a single procurement channel that supported a number of call-off methods including product catalogues, end-user requests, free text orders, and access to supplier's web shops. Lageson emphasizes the importance of the single channel:

We want to give suppliers a single point of contact, so they can deliver content, receive orders and have one business partner for all business processes.

■ **IBX Source:** This module, currently based on Emptoris, provides several capabilities ranging from planning procurement, requesting information (eRFI/eRFQ/eRFP), bidding, reverse auctioning to bundle buying. Lageson explains:

The product strategy was growing from the content and connectivity core to the next layer of a complete Source-Procure-Pay capability, becoming a full on-demand Supplier Relationship Management solution.

■ **IBX Pay:** This module, mostly based on the ePayment technology of trimondo, consists of the IBX eInvoice and the IBX Easy Payment tools. The first one links suppliers with buying organizations through a fully electronic invoicing interface, while reducing the workload and approval instances. The second tool is also capable of validating all the invoices against the authorized purchase orders, and if so desired, consolidates different invoices into one account.

■ **IBX Strategy:** IBX Strategy consists of a series of organizational models, best practice processes, sourcing and procurement strategies, as well as a skilled team of consultants with experience at implementing such strategies.

■ **IBX supplier network:** This network contains about 12,000 global suppliers, 1,400 catalogue suppliers and over 10 million line items. It may be accessed either by an internal eProcurement solution connected to IBX search engine or by using IBX complete eProcurement solution.

The revenue model

IBX business model is buyer centric, and IBX focuses its main efforts on working on behalf of the buyers. IBX helps the customers in transforming their current sourcing, procurement and payment business processes into more efficient ones leveraging IBX on demand solutions. When a buyer, for instance, has chosen IBX to provide support in transforming the procurement process, IBX among other things assesses the buyer's preferred vendor base, or helps the customer to assess it through a team of skilled consultants. Afterwards, the existing buying procedures of the company are optimized and taken to the procurement platform, while the system is fed with all viable call-off methods (catalogues, e-Forms, etc). Subsequently, IBX trains, activates and connects the suppliers to the platform. The revenue generated on the buyer side by IBX accounts for about 90% of total revenues. The seller side accounts for the remaining part of IBX's revenue. Peter Lageson explains:

We are of the opinion that the value that is created by means of the automated purchasing processes goes to the buyer in large parts. That's the reason why buyers should also be the ones paying for these services.

The main components of IBX revenue model consist of subscriptions and consulting fees, where over 80% of the total revenue is generated by recurring subscriptions, so called recurring fees. However, IBX expects consulting fees to increase over the next 3 to 4 years to 25% of total revenues.

The main business drivers in setting the subscription fees are (a) the number of users, and (b) the number of suppliers that the customer wants to have access to through IBX. IBX also typically awards discounts for long-term agreements (up to 5 years) and does not charge additionally for training and activation of suppliers, as those are included in the annual subscription.

15 of the 80 companies buying through the platform account for almost 80% of the total revenue. These 15

companies include global corporations such as Ericsson, IKEA, Deutsche Post and others who have registered around 100,000 users with IBX. Peter Lageson explains:

> At the moment, the main growth driver for our company is to go for the large corporate market. Implementing our system entails a big change management effort and only the big corporations are able to implement this at this point. We expect that the mid-market and public sector will become more interesting in 3 to 4 years.

Financial development and cost structure

IBX has shown a steady annual growth of 30% since it started operations back in 2000. In 2005, IBX became EBIT positive and reached a 1.8 million Euro EBITDA. The total revenue in that year was around 20.3 million Euros, which represented an increase of around 7 million Euros compared to 2004 (see Exhibit 6). This 60% growth over the previous year can be explained in large part by the acquisition of trimondo and the addition of major accounts such as IKEA. Peter Lageson added:

> This is our strategy: we would like to continue to grow organically at about 30% and at the same time add 30% through acquisitions in Europe.

Thanks to the subscription model, which helped the company to close 3-to-5-year agreements, IBX has secured an order stock for 2006 of 22.6 million Euros, which represents a 14% guaranteed growth over 2005. The budget for 2006 has reached around 27 million Euros with an expected EBITDA of around 3.2 million

Euros. The main revenue components, core recurrent and core non-recurrent fees are as high as 80% and 20% respectively. For every Euro of revenue, IBX reports 60 cents of costs; with its cost structure as follows:

- **IT operations** (hardware, software, third party costs) **10.7%**
- **External costs** (consultants, legal support) **10.7%**
- **Marketing** **3.8%**
- **Personnel** **74.8%**
- **Total** **100.0%**

Transaction volume

> The fact that we handled 4.4 Billion Euros in 1.2 million purchase orders in 2005 is evidence that we can help customers to capture the procurement spending in a very successful way. We have the means to actually grab the purchasing volume and this is what is creating compliance and ultimately savings to customers.
>
> Peter Lageson

This enormous transaction volume also opens up an additional business opportunity to IBX: By using the eProcurement system, all buyer requisitions reach the respective supplier only after approval of the relevant management instance within the buying organization, while binding the necessary monetary resources to proceed with the transaction. This guarantees that every invoice issued by suppliers will be backed up by the necessary funds, thus diminishing the financial risk for the vendors. This transactions information could be

Exhibit 6 IBX revenues and EBITDA 2002–2005

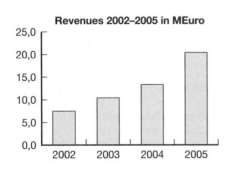

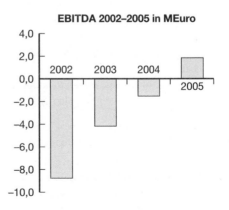

Source: IBX.

sold to financial institutions in order to create additional factoring services for IBX customers, which would benefit by getting paid more quickly. IBX expects to execute this concept in the next 4 to 5 years.

Implementing the business model

Using an 'Anchoring' marketing strategy to build the IBX brand

> We have quite an ambitious approach to marketing. Our marketing is mainly set up to create awareness among decision makers. However, the really good sales cases are the ones that came through word of mouth, like IKEA that came in through references. The essence of this business is that trust is very important. Seeing the effect of getting the IKEA brand was amazing from the marketing viewpoint, you get invited to companies that you just don't know how to get through the door.
>
> **Peter Lageson**

The collaboration with Ericsson during the start-up phase of IBX not only secured the transaction volume for a successful start, but it also enhanced the IBX image in the market place. Through the association with Ericsson, IBX became trustworthy from the outset. After recognizing the advantage of having a reputable local buying organization such as Ericsson in Sweden vouching for the platform image, IBX implemented an 'Anchoring' strategy for the rest of the Nordic region. Through customers like Novo Nordisk in Denmark, who joined as an IBX shareholder, Fortum in Finland, and the Norwegian Government, IBX secured credibility and solid initial transaction volume in the Nordic region.

Building on the initial success of this anchor strategy, IBX decided to enter the German market by offering Deutsche Post and Lufthansa a small participation share, and later on by acquiring trimondo.

Choosing between a transaction- vs. a subscription-based revenue model

When deciding the type of revenue model to adopt, IBX had to choose between the following two alternatives:

- a **transaction-based model**, which consisted of charging a fee for every transaction made through the platform, or
- a **subscription-based model**, where users paid an annual fee for the usage of the platform regardless of the volume of transactions made during that period.

At the end, IBX opted for the subscription-based model. Although a transaction model can be very appealing to customers initially because they only pay for the services that they actually use, and also to the platform operator because it can earn high revenues if fees are a percentage of the negotiated volume, customers feel that the long term costs of the solution could be very high and not controlled. Most customers are typically facing a make versus buy decision and want to know that the solution becomes cost efficient long-term as in the case of a subscription model.

The subscription model also provided IBX two decisive advantages. First, it provides a better cash flow since the fees do not depend on a transaction volume that might or might not be realized. Second, the cash flow is stable and predictable because of the long-term subscriptions. Ultimately, this creates a more sound foundation to build the company on.

Additionally, since it is the buying organizations that pay the subscription fees, suppliers do not feel pressured to invest in a technology that they did not choose; a fact which increases the commitment of buyers and suppliers to the new process. Peter Lageson explained:

> What is interesting with Lufthansa, IKEA, Skanska and Ericsson, is that they made the full investment and got the sponsorship and the management commitment to go through the necessary changes. This type of commitment is absolutely decisive for success.

It also became clear to IBX that the advantage in a transaction-based model (which other platforms such as mondus.com have used) of charging fees as percentages of auctioned purchase volume, was just superficial. Large companies like Deutsche Post or IKEA with a huge purchase volume did not want to see their suppliers' prices increase by 1% due to the IBX transaction fees. Transaction-based fees also would have increased the danger that the involved parties start closing transactions outside of the platform in order to avoid paying for these fees. Peter Lageson comments:

> We were purchasing people ourselves and we understood that buying organizations would not accept this intermediation. Some of them even argued: Why should I pay one or two percent to a third party on a continual basis? Thus, even if you have a transaction model today, you will be forced by the buyers to impose a cap at some point, so, in all reality, you are back to a subscription model.

Generating compliance among users

> Traditionally the purchasing department is about negoti-ation and contracting, but I think this is completely wrong. If you close a framework agreement and bring down agreed prices by 10%, you will only achieve these 10% savings if you have 100% compliance. But if your compliance is only 50%, then you'll only get 5% of these savings. The rest is maverick buying[25] and, ulti-mately, you may end up without any savings.
>
> Peter Lageson

Before the advent of e-procurement systems, it was common that end users in a given company would order MRO items from suppliers that did not belong to the preferred vendor base or were not even registered with the company. This so-called maverick or off-con-tract buying increased the expected spending of the company since these vendors typically had higher prices than the preferred vendors.

That is one reason why eProcurement became popu-lar with companies since it introduced an automated process that made off-contract buying difficult, resulting in increased savings. But, as IBX correctly recognized, making every one buy through the system does not guarantee that every one buys from the cheapest vendor, especially if a company has more than one supplier for the same items. Thus, it is possible that the expected sav-ings potential of increasing the contract compliance could be up to 80% or 90%, while the process effect only delivers up to 20% savings. Lageson explained:

> Normally, after closing a framework agreement, the pre-ferred vendor had to 'market' the idea inside the buying organization, because the agreement didn't guarantee that end users were buying from this supplier as they should. But if the compliance can be assured or at least increased within the procurement system the competi-tion rises, because suppliers then know that it is a life or death situation with the account, and then you get an enormous effect on prices.

Therefore, IBX decided to develop a model that allowed its customers to add any kind of suppliers, even if they did not offer the lowest prices. This model called 'green, yellow, and red' ranked a company's suppliers accord-ing to their price levels and closed agreements with the buying organization, where:

- **Green suppliers** comprised preferred suppliers with approved prices;

- **Yellow suppliers** included preferred vendors with-out specified products; and

- **Red suppliers** were any ad-hoc suppliers.

This model had two main advantages. First, it allowed buying organizations to gradually shift spending from ad-hoc suppliers to preferred ones, focusing the pur-chase volume on just a few. Second, this gradual change in the company's purchasing behavior helped the organization to avoid engaging in two fights simultane-ously (1) changing the buying behavior from manual to electronic, and (2) altering the pattern from old sup-plier to preferred vendor.

The benefit of higher compliance, which can be increased to levels of up to 80%, is not only reflected in a diminished level of maverick buying, but also in gained bargaining leverage vis-à-vis suppliers. The bar-gaining position improves mainly because suppliers are more interested in closing agreements, where agreed purchase volumes are actually being adhered to. This is the main reason why IBX does not encourage its cus-tomers to engage in bundle buying initiatives, because even if large companies managed to put their purchase volumes together, suppliers already know how high their compliance to framework agreements would be; a fact that impedes buyers to reach the desired leverage. Peter Lageson comments:

> Therefore, these companies should focus on ending the implementation of the eProcurement system and restructure their own purchasing behavior first, as sup-pliers know that they won't allocate all the volume.

Competition

Indirect competition

IBX confronts a number of direct competitors, but other players in the industry also represent an indirect or a future competitive threat. Companies such as Ariba, SAP and Oracle are the three major licensed eProcurement software providers. They pursue a strat-egy of selling their software licenses to B2B platforms on a regional basis without any contact at the opera-tional level. Nevertheless, Ariba has shown interest in moving from initially being a software vendor, to becoming a software service provider and to then becoming a third-party platform, thus entering in direct competition with companies such as IBX. Other smaller eProcurement software providers or niche solu-tion providers (such as POET or Healey-Hudson) play

---

25 Any company or employee purchase that does not meet a company's purchasing policy. This includes using off-contract methods of procurement and non-authorized purchases.

more of a complementary role than a competitive one. These can offer just a fraction of what B2B platforms do and are mostly used by companies that do not require a complete solutions portfolio.

According to IBX, ERP vendors like SAP or Oracle have also recognized the growth potential in the eProcurement solutions market. Their main advantage consists of their vast pool of existing customers, particularly large enterprises that have shown an increased interest in eProcurement. Their limited expertise in operating such platforms has been overcome through strategic alliances with other B2B platform operators and software providers. In fact, these vendors have entered into partnership with supplier networks and are reselling or recommending them as integrated parts of their supplier relationship management (SRM) solutions.

Direct competition

In the B2B platforms market there are four leading supplier networks, including IBX, cc-hubwoo, Perfect Commerce and Quadrem that provide services for supplier enablement and host search engines connected to eProcurement solutions. Additionally, they also offer end-to-end connectivity for order documents, acknowledgement and invoices, as well as content management. These four companies are grouped according to their business models, where Quadrem and cc-hubwoo show a supplier-centric transaction based model, while IBX and Perfect Commerce are considered to be buyer-centric, subscription based platforms[26] (see Exhibit 7).

While the main competitor of IBX in regional terms is cc-hubwoo in Europe (especially in Germany and France), Perfect Commerce and Quadrem concentrate their business operations on the North American and Asian markets respectively. Quadrem also differentiates itself as the only vertical platform, specialized in the mining, metal and mineral industry, concentrating 95% of its business on that industry. Peter Lageson elaborates on Quadrem's positioning:

> Quadrem seems to be the most successful example of a vertical platform, but they also focus on indirect materials rather than the sensitive direct flows.

After the competition in the American market had increased significantly during and after the dot.com bubble, numerous American platforms have tried to enter the European market to benefit from its higher price levels. This was, for instance, the case with Perfect Commerce, which on February 7th, 2006 announced the acquisition of the former e-business star CommerceOne. This strategy not only allowed Perfect Commerce to own the eProcurement solutions developed by the software provider, but also to expand its operations in Europe through the acquired customer database.

In terms of growth, only IBX and Quadrem have shown a steady annual growth rate of around 30% in terms of revenue, while Perfect Commerce grew at a pace of less than 10% and cc-hubwoo at just 3%. It is worth mentioning that although cc-hubwoo was 30% larger than IBX, it has only been growing through mergers and not through customer acquisition. Market observers are expecting a continued consolidation; hence, IBX has already looked towards the Benelux and UK markets. Peter Lageson explained:

> It is an international game; we don't compete on a local level anymore. Before, there were a lot of local players with a 3–4 million Euros turnover that could get a big customer and do OK. Today, we are basically facing Ariba and cc-hubwoo, and we see that Quadrem and Perfect Commerce are around and we are running into the Accentures and IBMs of this world. It's another level of competition compared to a couple of years ago; it's much more international.

---

26 Taken from 'On demand and end-to-end', *Efficient Purchasing*, Vol. 1, Issue 1, p. 50, 2005.

Exhibit 7 Leading B2B platforms

● = 100%	Software	Professional Services	ASP			Content and Connectivity	Market		
			Source	Procure	Pay		US	Europe	Asia
cc-hubwoo	○	◕	◕	●	◕	●	◑	●	●
IBX	○	◑	●	●	◕	●	◕	●	◕
Perfect Commerce	◑	◕	●	◕	◕	●	●	◔	◔
Quadrem	○	◕	●	◕	◕	●	◑	◑	●

Source: Beer, Johan (2005), 'Leveraging the network: On demand and end-to-end', Efficient Purchasing, Vol. 1, Issue 1, pp. 50–51.

Success factors

> The success of IBX is a combination of many factors: the right time, the right people, the right founding companies, the right investors, the right business model and ultimately, fewer mistakes made.
>
> **Peter Lageson**

IBX started with strong industry support. In spite of the crash of the Internet bubble that led to the demise of many B2B initiatives, IBX was able to survive and grow. Peter Lageson is convinced that the leading market position of IBX comes as a result of the company's relentless focus on the most decisive features of B2B platforms. He elaborates:

> Deep knowledge in purchasing and liquidity are the most important success factors now and back then. The morning after we started, we had almost one billion Euro transaction volume and around 80 suppliers from Ericsson ready to use. That's real liquidity.

Liquidity not only assured transaction volume, which in turn guaranteed revenues to IBX, but it also was a sign of quality to the market. By pursuing liquidity, especially through their anchor strategy, IBX opened new doors in various markets.

IBX's success is also due in large part to the company's ability to forge strategic alliances with the right partners. IBX would have had opportunities to collaborate with firms such as Accenture and IBM. However, there were some aspects that demonstrated to IBX that such collaborations could end up in competitive situations. Choosing SAP as a partner underpinned the IBX position. Both have complemented each other's role: SAP provides the software and IBX the solutions and deep understanding of the purchasing processes. Stefan Geilen, Head of Organization, Standards & Tools at Deutsche Post Corporate Procurement, commented:

> We chose to work with IBX because of their high global competence in the field of procurement processes – and their comprehensive SAP experience.[27]

Industry knowledge has also played an important role in IBX success. Through its expertise, IBX has managed and solved complex situations, showing that it can handle the required tasks year after year, thus winning customers' trust. According to Peter Lageson, the tricky part has been to transform this industry knowledge into a brand. As IBX looks ahead and wants to position itself as a source of sourcing and procurement knowl-edge, the strength of the brand and customers' trust become increasingly important. Lageson explained:

> Today, IBX doesn't need to rely on its owners anymore. But, during the early years, they guaranteed the quality and the liquidity. Our brand is now positioned as a cross-industry solutions and services provider for efficient purchasing. We are working with the most renowned companies in the world, in the biggest industries. We have won the confidence of IKEA, Ericsson, Lufthansa and Deutsche Post. Their endorsement is immensely valuable as we continue our expansion into new markets and new industries.

IBX started as a buyer-centric platform, which means that neutrality towards the suppliers was never an objective. However, neutrality became an issue on the buyer side in the early years, as many buyer organizations thought that IBX would give preferential treatment to Ericsson. Peter Lageson recounted:

> When Volvo joined [the platform], which was of the same size as Ericsson, the market understood that IBX wouldn't prefer any large corporation over another. Solving this issue helped us to increase confidence among new companies to join as customers.

Beside the key success factors that IBX was able to exploit, external organizations decide to join the platform mainly because of the multiple benefits that IBX offers on both the buyer- and the seller-side.

The main advantages that buyers on the IBX platform benefit from include the following:

- **Contract compliance effect** that has substituted maverick buying is the most important benefit of using eProcurement solutions. IBX has managed to increase average levels of compliance of around 30% to 50% up to 80%. This has led (1) to the realization of savings potential (price cut-offs) reached through framework agreements by each buying organization, and (2) to an increase in the bargaining power of buyers vis-à-vis their suppliers because of the guaranteed purchasing volume.

- **Process optimization** that increases the savings potential by up to 20% thanks to IBX's eProcurement solution. This optimization cuts the purchase management cost, reducing the cost per order from 70-90 Euros down to 30-40 Euros.

- **Process transparency,** through the use of the IBX platform. Buying agents can track and trace the

---

27 Taken from www.ibxeurope.com.

complete purchase process and control different aspects such as delivery and internal distribution. Additionally, IBX delivers statistics on buying patterns and helps identify process areas that can be further optimized, especially for commodities that are hard to control (such as professional services).

■ **High interoperability.** IBX supports its operations with XML messaging technology, which makes it easy for the platform to connect to other systems not using SAP technology. This was the case of Skanska, which uses an Oracle-based ERP system. Front-to-back supply chain integration was then assured and provided to all buying organizations for data processing and integration of purchase orders, order changes and invoicing.

■ **Price reduction through online negotiations.** The eSourcing solution of IBX allows buyers to obtain lower prices at reverse auction events, where suppliers compete to capture their purchase volume by offering better prices and conditions. These events occur online, reducing the sourcing cycle duration by almost 30% when compared to the off-line method. According to IBX, at reverse auction events, customers achieve savings ranging from 5% to 40% depending on whether the categories have been sourced previously or not.

■ **Bundled volume purchases.** IBX also enables buyers to launch joined auction events, where buying organizations bundle their purchase volumes in order to attain better price levels.

As a buyer-centric business-to-business platform, IBX concentrates its efforts on creating added value for its main customers, the buying organizations. Nonetheless, there are also some important benefits for suppliers using the platform; these include:

■ **Reduced cost of sales.** Suppliers benefit from an automated purchase order system that reduces the error percentage on incoming purchase orders, which can be as high as 40% due to inaccurate or incomplete data.

■ **Deeper market insight.** Suppliers are provided with additional statistics and information that help them monitor customer demand and market changes. Suppliers can thus identify market needs, set price levels accordingly and also quickly react to newcomers and low-cost vendors.

IBX's next challenge: Expanding the business model into Europe and into the direct vertical market

The five-year contract that IBX closed in 2004 with Skanska, one of the world's largest construction companies with around 54,000 employees, not only delivered average annual revenues of 2.5 million Euros for outsourcing their material flows, but also entailed a great challenge for the IBX business model. Skanska trusted IBX to build a vertical direct materials solution according to the distinct needs of the construction industry.

Together with HOCHTIEF, Skanska had already worked on an initiative called AEC global, an eProcurement platform that never got into operation. IBX attained understanding of the desired purchasing processes and understood that the construction industry was highly project centric (see Exhibit 8). The construction industry handles roughly 80% of the purchase volume through project sourcing, in contrast to other companies in the manufacturing industry that procured the same percentage from framework agreements. To meet the specific needs of the construction industry, IBX has built a specific project-centric request solution to launch requests for information, proposals and quotations as well as to run online auctions. Based on this technology, the IBX source solution was developed and rolled out throughout Skanska. Through this deal, IBX is successfully penetrating the construction industry as a vertical B2B platform for tracking direct and indirect material flows.

Dealing with the governance question

From the outset, IBX was aware of the governance problems that other vertical B2B initiatives such as Covisint, Eutilia[28] and Forrest Express[29] had encountered. In particular, Covisint, which was founded by Ford, General Motors, and DaimlerChrysler (and later joined by Renault, Nissan, and Peugeot Citroen) as an exchange in order to obtain significant component price reductions as well as to become a *de-facto* standard for eCommerce platforms in the automotive industry[30], faced serious governance issues.

---

28 An eMarket for the European utility companies founded by EdF, Electrabel, Endesa, Enal, Iberrola, National Grid, Nuon, RWE, Scottish Power, United Utilities and Vattenfall (www.eutilia.com).

29 Paper Exchange founded by Georgia Pacific, International Paper and Weyerhaeuser.

30 Taken from 'Shaping IT Standardization in the Automotive Industry', *Electronic Markets*, Vol. 15, Issue 4, p. 339, 2005.

Exhibit 8 Overview of the IBX solution for Skanska

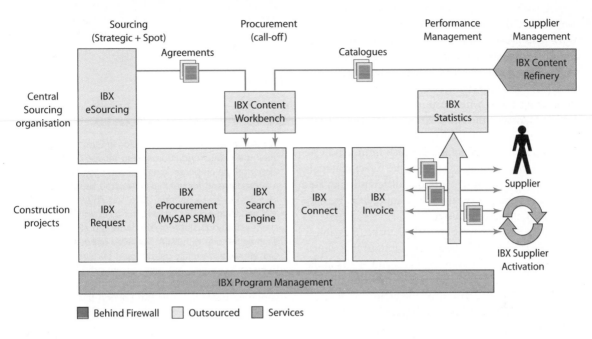

Source: IBX.

This platform was created in 1999 to broker 500 billion USD in purchase volumes. By the time it was sold to Freemarkets[31] in December of 2003, Covisint had already burned 350 million USD investment funds from the carmakers. Ultimately, it came as no surprise that this platform, which had received praise for its liquidity and the bargaining power of its owners, failed. In December 2002, Gerry Kobe, Executive Director for Automotive Industries, wrote:

> Today the B2B exchange is floundering. The investment is nearly gone; suppliers have been burned by OEMs[32] in manipulated online auctions; brokered sales are a fraction of what was expected and competition has eroded the value of the auction service itself. Covisint has reduced its workforce by 35% and is relocating to smaller and cheaper office space. Covisint is slowly dying; it's as simple as that.[33]

The development of such a standardized portal became more complex than expected due to problems of (1) governance between the three giant founders, (2) choice of technology standards, and (3) adaptation of internal process to the Covisint solution. The OEMs also did not allow the suppliers to get directly involved in the devel-

opment of the platform. This resulted in serious technology conflicts during the roll-out phase since Covisint did not match the suppliers' existing IT systems. This situation coupled with the growing mistrust towards the carmakers led to an unexpected reaction of the first-tier suppliers. Bosch GmbH, Continental AG and INA Werk Schaeffler oHG launched in April 2000 SupplyOn as a competing platform.

In the end, Covisint did not reach its goals. It reduced costs only on the buyer side, while positioning itself as an intermediary, charging subscriptions as well as transactions fees, and therefore generating more costs than value to suppliers. Although more buying organizations joined the platform, Covisint did not manage to attract enough suppliers to reach a 'critical mass' of transactions. At the same time, its inability to master basic technical integration impeded the creation of switching costs on the vendor side.

31 Freemarkets was bought by Ariba in January 2005.
32 Original Equipment Manufacturers.
33 Quoted in 'Covisint in Europe: analysing the B2B auto e-marketplace', *Int. Journal Automotive Technology and Management*, Vol. 5, Issue 1, p. 31, 2005.

Contrary to the Covisint approach, IBX from the outset assumed complete responsibility for Ericsson's eProcurement transactions and for its suppliers' network. This meant that IBX had to customize its services both for suppliers and buyers, thus making it a customer-driven B2B platform. Such cooperation never took place at most vertical B2B platforms, which hired developing teams with no purchase experience and having to force at the end their purchase departments to bring in the requirements. Additionally, IBX started as an indirect material initiative, which from a strategic perspective was not as sensitive as the direct materials since the latter represent a strong differentiating element of buying organizations, especially if they compete in the same industry.

IBX used its cooperation with Skanska to establish an eProcurement and eSourcing standard that coped with the distinctive needs of suppliers and buyers in the construction industry. IBX was convinced that by developing a strong vision of the right processes, it would avoid within the platform governance problems between competing construction companies. IBX's intention was to deliver a proven business model with customization capabilities while not letting the incumbents control any discussion regarding best practices, purchase processes or priority issues. According to Peter Lageson, IBX entered the construction industry with a strong message:

> We may accept change but thanks to our experience with Skanska, we are coming with an established and 80% proven business model. We know the right processes, so we can take the arguments, fight back and customize the remaining 20%, if needed. This way and because we are strong in our own thinking, we hope and believe that we create trust with the new prospects.

Next steps

IBX is not yet satisfied with the position they have achieved, as Hans Ahlinder, CEO of IBX explained:

> We plan to continue our expansion in Europe. […] We are seeing a clear trend. Purchasing moves up higher and higher on the corporate management agenda and there is a large demand for purchasing-related services in all the markets where we operate. 2005 was an amazing year for IBX and I expect continued strong growth in 2006. The successful acquisition of trimondo and strategic deals, such as the one with IKEA, validated our business model. Our efforts have really paid off and our services and on-demand solutions will play an important part in our continued growth. […] Germany and Scandinavia are important markets for us but beyond this, we want to expand with a focus on France and the UK.[34]

Clearly, IBX still faces many challenges. It remains to be seen whether its business model will be able to cope with the challenges of moving into a vertical B2B platform and whether its success factors are only fit for the horizontal market. In a way, the jury is still out and the market will have the last word.

---

34 Taken from www.ibxeurope.com.

eBay® customer support outsourcing

If we are to continue outsourcing, and even consider expanding it, why should we keep paying someone else to do what we can do for ourselves?

Kathy Dalton leaned forward in her chair. She read the message on her computer screen and let the words sink in. 'Why had she not anticipated that? After all, she was adept at asking insightful questions.' She felt her heart rate quicken.

She would have stared out her office window and pondered this question, but she didn't have an office. In keeping with a well-established Silicon Valley tradition, everyone at eBay, including CEO Meg Whitman, occupied a cubicle. Dalton, an attractive, 38-year old executive had joined eBay in late 2002 after years of call center experience for major long distance carriers. Now, nearly two years later, she couldn't think of doing business any other way. She liked being in the center of the action. Sitting in a transparent cube, surrounded by hundreds of service representatives, added to her already high level of energy, and kept her in touch with eBay's internal and external customers.

Dalton reflected on the email she had just received from her boss, Wendy Moss, Vice President of Global Customer Support. She knew she would pick up the phone soon, call Moss, and ask her clarifying questions about her email. Her mind raced through the details of the proposed outsourcing strategy she had submitted to Moss last week. She quizzed herself:

■ 'Did my team and I make a strong enough case for proposing almost a 100% increase in the amount of volume to be outsourced?'

■ 'Will eBay management concur with our recommendation to begin outsourcing potentially sensitive risk-related inquiries for the first time?'

■ 'How will senior management react to the addition of a second outsourcing vendor?'

■ 'Did we cover adequately the types of proposed volumes targeted and how these would be transitioned to the outsourcing vendors?'

■ 'In the event of a major vendor problem, systems issue, or natural disaster, how executable is our back-out plan?'

■ 'Will the data in our proposal allay the growing concerns among executives about offshore outsourcing altogether?'

She wondered, 'How would eBay senior management react to our proposal to reorganize and expand outsourcing in a new three-tiered approach?' 'And, would they even consider expansion in light of recent headlines about companies reducing the amount of work outsourced to India because of quality issues?'

Professors Scott Newman, Gary Grikscheit, Rohit Verma and Research Assistant Vivek Malapati prepared this case solely as the basis for class discussion. The information presented in this case is based on publicly available information and insights gained through numerous interactions between University of Utah MBA students, their faculty advisors, and local eBay managers during a field study project (sponsored by the University of Utah and approved by the eBay Salt Lake City Service Center). The case contains writer-compiled, disguised information and is not intended to endorse and/or illustrate effective or ineffective service management practices. Certain sections of the case study have been fabricated based on current service management and customer service literature to provide a realistic and stimulating classroom experience. The numbers in the case are available from public information, or estimates, or are fictitious. This case was the winner of the 2006 CIBER-Production and Operations Management Society International Case Competition.

This last question had perplexed her for several months. Not only was it a personal issue for Dalton – she felt her job security at eBay depended largely on the company's continuing commitment to offshore outsourcing – but one she recognized as a business practice whose time perhaps had come and gone. Several leading consultants were claiming that offshoring had lost much of its cachet in recent years as companies were coming to grips with the real costs, logistics, management commitment and service quality associated with third-party partners in India, the Philippines and elsewhere. In her proposal, Dalton had reinforced the benefits to eBay of continuing to outsource outside the United States and to weave into her new strategy more 'nearshoring' alternatives as well.

Dalton was scheduled to fly to San Jose in just two weeks to present her outsourcing strategy to Whitman and her executive staff. Now, here's Moss' email, questioning why she had not addressed the option of cutting out the middleman and building eBay-owned outsourcing locations in other countries.

A little history

eBay called itself 'The World's Online Marketplace®.' For the sale of goods and services by a diverse community of individuals and small businesses no venue was more appropriate. eBay's mission was to provide a robust trading platform where practically anyone could trade practically anything. Sellers included individual collectors of the rare and eclectic, as well as major corporations like Microsoft and IBM. Items sold on eBay ranged from collectibles like trading cards, antiques, dolls and house wares to everyday items like used cars, clothing, books, CDs and electronics. With 11 million or more items available on eBay at any one time, it was the largest and most popular person-to-person trading community on the Internet.

eBay came a long way from being a pet project for founder Pierre Omidyar and holding its first auction on Labor Day in September of 1995. Omidyar developed a program and launched it on a website called Auction Web. According to eBay legend, he was trying to help his wife find other people with whom she could trade Pez dispensers. Omidyar found he was continually adding storage space to handle the amount of email generated, reflecting the pent-up demand for an online meeting place for sellers and buyers. The site soon began to outgrow his personal Internet account.

Realizing the potential this web service could have, he quit his job as a services development engineer at General Magic, a San Jose based software company, and devoted full time attention managing Auction Web. As traffic increased, he also began charging a fee of $0.25 per listing to compensate for the cost involved in maintaining a business Internet account.

In 1996, Jeff Skoll, a Stanford Business School graduate and friend of Omidyar's joined him to further develop Auction Web. They changed the name to eBay, short for East Bay Technologies. In mid 1997, a Menlo Park based venture capital firm invested $5 million dollars for a 22% stake in eBay. Omidyar knew that the venture capital would be critical in building infrastructure and attracting top-tier management to the company.

In early 1998, Omidyar and Skoll realized eBay needed an experienced CEO to lead and develop an effective management team, as well as to solidify the company's financial position with an IPO. In March of that year, Whitman accepted the position of president and CEO. A graduate of the Harvard Business School, Whitman had learned the importance of branding at companies such as Hasbro and Walt Disney. She hired senior staff from companies like Pepsico and Disney. She built a management team with an average of 20 years of business experience per executive and developed a strong vision for the company. Whitman immediately understood that the eBay community of users was the foundation of the company's business model. A central tenet of eBay's culture was captured in the phrase 'The community was not built for eBay, but eBay was built by and for the community.' It was not about just selling things on the Internet; it was about bonding people through the web site.

Business model and market share

Unlike many companies that were born before the Internet and then had to scramble to get online, eBay was born with the net. Its transaction-based business model was perfectly suited for the Internet. Sellers 'listed' items for sale on the web site. Interested buyers could either bid higher than the previous bid in an auction format, or use the 'Buy It Now' feature and pay a predetermined price. The seller and buyer worked out the shipping method. Payment was usually made through PayPal®, the world's leading online payment company, which eBay acquired in 2002. Because eBay never handled the items being sold, it did not incur warehousing

Exhibit 1 Income statement and balance sheet, abridged

eBay's Income Statement (in '000s Dollars)	12/31/2004	12/31/2003	12/31/2002
Net revenues	$ 3,271,309	$ 2,165,096	$ 1,214,100
Cost of net revenues	614,415	416,058	213,876
Gross profit (loss)	2,656,894	1,749,038	1,000,224
Sales & marketing expenses	857,874	567,565	349,650
Product development expenses	240,647	159,315	104,636
General & administrative expenses	415,725	302,703	171,785
Patent litigation expense		29,965	
Payroll expense on employee stock options	17,479	9,590	4,015
Amortization of acquired intangible assets	65,927	50,659	15,941
Total operating expenses	1,597,652	1,119,797	646,027
Income (loss) from operations	1,059,242	629,241	354,197
Interest & other income, net	77,867	37,803	49,209
Interest expense	8,879	4,314	1,492
Impairment of certain equity investments		−1,230	−3,781
Income before income tax – United States	820,892		
Income before income tax – international	307,338		
Net income (loss)	778,223	441,771	249,891
Net income (loss) per share-diluted	0.57	0.335	0.213

eBay's Cash Flow (in '000s Dollars)	12/31/2004	12/31/2003	12/31/2002
Net income (loss)	$ 778,223	$ 441,771	$ 249,891
Cumulative effect of accounting change		5,413	
Provision for doubtful accounts & auth cred	90,942	46,049	25,455
Provision for transaction losses	50,459	36,401	7,832
Depreciation & amortization	253,690	159,003	76.576
Stock-based compensation		5,492	5,953
Amortization of unearned stock-based compens	5,832		
Tax benefit on the exer of employ stock opts	261,983	130,638	91,237
Impairment of certain equity investments		1,230	3,781
Minority interests	6,122		
Minority interest & other net income adj		7,784	1,324
Gain (loss) on sale of assets			−21,378
Accounts receivable	−105,540	−153,373	−54,583
Funds receivable from customers	−44,751	−38,879	−11,819
Other current assets	−312,756	−13.133	10,716
Other non-current assets	−308	−4,111	−1,195
Deferred tax assets, net		69,770	8,134
Deferred tax liabilities, net	28,652		
Accounts payable	−33,975	17,348	14,631
Net cash flows from investing activities	−2,013,220	−1,319,542	−157,759
Proceeds from issuance of common stock, net	650,638	700,817	252,181
Proceeds (principal pmts) on long-term obligs	−2,969	−11,951	−64
Partnership distributions			−50
Net cash flows from financing activities	647,669	688,866	252,067
Eff of exch rate change on cash & cash equivs	28,768	28,757	11,133
Net incr (decr) in cash & cash equivalents	−51,468	272,200	585,344
Cash & cash equivalents, beginning of year	1,381,513	1,109,313	523,969
Cash & cash equivalents, end of year	1,330,045	1,381,513	1,109,313
Cash paid for interest	8,234	3,237	1,492

Source: Case writers' estimates, compliations, and public records.

expense and, of course, did not hold any inventory. For a company with almost $8 billion in assets, not a single dollar was invested in inventory (Exhibit 1).

In 2004, eBay reported revenue of nearly $3.3 billion. Revenue was mainly generated from two categories. The first, called the Listing Fee, involved a nominal fee incurred by the seller in posting an item for sale. This fee ranged from $0.25 to $2.00. The second, the Final Value Fee, was charged to the seller as a percentage of the final price when a sale was made. This amounted to between 1.25% and 5% of the selling price, depending on the price of the item. The Final Value Fee on a $4.00 Beanie Baby would be $.20, representing a 5% fee. The same fee on a mainframe computer selling for $400,000.00 would be 1.25%, or $5,000.00.

Being first-to-market in the e-commerce world was frequently an insurmountable competitive edge. eBay capitalized on being the first online auction house. Early competition came from companies like OnSale, Auction Universe, Amazon, Yahoo! and Classified2000. These companies battled eBay on a number of fronts, mainly pricing, advertising online, and on attempting to lure key eBay employees away to join their ranks. eBay's biggest and most formidable competitive threat came from Amazon.com when it spent over $12 million launching its person-to-person auction service in 1999. eBay withstood all of these challenges. Amazon's efforts ultimately failed because it could not generate enough site traffic. Auction buyers went where the most items were available for sale, and sellers went where the most buyers were found for their products. eBay had more buyers, more sellers, and more items – more than 1.4 billion items were listed on the site in 2004! These numbers dwarfed the nearest competitor by a factor of over 50. eBay enjoyed a dominant 92% market share of the domestic online auction business, and a 74% share of the international market (Exhibit 2).

Exhibit 2 Online auction market share

	2001		2002		2003		2004	
	U.S.	Int'l	U.S.	Int'l	U.S.	Int'l	U.S.	Int'l
eBay	83%	41%	87%	50%	90%	65%	92%	74%
Yahoo	7%	28%	6%	25%	4%	16%	3%	11%
Amazon	6%	10%	4%	8%	2%	5%	1%	2%
Overstock	N/A	N/A	1%	1%	2%	2%	2%	2%
uBid	1%	1%	1%	1%	1%	N/S	1%	N/A
All others	3%	20%	1%	15%	1%	12%	1%	11%

Source: Case writers' estimates, compilations, and public records.

eBay's Customer Support organization

In December, 2004, Dalton was an operations director in eBay's Customer Support organization. She had several major responsibilities; the most critical one was customer support outsourcing, both domestic and offshore (Exhibit 3). This role occupied approximately 80% of her time. Upon joining the company, she had relocated to Salt Lake City, Utah, the site of eBay's largest customer service center. Utah's four seasons and mountainous terrain suited her. She loved to ski knee-deep powder in the winter and navigate forest trails on her mountain bike in summer. While thoughts of early season skiing had entered her mind, she had in fact spent the last three weekends in her cube and in conference rooms with her managers hammering out the strategy she had passed on to Moss for review.

World wide, eBay's Customer Support staff consisted of an estimated 3,000 FTE, comprising roughly two-thirds of the corporate work force. eBay operated major service centers in Salt Lake City, Omaha, Vancouver, Berlin, and Dublin. Smaller company owned Customer Support groups were located in Sydney, Hong Kong, London, and Seoul. The majority of these employees spent their workdays responding to customer emails. In 2004, eBay answered over 30 million customer inquiries, covering everything from questions about selling, bidding, product categories, billing, and pricing to thornier issues involving illegal or prohibited listings and auction security (Exhibit 4).

The Customer Support organization was made up of two major units – 1) General Support, and 2) Trust and Safety. Historically, most of the customer contacts were handled by the General Support unit. The communications consisted of questions regarding bidding on auctions, listing and selling items, and account adjustments. By mid-2004, however, nearly 45% of inquiries were directed toward the Trust and Safety function. Here, hundreds of employees were responsible for ensuring that the items listed on eBay were legitimate, legal, did not infringe on copyrighted, patented, or original material, and that they fell within the company's policies (i.e., no firearms, tobacco or alcohol, human body parts, etc.). It also enforced eBay's guidelines for proper member behavior by policing activities such as shill bidding, merchandise misrepresentation, and outright fraud.

Exhibit 3 eBay organization chart

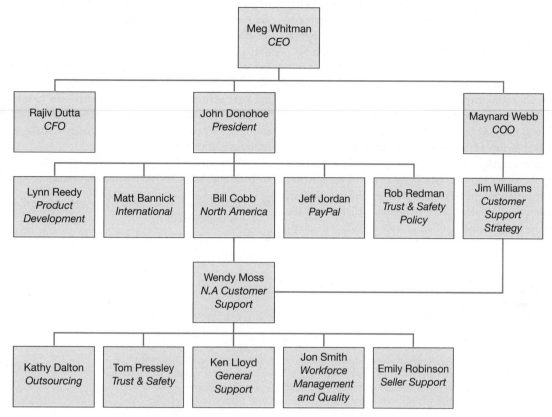

Source: Case writers' compliations, and public records.

Exhibit 4 eBay Customer Support volumes by channel (in millions)

	2001	2002	2003	2004
General Support				
Email	8.1	12.1	14.6	16.1
Phone	0.1	0.3	0.4	0.8
Chat	NA	NA	0.4	0.4
Total	8.2	12.4	15.4	17.3
Trust & Safety				
Email	4	6.8	9.8	12.6
Phone	0	0	0	0
Chat	NA	NA	0.1	0.6
Total	4	6.8	9.9	13.2
Combined GS and T&S				
Email	12.1	18.9	24.4	28.7
Phone	0.1	0.3	0.4	0.8
Chat	NA	NA	0.5	1
Total	12.2	19.2	25.3	30.5

Source: Case writers' estimates, compliations, and public records.

PowerSellers

Approximately 94% of eBay's customer service volume was email-based. However, live chat and phone inquiries were growing as the company opened up these channels to more customers, based on their profitability. Live chat volume was predicted to increase to 1.5 million communications in 2005, up 50% over 2004. Phone calls handled in 2005 were anticipated to reach 1.4 million, almost double the number in the previous year. This phone volume was expected to come primarily from 'PowerSellers,' who represented less than 7% of eBay users, but, due to the volume of merchandise they traded on the site, accounted for nearly 90% of the company's profit.

Phone and live chat access to Customer Support was designed to enlarge the pool of PowerSellers. Dedicated service representatives received additional training in upsell, cross-sell, and auction display techniques to share with sellers to increase the number of items they sold and qualify them for higher PowerSeller monthly sales volume thresholds (Bronze, Silver, Gold, Platinum, Titanium). Once attained, these thresholds qualified sellers for dedicated phone and chat support, as well as for the coveted PowerSeller logo (Exhibit 5).

Trust and Safety

No other company was able to harness the ubiquity of the Web and marry it to the auction concept as successfully as eBay. At the same time, eBay had to confront challenges never faced before, particularly in the arena of auction security and fraud prevention. Caveat emptor, 'let the buyer beware,' had been a rule in the auction world since the middle ages. With the advent of eBay, buyers had to deal with unknown sellers over the Internet, sight unseen, often in a totally different country, without the ability to personally examine the goods, and with little information about the seller except some written feedback from other buyers who had previously done business with him or her. It was absolutely critical for eBay's survival to create and nurture an environment of trust where millions of people around the globe could feel secure in trading online. The Trust and Safety Dept. was given this task. Procedural complexities, the differing legal environments and customs between countries, as well as the sophistication of online identity theft scams combined to make Trust and Safety a challenging business unit to manage.

Dalton wrestled with a number of questions related to Trust and Safety and its potential for outsourcing:

- 'What kind of Trust and Safety volume could be safely outsourced?
- 'What kind of Trust and Safety volume could not be outsourced?'

Exhibit 5 **PowerSeller criteria**

To qualify, members must:

- Uphold the eBay community values, including honesty, timeliness and mutual respect
- Average a minimum of $1000 in sales per month, for three consecutive months
- Achieve an overall Feedback rating of 100, of which 98% or more is positive
- Have been an active member for 90 days
- Have an account in good financial standing
- Not violate any severe policies in a 60-day period
- Not violate three or more of **any** eBay policies in a 60-day period
- Maintain a minimum of 4 average monthly listings for the past 3 months

PowerSeller program eligibility is reviewed every month. To remain PowerSellers, members must:

- Uphold eBay community values, including honesty, timeliness, and mutual respect
- Maintain the minimum average monthly sales amount for your PowerSeller level
- Maintain a 98% positive total feedback rating
- Maintain an account in good financial standing
- Comply with all eBay listing and marketplace *policies* – Not violate any severe policies in a 60 day period and not violate three or more of **any** eBay policies in a 60-day period

PowerSeller Levels

There are 5 tiers that distinguish PowerSellers, based on their gross monthly sales. Some benefits and services vary with each tier. eBay automatically calculates eligibility each month and notifies qualified sellers via email.

Gross sales Criteria for each PowerSeller tier

Bronze	Silver	Gold	Platinum	Titanium
$1,000	$3,000	$10,000	$25,000	$150,000

Source: eBay web site, case writer's estimates, compilations, and public records.

- 'How could she and eBay determine the credibility and quality of the potential outsourcing vendors?'
- 'How could she guarantee the vendors' ability to safeguard the eBay information entrusted to them?'

A number of eBay's executives had expressed concern and outright hostility to the idea of outsourcing any Trust and Safety volume. Rob Redman headed up the Trust and Safety Policy group in San Jose. He and other executives worried about outside vendors handling the sensitive type of customer inquiries common to this unit, especially when personal information such as Social Security numbers and credit card account numbers could be accessed. In addition, many of the jobs within Trust and Safety required direct and ongoing contact with local, national, and international law enforcement agencies in the hunt for and prosecution of fraudsters. Redman believed outsourcing vendors would never be as skilled at developing and nurturing these key liaisons as eBay's own personnel, and he had made this known to Whitman, Moss, and Dalton on numerous occasions.

Underneath her confident exterior, Dalton worried about these issues as well. She did not have any hands-on background in Trust and Safety herself. Still, she was intrigued by the possibility that several categories of inquiries within the department might be outsourced without undue risk.

Outsourcing beginnings

By late 1999, eBay had enrolled 4 million registered members, nearly all in the United States. Five years later, the eBay community had burgeoned to over 135 million members, living in every country in the world. If eBay were its own country, it would have been the 9th largest on earth, behind Russia.

To stay abreast of the growth of its customer base, eBay significantly increased the resources dedicated to its Customer Support group. In the very early days of 1995-1996, founder Omidyar would reserve part of his Saturday afternoons in a local San Jose park to respond directly to member questions. He soon could not manage the volume himself so the first customer service staff was organized. A measure of the power of the eBay community was the fact that these first service staffers were not employees at all, but members who had shown a penchant for helping other eBayers. These people worked on a contract basis out of their homes responding to customers' emails. At one time, there were close to 75 such employees, called 'remotes,' living in 17 different states across the country, handling an average of five emails per hour at all hours of the day and night, often while sitting in their pajamas!

In early 1998, eBay Customer Support took another step to simplify management and improve the consistency and quality of service. The company hired a small corps of 'in-house' customer service personnel in the San Jose, California headquarters to supplement its remote contractors. The 'remotes' had been a creative solution for a time, but one that could not be scaled as the technology, logistics, and training requirements of the Customer Support group increased in sophistication.

Kana

One such technological advancement occurred when eBay purchased the Kana email management system later that year to provide service personnel with a variety of 'canned' responses and performance statistics similar to an Automatic Call Distributor. Kana allowed representatives to answer common questions, such as 'How do I list an item for sale?', 'How do I leave feedback?' or 'What do I do with an item I received that is damaged in shipment?' with a few quick keystrokes to input the code number of a pre-scripted email reply. The representatives then took a moment to personalize the email with their name and the recipients' names.

The Kana technology enabled service employees to be trained more quickly and effectively. Most importantly, it reduced response time to customer inquiries and increased the accuracy of information the customer received. It doubled the service representatives' email productivity from 5 responses per hour to 10 and over. Without Kana, there was no way that eBay could have ever considered outsourcing even a portion of its overall Customer Support volume, let alone as Dalton's new strategy proposed, increasing it to over 50%.

By early 1999, nearly twice as many in-house representatives were employed as compared to the 'remotes.' This staffing strategy had paid off in improved productivity and in the rising customer satisfaction scores received from the hundreds of customers polled by mail each month (Exhibit 6). More in-house staff was needed, and a search was begun to build a dedicated center for Customer Support outside of California in a more cost-efficient locale. Three potential sites were considered – Salt Lake City, Tucson, and Albuquerque. In the end, the Utah location was selected due to the availability of a

Exhibit 6 eBay Customer Support productivity and quality

	1998	1999	2000	2001	2002	2003	2004
Emails Productivity/Hr	4.7	9.5	11.1	13.8	15.3	16	16.1
Emails per FTE/Month	571	1254	1475	1980	2078	2225	2280
Email Quality %	N/A	83%	89%	91%	94.5	95%	94%
Customer Satisfaction %	N/A	N/A	84%	86%	87%	88%	88%

Source: Case writers' estimates, compilations, and public records.

ready-made facility, as well as a communications infrastructure, generous incentives offered by the state, and the educational level, work ethic, and foreign language capabilities of the potential employees.

Designed originally for around 300 personnel, the Salt Lake facility was enlarged to accommodate over 1,000 by year-end 2000. In addition, a staff of 125 was added in both the newly opened Berlin and the Sydney locations to handle customer service inquiries. Still, with the worldwide popularity of eBay growing at a rate of 250,000 new members each month, it was apparent by 2001 that eBay could hire only so many of its own service personnel and build only so much of its own brick and mortar contact centers, and that even trying to do so would not keep up with the demand (Exhibit 7). Alternatives like outsourcing had to be explored.

Outsourcing pilot

eBay had made headlines for years for its innovation in the online auction space, its market leadership, its product and technological ingenuity, such as member feedback, the Buy-It-Now feature, item search capabilities, Kana, and for its irresistible pace and can-do attitude. eBay did not manage itself by 'the seat of its pants,' contrary to what others may consider to be a trademark of dotcoms. Far from it, the company was thoughtfully led, financially disciplined, and extremely customer conscious. These were the underpinnings of its tremendous success. eBay let others serve as lab mice, test and bleed, stub their toe, and work out the wrinkles. Then, and only then, it stepped in and adopted the 'latest and greatest' business practices.

Such was the case with outsourcing the elementary portions of its Customer Support operation. Leading companies like American Express, GE, and Citibank had been outsourcing some of their customer service functions for 10–15 years domestically, and for at least half that time offshore before eBay felt comfortable in considering outsourcing. By mid 2001, outsourcing surfaced as a viable way for eBay Customer Support to

scale to demand, avoid capital outlays, reduce unit costs, and leverage its investment in technology and management talent.

But, the senior staff in San Jose, including Whitman, was concerned about the potential reaction of the eBay community. If you traded on eBay, you were not a customer. You were a member of a passionate and vocal community of users, who felt strongly (and rightly so) that eBay's success was directly attributable more to them than to any business savvy of headquarters staff in San Jose. How would the community react to knowing

Exhibit 7 Growth in eBay users and revenues

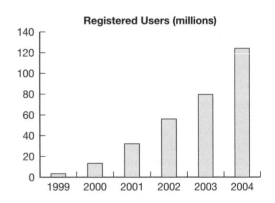

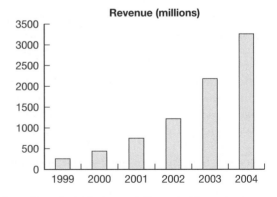

Source: Case writers' estimates, compilations, and public records.

that some customer support inquiries were answered by staff not employed by eBay, or not even residing within the USA?

Another concern at headquarters was the lack of talent inside eBay who had experience with outsourcing. For eBay to uphold its philosophy of 'prudent adoption,' it needed a team of managers who could thoroughly investigate how other companies had successfully outsourced, and then actually run the day-to-day operation.

In December, 2001, eBay hired Jim Williams, an Executive Vice President from Precision Response Corporation (PRC), one of the country's top echelon outsourcing vendors, and gave him responsibility for customer service worldwide. Williams brought instant credibility to the outsourcing initiative. His knowledge of the industry from the providers' point of view rein-

forced the research already compiled on other companies that had been successfully outsourcing elements of customer service in India and the Philippines for years. Furthermore, his intimate association with PRC, its management team, its training and technological capabilities, made Whitman and her executives comfortable utilizing PRC as eBay's first global outsourcing partner.

When it came to the issue of how the eBay community would react to the new venture, Williams had an answer for that, too. He proposed rather than launch a pilot in India, to begin with a small test near PRC's domestic headquarters in Fort Lauderdale. He essentially hand picked the most talented customer service representatives at PRC to handle the eBay business. By February, 2002, all preparations for the pilot were completed, and eBay's first ever outsourcing effort was launched (Exhibit 8).

Exhibit 8 eBay Customer Support timeline

1995: beginning of auction web

1996: first remote service representative hired

1997: eBay name introduced

1998: 'Number of remotes exceeds 75
First in-house reps hired in San Jose
Kana system introduced

1999: Trust and safety launched
Salt Lake City service center opens
Customer support staff exceeds 200

2000: San Jose service center absorbed into Salt Lake City
Salt Lake City service center grows to over 800 employees

2001: First outsourcing strategy devised
Jim Williams hired

2002: Domestic outsourcing piloted at PRC in Florida
First emails sent to India for handling
Kathy Dalton joins eBay
Customer support staff grows to over 1200 with purchase of PayPal

2003: Outsourced monthly volume exceeds 250,000 emails
Outsourcing pilot launched in Philippines for phone volume

2004: Outsourced volume exceeds 30% of total inquiries
Customer service staff exceeds 3000 serving 19 countries
Dalton proposes to expand outsourcing to 50% of total volume.

Source: Case writers' estimates, compilations, and public records.

Expansion of outsourcing

Dalton reflected on the progress made in outsourcing over the last several years. The outsourcing pilot program begun in Fort Lauderdale in 2002 had been relatively seamless. The plan had been to run the pilot for six months before attempting to route volume offshore to one of PRC's service centers in Bangalore, India. Yet, the service quality and email productivity results from the vendor were on par with eBay's own staff after only three months. Williams and his Customer Support team decided to cut the pilot short and sent the first emails to India in June, 2002.

The eBay community's reaction to outsourcing portions of its customer service was essentially only a small ripple in a big pond. There had been some issues with the written English of the agents in India. A handful of complaints found their way to Whitman's desk. Still, the service quality and productivity metrics of the outsource providers, both domestic and foreign, rivaled and frequently surpassed the same measurements of eBay's own employees (Exhibit 9).

And, who could argue with the cost differential? While eBay honored its community, it was also a publicly-traded company with shareholders who were accustomed to a compounded annual growth rate in revenues of over 65%. The domestic outsourcing cost per contact for the volume handled in Fort Lauderdale was not that much less than eBay's own staff results. This was perfectly acceptable, because a significant driver for outsourcing to another location within the U.S. had been, in addition to initially testing the outsourcing model, to avoid the capital outlay of building more plant and equipment for Customer Support.

The unit cost for the email volume being sent to India was another matter. It was literally half the cost per contact handled in the United States. An occasional complaint letter to Whitman about the way an email response was worded by one of the service reps in India was not taken lightly, but still considered a small price to pay for the level of operational savings. No question about it, after both the domestic and offshore outsourcing performance of 2002, eBay executives were satisfied that outsourcing would remain a component of its customer support strategy. Dalton wondered, 'What are the limits?'

Throughout 2003 and most of 2004, eBay had increased the volume of customer service sent offshore. Through analyses of email complexity and available canned responses in Kana, about 40% of the General Support volume, representing close to 500,000 emails a month, had been earmarked as 'outsourceable.' As additional service staff was hired and uptrained in India, the throttle was opened and more email was directed overseas for handling.

Dalton grabbed the hard copy of the strategy document she had submitted to Moss last week. She focused on several pages which highlighted the outsourcing expansion since her arrival at eBay. In a business as fluid as eBay's, it was realistic to expect that the original outsourcing strategy devised in 2002 would change over time. Indeed, even with eBay's penchant for hindsight learning from others' mishaps, Dalton's three-tiered strategy had only evolved after some operational missteps and plenty of analysis of test results.

Customer Relationship Management

One such misstep occurred in late 2003, when eBay conducted an outsourcing pilot in the Philippines for phone volumes. Less than 2% of eBay's volume arrived via telephone, but it was an expensive piece. The hope had been to cut eBay's phone unit cost in half, to just around $2.00. It did not play out that well in reality. During the pilot, both the accents of the Philippino

Exhibit 9 Metric comparison for eBay in-house and outsourcing vendors (comparison for similar volume types)

	Jul-02		Dec-02		Jul-03		Dec-03		Jul-04		Dec-04	
	In	Out	In	Out	In	Out	In	Out	In	Out	In	Out
Email productivity/ Hr	14.8	13.1	15.2	14.7	15.5	15.4	15.7	16.1	15.8	16.3	15.8	16.3
Emails per FTE/ Month	2050	1963	2181	2095	2202	2189	2240	2255	2250	2291	2250	2285
Email Quality %	94%	88%	95%	94%	95%	95%	94%	95%	93%	95%	93%	96%
Customer Satisfaction %	87%	83%	87%	86%	87%	88%	88%	88%	87%	88%	87%	89%
Email Unit cost ($)	1.59	0.87	1.55	0.86	1.56	0.85	1.49	0.82	1.48	0.81	1.48	0.81

Source: Case writers' estimates, compilations, and public records.

agents and their language comprehension were issues. Logistical issues with phone lines and data servers plagued the start-up. The biggest concern, however, was that eBay at the same time was taking its first major steps into Customer Relationship Management (CRM).

The company's marketing group had just completed a thorough segmentation analysis of its community members and saw potential opportunities in building deeper service relationships with its more profitable customer segments. Over 40 distinct customer segments were identified, and strategies for increasing profitability were then prepared for each segment. One of the proposed strategies was to offer dedicated live phone support to certain segments, particularly PowerSellers and potential PowerSellers.

With its focus on optimizing the phone touch point to generate revenue, senior management wanted to keep its phone support group in-house, rather than outsource it to third parties offshore. Management reasoned that this not only allowed for more efficient roll out of profit enhancing marketing programs, but also provided job enrichment and new career paths to eBay's own employees. In line with being more accessible by phone to high value customers, Customer Support shut down its phone outsourcing pilot in the Philippines in early 2004. Whether the pilot could have eventually been successful was unclear.

The same logic was used for eBay's live chat channel, which represented 2% of total volume or about 45,000 chat sessions a month. The original plan was to outsource this volume overseas as well. However, with the vision of using the chat channel to cross sell products and increase seller volume, it was determined to service chat line customers in-house too. These CRM-led constraints for the phone and chat channels helped fashion the new outsourcing strategy that Dalton had proposed to her boss last week and that she was scheduled to present to Whitman.

New outsourcing strategy

When she was given the responsibility for outsourcing in July of 2004, Dalton dug deeply into the existing operation to understand the issues as well as the opportunities and threats facing the department. She identified three major opportunities for improvement. She needed to figure out how to analyze each one and implement programs within 12 months, which was the

timeframe she and Moss had agreed was feasible.

The first opportunity she saw was to increase the percentage of outsourcing from 30% of overall volume to at least 50%. She calculated that this would save an incremental $3.9 million a year. What made this endeavor particularly difficult, however, was the CRM initiative that required her to keep the growing phone and chat volume with in-house service representatives only.

The second opportunity would help her to accomplish the first. It was to target for the first time specific volume types within Trust and Safety and demonstrate that these could be successfully handled by a third party outsourcer. Several within Whitman's executive team felt strongly that it was too risky to outsource any of this volume and Dalton knew she would be in for a fight. She deemed it a worthwhile fight because, according to her analysis, between 20% and 25% of Trust and Safety's monthly volume was straightforward enough to be included in the outsourceable pool.

The third area of opportunity was to seek an outsourcing partner in addition to PRC with which to contract. Dalton was concerned that eBay had for two years used only one outsourcing vendor. She reasoned that adding a second one would benefit eBay by instilling competition both in pricing and performance metrics between the two vendors, as well as providing a measure of redundancy in the event of system outages.

She and her staff had wrestled with these three problems over the ensuing months. Selecting a second vendor that could meet eBay's criteria proved challenging. The candidate company had to have both domestic and international presence, had to have a proven track record in servicing large quantities of phone, chat and email inquiries, and be willing to rival PRC's already attractive per unit pricing. Finding a vendor that had sufficient email experience proved the toughest challenge. Dalton and her team finally settled on I-Sky, a medium-sized vendor, but one that could deliver impressive email results out of its several service centers located in more rural parts of Canada.

Three tiers

In order to increase the outsourcing to 50% of total volume, at the same time take advantage of the opportunity for including Trust and Safety volume in the mix, Dalton had devised a strategy comprising three levels or tiers. Each tier represented a progressively more complex type of work, both in terms of the nature of the customer inquiry and the channel through which it accessed Customer Support (Exhibit 10).

■ **Tier One** – was comprised of email only volume involving the most basic of General Support type questions. These were typically simple bidding and selling questions that could be answered using a template of responses from Kana. Since these were less complex customer inquiries, training for the service representatives was less demanding, and could be conducted over a three-week period. Most of eBay's Tier One volume was already being handled by PRC's two outsourcing facilities in India. Dalton analyzed all remaining inquiry types to find an additional 260,000+ emails per month that could be safely off loaded to India as well. If these volumes could be found, she thought she might be able to negotiate with the vendor for a price reduction from $.81 to $.72 per email.

■ **Tier Two** – was designated for General Support email volume that was considered a bit more complex than Tier One work. This accounted for more billing-related and account adjustment questions, where more in-depth training was needed for the service representatives. eBay had outsourced a small portion of this volume, but only to PRC's Florida center, where English was the native language. Now, utilizing I-Sky's locations in Canada, Dalton proposed another option for handling this volume. These locations could satisfy the native English requirement, and prove very effective from a cost standpoint. Though not as low cost an environment as India, the Canadian Tier Two locations were on average 22% more economical in cost per email than PRC's domestic facilities and eBay's wholly owned service centers.

■ **Tier Three** – was reserved for more complex General Support questions, those that required flexibility and some judgment on the part of the service employees. Also, it was in this tier that Dalton proposed that some simple Trust & Safety inquiries be handled. She was careful not to select work that was overly sensitive in terms of customers' personal information or that necessitated detailed investigative work. Types of inquiries that qualified included reports from eBay users on spam or potential scam sites, and on listing violations or member misbehavior, such as not paying for items received, and shill bidding. This tier consisted mainly of email volume, yet Dalton designed it so that some simple phone and chat inquiries were included as well. While this was contrary to eBay's CRM philosophy that phone calls and chat sessions be kept in-house with experienced eBay service agents, she asserted that top reps at both PRC and I-Sky could be taught to service this volume just as adeptly as eBay's own.

Tier Three was to be handled by outsourcing centers exclusively in the United States, located in close proximity to eBay's own contact centers. This 'nearshoring' arrangement ensured that no language barrier existed, and that Dalton and her managers were within close proximity if the outsourcer needed extra support and training.

Exhibit 10 Proposed outsourced volume and unit cost by tiers

	Current (Dec. 2004)			Proposed (Dec. 2004)		
	Monthly volume	% of Total Volume	Unit Cost	Monthly volume	% of Total Volume	Unit Cost
Tier One Trust & Safety	510000	21.30%	$0.81	775000	32.40%	$0.72
Tier Two Gen'l Support	68000	2.80%	$1.45	186000	7.80%	$1.15
Tier Three Gen'l Support Trust & Safety	20000 NA	0.80% NA	$1.48 NA	25000 210000	1.04% 8.80%	$1.33 $1.33
Total	598000	24.20%		1196000	50.00%	

Source: Case writers' estimates, compilations, and public records.

In her recommendations to Moss last week, Dalton had made sure her boss understood that the arrangement for Tier Three volume would save the company only about $500,000 per year from a pure cost reduction standpoint, but that it did pay off in keeping Customer Support from having to invest in additional plant and equipment, as well as reducing the risk of spreading its management talent too thin. Plus, it opened the door to outsourcing approximately 20% of Trust and Safety work types, which was essential to meeting the goal of offloading upward of 50% of eBay's entire support volume.

Moss had readily acknowledged and appreciated Dalton's explanation on her team's strategy behind the logic for Tiers Two and Three. She was more inquisitive, however, about the Tier One work being serviced in India. The payoffs there in reduced operating expense were impressive, saving the company almost $3 million annually, and Dalton had sensed right away Moss's interest in bringing more dollars to the bottom line. Moss had quizzed her in detail last week on PRC's Indian-based operations and I-Sky. How experienced, how financially muscled, how well led, how competitively positioned, how quick to market were these two companies? What kind of presence did Customer Support have in these centers? Were eBay managers always on site in India training new hires, sampling emails, admonishing the 'eBay way'?

As she recounted these queries in her mind from last week's meeting, Dalton admitted that the question her boss had posed in her email was really no surprise at all. Customer Support was heavily invested in making the Indian operation a long-term service and financial win. But, why line someone else's pockets along the way? What Moss wanted to know, and what she had anticipated that Whitman and her staff would likewise want to know, was the feasibility of doing exactly what Dalton's outsourcing group was doing in India, but doing it without the middle man. 'Imagine if Customer Support was saving approximately 45% per email by offshore outsourcing, how much more could be saved by running our own sites in India?' Moss's email concluded.

To BOT or not to BOT

Fortunately, Dalton had done research on the subject of developing eBay-owned and managed sites offshore, though not in real depth. She had figured that opportunities would exist for her and her staff to still work out the minor kinks with the present outsourcing strategy. 'Chalk up another one to the exhilarating eBay pace,' she thought to herself.

She wanted to call Moss in San Jose and discuss her email and the next steps in preparing for the upcoming presentation to Whitman. But, first she opened her file drawer and pulled out a folder labeled across the top with the letters 'BOT.' It had been several months since she gathered the contents. Before she knew it, an hour elapsed and she remained focused on sifting through the packet of information, occasionally pausing to run several scenarios through a quickly composed Excel spreadsheet.

After another 45 minutes of analysis she was ready. She printed the spreadsheet and quickly surveyed it for clarity. It was not as detailed as it would need to be in the coming days, but it would help her frame a conversation with Moss about the question she asked in her email, the one she asked on behalf of Whitman:

- 'Why should we keep paying someone else to do what we can do for ourselves?'

In her spreadsheet, Dalton outlined and quantified three alternatives (Exhibit 11). The first alternative was the Tier One of her proposed three tiered strategy – maintain the relationships with eBay's offshore outsourcing partners, continue to improve the operation in India, and identify incremental volume to outsource in order to drive email costs lower. She viewed this scenario as the least risky of the three alternatives.

The second alternative was to eliminate the outsourcing vendors altogether. In this option, she proposed that Customer Support not renew its contracts with the vendors, and instead purchase or lease land or an already established facility in India and build its own operation. Dalton knew this alternative presented the most risks to eBay, including capital outlay, real estate commitments, governmental compliance, communications infrastructure, and in country management resources. Yet, according to her spreadsheet assumptions, this alternative promised the biggest potential payoff long-term in unit cost reduction, something that eBay's Executive Staff prized highly.

She believed her third alternative, called 'Build, Operate, and Transfer,' or 'BOT' for short, was the most creative and represented a hybrid of the first two. She recommended that eBay contract with a third party vendor that would acquire or build an operations

Exhibit 11 Dalton's spreadsheet

		Cost/ Hr/ Seat (250 Seats)	Cost/ Hr/ Seat (500 Seats)	Cost/ Hr/ Seat (1000 Seats)	Avg. Initial Investment/Seat (one-time cost)	Avg. Transfer Cost/Seat (one-time cost)
Scenario #1 Outsourcing to 3rd party vendors	*email, phone, chat*	$ 10.17	$ 9.56	$ 8.60	$ N/A	$ N/A
	email only	$ 6.24	$ 5.38	$ 4.66	$ N/A	$ N/A
Scenario #2 Build eBay owned center	*email, phone, chat*	$ 9.73	$ 8.85	$ 7.77	$ 12,000	$ N/A
	email only	$ 5.30	$ 4.68	$ 4.14	$ 11,000	$ N/A
Scenario #3 Build, Operate, Transfer	*email, phone, chat*	$ 9.88	$ 9.03	$ 8.10	$ N/A	$ 3,500
	email only	$ 5.34	$ 4.96	$ 4.40	$ N/A	$ 2,900

Source: Case writers' estimates, compilations, and public records.

center, staff and manage it, and then after a specified period of time of perhaps a year or two, transfer full ownership to eBay. This option appealed to her more than the second one because the vendor would bear the initial risks for the start-up phase, which she considered the most challenging and expensive. eBay could limit its cost exposure up front until the operation was ramped up and running. She planned to tell Moss that the most critical points of the BOT alternative were to negotiate the appropriate level of management fees with the outsourcing vendor and to work out the intricacies of the actual transfer of ownership down the road.

Dalton's biggest concern, however, was the fact that to date she had not been able to find any example of a domestic company utilizing a BOT approach with a vendor in India. To her knowledge, eBay would be the first customer service operation attempting such a strategy. As she prepared to pick up the phone and dial Moss's number, she was haunted by eBay's well entrenched mantra of not being on the 'bleeding edge' with any new unproven experiments.

The exploration and production enterprise portal of the Royal Dutch/Shell Group

Everything you do with IT you can potentially provide through a portal.[1]

Ben Krutzen of the CIO Team at Shell Exploration and Production

On June 14, 2004, at 9:55 a.m., a flashing screen and a sharp noise alerted Eldert van Schagen, Knowledge Manager at Shell Exploration and Production, that his video conference was about to begin. While putting his headset on, he thought about the old days, when he would either forget about his call or be obliged to go to a separate room for the call. Now with the latest applications on their EP-One portal, he didn't even have to leave his desk. Through EP-One, Mr. Van Schagen can work from home and remain in close contact with his colleagues and his business.

The projects

Shell's Exploration and Production (EP) division is implementing four major portal projects as part of a global initiative to standardize business processes. The oil giant is reorganizing its upstream business, moving from 41 country organizations to five regional operations. The globalization of the company and its processes has a major impact on IT, says Ben Krutzen, CIO at Shell EP. Portals are providing a valuable delivery mechanism to support those changes, he says.

Project **GeoPortal** covers users of complex technical applications that perform on-screen modeling. The aim is to improve information sharing and collaboration between the specialists working on the systems, without having to physically meet. 'To leverage people, you have to bring the work to wherever those people are,' said Ben Krutzen.

Project **EP-One Portal** covers document management and discussion forums to improve collaboration across the whole organization. 'We identified a need to access information and applications more easily,' said Ben Krutzen.

Project **Facility Services** covers the use of some 16 separate back end systems, integrated via the portal and providing the users with a wide range of services, interconnected via the portal. These services range from ordering lunch and making travel arrangements to organizing a conference and booking videoconference rooms at several locations simultaneously.

And Project **Wells Portal** aims to provide a more efficient process for managing the delivery and maintenance of oil and gas wells. The system allows Shell to document and publish a global process for wells, to ensure that process is correctly followed, and to improve collaboration between staff. 'We think we can apply this across the board in Shell Group and it could even be used in a lot of other industries,' he said.

Shell Exploration and Production

One of the largest corporations in the world, the Royal Dutch/Shell Group, was founded in 1907 when N.V. Koninklijke Nederlandsche Petroleum Maatschappij merged with Shell Transport and Trading Company

---

1 Quoted from www.vnunet.com/News/1141860, dated 26 June, 2003.

This case was written by Guus Pijpers, Managing Director of ePortals, and Tawfik Jelassi, Professor of e-Business and IT at the Ecole Nationale des Ponts et Chaussées, School of International Management, Paris. It is intended to be used as the basis for class discussion rather than to illustrate effective or ineffective handling of a management situation.

The case was made possible by the cooperation of Shell.

437

plc. Today, Shell is a diverse group of energy companies with operations in over 140 countries. Its businesses include oil and gas Exploration and Production, Power Generation, Manufacturing, Marketing and Shipping of oil products and chemicals, and Renewable Energy projects including wind and solar power.

Shell companies continue to face the challenge of exploring for and producing oil and gas against a background of fluctuating prices but they have responded with innovative technical solutions. Research efforts are directed towards ever more sophisticated technologies that can increase cost efficiency while improving safety and environmental performance.

With high oil prices forecast over the next few years, the business environment is likely to be extremely competitive. Shell companies believe that they are well placed, and that their managerial, financial and technological strengths equip them to be a preferred partner for oil and gas developments anywhere in the world.

Exploration and Production is the foundation of the petroleum industry. Sometimes known as the 'upstream' business, it extends from the search for hydrocarbons, through to the delivery of oil or gas to the refinery, processing plant or tanker for shipment. Shell companies have been exploring for and producing hydrocarbons for over a century. Today, they have interests in Exploration and Production ventures in over 40 countries and employ around 25,000 people. As operator, Shell is responsible for producing oil and gas in 21 countries. No other company has a comparable operating experience.

EP manages a diverse portfolio: the four largest sources of Shell equity crude oil are in different regions of the world – the USA, UK, Oman and Nigeria. Some EP interests date back to the beginning of the century, reflecting the long-established relationships of Shell companies in some countries. These companies strive for improved efficiency, developing innovative ways of boosting the productivity of existing oil and gas fields and of finding and developing new reserves.

Their staff and contractors in the Exploration and Production business participate in a broad range of activities. Typically they may draw up contracts, survey and drill, assess exploration data, plan the development of an oil or gas field, run production operations, carry out maintenance, or decommission after an operation has run its course.

Strategically, in 2003, the EP business has set out to maximize its strengths by growing its involvement in its 'heartlands', or areas where it has a strong presence, such as in northwest Europe, Nigeria, Borneo, and the Gulf of Mexico. It is also looking to develop new 'heartlands', for example, in Canada, Russia and Kazakhstan. And it has set out to capitalize on its competitive edge in technology, deep-water activity, experience in Nigeria, and its gas portfolio. Significant progress in 2003 has shown the strength of the business in building relationships, creating and delivering projects, applying technology, and in integrating operations.

The aim of EP is to work with stakeholders, such as governments, employees, contractors and suppliers, shareholders, customers, local communities and site neighbors, and the public at large, who all have legitimate interests in what Shell does. Shell strives to ensure that the oil and gas fields that are being developed, and the infrastructure of pipelines and treatment facilities that are being built, are in line with stakeholders aspirations as well as those of Shell.

Maintaining the competitive edge, and achieving the prime Shell upstream objective of sustained growth in the value of the business requires constant effort, and Shell's strategies are aimed at achieving this objective. Recently, project-screening criteria have been tightened to make sure that only economically robust projects are approved. There has also been more emphasis on customer focus and increasing the sector's response time by bringing new technologies to the field as quickly as possible.

Research & development

Research, development and the deployment of technology for Shell's global Exploration and Production businesses are managed by Shell Technology EP, a division of Shell International Exploration and Production. Two companies, one based in Rijswijk (near The Hague in The Netherlands) and the other in the United States (Bellaire in Houston, Texas), work together to provide a wide range of products and services to Shell companies in the sector.

For more than 80 years, Shell's EP business has had central laboratories to ensure that knowledge is gathered and shared among all Shell's Operating Companies. The Exploration and Production of oil and gas requires the technology and skills of many disciplines from the fields of geosciences, engineering, computing, environmental science, economics, and management. The challenge for the future is to get smarter: to recognize the gains, which will really give the highest financial returns while contributing to sustainable development.

Shell continues to invest in radical and revolutionary ideas and to closely monitor the progress and success of selected opportunities. Shell continues to search for new technologies and techniques to make its business more successful. Many ideas come from Shell employees and the employees of its partners.

EP-One

The Exploration and Production business has become an increasingly knowledge-driven business and, as a result, information and knowledge management is a core element in Shell's EP business strategy. The business drivers of this strategy require not only a standardization of business processes, workflows and supporting tools, but also a transparent and simplified access to process data and business information.

In August 2000, a workshop was organized with a representative cross-section of worldwide EP information users to discuss several issues:

- Team members are located in different locations and/or time zones.

- Team expertise is scattered and not always shared.

- Information is difficult to access and/or to find.

- Decision-making is compromised by time constraints and often based on incomplete information.

- Team members suffer from information overload.

This workshop made several statements: 'Information for EP users is a vital and essential asset in achieving EP's business objectives. For our EP sector to remain competitive, it is essential that the importance of information gathering and transfer be fully understood. Improved access to information will lead to less duplication of effort, fewer errors, increased efficiency and effectiveness, reduced lead times, and most importantly, to improved risk management and decision-making. In addition, it will free up staff for higher value-added activities'. The vision of the attendees was formulated as:

> The EP-sector must have a common vehicle for sharing information on a global scale to support a high degree of collaboration between its component parts.

As a result of this vision, senior management within Shell EP revitalized the existing Information Management function. The newly defined policy placed high emphasis on an important project, called EP-One

(**E**xploration and **P**roduction **O**nline k**N**owledge **E**nvironment). The main objective of this project was to deliver tools 'to extract, structure, and share the knowledge of the workforce and transform it into a true asset of the business'. In a knowledge-intensive organization such as Shell EP, timeliness and correctness of relevant and reliable information is a major success factor. 'Getting the right information at the right time from the right people or system is key', says Eldert van Schagen, Project Leader EP-One pilot project and Knowledge Manager Shell EP.

To meet the users' demand, a portal[2] was suggested which, in line with the overall EP vision, would provide users with a single web-based interface to access corporate information, hosted by various systems and databases, scattered throughout the company and beyond. The architecture would provide an open platform that could be extended to reach into any information repository using well-defined interfaces and tools. The portal should not only be an information portal, but also include applications and collaboration.

The business drivers for the portal were identified as (1) a significant improvement in informed decision-making, (2) a reduction in response times, and (3) a major improvement in the competitive edge. The portal should support using existing knowledge (scattered over many dispersed groups and individuals) to develop new technologies (such as new drilling techniques). A key value is that the portal is linked to the personal workflows and systems of employees. A recent IT Leadership Team Briefing Paper states:

> Our vision is that the Portal will be the single user interface that provides access to all EP knowledge, information, and data systems, and to all EP applications.

> Portal technology provides an excellent means to help meet current business goals and strategies. It will establish and enforce discipline in the management of the architecture and the application portfolio across the Group.

---

2 A portal is a concept for a personalized web site that serves as a single gateway to a company's information and applications for employees as well as for customers, business partners, and the general public. Elements of a portal are among others: access, search, categorization, collaboration, personalization, expertise and profiling, application integration, and security.

   A portal serves as an extra layer on top of all information systems, application, information sources, and appropriate corporate computing resources to give users access from any Internet-capable device to all internally and externally stored information so they can make informed business decisions.

Portals provide a framework to simplify large-scale development of software to user desktops; they provide functionality for integration of applications, data & information sources; and they provide 'user-roles' to be defined to simplify access administration, search functionality, and personalization.

Pilot project

When the EP-One project was started, a clear decision was made not to have this project be driven by IT. The pilot, conducted in 2001, needed a team-centric approach. For a number of teams the information requirements were analyzed, and specific portals were built. As EP R&D, currently approximately 2,000 employees were recognized as the first users that would benefit from a portal. Hence, the R&D business processes were analyzed. As a result, librarians were identified as the key users that could give input into the project providing both skills and content expertise. This would give the EP community a good example of the kind of expertise held by the library professionals.

EP Global Library

The Shell EP Global Library offers services to Shell EP communities all over the world from three locations: Houston (USA), The Hague (The Netherlands) and Rijswijk (The Netherlands). The vision of the EP Global Library is to provide global access to all the information Shell EP requires via web-based catalogues, a growing volume of electronically accessible information, and direct links to relevant information centers to encourage the free flow of information. Besides book collections, paper and digital magazines, and literature searches, the EP Global Library also manages the archive of Exploration and Production reports. These reports contain the knowledge and experience of the experts of the Shell Exploration and Production division.

The EP Global Library wanted to play a central role in the information chain. The recent revolution in IT has had its impact on the role of libraries. In the paper-based world the biggest value of a library was the collection and in a growing digital world, a physical collection is still part of the library's value. However, the core value now lies in managing information, both on paper and in digital form. Paper and digital resources are managed in the same cohesive manner and are supported by services necessary to allow users to retrieve and exploit resources.

To this end, the portal was a key enabler in achieving the vision of the EP Global Library. The portal facilitated the services of the EP Global Library for all its users and provides the library with the following benefits:

- Single sign-on to all available online sources, which reduces the number of user accounts and passwords for end-users and maintenance tasks for the librarians.

- A single interface to information across different sources inside and outside of Shell.

- A customized interface and content sources for different groups of users with different information needs.

- Capabilities to access information in its context, a major feature of the portal to be implemented.

- Library staff can zero in on the tasks that really add value to its role within the company, cutting down on administrative tasks and processes.

In the EP-One Portal pilot project, librarians provided their experiences and capabilities in structuring information and helped in defining and implementing procedures on how users search for and use information. Specifically, library staff developed an Exploration and Production taxonomy and thesaurus. This taxonomy guides users browsing through the first layers of information, and then offers a search engine to find specific information. The search engine uses the thesaurus to help users in building a correct query.

The pilot project (see Exhibit 1 for an example of the initial screen) offered end users (1) a large number of applications to relevant information resources (e.g., Shell's Intranet, the Internet, internal databases, and e-mail), (2) an integrated search to various resources (e.g., global EP-libraries, industry extracts and databases, R&D journals, collaboration tools as LiveLink (a document management system), and Internet sources), and (3) access to various resources (e.g., eMap, 'Who = Who' information, Health, Safety & Environment databases). The EP Global Library already had several licenses for electronic content sources, which previously were only accessible via Shell's Intranet. The portal provided further access to well and petroleum engineering information, geological, geophysical, well bores, seismic and concession data, and production data.

EP-One business case

The EP-One Portal pilot project was accompanied by a business case to assess the efficiency and effectiveness of

Exhibit 1 Shell's EP-One Portal

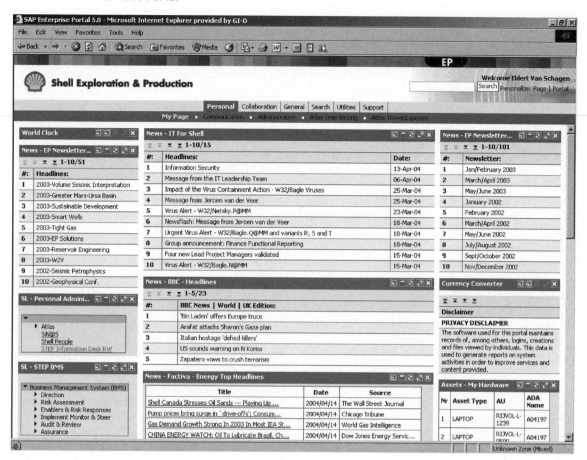

Knowledge Management in EP. For a portal project, using new, innovative technologies, an ROI or a proper cost/benefit analysis are hard to make. In the EP pilot project, a unique method was used to assess the real added value from a user point of view. In the pilot environment, two groups of knowledge workers were identified. Each had to answer a question, one group supported by the portal, the other group without portal support. The portal supported group needed minutes to give a perfect answer; the other group needed several hours. An independent group reviewed both answers as being of similar relevance.

As Bruno Best, Head of the Wells Cluster within Shell EP, states:

Some time ago, I needed to know more about the credibility of a subcontractor of a well in India. To get the required information normally takes a couple of hours. Retrieving this information using the portal was very easy:

- Launch eMap.
- Click on the well (or a well nearby).
- Click on the associated well information.
- Drag and drop this data to the GIS Iris database (a Geographical Information System; this system contains metadata on the coordinates and links of the well data and displays the information on maps with zoom functionality) and get the well header data.
- Drag and drop well header data on to an external, New York based, contractors database and get name of the contractors and the subcontractors.
- Drag and drop subcontractor data on the search field and get the required credibility information.
- This took no more than 3 minutes, instead of a couple of hours! We often have to collect such information. It appeared that the subcontractor was involved in law suits, so we decided not to give him a contract to drill more wells.

General management requested further evidence of the business value of the portal before deciding on the actual implementation. A pilot experiment, in which 200 users from EP (mostly scientists, engineers, and knowledge workers) participated, showed savings of at least 10% in FTEs[3] as reported by responsible business managers. They were asked to estimate the business impact of the EP-One portal to justify further investment in portal technology. The managers estimated direct personnel cost savings of $3.2 million per year (400 users out of 2,000 users are heavy users, average yearly salary costs: $80k). Furthermore, the 10% savings in FTEs resulted in 40 extra years of R&D capacity, a resource of high value in this industry.

In addition, significant indirect benefits were expected, among others reduced costs for the use of external databases (licenses), better decision-making, faster roll-out of new technologies, fewer lost opportunities, more time for value-added activities, improved collaboration, better risk management, prolonged life of existing information systems, fewer costly errors, and less time wasted with re-work. Furthermore, one of the goals was disclosure of information: worldwide access to all library information without the need to be at a specific physical location. Expectations more than offset actual portal costs, which are estimated at less than $150 per user per year (35% support, 35% licenses, 18% hardware, and 12% overhead). Several months after the EP-One portal went live in January 2003, 75% of the users reported the portal to be good/excellent and 70% confirmed savings of more than one hour per day because of portal usage.

Several other business cases were made for the EP-One portal. 3D graphical outputs were regarded to be one of the key values of the portal. Also, the portal helps to train new personnel much faster. Training time for new users in the EP field takes now about one month and the productivity of EP personnel using the portal has doubled in the first year. The return on investment taking into account the implementation costs and direct and indirect savings is estimated to be one to one and a half years.

Apart from cost savings, EP's policy towards knowledge management is placing emphasis on the portal as a strategic investment. A portal as such is only part of the productivity gains management can establish. The pilot studies and subsequent portal usage metrics clearly showed that the 'search and find' facilities were the major drivers to reach gains in employee productivity.

Shell EP was very well aware their EP-One portal would contradict the adagio 'we will build it and they will use it'. Therefore, EP stimulates the usage of the portal by actively 'selling' the portal to the business clusters by creating short, tailor-made reference guides and introductory courses (Exhibit 2 provides samples of portal training material). Furthermore, extensive one-to-one sessions were organized, 'walk in' sessions, lunch sessions and classroom courses. Communication was considered key in creating higher user acceptance. Leaflets, brochures, newsletters, and posters were all part of the communication strategy (Exhibit 3). A central help desk, coined Business Support Desk, was established early in the process to help users become familiar with the portal and its components.

Compelling evidence in efficiency gains are found in the ownership of content. A number of documents have high strategic and economic value for Shell, therefore, any document within Shell needs an internal classification code (e.g., 'internal use only', 'confidential'). When such a document is disseminated via the portal, the creator of the document is responsible for the right labeling. These classification codes in a portal environment are used to assess if a certain type of user or user groups are allowed access. This is important because within the Shell community, certain countries put strict limitations on the exchange of information (e.g., US Export Controls[4]). These countries are called the Generally Embargoed Countries. The actual filtering is done by combining the classification code, the user rights, and the IP-address where the user logs on to the portal. As a result, an end user might see different information in the U.S. than in, for instance, Nigeria or the Netherlands.

People are key

Within EP, people are the key resource. The knowledge management objective of EP is to store human knowledge in databases so that it can be used even after employees have left their jobs. With a rather high turnover rate of personnel, employees either stay only two to three years in one position, leave the company, or retire. Several knowledge features are implemented in the portal and its corresponding processes:

■ Knowledge on personal networks is available in the worldwide 'Who = Who in EP' system.

---

3 FTE: Full Time Equivalents.

4 The Bureau of Industry and Security of the United States has as a mission to advance U.S. national security, foreign policy, and economic interests (http://www.bxa.doc.gov/).

Exhibit 2 Portal training material

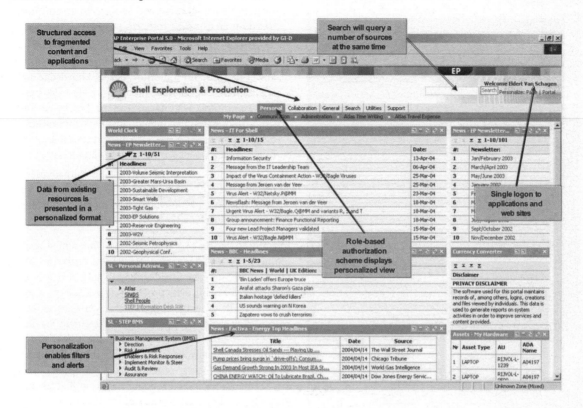

- Knowledge on procedures and working processes is stored in the Global Document System, covering many EP documents, including geographical maps, and various links with internal and external libraries.

- As of Autumn 2003, the latest actual knowledge is covered in twelve forums (twelve Communities of Practice; CoPs), supporting the formation of project teams, having 23,000 listed members of closed discussion groups (supervised by moderators).

- Additionally, various internal focused discussion groups exist on themes like 'Finance', 'GEO', 'Procurement Global Network', 'Benchmarking Global Network', 'Business Intelligence Global Network', and 'TaxNet'. All communities are virtual and use LiveLink software or dedicated tools. The size of a community is typically between 100–1000 persons. The forums support knowledge development in EP, but are also important for business managers in supporting the formation of project teams across EP.

These discussion forums are the most important tools to obtain answers to business questions.

Portals have a direct impact on the way people perform their tasks. The workflow changes, a user can customize the 'look-and-feel' of a portal, readily access information, which leads to more self-efficiency on the user side, and various tools help the user to minimize tedious administrative tasks. Uniformity in interface design is the single key issue in the acceptance of the portal. The information presented via the portal is aimed to be 80%–90% generic, business-specific information; the rest is information relevant to the individual. The technology behind the portal takes care of the interfaces to various information systems, internal and external. The sheer complexity and the number of different systems used within Shell and its partners make it almost impossible to standardize on one technology or one supplier solution. A portal can deal with this large variation.

443

Exhibit 3 Portal marketing material

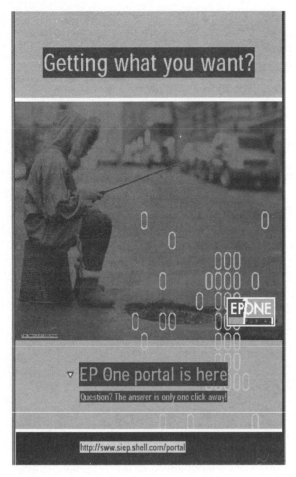

New developments

The portal pilot project revealed that functionality building on the user's point of view and Internet experiences is key. Content to be made available to the end user should also not be too personal or regarded as intrusive. Finally, lack of time to learn yet another new tool was also seen by the pilot users as hampering successful deployment of a Group-wide portal.

With the success of the pilot project came the recognition of the importance of portals for Shell EP. The project team that successfully launched the EP-One portal was also asked to provide the next business processes that were eligible to be accessed and connected to the EP-One portal. Based on the experiences gained to date and the strengths of a portal, the project team highlighted that the portal supports and facilitates most of all business-to-employee scenarios. Three different views were recognized:

1 From an IT perspective, a portal provides a framework to deliver content and services to an end-user based on an assigned role (e.g., employee, manager) by integrating back-end systems.

2 From a business perspective, a portal provides a mechanism to push and pull information, knowledge and applications. By using this mechanism effectively business-to-employee scenarios can be facilitated and supported. Examples include business communication, employee self services, management self services, facility management services, and work processes.

3 From an end-user perspective, a portal provides a readily available, easy-to-use environment to access information and knowledge and a place to arrange their daily workload.

Integration via the portal should therefore aim at combining IT systems, people, and business processes. The project team subsequently identified Facility Management Services as a key business process that was 'portal'-ready. Moreover, HR-processes like employee self-services were perceived as too personal. Facility Management Services on the other hand was close enough to the end user to be helpful for their daily work. In addition, the processes that were currently being processed via the portal were extended with additional functionality as well as streamlined into the latest ideas on issues like look-and-feel and ease-of-use.

One striking example that was requested by users exposed to the EP-One portal is the digitizing of maps. Shell EP has over a million maps of various areas. To date, these maps are archived at various libraries of Shell all over the world. In the past, request for such a map could take days to weeks. Although some of these maps are old, they contain crucial information about possible oil or gas fields (e.g., potential wells in Iraq). A small function was developed that can be accessed via the portal to request a map to be digitized. This process is done once and includes setting relations of the map with relevant aerial information as well as indexes to documentation. After this digitizing process, the map is available worldwide, through the portal for authorized personnel.

Another user change request was related to the Communities of Practices (CoPs). For a user who has subscribed to a couple of these CoPs, being informed and participating in the discussions takes time. However, not all discussions are relevant for everyone and when time passes by, relevance is diminished for some discussion threads. The portal application has been changed in such a way that the profile of a user is taken into account when new discussions are shown.

Project facility services

Shell EP is moving a number of people from London and The Hague to Rijswijk, the Netherlands, where a number of new buildings were erected for the new staff. The project is appropriately called EPiCentre. Facility Management understood its department would either be doubled in personnel or they had to come up with intelligent solutions. Moreover, the typical end user in the new site is a highly-educated professional who does not want to deal with menial, administrative tasks. The portal provided the solution to many of the requirements of Facility Management for an advanced, up-to-date environment where every end user could register his service call, be it a request, problem or just a question.

The entry of the service request is done once, at the user side, and automatically transferred to the engineer of Site Services to execute the request, no more helpdesk or staff in between. An underlying facility management system gives an end user insight into the status of his service call. An evaluation of this process highlighted that a number of steps could be omitted, fewer errors were made, and end users were very satisfied with the feedback, which they hardly ever had in the old situation. Moreover, thanks to the portal and the associated workflow, Facility Management could serve the double amount of site users without extending their number of staff.

A key issue in the development of the Site Services Rijswijk component of the portal is close involvement of the early users. Typically Personal Assistants make regular use of site services such as travel requests, meeting room arrangements, catering services, or IT services. Early participation and obligatory feedback in the prototyping phase of the project resulted in high commitment of these employees and a full-fledged version of the site services functionality (see Exhibit 4 for a closer look at the main screen of Site Services Rijswijk and Exhibit 5 for an example of the Travel request screen).

Exhibit 4 Site Services Rijswijk

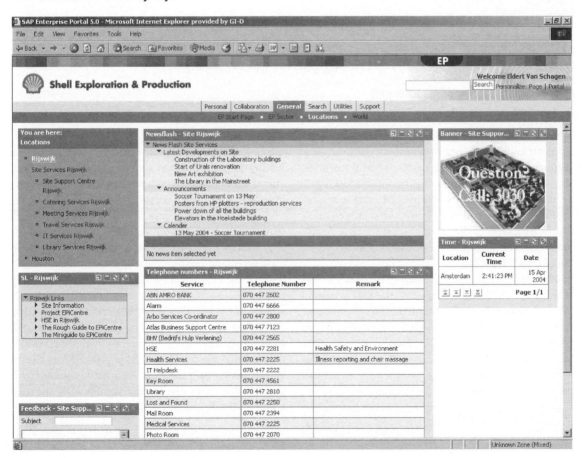

Exhibit 5 Example of portal screen for a travel request

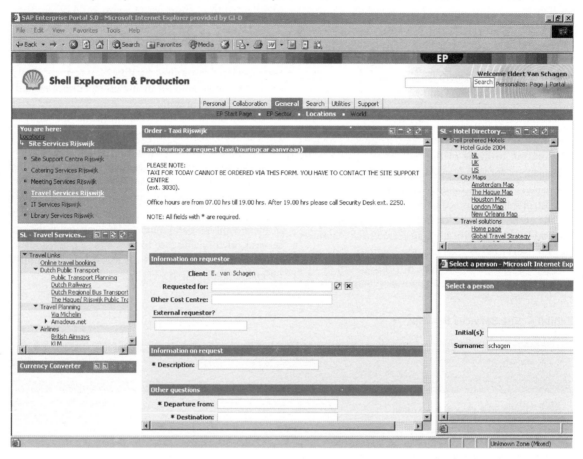

As an example of user involvement, the functional requirements for the meeting rooms of Management are shown in Exhibit 6. The key objective of this function is to make reservations for well equipped, easily accessible meeting rooms (Exhibit 7a) and video conferencing rooms with state of the art, high-performance equipment (most of the time corresponding online request is available in Exhibit 7b).

The Meeting Services functionality combines a large number of back office systems, e.g., the mail system of every single attendee, facility management system for the reservation of the physical locations, the catering system of the catering company, travel management system. The Meeting Services functionality combines various systems into one single screen, checks, using a number of business rules, the availability of the requested services, and through the portal, each of the back-end systems receives a complete order to deliver the requested services on the mentioned date. In this way, the portal serves only as an intelligent entry point to each individual system and, after the meeting has been authorized, expects the meeting to be booked and finalized.

Site Service Rijswijk proved to be one of the projects that (1) was on time and within budget (two months after starting in August 2003), (2) included an extensive user acceptance testing period, and (3) dramatically reduced the number of former Intranet sites of Facility Management (from 40 web sites to only 4 different screens in the portal, covering the same functionality). An interesting finding in this respect is the time it took to book an international meeting, which previously took on average ten days. The portal reduces this to approximately four days and Personal Assistants claim that it will further decrease to one day once they are familiar with the environment.

Exhibit 6 Functional requirement for Management Meeting Room

The functional requirements are described for the following aspects:
- Events
- Video conferencing (10 to 15 within the new EPiCentre, also to be used as general meeting room)
- General meeting rooms (6 standard and a big one within the new EPiCentre)
- Overall

Events
- Internal (on site) events.
  - Maintaining and setting up all audiovisual equipment (including ensuring that it works properly).
  - Maintaining and setting up the rooms (e.g., chairs, tables, stands, flip charts, video walls, projection screen, poster board, blinds, podium).
  - Maintaining IT equipment & support
  - Arranging and organizing the catering.
- External (off-site) events.
  - Maintaining and arranging all audiovisual equipment (including transport) on request.
  - Setting up the rooms and arranging and organizing the catering is by external organization in close consultation with the Events team.

Video conferencing (10 to 15 within the new EPiCentre, also to be used as general meeting room)
- Arranging (automatically and therefore proactively) for scheduled conferences.
  - A well equipped conferencing room.
  - With standard placing of tables & chairs (setup of tables & chairs in another composition on request).
  - In 99% of the cases scheduled video conferences must be clean and presentable.
- Resolving problems (technical, operating).
  - Upfront by offering instructions to new users (in 99% of the cases conferences must start without technical failures).
  - Between 8 AM and 7 PM continual assistance available for videoconference equipment.
  - 24hr assistance available by phone (ACT – Houston; 100% availability).
- On special request there will be a 'steward on site after regular business hours.

General meeting rooms (6 within the new EPiCentre)
- Arranging (automatically and therefore proactively) for scheduled meetings.
  - Well equipped meeting rooms.
  - With adequate placing of tables & chairs.
  - Always clean and presentable before scheduled meetings will start.
  - In 99% of the cases scheduled conferences must be clean and presentable and start without technical failures.
- Meeting rooms are standard equipped with
  - Video.
  - DVD.
  - Beamer.
  - Amplifier & boxes.
  - Whiteboards.
  - Speakerphone (on request).
  - Flip Charts (all rooms).
  - Electronically white board (1 room).
  - 2 beamers, also appropriate for groups videoconferencing (1 room).
  - 1 network connection (direct access to beamer), more connections available on request.
  - Computer (GID) available (direct access to beamer).
  - Small refrigerator available (with soft-drinks on account) and water coolers.
  - A printer/fax/copier available in the direct surrounding of the meeting rooms.
- Resolving problems (technical, operating).
  - Upfront by offering instructions to new users.
  - Between 8 AM and 6 PM continual physical assistance for audio visual and facilities assistance (response time 5 min in 99% of the cases)
  - After 6 PM assistance by phone.

Exhibit 6 Functional requirement for Management Meeting Room (continued)

Overall
- Booking of meeting rooms and all additional related services can be done simultaneously.
  - Management meeting rooms will take care of the back office coordination, i.e. with provider of videoconference applications, catering, suppliers of additional equipment.
- At the time of booking the client will be informed of the additional services.
- In case of extensions of meetings/conferences catering services can be ordered.
  - After 5 PM for simple dinner (i.e. bread and pizza) by just one phone call.
- On special request
  - There will be a 'meeting room facilitator' on site after regular business hours
  - A host will be available to guide people from the reception to the meeting room and serve them during the day if necessary.
  - Cups and saucers will be presentable (and not disposal).
  - A 'workshop kit' (tape, stickers in several colors, etc.).
  - IT & VC support.
  - Catering services can be ordered.

To be influenced by the customer
- Determining the guidelines for usage of the facilities.
- Consumption of the standard facilities (i.e. standard meeting rooms).
- Consumption of additional services (i.e. dinner facilities).

Not to be influenced by the customer
- Number, locations and standard equipment of the meeting and videoconferencing rooms.

Exhibit 7a Example of portal screen with Management Meeting Room information

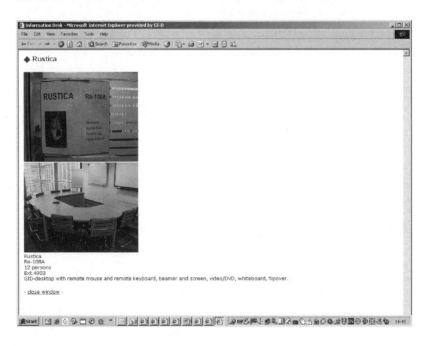

Exhibit 7b Example of portal screen with Management Meeting Room request

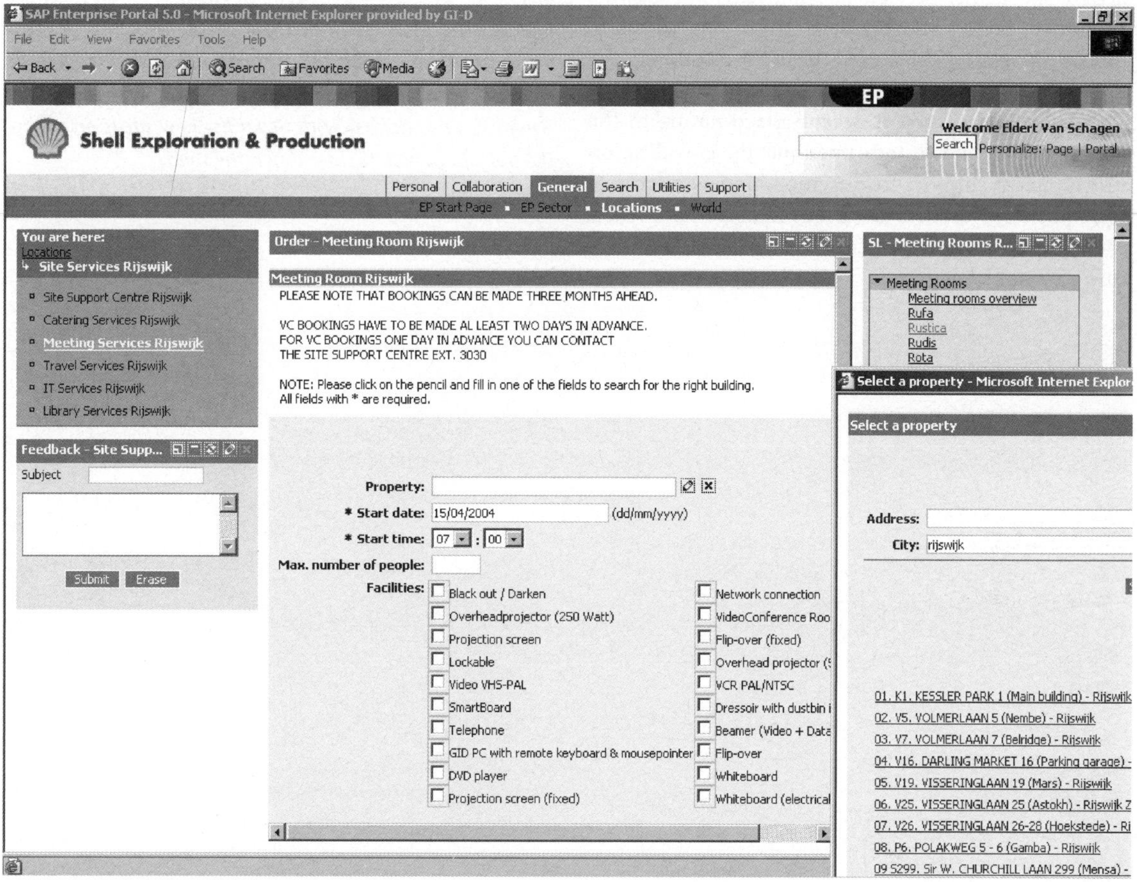

Future outlook

The EP-One portal is an important EP resource. The portal is intended to become the main access to EP knowledge resources and communities. It is regarded as an interface between data sources and many different users, each having an individual profile and information needs.

As a Business Information Manager within EP reports:

> Our portal implementation is the basis of our e-Business. It's the fabric that enables our employees and (Shell and Shell partners) customers to connect and collaborate with each other in an efficient manner, rather than reinventing the wheel each time a project is proposed. Securing the highest levels of efficiency gets harder and harder as your business processes become better managed.

During the roll-out of the portal to the whole EP community, the metrics that were already being used from the start of the pilot are used, analyzed, and reported to senior management. The information gathered serves also as a tool to identify future information needs, along with user requirements and problem support issues.

In early 2004, Shell EP reviewed its portal policy to see what next steps would give the highest benefits to the company, its employees, and their stakeholders. A number of savings were identified in (1) a further reduction of staff, (2) a substantial reduction in time to acquire a certain service, (3) a reduction in travel time, (4) further improvement in intelligent search and find mechanisms, and (5) an extended standardization in processes and services.

One of the most important issues remains the global presence of Shell in connecting employees worldwide to one another and to leverage their knowledge base. If the portal would grow to be the Enterprise Portal for Shell (85,000 users) and all stakeholders, several other organizational issues have to be addressed first. The current four major portal projects, EP-One Portal, GeoPortal, Facility Services and the Wells Portal, were developed rather independent from one another, although the latter three used the architecture and the rules and guidelines as was defined for the EP-One portal. Given the current decentralized nature of the Shell divisions, and, at the same time, the globalization efforts, fierce support from senior management is a prerequisite. Awareness at various managerial levels is available, due to increased cost savings and an enthusiastic group of loyal users.

'Good morning Eldert, how's life in the Netherlands these days?', he heard his colleague Seyal saying through his headset. As Eldert van Schagen clicked on the 'Accept' button to establish visual contact with his colleague, he was sure that next time he was over in sunny Brunei, he would have to discuss with Seyal his new ideas on taking the portal one step further down the road.

e-Government in Estonia
Establishing the world's leading information society

Introduction

> If the Internet were reborn as a country, it would be Estonia.
>
> **Mark Malloch Brown**, Administrator of the United Nations Development Program[1]

E-stonia, as the country of Estonia has smartly branded itself, is obsessively connected. When driving through Estonia, one can see big blue road signs marked with '@', pointing to the hundreds of free public Internet access points. Estonians have even equipped trains and inter-city buses with wireless Internet (see Exhibit 1). Per capita Internet access in Estonia exceeds that in Britain and Germany, close to 90% of bank transactions take place online or via mobile phones, and government ministries and agencies do much of their communication and information exchange online.

---

1   Quoted in 'If it works, you can break it', Forbes.com, 20 December 2004.
2   After John W. Heywood, Fulbright scholar in e-Governance Academy in Estonia in 2005–2006. [URL] http://starfid.com/papers/Estonia_The_Internet_and_Wireless_Development_A_Brief_History_and_Looking_Forward_Final.pdf *or* http://estonianwifi.blogspot.com/.
3   See Online Availability of Public Services: How Is Europe Progressing? (conducted by Capgemini in June 2006), European Commission's Information Society Benchmarking Report 2005, Global Information Technology Report 2004–2005 (published by the World Economic Forum), Top 10 Who are Changing the World of Internet and Politics (compiled by the global eDemocracy Forum in 2005).

Having spent over the last decade about 1% of the state budget on public sector IT development, Estonia has established itself not only as a 'wireless miracle'[2], but also as a recognized e-government champion in Europe and world-wide[3]. Putting into practice the information society concept, the Estonian government seems to have struck the right balance between the

Exhibit 1   Area of wireless Internet in trains

Source: wifi.ee.

This case study was written by Maria Štšekotovitš, Master of International Business student, under the supervision of Albrecht Enders Assistant Professor of Strategic Management, Harald Hungenberg, Chaired Professor of Strategic Management (all three from University of Nuremberg, Germany), and Tawfik Jelassi, Dean and Professor of e-Business and IT at the School of International Management of Ecole Nationale des Ponts et Chaussées (ENPC, Paris). It is intended to be used as the basis for class discussion rather than to illustrate effective or ineffective handling of a management situation.

This case study was made possible by the cooperation of Margus Püüa, Head of the State Information Systems Department at the Estonian Ministry of Economic Affairs and Communications.

development and supply of electronic services and citizens' capacity to adopt and use public-sector IT solutions. When asked about the secret of Estonia's Internet deployment and up-take success, Karen Rits, Head of the Information Society Unit at the Estonian Ministry of Economics and Communications, said:

> We have always had strong political support notwithstanding which parties have been in power for information society-related developments. Being a small country with relatively limited resources has forced us to be as cost-efficient and transparent as possible. What we consider important is the fact that the state has been increasingly active in developing e-services that do not only generate revenues for the state itself, but also provide benefits for individuals.[4]

Country background

Estonia, one of the smallest countries in Europe, is located in the northeastern part of Europe, on the eastern shore of the Baltic Sea. Roughly the size of the Netherlands, its population of approximately 1.32 million people is twelve times smaller. Yet, Estonia is widely viewed as the most advanced of all the former East-European countries, a perception that the country has worked hard for.

Like other European countries in the former Eastern bloc, Estonia had the chance 17 years ago (right after the fall of the Berlin Wall) to start over, from scratch, to re-invent itself. In the early 1990's, government officials – who where then on average about 30 years old – succeeded in transforming the country from a centrally-planned economy to a free-market economy, and pulled it off more quickly than any other nation in the former Soviet Union bloc. The government made several key decisions including the liberalization of markets, introduction of a currency board[5], flat tax[6] and zero tax rate for profits that are re-invested, sensible privatization, open-door policy to foreign capital, absence of trade tariffs (until 2004 when the country joined the European Union), or easy and cheap incorporation of new ventures. These decisions, which enabled the country's transformation to a free-market economy, have proven, over time, very successful.

The country has early recognized a clear link between information and communication technologies (ICT) and higher productivity. It watched Finland's major technological innovations (e.g., at Nokia) that were taking place 80 km across the Gulf, as Helsinki's TV feeds were transmitted wirelessly and reached Estonia. At that time, most people in Estonia did not even have a phone, not to mention a personal computer!

When the newborn Republic of Estonia liberalized its economy, technologically advanced Finnish and Swedish companies were the first to enter the market, taking advantage of Estonia's cheaper, yet talented, workforce. In 1992, the Estonian government decided to handover 49% of the Estonian Telephone Company (ETC) to Finland's Sonera and Sweden's Telia[7]. These telecommunication operators paved the way for bringing innovations to the Estonian market. They set up the first mobile phone network, and built optic fibre lines. Swedish Swedbank and SEB acquired shares in (and later completely bought out) Estonia's Hansa Bank and United Bank, contributing to the development of a strong banking system, and introducing Internet banking services in the mid 1990's.

The government considers IT and the Internet as a key pillar of Estonia's future economy. Since 1994, it has been allocating approximately 1% of the annual national budget to IT development. It has also taken foresight actions facilitating ICT and establishing an IT-friendly business culture. The country has also attracted significant foreign investments in the ICT sector, and helped the emergence of private initiatives and start-up ventures. The government promoted ICT use by citizens in society and invested heavily in education. Ivar Tallo, Director of the e-Governance Academy, said:

> We had to ask where we should best invest our scarce resources. It was clear that we couldn't do everything, so we chose to help the next generation to get the ICT skills necessary to help them when they get into the labour market.[8]

A technology awareness and promotion campaign, the Tiger Leap program, began in 1998 with the slogan: 'The Internet connects people, not computers.' Under the patronage of the former President of the Republic Lennart Meri, this initiative aimed at reshaping through

4 Quoted in 'Good things come in small packages', The Guardian, 23 November 2005.
5 In 1992, Estonian kroon was pegged to Deutsche Mark at the rate of 1 DEM = 8 EEK (now 1 EUR = 15.675 EEK).
6 In 1994, ignoring IMF advice to increase graduated tax rate, Estonia implemented a flat income tax of 26%, which turned out to energize what had been a stagnant economy. In due course, flat tax was reduced to 22% in 2007 and is planned to be reduced to 20% by 2009.
7 A Concession Agreement, signed between the Government of Estonia and ETC in 1992, granted exclusive rights to ETC for the period of eight years for the provision of basic services. In return, ETC was obliged to digitalize the existing network and to cover rural areas with telephone lines.
8 Quoted in 'Building government from scratch', PCTM Magazine, 10 March 2006.

technology the Estonian educational system. Tiger Leap brought computers to Estonian schools and connected all of them to the Internet. To meet the growing need for high-level IT professionals, the government established in 2001 the Estonian Information Technology College. At the same time, the private sector has taken several initiatives for further developing the country's ICT infrastructure. Furthermore, private companies (including banks, telecom operators, and ICT firms) organized and financed a project, called Look@World, aiming at considerably increasing the number of Internet users. Since 2001, this project enabled approximately 10% of Estonia's adult population (mostly senior citizens, 'blue-collar workers', and Internet sceptics) to acquire basic PC and Internet skills.

Furthermore, over the last decade, the country has experienced a major technical transformation. Almost 90% of the population use online banking, 86% of citizens file their income taxes electronically, everyone has one or more mobile phone and uses it to pay a bill or a parking fee[9]. Moreover, Estonia is now a technology producer and the reputation of Estonian IT specialists does not fall behind that of their Indian colleagues.[10] Rapid maturity of the ICT sector has contributed significantly to the economic growth of the country, which has been since 2001 on average 9.1% annually.[11]

Citizens' positive attitude and eagerness towards technology explain in part Estonia's successful IT revolution. Toomas Somera, an Estonian communications executive, said:

> If a Frenchman loves to sip wine with his friends and a German enjoys his beer, then an Estonian likes to sit behind his computer on a dark evening, surfing the Net and at the same time talking on his mobile phone.[12]

Building e-government

The history of e-government in Estonia goes back to the beginning of the 1990's. Margus Püüa, the Head of Department of State Information Systems (RISO) at the Estonian's Ministry of Economics and Communications, which is now responsible for the development and implementation of state IT strategies, explained:

> When the Soviet [Union] time was over, we had to start building all the state structures and everything practically from scratch. There was nothing to take with us and it was good, as we didn't have the burden of legacy systems. Other countries have huge problems with legacy IT systems: they need new versions, which have

to be adapted to older versions. When we started to develop IT systems for the state, we were able to use the most up-to-date technology. At the beginning, when ministries organized their work, we just couldn't wait to build a centralized system. However, decentralized development was the fastest way to solve the problem and everyone started to work on their own, developing computerized information systems that would meet their specific needs.[13]

By the end of the 1990's, different IT applications of ministries and agencies were developed. Margus Püüa said:

> What we needed next was to inter-connect these decentralized information systems and databases to the common data resource as to make them accessible to wider user groups. Furthermore, we needed a secure mechanism for online user authentication and a secure environment for government-citizens interactions and document exchanges. [...] It's hard to say whether we had this vision from the very first day, but relatively fast we started to develop systematically these main components.

In 1998, Estonia made the strategic decision to become an information society when its parliament (the '*Riigikogu*') approved the 'Principles of the State Information Policy'. The implementation of the information policy then became the 'lighthouse' guiding the development of ICT infrastructure and electronic services in the public sector. This development proceeded in three stages. The first involved the modernization of government agencies' document management and included redesigning and computerizing the entire document 'life cycle', from the initial capture of a record, to its signing, registration, processing, archival and preservation.

The second stage focused on modernizing public sector databases. For example, the X-Road project[14] included the implementation of an integrated Internet search system, which enables authorized users a quick and easy extraction of data from numerous databases.

---

9 Usage of mobile parking constitutes approximately 50% of total income gathered from parking fees.

10 Estonian programmers Ahti Heinla, Priit Kasesalu and Jaan Tallin were the prime code writers of the world famous peer-to-peer file sharing service KaZaa and global system of Internet-telephony Skype. In fact, Skype's research and development division is based in Tallinn, the capital of Estonia.

11 Statistics Estonia, Estonian Telecom Company (2006).

12 Quoted in 'Online biz is booming in Estonia', Wired.com, 21 April 2003.

13 Unless stated otherwise, quotations from Margus Püüa were gathered during interview made via Skype in May 2007.

14 This and further mentioned projects will be discussed in detail in the following sections.

The third stage involved the development of several projects including an electronic ID card, e-signature, e-Citizen, TOM, e-Tax Board, and the digitization of public libraries. These projects, along with others in the field of justice and court affairs as well as public procurement, helped to develop Estonia's Internet-based ICT infrastructure. Partners from the private sector were also included in the development of these various IT projects.

By 2002, the e-government technological infrastructure became operational; however, e-services for citizens were still under development. Margus Püüa explained:

> We started simply providing information, then we moved to information exchange, and now we have reached the stage of integrated e-services.

In 1994, the first government website went live providing public information to citizens. In 1998, a new portal called the 'Estonian State Web Centre' and containing all the web pages of governmental institutions went into operation; it offered citizens official forms that they can download. Furthermore, the official database of Estonia's current legislation 'State Gazette' became available online. The Government Communication Office opened a virtual briefing room, providing information on activities and decisions of the Ministries' Cabinet.

In 2003, in the context of the e-Citizen project, the government set up a common integrated ICT environment to enable mutual information exchange. Furthermore, with the introduction of the Citizen's Portal, it started the development of numerous e-services for citizens, businesses and public administration.

The evolution of Estonia's ICT to an integrated infrastructure enabled connecting, through a single interface, different information systems and the provision of comprehensive e-services. Introducing e-services in all state agencies became one of the main objectives of the revised 'Principles of State Information Policy' for the 2004–2006 period.

While transforming the public sector, policy makers realized that sophisticated e-services achieve little benefits if citizens cannot access them. Thereafter, they gave a lot of attention to the deployment of the Internet. By 2001, all public libraries in the country offered free Internet connections and the first Wi-Fi hotspots were installed. Wireless Internet access has quickly become available throughout the country. Within five years, the number of Public Internet Access Points (PIAPs) exceeded 1,100 and wireless Internet connection, mostly free of charge, can be found in post offices, shopping centers, ferry terminals, bus stations, conference halls, high schools, universities, gas stations, bars, cafés, and even castles[15]. In addition, the government started a project called 'Village Road 3' (a follow up on the 2001 projects which connected local governments and public libraries to the Internet) to improve access to permanent Internet connections in sparsely populated rural areas. Through this project, the government wanted to achieve quality Internet coverage of 100% of Estonia's territory. The country's broadband strategy adopted in 2005 aimed at bringing by 2007 cheaper and faster Internet connections into households all over the country.

The high Internet penetration rate helped the deployment and use of e-government applications. Linnar Viik, a technology consultant, explained:

> In the country side, the Internet is even more practical than in urban centers. It saves users there a lot of time and effort since they would otherwise have to travel a long way to take care of administrative chores. And that's the kind of thing Estonians like, pragmatic as they are.[16]

Today, developments in wireless technology and the prospects of WiMAX[17] represent a springboard to achieve a greater Internet penetration, which will further enhance e-services access and usage. Ivar Tallo, an IT expert and the Director of e-Governance Academy, recalled:

> There was an element of muddling through in all of this. Everyone speaks about national e-government strategies these days, but we never had a national strategy. The development of the information society was dependent on the cooperation of the public and private sectors along with NGOs [Non-Governmental Organizations]. What is a national ICT strategy anyway? Is it a master plan for the near future; a means of allowing interest groups to influence the state policy; or a declaration of joint values on introducing ICT into policymaking? The way you answer this question depends on whether you are a policy maker, a member of parliament or an ICT enthusiast.[18]

---

15 WiFi Internet access is available in Laitse Castle and Narva Castle.
16 Quoted in 'From Soviet farms to IT can-do', The Europe Journal/FAZ, 9 May 2006.
17 WiMAX (Worldwide Interoperability for Microwave Access) is a standards-based technology enabling the delivery of last mile wireless broadband access as an alternative to cable and DSL. It aims to provide wireless data over long distances, in a variety of different ways, from point to point links to full mobile cellular type access.
18 Ivar Tallo, 'Building government from scratch in Estonia', PCTM Magazine, 10 March 2006.

For Ivar Tallo, the process of creating a national ICT strategy for a government is more important than the strategy itself. He said:

> It helps raise awareness of the importance of ICT among decision makers. In the case of Estonia, it helped policy makers realize that it was a pre-condition for development and a function of the reform of our public sector administration. [...] So instead of formally developing an 'ICT master plan', we defined some information policy principles, and the government proceeded with a project-based development approach.

In 2006, Estonia's e-government services availability[19], as measured by the European Union, reached 76% while the average of the 25 EU member states was 50%. In 2006, 29% of Estonians aged 16 to 74 years and almost 70% of firms used the Internet to interact with governmental agencies. The number of users is expected to grow, as new e-services are launched and citizens are realizing the benefits of online communication with governmental institutions.

ICT infrastructure: A cornerstone for e-solutions

The cornerstone of Estonia's information society is a modern e-state infrastructure, commonly known as 'X-Road'. Digital signatures and ID cards are the basic elements enabling the creation for citizens of high-quality integrated e-services, and the reduction for the government of traditional interaction costs.

Data exchange layer X-Road

It is in the framework of the X-Road project that the architecture of Estonia's e-government was developed. The Ministry of Economic Affairs and Communications initiated the X-Road project in 2001 with the aim of connecting governmental databases and information systems to a common data resource accessible on the Internet. At the same time, necessary software, hardware and organizational methods for standardized usage of national databases were developed. After the successful start of processing database inquiries over the Internet, the X-Road environment was expanded to securely send over the Internet all kinds of XML-format[20] electronic documents; it also became a skeleton of all e-government services.

Technically, the X-Road architecture consists of several servers, software as well as numerous databases and information systems (see Exhibit 2). The X-Road security server is a standard software solution installed by all governmental agencies willing to use the system; it organizes the traffic on the X-Road. The latter's certification authority certifies, with the help of a special hardware module, all security servers. The data of certified security servers is transmitted to other security servers via central servers. The security server encrypts and decrypts incoming and outgoing messages, compiles logs, checks the rights of institutions to use the services and prohibits unauthorized access. Local and central monitoring stations monitor the X-Road system, see the actual state of security servers and generate statistics about the services used.

X-Road allows different information systems and databases to interact directly with each other and the Estonian Informatics Centre ensures the inter-operability of these systems. Different ministries house and manage various systems and databases; they have the exclusive right to update the stored data while other institutions or persons can only use or duplicate information. X-Road integrates the data from different ministries and develops (within a few hours or days) new services[21] for the public and business sectors, at costs ranging on average from 1,000 to 10,000 euros[22].

X-Road allows authorized governmental agencies, legal entities and users at large to search over the Internet data from national databases. Every citizen can use the system via the Citizen's Portal; however, such usage presumes a successful authentication of the user either through the Estonian ID card[23] or by using the electronic authentication of the main commercial banks in the country. Obviously, a citizen cannot read the data of another citizen, nor can an official read or write data that does not concern his/her tasks. The responsibilities, i.e., the owner of some specific data and the rights of different user groups (in terms of information access and usage), are well defined and recorded in the law.

---

19 This indicator shows the percentage of the 20 basic services, offered to citizens and businesses, which are fully available online, i.e. for which it is possible to carry out full electronic case handling. Source: Eurostat.

20 The Extensible Mark-up Language (XML) is a general-purpose mark-up language. Its primary purpose is to facilitate the sharing of data across different information systems, particularly via the Internet.

21 E-services will be discussed in detail in the following sections.

22 Here and further in this section, the information is provided by the Estonian Informatics Centre.

23 ID card principles and functions are described in the next section.

Exhibit 2 Overview of the X-Road system

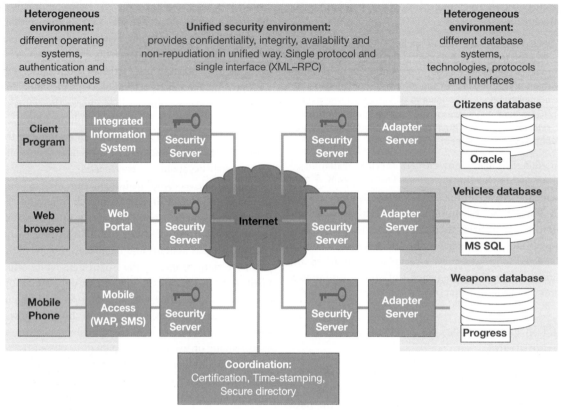

Source: Cybernetica Ltd.

Exhibit 3 offers an overview of the Estonian government's information system. So far, 69 databases (on population, businesses, registered cars, driving licenses, passports, land slots, buildings, ships, health insurance, pension, etc.) are inter-connected by the X-Road and offer more than 700 e-services. The number of X-Road enquiries averages 2.5 million per month and in 2006, more than 12% of Estonia's population through different portals' X-Road services[24].

X-Road is unique in the sense that it is not just a pilot system but also a nation-wide information capability covering all Estonian citizens, public institutions and private companies. The system is scalable and the Estonian public key infrastructure[25] (the national ID card and digital signature) is its major backbone.

ID card

To achieve significant savings from the implementation of e-services, both in terms of time and money, the government initiated in 1997 the 'compulsory national

ID card' project. It introduced a smartcard for personal identification, digital signature and electronic certificates. On December 18th 2001, Riigikogu established the ID-card as a compulsory identity document, and the Estonian passport is thus only a travel document for trips abroad. In January 2002, the first ID cards were issued to Estonian citizens and foreigners living in Estonia with a resident permit for at least one year. Between 2002 and mid-2007, the number of cards issued has exceeded one million and more than 80% of the Estonian population holds now an ID card.

---

24 X-Road services are explained further in the next section.
25 PKI (public key infrastructure) enables users of a basically unsecure public network such as the Internet to securely and privately exchange data and money through the use of a public and a private cryptographic key pair that is obtained and shared through a trusted authority. The public key infrastructure provides for a digital certificate that can identify an individual or an organization and directory services that can store and, when necessary, revoke the certificates.

Exhibit 3 Estonia's information system

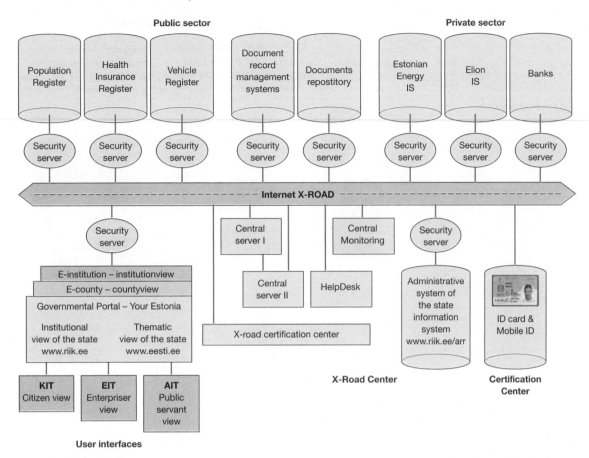

Source: Estonian Informatics Centre.

The ID card contains only personal data that is necessary for the identification of a citizen or a resident (see Exhibit 4). The data contained on both sides of the card, except the photo and the hand-written signature, is stored in electronic form on the chip, in a special publicly readable data file. All other information is stored in different information systems, and the card serves as a key to access personal data in the database.

Additionally, each issued ID card contains two X.509 certificates: one for user authentication and one for digital signature. Associated with the certificates are two private keys that are protected by two separate PIN codes. According to the Estonian law, the certificates are suspended if the card is lost and verifiers query the certificates' database.

The certificates contain only the holder's name and a personal code (11-digit national ID code) and are by nature universal. While names may overlap, the ID code is unique. The certificates lack restrictions on their field and, therefore, the card can be used in the public as well as private sectors, and also between individuals. In addition, the authentication certificate contains the cardholder's government-assigned e-mail address, which uses the following format: Forename.Surname@eesti.ee.

The Estonian Citizenship and Migration Board (CMB) is responsible for the Estonian ID card scheme; however, the process itself is managed through a public-private partnership between CMB and the following two private organizations:

Exhibit 4 Estonia's ID card and its main security elements

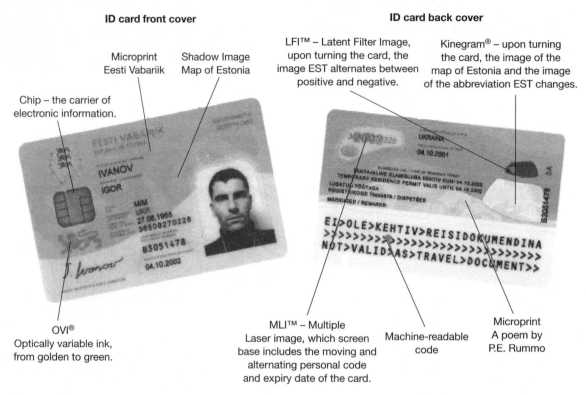

ID card front cover

Microprint
Eesti Vabariik

Shadow Image
Map of Estonia

Chip – the carrier of
electronic information.

OVI®
Optically variable ink,
from golden to green.

ID card back cover

LFI™ – Latent Filter Image,
upon turning the card, the
image EST alternates between
positive and negative.

Kinegram® – upon turning
the card, the image of the
map of Estonia and the image
of the abbreviation EST changes.

MLI™ – Multiple
Laser image, which screen
base includes the moving and
alternating personal code
and expiry date of the card.

Machine-readable
code

Microprint
A poem by
P.E. Rummo

Source: www.id.ee.

Certification Centre Ltd. (Legal name AS Sertifitseerimiskeskus, hereinafter 'SK') – a joint venture formed in 2001 between Estonia's two largest banks (Hansa Bank and United Bank) and telecommunication organizations (Estonian Telephone and EMT). SK is responsible for developments related to the ID card, digital signature, and other PKI infrastructure elements in Estonia. It is also responsible for issuing authentication and digital signature certificates to Estonian ID cards.

TRUEB Baltic AS – a subsidiary of the TRUEB financial services organization, headquartered in Switzerland, is responsible for manufacturing the ID cards.

SK and its partners have developed a secure, reliable, easy-to-use digital signature architecture named DigiDoc. DigiDoc is based on the Technical Specification TS 101 903 from ETSI, also called XAdES. It allows creating, handling, forwarding and verifying digital signatures, and supports file encryption/decryption.

In DigiDoc, the validity of the signer's certificate is obtained at the time of digital signature in the form of OCSP response[26] and stored within the signed document. (See Exhibit 5 for an example of the validity confirmation). Furthermore, the created signature is sent within the OCSP request and received back as part of the reply. This allows interpreting the OCSP positive reply as 'at the time I saw this digitally-signed file, the corresponding certificate was valid'. As the Estonian public sector is legally obliged to accept digitally-signed documents, the 'time-stamp feature' is especially important when sending documents to governmental agencies and, above all, to courts of law. A 2003 ruling by a district court made digital signatures valid in the Estonian court system.

DigiDoc components can be easily integrated into existing applications in order to allow for digital signature capabilities. People can use Estonian ID cards and

---

26 The Online Certificate Status Protocol (OCSP) is an Internet protocol used for obtaining the revocation status of an X.509 digital certificate.

DigiDoc to give digital signatures in any form of communication. DigiDoc Client and DigiDoc Portal are available free of charge as standard applications for end-users. This technology has become a *de-facto* standard in Estonia. More than two million digital signatures have been made using DigiDoc. The system is used by the private sector and most of the public sector, including courts, central government, and local municipalities.

Legal entities can use SK's 'Business ID' product, which includes authentication and digital signature certificates issued to an organization, a chip-card as well as a set of procedures defining its use. As an example, some organizations are using this product as a digital stamp.

In May 2007, a Mobile-ID service was launched. It enables highly secured identification of a person and digital document signing via a mobile phone, and thus helps to give greater freedom for performing transactions. It presumes a new type of SIM card, but works with most of the mobile phone models that are in use today.

Besides its prime functions as an authentication method and provision of digital signature, Estonian citizens can use many other ID card applications. These include:

■ To buy an e-ticket for public transportation (in Tallinn and Tartu)[27]

■ To read their information in the population register

■ To check the status of health insurance

■ To check the telephone bill

■ To sign and encrypt e-mails

■ For drivers permit verification

■ Additional features can be consolidated into the card (e.g., work passkeys and bank cards).

The ID card is a very secure authentication mechanism. Margus Püüa proudly explained:

> In Estonia, there is a very tight connection between the certificate placed on the ID card and the Population Register. If someone uses such certificate, we guarantee at the country level that the person behind it is that true person. This is called qualified certificate. Only a few countries in the world have such capability. If two persons want to communicate, they must meet; however, by exchanging certificates we make sure they are those who they personate, and then they can trust each other. In Estonia, you can trust everyone, because the state gives you this identification guarantee. And that's the foundation for building personal services for citizens.

------

27 ID ticket revenue accounts for over 65% of the overall ticket revenue in Tallinn. According to SK, more than 2 million ID-tickets have been sold in Estonia since its introduction in March 2004.

Exhibit 5 Validity confirmation sheet

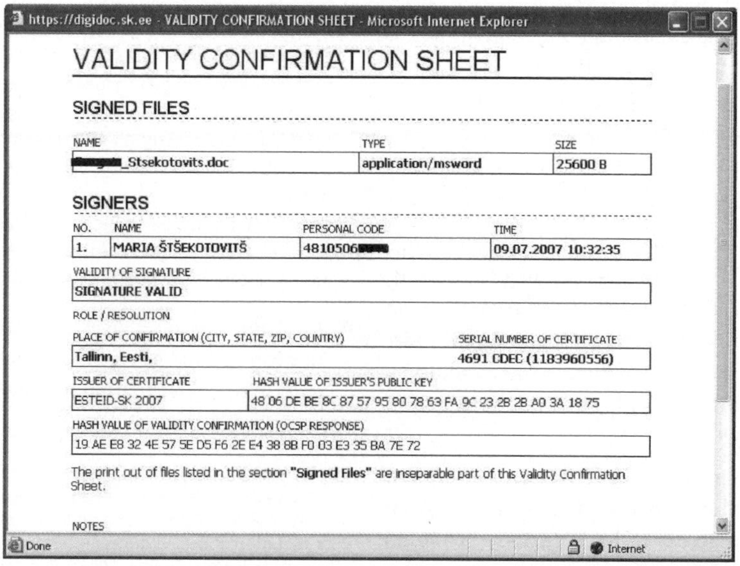

Source: Screenshot from digidoc.sk.ee.

Doing business in the 'virtual office'

The concept of a 'virtual office' evolved within the framework of the nation-wide e-Citizen project started in 2003 and aiming at creating an Internet portal to become the main channel for e-government services. Later it developed into a unique solution, enabling citizens to participate in the information society. According to Margus Püüa,

> the idea was to develop a secure environment, where every person could save his or her government-related documents and where he or she can look up the data that government holds about them. We started with the principle that people don't ultimately care whether the service comes from the state, the local government, or even from some private contractor.

Being a single entry point to online public information and services, Citizen's Portal (KIT) is organized as a virtual common space, where authorized users can play three possible roles: that of a citizen, an entrepreneur and an official. For citizens, the portal serves as a secure personalized 'virtual office' through which they can, in their different roles, manage their affairs (e.g.; use public services) and communicate with the government, businesses and other citizens.

A citizen's communication with all other information systems in the state occurs via his personal information system (virtual office). State information systems (or that of enterprises connected to the system) have an obligation to communicate with the citizen's office and reflect the state of processing his/her affairs to that office. That means the citizen no longer needs to search for services, but has the opportunity to order services and to follow up the processing of these without leaving his or her 'office'.

So far Citizen's IT environment has developed the following capabilities:

- **E-Forms**. There are over 400 official applications and forms in PDF-format that can be printed out, and about 80 forms that can be filled in directly on the screen and submitted online. Thus, a new passport can easily be applied for by post, on condition a person possesses already an identification document issued by the CMB.

- **Direct X-Road services.** The X-Road environment comprises several national databases and registries that citizens can access to look up their personal data.[28] For example, in the database of the Health

Insurance Fund, a citizen cannot only control the validity of his or her health insurance, but also directly apply for the EU health insurance card by pushing the proper button on the screen. In other registries, the user can control the validity of his/her driving license and, if needed, apply for a new one, or register residency, or apply for parental leave benefit. Students can send their admission application to the higher education schools directly from the Admission Information System (SAIS), also part of the X-Road portal.

The system also allows a citizen to make possible corrections of his/her personal data (nationality, education, mother tongue, field of activity, etc.) and see who made enquiries about him or her. Anna Ivanova, a woman in her fifties, has shared her opinion on the X-Road system:

> I was quite impressed, if not to say shocked when my daughter first showed me what kind of information our government holds on me. I guess it is because all the data is gathered in one place: what kind of car I have, apartment I own, where I live, that I am Russian by nationality, that I have two children, and other more sensitive information. Now I think it's a good idea that I can see how this data is used. I wouldn't like it if someone misuses my personal data.[29]

- **Digital signing environment.** It represents the authentication and transmission system of digital documents. Raini Ots, an advocate in Tallinn, said:

> For me this digital signing environment is very practical. For example, when you deal with a court, it is very important to follow the procedure and meet all the deadlines. If I am working outside the city, I don't need anymore to rush and submit my client's application or an appeal to the court. I log on to my 'virtual office' with my ID card, upload the document, sign it digitally and send the appeal directly to the judge's office e-mail address. [...] I can also receive digitally signed document or send them for signing by entering the personal 11-digit code of the recipient.

- **Location-based services.** Citizens can retrieve information from government agencies or private enterprises participating in the system. For example,

---

28 According to §10 of the Estonian Personal Data Protection Act, each individual has the right to know what information state holds on him or her and how this information is used.

29 Quotation collected during interviews with Estonian citizens made in Estonia in June 2007.

Estonian Energy Ltd. provides information about planned interruptions of electricity supply in specific areas. Also, city authorities post information on city roads closed for re-construction or repair, as well as changes of public transportation routes.

- **Notification**. The system allows participating departments to send text messages (SMS) to citizens on topics ranging from emergency alerts to notification of when vehicle licences are ready. According to Margus Püüa, the notification service is the most popular one amongst students:

For the third year running, Estonian students can look up their national examination results in the Citizen's portal. They can also order result reports by e-mail or SMS. This year 80% of students have used this service.

- **Official e-mail address.** The official address (Forename.Surname@eesti.ee) is a citizen's lifetime address and is supposed to be the main communication channel between citizens and the government. A citizen can configure the system to forward incoming messages to his/her current e-mail account.
- **Election information.** A citizen can loop up the location of his polling station, its opening hours or during elections, go directly to the e-voting space to cast his/her e-vote.

Since the Citizen's portal is connected to the Internet applications of the main Estonian commercial banks, users can carry out payments for specific services like state duties or customs and money transfers usually occur in less than two hours. To access the citizen's portal requires authorization either with the ID card or via e-banking PIN. However, signing documents digitally is only authorized through the ID card.

Citizens and foreigners residing in Estonia use the Citizen's portal based on data held in the Population Register. Business users are authorized to use the Entrepreneur portal (EIT) based on data held in the State Commercial Register, which enables them to access transactional business services. The development of EIT was initiated in 2005; currently, the most popular service is the application for alcohol sale license.

In addition to the 'virtual office', residents can use the Government and information portals (described below) which do not require a prior user authorization.

The **Government Portal** (www.riik.ee) encompasses several closely integrated government portals. It offers citizens and business users a single access point to

public information about state agencies' functions and services. The aim of the portal is to provide government-related information and services based on the X-Road technology, geographic information systems, and mobile solutions.

Thematically structured, the **Information portal** (www.eesti.ee) gives practical information about the rights and obligations of the people living in Estonia, in addition to tips about dealing with Estonian state institutions. The topics range from consumer information to legal help, from human rights to work and entrepreneurship. The portal offers forms and references to legal acts, useful web pages and links to specific services that can be carried out in the Citizen's Portal. Additionally, the portal presents content related to a citizen's life cycle (whether he/she is a child, a juvenile, a working person, a senior citizen, or an individual with special needs). Margus Püüa said:

E-services must solve a citizen's problem, because that's the only way to entice people to use them.

An integrated e-service example that required cooperation between different agencies is claiming parental leave benefits. Margus Püüa explained:

Just a few years ago, a new parent had to physically go to five agencies to obtain five certificates with eight signatures in order to receive his/her parental leave benefits. Eighteen data requests were made to five information systems, and were then followed by a computation at the end. Today, this procedure can be done via the Internet, from a parent's 'virtual office', in just three minutes and one mouse click.

In the case of the 'parental leave benefit' service, the real-time interaction takes place between five information systems, namely the Citizens' Portal, the Register of the Social Insurance Board, the Population register, the Information System of Health Insurance Fund, and the Information System of Tax and Customs Office. Such automated interaction of systems considerably saves time (and money) for both parties: citizens and state officials. Other popular examples of integrated e-government services include the use of the ID card as a bus ticket, the mobile phone to pay for municipalities' parking, and SMS to obtain exam results.

Another integrated e-service, which was introduced early 2007 and has become very popular, is registering a new company online. The service is so far limited to registering a private limited company with a share capital at least 2,555 euros or a self-employer new venture.

Users enter in the system the required data, confirm the application with a digital signature, pay state duties and share capital using e-banking, and submit the application online to the Centre of Registers and Information Systems (RIK).[30] The new company is registered within 12 minutes (for the simplest case) or by the following business day at the latest.

Best practices in Estonia's public sector

> Estonia is one of the smallest countries in the world. We have to be efficient and optimal in dealing with our administrative burden. Online solutions are a great opportunity to bring the government closer to people.[31]
>
> **Siim Raie**, General Director, Estonian Chamber of Commerce and Industry

In a relatively short time, Estonia has developed an impressive array of e-government services, some of which are described below.

e-Cabinet

> Check out the world's most high-tech cabinet room. This e-cabinet doesn't just look cool. It is cool – and it promotes efficiency and saves money, too.
>
> *Newsweek*, 11 March 2002

In August 2000, the Estonian government outfitted its Cabinet meeting room with sleek PCs terminals and cordless keyboards that ministers activate with their ID card (see Exhibit 6). This new electronic environment, coupled with the use of digital signatures on official documents, has virtually eliminated paperwork. Ministers go over draft bills and regulations, put in their comments and suggestions, and vote online. Cabinet sessions that used to take most of a day, now take half an hour!

Apart from a single copy needed for the state archives, the official record of cabinet meetings is no longer printed on paper but exists solely on the web and citizens can download it from the government's website. Moreover, the Prime Minister's press conference (which takes place every Thursday at 12:00 noon at Stenbock house) is broadcasted real-time via the Internet and citizens can watch it either live or on demand later on.

The new web-based document system automated the preparation process and the proceedings of the

Exhibit 6 e-Cabinet meeting

Source: The State Chancellery.

Cabinet meetings; it also enabled ministers to participate in the meetings from any location. The State Chancellery said:

> It is something, which has made decision making at the ministerial level much more transparent.[32]

Total investment into the e-Cabinet project amounted to 200,000 euros, but the system is saving some 192,000 euros per year in paper and photocopying costs.[33] Furthermore, the e-cabinet project enabled civil servants to rethink the role that technology can play in their work environment and how to create a paperless administration. As a result, citizens can now deal directly with the administration's back office, without having to go through an intermediate civil servant.

e-Democracy

In June 2001, in response to Prime Minister Mart Laar's request, the government launched its direct democracy portal 'Today I Decide' (TOM, or '*Täna Otsustan Mina*'). This project aimed at creating a tool that would allow people to have an impact on government work by being able to speak up about all spheres of life. It was the first attempt to launch a discussion between the government and Estonia's citizens and residents about possible applications of ICT and the Internet.

---

30 For more information read the Manual for Company Registration Portal, available here: https://ekanded.eer.ee/help/help_eng.html.
31 Quoted in 'Good things come in small packages', The Guardian, 23 November 2005.
32 Taken from the State Chancellery webpage.
33 Ibid.

Eventually, TOM gave birth to e-democracy in Estonia.[34] Kristiina Ojuland, Estonia's Minister of Foreign Affairs, said:

> The system [TOM] has been built up on the principle that everyone who has something to say to the government can write it into the system. In the ministries, there are people who look into the proposals to see if there is anything serious. It does have a negative side if people write stupid things.[35]

The TOM portal has led to a number of changes in Estonian laws; for instance, the proposal to move the clock forward in the spring and backward in the fall. Tex Vertmann, who served from 2001 to 2004 as IT advisor to the Prime Minister, commented:

> The Parliament had made a stupid change in the weapons law. Students and sportsmen weren't allowed to carry swords or guns anymore. The sportsmen and members of student fraternities proposed that they could carry their swords on the streets again. The law was subsequently amended.[36]

By April 2007, TOM had 6,800 registered users but the number of its visitors is much higher. The portal has been in use since its introduction; however, its popularity has been decreasing due to a lack of political interest caused by changes in Government leadership and a shortcoming in the initial design. Margus Püüa considers TOM an interesting idea but thinks that citizens should play a different role in the law making process:

> We are looking at this as if people want to participate in making legislation. I think the approach should be different. Politicians should put forward their ideas and ask questions to citizens. When I wake up in the morning, I don't feel like saying anything [to law makers] but if a politician asks me something, I'll reply with pleasure. TOM doesn't work yet like this.

e-Voting

> In many countries, e-government is more political rhetoric than hard reality. But not in the tiny Baltic nation of Estonia, where democracy is running about as close to real-time as you can get.[37]
>
> **Clark Boyd**, BBC News

In October 2005, Estonia became the first country in the world to enable its citizens nationwide to vote over the Internet for a political election – municipal government election. Citizens could vote electronically ahead of the polling day with a possibility to change their vote on the Election Day at the polling station, in which case

the previously given e-vote becomes void. Arne Koitmäe, Member of the Secretariat of Estonia's National Electoral Commission, said:

> The goal is to make things easier for people, to increase participation. No one has managed to prove that e-voting actually raises participation, so that remains unanswered. But this gives people another possibility.[38]

The premise of e-voting is the secure authentication (with the ID card) of the voter's identity. Once authenticated on the special website, voters cast their ballot through an encrypted system and then affix their digital signature before transmitting their vote. In e-voting, the system takes into account all the major principles underlying the paper-based voting procedure (see Exhibit 7).

Although the older generation is still sceptical about entrusting their vote to a computer, younger people, like Liisa Lumiste, have embraced e-voting with enthusiasm. Liisa said:

> It's quite practical and very convenient. The most important is not how and where to cast your vote, but to do it.[39]

The number of e-votes cast during the 2005 local elections amounted to 9,287 representing 1% of the total votes and 7% of the advanced votes. This relatively low percentage did not stop the government from declaring this first experience a success, since systems and procedures worked well and there were hardly any security problems. This achievement led the government to make e-voting optional during the parliamentary elections of March 2007, when 3.4% of the 940,000-strong Estonian electorate cast their vote electronically.[40]

---

34 The portal has helped Estonia to gain international recognition for its e-democratic initiatives; the European Commission has presented the Estonian Prime Minister's Office with an award for implementing TOM. TOM is also regularly listed among international best-practice initiatives in e-democracy.

35 Quoted in 'Talk time: Kristiina Ojuland', The Guardian, 11 March 2004.

36 Quoted in 'Estonia – the state of the e-state', The Baltic Times, 22 July 2004.

37 'Estonia opens politics to the web', BBC News, 7th July 2004.

38 Quoted in 'Online voting clicks in Estonia', Wired.com, 2 February 2007.

39 Quotation collected during interviews with Estonian citizens made in Estonia in April 2007.

40 This time, an additional feature was added to the process: voters could request their elector cards to be sent to them electronically, eliminating thus the need for the paper card and doing one's bit for the environment.

Exhibit 7 e-Voting: envelope scheme

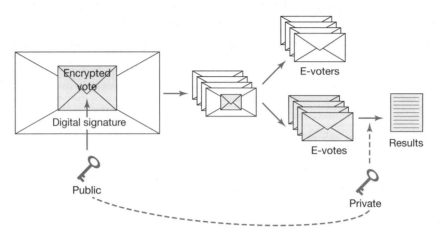

Source: Cybernetica Ltd.

Peeter Marvet, a representative of e-Estonia, said:

> Voting online does not change the essence of the democracy, but it appears to be a powerful means to promote e-administration. It is a paradox, but our lack of long democratic tradition might be a chance for faster progress into the present era. My conviction, which is shared by many people here, is that the more new technologies in the public sphere the more transparency, and in the end – more democracy.[41]

Margus Püüa of RISO believes that the mechanism of e-voting may be best used on the municipal level, where residents can actually participate in the local administration:

> On the local level, we can come to know everyone's opinion on this or that question very fast and very cheaply. It is very convenient. [...] I don't think that people care that much about what happens at the state level, but rather what happens in their house, in the neighbourhood, their kindergarten, school, and grocery store. They want to know right away, what happens there and they want to express their opinion.

e-Tax Board

The Tax and Customs Board (TCB) launched in 2000 its electronic system called e-Tax Board. With time e-Tax Board has become one of the most popular e-solutions among ordinary citizens. In 2007, 86% of private income tax declarations were submitted online, using safe and easy Internet application.

Priit Rebane, an employee of a construction company in Tallinn, appreciates the convenience that e-Tax offers; he said:

> There was a time when I had to get permission from my boss to leave my job earlier to go to the Tax Board. They were open until 5 p.m. and there were always hundreds of people before you in the line, loud and impatient, making you nervous. There I had to wait at least a couple of hours for my turn to speak with a tax consultant. I would show my tax declaration application, salary and social tax references and dozens of other documents, to help me fill in the tax return... Some months later, I would at last get the refund. Thanks God, that's all past. Now I just need a few minutes for the whole process. I log into the e-Tax Board system with my bank identification or ID card. The main fields like my salary, social tax and pension deductions, or unemployment insurance are already filled in. I add some more information, like payments I made for my son's education, and then press the 'send' button. It's as simple as that![42]

Taxpayers can file in, view and correct their tax returns online. The main services that e-Tax Board currently offers include the following:

41 Taken from Peeter Marvet's personal blog www.tehnokratt.net.
42 Quotation collected during interviews with Estonian citizens made in Estonia in April 2007.

- Personal income tax return, tax demand notice, social tax balance for private persons;

- Income tax and social tax returns, value-added tax (VAT) return, overpaid VAT refund claim for legal persons; and

- Tax decisions, tax balance and calculation, requests and applications, and tax debt information.

The extension of e-services played a key role in increasing the popularity of the e-Tax Board system. It included adding more languages, simplifying the tax filing process, speeding up the service, and adding an automatic checking procedure. Furthermore, the system enables taxpayers to receive their tax refund within 5 working days.

For businesses, TCB developed an e-application for customs and excise duties (called e-Customs) in cooperation with the European Commission to ensure inter-operability with the common EU custom systems. After TCB introduced in May 2006 the new system for processing customs declarations, there was a significant increase of its usage and within five months, corporate customs declarations were filed 100% online.

Due to its innovative approach, Estonian taxpayers view TCB as one of the most reliable government authorities. Having invested several years ago some 150,000 euros for the implementation of its e-application, TCB has since made significant time and cost savings. In 2007, there were 455,000 personal income e-tax returns, which saved 135 days of data entry corresponding to 6 months of manual work.[43] According to Dimitri Jegorov, the deputy director-general in charge of the service, Estonia is still today one of the leading countries in the world for the popularity of its electronic submission of tax returns and customs declarations.[44]

Security and privacy issues

E-government in Estonia relies on appropriate legislation[45] as well as specific standards and procedures such as security requirements for databases, services, and state procurement. This foundation enabled the state to provide secure e-services and establish trust among online users. In developing these services, the government used modern ICT technologies and novel methods for testing the new applications. Kristiina Ojuland, former Minister of Foreign Affairs, said:

> We have hired hackers whose task was to test for example the [e-voting] system by breaking into it in order to inflict damage.[46]

Another system security aspect is ensuring that users protect their PC from external dangers. Margus Püüa said:

> Although the number of people using firewalls and anti-virus programs has been growing, it's still low. Moreover, many people are careless about their passwords. Phishing scam is just one way [for hackers] to steal your personal information.

To increase citizens' awareness, the government set up in 2006 a special website that provides information on how to protect one's computer from cyber-criminals and avoid Internet fraud, especially when shopping online. It is the first project of a nation-wide initiative called 'Computer Protection 2009', which was launched by the Ministry of Economic Affairs and Communications in cooperation with the largest banks and telecom operators in Estonia. The initiative, carried out by the Look@World Foundation, aims at making Estonia by 2009 the country with the most secure information society in the world. To this end, the government launched several sub-projects including the promotion of secure ID card-based authentication in the use of e-services.

During past years, Estonia has become a 'test site' for e-services; several IT companies have tried their products first in Estonia before launching them in other countries. Margus Püüa explained:

> We can try and test everything here. Bad guys also do that. Most of the cyber-attacks are first tested in Estonia, because if you succeed here then it will definitely work elsewhere!

The government is also enhancing privacy protection and network security with the launch in May 2006 of CERT[47] Estonia. This unit aims at raising awareness and helping Internet users implement preventive measures that reduce damage from network security

---

43 According to information provided by the TCB.
44 Ibid.
45 There is no specific e-government law in Estonia. The legislation affecting the development of e-government concerns freedom of information, data protection/privacy, e-commerce, e-communications, e-signature/e-identity, e-procurement, and other legislation, like Databases Act.
46 Quoted in 'Talk time: Kristiina Ojuland', The Guardian, 11 March 2004.
47 Computer Emergency Response Team.

incidents. In April 2007, a series of DDoS[48] attacks disrupted Estonia's most vital computers, including the websites of the presidency, the parliament, most government ministries, political parties, as well as some of the biggest banks, news organizations and communications firms. The government took emergency measures and blocked access to the government's websites from the outside world. These actions had serious consequences, including a huge economic loss. For specialists, this unprecedented breakdown in terms of scale and duration (three weeks) was a major learning experience[49]. Since this breakdown, Estonia has set up a centre of excellence on cooperative cyber-defence aimed at dealing with the legal aspects of fighting cyber-terrorism.

Challenges faced and measures taken

The Estonian government overcame several hurdles to create integrated public e-services. Though it developed the basic e-government infrastructure in a relatively short time, the major challenge was to ensure the interoperability of information systems, registries and interfaces, and to integrate them into a single portal serving citizens, businesses and other organizations. Another challenge was to promote the use of ID cards since although 950,000 citizens had them, only 60,000 ID cards are actively used for online authentication. Hurdles for achieving a broader use included changing people's habits and equipping usage points with ID card readers. Furthermore, harmonizing e-identity standards, achieving digital signatures interoperability with other countries as well as ensuring the interoperability of X-Road with pan-European information systems has been a major challenge.

To overcome the above challenges, the Estonian government took a series of steps to ensure the interoperability of information systems. In 2004, it elaborated 'The Government IT Architecture and Interoperability Framework' in cooperation with state and local government agencies as well as private sector IT experts. The framework defined a set of recommendations and guidelines, which described the way in which organizations should interact with each other. Adhering to the framework's policies and specifications is mandatory to all parties. Beside inter-organizational agreements and technical inter-operability (allowing different systems to work with each other and seamlessly exchange data), the major area of concern was

semantic interoperability. The latter refers to the IS capability to adequately use data received from other IS applications in spite of their varying software systems, application objectives and organizational contexts. To resolve these issues and facilitate data identification, RISO focused on creating a semantic repository.

To bolster the mass-market use of the ID card, the government took several initiatives to make PKI the main authentication method and to phase out old authentication technologies (such as password-based cards). These initiatives include Internet-based Parliamentary elections, online declaration of taxes, and lowering the amount of online money transfers for those not using the ID-card. Another initiative within the 'Computer Protection 2009' project consisted of significantly lowering the price of card readers to 5 euros for retailers, and even giving them to banks free of charge so they can be used with e-banking applications. Since the start of the 'Computer Protection 2009' initiative, the number of active ID-card users has doubled and is expected to reach 100,000 by the end of 2007.[50] The aim is to reach 400,000 ID card and Mobile-ID users by 2009.

Achieving cross-border and cross-organizational interoperability, managing multiple systems, standardizing digital signatures are current challenges for the Estonian and other European governments. In 2003, Estonia has reached an agreement with Finland regarding legally binding digital documents. To harmonize electronic identity standards with its neighboring Latvia and Lithuania, leading banks, telecommunication operators and certification service providers from all three countries founded in 2007 the Baltic WPKI[51]. The European Union has also been exploring digital ID usage in government and business applications between its member states, and harmonizing standards for cross-border use of digitally signed documents.

In Estonia, the government has deployed X-Road for a wider use. Its further objective is to integrate X-Road with pan-European information systems. To this end, Estonia participates in several pilot projects including IDA eLink, GUIDE, Electronic Exchange of Social

---

48 In 'distributed denial-of-service' attacks, a target site is bombarded with so many bogus requests for information that it crashes.
49 'In Estonia, what may be the first war in cyberspace', The International Herald Tribune, 28 May 2007.
50 Andres Käärik, Council Chairman of the Look@World Foundation, quoted in www.delfi.ee.
51 Wireless Public Key Infrastructure is the name of the highly secure technology used in the services.

Security Information (EESSI) and the Schengen Information System.

Future outlook

In 2006, the Estonian government approved a new '*Information Society Development Plan*' for the period 2007–2013. The plan calls for using IT to improve citizens' quality of life and increase their involvement in public life, with the ultimate goal of achieving a completely paper-less public administration. The state intends to continue with the creation of a unified service space, which will enable citizens to access all public services through a 'one-stop' concept, as well as with the development of public sector e-services for citizens and enterprises.

For Margus Püüa, using IT to increase the well-being of society pre-supposes that besides developing Internet connections and various e-services, the government aligns processes and business procedures with the new technological capabilities. Moreover, he believes that quite often the biggest problem is not the technical implementation of new applications, but rather the legal aspect surrounding them:

> It's not uncommon that a given law says that a citizen must provide a certain data, while another law says that a civil servant must extract this same data from the state records. That's stupid!

Regarding the future, Margus recognizes the importance of the existing X-Road and the PKI infrastructure for the creation of a fundamentally new approach to deliver public e-services to citizens. He said:

> Our dream is that with e-state version 2.0, when I take to the public servant a dozen of references and filled-in documents, he says that he doesn't need them since he can check all of them electronically. With e-state version 3.0, I won't have to go to the state servant anymore since as the e-service will find me over the Internet.[52]

_____

52 Quoted in 'Millal tuleb e-riik 3.0?', DELFI.ee, 21 June 2007.

Online file-sharing
The music industry's paradigm shift

This will be decided not in the courts, but around American dinner tables.

Cary Sherman, President of the RIAA[1]

I am all for destroying their machines ... [damaging an accused pirate's machine] may be the only way you can teach someone about copyrights.

Orin Hatch, Chair of the US Senate Judiciary Committee

In the late 1990s the music industry experienced an unparallelled period of growth. The coming of age of the compact disc (CD), and the economic boom at the time, made music a worldwide boom industry. Unfortunately, the same technology boom that was driving consumer spending was also driving a new technology that would threaten, if some observers are to be believed, the very livelihood of the industry and the musicians and artists who provided the content that made the industry so successful.

Between May and November 2003 the RIAA issued over 911 subpoenas to Internet service providers demanding the names of clients who were still offering music on file-sharing networks. In June 2003 Jesse Jordan, a 19-year-old college student, was one of the first individuals to be hit with a lawsuit by the RIAA. Mr Jordan settled the suit by paying $12 000 to the RIAA. On 29 September 2003 Alan Davis was sentenced to six months in jail for criminal music copyright infringement, and on 2 October 2003 four individuals pleaded guilty to criminal copyright infringement charges.

Many people are passionate about music: the people who buy it, the people who write it, the people who perform it and usually the people who sell it. A considerable body of economic theory also shows that the usual relationship between price and utility changes significantly when consumers add such an emotion to their purchasing decision, and for decades this has driven almost continuously rising revenues and profits for the music industry.

In late 1998 everything changed. Shawn Fanning, a young computer whizz-kid, put the Internet, music lovers and traditional file-sharing together in an explosive cocktail that took on Fanning's hacker handle for its name: Napster. File-sharing, over Usenet, bulletin board systems, cassettes and eight-tracks, had been around for years, although the level of activity had never really posed a major threat to the record industry in its established markets.

Fanning's ignition of the taper was his decision to create a system that was 'presence aware' and that actively encouraged users to share their own material: any user logging on to Napster could now see what was being shared by all the active users (replacing the frustration of trying to download something that was on a computer that was not connected) and could painlessly share their own files without having to endure a complicated process to do so.

Napster would never have taken off without the creation of an acceptable compression algorithm to shrink

---

1 RIAA, Recording Industry Association of America.

This case was prepared by Timothy Lennon and Leslie Diamond, MBA participants (2003), and Tawfik Jelassi, Professor of e-Business and IT, all at the School of International Management at the Ecole Nationale des Ponts et Chaussées, Paris, France. Case released in 2004.

music files from around 10Mb^2/minute of music to 1Mb/minute – the Motion Picture Expert Group's MPEG-1 layer 3 format (better known as MP3)[3]. Nor would such an innovation have worked without the growth in mass, inexpensive bandwidth, or the fall in mass-storage prices. Nevertheless, the ability to share music on a scale not seen before sent shockwaves through the music industry. Early on, music CD sales began to decline as what the industry describes as the 'LP/CD upgrade cycle' – the music industry cash cow that has seen music buyers upgrade old collections from eight-track to LP,[4] to cassette, to CD – faltered.

In the best traditions of the music business and the people who work with it, the industry began to eat itself: Metallica sued Napster and immediately became the target for industry alumni and other bands, with some making recordings attacking Metallica and others joining the RIAA suits against Napster and the clones that soon began to spring up.

The sharing of music has been around since music itself, but its frequency has increased dramatically as new media have become available to the general public. The advent of the cassette, for example, led to a long and eventually unsuccessful record industry campaign with the tagline 'Stop home taping; it's killing music'. More recently, those who wanted to share their music moved to dialling directly into one another's computers using bulletin boards.

With widespread Internet availability, however, major changes began to take place. Initially, music aficionados would use File Transfer Protocol (FTP) servers and their own homepages and websites. For nearly three years after 1995, this was recorded as the most common method for sharing music.

In 1998, however, Shawn Fanning's Napster finally put together the components needed to make file-sharing a major force. Fanning was helped by a motley crew of dot.com wannabes, including his uncle, to turn Napster into a runaway success, with millions of world-wide users sharing huge numbers of songs.

Not surprisingly, it was not long before the lawyers were on the scene: the RIAA sued Napster for $100 000 for each song that was copied, on the basis of infringement of copyright. By early 2000, Napster had entered into a relationship with German media giant Bertelsmann. Hoping to provide a legitimate service to the millions of people who had downloaded the Napster client, they attempted to block sharing of hundreds of thousands of songs on a list provided by the RIAA. This failed and the RIAA sued again. Combined with other woes, such as the blocking of Napster traffic by some universities – the biggest source of such traffic – this proved to be the final straw: in late 2001, Napster had closed down.

In January 2002, Bertelsmann, which had invested US$85 million in the company, offered to buy the remains for $20 million. In-fighting followed, and the tattered remains of the business, including the brand name and rights thereto, were sold to Roxio.

The rise of peer-to-peer

The fall of Napster was not the end of the story for savvy Internet users who wanted to listen to music. While the RIAA was smothering Napster in legal judgements, America OnLine (AOL) was purchasing a small company called Nullsoft, one of whose projects was to become the Gnutella network. AOL quickly cancelled the project, but by then it was too late and the code and design were in the public domain.

Gnutella was the first of the peer-to-peer (P2P) networks. With no central server or presence that could be shut down by litigious copyright owners, it was a supposedly safe way to share one's files. All that was required was that someone wrote the client software, which would allow Internet users to connect to this network. This was accomplished quickly and, just as quickly, competitors began to spring up.

Most file-sharing applications allow the user to share files of all types as well as MP3s. They run on Windows, Macintosh, Linux, Sun and other computing platforms. The applications operate essentially along the same lines, whereby they offer:

- searching ability (by artist, genre, or other meta information);
- multi-tasking (it is possible to operate multiple searches and multiple downloads at the same time);
- integrated file libraries;

---

2 Mb, megabyte. One byte represents one character or piece of information; there are 1 048 576 bytes (1024 ¥ 1024) in a megabyte.

3 MP3 is a compression algorithm that allows data to be compressed and expanded 'on the fly', given sufficient computing power. However, the algorithm is 'lossy' to provide better compression; it strips some of the data from the original source, thus making any MP3 file an imperfect copy of the original.

4 LP, long-play disc.

- browsing abilities (when someone else is online, it is possible to browse the contents of their shared folders);

- interchangeable colour schemes ('skins');

- availability in different many different languages;

- speed of downloads (most sharing systems allow users to download a track from multiple locations and attempt to optimize use of bandwidth and download times).

These systems not only allow for sharing music but also encourage users to publish their original works and share these works with the general public. Because the systems allow multiple users to exchange the same information, the effect is that the information is more easily accessible and quicker to obtain.

The user downloads the desired program, be it Kazaa, Gnutella, Morpheus, Grokster, etc.; with that program, the user is allowed to search other users' hard drives that they have made available and that are running on the same program. For example, a user using Kazaa or the Kazaa Media Desktop (KMD), which is owned and operated by Sharman Industries, can search the shared files on the hard drive of someone else who is running KMD. For example, Dorothy and Albert, as well as a lot of other people, are running KMD. Dorothy searches for 'Where did our love go?' by the Supremes. Dorothy runs the search, the program finds the song on Albert's hard drive, and Dorothy downloads it to her computer. As sharing is the name of the game and the ability to swap content (music or other) is key, the program requires the user to set up a folder ('My shared folder') in which the user stores material that he or she wants to share. The file-sharing services urge users not to make their entire hard drive or 'My documents' folder available and to keep the folders from which they would like to share information separate and well marked to avoid unwanted infiltrators. (A report in 2002 found that most users had little idea as to precisely what they were sharing, evidence borne out by some of the users named by the RIAA's latest legal cases.[5])

The philosophy behind the file-sharing programs is to make available and share information. Users are encouraged to share responsibly at least as much information (content) as they download. Kazaa rewards those who actively participate in downloading as well as making content available by rating each user's participation level. The level of participation is then used when a user is searching for information. When a file is requested by another user and it has already been requested by someone else, the user with the highest participation level will be given priority. (This would matter, of course, only in terms of a highly desired file.)

To date, the most popular of these is the FastTrack network, which can be accessed using clients offered by Kazaa and Grokster. As of 26 May 2003, Kazaa had become the most downloaded piece of software ever on the Internet, with 203 million copies downloaded.

Since Gnutella and FastTrack, a number of alternative networks have emerged, all operating on a similar business model. On any given day, millions of people are typically active on these networks, as shown in Table 1 (numbers obtained 7 December 2003 at midday).

Table 1 Peer-to-peer networks and user numbers

Network	Users
FastTrack	3 941 240
eDonkey	1 598 842
iMesh	1 311 015
Overnet	688 128
MP2P	279 254
Gnutella	191 650
DirectConnect	189 899
Ares	57 446
Filetopia	4,284
Total	*8 261 758*

Source: www.slyck.com, 7 December 2003.

P2P revenue streams

Currently, the companies selling or offering clients to P2P networks have three revenue streams:

- Subscriptions from users who choose to purchase the clients.

- Advertising revenue from partners who advertise through the P2P clients (typically using a product like Cydoor or Gator[6]).

- Payments from Altnet for hosting specific files.

---

5 Brett Glass, 'Kazaa and others expose your secrets', www.extremetech.com

6 Both Cydoor and Gator are considered by hardcore users as 'spyware': they install small software clients, which watch a user's surfing behaviour in an attempt to target the user with more appropriate advertisements.

Subscriptions

The number of subscriptions purchased for P2P clients appears to be low, with as few as 1% of completed downloads resulting in a subscription. However, this still represents some 2.5 million subscriptions (based on a P2P community of roughly 250 million people),[7] based on typical subscription fees of $20–35. Given the reluctant attitude towards paying for services that is held by many Internet users, it is hard to see how subscriptions will provide meaningful revenue streams for the P2P companies. However, the issue of subscription was recently caught up in the RIAA subpoenas: one of the first people to be targeted was a 12-year-old New York girl, whose mother believed that since she had paid Kazaa a $29.95 subscription, her daughter was free to use the software (and the material downloaded using it) as she wished.

Advertising

Of the three revenue streams, the second seems to be the hands-down winner in terms of generated revenue. Figures are not directly available because online advertising rates fluctuate hugely and P2P companies are shy of releasing such figures; however, recent speculation suggested that a number of the key figures involved in the creation of various P2P networks have made handsome returns from their creations:

> Niklas Zennstron and Janus Friis [founders of Kazaa and FastTrack] ... may be sharing up to US$70m ... on an annual basis. ... Elan Oren formed iMesh in 1999 ... Slyck estimates that iMesh has earned the Israeli owner a cool US$100m.[8]

Anecdotal information – as well as any examination of the essential technology involved – suggests that a P2P network once set up can be extremely profitable. Providing a network has sufficient users to interest advertisers, then the incremental revenue from customers is almost entirely profit.

Altnet

Streamwaves, the first music service backed by major record companies, approached Kazaa to find a way in which file sharers would pay for downloaded music. Streamwaves' Altnet pays Kazaa for the right to place its clients' files on the top of search results. Those files are scrambled to deter piracy and in some cases require users to pay to play them. Under the deal, Kazaa users who search for many major-label artists will find a link to Streamwaves at the top of their search results.

Clicking on that link will launch Streamwaves' software, providing samples of songs by the artist and related performers from an online jukebox. Streamwaves streams music to users rather than offering downloadable tracks. Altnet's files are protected by electronic locks (i.e. DRM,[9] see later) that control how files are opened and used. Altnet also offers to pay users to share files authorized for distribution. They are able to accumulate what are called 'peer points' which could amount (in theory) to $250 000 worth of prizes each month to those who transmit the most files to other Kazaa users. But the only files that earn points are Altnet files; the non-paid-for downloaded files from Kazaa cannot be used. Hence, Altnet is using honey to try and rid Kazaa of what the RIAA terms illegally downloaded files while the RIAA's vinegar seems to be antagonizing users.

Future revenue streams

Partly because of its close association with Kazaa and Sharman Networks, Altnet is not an option that is liked by most of the P2P industry, who set up their own lobbying group, P2PUnited, in mid-2003.

Other P2P companies are looking at similar revenue models that do not embrace such proprietary solutions. In a recent interview, Limewire's CEO Greg Bildson described his company's attempt. Called 'Magnetmix', it allows artists to cheaply publicize their content without the expense of hosting that content, and offers users a higher value-added experience beyond simply searching for a specific item and downloading it.

Because P2P networks essentially allow users to share data easily, and with a low cost to them, they are already making small inroads into areas such as online gaming, telephony solutions and software distribution. How the networks – the people who make the software – succeed in making money from such services remains to be seen; perhaps the type of data-sharing envisaged in these applications will become such a seamless, unseen part of users' operating systems that the software vendors will be swallowed up by operating system suppliers.

---

7 Over 500 million downloads have been made of P2P clients, but there is no agreed methodology for assessing the actual number of people on all the file-sharing networks.

8 Ciarán Tannam, 'P2P millionaires on the increase', www.slyck.com, November 2003.

9 DRM, digital rights management: software that controls how DRM-protected material can be used, by restricting copying, etc.

Music industry background

The music industry as we know it was started by Thomas Edison, whose invention of the first phonograph in 1877 paved the way for music to be reproduced in one's own home. From these early beginnings, records came into popular usage from the turn of the 20th century, and the industry experienced its first boom.

This continued until the 1920s, when radio became a mainstream medium. Fearing the loss of their livelihoods and their monopoly, the musicians' unions forbade their members from recording for radio or licensing their material to the nascent radio networks. This all changed when Louis Armstrong and a host of largely black, non-unionized musicians began to record for radio: their rapid rise to popularity convinced the unions and the recording companies that radio – far from threatening their livelihoods – was driving an overall growth in the market for music consumption.

Especially in the USA, industry growth continued with little interruption throughout the inter-war years and the Second World War. Throughout this period, the record was the sole mass medium for people to listen to their music on demand. In 1940 RCA Victor awarded Glenn Miller the first ever gold disc for selling one million units of 'Chattanooga Choo-Choo'.

The invention of the cassette in 1964 spelt the beginning of a long, slow decline in sales of records. Since their original design, with a mono soundtrack recorded at 78 rpm, and made from thick bakelite (an early type of plastic), records had moved on to stereo and quadrophonic recording (although the latter was a commercial failure) and were now available as full LPs on 33 rpm.

Philips chose to license widely its cassette technology, driving rapid uptake and incurring the wrath of music industry executives, who treated the cassette as the second coming of radio, believing that it would drive piracy and shrink the overall music market. In fact, although piracy grew as a result of the introduction of this new technology, the overall music market grew sufficiently to far outweigh this loss of revenue. Furthermore, extensive independent research suggested that although cassettes allowed consumers to share music in a fashion that had not previously been possible, this sharing of music broadened general tastes in music consumption and led indirectly to an overall growth in per-capita consumption of music.

In 1978 Philips demonstrated the compact disc, sounding the beginning of a long but initially slow decline in cassette sales. Just as the cassette was eating away at vinyl sales, so would CDs eat into the market share of both vinyl and cassette. Surely enough, in 1988 CDs sold more units than vinyl, and by 2002 the IFPI[10] estimated that CDs provided 89% of global music industry revenue (see Table 2).

In 1991, Sony introduced the Mini-Disc (MD), hoping to replace the cassette with a medium that offered the flexibility of the cassette with the technology of the CD. Despite Sony's earlier success with the

Table 2 Global value of music industry sales by format

Media		Value share (%)
CD		89
Others		11
of which	Singles	40
	DVD video	27
	Cassette	24
	VHS video	6
	Vinyl	2
	Other audio	1

Source: IFPI Recording Industry World Sales Report, April 2002.

Walkman, which revolutionized the consumer electronics and music markets, the MD has been less of a trend-former, being rapidly overtaken by recordable CDs and MP3 players.

The music industry today

Throughout its history, the music industry has seen extensive mergers and acquisitions activity. From the humble beginnings at the turn of the twentieth century, the music industry is now a sprawling multi-billion euro monster. In 2002, the world music market was worth US$32.23 billion, with the USA the largest single market (see Tables 3 and 4).

Much of this activity is either controlled by, or at some point touches on the businesses of, five major players: Sony Music, Universal Music and Distribution, Bertelsmann Music Group (BMG), AOL Time Warner and EMI. Around one-quarter of the market is controlled by so-called 'indie' labels – labels independent of these groups (see Table 5).

---

10 International Federation of the Phonographic Industry.

Table 3 International music markets and sales breakdowns

Market	% of world sales
USA	39
Japan	16
UK	9
France	6
Germany	6
Canada	2
Italy	2
Spain	2
Australia	2
Mexico	1
Others	15

Source: IFPI Recording Industry World Sales Report, April 2002. NB Slight errors introduced due to rounding.

Table 4 Regional summary of market changes, 2001–02

	Unit change (%)	Value change (%)	Value (US$ billions)
World	−8.40	−7.20	32.2
North America	−10.10	−8.20	13.2
Europe	−4	−4.10	11.1
EU	−2.90	−3.90	10
Asia	−12.80	−10	6
Asia (excluding Japan)	−15.20	−13.40	1
Latin America	−5.40	−9.80	1
Australasia	−2.80	−5.40	0.6
Middle East	−20.50	−15.50	0.2
Africa	−3.10	1.40	0.1

Source: IFPI Recording Industry World Sales Report, April 2002.

Table 5 Worldwide market share ('Big Five' and independents), 2002

Company	Worldwide market share (%)
Universal	25.9
Sony	14.1
EMI	12
Warner	11.9
BMG	11.1
Independent labels	25

Source: Forbes Magazine, August 2003.

Making music

The process of making and selling music seems, in many respects, very simple. However, a look at the industry's value chain[11] and a look at the cost breakdown of a typical CD (see Table 6) shows how many people can be involved in the production and sale of a single or LP: depending on the agreements signed by an artist and the other creative people and businesses who have an input into a recording, a contract can look more confusing than the King of Spain's early attempts to 'share' the wealth of the New World with those who had travelled there and enslaved the locals on his behalf.

The complexity and opacity of this system is perhaps one of the reasons that so many musicians are publicly disgruntled with the music business. Even before The Beatles formed Apple in the late 1960s, there had been high-profile defections from major record companies. However, this was only one high-profile example of a number of ways in which artists 'get back' at the industry majors:

- Mariah Carey signed a £70-milion deal with EMI's Virgin subsidiary in 2001. After the failure of the first album ('Glitter'), EMI paid Carey £19 million to extricate itself from the contract.

- Prince took to using a symbol for his name, then called himself 'the artist formerly known as Prince', then just 'Artist' in order to make his point to his then label Warner Bros. about the music he wished to pursue.[12]

- George Michael fell out publicly with Sony and ended up in court. After losing the case, Michael reached an agreement with Sony so that the latter could avoid expensive and embarrassing litigation: he moved to Virgin/Dreamworks and Sony received a lump sum payment.[13]

- Courtney Love famously took the industry to task in 'Courtney Love does the math[s]', published online in *Salon* magazine. She wrote: 'Piracy is the act of

---

11 R. Schulze, (1994) quoted in Shuman Ghosemajumder, *Advanced Peer-based Technology Models*, MIT Sloan, 2002, identified up to 15 different organizations that might seek a share or payment from an artist's work, from recording studios, managers, agents and distributors to sound engineers, retailers and marketers (obviously, some organizations might perform a number of these functions).
12 Ann Harrison, *Music: The Business*, Virgin Books, 2002.
13 Ibid.

stealing an artist's work without any intention of paying for it. I'm not talking about Napster-type software. I'm talking about major label recording contracts.'

■ Robbie Williams signed a US$80-million deal with EMI in 2002, including the record company in his merchandising, concerts and other commercial activity.

■ Janis Ian attacked the industry in May 2002 for its negative approach to file-sharing and the opportunities she said it offered (www.janisian.com).

In a 1999 report, one consultancy reported that any given album release in the USA had a 0.4% possibility of becoming a million-selling release, with a majority of the 30 000–40 000 albums released there each year losing money.[14] Courtney Love did her maths well from an artist's point of view, but she ignored the unpleasant reality that record companies simply do not know who will be a financial success and thus they need successful acts to subsidize less successful acts.

To the uninitiated, for example, a £250 000 advance is a lot of money. However, when one 'does the maths', the economics of the record industry start to become a little clearer. The record company is advancing £250 000 to a promising artist or band to get their first album. The band then needs to cover its living expenses for up to three years and to make some or all of the following payments: legal costs, accountancy costs, management fees, studio fees for album, tax, and cost of video production.

At this point, if the band fails to come up with material that the record company feels able to release, then the company is out of pocket by £250 000 in cash, plus whatever value it puts on management time and other resources it has devoted to helping the band members get their act together.

Assuming that the album is 'up to standard' – in any case, this is a highly subjective judgement – the record company now needs to commit time and money to the promotion and marketing of the album: another black hole into which limitless cash could be poured.

The music industry's response

Shutting down the file-sharing services

The RIAA joined forces with the film industry in 2001 by filing a copyright infringement suit against the larger P2P networks (including Morpheus and Grokster). Napster used a central server in order to co-ordinate

and distribute the music and hence was held responsible for the infringement of the copyrights by the users of the service. File-sharing programs like Kazaa, Morpheus and Grokster use a decentralized network, where files are distributed from and by the user(s). Napster, being incorporated in the USA, was wholly vulnerable to legal action, whereas file-sharing services like Kazaa and iMesh are incorporated offshore and therefore inaccessible to US courts. Therefore, it is not as easy to file a law suit against the decentralized services as there is no one to sue. (Kazaa is based on software that was commissioned by two Scandinavian businessmen; the programmers are Estonian; and the right to license the program was acquired by an Australian-based company, Sharman Networks, which has no direct employees and is incorporated in Vanuatu, a tiny island in the South Pacific.)

Under the 1998 Digital Millennium Copyright Act, a federal judge in Washington, DC, was able to rule in January 2003 that Verizon Communications Inc., a provider of landline-based and wireless communications, was forced to identify an Internet subscriber accused of illegally making available 600 songs from well-known artists. Verizon subsequently appealed against this ruling and won, partly on the basis that an ISP is not responsible for data held on its client's computers.[15]

Suing the users

Realizing that it may be too difficult to prove that the music file-sharing programs were committing copyright infringement, the RIAA decided to file suits against individuals who use file-sharing software and has hence announced that it would begin preparing hundreds of lawsuits against individuals, demanding $150 000 per song downloaded.

In April 2003, the RIAA filed lawsuits against four students at three different American universities, accusing them of operating music file-sharing programs like Napster. The RIAA's aggressiveness is antagonizing not only university officials but one of their largest target audiences (students) as well. The President of Michigan Technological University, one of the universities cited in the suit, stated in a letter to the RIAA:

---

14 Ashish Singh, *Cutting Through the Digital Fog*, Bain & Co., 2003.

15 www.eff.org/cases/Riaarvrverizon/opinion-20031219.pdf

Had you followed the previous methods established in notification of a violation [copyright infringement], we would have shut off the student and not allowed the problem to grow to the size and scope that it is today. I am very disappointed that the RIAA decided to take action in this manner.

Many file-sharing users tend to be students using high-speed campus computer networks, and many colleges believe that blocking P2P networks would be contradicting academic freedom. Record industry executives and online music companies are now working with colleges and universities to find ways in which to offer legitimate sources of free or deeply discounted music to students in order to stop the use of unauthorized file-sharing, although colleges and universities would then be obligated to block unauthorized downloads. Discussions are still in the early stages.

Other means

The record industry has also pursued less conventional ways to combat music file-sharing by harassing music file-sharing systems and users alike by posting corrupt or empty files. The industry has actually looked at legal ways to 'lock up' any computer that uses the file-sharing software. So far, the Big Five of the music industry have refused to partner with any of the file-sharing programs. Ever since 1999, Napster and its successors have made numerous attempts to reach some form of concord with the industry, including an ill-fated attempt by Napster to filter out illegal content and more recent efforts by Kazaa and Grokster to offer distribution deals to the industry.

Despite efforts thus far, the industry has behaved in what appears to be an extremely reticent manner, refusing to accept that file-sharing services have any form of future and refusing almost point-blank to deal with them.

The Big Five have asked major recording artists, such as Eminem, Madonna, Elton John and Luciano Pavarotti, to speak out against music file-sharing and to deliver personal messages in the media. Some high-powered musicians have even testified at US Federal and State Government hearings on illegal file-sharing. On the other hand, some artists, including Courtney Love, Joni Mitchell, Jimmy Buffet and Janis Ian, have been outspoken as to how the music industry has been taking advantage of artists all along and now the tide has turned. In 'Love's manifesto',[16] Courtney Love sets out explicitly how she believes the music industry has profited from artists and how the artists have not received their due.

The music executives who are recruiting these big stars to come out against file-sharing are also the same people who are desperately trying to work out how to turn this around so that they too may profit from the Internet distribution systems. Adding to the soup, some of the Big Five are also part of organizations that are selling computers with CD burners and other equipment for copying music (Sony is an excellent example of this).

Signing up universities

The rejuvenated Napster (now a division of Roxio) signed in December 2003 a deal with Pennsylvania State University, allowing the students access to the new Napster and most of its library, although the service makes heavy use of Windows-embedded DRM technology. Precisely what the cost is to Penn State, or what the contract between the university and Roxio contains, or even whether such a deal is for publicity purposes or is repeatable, are all still in debate.

Legal file-sharing services

The music industry has launched alternatives to the P2P networks, supporting legal online music services such as MusicNet, eMusic, Pressplay, Rhapsody, iTunes and Buymusic.com. MusicNet has been touted as the industry's best response to music file-sharing. For $9.95 a month, a user can download 100 songs streamed to them. Of course, these services are not as popular, not only because they are paying services but also because some of them offer monthly subscriptions rather than selling individual songs and albums. How is the music industry going to get the public to purchase something that they have been able to obtain for free?

Online retail

Through their control of most of the popular catalogues, the music majors are busy trying a number of different ways to sell to online users, as described later. With a tiny number of exceptions, these follow their current model, using a third party to interact with music buyers.

---

16 Courtney Love, 'Courtney Love does the math', 14 June 2000, *Salon.com magazine* (San Francisco and New York), http://dir.salon.com/tech/feature/2000/06/14/love/index.html

DRM

A key element of a number of industry responses is the use of digital rights management (DRM) technology. A simple concept, good DRM is very difficult to get right, as Sony has found out with its ATRAC-3 system. Essentially, the technology allows the vendor of a piece of digital media to decide:

- how long the user can listen to the music for (e.g. one week);
- whether, and how many times, the track can be duplicated;
- what media the track may be duplicated to;
- whether the track can be translated into another format (e.g. from WMA to MP3).

At present, however, DRM systems are proving generally to be cumbersome and complicated. For example, if you download tracks from some music services, you are unable to install them on your MP3 player unless it is on a list of approved and tested equipment. Or perhaps you have two computers and wish to use the track on both: most DRM systems will not allow this, despite the fact that such use clearly falls within applicable copyright and reproduction laws in both the USA and Europe.[17]

Other revenue sources

Traditionally, record labels have largely only earned money from the sale of recorded music. EMI Group was the first of the Big Five to make an all-encompassing deal with Robbie Williams, the British pop star. EMI paid Robbie Williams around $80 million to become a full partner in all of Williams's earning: publishing, touring, merchandising and record sales.

In a presentation on 3 May 2003, EMI Executive Vice-President John Rose stated that EMI is actively looking for a strategy but it is still relying heavily on law enforcement rather than looking to partner with any of the file-sharing programs. Some of the strategies that he mentioned include the following:

- Tighter pre-release management.
- Keeping a tighter internal inventory so as to avoid leaks and letting songs and/or content reach the Internet too quickly.
- Becoming better informed about customers.
- Making it more difficult to rip and burn CDs by embedding the CDs with technology that limits the customer's ability to copy the music.

All of these ideas are well and good, but none of them is aggressive enough or will react fast enough to the changes occurring in the industry. Any technological encryption will probably be broken relatively quickly, which means spending more and more time and personnel to constantly re-invent ways in which to make CD copying more difficult.

The music industry realizes that it must change its business model. Besides Streamwaves' partnership with Kazaa, the music industry has been very reluctant to form any sort of partnership with the file-sharing companies. Mr Rose stated that it must now seek new revenue sources such as Internet and physical sales, DVD music videos, Internet radio, turning telephone ring tones into ring 'tunes', and digital downloads. EMI realizes that it must fully integrate digital distribution into its business model.

Response from other parties

The advent of file-sharing appears to be affecting the industry far more than earlier incarnations of music-sharing, such as cassettes and eight-track tapes. Who are the other parties who are involved here?

Artists

For some artists, the advent of the Internet has revitalized their careers and their finances. The most frequently quoted case is that of Janis Ian, who has famously published two articles providing what she describes as 'an alternative view'.[18]

The Internet has allowed artists to take more control, at lower expense, of their promotion and marketing, where they are allowed to do so by their contract, and for some this is a huge boon: they can gather more of the revenue from their products – whether this is a music download or a mail-order CD – than was possible previously. A look at the available analyses of CD costs shows that record companies, distributors and record shops, whether online or on the high street, take a large part of the actual consumer cost of a CD (see Tables 6 and 7).

---

17 The most famous attempt at DRM was the SDMI (Secure Digital Music Initiative). The creators (in 2001) offered a US$1-million prize to whoever could crack it: a group of Princeton researchers took 48 hours and were promptly sued into silence.
18 www.janisian.com

Importantly, artists from both ends are threatening the semi-hegemony enjoyed by the Big Five record companies. Where people like Janis Ian are taking their own responsibility for selling a broad catalogue to a compar-

Table 6 Revenue shares from an £11.61 ($16.98) CD

Company overhead, distribution, shipping	£2.29	19.72%
Pressing album, printing booklet	£0.51	4.39%
Retailer mark-up	£4.26	36.69%
Advertising, retail discounts	£0.58	5.00%
Artist royalties	£1.36	11.71%
Marketing	£1.47	12.66%
Signing and producing record	£0.74	6.37%
Label profit	£0.40	3.45%
Total	*£11.61*	*100%*

Source: Billboard, CNN.

Table 7 Estimated revenue breakdown for a $0.99 music file download

Telecoms company (bandwidth)	$0.02
Publishing	$0.08
Retailer margin (e.g. MSN)	$0.12
Service provider	$0.21
Artist royalties	$0.09
Marketing	$0.20
Overhead/A&R	$0.19
Corporate profit	$0.08
Total	*$0.99*

Source: *Financial Times*, 1 September 2003.

atively small audience, groups such as Simply Red are also taking responsibility for their own products; for example, the release of Simply Red's latest album is being handled entirely 'in-house' by the group, thus depriving their former label of millions of euros in potential revenue.

Of course, for any artist, the greatest fear is that of anonymity, and the Internet does not necessarily offer a cure for this. Shuman Ghosemajumder found that many artists who had submitted work to MP3.com had received almost no sales as a result, or had sales that were derisory in terms of their effort and expense. He also pointed out that in 1993, 90% of UK artists generating income from copyright received less than £1000 for the year, with 31% receiving less than £25.

Although it is difficult to establish clearly how the Internet, along with the easy portability and downloading

of music, is affecting some artists, it seems sure that the two sides who are using it successfully are either the most well-established, well-known groups, or the lesser-known but still long-established groups with a clear fan base.

Service companies

It is extremely difficult to get any figures relating to the amounts of money that the industry spends on efforts to eradicate the online sharing of music. Particularly in developed markets, where this is perceived as a problem, there are a number of businesses that appear to be making healthy profits from working with music companies to create 'spoof' recordings, to flood P2P networks, to target users on the networks, and of course to try to drag sharers to court.[19]

Consumer electronics companies

The uneasy relationship between the music industry and the companies who make the equipment on which people listen to their product is best epitomized by the marriage of Sony's music and consumer electronics divisions. Jealous of Apple's iPod, senior staff at Sony seem to have spent much of 2002 trying to work out how to keep their businesses ahead in both markets.[20] Sony's dilemma is encapsulated in devices like its USB-compatible MiniDisc: unlike many other devices designed to carry music around in a quickly erasable/rewriteable format, Sony's latest generation of MiniDisc players uses a copy-protection system that some may consider to be somewhat cumbersome or unfriendly.

Other companies, such as Philips, Apple, Samsung, Nokia and Creative, have been happy to create a bewildering array of players for MP3 tracks, allowing consumers, in some cases, to carry around more than 7000 songs (30 Gb or more of data) on a small player.

Recent initiatives have supposedly brought together many of the key players, in an attempt to agree secure standards for such devices.[21] However, this activity has not stopped the design of more and more sophisticated and user-friendly MP3 players. In fact, as pointed out in

19 'Spoofs' are corrupted or unusable files that record companies pay intermediaries to host. The purpose is to render music downloading a less pleasant, more frustrating experience. The most famous was the 'release' of tracks from Madonna's new album in mid 2002; rather than the actual tracks, the MP3 contained an endlessly repeated clip of Madonna saying: 'What the **** are you doing?'

20 Frank Rose, 'The civil war inside Sony', *Wired*, February 2003.

21 '17 leading companies form a working group to simplify sharing of digital content', Philips press release, June 2003.

Rose's article, the relative sizes of these two industries suggest that the leverage of music companies is limited: although they control the content creation, the availability of software to 'rip' anything produced by the industry secures consumer electronics companies from any accusation of open complicity in file-sharing. Ripping, in this context, means the duplication of a digital stream, and commonly refers to the uploading of a CD's contents to a hard drive, hence Apple's advertising campaign in late 2000 featuring the catchphrase 'Rip, Mix, Burn': tracks could be 'ripped' or copied, mixed (i.e. gathered in the order chosen by the user) and 'burnt' (transferred) to a new (blank) CD.

Online music retailers

The music industry has certainly not stood still in its response to people sharing music online. A number of efforts have been made to attract people to the purchase of music online, with varying degrees of success, and there have been a number of reviews of the different services. To make comparison easier, we examine some of the newer online businesses to look at the options being explored by the industry.

The iTunes music store

Launched in May 2003, the iTunes music store is a composite part of Apple's iTunes software. Available to all Macintosh users (less than 10% of the worldwide PC community), iTunes is a program for managing music and audio files on a Macintosh.

Apple has managed to get a number of major record companies on board, leading to a fairly broad content availability (of around 200 000 titles in July 2003). This content is easily accessed through a simple interface that is based heavily on the album-cover images (see Exhibit 1). To use the music store, one simply connects, clicks on the tracks one wishes to purchase, and either downloads them immediately (at 99 cents each) using a 1-Click[22] payment interface, or stores them in a 'basket' for group purchase later on.[23]

Music is downloaded as 128 Kbps AAC[24] format files and is almost infinitely transferable, whether to another computer or to an MP3 player or writeable CD. This was an issue with some respondents to CNet's review of the music store, which pointed out that for a track to be CD quality, it should be recorded at bit rates of at least 192 Kbps. The other main issue is, of course, the fact that the service is available only to Apple users. Nevertheless, in

---

22 An online payment interface that allows consumers to purchase items with a single click once they have set up their credentials on that website.

23 In November 2003, Steve Jobs, Apple's CEO, cast doubt on the economics of this price point, claiming that with over ten million downloads, Apple had failed to turn a profit on the service, with 'almost every cent going to the music companies'. Even so, Wal-Mart's offer of tracks at 88 cents each set a new base price in late December 2003.

24 Kbps, kilobits per second: a measure reflecting the amount of sound data captured – the higher the figure, the greater the fidelity to the original recording. AAC, Advanced Audio Coding, or MPEG 2 layer 3.

Exhibit 1 The iTunes music store

Source: Download via www.apple.com/itunes, May 2003.

December 2003 Apple reported that 25 million tracks had been downloaded from the store since its inception.

BTOpenWorld's dotmusic on demand

dotmusic (www.dotmusic.com/ondemand) is a relatively new player built for the European market (iTunes is currently available only in the USA). It is wedded to Microsoft's WMA[25] music format. This goes to the extent of requiring users to have Windows, Internet Explorer and Windows Media Player all installed before they can use the service.

Users of the service have a number of options when joining, from paying for individual tracks (ranging from 99p to £1.49) to a full subscription (at £9.99 a month), which includes unlimited streams and unlimited downloads (see Exhibit 2). The dotmusic streaming service includes a number of radio stations (whose content is changed every fortnight) and also all of the music available on the website. (Since streams tend to be at much lower bit rates than downloads, they are good for previewing whole tracks or albums, or simply listening to something online. The quality is not usually acceptable, however, for a reusable format, i.e. burning on CD.)

The site claims to contain around 170 000 tracks (in May 2003) and is operated on behalf of British Telecom by OD2, which also operates Freeserve's[26] music service

Exhibit 2 Dotmusic pricing options

Source: www.dotmusic.com/ondemand, May 2003.

on many of the similar basics (WMA, similar track selection, subscription service, etc.).

eMusic

A subsidiary of Vivendi Universal (the parent company of Universal music) and founded in 1998, eMusic had 70 000 subscribers by December 2003. The eMusic service offers unlimited downloads for a monthly subscription, using 128-Kbps MP3 files as the standard music format. As the website says:

> Since it was founded in 1998, eMusic has been a pioneer in the digital distribution of music. In July of 1998, eMusic became the first commercial site to begin selling singles and albums in the popular MP3 format. In the Fall of 2000, eMusic became the first company to launch a downloadable music subscription service.[27]

The site had around 70 000 subscribers for its 250 000 songs in December 2003, but it did manage to generate some negative publicity in May of that year, when it advised some customers that downloading several thousand tracks over a single month was not considered to be 'fair use'.

For many commentators, eMusic's service is the future for a large part of the music industry, offering users effectively unlimited music for a constant revenue stream. Perhaps the poor support of the service by music companies demonstrates their fear that music consumers are moving further from their marketing reach and that consumers will become further accustomed to getting more music for the same outlay.

Other services

Exhibit 3 shows the results of a CNet review carried out in 2002, and compares some of the biggest services then available. As is clear from this exhibit and from the other services described above, there is a huge range of options in terms of the way that one can download and listen to music online.

Looking carefully at the different services available, it is clear that while the industry has learnt a lot from the operation of other online businesses, it is still seeking a model that customers 'like' – so far, downloadable music as a business has no Amazon.com trailblazing the way it deals with customers. Almost all of the services looked at are seeking a way to make customers more 'sticky', and

25 WMA, Windows Media Audio, Microsoft's proprietary music compression format, which contains a number of DRM features.
26 www.freeserve.com/entertainment/music
27 www.emusic.com

Exhibit 3 **CNet's 2002 comparison of online music purchasing services**

	BurnItFirst	eMusic	FullAudio Music Now	Pressplay	Listen.com Rhapsody 1.5	RealOne MusicPass
Free trial	Yes, but 30-second previews only	Yes; 30 days, 50 downloads	Yes; 30 days, 100 downloads	Yes; 3 days, unlimited streams and downloads	Yes; 7 days	No; 14-day SuperPass trial includes video content but not music
Number and price of plans	One plan: $9.95/month	Two plans: $9.95 (12-month commitment) and $14.95 (3-month commitment)	Two plans: $7.49 and $14.99	Three plans; $9.95 or $17.95 per month, $180 per year	Four plans: $4.95 to $9.95	One plan: $9.95/month (plan with video content also available)
Number of songs streamed in each plan	No full streams, but unlimited number of 30-second streamed previews	No full streams, but unlimited number of 30-second streamed previews	No full streams, but unlimited number of 30-second streamed previews	Unlimited	Unlimited	100
Number of downloads in each plan	20	Unlimited	50/100	Unlimited (downloads that expire with membership); 0/10/120 (permanent downloads)	None	100
Downloaded songs accessible after membership	Yes	Yes	No	Yes, 10 per month with middle plan, 120 per year with highest plan	NA	No
Can burn songs to CD	Yes, three times each	Yes	No	Yes, permanent downloads only	No	No
Can transfer tunes to a portable player	Yes, some players	Yes	No	Yes, permanent downloads only	No	No
Songs are copyright-protected	Yes	No	Yes	Yes (the unlimited downloads expire)	NA	No
Quick whole-album downloads	Yes	Yes	No	Yes	NA	No
Approximate number of tracks in catalogue	2 100	220 000	50 000	100 000	135 000	75 000

Source: www.cnet.com, May 2003.

many seem to be almost experimental, considering the different ways in which customers can interact. It was found that customers can get their music in a number of different ways:

- Streaming[28] audio, based on song or playlist selection.
- Streaming audio based on radio channels created by the services (e.g. MusicMatch MX).
- Downloadable tracks that are non-transferable and that expire with a period of time or with membership.
- Downloadable tracks that are transferable in specific fashions to specific devices.
- Downloadable tracks that have no DRM system and are infinitely transferable (i.e. to CD, MP3 player, etc.).

Other proposals

The music industry provides a heady combination of big business and high emotion: consumers respond to purchasing music in a different way to purchasing washing machines. Largely as a result, there is no shortage of advice available to the industry, ranging from Orin Hatch's quickly withdrawn proposal at the beginning of this case study to advocates of free goods supporting the complete destruction of the music business as we know it.

Some of the more (and less) possible suggestions being proposed, aside from those discussed above, include:

- Licensing P2P companies and paying the proceeds to artists.
- Requiring compulsory DRM installation on equipment.
- Banning P2P networks.

Next steps

With the two sides of the debate so polarized, a solution seems a long way away. Record companies seem loath to abandon what they see as decades of growth based on their existing distribution and business models, and the P2P companies – along with their users – are continuing to refuse to share the revenue with what they consider to be the overbearing and stifling Big Five.[29]

Certainly in the USA, it is clear that action in the courts will continue apace, and recently the IFPI announced that it was planning to begin similar actions in Europe. It is clear that such action has an effect – however temporary – on the downloading of music. However, the negative effect that this action is causing for the industry, as well as the prospect that P2P services will be around for the indefinite future (in 2001, Intel's Andy Grove described P2P as 'the future of computing'), call for a far more permanent and customer-friendly solution.

Consumers may have more and more leisure euros to spend, but the music's share of that cash has been falling. The two divergent but interconnected questions that observers worldwide are trying to decide are the following:

- How do you carry on giving consumers the music they want while paying the people who actually make it?
- Where do the P2P businesses go from here?

---

28 Streaming refers to a constant digital stream between the service provider and the customer, operating in a very similar fashion to a radio station. Sound quality tends to be lower, but streams are effectively available on demand.

29 One mailing list included the following anecdote: 'Wayne Rosso yelled to a room packed with people anxious to be involved in legitimate online music distribution at the iHollywood Conference – "I'm not going to pay you guys a damn thing!"' (referring to a conference held in December 2003).

open BC vs. StayFriends
Germany's biggest Internet-based social networking sites

Introduction

> April's top 10 social networking sites collectively grew 47 percent year over year, increasing from an unduplicated unique audience of 46.8 million last year to 68.8 million in April 2006 and reaching 45 percent of active Web users.
>
> **Nielsen/Netratings**, New York, May 2006[1]

In recent years, the World Wide Web has undergone major technological changes that significantly altered its capabilities, leading to the advent of *Web 2.0*[2]. New Internet applications include social and business networking websites, web-logs (or blogs), wikis,[3] podcasting,[4] RSS[5] text feeds and new file sharing tools. However, Lars Hinrichs, Chief Executive Officer of the business networking portal openBC,[6] is cautious about these recent developments:[7]

> Actually, I am not too fond of the term 'Web 2.0'. It is a buzzword, often used without a real meaning. Web 2.0 is not just about technologies like AJAX,[8] wikis or RSS. It is about putting the customer in the center of attention.

Sociological research about networks had led to the theory of the 'Small World Phenomenon'. The idea that, on average, any two individuals are indirectly connected through only six people in between, fueled discussions among networking visionaries and led, along with the technological developments, to the mushrooming of numerous networking portals, both social- and business-orientated. Prominent examples include 'MySpace' or 'Facebook'[9] on the social side and 'LinkedIn' or 'plaxo'[10] on the business side.

Social and business networking sites can actually make exchanges of information and their corresponding real-life connections visible. This allows people to profit not only from their direct personal network, but also from the resources of people they formerly did not

---

1 http://www.nielsen-netratings.com/pr/pr_060511.pdf.
2 The term 'Web 2.0' originated from a series of conferences about new web technologies of the same title. These conferences were initiated by Tim O'Reilly, an internationally renowned expert on internet and open source technologies.
3 A wiki is a tool for collaborative authoring that allows the visitors themselves to easily add, remove, edit and change available content.
4 A podcast is a multimedia file that is distributed by subscription over the Internet using syndication feeds, for playback on mobile devices and personal computers.
5 RSS (Really Simple Syndication) is a web feed format enabling users to automatically include content of these sites on their own web site or read and organize content with RSS-aware software.
6 URL openBC/XING: http://www.openbc.com; http://www.xing.com.
7 Quotes from Lars Hinrichs and other openBC employees are taken from interviews at openBC headquarters in September 2006 in Hamburg, Germany.
8 AJAX (Asynchronous JavaScript and XML) is a web development technique for creating interactive web applications by enabling web pages to reload small amounts of data from a server, instead of reloading the entire web page each time the user requests a change.
9 URL MySpace: http://www.myspace.com, URL Facebook: http://www.facebook.com.
10 URL LinkedIn: http://www.linkedin.com, URL Plaxo: http://www.plaxo.com.

This case study was written by Hans-Peter Denker and Sebastian Mauch, Master of Business Administration students, under the supervision of Albrecht Enders, Assistant Professor of Strategic Management, Prof. Dr. Harald Hungenberg, Chaired Professor of Strategic Management (all four from University of Nuremberg), and Tawfik Jelassi, Dean and Professor of e-Business and IT at the School of International Management of Ecole Nationale des Ponts et Chaussées (ENPC, Paris). It is intended to be used as the basis for class discussion rather than to illustrate effective or ineffective handling of a management situation.

This case study was made possible by the cooperation of Lars Hinrichs, Chief Executive Officer, OPEN Business Club AG and Michel Lindenberg, Chief Executive Officer, StayFriends GmbH.

even know about. On online networking sites, users create their individual profile displaying personal and contact information, and they have the possibility to upload photos or multimedia content. Users can communicate or share content through the platform using online groups or messaging functions, keep track of their existing network and invite others to the site, thus making the community grow constantly.

On business networking sites, users additionally indicate previous experience, education, and other relevant business data, which allows them to benefit from business opportunities through contacts made via the platform.

Company background

StayFriends

> Our overall goal is to make people think of StayFriends, when searching for old friends, like they think of Amazon, when searching for books. Our strategy is to become a portal that users revisit not every day or every week, but once a year. StayFriends must remain a site where it is OK to be registered for 20 years.
>
> **Michel Lindenberg**, CEO StayFriends[11]

History

Michel Lindenberg, founder and CEO of StayFriends,[12] first got the idea of launching his venture from his private English teacher in January 2002. Upon her return from a trip to the UK, she told him about the British website Friends Reunited,[13] which, at the time, was experiencing significant growth rates and media attention. In 2002, the member base of Friends Reunited doubled from 4 to 8 million subscribers. Friends Reunited is a social networking site that facilitates searching for former classmates and reconnecting with them. When analyzing the idea of opening a German site, Lindenberg's first thought was that there had to be players in this market. True enough, there were already four platforms offering what seemed to be exactly the same service: Passado, Schülermails, Abjadaba and Unicum.[14] When taking a closer look at them, however, he stumbled on an oddity:

> The biggest player at that time had only 10,000 members. Numerous questions immediately came to my mind: Had the service just started? Were they doing something wrong? Or was there simply no market for this kind of service in Germany? I couldn't stop thinking about it.

After three months of further pondering and observing the existing players, it turned out that none of them had reached a critical mass of users yet. Instead, the number of subscribers to the sites was growing only moderately. Michel Lindenberg, therefore, decided to take up the challenge. He gathered a team of 28 volunteers who accepted to contribute to the project in addition to their regular jobs. The launch of the platform was planned for 23 June 2002, but got postponed, due to technical problems. Lindenberg remembers:

> When driving to work that day, I heard on the radio that Stern[15] was about to launch its site 'Stern-Klassentreffen.de'[16] on the very same day StayFriends had planned to go online. It made the front page of the magazine and was featured in a six-page article. At that moment, I thought StayFriends was dead before it had even been born!

Although the StayFriends team was afraid of the huge media power of Stern, which has a readership of 7.6 million per week, they decided to go ahead with the launch of their website. After all, they did not want to give up on what could become a success. StayFriends went online on 8 August 2002, and today, the Erlangen-based company is Germany's market leader in the field of social networking with 3.5 million members[17].

Financing

After the initial start-up phase, a more professional way of managing the venture and raising additional funds were needed. A private investor acquired a 50% share of the company. In order to limit risk, a company with limited liability under German law (StayFriends GmbH[18]) was founded.

In January 2004, StayFriends was acquired by Classmates.com,[19] an online portal specialized in social networking with today more than 40 million members. It is owned by the US company United Online Inc.[20]

---

11 Unless stated otherwise, quotations from Michel Lindenberg were gathered during interviews in July 2006 at the StayFriends headquarters in Erlangen, Germany.
12 URL StayFriends: http://www.stayfriends.de.
13 URL Friends Reunited: http://www.friendsreunited.co.uk.
14 URL Passado: http://www.passado.de, URL Schülermails: http://www.schueler-mails.de, URL Abjadaba: http://www.abjadaba.de; Unicum is a free monthly German magazine for students; URL: http://www.unister.de.
15 Stern is a major weekly German news magazine.
16 Klassentreffen is the German term for class reunion.
17 Taken from Stayfriends.de homepage.
18 GmbH: Gesellschaft mit beschränkter Haftung.
19 URL Classmates: http://www.classmates.com.
20 URL United Online: http://www.unitedonline.net.

United Online is a provider of Internet access via dial-up connections, but also offers e-mail, web-hosting and community-based networking services. In 2005, United Online generated a net income of $47.1 million (€39.2 million). By the time StayFriends was overtaken, about 230,000 members were registered on the site (see Exhibit 1 for the evolution of subscriber numbers). The acquisition price was not disclosed.

openBC

> Networking is increasingly important, not only on an individual level, but also for businesses and organizations. Staying in contact has become a crucial factor in the financial and professional worlds. openBC provides the social infrastructure and extended applications to give networking a professional character – in many of the world's languages.
>
> **openBC philosophy**[21]

From idea to concept

After reading 'The Tipping Point'[22] Lars Hinrichs was thinking about ideas, products, messages or behaviors that can spread across the globe like viral pandemics. He was convinced that a business network connecting professionals would spread out in exactly the same way, leading to vastly increasing benefits for its users and simultaneously catering to social needs. The book had taught him three lessons: Information can spread virally (a) if it possesses a certain degree of stickiness,

(b) if it is delivered in the right context, and especially (c) if it is transported by the right people. Lars Hinrichs was convinced that he was one of the latter:

> I have always been curious about my friends' and colleagues' e-mail address book. I wanted to know the people they knew. And I had a large and high-quality professional network. After I read the book [The Tipping Point], one thought immediately struck my mind: 'Wait a minute. I can be a Connector myself!'

In spite of his enthusiasm, Lars Hinrichs kept in mind his personal experiences with dot.com failures in 1999 and 2000. He knew that his new online networking platform needed to create substantial value for its users and that it needed to be more than an entertaining source of Web 2.0. Such a value could appeal to some of the 4 million unemployed Germans who had been suffering from a bleak economy. Job vacancies were scarce and often staffed without even posting an offer. A good network was vital to find job opportunities, as a user concluded in his testimonial about openBC:

> A network is something you better build up before you need it. Through my pool of contacts, I have recently found new jobs for a couple of people in Frankfurt and Düsseldorf.

---

21 Taken from openBC website.
22 Gladwell, Malcolm: 'The Tipping Point: how little things can make a big difference', Great Britain, 2000.

Exhibit 1 Development of openBC and StayFriends membership figures

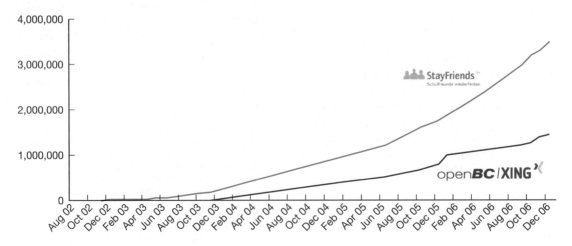

Source: openBC, StayFriends homepage.

History

> I knew right from the start that this will be the next big thing. One week later, the first very rudimentary version of openBC was launched – basically from my living room and with my direct network of 472 users.
>
> **Lars Hinrichs**

Lars Hinrichs neither had sufficient funds nor the technical expertise needed for setting up the platform all by himself. What he did have, however, was a vision, and he wanted to implement it as quickly as possible. Four of his friends, who were particularly IT savvy, contributed their programming skills.[23] Lacking the financial resources to reimburse them, Hinrichs offered them shares in the soon-to-be-founded company. The 'OPEN Business Club' was launched as a limited liability company under German law (GmbH). On 1 November 2003, openBC went live. While not having a sophisticated design, the platform aimed at fulfilling four user needs:

- **Find & search:** To provide search tools for different business needs

- **Enable business:** To set up a platform usable for carrying out transactions

- **Manage personal information:** To provide up-to-date contact details

- **Communities & events:** To encourage online activities as well as offline events

During its first year, the number of openBC members grew rapidly (see Exhibit 1), and the platform became operational in 16 languages, requiring substantial translation work. Server capacity had to be ramped up frequently in order to provide the processing power needed to manage the 100,000 members the platform had attracted by November 2004. However, as Dr. Stephanie Busch, Director of *Operational Services* at openBC, recalls, this rapid growth took its toll:

> Lars [Hinrichs] had been swamped by the ever-increasing workload. In the beginning, it was difficult for him to let go of certain matters, especially because he wanted to be involved in everything. But very soon he realized that there were not enough hours in the day to accomplish all that by himself.

By the time Dr. Busch joined openBC, venture capital talks with Wellington Partners[24] had started. This was yet another reason for adopting a more formal manage-

ment approach, which was implemented over the following months. Dr. Busch remembers:

> When I started working for openBC in May 2005, we had a paper-less office. Some of our employees didn't even have a formal employment contract, holidays were taken according to verbal agreements, and salaries were agreed upon by handshake. Now you go ahead and tell that to our investors! Of course, they wanted to have written contracts, but also formal target agreements and regular board meetings.

The deal between openBC and Wellington Partners was closed in September 2005, providing openBC with venture capital of €5.7 million to support the ongoing international expansion of the portal. However, up to now, the money has not actually been invested. All necessary investments in new infrastructure and, above all, in the internationalization of the platform were financed from cash flows.

As of 30 September 2006, openBC is Germany's leading business-networking portal with currently 1.45 million registered members worldwide. openBC caters to the needs of business members who share a common trait: the desire to manage their contacts and broaden their professional network.

Service concepts: StayFriends and openBC

Registration process

In order to use the service, new users of StayFriends, as well as of openBC, have to register. On both platforms, registration follows common Internet standards: entering first and last name, choosing a username and password, and providing an e-mail address. In order to avoid fake profiles, confirmed subscription models (also known as 'double-opt-in'[25]) are used. Users registering with StayFriends then specify the schools they attended.

---

23 Since 2001, they were actually running e-publica GmbH, a service provider for technical layout and programming of dynamic, data based web applications and websites, URL e-publica: http://www.epublica.de.

24 Wellington Partners invests venture capital in information and communication technology (ICT) and life science companies. The current portfolio has a volume of €400 million.

25 New entries are not displayed on the website until the original registration has been confirmed. After a new registration is made, an e-mail is sent to the indicated address of that new member asking him or her to first click on an Internet link contained in this e-mail before the new entry is shown on the website.

To complete the registration, they indicate their birthday and graduation year from each school they attended. Then, they get 'allocated' to their classes and may see if any of their former classmates have already registered. In order to complete the registration at openBC, new customers are asked for at least a minimum of business data such as position, company, and industry.

StayFriends membership and functionality

StayFriends does not charge users for registering. Users can acquaint themselves with the site and its services for free, and then decide later whether to become a full and paying member. StayFriends approach thus reflects a business model based on three pillars: first, users have to be attracted to the platform; then, StayFriends invites them to become members, and finally, existing members are converted into paying members. To support this business model, StayFriends offers two levels of membership with differing features:

Basic membership

All basic members have – without paying fees – the opportunity to create a personal page where they can upload pictures and where they can post information about themselves or their business. This information is then displayed as part of their profile. Further features available to basic members include:

- **People search:** The possibility to search for people by name, school, city and/or graduation year.
- **User profiles:** When looking at other user profiles, basic members only have access to a limited version of the profiles.
- **Message exchange:** Sending messages to other users is possible; however, in order to read incoming messages from other basic members, gold membership is needed. The receipt of a message that a user cannot read is aimed at encouraging him or her to upgrade to gold membership.
- **Class reunions:** Every registered member can announce a class reunion; members of the class in question are informed about the place and time of the reunion via e-mail.
- **Guest book:** All users can create a guest book where others can enter greetings or stories and upload photos.

- **Contact list:** All users can create a contact list; added users can be displayed in the form of a simple list, a gallery with names and photos, or a map of Germany indicating where the contacts are located. However, members added to a contact list are not informed about this fact.
- **Memories and stories:** Users may add memories of 'the good old days' to their profile.

Gold membership

In addition to the features available to basic members, gold members are, for a fee of €18 per year, provided with enhanced capabilities including:

- **User profiles:** Gold members may view other users' full profiles (see Exhibit 2).
- **Message exchange:** An unlimited number of messages can be exchanged via the StayFriends mailbox. However, actual e-mail addresses are not revealed (in order to keep communication within the platform and lead basic members to upgrade to gold membership).
- **Class reunions:** Gold members have access to all information about class reunions.
- **Guest book:** Gold members may read all entries in their guest books and have unlimited access to other users' guest books including photos.

Silke Glossner, a StayFriends user from Munich, comments on StayFriends added value:

> We recently arranged a class reunion via StayFriends. It was a great success. I am sure we wouldn't have been able to gather so many of our classmates 15 years after graduation without the help of StayFriends.

There is yet another way of earning a gold membership for free: by recommending StayFriends to others (tell-a-friend-mode). For every three successful invitations to register with StayFriends, the user gets a free gold membership for one month.[26] Through this feature, StayFriends wishes to create a snowball effect. However, the acceptance rate of this recommendation feature is fairly low because many users don't see a personal benefit from recommending StayFriends to others. Clemens Capeller, a StayFriends member, explains:

---

26 When this feature was first introduced, users got three months' free gold membership for five successful invitations. However, users found it tiresome to find so many new members, so the number has since been lowered.

Exhibit 2 Michel Lindenberg's StayFriends profile as displayed to gold members

Google AdSenses in the form of a skyscraper

Why should I invite people I already know? If I knew how to contact my classmates, I wouldn't need StayFriends anyway.

Michel Lindenberg elaborates on this point:

In order to grow through viral marketing, there must be a direct personal advantage. openBC for example has an immediate benefit: When you invite someone to openBC, you can add him to your contact list right away and expand your network. When you invite somebody to StayFriends, you hope that he or she invites somebody, who might then invite somebody else who was in your class...

Over time, StayFriends has built up an image of 'nostalgia', which has proven to be one of StayFriends major assets. One feature that clearly emphasizes the nostalgic 'look and feel' of the website is the interactive class photo: People can upload class photos and place little tags on their classmates. When clicking on it, the tag shows the person's name, and indicates whether the student in question is registered with StayFriends or not (see Exhibit 3). Users greatly appreciate this feature, as Rainer Nachtwey, a StayFriends member states:

What I like about the photos is that they are so full of atmosphere. It is so funny how people and styles have changed since. It's like stepping back into the past.

Users are encouraged to develop a kind of 'community spirit', by inviting classmates to help them fill in the names of those students they cannot remember. When an existing StayFriends member is identified in a new photo, StayFriends sends him or her a newsletter to inform him or her about it. This type of newsletter has proven to be one of the best mechanisms for persuading users to revisit the StayFriends homepage. Michel Lindenberg explains:

A crucial step has been to transfer communication from the user's private mailbox to the StayFriends platform. It makes a big difference to a user whether he receives a message from an old friend between two spam mails or next to a picture of his old friend. And then he is only a click away from sending a message to someone else from his class. It has had a major impact on our revenues.

At present, StayFriends users care more about new members they might know than about additional features. The main trigger for users to subscribe to the gold membership is the registration of a new classmate. Thus, the focus of activities for the near future lies in customer acquisition, since a decline in new registrations will have a negative impact on conversion rates and ultimately on revenues.

Exhibit 3 Stay Friends' interactive class photo

 Registered – Click for a direct link to the user s personal page

 Not registered but identified and named

 Neither registered nor named

Source: StayFriends website.

With increasing market saturation the importance of new members will decrease. Additional features will then gain importance. More features would also help to further foster customer loyalty. Currently, users sometimes have difficulty in assessing the long-term value of StayFriends. Silke Glossner, a StayFriends member says:

> StayFriends is great! Thanks to the platform I have found so many of my former friends! But now that I have found them and we have exchanged e-mail-addresses and phone numbers, I don't think I will renew my gold membership.

But Karsten Giernalczyk,[27] Business Development Manager at StayFriends, is confident of the future success of StayFriends:

> One million students finish school every year. So there will always be new members to acquire even if it is not such a big target group. Second – and this is even more important – people will lose contact again. They move, change their e-mail-address, phone number, etc. And a school friend is not necessarily somebody you are in touch with every week – so people will forget to inform them about these changes.

openBC membership and functionality

> Our business model is about connections, not only profiles. The true value lies in the connections between people. It is not the two dots on the map but rather the road that connects them.

Eoghan Jennings, CFO, openBC

Users registering at openBC select one of two membership alternatives (for comparison and overview see Exhibit 4). A free basic membership enables users to use functions of the platform, such as publishing their profile, making and maintaining new contacts, engaging in group discussions, and thus gradually building up their individual business network. In addition to the features covered by the basic membership, users can opt for a premium membership at €5.95 per month. Premium members can draw from the full networking potential of the platform,

---

27 Unless stated otherwise, quotations from Karsten Giernalczyk were gathered during interviews in July 2006 at the StayFriends headquarters in Erlangen, Germany.

featuring extended search, contact management and communication options. The most important basic and premium membership features include:

Personal profile

Users can provide information about previous employers, education, their wants and haves, and personal interests (for a sample profile page, see Exhibit 5). Essentially, the profile page resembles a curriculum vitae. Adding a personal picture is a very popular feature and increases the click rate on profiles by approximately

35%. The profile page can also show information about a user's status within the openBC community; for example, their profile statistics in terms of activity and their number of contacts and page hits.

Searches

Basic membership enables users to reconnect with people they already know by name, or find members in the same city or industry. In order to use openBC for commercial purposes, for example, as a tool for head-hunting or creating business opportunities, more

Exhibit 4 Comparison between basic and premium membership features*

	Free membership	Premium membership
	Search	
Find & search **Enable business**	– First name – Last name – City – Industry	– Organisations & universities – Companies & positions – State/province/country – Interests & knowledge, etc.
	Power search	

	Not available	– Members who...
		    ...viewed your profile
		    ...match your wants and haves
		    ...have clicked on your home page
		    ...have viewed your "About me" page
		– (Former) Colleagues or alumni
		– Contacts of your contacts
		– Birthdays of contacts. etc.

Manage personal info	**Personal messages**	
	Not available	20 messages per day
	Number of contacts	
	Unlimited	Unlimited
Communities & events	**Number of participants**	
	10	Unlimited
	Export guest list	
	Not available	Available
	Premium World	
		Available
Membership fee per month	Free of charge	Eur 5.95

*Premium features are available in addition to basic features, which are available to all openBC members.
Source: openBC/XING website.

Exhibit 5 Lars Hinrichs' profile page on openBC and XING

Source: openBC/XING website.

detailed search functions of the premium membership are needed. These power searches enable premium users to see who has recently changed the company or position, or who matches their own wants and haves. The most popular feature by far is a power search as well, however, one with a rather social component: the search for members 'who clicked on my profile'. This 'backward voyeurism' seems to fascinate members at openBC tremendously, as an openBC user confirms:

> If I think about the feature that I miss the most after my premium membership expired, I can definitely say that it is the 'Who clicked on my profile?'-statistic. I am very curious about who is interested in me – I think everybody is.

Another networking tool in the power search is searching for one's own second-degree contacts, thus enabling members to leverage the value of their personal network by accessing the otherwise inaccessible greater network of their contacts' contacts.

Messaging and contacting

openBC provides various options for interacting with other members. Personal messages facilitate fast communication over the platform and are available for premium members only. Basic members can, however, reply to messages received from other members. A mailbox keeps track of incoming and outgoing messages. Skype[28] functions are integrated into the platform and are accessible to all members. This feature enables members to view the current online/offline status of a contact, call members directly from their contact page, leave voice mail messages or send files to them. openBC also offers a guestbook to all members.

Invitation and contact confirmation

All members can send different types of invitations to other professionals for joining the platform. A customized invitation can be sent to one or several users asking them to register. Using the openBC-plug-in, which is compatible with several popular mail applications, users can compare, for example, their Microsoft Outlook address book with their openBC contact list

and invite people who have not registered yet. Users can send contact requests to any other user on the platform they want to add to their contact list stating a reason for their approach. The person being contacted then receives a notification and can choose whether to confirm or deny the request. He then may specify for each contact which contact information he wants to share. Confirmed contacts then appear on a user's contact list. The contact path (see Exhibit 6) is a tool openBC uses to visualize the relationship of two users over several degrees of separation. This tool is one of the key achievements in the development of the platform and posed one of the greatest challenges, as Eoghan Jennings, CFO at openBC, recounts:

> It looks so simple, but it was hard work because it is calculated in real time. If we had not continuously improved the software and the algorithm, by now the contact path would take half an hour to load. Leaving it out was never an option, though. It visualizes connections to people you otherwise would not even know about – and that's a huge new pool of potential contacts for your business.

Members are able to browse through several degrees of contacts searching for business opportunities or expertise. The 'introduction' feature is intended to facilitate tapping into new contact pools. A member can introduce two of his own contacts who did not know each other before, thus enabling them to connect and possibly do business together.

Groups and events

As of October 2006, openBC hosts more than 4,700 groups covering almost every imaginable aspect of business, as well as social or after-work aspects. Groups also vary in terms of entry restrictions due to a specific focus or regional limitations. Active members of the openBC community, who had started local online groups on the platform, soon took them to the real

---

28 Skype is an online communication service provider for Internet telephony. Calls between Skype users are free of charge, only calls to landline or mobile phones are charged. URL Skype: http://www.skype.com.

Exhibit 6 openBC contact path

 Hans Denker
Universität
Erlangen-Nürnberg

 Sebastian Mauch
Friedrich-Alexander-Univers
Erlangen-Nürnberg

 Eoghan Jennings
Open Business Club AG,
openBC

 Lars Hinrichs
Open Business Club AG,
Xing

Source: openBC/XING website.

world. Regular offline networking events have been taking place all over Germany. Lars Hinrichs is astonished about their rapid development:

> Munich had 2,000 members in no time. They started up monthly networking events and even charged a registration fee for some of them. Once in a while, I would join a local event and pretend to be a technician, working at the openBC customer support department. I got interesting testimonials from users telling how often they used openBC and what kinds of deals they had already closed with the platform's help.

openBC provides event management functions such as a 'calendar and invite function' for own events and reminders for events in a member's own city or region. These functions are upgraded with premium membership, increasing the number of events and possible participants and providing the functionality to export participation lists to Microsoft Outlook.

openBC also receives numerous comments from groups where members discuss the functions and performance of the platform. Frequently, new features are developed in response to users' inputs. openBC introduced a formalized feedback process for valuable inputs in order to honor good ideas when a feature is introduced.

Customization

Members can selectively filter the information they receive when accessing the portal. For private users, features like a list with upcoming birthdays of their contacts might be more interesting than a constantly updated list of new contacts or a list of upcoming business events. Thus, each start page can be customized according to individual needs and interests while still adhering to a professional look and feel. Various e-mail notifications and RSS feeds enable members to keep track of new messages and group posts.

Data validity and privacy

> openBC is the keeper of the Holy Grail of user-generated content. That is why their business model is built upon trust and how they deal with this content. Essentially they are 'a trust for trust'.
>
> **Hanno Zulla**, e-publica GmbH, Germany

Any website handling a large number of personal user files faces the problem of fake profiles. With openBC and StayFriends, fake user accounts do occur as well, but pose no serious threat to the integrity of the plat-

forms as a whole. Both routinely check new entries for certain key words. If an entry contains, for example, obscenities, VIP names, or looks irregular in any other way, it is automatically reported and screened manually. The number of entries deleted from both databases is relatively small, though. At StayFriends, for instance, only 4.2% of all user entries had to be deleted so far, either because people wanted their profile to be deleted, or because StayFriends could not validate the entry.

People in Germany are very concerned about their privacy, and German courts strictly enforce data protection laws. Any abuse of personal data would also mean a huge loss of trust, which could ultimately endanger the whole concept of any social networking site. Michel Lindenberg explains StayFriends policy regarding privacy:

> The police calls us about once a month and asks for some people's personal data, like their e-mail-address or the exact time people logged in or out. But as long as we are under no legal obligation to do so, we do not pass out any personal information.

Generally speaking, a legal obligation to hand over personal data to law enforcement authorities can only be issued by court order. In order to further protect privacy, StayFriends users can specify that certain sensitive data (such as date of birth, address or telephone number) is not to be displayed on their personal page.

For openBC, data privacy is an even more important issue as people enter a lot of sensitive personal data. Therefore, a high level of consumer trust and seriousness is essential for the business model. The vast database of business professionals with a high depth of contact details, as well as the various contacting tools, provide ample opportunity for inappropriate posting or advertising, spamming and Multi-Level-Marketing (MLM[29]). As Lars Hinrichs explains, openBC has shifted some responsibility in reporting incidents of spam and MLM to its users:

> You know, basically, we have 1.5 million policemen out there on the platform who watch out for one other.

Users can also fully manage data privacy. They can set detailed preferences for entries in their guestbook, their

---

29 Multi-Level-Marketing is a questionable sales structure where vendors are compensated based on their sales of products or service, as well as the sales achieved by those they bring into the business. Fraudulent MLM schemes can usually be identified by high entrance fees or requirements to purchase expensive inventories.

current Skype online status, group memberships, the reception of personal messages, and the visibility of their own contact list to others. In addition to these options, members can specify for every single contact, which information they want to make accessible to them. Each time a contact is confirmed, a member can choose to apply predefined clearances for certain types of information or specify exactly which information a contact is allowed to access. In group discussions, voluntary moderators supervise the compliance with business conduct guidelines and general rules of 'netiquette'.[30] Users breaking these formal or informal rules on openBC receive a warning letter and are, in serious cases or repetitions, permanently expelled from the platform. Data privacy toward external organizations or individuals is also taken seriously. Visibility of one's own profile and group articles toward search engines can be chosen freely, with openBC as with StayFriends.

Business strategy

Customer perspective
Target group comparison
StayFriends main target group consists of people who went to a German school, either in Germany or abroad, and who are now looking to reunite with their former classmates. Thus, virtually every German who has finished school and has access to the Internet is a potential StayFriends' user. So far, 3.5 million users have subscribed to StayFriends. In 2005, the average number of new registrations was about 82,000 per month. In the first half of 2006, this number increased to almost 122,000. There are roughly 1.4 million classes registered with StayFriends. On average 2.5 students per class are members of the platform.[31]

openBC follows a rather pragmatic approach concerning its target group. The fairly straight and simple page design and navigation concept (see Exhibit 5) as well as the lack of any advertising on its website provides seriousness that fits the needs of a professional target group, as are the many different contact and search functions. Apart from business professionals, openBC also plans to extend its reach to other target groups, such as scholars and scientists.

Marketing and customer acquisition at StayFriends
From the very beginning, StayFriends attempted to create viral growth by leveraging user recommendations, for example with monthly sweepstakes. Each successful recommendation equaled an entry into a lottery draw

for the referring user. In the beginning, the StayFriends' team counted on the viral effect of the platform, but Michel Lindenberg soon became disillusioned:

> When we started, everybody thought that the most interesting trait of our business model was the viral aspect. It does not require a lot of marketing – you just make a certain start-up investment and then it is supposed to work by itself. Today, I know that the viral growth in this business is not sufficient as the main growth engine for this type of business. You have to do online advertising campaigns. I underestimated the amount of money you have to spend in order to reach a critical mass of members.

Currently, StayFriends spends about €100,000 on customer acquisition per month.[32] The reason behind that is the twofold importance of additional users. On the one hand, the registration of a new user is a trigger for existing users to upgrade to a gold membership. On the other hand, new users are tomorrow's existing users, enlarging the customer base and thus making the platform more attractive to new visitors.

Although some users come to the platform via links on people's private homepages, the tell-a-friend-mode, and 'Walk-Ins'[33], StayFriends mainly acquires customers via three different paths:

Advertising
About 20% of StayFriends users are acquired via advertising.[34] Over time, StayFriends marketing team built up advanced skills in designing online advertising campaigns and learned that minor details can have a major impact for StayFriends. Banners, for example, need to contain keywords like 'school' to prevent people from confusing StayFriends with a dating site. For the future, StayFriends management will have to rethink current customer acquisition activities, as costs for online advertising are increasing more and more. But as of today, Michel Lindenberg is convinced of StayFriends banner advertising campaigns:

> Our banners are not very sexy. In fact, they are so unsexy that some portals even refused to display them.

---

30 Netiquette (neologism, a morphological blend formed from 'Internet etiquette') includes general conventions of politeness recognized in electronic communication, such as Usenet, mailing lists, or virtual communities.
31 This low average number can be explained in part by statistics: quite often, especially for elementary schools, only one person is registered per class. Statistical information was collected from the Stayfriends.de website.
32 Calculated on the basis of statistics from Nielsen Ad-Relevance.
33 Visitors typing the URL directly into their browser.
34 Own research based on Alexa.com.

But they work! The secret is to make them blink, load quickly and be understandable at first glance.

StayFriends has also gained some experience in offline advertising. StayFriends employees attended school parties and offered people to register on the spot. Also advertising in yearbooks was tried out. However, the relatively young target group of those still attending school turned out to be reluctant to pay for StayFriends service. Another attempt was made with newspaper advertising, where coupons for free gold membership were inserted in a newspaper. Registration numbers on the coupons allowed the results of the campaign to be directly measured. However, the results of this campaign were not at all comparable to online advertising. People seemed unwilling to cross the divide between print and the Internet. Thus, StayFriends experiences with offline advertising proved rather disappointing. The plus of this cooperation for StayFriends is the de-facto built-in targeting: Amazon's customers have Internet access and buy online. But Michel Lindenberg remains cautious:

Everything we have done so far regarding offline advertising has not met our expectations. By now, we are very careful with offline advertising. There is no reliable method of testing performance in advance and the path from a flyer to an online registration form is a long one.

Content integration

20% of all users were acquired through the integration of StayFriends service into Internet portals.[35] In May 2003, StayFriends signed a cooperation agreement with the German weekly news magazine 'SPIEGEL' concerning the 'SPIEGEL-Online-portal',[36] one of the most renowned and most popular German online sites.[37] Michel Lindenberg emphasizes its importance:

Signing this agreement was kind of a breakthrough event. Especially in the early days, the integration helped us to significantly improve our credibility and trustworthiness.

The biggest cooperation to-date was struck with T-Online, one of Europe's biggest Internet service providers with over 13 million private users.[38] In March 2004, a partner-integration was officially launched with StayFriends, which in the meantime had been acquired by Classmates. Since then, StayFriends service has been integrated into the T-Online layout and is now accessible directly via T-Online's portal.[39] The crucial advantage for StayFriends is the broad reach of T-Online and its positioning on the start page of users' Internet browsers in Germany. The long-term agreement with T-Online positioned StayFriends to achieve higher conversion rates, which are mainly due to two facts: First, when using the service, users stay within their trusted portal; second, willingness to pay correlates inversely with Internet-affinity for e-commerce services.[40] The less Internet-savvy people are, the higher is their willingness to pay. Portals like T-Online or AOL[41] offer user-friendly services and are popular among less sophisticated Internet users. Thus, their willingness to pay for StayFriends service is above average. As StayFriends delivers content and T-Online provides visibility and coverage, both partners benefit from the additional traffic, as Burkhard Grassmann, COO for media at T-Online[42], confirms:

We are happy about the cooperation with Classmates, whose service has more than 38 million members worldwide and connects school friends and old acquaintances. Via StayFriends we can offer visitors to our German sites access to this community. The partnership offers T-Online new revenue potential through non-access business.

Similar cooperation agreements were reached with AOL and GMX[43], although their terms are not as advanced as those with T-Online. Nonetheless, AOL users represent the user group with the highest likelihood of upgrading to gold membership, even outpacing T-Online users.

Search engines

The third important customer acquisition path is search engine optimization (SEO). Search engine results are displayed according to a ranking that basically reflects the importance of a website. The rank is determined by an algorithm considering such factors as the number of links referring to the website in question. As top ranked

---

35 Own research based on Alexa.com.
36 URL SPIEGEL-Online: http://www.spiegel.de; http://stayfriends.spiegel.de.
37 SPIEGEL's readership consists mainly of men aged between 20 and 59 years. More than 42% of its readers have the Abitur (Diploma from a German secondary school allowing admission to university or matriculation) – i.e., more than twice the percentage in the general population.
38 As of 2003.
39 URL T-Online: http://www.t-online.de; http://stayfriends.t-online.de.
40 According to a recent study published by Stern: 'Markenprofile 11: Die Rückker der Qualität', URL: http://www.gujmedia.de/_components/markenprofile/index.html.
41 AOL LLC (formerly America Online, Inc) is an American online service provider, bulletin board system, and media company operated by Time Warner. URL: http://www.aol.com.
42 Quoted in a StayFriends press release of 18 March 2004.
43 GMX (Global Message eXchange) is a free German e-mail provider with its own web portal. URL: http://www.gmx.de.

search results are 'clicked' more often, the position and the number of search results for certain keywords are crucial for increasing the number of visitors to a homepage. StayFriends currently conducts SEO with Google – which has a market share of roughly 90% in Germany.[44] The website is optimized for Google searches on the names of StayFriends members[45] and the names of the schools. Opening the StayFriends directory to Google doubled the member base growth rate almost over night. Today, 40,000 people searching for names visit the StayFriends website every day.

In order to increase the visibility of the website in search results, StayFriends furthermore conducts search engine marketing (SEM) in the form of Google AdWords.[46] For a small fee, the latter allow companies to have a link to their website featured whenever a user searches a keyword specified by the company. Today, StayFriends uses Google AdWords for example for the keywords 'finden' (to find), 'Schulfreunde' (school friends), and 'Klassenkameraden' (classmates). Currently, the search engine marketing and the Google search engine optimization account for 20% of all new StayFriends users.[47] Michel Lindenberg would like to expand the cooperation with Google. His vision is to convince Google to refer to StayFriends as a specialized player when it comes to searching for people on the Internet.

Marketing and customer acquisition at openBC

Internet users are the least loyal customers you can imagine. You need to have something to make them happy, or a reason why they can't switch [to another website]. openBC has both. We didn't have to invest heavily in customer acquisition – our members are the best sales force [for us] that you can imagine!

Lars Hinrichs

For openBC, the viral effect of word-of-mouth marketing is the main factor driving its growth. The initial strategy of the platform was to reach a critical mass of members as quickly as possible in order to increase customer value and lock-in. For a while, this approach worked well, especially since members benefited from having as many business contacts on the platform as possible. openBC grew through these 'network externalities' since every member had a motive for inviting more members to the platform. However, despite its vast potential, viral growth has its limitations. Dr. Stephanie Busch elaborates:

In many of our regional markets, we have achieved a critical mass and can observe high growth rates. It is hard to generalize, but usually by the time the first thousand users have registered, a steep increase in user figures can be detected due to network externalities. In our domestic markets (Germany and Switzerland), however, we are currently facing a new challenge. Eventually, market penetration will reach a point where the majority of the target group is either registered or, for some reason, simply is not interested [in joining the platform]. So what comes after viral growth?

In the beginning, openBC mainly relied on viral marketing for customer acquisition. However, every viral spread will slow down eventually. Activity on the platform (see Exhibit 7) declined after the initial networking hype. Already from the start, openBC offered incentives to users for attracting new members to the platform. For ten successful recommendations, members receive a free premium membership for one month. The same incentive is offered to the user for every recommended user who decides to become a premium member. Due to the high transaction costs and in order to increase customer loyalty, openBC also gives incentives for longer membership and payment intervals. Signing up and paying at once for a one-year premium membership is rewarded with an additional month of free premium membership. Signing up for two years is rewarded with three months of free membership.

In September 2006, openBC launched its 'Premium World'. This offer features special rates for travel, business newspapers, car rentals and other products and services available only for openBC premium members. Participating companies, including The Financial Times, American Express, BMW and Skype, can tap into openBC's member pool, which constitutes an attractive target group for these companies. However, it is the openBC members who initiate the contact with the

---

44 According to a press release of heise online dated 18 September 2006; URL: http://www.heise.de/newsticker/meldung/78315.
45 StayFriends-users may choose whether they want to be found in Google's search results if somebody searches for their name or not.
46 Google AdWords is an advertising form consisting of a headline, two context lines and a hyperlink. For certain keywords the advertiser can display his AdWords next to Google's search results for the keyword. For AdWords StayFriends pays per click. For a new user acquired via this path StayFriends pays on average 48 cents.
47 Own research based on Alexa.com.

Exhibit 7 openBC user activity (measured by contact page hits) May–October 2006

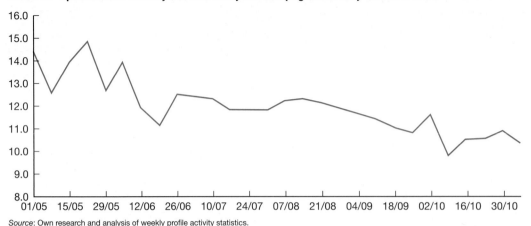

Source: Own research and analysis of weekly profile activity statistics.

companies, since openBC follows a no-advertising-policy. For openBC, this deal creates additional value for premium members, increases their loyalty, and provides greater visibility for the platform since participating companies mention openBC in their communication to their own customers (e.g., in their newsletters). Thus, for openBC this is a lever for increasing market penetration and attracting new customers to the platform.

Company perspective
Costs

The fixed costs of a social networking site include personnel and IT costs for the infrastructure that is necessary to host databases, run computer servers and manage the online platform. For openBC, these costs represent the largest part of overall expenditures. At StayFriends, costs for data hosting and traffic handling amount to €20,000 per month; however, the main cost driver is customer acquisition. In contrast, openBC does not spend much on customer acquisition, except for building up a local presence in a given market, where investments are made depending on the existing equipment of the country manager. Overhead expenses cover costs for legal and tax advice, financial control, and office equipment.

The most important variable costs are transaction costs. StayFriends users can choose among different payment methods: credit card, direct debit, bank transfer or via firstgate ClickandBuy.[48] Transaction costs range from 6–10% of the gross amount, depending on the payment system used. openBC users can pay via

credit card or direct debit. Unit transaction costs for payment via credit card amount to 2–3% of the transaction value. For direct debit, openBC pays 10–50 cents per transaction, regardless of the transaction size. Overall, openBC transaction costs currently amount to more than one Euro per transaction.

openBC revenues

According to Lars Hinrichs, openBC has been cash flow positive since its third month of operations, with expected revenues of €10 million in the fiscal year of 2006 (see Exhibit 8). 90–95% of revenues are generated from fees of €5.95 per month for premium memberships. In May 2006, openBC introduced 'premium groups' as an additional source of revenue. These closed, branded areas on openBC enable organizations to present their group with individual corporate identity inside openBC, using the infrastructure and all the amenities of an international networking portal. openBC charges an annual fee for the setup and maintenance of a group. Several large communities (e.g., the SPIEGEL Graduate Network) and corporate (e.g., Accenture[49] Alumni) or academic alumni organizations (e.g., AIESEC[50]) have been using this service. Revenues from premium groups currently account for 5–10% of openBC's total revenues.

Earlier, openBC generated additional revenues by selling its platform technology as a white label product.

---

48 People must first register with the service firstgate ClickandBuy and can pay via debit advice, credit card, invoice or prepayment. URL ClickandBuy: http://clickandbuy.com.

Exhibit 8 openBC revenue development financial year 2003–2006

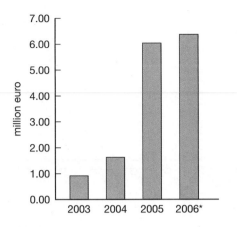

million euro

Source: openBC/XING, FY from July 1 to June 30, * FY 2006 shortened, from July 1 to Dec. 31 2006.

Companies with large alumni organizations interested in contact management and networking functions were offered so-called private clubs that were not directly integrated into openBC. This approach was eventually abandoned since it did not yield enough revenues and interfered with membership on the website. Another possible revenue stream is the sale of advertising space on the platform. However, Lars Hinrichs categorically rejects advertising as a potential revenue source:

> Advertising as a source of revenue is like a fire. Once you get it going, it keeps getting hotter. But when it does not get enough to feed on, it dies down to a faint smoldering.

The only way for openBC to generate sufficient cash flows immediately was to charge for the premium service right from the start. To accomplish that, pricing was a crucial decision for Lars Hinrichs to make:

> Actually, I had planned to charge around €18 per month for the premium membership, which would have been just about the mean of all dating sites that I used as a benchmark.

However, Hinrichs realized that there was a fundamental difference between dating sites and the business model he had in mind. Most dating sites have a churn rate of 100% in six months. However, Hinrichs expected users to stay with openBC for a couple of years, which would have been too expensive in terms of customer lifetime value. He based his calculation on the assumption that, unlike portals which explicitly focus

on a young target group like students, openBC would address a target group that is more stable and predictable in its needs and preferences. He then aimed for a monthly fee of around €12 when he stumbled on an odd phenomenon:

> I came across a fascinating study about the effect on pricing of the introduction of the Euro currency in 2001. One Euro roughly converted to DM 2, a calculation that customers simply didn't do for products priced at less than €10. Prices below that barrier were perceived as a one-to-one conversion, which essentially cut the perceived price in half.

Still, the pricing model remains an often-debated issue at openBC. China is the first regional market where prices have already been adapted in order to reflect local purchasing power. Prices were reduced by two thirds from CNY[51] 165 (€16.50) for three months to CNY 55 (€5.50). However, differentiating prices for local markets is just the least that can be done, especially compared to other industries (such as airlines), where sophisticated yield management has been used to differentiate prices and increase revenues. CFO Eoghan Jennings comments:

> What we see on openBC is a typical example of the free-rider phenomenon. We support basic members who don't generate revenues. At the same time we leave potential revenues from professional members (such as headhunters) on the table, since these users benefit immensely from the platform. Thus, they would be willing to pay thousands of Euros for our services.

StayFriends revenues

StayFriends has two sources of revenues: fees for gold membership and fees for advertising space on StayFriends homepage (see Exhibit 9 for StayFriends net revenues). In both cases, revenues depend on three factors: (1) the base of existing users, (2) the stream of new users, and (3) the fine-tuning on StayFriends homepage. The lion's share of StayFriends revenues is generated by membership fees.

---

49 Accenture is a global management consulting, technology services and outsourcing company, URL Accenture: http://www.accenture.com.
50 An international student organization, URL AIESEC: http://www.aiesec.net.
51 CNY ('Renminbi') is the official currency of the People's Republic of China, 1 Euro equals 10.10 CNY as of November 22, 2006.

Exhibit 9 **Evolution of StayFriends net revenues**

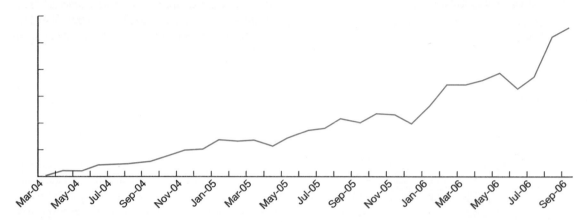

Source: StayFriends (absolute figures were not revealed).

Initially, StayFriends offered its full service for free, aiming at attracting as many users to the platform as possible, in order to quickly reach a critical mass. The original idea was to offer services for free for one year and then to charge €5 per year. This price was chosen because Friends Reunited was charging £5 (€7.4) per year in the UK in 2002. At the end of the first year, some 100,000 people had registered. As StayFriends managers considered this number too small to result in a sufficient number of search matches, they decided to postpone the implementation of the revenue model. It was only after 250,000 users had subscribed to the site by March 2004 that StayFriends started charging fees. However, at that point, the market leader in Germany, Passado was charging €12, and in the UK Friends Reunited had raised their fees to £10 (€14.8) per year. Hence, Classmates, StayFriends parent company, recommended Michel Lindenberg to charge a higher price than €5, which had originally been planned.

StayFriends therefore conducted a pricing experiment among its users to determine the optimal price and eventually introduced a more sophisticated pricing model:

- Basic membership: Free of charge
- Gold membership:
  - €18 per year for the initial subscription
  - €15 if the subscription is made within 24 hours of registration
  - €12 annual renewal fee

However, not all users are happy with this pricing system:

> I really think that StayFriends offers a great service. But charging 18 Euros for reading messages and viewing pictures? You must be joking! With all the advertisements on the site the service should be for free.
>
> **A Ciao user** (who does not want to be identified)

When StayFriends started its service in 2002, the homepage did not display any advertisements (except for the monthly sweepstakes). The goal was to reach a critical mass of members as fast as possible. Advertising banners were integrated on the StayFriends homepage shortly after the introduction of the new pricing model in March 2004. The short-term target is to raise advertising-generated income to 10% of total revenues. However, in order to generate substantial advertising generated income, it is important to create traffic on the site. So far, StayFriends has 30 million page impressions per month on its internal and external sites.[52] Furthermore, Stayfriends is also concerned that too many advertisements would deflect customers' attention. At present three different types of advertisements are included on the website:

- **Google AdSenses**[53] are used in the form of a skyscraper (see Exhibit 2).

---

52 Internal sites can only be accessed by StayFriends members after they have logged in. Statistics taken from Alexa.com.
53 Website owners can register at Google AdSense to enable advertisements on their sites. The ads are administered by Google and generate revenue on either a per-click or per-thousand-impressions basis. Google customizes the content of the advertisements, so that the contents of the advertisements are relevant to the website they are placed on.

- **Login- and logout-sites** (and to a limited extent the menu) are used to display advertisements.
- **StayFriends Newsletters** in which a limited amount of advertisements is integrated.

Internationalization

Compared to many other platforms, I appreciate the international dimension of openBC. Whether you're in Minneapolis or Munich, you can find like-minded people who are up to something. It reinforces how small the world truly is! openBC has built a site with a multi-cultural user in mind.

Melanie Menzel, openBC user, Germany

The most obvious barrier for the internationalization of openBC is language. openBC started out with a German and an English version of the portal in 2003, but quickly introduced other important languages such as French or Spanish. At the moment, services are offered in 16 languages, supporting various alphabets such as Korean, Cyrillic or Chinese. openBC's Member Relations division, run by an ethnically diverse staff, provides support in all 16 languages of the platform. However, translation is only part of the challenge. Maren Gintzburg, Vice President of openBC Member Relations, clarifies:

In general, the market potential in any country is rather huge. However, you shouldn't make the translation and then wonder why nothing happens. For example, nothing would have happened in China if it wasn't for our very capable country manager...

A separate international division at openBC includes 12 country managers who promote the platform in their respective regional market in addition to their regular job outside of openBC. These country managers are highly connected business professionals with experience in their particular field of expertise, but above all with a huge network of other 'high net worth' entrepreneurs, freelancers and executives. Eoghan Jennings explains:

The intuition in acquiring our country managers – that's our special sauce, our business secret. We developed techniques in identifying the right people. And of course we have a good network – our platform.

A country manager first plans offline events, sets up regional groups, and invites new members to the platform. Instead of receiving a salary, they get a fixed percentage of the premium member fees of the new users they acquire. The idea is to reach a critical mass,

thereby creating a 'micro tipping point' in each regional market rather than relying only on cross-border connections of a few international 'super networkers'. This approach has worked in countries such as Germany and Switzerland.

StayFriends has slightly different goals to further internationalize its activities. Besides generating additional revenues by offering attractive advertising packages for companies interested in addressing multinational target groups, StayFriends wants to benefit from economies of scale by leveraging expenses for platform development and maintenance. In May 2004, StayFriends parent company Classmates acquired the Swedish social networking site Klasstraffen.[54] The site was founded in March 2000 and offered largely the same service as StayFriends in Germany. The strategic goal behind Classmates' acquisition of StayFriends and Klasstraffen was to strengthen its presence in Europe in order to build up a bridgehead. After the acquisition, Klasstraffen.se was renamed StayFriends.se and the design and backend-processes were switched to the well proven German StayFriends design. Michel Lindenberg recalls:

The more professional StayFriends appearance also allowed us to transfer the revenue model to the – until then – free Klasstraffen service.

StayFriends plans to further expand international activities. Currently, StayFriends management is negotiating with the French social networking site Trombi[55] about a possible take over.

openBC is continuing its internationalization strategy although in some countries it is facing some challenges. In Russia, for instance, the platform faced insufficient infrastructure due to rather low Internet penetration. However, the influence of the country manager cannot be overestimated, as Dr. Busch explained based on the experiences of the successful market entry in China:

We founded a joint venture with a well-connected Chinese businessman. We were quite surprised when he told us to reconsider the timing for our first offline events, which were scheduled to take place during the week. The reason was that Friday is the only day allowed for networking events due to the strong contrast between the fast-paced, hectic urban life during the

---

54 URL Klasstraffen: http://www.klasstraffen.se, http://www.Stay Friends.se.

55 URL Trombi: http://www.trombi.fr; Trombi derives from the French word *trombinoscope*, which is a company notice board with, for example, employee photos.

work week and the family-orientated and traditional weekend. But this taught us an important lesson: Multicultural thinking is essential in our business.

Competitive perspective

There is this MySpace-hype in the US and it is likely to reach Europe and Germany as well. Some of the existing portals will stretch their business model and try to participate in order to gain market share. But I don't think one player will take it all. No platform will be able to cover all customer needs. Once the hype is over – in one or two years – StayFriends, openBC and a limited number of other players will survive. They will continue to plough their paths alongside the social networking hype because they are already specialized.

Karsten Giernalczyk

openBC vs. LinkedIn

LinkedIn, founded in 2003 in the USA, is openBC's direct competitor in the market for international business networking websites. It provides registered members a portal to keep track of their professional contacts, find or post jobs, or search for business opportunities. As of today, the portal has accumulated over 6 million members. Just like openBC, growth at LinkedIn occurred almost exclusively via word-of-mouth. The company reached its break-even point in April 2006, after conducting two venture capital rounds which generated €11.2 million.[56]

LinkedIn and openBC are quite different in several aspects of their business model. Unlike openBC where registered users can contact other members (depending on individual privacy settings), LinkedIn has established an extensive gate-keeping system. Users cannot directly contact anyone outside their immediate circle of contacts, but must instead request a referral endorsement from the mutual colleague. LinkedIn has started to build up online groups of its own; however, it is no match for its German competitor in terms of user-generated content, online groups and offline activities. LinkedIn co-founder Constantin Guericke elaborates on the reason for the comparatively low figures in page views:[57]

On LinkedIn, we don't do much in the way of page view drivers such as browsing, messaging and discussion groups because our goal is not to help people network, but help them get business done. The fewer clicks the better.

At LinkedIn, users can opt for one of four membership models, including a free basic membership. A $19.95 (€15.20) 'Business' membership offers all main func-

tions, however, with limitations, for example in the number of messages per month. For $50 (€38.20) per month, 'Business Plus' users receive the same functions but with a higher number of messages. The $200 (€152.81) monthly fee for a 'Pro' account includes more contact volume in terms of messages, referrals and introductions. However, even at this level, communication through the platform is still limited to 50 'InMail'[58] messages. For commercial customers, services of up to $2,000 (€1,528.13) are offered. Furthermore, LinkedIn charges for certain individual tasks, for example $125 (€95.51) for posting a job offer on the platform, or $10 (€7.58) for purchasing additional InMail messages. Further revenues are generated from advertiser-supported services.

LinkedIn has been trying to further enlarge its user base. In October 2006, the platform launched a service-directory similar to the yellow pages. This way, new target groups such as lawyers, blue-collar workers, and service providers could be integrated into the platform in addition to the mostly executive users.

StayFriends vs. Passado

For a long time, StayFriends most direct and biggest competitor was Passado. Founded in 2001, Passado started by offering tools for searching for friends from schools and universities. This business model was then modified a number of times as other platforms offered additional features. Friends Reunited, for instance, successfully implemented a dating service under the Friends Reunited brand. Passado also tried to integrate new features. The first attempt was adding more search features, such as hobbies, interests, and universities. Search results could be limited by city, gender and/or age.

In July 2003, Passado negotiated with T-Online about the possibility of partnering on a common service, but the parties failed to come to an agreement. In September 2003, Passado acquired the database of Stern-Klassentreffen, which had filed for bankruptcy. StayFriends closely monitored the development of Passado's subscriber numbers and strategic moves.

---

56 $ 4.7 million (€ 3.6 million) of venture capital was provided in November 2003 and $ 10 million (€ 7.6 million) in October 2004 respectively by US-based Sequoia Capital and Greylock Partners.
57 Source: http://blog.thylmann.net/2006/01/10/linkedin-versus-openbc.
58 'InMail' is a message option on LinkedIn for direct communication between users over the platform.

Today Passado is active in seven countries, with a total of 4 million users. Target groups differ slightly from one country to another. In Spain, for example, Passado targets a relatively young user group, namely teenagers still attending school. Among younger target groups, the willingness to pay fees is lower due to a much lower disposable income. Thus, Germany, where an older target group is addressed, is the only country in which, at least until recently, a pricing model similar to that of StayFriends could be implemented successfully. Viewing profiles was free, but users were charged €12 per month for advanced features such as contacting other members. When StayFriends introduced its fee of €18, Passado also raised its price to €18.

In May 2005, Passado modified its business model by enlarging its services, which hitherto had been solely socially orientated, to include business-related areas, such as search for companies. The goal was to participate in the increasing success of business platforms such as openBC. In March 2006, Passado started offering its services for free. Karsten Giernalczyk explains:

> The idea behind this was probably that charging members was considered a factor which limits viral growth – and one which Passado could easily remove as it did not have a lot of paying customers anyway. The problem, however, is that you then have to invest time and money in letting people know that your service is now free. Passado did not make that effort.

Willingness to pay is not only a matter of price but also of finding the right trigger, as Michel Lindenberg states:

> Simply offering a low price will not make people buy. Our service is meaningless to them unless there is someone they want to reconnect with. When you are told that a friend of yours has joined your class, 18 Euros can still be an attractive price – more than a one Euro charge could ever be without that trigger.

From direct to indirect competition

Several other business networking platforms with different business models have appeared in the US and in Europe. Spoke Software, Inc.[59] is using an installed software tool rather than a web application. This tool provides access and numerous search options for a database featuring more than 30 million professionals at 900,000 companies. Although, at first glance, Spoke resembles rather a directory than a real network, several functions provide important networking potential for users, for example, showing the 'path strength' to other users or the visualization and analysis of intra-organizational networks via e-mail traffic. The pricing model is similar to openBC, with a basic and a premium membership, but more expensive with premium membership starting at $55 (€41.70) per month.

The US site plaxo has attracted more than 15 million members through advertising and word-of-mouth. plaxo offers a free basic membership and a premium membership at $49.95 (€37.87) per year. The main focus of the plaxo business model is contact management. In addition, plaxo offers several offline services related to contact management, such as data recovery assistance and insurances against data loss.

In addition to the above mentioned open networks that can be joined by anyone, several business networking sites have opted for a different approach in an attempt to keep their network exclusive and elitist. CAPup![60] is a German closed executive network offering its users both the online platform and offline-events. ASmallWorld[61] follows a similar approach emphasizing elite networking ambition by appealing to high-society members and celebrities. These networks had only limited economic impact due to their small user base and lack of a viable revenue model.

Both openBC and StayFriends have a few direct competitors that provide similar services and make money in similar ways. But Johannes Haus of Business Development at openBC had his doubts about whether this picture was complete and comprehensive enough to truly understand and challenge competition. He remembers:

> If you define our industry as international business networking, then the list of competitors is rather short. But once you ask: 'What do our customers use openBC for?' the picture gets totally different.

Through a survey of customer perspectives, four key use areas were identified and depicted in a competition radar screen (see Exhibit 10). The position of a (potential) openBC competitor on the screen depends on the direction (i.e., the general function which the entrant could substitute or provide in a superior way), the distance (depending on specific market focus and resource set), and size (e.g., determined by market attractiveness and bargaining power).

---

59 URL Spoke: http://www.spoke.com.
60 URL CAPup!: https://www.cap-up.com.
61 URL ASmallWorld: http://www.asmallworld.net.

Exhibit 10 **openBC competition radar**

Source: openBC/XING.

Future outlook

The market for social networking sites is still growing and new Internet portals are launched almost every week. However, the key question is whether social networking sites have found a sustainable business model. While some sites generate revenues from online advertising, others charge their members for using the online service. The main drawback of the former model is its dependence on attracting strong traffic to their website; for the latter, it is their dependence on securing a loyal community of users. Regarding future developments, there are three different scenarios that could influence the upcoming business environment.

Collaboration of direct and indirect competitors

This scenario implies the market entry of a large-scale firm that is also an indirect competitor. This could be Google, for instance, which has the financial means to make acquisitions or to invest in the development of a social networking site and build up a community. However, building a community is crucial, since it is an important traffic generator and value driver for a portal. Generating strong traffic to a site would obviously contribute to achieving a critical mass of users. Karsten Giernalczyk of StayFriends is well aware of this threat:

> Companies like [the major German media company] Bertelsmann could say 'this is the next big thing' and

pump in 100 million Euros. Having an opponent with so much money in the market would be painful. However, these people are no rookies – they see it's a low margin business and that we are well positioned with a parent in the background with deep pockets.

Entry of an indirect competitor with a large community

A large community does not necessarily require a strict business focus to lock-in users. There are portals with a large although loose and casual network of users who have a common business-related interest (such as business book communities on amazon.com). These portals could be interested in generating new revenues by setting up a similar network. However, Karsten Giernalczyk considers this scenario unlikely:

We don't expect T-Online or one of the other big portals to enter the market with their own service, because we know there is no viral growth in this business. Thus, they would basically be limited to their own traffic – they could never compete with us.

Disruptive entry of a new player

With many changes currently taking place on the technological side of the Internet, a disruptive innovation could occur in different areas. A large number of 'mash-ups' already use various new technologies in order to create a surplus by simply combining the content of different providers to create something new. This scenario could also contain 'meta-network services', i.e., administrating a number of separate networks a user participates in and providing a single interface through which members keep their data up to date and communicate with their different networks. Johannes Haus of openBC assesses this scenario:

It's really hard to predict what potential new entrants could come up with, there is so much going on in the new Web. We think that this scenario is the most dangerous one since there is so little we can do to be prepared for it.

Lars Hinrichs did not intend to wait and see which one of these scenarios would strike first or what would happen to activity levels on the platform, which had been declining for more than half a year. He assumed that this was the result of the decelerated growth rates of 2006. Instead, he had his own plan about what openBC should do next. In July 2006, openBC announced a re-launch of the website including a complete redesign of the platform, which was carried out

through a design contest. All openBC members were able to contribute to the new networking platform (for the new design, see Exhibit 5). The platform design had been on Hinrichs' agenda for a while. However, Lars Hinrichs was also unsatisfied with the recognition the name 'openBC' and the associated brand had been receiving internationally:

The feedback we got for the brand 'openBC' had always been unsatisfactory outside of our German-speaking markets. The more we expanded internationally, the more voices were uttered criticizing our design and navigation approach. We realized that users' habits varied quite a lot from one country to another.

The team came up with a new name:

XING aimed at avoiding any misunderstandings about the site and paving the way for a more international platform with a broader target group, both geographically and in terms of business scope. On 16 October 2006, the legal organization of openBC was changed to a public company (AG[62]), with a board of directors (for an organizational overview, see Exhibit 11). This organization is commonly chosen for companies that intend to go public in the future. On 9 November 2006, the initial public offering (IPO) was announced to take place within the following six months. The shares would be traded on Germany's Prime Standard[63] at the Frankfurt Stock Exchange. The IPO was to be carried out with Deutsche Bank and the US investment bank Lehmann Brothers and was estimated to yield around €100 million. Yet, Lars Hinrichs had some doubts about what the future would bring for openBC/XING:

One fear for the future of XING is that, one day, our biggest strength could prove to be our Achilles heel: the power of viral growth. Right now, we have a positive network effect. But what if, one day, this effect turns negative? The same effect and mechanisms that have led us to become one of the world's market leaders in business networking might as well lead us to our doom. However, I consider this to be a rather insignificant threat, as long as we keep on with our successful expansion and customer acquisition strategy.

Michel Lindenberg is confident that StayFriends has achieved a solid position in the German market and of having a member base which continues to grow. However, he knows that growth rates will someday

---

62 AG: Aktiengesellschaft.
63 Prime Standard is a market segment of the German Stock Exchange that lists German companies which comply with international transparency standards.

Exhibit 11 openBC/XING organizational chart (total staff: 67, as of 31 December 2006)

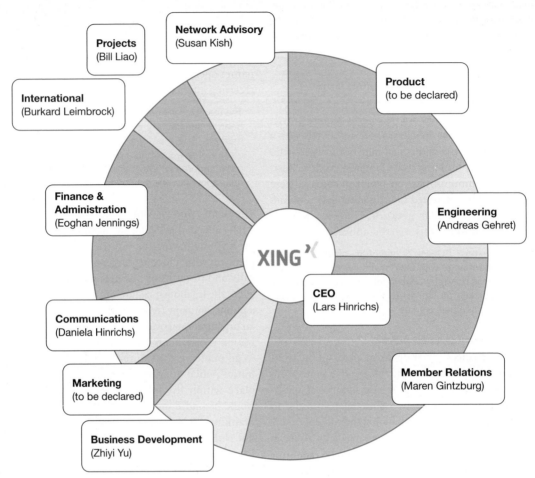

Source: openBC/XING.

decline and that other trigger mechanisms will have to be found to convert basic members into gold members. He is pondering new ideas, especially with regard to possible future developments:

> We care about our costs and about whether we are effective. We care about growth as well, but we want to make sure we earn back the money we spend. However, with United Online and Classmates in the background, we could acquire players in Germany or launch a dating site under the umbrella brand of StayFriends. Maybe we should be thinking in even bigger dimensions…

Spreadshirt
Mass customization on the Internet

Introduction

Spreadshirt has an unrealistic business model which is characterized by arbitrary investment planning and declining market development.

Jury statement at the NUK Business Plan Competition[1] in February 2002 in Cologne (Germany)

Today, five years after the Cologne event, the jury's decision could be questioned, especially with Spreadshirt being now the European market leader in micro-merchandising[2] and one of the top three players worldwide with an accumulated sales amount of more than 5 million customized merchandising articles. 2006 turnover was EUR 15 million, and the company currently employs more than 250 people in Europe and the United States.

Company background

Idea

Spreadshirt's CEO and founder Lukasz Gadowski[3] has always been interested in entrepreneurship. He founded his first company during his third semester at the University of Paderborn (in North Rhine-Westphalia) where he studied business administration and information technology and worked for Campus Consult, one of the largest student consultancies in the world.

I was very much involved with Campus Consult from the first day on. So I didn't spend a lot of time in the lecture rooms. Instead, I carried out consulting projects, participated in internal seminars, and was a member of the management board. But particularly through the consulting projects I learned what was really going on in the business world.

Lukasz Gadowski, CEO Spreadshirt

Along with other Campus Consulters (that is how the members call themselves), Gadowski did market research projects, built and sold websites and content management systems. They founded a limited liability company and started selling and implementing controlling software; however, long-term success was not in sight. One semester later, Gadowski founded a mobile commerce company, but again it did not succeed. Market conditions were not favorable since it was right after the Internet bubble burst. He remembered the idea he had been thinking about for some time:

---

1 NUK: Netzwerk und Know-how (Engl.: network and know-how). The annual NUK Business Plan Competition is organized by the non-profit association NUK Neues Unternehmertum Rheinland e.V. based in Cologne (Germany).
2 Micro-merchandising enables consumers to create their own merchandise by putting their own logos, slogans, and designs on apparel and other articles.
3 Lukasz Gadowski was born in 1977 in Upper Silesia (Poland) and emigrated with his family to Germany at the age of seven.

This case study was written by Sebastian Bartz, International Business Master student, under the supervision of Dr. Albrecht Enders, Assistant Professor of Strategic Management, Harald Hungenberg, Chaired Professor of Strategic Management (all three from University of Nuremberg), and Tawfik Jelassi, Dean and Professor of e-Business and IT at School of International Management of Ecole Nationale des Ponts et Chaussées (ENPC, Paris). It is intended to be used as the basis for class discussion rather than to illustrate effective or ineffective handling of a management situation.

This case study was made possible by the cooperation of Lukasz Gadowski, Chief Executive Officer, Spreadshirt and Konrad Marx, Country Manager (Germany, Austria, Switzerland), Spreadshirt.

In 2000, one of our first clients was a small textile printing company in Hesse. Through this project I got to know the printing technology and market. And the Spreadshirt idea popped right up. [...] I was also inspired by the Amazon affiliate program that enabled people to put adequate books on their websites. So if it worked with books, why should it not work with shirts?

Lukasz Gadowski

Realizing that his strengths lay within management rather than IT, Gadowski first went to the University of Mannheim (Baden-Wuerttemberg) to study business administration, but later decided to pursue a diploma program at the Leipzig Graduate School of Management[4] that is renowned for its entrepreneurial focus.

Foundation

In the summer of 2001, the first website bearing the name *Spreadshirt* was launched. Gadowski explains where the name stems from:

I chose this name because the business model was to spread shirts via the Internet. Furthermore, the company itself would be spread on the web through all the shop partners, which would also spread the word about us. I didn't want a central portal where people could only go to order their shirt. I wanted thousands of other mini-entrepreneurs to create their own products in their own shops using my platform.

The first website version, however, did not allow users to create their own shop by themselves. Gadowski had to do it manually and thus concentrated on the most important customers – requiring at least 100,000 page impressions[5] per month in order to set up a Spreadshop for them.

Late in 2001, one of the first Spreadshop owners, Michael Spiess, joined Gadowski, and both founded Spreadshirt GbR[6] based in Leipzig. Henceforth, Spiess took charge of the IT development while Gadowski was responsible for marketing and business processes. In May 2002, the first fully automatic version of the website went online. Now, people interested in a Spreadshop could open it themselves online and offer merchandising articles they designed. This was the enabler for the subsequent growth in the following years. In order to finance this growth, Gadowski attempted to raise some capital:

Throughout the year, I was trying to get in touch with business angels in order to convince them of our busi-

ness model. However, I never succeeded. Very often, I was already turned down by the secretary saying: 'We don't do Internet anymore.' It was such a waste of time.

Growth

Spreadshirt's growth had to be financed internally, resulting in a business that hit break-even right from the start. The innovative business model even won a business plan competition in Saxony in October 2002.

The FutureSAX 2002 award was very important to us because it generated a lot of attention right from the beginning. Furthermore, the 2004 HP Business Vision Award meant a lot to us because it was the first international one we received.

Lukasz Gadowski

By the time Gadowski finished his studies at HHL in June 2003, Spreadshirt registered already more than 5,000 shop partners. Since the number of orders and sales volumes grew exponentially, Gadowski and Spiess hired more staff – especially for customer service. Potential candidates were found quickly via placards or Internet ads. The first job interviews took place in the HHL lecture rooms because at the time the company had no office. All candidates had to pass several tests like writing service emails, figuring out brainteasers, solving math problems, and designing t-shirts. A lot of students were grateful for the opportunity to work for a dynamic and successful start-up. There were not many student jobs in Leipzig that offered such a broad range of interesting tasks.

In May 2004, counting more than 25,000 shop partners, Spreadshirt opened its own production and logistics center with a surface area of 130 m^2 next to their office building in the west of Leipzig. It enabled the company to be independent from the former fulfillment partners and to produce as well as pack the articles for faster shipping – now within 48 hours. Also, the Spreadshirt Designer, an online customization and order tool was launched, first in German, then in English, French, Spanish, Dutch, Italian, Norwegian

---

4 In German: Handelshochschule Leipzig, HHL (Saxony).
5 A page impression is a request to load a single page of a website. It serves as an indicator for a site's traffic and thus is often used to evaluate the expected revenues from advertisements on the page.
6 GbR – Gesellschaft buergerlichen Rechts (Engl.: civil-law association).

and Swedish. Now most European and North American customers are able to customize their own articles directly at Spreadshirt without having to open a shop themselves or having to search for an existing shop that might have a similar article as desired.

Later that year, former HHL colleague Michael Petersen returned to the company and joined Gadowski and Spiess on the management board after having worked for McKinsey for some time.

> I knew Michael from HHL. Very often, we had worked together and felt that we got along very well. It was also planned that he would start working at Spreadshirt after his studies. However, he was a little sceptic about our sales forecast and thought we wouldn't achieve our goals. And when he got the offer from McKinsey, he accepted it, but we kept in touch. Before Michael went to McKinsey, he had two months time to help us out. There he really saw his impact on the company. He never forgot that and eventually returned.

> **Lukasz Gadowski**

At the same time, Spreadshirt Inc. was founded in Louisville, Kentucky, as a 100% subsidiary of the Spreadshirt GmbH – the limited liability company that had been created out of the GbR in December 2003.

The years 2005 and 2006 were characterized by winning awards and relocating facilities:

- **Personal awards for Lukasz Gadowski**
  - 2005, Saxony's Founder Champion of the year
  - 2005, Entrepreneur of the year of Middle Germany
  - 2006, Internet Entrepreneur of the Year
- **Awards for Spreadshirt**
  - 2005, German Internet Prize
  - 2005, FutureSAX Business Plan Competition
  - 2005, Nomination for the renowned German Founder Prize
  - 2006, Red Herring 100 Europe Award (Europe's 100 most innovative companies)
- **Relocation activities**
  - Spring 2005, Spreadshirt Inc. moved from Louisville, Kentucky to Greensburg/Pittsburgh, Pennsylvania
  - Fall 2005, Spreadshirt moved into the new production and logistics center in Taucha, just east of Leipzig, tripling its production capacity

- Spring 2006, Spreadshirt also relocated its Leipzig headquarters to a neighboring building, which allowed the company to house all its departments on a 1,200 m^2 surface area.

In July 2006 as the first European company in its industry, Spreadshirt closed a deal with London-based Accel Partners who invested several million euros of venture capital. Gadowski makes an interesting comment about this in his personal blog[7]:

> We don't really need venture capital, and above all, not that much. But a little bit of it makes sense, especially when you're expanding internationally and simultaneously trying to enhance product development. However, the major part of the money is cushion which will be used in case of catastrophes or for seizing certain opportunities just as acquisitions.[8]

In October 2006, the business organization *Entrepreneurs for Growth*[9] published its new list of Europe's 500 strongest growing mid-sized companies. It includes the most successful businesses in 28 European countries and is sponsored by KPMG and Microsoft. In total, these 500 companies have shown a 57% staff increase and a growth of 67%. Spreadshirt has ranked among the top 1% of this list and even finished number one in Germany. Between 2002 and 2005, the Leipzig-based online merchandiser increased its turnover from about EUR 100,000 to more than EUR 8 million, and its staff from 2 to 200.[10]

> Spreadshirt's superior ranking among the top 5 strongest growing mid-sized companies in Europe is very impressive. This award shows that business success can stem from Germany.

> **Rezzo Schlauch**, Chairman of Spreadshirt's supervisory board

At the end of 2006, Spreadshirt operated three production plants, four marketing and sales offices, and one development center in Europe and the United States (see Exhibit 1).

---

7 http://www.gruenderszene.de.
8 http://www.gruenderszene.de/?p=19.
9 For information on the organization visit: http://www.entrepreneursforgrowth.org.
10 http://www.spreadshirt.net/26_10_2006.1004.0.html.

Exhibit 1 Spreadshirt's production facilities and offices

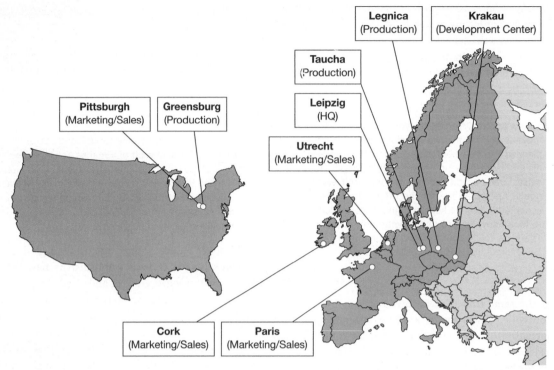

Source: Own illustration.

Business areas

Exhibit 2 gives an overview of Spreadshirt's different business areas. The original ones on the left have a mass customization approach and would probably be considered the core business. However, the three remaining business areas (La Fraise in particular) also contribute significantly to the company's success.

Spreadshirt.net

The award-winning Spreadshirt business model differs substantially from the traditional textile print shop around the corner although, at first sight, it may appear as if Spreadshirt, too, only refined shirts and other articles. However, the company uses the Internet to enable virtually anybody to become an entrepreneur and sell merchandise; or as Gadowski puts it simply: 'We enable users to do their own thing.'

He is referring to the so-called Spreadshop system that has been offered at spreadshirt.net from the beginning:

Our business model is that we offer everybody the possibility to open their own shop and to start selling customized merchandising articles within minutes. Since shop management is done online, all you need is an Internet connection to get started. Spreadshirt takes care of all the rest: the shop software, inventory management, printing, packaging, shipping, payments, and after-sales service. Thus, our value creation lies within the order fulfillment where we generate revenues per unit.

The process of opening and operating a Spreadshop works as follows (Exhibit 3 visualizes the process): Potential shop partners need to register online before they can start creating and selling their own merchandise. Currently, there are about 80 different types of merchandising articles and several hundred designs to choose from. Additionally, shop owners can upload their own vector or digital graphics. At the end, they determine the margin for every customized article, i.e. a price equal or above the base price charged by Spreadshirt (currently EUR 12.90 for the Men's Slim Contrast Tee, EUR 9.90 for the mug, EUR 3.00 per

Exhibit 2 **Spreadshirt's business areas**

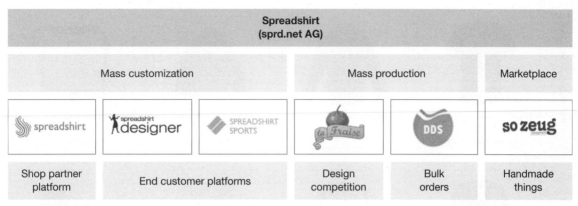

Source: Own illustration.

Exhibit 3 **The process of opening and operating a Spreadshop**

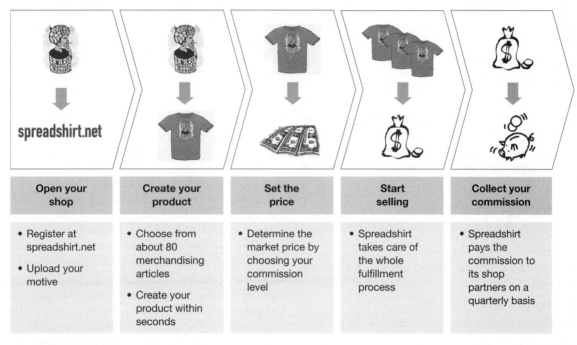

Source: Spreadshirt.

motif or text). The assortment (see Exhibit 4 for examples) ranges from classic t-shirts, casual, trendy apparel, and sportswear, to accessories and gifts including mugs, mousepads, badges, and bags. Commission levels are uncapped and earnings are paid out quarterly. Also, shop partners have the option to personalize the shop itself in terms of colors or fonts, for example.

By December 2006, the company had about 200,000 shop partners including private individuals, associations, companies, sports teams or artists. Very often these are people interested in a specific niche which they want to promote online, or webmasters who simply want to earn some extra money with their website.

Exhibit 4 Spreadshirt merchandise assortment examples

Spreadshirt.net / Designer	Sonar Retro Shirt — Promodoro Lady Leisure Jacket — Winter Cap — Messenger Bag
Spreadshirt Sports	Nike Park Plus Jersey — Adidas Avantis Jersey — Jako Short Cardiff — Puma Stirrups

Source: Own illustration.

Once a regular Spreadshop is set up and is running successfully in terms of sales, a shop partner may consider upgrading it to a premium shop. For EUR 10.00 a month, a premium shop operator benefits from several advantages:

■ Offering the shop in 13 languages,

■ Running the shop without Spreadshirt advertising,

■ Having almost unlimited motif uploads,

■ Including a personal logo on invoices and delivery notes,

■ Offering limited editions, and

■ Offering sales discounts to best customers.

Some of Spreadshirt's most famous premium shop partners include: Harry Potter, BoingBoing (see Exhibit 5 for screenshots), Eurosport, RyanAir, Napster, Tiscali, LinkedIn, Texas Instruments, RTL, and Coca-Cola.

The success of spreadshirt.net is due to the easy handling of the shop by its owners and users as well as the completely risk-free profit opportunity it offers. Regular shop partners do not encounter any fixed costs, thereby do not need to sell any articles. Only when items are sold, are they paid the individually selected commissions. Like Spreadshirt itself, every regular shop

hits break-even right from the start. Premium shop sales, however, will have to compensate the monthly fee charged for the extra functions.

Spreadshirt Designer/Spreadshirt Sports

The Spreadshirt Designer allows online users to create their customized apparel, accessories and gifts without opening a shop. Personalized designs and texts are printed on any item in the Spreadshirt assortment. It is an on-demand solution that does not require any minimum order quantity. The company does not define a typical Spreadshirt Designer customer; anyone looking for a gift can use it.

A special form of the Spreadshirt Designer is Spreadshirt Sports. Here, the product line is adapted to the needs of people interested in sports. Among the different types of t-shirts, users also find several jerseys, shorts, and socks that are not available at the regular Designer.

Konrad Marx, Spreadshirt's D-A-CH[11] Country Manager, comments on the importance of having the Designer and Spreadshirt Sports next to the Spreadshops:

> The shop partner platform is the core of Spreadshirt's business. It is the main reason why we were able to

---

11 Germany, Austria, Switzerland.

510

Exhibit 5 Big account Spreadshop screenshots

Source: Screenshot taken from http://harrypotter.wbshop.com.

Source: Screenshot taken from http://www.spreadshirt.com/shop.php?sid=3533.

grow exponentially in the past. However, the designer shops are important, too. Internally, we call them the 'own shops' that independently promote our customized merchandising articles. They account for more than 40% of the sales. But they have a big disadvantage: Online shirt designer platforms are dime a dozen on the market. So every one of them has to buy customers through marketing campaigns and hope they will stay loyal and come back. In contrast, shop partners are businesses themselves. They want that their products sell. We only provide the platform for it.

The three business areas presented above resort to the same fulfillment process displayed in Exhibit 6. After receiving the individual order, production preparation takes place, depending on the printing technology used. In the case of flex or flock printing, the motifs are plotted on colored plastic foils and then separated from the foil rests. In the warehouse, motifs and their corresponding merchandising articles are brought together and a first quality check takes place. Thereafter, the motifs are transferred onto the articles. Flex and flock motifs, for example, are pressed onto a garment under strictly controlled conditions of heat and pressure. In a second quality check Spreadshirt employees meticulously examine the operations' outcome and take action where necessary. Then, the customized articles are packed and ready for shipping. International after-sales customer service is done by native speakers from Leipzig headquarters.

The Derby/La Fraise

The Derby is a continuous online t-shirt design competition, which was introduced by Spreadshirt in April 2006. All amateur and professional designers are encouraged to upload their motifs which are then subject to popular voting. Every two weeks, the winning designs are eventually awarded a certain amount of money, produced in a limited edition, and offered to the public in the Derby online shop. The Derby customers are typically fashion-oriented individualists who do not fall for brands and want something special.

After only two months in business, Spreadshirt decided to back up its Derby by going offline and opened its very first bricks-and-mortar shop in Berlin[12], called *The Derby Store*. Since then, the Derby winner shirts could not only be ordered online, but also picked up at the store. CEO Lukasz Gadowski explains this move:

> The Derby Store is an additional channel that distinguishes us from our competitors. Furthermore, our shop partners and design contributors at The Derby like the shop. Now we are able to present their motifs offline. We can even imagine expanding this [physical] channel. But this is not our priority number one right now. We'll only open more stores in case of special opportunities.

In July 2006, it became clear what Spreadshirt would use a part of its venture capital for: The Leipzig-based merchandiser acquired Europe's number one online t-shirt design competition La Fraise. Patrice Cassard had launched La Fraise in 2003 from his apartment in Saint-Etienne (France). With only EUR 10,000 to get set up, he began selling t-shirts aiming at the geeks & gamers community. Within only a short time period, he started

---

12 The Derby Store is located at Gabelsbergerstraße 16, Berlin Friedrichshain.

Exhibit 6 Spreadshirt's mass customization fulfillment process

Order receipt	Preparation	Warehousing	Operations	Logistics	Customer service
• Digital receipt of motive(s) and article(s) • Receipt of payment • Forwarding to production	• Preparation of the printing depending on the printing technology • Technologies: flex, flock, digital, offset, transfer	• Optimization of stock • Avoid running out of stock • Minimize working capital	• Transfer of the motive onto the article • E.g. pressing of the flex motive onto a shirt	• Attractive shipping conditions • Shipped by Deutsche Post, DHL	• Multi-lingual service center based at Leipzig HQ • Currently: service by email by native speakers

Source: Spreadshirt.

receiving the first submissions from community designers visiting the online shop and blog – the design competition was born. Cassard explains how it works:

> Designers submit their drafts directly on the website. The following week, the designs are subject to the visitors' votes. At the end of the grading period, and in concordance with several criteria, we award a EUR 1,000 cheque to the selected designer and print a limited edition of 500 shirts. Usually, we pick between 16 and 20 new designs every month.[13]

This model strongly benefits from viral effects because users generate the content and each one of them has the incentive to gain new users, e.g. by saying: 'Hey, can you vote for my design please? Thanks!' Also, users have a different relation to the shirts produced – after all, they have voted and thereby influenced their fate. Most important to the leveraging of viral effects is the quality of the products, i.e. the quality of the designs. And thanks to the active and professional community of more than 70,000 users, the designs are usually very fancy, funny as well as graphically appealing.

Cassard knows the reason why the community is so active in contributing content:

> I always made sure to take their opinions and comments into account. The website is all about its community. It isn't limited to marketing but is an everyday reality. In a way, a sort of huge board of directors…[14]

According to Gadowski, the success of La Fraise is due to several factors:

> One thing is that it came to market relatively early. Also, its website is really simple and pleasing. Last but not least, there is Patrice [Cassard] who composed the very popular 'boss blog' of La Fraise and who simply has the talent to build a community.[15]

After months of meetings with Spreadshirt, Cassard decided to sell his company and signed the contract in July 2006.

> Patrice's motivation [to sell La Fraise] was probably to do something different. Furthermore, there is a big difference between starting an enterprise and running it on a day-to-day basis. The latter makes different demands on the organization, administration, and logistics. Not everybody wants to be bothered by this.[16]

Lukasz Gadowski

For Spreadshirt, however, acquiring La Fraise was an important move into this new market segment of online t-shirt design competitions. In addition, La Fraise would foster Spreadshirt's shop partner business. Designers, whose drafts do not make it to market, will most likely open up their own Spreadshop and sell their work there. This leads to additional shop partners and additional sales for Spreadshirt.

> We are proud and feel honored that Patrice decided to sell [La Fraise] to us. That's indeed a great sign of confidence. And such a takeover is by all means delicate because, after all, it's a community business. […] Thus, there was some turmoil [within the community] after Patrice's announcement [of the deal], but which he was able to 'blog-manage' with calmness.[17]

Lukasz Gadowski

---

13 http://blog.spreadshirt.net/uk/index.php?itemid=6222& catid=32.
14 Ibid.
15 http://www.gruenderszene.de/?p=20.
16 Ibid.
17 Ibid.

For a moment, Spreadshirt was thinking to keep both design competitions – The Derby and La Fraise. But it became obvious that one of them would eventually lose. In terms of usability and high profile, La Fraise was the better platform, so it was decided to phase out The Derby and to refactor and internationalize La Fraise instead.

DDS

The DDS[18] is the bulk order service of Spreadshirt which offers the whole range of merchandising articles for quantities starting at 25 pieces. Ironically, it was never intended to engage in such a business as Konrad Marx explains:

> We didn't plan to take part in the classic textile printing business because of the fierce competition. There are thousands of textile printers in the world and probably around 30 in Leipzig alone. Usually, the customer invites offers from 10 companies and decides upon the price. However, we received so many requests with order quantities of 100, 200 or more, and many of our proposals were even accepted by the customers – which surprised us. Then, the requests became so relevant that we decided to form a separate unit to deal with this business. So we hired a bunch of people who created the DDS in early 2004.

Orders fulfilled by the DDS – which very often come from larger corporations – do not resort to the company's own production capacities, since these are reserved for small scale orders where delivery time and flexibility are essential, but are sourced out to partner print shops. The same measure holds true for the La Fraise limited editions that do not require a mass customization approach either. Spreadshirt benefits from a strong bargaining position with its textile suppliers because of its huge purchasing volume. Therefore, Spreadshirt is able to compete on the price.

> We probably have the best purchasing conditions of all textile refiners in Germany. Thus, small print shops cannot compete with us at all. On top of that, we hardly need to actively acquire any customer because most of the requests come from our shop partners. Our competitors do not possess this enormous customer network. And there is another beneficial side effect: The more articles we process at DDS, the better our conditions get because the typical orders are always significant in quantity. Recently, for example, we sold 15,000 shirts to General Motors.

Konrad Marx

Sozeug

Sozeug is a German online platform for buying and selling handmade things which went online in March 2006. But according to its founder Hannes Diedrich, it differs considerably from established online market-places such as Ebay or Amazon. At Sozeug, designers, artists, and others do not just buy or sell products. Instead, they are the focus themselves, acting and communicating with each other – corresponding perfectly to the first of the 95 cluetrain theses: 'Markets are conversations.'[19] People can leave comments or write messages to each other. The products for sale online, and thereby their creators, are linked via tags. Thus, the conventional hierarchical structure is replaced by a more flexible mode.[20] Revenues are not generated by charging the offering of a product, but by a 7% sales commission to the company.

Diedrich came up with the Sozeug idea after observing many designers in Berlin who had at best their own small stores, but mostly sold their self-made products at the weekly market. On the one hand, he realized that this is a business that works. On the other hand, he thought an online platform would connect supply and demand on a much larger scale. Also, he found out about Etsy[21] and decided to launch a similar enterprise in Germany. In October 2006, Diedrich posted a comment in his corporate blog carrying the title 'Friendly Takeover':

> I'm happy to announce that, henceforth, Spreadshirt [...] will take over sozeug.net. [...] Spreadshirt's experience and knowledge only promise the best for the future of sozeug.net. Some exciting things have already been planned...[22]

Hannes Diedrich

One may wonder why Spreadshirt decided to buy a company that does not have anything to do with textile printing or merchandising. Additionally, Sozeug may seem somewhat irrelevant to traditional online shoppers. But it has a quite homogeneous community – possibly a *creative class* – that Spreadshirt is obviously interested in. Sozeug shows what social shopping could look like in the future.

---

18 DDS stands for Deutsche Druckservice (Engl.: German Printing Service).
19 http://www.cluetrain.org.
20 http://www.sozeug.de/pressematerial/sozeug-pm230306.pdf.
21 http://www.etsy.com.
22 http://sozeug.net/blog/2006/10/09/freundliche-uebernahme/.

Organization

Organizational structure

Spreadshirt is organized in a matrix structure shown in Exhibit 7. Its second management level represents a functional and a regional specialization. Thus, every organizational unit reports either to its area manager, country manager, or both.

Interestingly, Spreadshirt does not have an explicit organization chart. According to Konrad Marx, the company simply does not need it:

> The responsibilities of every single employee are put down on our Intranet. [...] The whole organizational chart is written down if you will. You can read who is responsible for what and who is everyone reporting to. Basically, you don't need anything else.

At Spreadshirt, there is the so-called *owner principle* of responsibilities. Everyone can assume as much responsibility as desired. At all times, there is a list of project proposals posted on the Intranet. Everybody can take what they want. The area or country manager then simply activates the budget for it. If someone seizes a project, nobody is going to mind as long as the project is managed in a professional way. However, if the project does not advance well, others will try to get it.

Open Logo Project

In December 2005, Spreadshirt launched the Open Logo Project (OLP) in order to refresh its corporate design. As the name suggests, the design development process was not conducted confidentially with a professional design agency as most companies do it. Instead, Spreadshirt set up a blog platform[23] and invited everybody to submit design proposals. Andreas Milles, Spreadshirt's so-called *Brand Evangelist*, comments on the decision:

> For our new corporate design we didn't want any longwinded bids. After all, we've got our numerous shop

_____
23 http://olp.spreadshirt.net.

Exhibit 7 Spreadshirt's organizational structure

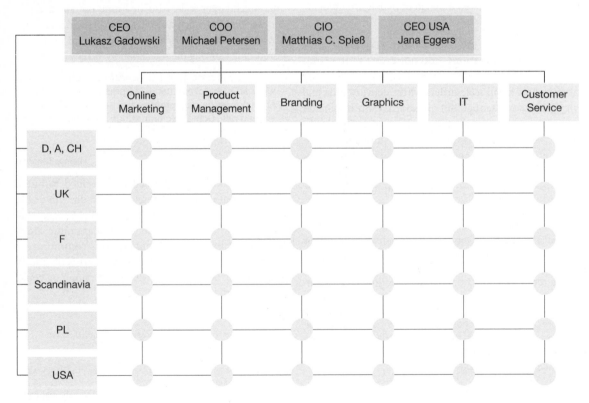

Source: Own illustration.

partners. And what's more obvious than resorting to the ideas and the joy to create of our online community?[24]

As Milles states, the OLP was aimed at the vast international Spreadshirt community which, at the time, represented more than 100,000 shop partners, many of whom were either professional or amateur designers. Before giving the starting signal, Spreadshirt framed several important guidelines for the project (see Exhibit 8).

Besides defining the OLP's objectives and requirements, Spreadshirt explained how it would proceed with the submissions and what the awards for the winners would be.

> Spreadshirt will choose up to 10 winners from all entries. The grand prize of EUR 5,000 (USD 6,000) will be split among the winners. In addition, there will be a special prize for the most original design. Copyrights must be passed on to Spreadshirt before any prizes are distributed. Until prizes are awarded, all designs remain your property. Spreadshirt employees are excluded from entering the competition.[25]

Andreas Milles

The design collecting period ended in February 2006. The response to the project was enormous: Within only two months, 600 participants submitted a total of 1,100 designs. All proposals were published on the official website for the community to comment on. An average of 1,500 users viewed this website every day. The OLP was posted more than 140 times in other blogs. Therefore Spreadshirt estimated that several hundred thousand people have read at least one of the blog entries making the project a great success.

Following the design collecting period, the OLP team had the difficult task of narrowing down the vast amount of proposals to a maximum of ten as they had announced before. Eventually, six concepts made it to the finals.

> We picked 6 drafts of which we thought they'd have the potential to represent Spreadshirt in the future. We could also have picked more designs because we had received so many sophisticated concepts. But in the

---

24 http://www.spreadshirt.net/28_03_2006.809.0.html?lang= de&locale=DE.

25 http://olp.spreadshirt.net/wordpress/?addon=brief.

Exhibit 8 Guidelines of the Open Logo Project

	Logo / Trademark	Color Scheme	Text Logo
Objectives	The logo should: • Look and function like a label • Show our internationality and make sense internationally • Reflect what Spreadshirt offers	• Finding a color "atmosphere" that represents and characterizes Spreadshirt internationally	• Developing an international text logo • Definition of a font to use in-house and for advertisements and claims
Requirements	• High international recognition, able to function as an independent icon • Cross-media usability: optimized for intergration/ recognition online, also in smaller presentations • Simple and flexible combination possibilities with a claim • Positive and negative presentation options • Single-color reproduction possibilities	• Cross-media, credible international application • Clear specifications in pantone/CMYK/RGB color systems • Broad acceptance • Expresses the Spreadshirt values: reliability, speed, freshness	• Matches with the logo • International recognizability • Memorability, can function independently

Source: Spreadshirt.

end, we just had to make a decision: We picked 3 drafts that had a fresh and dynamic signet, a very clear and strong logo. On top, we picked 3 more drafts that had a very interesting concept as well as the potential to be developed further.[26]

Andreas Milles

These six designs were then presented and discussed in a number of forums and weblogs for the international community to vote on their favorite one. Two weeks later, the winner – with 25% of the votes – was chosen: Maxime Colin, Junior Art Director from Lyon (France). Ironically, Colin was an actively contributing designer to La Fraise, which Spreadshirt acquired only a few months later. He had submitted the design called *The Fingerprint* (see Exhibit 9) which not only the community liked, but also Andreas Milles: 'The result [of the voting] thrills us. *The Fingerprint* is a perfect metaphor for Spreadshirt.'[27]

Colin's logo concept managed to combine various important issues of Spreadshirt and its business model: First, the fingerprint clearly symbolizes uniqueness, which is exactly what Spreadshirt's mass-customization approach enables. At the same time, it also represents the first capital letter 'S' of the company's name; or as Colin puts it: 'That's the logic link between the design and the [...] word'.[28] Third, the logo also symbolizes the viral effect, resembling water circles that spread when something hits the water surface. The curves make it look very dynamic – which the young company really is. Colin was awarded EUR 1,000 and a design tablet worth EUR 2,500.

> Through the OLP we've learned how our customers perceive us, and what they think is important about Spreadshirt. What I liked best about the OLP was that a very interesting international community was created.[29]

Andreas Milles

Exhibit 9 *The Fingerprint* – **The winning design of the Open Logo Project**

Source: Spreadshirt.

Exhibit 10 **The five different versions of *The Fingerprint* used by Spreadshirt**

| Leipzig | Taucha | Greensburg | Paris | London |

Source: Spreadshirt.

The original draft was subsequently enhanced into four additional versions of the fingerprint – shown in Exhibit 10 – that are used at random for any occasion. Their names only distinguish them from each other.

Business strategy

Spreadshirt's long-term goal is 'to become the global market leader for customized merchandise.'[30] Since Spreadshirt already is the European market leader and has grown tremendously during the past years (see Exhibit 11), the company seems to be on track. Gadowski anticipates that Spreadshirt will have become number one worldwide by 2010.

> Success stems from many factors: we are just different and we execute well. We have a strong long-term perspective and we think about real customer value. We have a good software and, above all, excellent people. That's probably why so many companies have failed and we're still around. [...] Also, right from the start, we've approached the right customer segment and got something across – a message that was commercial but that people could identify with.

Lukasz Gadowski

The Spreadshirt people

For Gadowski, it is the Spreadshirt people who make the difference. That is why it has always been of utmost importance to him to identify the ones that fit.

> We really expect much from our employees – during the interviews and on the job. Our motto is: 'Good is not good enough.' This means that everybody, including the service personnel, has to contribute more than just the ordinary. Especially during the first two years, we have

26 http://olp.spreadshirt.net/wordpress/?p=1485.
27 http://www.spreadshirt.net/28_03_2006.809.0.html.
28 http://olp.spreadshirt.net/wordpress/index.php?p=1113.
29 http://companice.twoday.net/stories/1818009/.
30 http://www.spreadshirt.net/About_Us.124.0.html.

Exhibit 11 Spreadshirt growth summary (2002–2006)

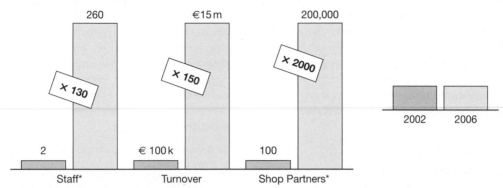

* Figures taken from January 2002 and December 2006.

Source: Own illustration.

been rigorous with our staff. I've even fired people who did their job quite well. So I guess, even today, there are still some people in Leipzig who think I'm a lunatic.

Lukasz Gadowski

Gadowski believes that if a company in its early stages is not able to pay exceptional people, it must wait until it is. A start-up cannot afford to work with average staff for a very good reason:

Excellent people replace [corporate] rules. You can't set up as many rules as you would need. That's why you definitely need excellent people.[31]

Lukasz Gadowski

In order to find excellent employees, Spreadshirt has developed a multi-level recruiting process. Incoming applications are analyzed and promising ones immediately forwarded. Before inviting a candidate to a personal interview, a telephone conversation is arranged to evaluate the applicant's basic social fit. The first personal interview usually takes place with participation of Human Resources staff and two or three department managers. If the candidate is convincing, a second personal interview is conducted only days later, led by a division manager and/or a member of the management board. Thereafter, the final decision is quickly taken and communicated to the applicant. Although Spreadshirt is currently having trouble to fill all the vacancies with excellent people, the Leipzig area offers a well-educated labor pool.

Sometimes venture capitalists are sceptical and ask me: 'Do you get the talent in Leipzig?' They think the only place where you can do business is Silicon Valley. That's nonsense!

Lukasz Gadowski

After a new employee has joined the team, the so-called *Spreadshirt Academy* program fulfills important on-boarding functions, ensuring immediate knowledge transfer during the first days on the job. It consists of different modules that a mentor can combine. Each module contains a set of tasks whose execution creates interaction with other Spreadshirt people. Some introductory tasks only require getting a login and a password. Others, for example, assess the knowledge about Spreadshirt's products and competitors in the form of a written test. Furthermore, newly hired employees working at the Leipzig headquarters carry out a so-called *Production Day* in order to learn how the customization is done. They take part in each stage of the entire fulfillment process, from plotting the motifs on the flex and flock plastic foils to the packaging of the refined articles for shipping.

As job motivation is crucial, Spreadshirt regularly organizes informal get-togethers in bars or other locations. There, employees get the chance to talk about other than work-related issues. More professional topics are addressed in the monthly general assembly

---

31 http://www.connectedmarketing.de/cm/2006/11/besuch_in_leipz.html.

where latest news is spread and future objectives announced. Good communication as one motivating factor is also guaranteed by frequent intra- and inter-departmental meeting sessions. Moreover, the company intends to motivate in monetary form: Most of Spreadshirt's employees receive a performance bonus beside their base salary. For the sales staff, performance is quite easily quantifiable, but for others it depends on the quarterly 360 degree feedback based on the following six criteria:

- Responsibility,
- Results/Effectiveness,
- Efficiency,
- Organization,
- Innovation, and
- Leadership.

Also, in the future, there will be chances for an employee share pool to be set up, whereby identification with the enterprise is planned to be intensified.

The Spreadshirt processes and systems

> What I really like about Spreadshirt, and what you can hardly see from the outside, is that in terms of management processes we perform better than many other SMEs. Especially job candidates often arrive with the expectation that we're only a start-up and everything must be chaotic. But then, they're surprised.
>
> **Konrad Marx**

Project management, for example, is very important at Spreadshirt. Everything that takes longer than one day requires a project plan which is created on the company's Intranet – based on a Wiki[32] platform – and defines the main project parameters:

- Project team and leader,
- Project objectives,
- Milestones,
- Deadlines,
- External contacts,
- Internal/external dependencies, and
- Possible risks.

There is also a mandatory debriefing in order to share all the lessons learned from the project. Furthermore,

Spreadshirt employs sophisticated performance measurement systems. *Marketing Overview*, for example, gives control over the use and efficiency of marketing channels. *Cockpit* is used regularly to provide relevant key performance indicators on a monthly basis. Additionally, *SpreadReports* is a reporting system (based on open-source SQL) that supports various queries to Spreadshirt's database (see Exhibit 12).

Competitive advantage

> Our competitive advantage is just a better service level. No other competitor is able to deliver as fast as we do. [...] More than 80% of the articles ordered are ready for shipment within 24 hours; the rest within 48 hours at the latest. [...] The secret lies within our back-end. It's our people, our processes, and our management.
>
> **Konrad Marx**

Capitalizing on its staff's competencies and skills, Spreadshirt pursues a strategy of differentiation in terms of quality and time, based on its strong

---

32 A wiki is a website that allows visitors to add, remove, edit, and change content. It also enables linking among any number of pages. This ease of interaction and operation makes a wiki an effective tool for mass collaborative authoring. For more information visit http://en.wikipedia.org/wiki/Wiki.

Exhibit 12 SpreadReports screenshots

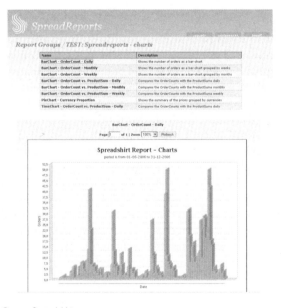

Source: Spreadshirt.

Exhibit 13 Spreadshirt's worldwide market penetration in the past

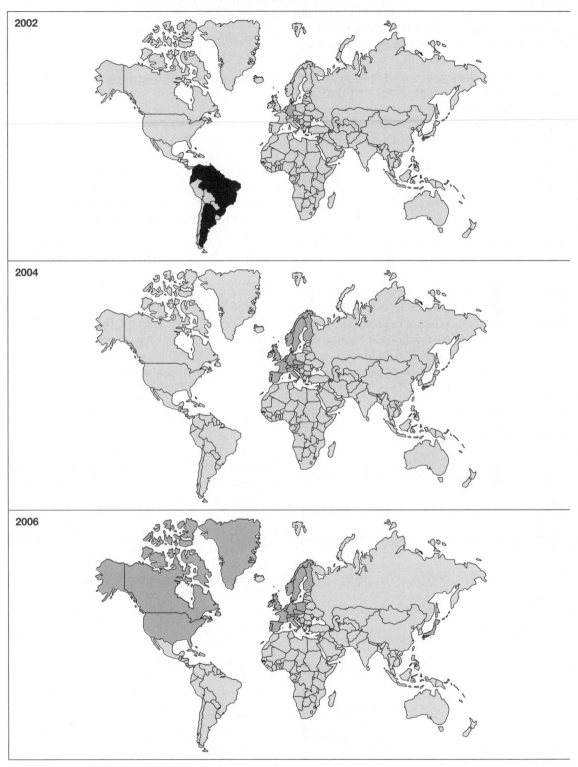

Spreadshop platform. The well-designed processes enable the company to achieve short fulfillment times. Also, Spreadshirt has been expanding its markets and business areas. Exhibit 13 shows its market penetration for the years 2002, 2004, and 2006.

In order to enter the Eastern European micro-merchandising market, the company took over the Polish market leader Butik[33] in the fall of 2005, enabling the Eastern European shop partners to operate on the Spreadshop platform. Lukasz Gadowski stresses the strategic importance of this move:

> We've acquired Butik for strategic reasons. We didn't want a direct competitor to grow up in a neighboring country having a totally different cost structure combined with an expansion strategy.

Exhibit 14 illustrates Spreadshirt's diversification strategy which relies on either organic growth or on acquisition of new businesses. This strategy was operationalized in 2004 and 2006 by the creation of the DDS, Spreadshirt Sports, the Spreadshirt Designer, and The Derby as well as the acquisition of La Fraise and Sozeug.

According to Gadowski, the choice of business partners depends on the industry Spreadshirt wants to step into. However, for business areas to become relevant, they should meet certain criteria. There should be:

- A marketplace,
- User-generated content involved,

Exhibit 14 Spreadshirt's diversification strategy

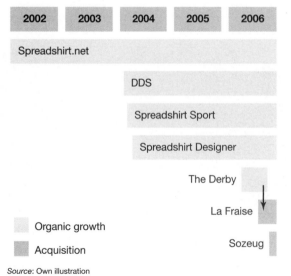

Source: Own illustration

- A community,
- Mass customization, and
- A fun or entertainment brand.

Core business competition

Spreadshirt's main German competitor is Shirtcity[34]. The Bavarian-based company was founded in 2002 and is active in all of Spreadshirt's core businesses: the online shop platform, the end customer business and the design competition. It also has a bulk order service. However, according to Gadowski, there are more important competitors to be watched closely (see Exhibit 15 for a table of Spreadshirt's most important competitors):

> In the beginning we observed Shirtcity a little. […] But today, we are rather keeping an eye on Cafepress and Zazzle in the US.

Cafepress[35], headquartered in Foster City (California), was set up in 1999. It was the first company to succeed with a business model similar to that of Spreadshirt. It offers print-on-demand and e-commerce services that enable individuals and organizations to create, buy, and sell customized merchandise online. The company has a network of 2.5 million shopkeepers who have created over 35 million unique products on customizable merchandise such as apparel, home and office accessories, posters and cards.[36] Currently, about 50 major accounts (such as Dilbert, Wikipedia, and Startrek) use the Cafepress platform for their own merchandising projects. Despite its large size, Cafepress has not yet entered the European or Asian markets. The website is only available in English and fulfillment is exclusively done in Kentucky. International orders, however, can be made with the goods being shipped out of the USA to their destination abroad. Unlike Spreadshirt, Cafepress neither offers a design competition nor a bulk order service.

The second major competitor of Spreadshirt, Zazzle[37], uses the same business model of on-demand manufacturing and an e-commerce platform that allows people 'to create, share and celebrate […] unique interests and passions'.[38] Zazzle started in 1999 producing on-demand products with automated

33 http://www.butik.pl.
34 http://www.shirtcity.com.
35 http://www.cafepress.com.
36 http://www.cafepress.com/cp/info/about/.
37 http://www.zazzle.com.
38 http://www.zazzle.com/welcome/first/aboutus.asp.

Exhibit 15 Spreadshirt's main competitors by origin and business area

	Shop partner platforms	End customer shops	Design competitions
Germany, Austria, Switzerland	• **Shirtcity** • Personello • eQuisto	• **Shirtcity** • Personello • Shirtalarm • Shirtinator	• **Shirtcity** • Cajong
Europe **(except D, A, CH)**	• Comboutique	• Comboutique • TShirtStudio • Divao	• Teetonic • Split the Atom • StyleTax • Koalala
USA	• **Cafepress** • **Zazzle** • Printfection	• **Cafepress** • **Zazzle** • Printfection	• **Threadless**

Source: Own illustration.

manufacturing systems; however, it did not go online until 2003. Today, customers can shop at zazzle.com and choose from existing designs and products, create their own customized merchandise, or publish their product in a gallery earning a 10% commission every time their creation is purchased. According to the website, Zazzle combines 'innovative manufacturing, a robust community, the largest online collection of customizable digital images and unmatched personalization tools to empower [customers] to create apparel, posters, cards, stamps and more.'[39]

The main international competitor to La Fraise is Threadless[40] – the initial project of Skinny Corp[41] which was launched in 2000. Today, the Chicago-based ongoing design competition is probably the most famous one in the world. Since La Fraise's founder Cassard was inspired by Threadless, the two concepts are very similar. At Threadless, the submitted designs get scored for seven days, usually receiving between 2,000 and 3,000 votes. Then, the four to six top-scoring designs are picked, printed in a limited amount, and sold online. The winning designers are awarded up to USD 2,000 in cash and prizes. Although Threadless may appear very US centric, its large and active community is actually international: 35–40% of all orders

and 50% of the winning designs come from abroad. The 2006 sales are predicted to be near USD 20 million, with a sales volume of over 80,000 shirts a month.[42]

Future outlook

Spreadshirt's future business strategy focuses on the following four factors:

■ Conquering the Asian market,

■ Pushing the offline model,

■ Creating new business areas, and

■ Growing through small acquisitions.

In order to expand on the Asian market, Spreadshirt is currently planning to build its own production capacities in Beijing in 2007. By doing so, the company will not only be able to operate in Japan (as it already does today), but also in China, Taiwan, and South Korea to achieve its 2008 worldwide market penetration goal (see Exhibit 16). According to Gadowski, by 2010,

---

39 http://www.zazzle.com/welcome/first/aboutus.asp.
40 http://www.threadless.com.
41 http://www.skinnycorp.com.
42 http://boetter.dk/podcast/category/customermade/.

Spreadshirt's turnover could be made up of 40% from Europe, 35% from North America and 25% from Asia.

Spreadshirt is continuously enhancing its products and processes in order to sustain and further strengthen its market position. The focus is put on the Spreadshop platform. From January 2007 on, not only big accounts but also premium shop operators will be able to integrate the Spreadshirt Designer interface into their website, thereby increasing the customization features for buyers. There are also plans to further interconnect the tens of thousands of Spreadshops via an online social networking platform. Currently, shop partners can create their own profiles and send messages to each other. However, the objective is to set up a central motif database through which the participating shops' content becomes available to everybody.[43] This adds value to most of the partners as Konrad Marx explains:

> Imagine you're a shop partner, but you hardly have any traffic on your site. Now you can make all your designs available to the whole community. If somebody buys a product with your design, the earnings are split between you and the selling shop.

By these new initiatives, Spreadshirt aims at becoming a Web 2.0[44] business. Exhibit 17 illustrates the network effects generated through this business model as well as its distinctive features compared to a classic shirt shop and the initial Spreadshirt 1.0 business model. Likewise, it assigns the various success factors to each business type.

With the right technology, a classic shop can offer mass-customized products to its customers, either in bricks-and-mortar stores or online. Via its Spreadshop technology, however, Spreadshirt 1.0 capitalizes on viral effects by spreading the company's front office online. Konrad Marx explains how this may function in practice:

> Suppose you're a Harry Potter fan and one day you find out that the official online shop is run on a Spreadshirt platform which anybody can use for personal merchandising purposes. So you decide to open your own shop selling jerseys of your soccer club, for example. Then, one of your team-mates likes the idea, starts running a shop for his dog-breeding association, and tells his friends about it…

---

43 An early beta version has already been launched at www.spreadshops.de.

44 The term Web 2.0 suggests a new Internet generation after the bursting of the dot-com bubble in 2001 and became popular in 2004 when the first Web 2.0 Conference was held in San Francisco. For a definition of the term by its creator Tim O'Reilly visit http://radar.oreilly.com/archives/2005/10/web_20_compact_definition.html.

Exhibit 16 Spreadshirt's future market penetration goal

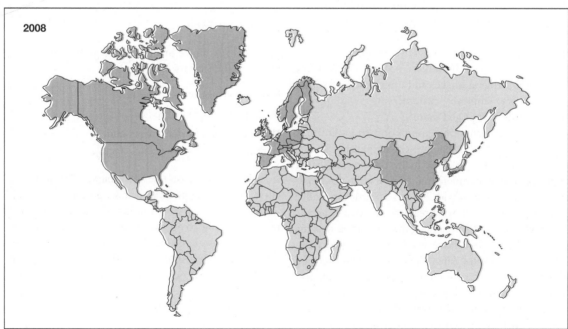

2008

Source: Own illustration.

Exhibit 17 Business model enabled success factors

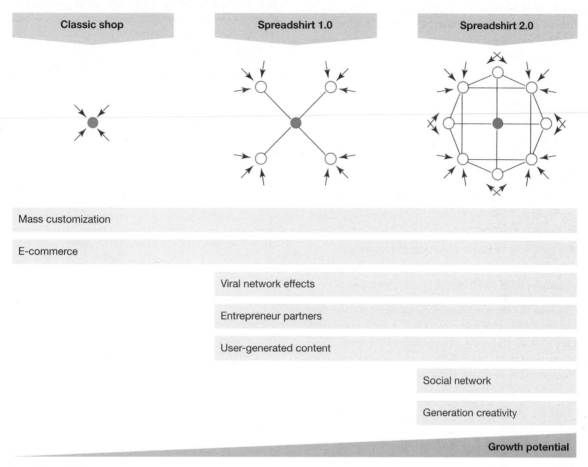

Source: Spreadshirt.

Through this approach, all shop partners become entrepreneurs and promote their ideas and designs within their social environment – or even beyond by using Google ads, for instance. In the end, such actions lead to higher sales for Spreadshirt because fulfillment can only be done with them. Furthermore, the Spreadshirt Designer tool allows users to generate their own content which many make use of, again leading to higher sales.

Spreadshirt's next step is to develop a Web 2.0 business model driven by the effects of a social network through which people do not only communicate with the hub, but also with each other. The other main pillar of Spreadshirt 2.0 is the *generation creativity* whose basic assumption is that people are creative, but that they do not (or rather did not) have the means to express their creativity. Spreadshirt 2.0 not only enables users to generate their own designs and thereby express their creativity, but also to find a market for their products through the Spreadshops' network. By this social network, shop partners can inform potential customers about their products and the ideas behind them, exchange experiences with each other and recommend certain designs, sell products at a self-determined margin and let Spreadshirt do the rest – all without any upfront costs. If Spreadshirt 1.0 is the showroom for one's creativity, Spreadshirt 2.0 is the marketing platform that will bring in visitors and potential buyers.

Growth opportunities are obviously far greater for Spreadshirt 2.0 than for the classic shop. There are far more individuals on-board, i.e. the tens of thousands of Spreadshop partners involved in creating value for customers. All of them have the incentive to promote their shops in order to achieve higher sales, thus leading to higher sales for Spreadshirt. Connecting them via a social platform will result in even higher growth opportunities. Intra-community communication should make trends emerge more quickly and spread further, again leading to higher sales for Spreadshirt. Users will be able to make recommendations about their designs and products, or about Spreadshirt. Peers trust each other much more than any company slogan.

Moreover, Spreadshirt sees future growth opportunities by:

■ Educating its shop partners – especially in terms of self-marketing,

■ Pushing its brand,

■ Promoting La Fraise design competitions, and

■ Acquiring more corporate customers, especially among small and medium-sized enterprises.

Through the above measures, Spreadshirt aims at doubling its worldwide sales in 2007 and 2008 respectively (see Exhibit 18 for its sales performance until 2006), while keeping its market focus and innovation drive. Regarding the company's future, Gadowski says:

What keeps me up at night are rather internal questions like 'How are we going to enhance our organizational structure, keep high quality levels and organize our product development?' We are not afraid that somebody attacks our markets and threatens our position. [...] One day, there might be someone who emerges with an innovation. But it will be up to us to respond quickly.

Exhibit 18 Spreadshirt's sales performance (in EUR million)

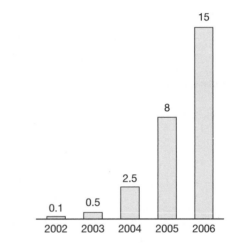

Source: Spreadshirt.

Second Life

Mercedes-Benz enters the Metaverse

The scene could be part of a picture book. Whitecaps burst at the island's cliffs while trees are blowing in the wind. The sun reflects on polished cars, consciously arranged in front of the modern architecture showroom, waiting for prospective customers. Mr. Milestone, leaning against the wooden information desk, asks himself whether there could be a better place to promote a new car than here. Even months after the launch of the new Mercedes-Benz C-Class, the stream of people visiting this sunny place has not waned. He decides to have a look around and flies to a special attraction, the test-track, where a group of people wearing Formula 1 racing suits are just preparing their tour.

Meanwhile in DaimlerChrysler´s German headquarters in Stuttgart (Germany), Sven Dörrenbächer, manager of the Division for Digital Communication, pushes the 'fly-button' and his avatar[1] – Mr. Milestone – takes off smoothly. Needless to say, this scene does not take place on the Balearic Islands or in the Maldives, but rather occurs on anyone's personal computer, as it is part of today´s virtual world Second Life. Initiated by the *BusinessWeek* headline 'Virtual World, Real Money' in May 2006, the world-embracing hype, including an exponential rise of its residents[2] (see Exhibits 1–3), spurred even 'Blue Chip' companies such as Mercedes-Benz to enter the Metaverse.[3]

> In Second Life Mercedes-Benz sets new standards, both visually and with regard to the content. At the same time we offer to experience the fascination of the brand and its products in this virtual environment.[4]
>
> **Dr. Olaf Göttgens**, Vice President of Brand Communications, Mercedes-Benz Passenger Cars

History of online games

The origin of online gaming can be traced back to the mid-seventies. The first role-playing game 'Dungeons & Dragons[5]' was published in 1974. In this and other 'pen-and-paper' role-playing games, the game world exists within the collective imagination of the players. Launched in 1978, 'MUD1[6]' established the online role-playing norms for a generation of developers.

Driven by gameplay, social and economic factors, technological savvy consumers and later on casual gamers moved into this sub-genre of gaming, the Massively Multiplayer Online Game (MMOG). This type of computer game enables thousands of players to simultaneously interact with each other in a virtual world, all connected via the Internet. MMOGs tend to be very time-intensive experiences, with players often

---

1 An avatar is an Internet user's representation of him or herself, whether in the form of a 3D-model used in computer games or a 2D-picture used on Internet forums and other online communities.

2 In Second Life, users were called residents. A resident is a uniquely named avatar who can log in, trade Linden-Dollars, and visit the community pages.

3 The term Metaverse (metaphysical universe) comes from Neal Stephenson's 1992 novel *Snow Crash*; it is a metaphor for the real world without its physical limitations.

4 Quote from Mercedes Press Release, February 15th 2007.

5 Dungeons & Dragons is a fantasy tabletop role-playing game. As of 2006, it remains the best-known and best-selling role-playing game, with an estimated 20 million having played the game and over US$1 billion in book and equipment sales.

6 MUD is an acronym for 'Multi User Dungeon,' a role-playing game inspired by Dungeons & Dragons.

This case study was written by W. Henning Blarr, Master of Business Administration student, under the supervision of Albrecht Enders, Assistant Professor of Strategic Management; Harald Hungenberg, Chaired Professor of Strategic Management (all three from the University of Nuremberg); and Tawfik Jelassi, Dean and Professor of e-Business and IT at the School of International Management of Ecole Nationale des Ponts et Chaussées (ENPC, Paris). This study is intended to be used as the basis for class discussion rather than to illustrate effective or ineffective handling of a management situation.

This case study was made possible through the cooperation of Dr. Olaf Göttgens, Vice President of Brand Communications Mercedes-Benz Passenger Cars, and Sven Dörrenbächer, Manager Global Advertising Passenger Cars, Mercedes-Benz and Maybach, Digital Communication, both of DaimlerChrysler AG.

Exhibit 1 The developement and structure of Second Life's residents

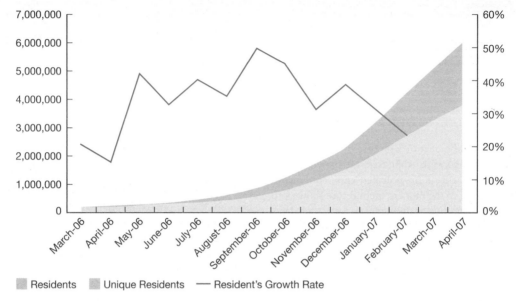

Source: Linden Lab, May 2007.

Exhibit 2 Second Life's residents by country

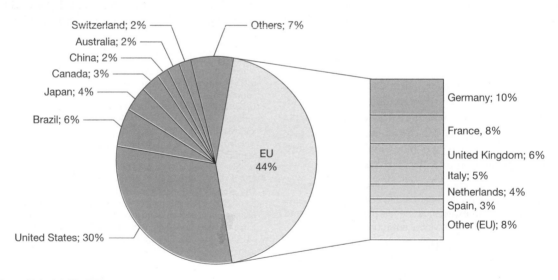

Source: Linden Lab, May 2007.

spending 20 hours or more per week in this virtual world. Typically, in these kinds of games, events continue to evolve during and after a player's visit. In addition to the online component, MMGOs differ from stand-alone video games in that they are mostly subscription-based, requiring users to purchase the software for a one-time payment and to pay an ongoing monthly subscription fee.

Exhibit 3 Residents logged-in to Second Life

Residents Logged-In During Last 7 Days	488,449
Residents Logged-In During Last 14 Days	688,615
Residents Logged-In During Last 30 Days	1,105,239
Residents Logged-In During Last 60 Days	1,761,927
Total Residents	**6,954,573**

Source: Linden Lab, Valuation day: June 1st 2007.

Today's market

The worldwide video game and interactive entertainment industry is expected to grow from about US$29 billion in 2005 to as much as US$44 billion in 2011.[7] The vast majority of the industry's revenues are generated either from the closed system (i.e., console-based market) or the open one (i.e., architecture-based PC market). The console-based market, led by powerful first party hardware developers (such as Sony, Microsoft and Nintendo), traditionally lagged behind the technological improvements found in the open, architecture-based PC world.

The market value for MMOGs in the Western world reached US$1billion for the first time in 2006,[8] and by 2011, the MMOG subscription market is expected to be worth over US$1.5billion. The dominant type of MMOG games are MMORPGs[9] (pronounced 'morpegs'), popularized by 'Ultima Online.[10]'

> These worlds are the modern, interactive, equivalents of Nordic myths and Tolkien fantasies. They allow players to escape into their imaginations, and to take part by, say, joining with others to slay a monster.[11]
>
> **Edward Castronova**, Associate Professor of Telecommunications, Indiana University

The term 'role playing' might be a bit misleading regarding MMORPGs. In computer game terms, a role-playing game is a game where the avatar has a set of statistics, e.g., power, intelligence, skills, or experience. During the last decade, many MMORPG products were launched with the target of bringing online role playing to the mass market but none has succeeded, while never in the history of MMORPGs were there more than five top-line products in existence at a given time (see Exhibit 4). 93.5% of the MMORPGs were placed in the fantasy genre, 4.1% in

---

7 DFC forecast in September 2006, including revenue from video game hardware and software, dedicated portable system hardware and software, PC games, and online PC and console games.
8 Screen Digest, March 2007.
9 Massively Multiplayer Online Role-Playing Game (MMORPG).
10 Ultima Online is a popular MMORPG by Origin Systems, introduced in 1997, still running today.
11 Quote from *The Economist*, September 28th 2006.

Exhibit 4 Lifecycle of MMORPGs

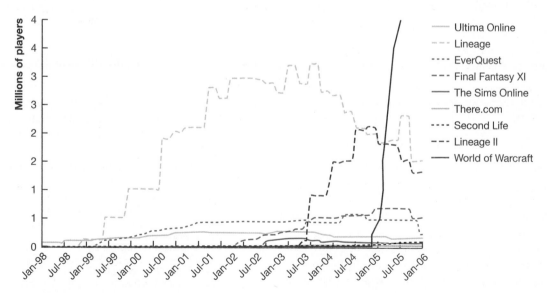

Source: mmorpgchart.com, June 2006.

the science fiction genre, 0.3% in the combat genre, and 2.2% in the social or other genres[12].

Games evolving into networks

While fantasy based games can be seen as the origin and historical driver of the MMORPG market, social games first became popular in 2002, when the best-selling PC game in history, 'The Sims,[13]' launched its online version, 'The Sims Online.' The game is a simulation of the day-to-day activities of one or more virtual people, called 'Sims,' in a suburban household. In contrast with other games, which tend to have a definite goal or objective, 'The Sims' focused entirely on the lives of virtual people, placing the player in control of their world and their daily activities.

Social interaction is a key driver of people's Internet use today. An explosion of collaborative creation with tremendous effort poured into many highly differentiated applications, pooled in the term 'Web 2.0.' Social networking has been for the last two years a central part of Web 2.0. Using the Internet, certain groups with common interests, requests, or desires can easily build up a community and get in contact with one another, whereby the decentralised structure of the web facilitates the meeting and interaction of people around the globe.

YouTube[14] and MySpace[15] have built large, loyal communities through entertainment and user-generated content. In March 2007, MySpace announced that its members numbered 160 million. Within MySpace, people create highly personalized homepages, loaded with message boards, blogs, photos, and streaming content, such as music and video. Social networking offers Internet users specific tools to connect, recommend, rate, or communicate within their group (see Exhibit 5).

> We ll become bigger than MySpace! Second Life will be as big as the whole Internet – I assume about 1.5 billion users.[16]
>
> **Philip Rosedale**, Founder and CEO, Linden Lab

The collaborative and community-related aspects of social games constitute the continuation of the idea of user-generated content in a 3D-world. Unlike the homepages on common social networking sites, virtual worlds are living spaces filled with other real people. Thus, they appear less than a game but more as an ambience to present content – made by the community's members. For many years, a wide range of virtual

Exhibit 5 The merger of social communities and online games

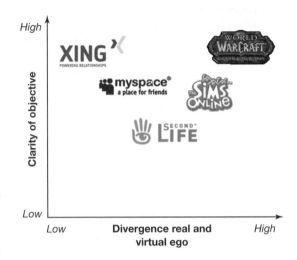

worlds, such as Second Life, Entropia Universe, There.com, and Active Worlds, have offered the player different places for his or her virtual life (see Exhibit 6).

Creating a Second Life

Today [June 23rd 2003], Linden Lab officially unveiled Second Life, a rapidly growing and constantly changing 3D-online society, shaped entirely by its residents. In Second Life, Linden Lab has pioneered real-time 3D-streaming technologies and advanced compression capabilities to create a persistent, contiguous landscape where residents can discover a world of exploration, socializing, creativity, self-expression, and fun unlike any other.[17]

The company behind Second Life

Linden Research, Inc. (commonly referred to as Linden Lab), was founded in 1999 by Philip Rosedale to create a new form of shared experience, where individuals jointly inhabit a virtual 3D-landscape and build the world around them. Philip Rosedale was Chief Technology Officer (CTO) of RealNetworks, where he

---

12 Quote from MMOGCHART.com, June 2006.
13 Sold 70 million units worldwide as of January 2007.
14 YouTube is a video sharing website where users can upload, view, and share video clips.
15 MySpace is a social networking website.
16 Quotes from *Vanity Fair*, February 2007 and Frankfurter Allgemeine Zeitung (*FAZ*), March 23rd 2007.
17 Quote from a Linden Lab Press Release, June 23rd 2003.

Exhibit 6 Today's popular virtual worlds

	Second Life	Entropia Universe	There.com	Active Worlds	Sony Home
Established	2003	2003	2003	1994	Fall of 2007
# of user	6.800.000	580.000	500.000	< 500.000	n/a
Earthlike	✓	✓	✓	✓	✓
In-game Economy	✓	✓	✓	✗	n/a
Costs	Basic membership for free	Basic membership for free	Basic membership for free	Basic membership for free	n/a
Requirements	PC/Mac	PC	PC	PC	Playstation 3

pioneered the development and deployment of streaming media technologies, such as RealVideo. Based in San Francisco (California), Linden Lab employs a senior development team bringing together expertise in physics, 3D-graphics, and networking. In February 2007, the privately held company had about 140 employees, including 28 engineers. Team members have previously worked at leading entertainment companies, such as Electronic Arts, Disney, THQ, Acclaim, Hasbro, and Mattel. Rosedale's fascination with automata and self-organizing systems had a deep impact on the initial form of 'Second Life'. Philip Rosedale explained:

> I always wanted the world to be LEGO somehow. I just wanted to make things as a kid. As I got older and computers came around, I just wanted to use computers to build stuff. I thought of a computer more as a hammer. I just wanted to do something cool with it.[18]

During a board meeting in 2001, Philip Rosedale thought of the real potential of the virtual world. While making a presentation, he asked a few Linden Lab engineers to play around in the virtual world as a background diversion. He said:

> We were watching this in the background, and we realized a city was emerging very, very fast. It was an incredible thing. Someone built a snowman and someone else built a sort of burning man, and you could see this jazz thing happening in real time. There had never been a canvas two people could paint on at the same time, much less three or four or five. That was a moment of change. We realized it is not necessarily about the wind working really well. It is about people making things together because the capacity this thing provides

is mysterious in the degree to which it allows people to do things together.[19]

An early prototype called Linden World was shown to attendees at Demo 2002, a conference that showcases information-technology start-ups. In 2003, the first public version of Second Life went live, burning through 2005 the US$8 million venture capital (VC) investment. Linden Lab implemented a distributed grid[20] for computing and streaming, which supports a large, scalable world with an unlimited amount of user-created and real-time content. Within these years, Second Life remained rather invisible, with the exception of a few mentions made on enthusiasts' weblogs. In March 2006, Linden Lab used some of the US$11 million additional investment from VC firms as well as from Amazon's Jeff Bezos, eBay's Pierre Omidyar, and the Open Source Foundation's Mitch Kapor, to hire a professional agency, Flashpoint PR.

A grid of the nearest neighbors

Online games are differentiated by their ability to put the dozens of frequently updated interactive content in front of users. The content (graphics, sound, geometry, animation, and behavior) associated with the player-created content are delivered to other players, typically in real time. The exponential increase of Second Life's residents led to slow response time during the peak

---

18 Quote from gamasutra.com, August 22nd 2006.
19 Quote from gamasutra.com, August 22nd 2006.
20 A grid is a collection of servers that run a virtual world.

Exhibit 7 A section of the Second Life world map – each field represents one sim

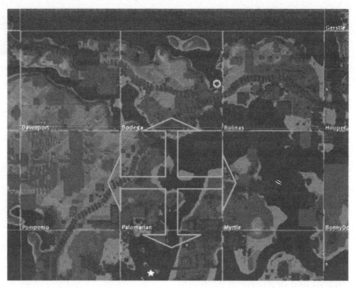

Source: Linden Lab.

periods. Second Life runs on servers, using micro-processors from either Intel or AMD, housed in facilities located in San Francisco and Dallas (Texas). These support 34 terabytes[21] of user-generated content, whereas the traffic load for accessing this content differs in the extreme from a conventional website's.

As existing products and platforms did not meet all the technical requirements, Linden Lab built from scratch the simulation, streaming, and rendering architectures of Second Life. The result is a topologically-tiled grid that connects machines of 'nearest neighbor'. Since Linden Lab is committed to open source software, machines run Debian Linux[22] and the MySQL[23] database. Therefore, each server represents one sim,[24] which means a virtual 65,536m[2] geographic area that supports between 50 and 100 avatars in one place at one time. In April 2007, Second Life possessed a total land size of 579 million square meters. Each server talks only to its four nearest neighbors (see Exhibit 7), so there is no scaling problem when the world becomes larger and larger. As objects move around the world, their representations are transferred from simulator to simulator, whereas players moving inside the game world maintain a streaming connection only to the machines nearby. As the virtual world grows, the number of back-end server machines grows with it. This streaming technology allows the world to be created and changed in a fluid, collaborative, and interactive manner, and it is possible to travel across the entire world. Due to today's technological restrictions, a streaming game has certain drawbacks compared to a stand-alone game.

In January 2007, Linden Lab opened up the source code for its client software, which runs on Linux, Mac OS X, and Microsoft Windows. In contrast, server source code is still not open sourced and might be licensed to other companies. For this platform-independent functionality, Linden Lab used OpenGL[25] and Havok[26] for Second Life's graphics, as well as the Ogg Vorbis[27] audio format and the JPEG 2000[28] standard, ensuring a progressive compression of texture data. In contrast to other MMOGs, Second Life was designed to be distributed only via the Web, using a small client to be downloaded on the official Linden Lab page and offering a quick download, installation, and launch for the user.

Earning real money

Linden Lab offered the residents its client software free as well as memberships in increments ranging from US$14.95 monthly and US$134.95 yearly to US$225 for a lifetime membership. To allocate limited resources,

21 34 terabytes equal approximately 1,563 CD-ROMs.
22 Debian Linux is server software suited for scaling with a small IT staff.
23 MySQL is a multi-threaded, multi-user database management system that allows the server farm to be scaled horizontally.
24 Sim is short for simulator.
25 Open Graphics Library (OpenGL) is a standard specification defining a cross-language cross-platform that produces 3D-computer graphics.
26 Havok is a middleware physics engine allowing interaction between objects or other characters in real time.
27 Ogg Vorbis is an open source audio codec, producing smaller files than most other codecs.
28 JPEG 2000 is a wavelet-based image compression standard.

Exhibit 8 Land pricing and use fees

Land	Size	Monthly Fee
1/128 Region	512m²	US$5,00
1/64 Region	1,024m²	US$8,00
1/32 Region	2,048m²	US$15,00
1/16 Region	4,096m²	US$25,00
1/8 Region	8,192m²	US$40,00
1/4 Region	16,384m²	US$75,00
1/2 Region	32,768m²	US$125,00
Entire Region	65,536m²	US$195,00
Island*	65,536m²	US$295,00

* Islands are generally priced at US$1,675 for 65,536m².

Source: Linden Lab, May 2007.

e.g., land, to the residents and to prevent the classical phenomena of runaway inflation,[29] Linden Labs introduced the 'Linden tax,' a tax on all objects payable in the in-game currency 'Linden-Dollar (L$).[30]' Initially, a complicated system, based on objects' creation costs and user value, that generated a weekly tax burden was chosen as the best method. Some residents decided that this tax system unfairly burdened major projects because people who put up skyscrapers or designed especially complex objects were charged more, even though these constructions created fun for others. They launched a series of symbolic protests, the 'Second Life Tax Revolt', by clothing themselves in American icons and holding Boston tea parties. Although some of the frustration could be linked to the general dislike of taxes, the revolt forced Linden Lab to announce some tweaks to the game's economic system.

In November 2003, the system of creating costs and taxes was replaced by a monthly subscription fee. Ever since, Linden Lab has offered for free the software client and basic membership which allows users to create and evolve their avatar and visit all places and events. If a resident wants to build a home or create his or her own objects, he/she needs to have a premium membership to buy[31] a piece of land from Linden Lab, allowing him or her to design a defined number of prims.[32]

Given that residents can own as much land as they want, they simply purchase more land if they want to build more. If a resident's land exceeds 512 square meters, he or she must pay a monthly maintenance fee. Since pricing is based on the processor, memory and storage needed for the user's piece of land, residents are in a way renting a server (see Exhibit 8). Premium membership is US$9.95 per month, US$22.50 per quarter, or US$72 per year (see Exhibit 9). Actually,

---

29 Runaway inflation means the decline in the value of goods and money because gems that were rare in the game's first month become useless rocks in its second year.
30 The Linden-Dollar (L$) is the Second Life in-game currency with an exchange rate of L$270 to US$1 in May 2007.
31 Linden Lab uses an auction system to sell large territories, thus offering the possibility for speculators to divide the land into small lots and resell them to residents.
32 A prim is the fundamental building block of all Second Life creations; e.g., a square, triangle, or circle.

Exhibit 9 The development of Second Life's premium residents

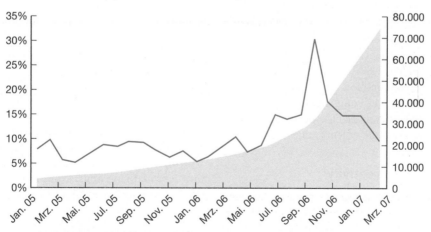

Premium Residents — Growth Rate for Premium Residents

Source: Linden Lab, May 2007.

Exhibit 10 Community standards set out six behaviours to avoid

Intolerance	• Combating intolerance is a cornerstone of Second Life's Community Standards. Actions that marginalize, belittle, or defame individuals or groups inhibit the satisfying exchange of ideas and diminish the Second Life community as whole. The use of derogatory or demeaning language or images in reference to another Resident's race, ethnicity, gender, religion, or sexual orientation is never allowed in Second Life.
Harassment	• Given the myriad capabilities of Second Life, harassment can take many forms. Communicating or behaving in a manner which is offensively coarse, intimidating or threatening, constitutes unwelcome sexual advances or requests for sexual favors, or is otherwise likely to cause annoyance or alarm is Harassment.
Assault	• Most areas in Second Life are identified as Safe. Assault in Second Life means: shooting, pushing, or shoving another resident in a Safe Area; creating or using scripted objects which singularly or persistently target another Resident in a manner which prevents their enjoyment of Second Life.
Disclosure	• Residents are entitled to a reasonable level of privacy with regard to their Second Lives. Sharing personal information about a fellow Resident – including gender, religion, age, marital status, race, sexual preference, and real-world location beyond what is provided by the resident in the First Life page of their Resident profile is a violation of that Resident's privacy. Remotely monitoring conversations, posting conversation logs, or sharing conversation logs without consent are all prohibited in Second Life and on the Second Life Forums.
Indecency	• Second Life is an adult community, but Mature material is not necessarily appropriate in all areas. Content, communication, or behaviour which involves intense language or expletives, nudity or sexual content, the depiction of sex or violence, or anything else broadly offensive must be contained within private land in areas rated Mature (M). Names of Residents, objects, places and groups are broadly viewable in Second Life directories and on the Second Life website, and must adhere to the guidelines.
Disturbing the peace	• Every Resident has a right to live their Second Life. Disrupting scheduled events, repeated transmission of undesired advertising content, the use of repetitive sounds, following or self-spawning items, or other objects that intentionally slow server performance or inhibit another Resident's ability to enjoy Second Life are examples of Disturbing the Peace.

Source: Linden Lab, May 2007.

80% of Second Life's revenues comes from land and maintenance fees, while the remaining 20% is generated through subscriptions.

According to Chief Financial Officer John Zdanowski, Linden Lab's revenues have reached approximately US$12 million in 2006, up from US$4 million in 2005[33] and the company became profitable in December 2006. Revenues have been increasing at almost the same rate as the system's usage.

Using residents' creativity

> The residents are creating a world that will be thousands of times more compelling than we could create ourselves.[34]
>
> **Philip Rosedale**, Founder and CEO, Linden Lab

Compared to pre-fabricated MMORPGs using a fantasy-based world and a strong storyline, Linden Lab turned the user-generated content into the center, forcing residents' creativity and social interaction. Second Life's virtual world attempts to model the surface of an Earth-like world. The sun rises and sets, objects fall under the effect of gravity; and grass blows in the wind, while the participants themselves determine what they want to do during their game. The law within this virtual world is represented by behavior guidelines, named 'The Big Six' whose violation result in suspension or, with repeated violations, expulsion from the Second Life Community (see Exhibit 10).

---

33 Quote from *Baseline Magazine*, March 1st 2007.
34 Quote from *Technology Review*, January 2006.

Linden Lab is a service provider, which means, among other things, that Linden Lab does not control various aspects of the service. As a result, Linden Lab has very limited control, if any, over the quality, safety, morality, legality, truthfulness, or accuracy of various aspects of the service.[35]

The goals of Linden Lab's Community Standards are simple: treat each other with respect and without harassment, adhere to local standards as indicated by simulator ratings, and refrain from any hate-motivated activity that slurs a real-world individual or real-world community.

Second Life is not a video game but a place where people make things.[36]

Philip Rosedale, Founder and CEO, Linden Lab

The new land model forced residents to be creative in building new, interesting places and allowed speculators and entrepreneurs to build stores and trade with other residents. Islands, whole cities (such as Frankfurt and Amsterdam) or sights (such as the Louvre, the Space Flight Museum, or the Burj Al Arab) can be designed. Second Life offers residents a huge range of beaches, bars, cafes, and clubs where to meet other residents or just hang out. Given that there is no fixed storyline or level to pass, exploring these places is an essential part of in-world's activities[37]. To travel across the entire world, the residents can walk, fly, or teleport[38].

Shifting the content creation to the user means that Second Life's residents[39] are able to truly create objects. The scripting language used, called Linden Scripting Language (LSL), is similar to C.[40] It determines how objects behave, controlling the waving of virtual hair or the driving of a virtual car. By using a built-in tool, residents create objects using a combination of prims, which are sized, scaled, and stretched as needed (see Exhibit 11). Similar to the real world where everything is built out of atoms, all objects within Second Life are constructed from some combination of prims (the in-world atoms), textures, and LSL scripts. As a user-created virtual world, Second Life's success is inextricably linked to the innovation and creativity of its players. Linden Lab estimated that in May 2007, an equivalent of 5,100 full-time content creators created, for Second Life on a voluntary basis, 34 terabytes of houses, clothes, and other items.

Linden Lab gave residents the intellectual property rights for their creations, thus allowing them to generate a real-world income. Second Life's residents can add

Exhibit 11 Transforming a prim into an avatar

value during the process of object creation, thus setting up in-world marketplaces and appearing as producers, consumers or both.

Economic opportunities

Second Life's prims alone have no costs except the computing, memory, and bandwidth resources they consume. Residents who apply more innovation, skills, or time to their creations are able to generate real in-game value. Since Linden Lab allows the residents to determine whether their objects may be copied, modified, or transferred, they actively trade them on virtual markets. Philip Rosedale said:

The growth of the community and expanding marketplace should yield a bigger income stream for the thousands of content creators who are making money within Second Life.[41]

To foster its economic growth, Linden Lab introduced in 2005 the LindeX[42], which allows Second Life residents to buy and sell L$ and exchange them for US$

---

35 Quote from the Linden Lab's Terms of Service, May 2007.
36 Quote from *The Economist*, April 20th 2006.
37 The world within Second Life is called 'in-world' by its residents.
38 Teleport means to transport instantly from one place to another by typing in the destination's coordinates.
39 Members of Second Life are called 'residents.'
40 C is a general-purpose, procedural, and imperative computer programming language.
41 Quote from Linden Lab Press Release, October 3rd 2005.
42 LindeX is Linden Lab's currency exchange, introduced in October 2005.

Exhibit 12 Estimated In-World business owners: Unique residents with positive monthly Linden-Dollar flow (PMLF)

USD Equivalent PMLF	11/06	12/06	01/07	02/07	03/07	04/07
< $10 USD	7,098	9,000	11,396	13,49	16,598	17,795
$10 to $50 USD	3,592	4,535	5,671	6,625	8,692	9,475
$50 to $100 USD	1,01	1,239	1,489	1,69	2,133	2,34
$100 to $200 USD	797	921	1,119	1,289	1,635	1,763
$200 to $500 USD	671	823	1,018	1,165	1,415	1,592
$500 to $1,000 USD	289	350	386	496	631	699
$1,000 to $2,000 USD	179	229	263	283	395	396
$2,000 to $5,000 USD	94	140	188	211	278	275
> $5,000 USD	58	90	97	116	152	139
Total Unique Users with PMLF	**13,788**	**17,327**	**21,627**	**25,365**	**31,929**	**34,474**

Source: Linden Lab, May 2007.

through the Second Life website. The LindeX exchange works by matching existing buyers and sellers of L$ currency together to automatically reach the best price for the currency. For buyers, fees are charged to their Second Life account, and for sellers, withdrawals of U.S. dollars generated through the marketplace are made either by credit card or through PayPal.[43] Unlike other MMORPGs, the L$ has actually appreciated against the US$. In May 2007, even Nasdaq CEO Bob Greifeld could imagine opening up a stock exchange in Second Life.[44]

Entering Second Life for the first time means arriving on 'Orientation Island,' which is the starting point for all new users. This special place features small stations that teach residents the basic operations of Second Life, such as camera zooming, basic chatting, and appearance mode features. Residents learn the importance of customization, by using the built-in avatar creation tool. It is therefore not surprising that clothing and avatar stores were the first businesses within Second Life. Meeting with other residents at clubs, parties, or other events is also very popular and constitutes another common business venture. Specialization abounds in this virtual world with residents acting as project managers, salespeople, agents, or event coordinators. Second Life's residents are able to choose places or stores based on text- and popularity-

searches or by recommendations from other residents. The ability to generate content provides an opportunity for those who come up with new ideas, as in the case of Anshe Chung, the avatar of the Chinese-born language teacher Ailin Graef, currently living in Germany. She buys plots of virtual land from Linden Labs, develops them into thematic communities with houses, beaches, or other features and then resells or rents those properties to other residents. She said:

> There is no real upper limit when it comes to people spending money on art, self-expression, and uniqueness. Well-off individuals have paid more than US$10,000 for virtual properties.[45]

Over the last three years, Graef created a lucrative real estate empire, including the China-based real-world company Anshe Chung Studios and claimed in November 2006 to be the first Second Life made, real-dollar millionaire! While some residents are just bumming around in the virtual world, a majority of Second Life inhabitants buy and sell their generated goods and services. In April 2007, more than US$7 million changed hands on the LindeX alone, giving 35,000 businesses a positive cash flow (see Exhibit 12). To

43 PayPal is an online system owned by e-Bay and allowing payments and money transfers to be made through the Internet.
44 Quote from *Reuters*/Second Life, May 8th 2007.
45 Quote from *BusinessWeek*, April 16th 2007.

foster new ideas, McKinsey & Co. launched in May 2007 a virtual venture competition, challenging young students to create an in-world business within 45 days. The winning team were promised US$20,000 in training and career counseling.

Although residents have been successful in starting small ventures and growing them, the corporate use of Second Life still lags behind. Real-world companies have been struggling to develop relevant business models for public virtual worlds.

Corporate use of games and social networking sites

The migration of people from watching TV to playing console and computer games during leisure time drew the attention of advertisers to the game industry. U.S. males aged 18–34, for example, spend 12.5 hours each week playing video games and only 9.8 hours watching TV. Gamers, different from TV-consumers, are highly focused and emotionally engaged individuals. Studies suggest that well-designed ads shown within games are more effective than ads broadcasted on TV or in films because in a game's immersive environment, players can directly interact with the product thus maximizing consumer acceptance. Paul Hemp, Senior Editor, *Harvard Business Review*, said:

> The first companies to seriously and thoughtfully exploit the potential of advertising and product creation in games will find themselves rewarded with lower costs for market entry and, ideally, enhanced customer relationships.[46]

The most common forms of video game advertising are 'Advergaming' and 'In-Game-Advertising.' While Advergaming involves designing an entire game around brand or product promotion, In-Game-Advertising means the placement of real-world marketing into existing console or computer games. For example, in the Sims Online, McDonald's installed virtual fast-food restaurants with automated employees working at the counter and serving (free) virtual burgers. According to a report from the U.S.-market-research company Yankee Group, companies spent US$165 million in 2006 for In-Game-Advertising, a figure that is expected to reach US$732 million in 2010. Since 2004, some large brands have already created their own independent virtual worlds for customers called 'Adverworlds.' Coca-Cola's 'MyCoke.com' envelops fans in everything Coke with games, music, and chat in a virtual setting.

The increasing size of social communities attracted companies to start advertising campaigns within these networks, a cost-effective method of direct advertising to their key demographic target. MySpace for example, with over 160 million members and instant exposure to adverts, can play a crucial role in product launches, brand building, and driving traffic to a new website. In 2006, Motorola promoted a new phone by opening a profile called 'My Very Thin Space.' One week after the launch, this profile accumulated 2,500 MySpace friends. While companies spend large sums to segment, reach, and influence potential customers using these forms of advertising, they rarely target those online alter egos. Bonita Steward, Manager of Interactive Marketing, DaimlerChrysler AG, said:

> When marketing online, you want sustained engagement with the brand rather than just clicking through to a purchase or a product information. Avatars create an opportunity for just this type of engagement.[47]

In virtual worlds, marketers can segment, reach, and influence the alter egos of their real-world customers. The amount of marketing and purchasing data that could be mined is quite high. Simply observing how inhabitants of a virtual world use a particular type of product or choose, say, their virtual vacation destination can generate valuable information. Everything within the virtual world can be tracked and logged into a database.

Henry Jenkins, Head of Comparative Media Studies Program at MIT, said:

> Marketing depends on soliciting people's dreams, and here [in virtual worlds], those dreams are on overt display![48]

MMORPG gameplay spurs its players to trade with in-world commodities to enhance avatars' statistics. Time-constrained users often make the rational economic decision to use real-world currency to advance their avatars, rather than time-intensive self-creating. Consequently, some users established secondary markets, so-called RMTs,[49] for the value created within these virtual worlds, assumed to be worth between US$250 million and US$880 million a year, according to experts.

---

46 Quote from *Harvard Business Review*, June 2006.
47 Quote from *Harvard Business Review*, June 2006.
48 Quote from *Harvard Business Review*, June 2006.
49 Real money trades (RMTs) are places in which people buy and sell online games' virtual assets for real money.

In Second Life, many residents have already imported real-world company logos as decorations, such as a neon Budweiser sign at a bar or a BMW car in front of a virtual house. While this world is not rife with original-branded buying opportunities, and companies must still field virtual products to sell, although there are interesting opportunities to do so, creative marketers see a new way to reach a desirable demographic. Unlike TV or movies, virtual worlds offer consumers a chance to experience some products, whereas some things cannot be replicated (yet), such as smell or taste. More and more people want to express their personal lifestyles to other residents, especially by using popular, real-world brands. As a consequence, virtual worlds are not only new channels for conveying information to the customer, but also opportunities for companies to create and sell their own virtual products.

Edward Castronova, Associate Professor of Telecommunications at Indiana University, said:

> Second Life is not the first virtual world in Cyberspace, but none appears so real. This [virtual] world became an extension to the real-world economy.[50]

June 2006 marked the first major influx of advertiser-backed brand presence in Second Life, when the clothing retailer American Apparel launched the first in-world version of a real-world retail store, offering virtual clothing items to its avatar clientele.

Mercedes-Benz' ways of online marketing

A specialized section of Mercedes-Benz brand communication is responsible for Web pages and online campaigns. In particular, they are scanning the market for new possibilities to communicate with the targeted customer group, thus keeping their eyes on the changes in people's daily use of mass media.

In November 2001, Mercedes-Benz launched the online game 'Mercedes-Benz Wunschwald', making it the first company to use this type of media for marketing purposes. Using this entertaining method, the game linked companies and users' created content and fostered a dialogue within the whole community. Launched during the Christmas holiday, Wunschwald combined the players' chance of winning with a charitable donation. Within four weeks, viral effects led 50,000 users to register, while the average player had an age of 36 and visited the webpage 7.2 times during the game's duration. Therefore, Wunschwald achieved the company's target to reach new customer groups.

Since June 2004, Mercedes-Benz has used the potential of the Internet to continuously attract and stay in contact with customers by offering a service called 'Mercedes-Benz Mixed Tape.' Based on the idea of the traditional compiled mixed cassette that spans all genres, the company started a webpage offering its visitors a free music compilation at regular intervals (approximately every 10 weeks). Using music as branded entertainment, Mercedes-Benz counted more than 27 million (international) downloads during the first three years, with average users in the mid-thirties. In July 2007, the company launched the 18th Mixed Tape compilation and announced the introduction of a new enhanced platform to their loyal customers in the autumn 2007.

Sven Dörrenbächer, manager of Digital Communication of DaimlerChrysler AG, explained its divisions' maxims in order to find new modes of communication:

> We want to use or create worlds authentically and communicate with our customers at eye level. Hence, a new concept has to be useful, relevant, innovative, concise and has to offer real added value. In this way, we can create a relevant benefit using digital lifestyles – the best premise to build up new customer-relationships. We can choose specific types of media that are more than just push-advertising services. Interrupting someone's favourite show with push-advertising is only the 2nd best solution. Our aim is to be someone's favorite show with a fascinating piece of branded content.[51]

In mid 2006, DaimlerChrysler received attention about the virtual world Second Life. The company compared the conditions within this world to other existing 3D-platforms, but the fit of residents' age groups (see Exhibit 13) and the possibility of creating a real-world aligned presence was perfect for choosing Second Life to make the first steps from 2D- to 3D-Internet. DaimlerChrysler assumes that 3D-presentation methods were an important stage of development for digital communication. Design is the most important feature that differentiates car manufacturers from one another. By offering a 360° car-configuration-service on its 2D-homepage, the company already implemented interactive ways of presenting a car's color, interior, or rims in high definition. For Mercedes-Benz, virtual 3D-worlds are the next step and a new, mid-term

---

50 Quote from 'Die Zeit,' January 4th 2007.
51 Statement made during an interview on April 21st 2007 with the case study authors.

marketing channel. Sven Dörrenbächer, Manager of Digital Communication at DaimlerChrysler AG, said:

> With the pending launch of the Mercedes-Benz C-Class in March 2007, we could combine our entrance into Second Life with this special market introduction.[52]

C-Class models have been among the most popular vehicles in the Mercedes-Benz product portfolio ever since the launch of the 190 Series – the so-called Baby Benz – 25 years ago. With the latest model changeover in March 2007, the fourth generation of the C-Class tries to continue this story. Germany is the most important market for the C-Class, accounting for approximately 30% of worldwide sales. Compared to other Mercedes-Benz models, the C-Class targets a wide band of customers, including younger consumers that already express their digital-lifestyle by using i-pods[53] or BlackBerrys.[54] Hence, a branded property in Second Life offers the chance to communicate with this and other new target groups. Developing the concept of the brand-presence, the digital communication team focused on two important key factors: gaining insights and experience of 3D-environments by initiating a one-one dialog with potential customers as at a real-world car dealer.

Step-by-step into the virtual world

In December 2006, Mercedes-Benz assigned the Frankfurt-based agency Neuland + Herzer to develop a concrete conception and implementation. Design and implementation of the virtual establishment was aimed at setting the pattern within Second Life and transfer-ring real-world brand values into the virtual world. The agency developed a concept that offers multiple enter-tainment choices, integrating existing marketing platforms like Mercedes-Benz Mixed-Tape. To create a certain buzz and use viral marketing, Mercedes-Benz opened its island step-by-step.

On February 15th 2007, the company launched both its Second Life island in the South West district (coor-dinates: 128.128.11) and the accompanying website www.mercedes-benz.com/secondlife. This page reports continuously about the company's virtual activities and gives visitors a short introduction to Second Life in general. The whole island spans 8 sims[55] and contains a virtual showroom in its middle, framed by a test track (see Exhibit 14). The subsidiary demonstrates a detailed 3D-architecture and reflects today's Mercedes-Benz architecture of the real world (see Exhibit 15). The island also includes a small brand-history museum, an area for vehicle presentation, a stage for events and big screens for showing current product films and TV advertisements as well as highlights of previous events on the island.

Arriving residents can take an interactive guided tour of the island's highlights and then choose to be teleported to the different stations. To welcome its guests to Second Life, Mercedes-Benz uses a dedicated avatar (see Exhibit 16). On the island, the avatar is the first point of call for advice, help, and any questions visitors might have. Furthermore, it answers any gen-eral questions on current Mercedes-Benz specials or vehicles. The service is available on weekdays between 3:00 pm and 11:00 pm, and can be individually called by using Second Life's instant messaging function or sending an email to secondlife@daimlerchrysler.com. Besides this, Mercedes-Benz offers its guests a racing outfit for their avatar.

On February 20th 2007, Mercedes-Benz officially marked the opening of its new presence in the virtual world and hosted a live event. The show's highlight was a live gig by Wagner Love, contributors to the Mercedes-Benz podcast and Mixed Tape compilation series. At 10 pm CET, the band from Frankfurt performed three titles on the stage of the Mercedes-Benz Island. Wagner Love is also featured on Mixed Tape 16 that was released on

Exhibit 13 Second Life's residents by age group

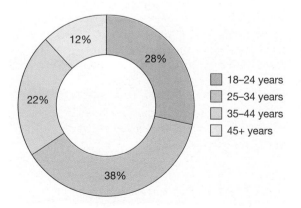

- 18–24 years
- 25–34 years
- 35–44 years
- 45+ years

28%
38%
22%
12%

Source: Linden Lab, May 2007.

---

52 Statement made during an interview on April 21th 2007 with the case study authors.
53 I-pod is Apple's brand name for a range of digital music players (DAP).
54 The BlackBerry is a wireless, business-oriented hand-held device.
55 Approx. 524.3 km².

February 27th 2007. One hour before show time, Second Life's over-crowding restrictions forced Mercedes-Benz to turn away new arrivals. Nevertheless, those who made it joined the concert and stayed around until the early morning hours. (See Exhibit 17.)

Since this music show, the island has also featured a Mixed Tape download station for added entertainment, offering visitors the latest compilation a week before the official release date. In order to reach Internet users who are not registered in Second Life, Mercedes-Benz deposited pictures and videos from this event at popular online communities, such as YouTube, Flickr[56] and MySpace.

Two weeks prior to its real-world launch[57], Mercedes-Benz invited Second Life's residents to an exclusive preview of its new C-Class car model. On March 16th 2007, a virtual model of this new car was unveiled as part of an event on Mercedes-Benz Island. The Second Life edition of the new C-Class came with 'Avantgarde' trim and an optional sport pack AMG[58]. With models available all over the island, visitors were encouraged to take a closer look at the new car and become acquainted with it.

---

56 Flickr is a photo sharing website where users can upload, view, and share photos.
57 The new real-world C-Class car was actually launched in Europe on March 31st 2007.
58 AMG is the tuning division of Mercedes-Benz.

Exhibit 14 Mercedes-Benz Island

Source: DaimlerChrysler, 2007.

Exhibit 15 The virtual Mercedes-Benz showroom

Source: DaimlerChrysler, 2007

Exhibit 16 The Mercedes-Benz avatar: Mr. Mercedes Milestone

Source: DaimlerChrysler, 2007.

Exhibit 17 The opening party on the Mercedes-Benz Island

Source: DaimlerChrysler, 2007.

At 8:00 pm, the avatar Mercedes Milestone started the event and provided short descriptions of the virtual edition of the C-Class. Later on, guests were invited to stick around for an after-show party with DJ Julian Smith, host of the Mercedes-Benz opening night and Mixed Tape concert. Mercedes-Benz then officially opened the test track to all visitors, allowing them to test drive the virtual C class car. The test track was similar to a German highway, while the topography and landscape of the island offered a variable terrain consisting of mountains and valleys alternating between the straights. Test drivers were also able to prove their driving proficiency under different weather conditions with rainy and snowy conditions simulated within seconds (see Exhibit 18). For using the test track, Second Life residents can rent a C-Class car for a limited time. This virtual edition of the C-Class includes a configurator that enables the paint and wheel rims of the vehicle to be customized. Eight different paint finishes can be selected, and three different wheel rims can be installed on the vehicle. All the changes made by the visitor using the configurator are immediately visible on the vehicle.

In Second Life, the C-Class is also for sale: users may purchase a customized version for their Second Life avatar. Sven Dörrenbächer explains the challenge of pricing in virtual worlds:

> The new C-Class raises the bar of virtual cars in Second Life. Compared to existing, unofficial Mercedes-Benz car models offered by Second Life residents, we consciously used high-quality graphics to design a 3D-model as real as possible (see Exhibit 19). In the real world, the brand has its value, and even in Second Life, there is a certain demand for a status symbol and luxury. But pricing in this virtual world means competing with speedboats, houses, jewelry, and of course plagiarism.[59]

Even though Second Life residents can fly or teleport from place to place rather than drive, cars are a popular and cheap commodity. Mercedes-Benz' competitor Toyota offers its Scion for about US$1; Nissan provides copies of its Sentra for free. An avatar brought to market the Dominus Shadow, a retro two-seater created with painstaking detail both inside and outside. At about US$40, it is the most expensive car to be sold in Second Life. Mercedes-Benz finally decided to offer its virtual C-Class for L$1,500, including an update option on the vehicle. As soon as new features for the C-Class are available in Second Life, owners are automatically informed about it. The next time they log in to Second Life, the updates can be installed and used immediately, free of charge.

Different companies and different concepts on Second Life

Aside from DaimlerChrysler's brand Mercedes-Benz, many other companies entered Second Life because the press gave the virtual world so much attention. Besides this temporary buzz, Second Life offers marketers an interesting way of connecting with a real-world brand using a cutting-edge platform. IBM, for example, started to use Second Life as a 3D-Intranet and plans to invest in it US$10 million in 2007. By May 2007, IBM had 4,000 employees active in the virtual world, up from 800 in December 2006. More than 230 IBM researchers, consultants, and developers already use

---

59 Statement made during an interview on April 21st 2007 with the case study authors.

Exhibit 18 The virtual C-Class on the test track

Source: DaimlerChrysler, 2007.

Exhibit 19 Acceptance of Real Life Brands in Second Life

Source: DaimlerChrysler, 2007.

virtual worlds to experiment with and develop social networking tools as well as to design new ways of learning and doing business. The company has more than 30 other virtual islands for conducting research, onboarding new employees, providing developer support, and conducting meetings with IBM staff and clients.

According to a research report[60] (see Exhibits 20 and 21), the majority of Second Life's residents think the presence of real-life engagements is positive. Consequently, many companies spanning various sectors of the economy or even the public sector have been using this medium. Today, Second Life is a sandbox of sorts, and the models may evolve and adjust over time through continued discovery. In June 2007, nearly no day goes by without another company announcing the launch of its presence in a virtual world.

Reebok

Reebok launched its Second Life presence in October 2006; its island is located near the Adidas store (Adidas entered Second Life in September 2006). It created a whole urban-style district fitting into the 'I am what I am' campaign. The main idea was that residents create virtual shoes for their avatars. Reebok allowed visitors to customize shoes from its sub-label RBK in the same way they can do in real life on the Reebok website. People can wear the same design shoes in the real-world and in Second Life. First, residents need to buy a blank pair of shoes and design them later at the 'Customizing Station'. The blank pair costs L$50 and the customization process costs L$5. The configurator enables customers to choose the paint of the base, the shoulder and the side-stripes.

Calvin Klein fragrances

Although smelling is not possible in the virtual world, Calvin Klein went ahead and launched in Second Life a virtual version of their new ck IN2U fragrances for men and women. This launch took place simultaneaously with the real-world launch on March 21st 2007 of the same fragrances. Since avatars cannot smell, the virtual perfume bottles enabled residents to spray each other with bubbles that 'initiate dialogue,' probably requesting the sprayee to engage in a Calvin Klein animation. Lori Singer, Vice President of Global Marketing at Calvin Klein Fragrances, said:

---

60 'Real Life Brands in Second Life' by Market Truths, April 2007.

Exhibit 20 Acceptance of real life brands in Second Life

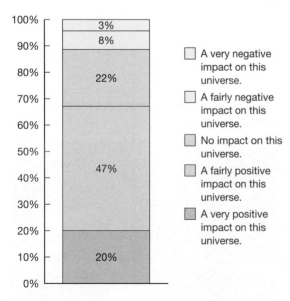

- A very negative impact on this universe.
- A fairly negative impact on this universe.
- No impact on this universe.
- A fairly positive impact on this universe.
- A very positive impact on this universe.

Source: Repères Study: Perception of the Presence of Brands in Second Life, April 2007.

Exhibit 21 Opinions regarding the presence of real life brands in Second Life

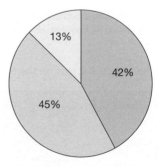

- The presence or absence of real life brands in Second Life does not matter to me.
- I would like more real life brands to settle in Second Life.
- I estimate that there are already too many real life brands in Second Life.

Source: Repères Study: Perception of the Presence of Brands in Second Life, April 2007.

ck IN2U speaks the language of a generation connected by technology — the aptly named technosexuals. They are the first generation to be defined more by their means of communication rather than fashion or music.[61]

There were also 'graffiti bottles' available from the Calvin Klein build, put together by the agency Rivers Run Red on their Avalon island in Second Life, where Calvin Klein held a L$1 million photography contest to accompany the launch.

The Coca-Cola Company

In April 2007, Coca-Cola officially entered Second Life, issuing an invitation to avatars as well as the public to submit ideas for a portable virtual vending machine, named the 'Virtual Thirst' campaign. This design competition invites people to submit designs to www.virtualthirst.com for a chance to win the prize of building and launching the ultimate vending machine. Design entries were accepted through a variety of formats and submission methods, including submissions within Second Life, YouTube and MySpace. The winner was invited to a trip to San Francisco to participate in the creation of a video documenting the creation of the winning design object. Michael Donnelly, Director of Global Interactive Marketing at Coca-Cola, said:

> The Virtual Thirst platform is something that could be extended into offline media and, moreover, into portable media games, wireless and other emerging platforms. The concept could eventually tie into or complement Coke's current campaign – The Coke Side of Life.[62]

Sony-Ericsson

Alongside its participation at CeBIT[63], Sony-Ericsson built a virtual trade-fair stand in Second Life. The Swedish-Japanese joint venture was represented at CeBIT and on Second Life from March 15th to 21st 2007; it was the first mobile-phone manufacturer to be present on Second Life. Martin Winkler, Head of Marketing at Sony-Ericsson (Germany), said:

> Second Life is a true-to-life interactive world that's full of adventures and that puts no limits on one's creativity. As an innovative brand, we naturally also want to present our products and the experiences associated with them in a creative and modern format like Second Life so that we can reach our customers in all worlds. We not only offer information about our products, but also offer interactive features that strengthen the experiential character.[64]

The company built a place called 'Sony-Ericsson Island,' offering products ranging from mobile phones to accessories. Furthermore, promoter avatars were available to offer individualized advice. Sony-Ericsson's stand offered special features for music fans. People could dance to beats from break dance to aerobic dance on the disco dance floor or lay back, relax, and enjoy some music in ball chairs. Additionally, there was a t-shirt stand where visitors received free branded digital shirts. As a special highlight, guests had a chance to win one of the mobile phones given away each day throughout the duration of CeBIT and sent out into the real world.

Starwood Hotels

Starwood Hotels, owner of the Westin, Sheraton, and W chains, became the first real-world hospitality company to enter Second Life. Prior to opening to the public in 2008, they assigned the Electric Sheep Company to install a virtual 'Aloft' prototype (see Exhibit 22). Since September 2006, Second Life's residents could wander through the lobby and rooms of this digital Doppelganger and were asked for ideas on changes to make to the design (see Exhibit 23).

> Brian McGuinness, Vice President at Starwood, said:

> This is the first time the company has created a complete mock hotel – digital or physical – to serve as 'a laboratory.' We are saving money. If we find that significant numbers of people do not like a certain feature, we do not have to actually build it. We do not have to have a painter here for 40 hours changing the color of a wall. We can reconfigure a detail. It is parallel to rapid prototyping.[65]

For Starwood, opening Aloft in Second Life was a way to test-market the hotel's design and rapidly prototype the evolving concept. For instance, staffers observed how people moved through the space, what areas and types of furniture they gravitated towards, and what they ignored. Although Starwood first stated that this would be an ongoing project, they left Second Life in June 2007, as they discovered that avatars do not need to sleep and such a presence is unable to sustain the residents' interest in the long run.

---

61 Quote from 3pointd.com, March 21st 2007.
62 Quote from marketingvox.com, April 17th 2007.
63 CeBIT is the world's largest computer expo. It is held each spring on the fairground in Hanover, Germany.
64 Quote from Sony-Ericsson Press Release, March 13th 2007.
65 Quote from *BusinessWeek*, August 23rd 2006.

Exhibit 22 The virtual Aloft Hotel

Source: The Electronic Sheep Company, 2007.

Exhibit 23 A room in the Aloft Hotel

Source: The Electronic Sheep Company, 2007.

Axel Springer AG

Bild.T-Online.de, the online edition of BILD, a German tabloid newspaper published by Axel Springer AG, created a weekly professional tabloid newspaper for the residents of Second Life, named 'The AvaStar,' which keeps its readers informed about the vast, diverse, and ever-changing virtual world. The 30 pages of content are structured into News, Business, Celebrity & Gossip, Style & Fashion, Travel, and Entertainment sections. Gregor Stemmle, Chief Executive Officer of Bild.T-Online, said:

> The AvaStar is the first mass medium in Second Life to be produced with a professional background. Using their experience in journalism and publishing, Bild.T-Online and Axel Springer are establishing a newspaper format for a broad readership and at the same time creating a very interesting publicity setting for advertising clients.[66]

The publisher set up a virtual office in Second Life with an actual editor-in-chief and twenty imbedded reporters and contributors from Second Life that use their expertise and knowledge to uncover stories from the virtual world. Axel Springer AG instructed consultancy and market research agency CScout to lead the whole project, including a futuristic publishing house located on AvaStar Island, designed and conceptualized by Sebastian Otaared from Pham Neutra and built by Aimee Weber.

Since December 21st 2006, the English and German versions of the magazine are available via newspaper vendors all over Second Life as well as at most popular places. After a free introductory period, residents have the option to buy a single issue (at L$150) or subscribe for a regular update.

Vodafone

Mobile telecommunications company Vodafone opened its Second Life island in February 2007 as part of the company's 'Make the most of now' strategy. Visitors were able to experience features, such as 'photographic ice skating,' 'butterfly flights,' and a 'sound garden.' The latter gives residents an audio experience, enabling them to make their own music depending on the direction in which their avatars move. David Erixon, Head of Brand Strategy and Manifestation at Vodafone, said:

> The launch of the island marks an important point in the evolution of Vodafone's 'make the most of now' brand strategy and we hope that it delivers something of real benefit to the Second Life community. In the long term we are looking to engage even more fully with the community, further opening up communication channels between real and virtual life.[67]

Additionally, Vodafone rolled out a communication service that enables residents to call each other via virtual mobile phones as well as punch out into the real world and speak to friends outside Second Life.

Randstad

On March 7th 2007, Randstad, a Dutch job agency, was the first human resources service provider to establish a presence in Second Life. The company cooperates with the University of Amsterdam on a research project

---

66 Quote from CScout Press Release, December 15th 2006.
67 Quote from *Marketing Week*, February 1st 2007.

about the influence of virtual worlds on social networks. Since the company offers virtual and real jobs, real-world and in-world job seekers were potential visitors. Christine Uphoff, Head of Marketing at Randstad (Germany), said:

> More and more people quit their real-world jobs and enter virtual worlds to earn money. There is a growing demand for personal services because many companies now need in-world staff. We reach people that seek a job in real life, but prefer this virtual channel to get information about temporary work.[68]

Randstad pays Second Life's residents in L$, the in-world currency, while employers pay Randstad a commission. The company offered Second Life's residents vacancies such as manager of the virtual presence at ABN AMRO; however, real-world vacancies have been so far confined to the Dutch market.

France's 2007 presidential election

All four major candidates in France's 2007 presidential election opened virtual headquarters in Second Life to engage residents in debates, attend political rallies, and take part in protests. Campaigns reported daily visit numbers of up to 20,000 for Ségolène Royal, 11,000 for Le Pen, 10,000 for Nicolas Sarkozy, and 7,000 for François Bayrou. Margaux Gandelon, François Bayrou's Second Life Coordinator, said:

> It is not a mass communication phenomenon, but we reach people who would not have gone to meetings or rallies. We talk to a lot of undecided voters and activists from other parties.[69]

François Bayrou's headquarters included a farm with cows, barns, and a tractor, reflecting his roots as the son of farmers and his hobby raising thoroughbreds. A visitor could find a Bayrou activist wearing an orange T-shirt emblazoned with 'Sexy Centrist' riding a horse. Just as in the real world, each campaign needed some staff to maintain their Second Life headquarters. Three Bayrou supporters spent 50 hours each over three weeks to construct the headquarters, the maintenance of which later required 10 people working 2 to 3 hours a day.

INSEAD

In March 2007, INSEAD announced that it had established a virtual campus on Second Life. It was designed to offer an innovative learning environment in which participants from around the world can collaborate in real-time and learn from the diverse experiences of fac-

ulty and peers. The school integrated Second Life into a range of programs, including its MBA, Executive MBA, and Executive Education. Miklos Sarvary, Director of the Centre for Learning Innovation at INSEAD, said:

> The Second Life campus underscores the value INSEAD places on entrepreneurialism. Our presence there is a natural extension of our dedication to provide participants with the most current, real-time technological advancements and deliver top leadership development programs, whether it takes place on a physical campus or in the digital world.[70]

A number of courses were set up, including an MBA class on entrepreneurship in which participants had the opportunity to develop a business plan and test it in Second Life. For Antonio Fatas, Dean of the MBA Program at INSEAD,

> as an international business school with participants from around the world, INSEAD embraces innovative approaches to learning that will enable us to develop leaders who are prepared to operate in a constantly evolving global business environment. We recognize the growing importance of the digital marketplace and want all of our participants to have the opportunity to experience it first-hand.[71]

A virtual world with real challenges

Many companies made the transition from the real world into the virtual world of Second Life. As the rationale behind these efforts is vast, most companies considered their investments and set goals for their virtual presence. Nevertheless, many branded islands were empty most of the time; after a first buzz, only few Second Life residents kept coming back. There is obviously a real danger that product placement will feel to residents like 3D-spam, and thus, Volkswagen's Head of Marketing Jochen Sengpiehl advised his colleagues to put their time and energy (back) into the real world, instead of wasting it in virtual ones.[72]

American Apparel, which established a Second Life presence as the first real-world company, refined and relaunched its store in spring 2007, hoping to be more appealing to residents. The company announced that the

---

68 Quote from *FAZ*, March 15th 2007.
69 Quote from *Washington Post*, March 30th 2007.
70 Quote from INSEAD Press Release, March 20th 2007.
71 Quote from INSEAD Press Release, March 20th 2007.
72 Quote from www.ibusiness.de, April 12th 2007.

new store would look less like a real-world location dropped into the virtual world and might also offer clothing options that are more attuned to what avatars are apt to like. Charlene Li from Forrester Research said:

> Many companies approach social computing as a host of technologies to be deployed as needed – a blog here, a podcast there – to achieve a marketing goal. But a more coherent approach is to start with your target audience and determine what kind of relationship you want to build with them, based on what they are ready for.[73]

Actually, there is no proven model for attracting meaningful traffic to brand integration, but companies participating in the virtual world should at least try to define their role, regarding some 'laws' (see Exhibit 24). Sven Dörrenbächer, Manager of Digital Communications at DaimlerChrysler AG, said:

> We designed our island as real as possible to force visitors to talk about our real cars. The users' motivation to visit Mercedes-Benz Island is the same as visiting a local car dealer. Two months after the launch, we counted tens of thousands of visitors, which on average stay about 15 minutes. Regarding the Second Life Traffic-Index,[74] this means a ranking in the top-level.[75]

Despite the fact that companies spend a great deal of money in Second Life, Linden Lab does not offer any special controlling or monitoring services other than some general, monthly figures. Without reliable data, it is difficult to trace the exact number of visitors and track their behaviors. Dörrenbächer continued:

> Actually, our figures are based on the monthly, general figures. Additionally, we count and observe our visitors manually or pose questions to selected focus groups. Beside these figures we concentrate on a high contact quality with personal dialogues with our guests to learn more about their demographic data and habits. However, the media coverage and the PR impact topped our invested money.[76]

Some companies used third-party software to solve the monitoring problem, but these were not used widely. Second Life's residents as well as the companies can easily create dummy avatars that are not backed by human beings to fake the statistics; Linden Lab concedes that these types of tools are not fully reliable. Glenn Fisher, Director of Marketing Programs at Linden Labs, said:

A couple of companies came in thinking about return on investment. I think it is early to be thinking about ROI. It is more about expanding marketing brand presences, from generating PR to exploring Second Life to establishing a presence of some kind.[77]

Sodom and Gomorrah

Anything one can do in the real world can also be done in the virtual. Second Life therefore mirrors the real world right down to the smallest details. Due to the continuous development and as an open environment accessible by almost anyone, a number of real-world difficulties have arisen around Second Life, in particular legal and moral issues.

Legal issues

Social media, especially a virtual world like Second Life, brings many intellectual property rights into question. Linden Lab has attempted to make the protection of intellectual property a cornerstone of Second Life, giving residents ownership rights for the content they create in-world. In November 2006, a software tool called 'CopyBot,' which can clone avatars, objects, and textures, stoked the ire of Second Life business owners who fear their creations could be illicitly copied and sold. Copying is a value killer; not only will the financial future of Second Life merchants be in danger, but also Linden Lab's business model. If the company's way of dealing with copyright fails, creators will stop creating and the growth of the online world will be stunted. Therefore, Linden Lab announced in November 2006 that using CopyBot or similar tools is a violation of Second Life's terms of service.

In the real world, fake Prada purses and knock-off Rolex watches are usually sold out of trench coats on

---

73 Quote from Business Communicators of Second Life: Forrester Social Technographics, May 2007.
74 The Traffic Index is Second Life's official traffic counter, which awards points based on how residents divide their time within each 24-hour period.
75 Statement made during an interview on May 2nd 2007 with the case study authors.
76 Statement made during an interview on May 2nd 2007 with the case study authors.
77 Quote from Marketing News, February 15th 2007.

Exhibit 24 Gartner's five laws for companies participating in virtual worlds

First Law: Virtual worlds are not games, but neither they are a parallel universe (yet). The initial reaction of many business leaders when faced with virtual worlds is to dismiss them as a mere 'game' of no benefit to the enterprise and something to be banned for wasting computer resources and time.

Second Law: Behind every avatar is a real person. Gartner said people can't be fooled by the fantasy elements in the virtual world. There are unwritten rules and expectations for behavior and culture are developing. Enterprise users must consider their corporate reputations.

Third Law: Be relevant and add value. There has been criticism of early corporate entries into the virtual world, Second Life, related to the showrooms usually being empty and lacking atmosphere. Most corporations will see minimal revenue gains in the market at this time.

Fourth Law: Understand and contain the downside. Enterprises face serious questions, such as 'Could activities in the virtual world undermine or influence my organization/brand in the real world?' with significant portions of the virtual economy based on adult oriented activities, questions of appropriate behavior and ethics also arise.

Fifth Law: This is a long haul. Gartner recommends that enterprises should experiment with virtual worlds, but not plan massive projects, and look for community benefits rather than commerce.

Source: Gartner Inc., April 2007.

street corners. In Second Life, residents started to create branded content as deco objects, but now, these counterfeit goods can be found in malls and department stores, selling unauthorized Louis Vuitton purses or Ray-Ban sunglasses. These shoddy products might mis-represent those companies concerned, which is one reason some lawyers say that these trademark violations are an issue in virtual worlds as well as on the street. Benjamin Duranske, founder of the Second Life Bar Association and a real-world lawyer, estimated there was trademark infringement in at least 1% of Second Life transactions, which is approximately 1.4 million per year. He assumed that a classifieds search for 'Gucci' products on Second Life generates 106 hits, while one for 'Louis Vuitton'

products generates 39 hits, although none of these companies has endorsed the virtual products.[78]

In February 2007, terrorists launched a bombing campaign in Second Life. People controlling animated avatar members of a self-proclaimed Second Life Liberation Army (SLLA) set off computer-code versions of atomic bombs at virtual world stores. The virtual bomb blasted in Second Life exploded in hazy white balls, blotting out portions of a screen and battering nearby avatars. In May 2007, this anti-capitalist and pro-democracy movement bombed the Australian broadcaster ABC's Island and turned it into a crater.

---

78 Quote from *Reuters*, May 29th 2007.

The media organization had to restore the whole island because most features had been totally destroyed.

Within Second Life, hundreds of casinos offer poker, blackjack, and slot machines to the residents. While the virtual world's decentralized nature makes it difficult to estimate the total size of the gambling industry, the 3 largest poker casinos are earning profits of US$1,500 each per month, according to casino owners. In April 2007, the FBI visited casinos in Second Life, but federal law enforcement officials have not yet taken an official stance on virtual gambling. Most lawyers agree that placing bets with Linden-Dollars violates U.S. anti-gambling statutes, which require that 'something of value' be wagered. However, the degree of Linden Lab's responsibility and the likelihood of a crackdown by law enforcement officials are actually far from certain.

Moral issues

Generally, Second Life's grid regions are rated either 'PG' or 'Mature'. Builds, textures, actions, animations, or businesses that are of an adult nature are regulated by the Terms of Service to only occur in simulators with a mature rating. Actually, Second Life has enough sex clubs and brothels to rival Amsterdam's red-light district.

In spring 2007, Second Life got headlines in becoming a haven for sexual deviants and misfits with a number of authorities around the world investigating sex crimes committed in the virtual world. Although residents on Second Life's Main Grid have to be 18 years or older, in May 2007, special attention has been given to sex-related activity involving avatars with a child-like appearance, the so called 'ageplay.' Cybersex in Second Life involving adults playing the role of children has been a controversial part of the virtual world for a long time. Parry Aftab, Executive Director of WiredSafety.org, said:

> Child porn is present on lots of social networks. You can get images of children to download to your iPod. You can order a live online molestation of a real child for viewing.[79]

Although Linden Lab announced that sexual ageplay was always banned in Second Life, longtime residents said it was widespread until January 2007, when the company started shutting down sexual ageplay areas. Role-play in general is integral to Second Life. Avatars appear to be men or women, elves, dragons, winged fairies, vampires, killer robots, and all varieties of other real and fanciful creatures. Even age-based role playing

can take on various forms: It can be as innocuous as people acting out a family dynamic or as potentially troubling as two adults engaging in sexual role-playing with one of the avatars made to look like a child. The line between twisted fiction and actual crime is blurred at this point with such virtual acts not considered illegal in the United States, home of San Francisco-based Linden Lab, but certainly against pornography laws in other countries. Even so, legal experts said such virtual behavior between adults is not likely to break the law, since there are no real children involved. Moreover, German TV news magazine, *Report Mainz*, uncovered a child sex pornography ring, where residents paid Linden-Dollars to see pornographic images of children and to buy sex with other players posing as children. ARD's[80] reporter Nick Schader said that he had been invited to pay L$500 for attending such a meeting. Peter Vogt, Chief Prosecutor at the German Central Office against Child Pornography, said:

> I am lost for words. We are trying to find out the identity of this person because what is being offered is nothing short of child pornography. In Germany, this crime is punishable from three months to five years in a real prison, not a virtual one.[81]

Linden Labs issued a statement on its official blog condemning the virtual depictions of child pornography. The company announced that it was cooperating with law enforcement and had banned two participants involved in the incident, a 54-year-old man and a 27-year-old woman. In addition, the company announced that it is introducing a much more stringent age-verification system to ensure that only adults can enter adult-content areas of Second Life.

The advent of the virtual Web

Three-dimensional virtual worlds are slicker, more realistic, interactive, and social than anything that is possible by using today's web browsers. For Ginsu Yoon, Vice President of Linden Lab,

> people always make the comparison of Second Life to a 3D-web, but one of the things that is quite different is that on websites today, you do not see people from different countries interacting much. People on the Internet tend to stay within their own culture because websites

---

79 Quote from Information Week, May 11th 2007.
80 The ARD is a large TV and radio broadcasting organization in Germany.
81 Quote from BBC.co.uk, May 9th 2007.

are still primarily a text-based medium. But Second Life is so immersive that it can transmit more than just text; it can transmit entire cultures.[82]

With the spread of virtual worlds and services, such as Google Earth[83], people may soon be spending more time communicating and shopping in complex 3D-Web environments. Analysts, such as Joe Laszlo of JupiterResearch, predict that virtual worlds are poised to become the next hot Web acquisitions for big media companies. Analysts at Gartner Group announced that 80% of active Internet users and Fortune 500 companies would have a Second Life by the end of 2011.[84] Gartner Inc. said:

> Today's multiplicity of virtual environments has developed through the convergence of social networking, simulation and online gaming. There are many new entrants, whose stability and scalability are not yet established. There is a significant probability that, over time, market pressures will lead to a merging of current virtual worlds into a smaller number of open-sourced environments that support the free transfer of assets and avatars from one to another with the use of a single, universal client.[85]

IBM is already cooperating with Linden Lab and currently working on standards to realize a 3D-Internet. It predicts that a breakthrough will become a reality when open standards for virtual worlds are set. Window Snyder, Head of Security Strategy at Mozilla Foundation, said:

> Instead of web sites like we have now, we will have 3D-representations in the virtual world. Users might walk through a 3D-online bookstore, talking to other shoppers and clerk avatars. In ten years, it will be more about this first-person avatar based 3D-experience.[86]

The first movers in virtual worlds that have built public or corporate virtual environments for marketing, learning, or training purposes may have a different perspective dealing with the long-term value of the virtual worlds. Ron Burns, Founder and President of ProtonMedia, said:

> What do learning, selling, and marketing have in common? They are all more effective when they happen within the context of a powerful, committed, and knowledgeable community. The best learning organizations and the best-marketed products all share networks of loyal advocates. Training an employee on a product or service is very similar to the process of selling that same product or service to a consumer, which is why in the near future, winning companies will be those that adopt Web 2.0 technologies to foster such communities.[87]

After his short trip to the test-track Mr. Milestone returned to the showroom, welcomed a new visitor and invited him to have a look inside the building. Hours later, after Mr. Milestone's in-world tasks were finished, Sven Dörrenbächer reflected in his German office on the eventful last weeks on the Mercedes-Benz Island and started to puzzle out new, innovative concepts.

---

82 Quote from the blog www.ugotrade.com, June 1st 2007.
83 Google Earth is a virtual globe program that maps the earth through the super-imposition of images obtained from satellite imagery, aerial photography and 3D globe.
84 Quote from a Gartner Inc. Press Release, April 26th 2007.
85 Quote from a Gartner Inc. Press Release, April 26th 2007.
86 Quote from Information Week, March 22nd 2007.
87 Quote from Marketingprofs.com, May 22nd 2007.

Mobile phone meets digital music at Sony BMG

Marc Dimolaidis flicked his wrist and hammered the tiny white football into the opposite goal of the table-top soccer located on the second floor of German Sony BMG headquarters in Munich. The 37-year old of Greek origin heaved a deep-drawn sigh and turned slowly to his office.

Equipped with a Master of Law (LL.M) from New York University and two years of work experience as an attorney in a law firm, the hobby broker and passionate windsurfer started his career at Sony BMG in the Legal & Business Affairs Department in 2000. Now in 2005, after successfully moving up the ladder, Marc co-heads Sony BMG eMedia, the department responsible for the distribution of digital music. Of course, he already had to manage several challenging situations within the last two years chiefly due to the fast moving nature of the music business. Nevertheless, this time Marc had a particularly hard nut to crack. He knew that he soon had to make a far-reaching decision which could substantially impact the performance of Sony BMG's German digital music business well into the future.

German music industry

The Blues is not over yet

2005 could not bring a turnaround to the crippled German music industry. Of course, crisis in the music industry was ubiquitous at that time due to illegal downloads and compact disk (CD) burning. German music industry revenues dropped at 4.6% compared to tremendous double-digit slumps in previous years. Music majors and analysts knew that the German music industry was not back on track and even far away from generating sales growth (Exhibit 1).

Exhibit 1 Music industry revenues

	Revenue in Mio. €[a]	Revenue in prices of 1995[b]	Revenue per capita in €[c]
1996	2.472	2.435.6	30.22
1997	2.587	2.502.1	31.55
1998	2.574	2.468.2	31.39
1999	2.500	2.383.4	30.49
2000	2.490	2.342.4	30.29
2001	2.220	2.049.9	26.97
2002[2]	2.054	1.872.4	24.93
2003	1.684	1.480.8	19.98
2004[3]	1.572	1.389.9	19.05
2005	1.500	1.300.6	18.18

[a] Retail prices incl. VAT
[b] Since 2002 incl. music videos
[c] Since 2004 incl. downloads

Source: BV Phono.

This case study was written by Thomas Engelbertz, Master of Business Administration student, under the supervision of Albrecht Enders, Assistant Professor of Strategic Management, Andreas König, Research Assistant at the Chair of Strategic Management, Harald Hungenberg, Chaired Professor of Strategic Management (all four from the University of Nuremberg), and Tawfik Jelassi, Dean and Professor of e-Business and IT at School of International Management of Ecole Nationale des Ponts et Chaussées (ENPC, Paris). This case study is intended to be used as the basis for class discussion rather than to illustrate effective or ineffective handling of a management situation. The facts and circumstances detailed in this decision-forcing case mainly relate to the year 2005.

This case study was made possible by the cooperation of Marc Dimolaidis, Co-Director of Business Development eMedia at Sony BMG.

Sales/revenues

Since 1996 music industry revenues in Germany, the 4th largest music market worldwide, continuously dwindled reaching its current trough in 2005 with €1.5bn. The uptake of digital music had minor effects on total revenues owing to its nature as a low-margin business. Therefore, the lion's share of 2005 revenues remained driven by longplay CDs (83%). Although this is the major format with 123.7m units sold, longplay CDs steadily lost ground (sales went down one third compared to 1996). Only 15.4m single tracks were sold in 2005. Within the last decade, single CDs and music cassettes (MCs) lost respectively two-thirds and three quarters of their sales volume, chiefly as a result of illegal downloads and technological innovations. Annual revenues per capita from music products were about 18€.

Players

The German music industry is comprised of four major music companies which together account for almost 80% industry market share and a large number of 'Indies' (Independent labels) gathered together under the patronage of Impala.[1] In 2004 Sony BMG led the majors with 26.3% followed by Universal with 24.7%. EMI and Warner were behind with 12.1% and

9.9% respectively. Indies had 26.9% of the whole market in Germany.[2] Marc Dimolaidis depicts the primary functions record companies are carrying out:

> As a music major, Sony BMG searches for talented artists, signs them and provides support during the recording and production process. We then promote and market our artists and handle physical or digital distribution.[3]

Although music majors serve as linchpin in the music industry, many other players are also involved in the value chain (Exhibit 2).

Sales and distribution

A positive working relationship with retailers is crucial to any music major. The latter sell and distribute their products, i.e. phonographic records, to the retailer who introduces the physical or digital products into the market. In general, phonographic records are spread

---

1 Impala represents indigenous European independent music companies, promotes their competitiveness and ensures better market access for independent labels.

2 Taken from International Federation of the Phonographic Industry (IFPI) annual report 'The Recording Industry in Numbers – 2005'.

3 Unless stated otherwise, quotations from Marc Dimolaidis are elaborated from information gathered during company interviews made in November 2006 in Munich.

Exhibit 2 Players in the traditional music industry

Songwriters	Artists	Music publishers	Producers	Record companies (music major)	Radio, TV stations	Retailers
Tunes	Singing	Rights purchasing	Studio recording	A&R, artist development	Air-time	Point of sale
Lyrics	Performing/ acting	Rights administration	Rights administration	Marketing & promotion, sales & distribution	Broadcast	Billing
One-time fee + royalties	Royalties (15-30% of retail prices)	Royalties	Royalties (15-17%)	15-25% of retail price	Air-time fees	20-30% of retail price

Players   Tasks   Revenue Model

into the market using multiple retail channels: Megastores (37.3%), Direct Mail (29.6%), Retailer (26.4%), Download (2.0%), Other (4.8%).

Customers

Recent studies published by German Gesellschaft für Konsumforschung (GFK)[4] show that merely 4.9% of all customers buying phonographic records generate 40.3% of total industry revenues. This group has been labeled as 'intensive buyers' and purchases more than nine phonographic records per annum. Besides, the average age of music buyers rises and is distributed as follows; 10-19 years (12.1%), 20–29 years (19.5%), 30–39 years (24.9%), 40–49 years (21.2%), 50 and up (22.3%). The composition of revenues, in terms of different music repertoires, shows the attractiveness customers attribute to the distinctive music genres. Pop music has the highest percentage with 37.1% followed by Rock (19.2%), Classical (7.9%), Schlager[5] (6.8%), Dance (5.3%) and Other (23.7%).

Problems – Piracy endangers the music industry

The following reverberating headline set the music industry's teeth on edge:

> For the first time in history the number of annually burned CDs exceeds the number of annually sold CDs.
>
> International Federation of the Phonographic Industry, 2001

This trend has continued. In 2005, the number of burned music CDs was 3.5 times the number of music albums sold (Exhibit 3). Increasing piracy highly correlates with decreasing sales and precipitated the outbreak of the music industry crisis. John Kennedy, CEO and Chairman of IFPI knows:

> The biggest challenge for the digital music business has always been to make music easier to buy than to steal.[6]

In 2005 the total value of music piracy amounted to €6.3bn which was 3.5 times the actual annual industry revenues. Private CD burning caused 89% of this damage. Illegal downloading made up 8% of the total value of music piracy.

- **CD-burning.** 44% of all purchased blank CDs are used for burning music. Taken together all sound medium storage used for burning music (CD, DVD, etc.) sums up to 439m units measured in CDs. More than 21 million Germans burn music. The average user clones 14 CDs per year.

- **Illegal downloading.** Music downloads in general have been boosted by 8.4% in the last twelve months. In absolute figures, 415m phonographic

---

4 Gesellschaft für Konsumforschung is Germany's biggest research institute. It is among the five top research institutes worldwide.
5 Domestic pop music.
6 In IFPI Digital Music Report 2005.

Exhibit 3 Blank CDs used for burning music and albums sold

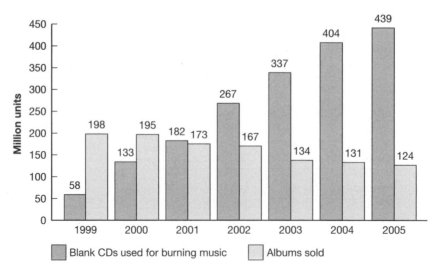

Source: GFK Panel Services.

Exhibit 4 Internet-based music downloads

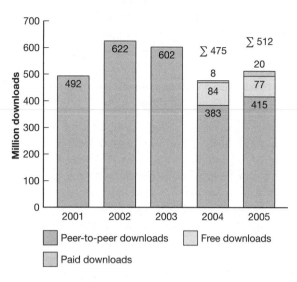

Source: GFK Panel Services.

records were downloaded from peer-to-peer platforms (Exhibit 4). 81% of all these downloads were illegal by nature.

Opportunities – Sheet anchor digital music

The digital services have given the industry the shot in the arm it needed – Stimulating the public's appetite for consuming music while giving them a superior legal alternative to the P2P[7] sites.

Chris Gorog, Chairman and CEO of Napster[8]

The majority of industry experts argue that digital music is poised for take off. It is gaining a strong foothold and growing rapidly. Several key factors drive the growth of digital music, including partnerships between record companies and online/mobile music services, growing broadband and mobile penetration, increasing sales of portable players and handsets, rising consumer awareness of legitimate services, the increased flexibility that is offered to consumers and the fight against online piracy. Thanks to Digital Rights Management (DRM)[9], music majors are starting to diffuse legal download tracks and bundles which cater to different purchasing behaviors. As a consequence, German digital music revenues, which split into revenues from online and mobile, soared by more than 200% to €50m in 2005.

■ **Online:** Download revenues rose by 230% from €11m (2004) to €26m (2005). 16.4m single download tracks (+154%) were sold compared to 1.3m bundles (+300%). Germany is the second most advanced digital music market in Europe with more than 20 services offering music downloads (e.g. Musicload, MTV, iTunes, AOL, etc.[10]). Consumers can shop in or browse online services that offer a bigger catalogue than the very largest physical megastore. Musicload is Germany's market leader with an extensive catalogue of more than 1 million tracks and 15.5 million downloads in 2005. Susanne Krian, Director of Marketing and Sales at Musicload, points out:

Internet music downloads gained momentum within the last years. Our recipe for success is 24/7 accessibility, a large repertoire, multiple payment methods and easy handling. Furthermore, we enable our clients to just buy specific single-tracks out of longplay records[11].

■ **Mobile:** Mobile music exploded in 2005 and revenues doubled reaching €24m. Music via mobiles has quickly evolved from ringtones to the use of full audio recordings in ringtunes, ringback tunes, full-track downloads and other multimedia applications. With the advent of 3G[12] technology, consumers can get a range of interactive content, including music tracks and videos, at higher speed and better quality. Along with 3G, the availability of high-speed downlink packet access (HSDPA) will help drive the mobile music market by cutting the time necessary for downloads. Mobile phone handsets have quickly evolved from talking devices into fully-fledged entertainment gadgets, and consumers are increasingly familiar with the concept of buying music through their handsets. Besides, mobile phones are also beginning to see much bigger storage capacity, longer battery life and increased functionality. Having said that, to become the mass market

---

7 Peer-to-Peer.
8 Quoted from IFPI Digital Music Report 2005.
9 DRM is a system for protecting the copyright of digital data by enabling secure distribution and disabling illegal distribution of data.
10 AOL, iTunes and Musicload capture 90% of the online sales market in Germany.
11 Quoted from www.zukunftsmusik.de, 2005.
12 3G is short for third generation of wireless technology, especially mobile communications. Among other upgrades, 3G allows broad bandwidth and high speed (upwards of 2 Mbps) in wireless data transmission.

phenomenon it promises to be, mobile music must continue to develop beyond master ringtones to full track downloads.

Marc Dimolaidis shares his view on future developments:

> Digital music grows by 30% p.a. Over-the-air fulltrack downloads will play a decisive role in the future.

Though the potential of digital music seems tremendously high to many analysts, Maarten Steinkamp, Chairman & CEO of Sony BMG G/S/A and President Continental Europe, is well aware that:

> The biggest challenge for the music industry is to integrate digital music into its day-to-day operations.[13]

Mobile music

Mobile music is a service that allows mobile phone users to select and access (download or stream) the full array of mobile music via wireless networks. The first major mobile music blockbuster was and still is the ringtone. A ringtone is a sound that indicates an incoming call. Ringtones make up two-thirds of the German mobile music market. 40% of the ringtone revenues are realtones and the remaining 60% are mono/polyphonic ringtones. The fact that mobile has produced such an unexpected and lucrative product in ringtones has also sharpened the music and wireless industries' focus on other mobile music products. However, mobile music is a general term that encapsulates the following products:

- **Polyphonic ringtone**: Polyphonic ringtone is the technical term for the traditional 'beep'. Polyphonic ringtones make use of polyphony[14]. To the detriment of music majors, they are not entitled to charge royalties for polyphonic ringtones as property rights of the composition lie with the publishing houses and not the producing labels.

- **Realtone**: Excerpt from pop song or mainstream music used as ringtone.

- **Ringback tone**: Song or sound that is heard on the telephone line by the calling party after dialing and prior to the call being answered at the distant end. Using ring-back tones customers can greet callers with tones of their choice instead of using traditional call signs.

- **Video ringtone**: Incoming call triggers play-back of music video substituting pure audible ringtone.

Video ringtones have come into vogue. Even this year's MTV Video Music Awards will for the first time ever award a prize to the 'Ringtone of the Year'.

- **Over-the-air fulltrack download (OTA)**: Wireless transmission of fulltrack single or record file to mobile device.

- **Music video**: Wireless download or stream of a music video to a cell phone.

According to industry experts, mobile music is heating up. A plethora of business analysts forecasts strong growth for mobile music and argues that it can step into the breach for declining physical CD sales. Whether mobile music revenues will skyrocket depends on the attainment of the critical mass of music-enabled handset owners (Exhibit 5) and 3G penetration rates (Exhibit 6).

However, some experts have strong reservations as to the extent to which demand for mobile music services can be stimulated in the short term. This opinion is based on the view that mobilizing music distribution confers only limited advantages to consumers and that few will accept the poorer search and download experience and higher prices charged for consumption over cellular networks. There are technological and commercial roadblocks that must be overcome if mobile 'iTune'-like services are to gain acceptance:

---

13 Quoted from Musikwoche, 21.11.2005.
14 Most ringtones use Musical Instrument Digital Interface (MIDI) sources which contain encoded sequences of single notes.

Exhibit 5 Multimedia handset penetration

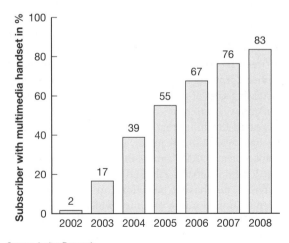

Source: Jupiter Research.

Exhibit 6 UMTS penetration in Germany

	UMTS users*
2002	0
2003	0
2004	293
2005	2,836
2006	6,842
2007	12,756
2008	20,520
2009	29,574
2010	39,220
2011	47,965

*In 1.000 users

Source: Pyramid.

- Questions remain as to whether sufficient latent demand exists for mobile music or if it could be created. It is questionable if consumers will view the advantages of anytime and anywhere.

- Competition from alternative access channels in particular fixed online music download services (both legal and illegal) is fierce.

- PC-to-handset transfer of songs already stored on personal computers is a main growth inhibitor.

- Prices are relatively high.

- Available mobile music catalogues are small and limit customers' choices.

Martin Fabel, principal at A.T. Kearney media practice, comments on technological barriers:

> Currently, the highest hurdles are the low cell phone storage capacity and the long time it takes to download music fulltracks followed by the lack of interoperability between devices, i.e. the possibility to transfer content. I guess these bottlenecks will be eliminated at the latest with the area-wide introduction of UMTS.[15]

Value chain

Marc Dimolaidis demonstrates the functioning of the mobile music value chain using the following example:

> Let's imagine the following situation: In the back of a cab, after the final encore of a breathtaking two-hour

Shakira show, my nephew Tim is still singing her song 'La Tortura'. He grabs his mobile, scrolls through the menu of the ringtone application that he downloaded some months ago, finds the Shakira section and downloads the tune. Behind the scenes, Tim's ringtone client application on his handset communicates with the ringtone server via the wireless network. The server debits Tim's post-paid account and streams the song data back to his handset so he can set it as his default ringer.

What looks quite simplistic at first glance, actually involves many players backstage.

Handset manufacturers

The makers of handsets continuously identify opportunities in tapping the large market of mobile users. They offer new products with dual phone[16] and MP3 player functionality. Close cooperation with music industry, carriers, content providers and end-users is essential to ensure the compatibility of hardware with protocols and networks. Handset makers steadily look for attractive new applications, which could leverage improvements in storage capacity and multimedia ability, to increase their handset sales to operators and end-consumers. As a result, a 59% replacement rate in Germany indicates that almost two-thirds of German citizens purchase a new cellular phone each year.

> Integrated MP3 players and increased storage capacity push the use of mobile music. It can be the next generation killer application the converging industries are on the look-out for.

> **Ralf Gerbershagen**, Head of Motorola Mobile Devices[17]

Music majors

The packagers of music have two main concerns that need to be addressed whenever they license their content for use in the digital environment.

- **Content protection**: Music content must be adequately protected by DRM solution.

- **Protection of existing revenue streams**: Revenues from digital products should not result in less physical sales set off by increased cannibalization.

---

15 Quoted from A.T. Kearney News Release (2004).
16 A dual mode phone is a handset which comprises the elements of a mobile and fixed phone.
17 Quoted from *manager magazine*, 'Mobile Music – Killerapplikation der Zukunft', 10.11.2005.

Regarding the business model, record companies do support the pay-per-track model as well as subscription models. Although initially unpopular in the area of mobile, unlimited subscription models can be expected to receive greater acceptance over time, especially since they provide a realistic alternative to illegal P2P file-sharing. From his out-of-the-box perspective, A.T. Kearney Principal Martin Fabel is convinced that:

> The Music industry is definitely capitalizing on upstream mobile data transfer.[18]

However, most of mobile music revenues could bypass music majors if the latter remain unable to manage their own retail channels in the long-run.

Content aggregators

Content aggregators such as Napster and iTunes are screening for business extensions of their almost traditional e-commerce products. With new DRM technologies, content aggregators are enabled to offer subscriptions in addition to one-off purchases, thus greatly extending their product offerings from PC to mobile devices. Cooperation with hardware providers such as Napster/Sony Ericsson and Motorola/iTunes are strategically important to achieve synergies that provide both entities with a far more complete product. While some wireless carriers are likely to set up their own mobile music portals, many probably will team up with content aggregators that have expertise, reputation and a huge digitalized back catalogue.

Mobile network operators

German telecommunication companies are simultaneously fighting on several fronts. They suffer from plummeting revenues by virtue of Fixed-Mobile Convergence[19], IP-revolution, no frills MVNOs[20] and Triple Play[21]. Industry consolidation and slow growth in new mobile subscriber additions has forced voice average revenue per user (ARPU) down, nudging wireless carriers to seek revenue from premium content services to maintain and grow overall ARPU.

> UMTS operators cannot achieve their expected revenues only by traditional voice revenues but by additional data and multimedia services.

Phillip Gerber, Principal at A.T. Kearney[22]

They seek the potential of increased ARPUs that result from extra demand for data services. It is in their interest

to support music downloads over the air to place margins on music subscriptions and single-track downloads.

> We have to look for new ways of revenue generation, entertainment related services for instance. We believe that there are two emerging killer applications within entertainment; one is music, the other is TV. We believe both have a broad market appeal and a fairly substantial customer willingness to pay. Within music, the emerging business model is paid OTA downloads.

Jens Schulte-Bockum, Corporate Strategy Director at Vodafone[23]

With a single track compressed by MP3 at CD quality weighing in at around 3.5MB, the key barrier to offering wireless music download services has historically been the fact that network transmission speeds and capacity have been inadequate for transporting large data files. However, as carriers have invested heavily, networks migrated from 2G to 3G. Rising wireless transmission speeds combined with advancements in audio file compression standards (principally MPEG-4 AAC) made the commercial launch of mobile music download services increasingly feasible. Now, demand for entertainment is being driven by wireless carriers' initiatives to market their broadband 3G mobile services, along with the concurrent introduction of MP3-player enabled handsets. Over the past two years, European mobile operators have been setting up their own digital music retail stores (incl. fulltrack OTA downloads) as extension and differentiator of their value added service portfolio. Operators seeking to benefit from mobile music usually choose one of two major strategic objectives: Churn[24] retention or revenue generation.

---

18 Quoted from A.T. Kearney News Release, 2004.
19 Fixed Mobile Convergence (FMC) is the integration of wireline and wireless technologies and services to create a single network foundation.
20 Mobile Virtual Network Operators (MVNOs) are companies that launch mobile service offerings using the network infrastructure of traditional carriers. No-frills MVNOs traditionally offer voice and SMS only charging very low prices for their services.
21 Combination of telephone, broadband and entertainment services (such as TV and Video-on-demand).
22 Quoted from A.T. Kearney News Release, 2004.
23 Quoted from an interview posted on McKinsey & Company Mobile Telecommunications Extranet (2005).
24 Churn is the average number of customers that leave a subscription service during a year.

In a nutshell, most analysts agree that operators seem to be in the driver's seat. With the network infrastructure necessary to transmit digital audio files over-the-air to mobile handsets, they provide the backbone for mobile music and already earn revenues from mobile music that surmount 5% of the total music industry's physical sales.

Consumers

87% of German citizens are interested in music. The majority is looking for music anywhere and anytime. However, mobile music will run up against one major problem, namely that the time, cost or convenience benefits of downloading music files over a cellular network might be insufficient to make music customers alter their purchasing habits. Emanating largely from segments with mid- to high-interaction needs and willingness to use advanced products, premium content users represent 9% of mobile subscribers (see Exhibit 7 for information on German mobile subscribers) and generate over 20% of total industry revenues. They are overwhelmingly post-paid customers and prefer unlimited subscription-based tariff schemes to pay-per-use models. There is mixed evidence of whether customers are willing or not to pay significant premiums for mobile music access.

Sony BMG

The announcement of Sony BMG Music Entertainment marks the beginning of a new and critically important era in the history of recorded music.

Sir Howard Stringer, Chairman and CEO Sony Inc.[25]

On 12th December 2003 the international media and entertainment giants Sony Corporation and Bertelsmann AG decided to combine their forces in the recorded music business and signed a binding joint venture agreement. Today, Sony BMG Music Entertainment is the second largest music major in the world.

Bertelsmann AG – the German media giant

In 1835, Carl Bertelsmann founded Bertelsmann AG as a small, family-run publishing house. Today, Bertelsmann which is still headquartered in Gütersloh (Germany) is a worldwide media company posting annual revenues of €17.9bn. It has six major business divisions: Television/radio, book publishers, magazines/newspapers, music labels and publishers, print/media services, book and music clubs. Bertelsmann relies on a strongly decentralized structure. Each business line is headed by its own board of directors and is said to enjoy extensive autonomy in strategic and operational decision making.

_____

25 Quoted from 'Sony Music Entertainment and BMG unite to create Sony BMG Music Entertainment', 5/8/2004, Company Homepage.

Exhibit 7 **German mobile subscribers**

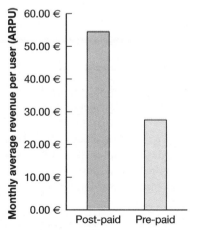
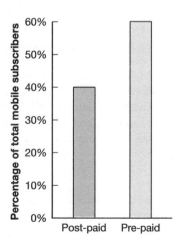

Note: Mobile penetration is at about 100%.
Industry pre-paid churn is 30% on average.

> Bertelsmann is an enterprise for entrepreneurs – a decentralized, international and innovative company that grants its executives the greatest possible freedom.

Gunter Thielen, Chairman & CEO Bertelsmann AG[26]

One decade after large parts of Bertelsmann's facilities were completely destroyed during a British air raid on Gütersloh the publishing house entered the music business in 1956. It united legendary artists like Peter Alexander and Zahra Leander under its first music label Ariola. Now, almost 40 years later, the audio division is comprised of Bertelsmann Music Group (BMG) and BMG Music Publishing. In fiscal year 2003, the two units together contributed revenues of €2,712m and €110m Earnings before Interest and Taxes (EBIT) to the consolidated financial performance of Bertelsmann AG. However, in 2003 BMG could only prevent drastic sales decline through the acquisition of Zomba[27] in November 2002.

Sony Corporation – Rebuilding from the ashes

In September 1945, Masaru Ibuka returned to Tokyo to start a new life in a war devastated city. He set up his own business in a tiny run-down room in the later called Tokyo Department Store in Nihombashi. Ibuka paved the way for today's multinational conglomerate Sony Corporation which has annual sales of US$64bn, 913 affiliates and a total workforce of 158,500 employees. Sony Corporation is one of the world's leading manufacturers of audio, video, communications and information technology products for consumer and professional markets.

With the acquisition in 1988 of one of the most famous US record labels, CBS Records Inc., Sony Corp. pursued its expansion strategy in the audio sector and ultimately stepped into the music business. Former all-American icon CBS was integrated into Sony's music business and renamed Sony Music Entertainment Inc (SMEI). At the end of 1997, Sony Music Entertainment Inc. posted a historical record income of US$441m. Since the advent of rampant piracy, CD burning and filesharing Sony Music Entertainment faced massive sales and profit declines culminating in a record loss of US$225m in 2002.

Sony BMG – Britney and Michael combine firepower and strengths
Two crashed weddings and a pair of newlyweds
At the beginning of the millennium, BMG was prey for possible take-over targets in order to fight declining industry sales.

- February 2000: According to New York Post, BMG, spurred by commitment and firepower from Bertelsmann headquarters, carried on negotiations with Sony Music Entertainment (SME) to merge their music divisions. Most business experts saw this step as a counterattack to recent talks between EMI (UK) and Time Warner (USA).

- Mario Monti, the Antitrust Commissioner of the European Union (from 1999 to 2004), and his antitrust authorities foiled a possible merger of British EMI and German BMG in April 2001. Since both companies were requested to sell specific parts of their respective businesses in order to reduce market concentration, it became clear that the sum-of-the-parts would be less than the agreed upon deal value. BMG and EMI then decided to end their talks.

- In summer 2003, BMG and Warner were already in exclusive talks when EMI joined the negotiations and submitted a bid for Warner, too. All players knew that only one merger had chances to be approved by the EU and US antitrust authorities.

- On 12th December 2003, Bertelsmann AG and Sony Corporation confirmed that they had agreed to combine their recorded music businesses BMG and SME under a 50:50 Joint Venture labeled Sony BMG Music Entertainment. The Joint Venture was subject to US and European antitrust authorities' approval. After six months of heated debates, the US Federal Trade Commission and its European Union counterpart gave their green light to the new entity.

> The creation of Sony BMG Music Entertainment is a historic opportunity for us to build a new music company that we believe can thrive creatively and financially in a highly challenging worldwide music market.

Rolf Schmidt-Holtz, Chairman and CEO BMG[28]

Nowadays, Sony BMG is headquartered in New York and equally owned by Bertelsmann and Sony Corporation. The new venture brought together Bertelsmann Music Group (BMG) and Sony Music Entertainment (SME). The deal did not include the companies' businesses in music publishing, physical distribution and manufacturing which remained under the wings of their traditional

---

26 Quoted from company homepage.
27 At that time, Zomba was one of the world's biggest independent music companies.
28 Quoted from company homepage.

owners. From Bertelsmann/BMG perspective acquisition costs totaled €558m[29] for the fair value of contributed assets and incidental costs. The bottom line was a €180m[30] gain for BMG as the fair value of the received assets exceeded the fair value of the assets that had been given up.

> A Japanese company with American management differs to a huge extent from a German-headed company. Compared to decentralized BMG, SME organization can be described as more centralized and formalized. It was more of a global player with focus on marketing of global superstars whereas BMG was very strong with local artists and repertoire.
>
> **Wolfgang Orthmayer**, Vice President Commercial Affairs Continental Europe Sony BMG[31]

Therefore, Chairman Schmidt-Holtz announced that the integration process would be 'no faster than in a year' and would incur integration costs of €115m[32].

The joint venture was to underscore Bertelsmann's commitment to music as a core business. Major aims of the merger were to compensate the steady decline in the global recorded-music business by adding market shares, and to further increase profits through cost-cutting initiatives. Savings of €350m per year were forecasted to be achieved.

As stipulated in their letter of intent, both parties made up an equal number of representatives at the Board of Directors where Rolf Schmidt-Holtz, former Chief Executive Officer of BMG, was appointed Chairman. Andrew Lack who previously served as CEO of Sony Music was at the helm of the newly formed company as Chief Executive Officer of Sony BMG.

The new entity capitalizes on shared know-how and a bigger artist roster (Exhibit 8). With revenues of almost €5bn, it now has 25.1% global industry market share and employs about 9000 people. Schmidt-Holtz summarizes:

> Together we will work to face the challenges of our industry.[33]

Sony BMG Germany – the Bermuda Triangle

Maarten Steinkamp, Head of Sony BMG Germany, recalls a lunch with Michael Smellie, COO of Sony BMG, which he had in New York City in 2004. He was asked whether he would be willing to head the German business unit. Steinkamp quickly answered:

> Hmm, nice country, bad soccer team, but...no thanks. Germany is the Bermuda Triangle for executives.[34]

---

29 Bertelsmann AG, Annual Report 2004, p.57.
30 Bertelsmann AG, Annual Report 2004, p.65.
31 Unless otherwise stated, quotes from Wolfgang Orthmayer were gathered in an interview from 2/11/2006.
32 Bertelsmann AG, Annual Report 2004, p.12.
33 Quoted from investor relations briefing, 12/12/2003.
34 Quoted from interview of Musikwoche, edition 34 (2004) posted on company homepage.

Exhibit 8 Sample artist roster

AC/DC, Aerosmith, Avril Lavigne, Beyoncé, Bob Marley, Christina Aguilera, Cypress Hill, Destiny s Child, Fatboy Slim, INXS, Julio Iglesias, Luther Vandross, Maroon 5, Mia, Miles Davis, Oasis, Revolverheld, Santana, Justin Timberlake, Toni Braxton, Usher etc.

However, he eventually agreed to become CEO of Sony BMG Germany. His goal still prevails today:

> We want to be the best and most successful music major in Germany – a Music-Powerhouse.[35]

After the merger, the newly formed entity Sony BMG Germany targeted an annual sales volume of €330m and aimed at improving the previous year's combined EBIT of €27m. Four percent of annual revenues came from digital music. The decision about the location of the corporate headquarters (in Berlin or Munich) caused a stir among German Sony BMG staff. At the end, the headquarters were moved to Munich, the base of its administration and IT backbone:

> Munich is the engine and heart of our company.

Willy Ehmann, Senior Vice President Music Division[36]

In April 2006, Steinkamp is to step down leaving his position to Edgar Berger (who previously served as President of Sony BMG Germany). During his tenure, Steinkamp has achieved the following accomplishments e.g.:

- Sony BMG Germany has become the most profitable business unit in Continental Europe. It achieved a 15% rate of return benchmarked to 1.5% in 2003.
- Compared to other country operations of Sony BMG, Germany is the best-in-breed in the post-merger integration process.
- It shifted its strategy from quantity to quality.
- It launched enhanced consumer centric services via price differentiation models and multi-channel distribution strategies.

> Our customers must have total access to our music – anytime and anywhere.

Maarten Steinkamp[37]

Though sales in the upcoming digital market more than doubled, the only thing he could not fight successfully was the drastic decline of total revenues by 15% compared to an industry benchmark of 5%.

> In the first two years following the merger, we could not manage to stop the erosion of our cumulated market share.

Wolfgang Orthmayer

For Steinkamp, two questions remained unanswered:

- How can Sony BMG Germany stop the continuous decline in total revenues?
- How can the German company leverage digital distribution channels and further exploit digital music growth opportunities?

Sony BMG eMedia

eMedia was founded in 2004 immediately after the announced merger was waved through by antitrust authorities. The department resulted from merging the former Sony 'eMedia' and BMG's 'Neue Medien'[38]. It was imperative for Sony BMG to establish a separate digital music entity to be able to seize upcoming digital business opportunities. Marc Dimolaidis, who reports to Ulrich Järkel, Head of Strategic Marketing (Exhibit 9), points out the importance of the new department:

> In fact, at this point of time, we are quite different from our physical [distribution] counterparts. They sell physical records to brick-and-mortar stores like Media Markt and Saturn. We on the other hand partner with portals and MNOs selling our rights and licences to them. We do not have to care about storage or return management and we are not limited by shelf space availability. Accordingly, a large part of digital revenues results from older or less known titles that you would rarely find in a brick-and-mortar store (so called 'long tail'[39]). Besides, we are not limited to the album or single format but we can create unlimited packages and configurations for the consumer.

Therefore eMedia is solely in charge of the whole range of digital music distribution. As Marc Dimolaidis explains, their vision is quite straightforward:

> We want to develop the digital music market and we want to achieve the best possible position in this fast-growing market.

In order to do so, eMedia focuses on three different categories of operations:

---

35 Quote taken from interview posted on company homepage.
36 Company homepage, 29.6.2006.
37 Quoted from interview in Musikwoche, edition 34 (2004).
38 'Neue Medien' is German for 'New Media'.
39 The term 'long tail' was made popular by Chris Anderson in 2004. Due to unlimited shelf space in digital stores, not only blockbusters (short head) but also products with low sales volume (long tail) can be offered for sale and thus increase total revenues.

Exhibit 9 Organization chart of the Strategic Marketing Department

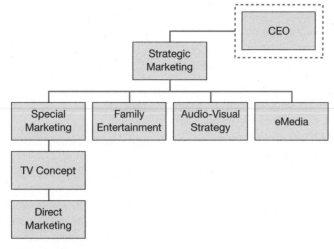

Source: SonyBMG.

- Its core business is the distribution of licenses to Internet portals (iTunes, AOL, Musicload, etc.) and MNOs (Vodafone, O2, etc.).

- eMedia scans emerging business opportunities and assesses their potential for developing new revenue streams. In 2005 for example eMedia started to sell secure digital memory cards, mobile phones and MP3 players armed with pre-installed content like e.g. the latest Kuschelrock[40] compilation. Or, it teamed up with companies like e.g. German bank giant Sparkasse and consumer brands like Ferrero to feed their customer loyalty programs and on-pack-promotions with digital music. By way of further example, it launched the web-portal 'Musicbox' for direct sale of mobile content and display of music videos to the consumer. eMedia also offered this portal as a turn-key solution to third party websites like web.de that wanted to boost their online presence.

- It develops and carries out all areas of Sony BMG's online sales marketing.

Climbing the staircase up to the second floor of Sony BMG headquarters in Munich, the visitor enters the spacious and illuminated office site of eMedia with its modern interior. The offices are arranged around a central spot which combines café lounge and tabletop soccer. Each employee finds his/her name engraved on compact discs on his or her door frame. Yellow painted walls are loaded with award winning records of famous artists like Christina Aguilera and Anastacia. Marc Dimolaidis likes the working spirit and team approach:

> We have a great working atmosphere. That is no coincidence. We set high value on teamwork and take care that our members get along with each other very well.

Mobile music at Sony BMG

BMG started selling its first mobile ringtones back in 2002 when mobile music was still in its infancy. Marc Dimolaidis smiles whimsically when he remembers:

> Well, we started with Vodafone. With hindsight that was so bizarre. In order to get started as early as possible, we charged them less than half of the amount [for licenses] we put down on their account one year later [2003]. Nonetheless, we were a pioneer and first in the market.

What does the mobile product palette look like today? Sony BMG eMedia signed licensing contracts with every major provider of digital music in Germany. Having done this, it distributes ringtones through a diverse set of channels, namely WAP, Web and TV.

However, beyond the distribution of ringtones, only Vodafone and O2 prominently market fulltrack over-the-air downloads. T-Mobile, Germany's largest MNO, has not really pushed such offers so far.

Distribution of music via licensing certainly contributes the bulk of revenues but there is a number of

---

40 Compilation of soft rock music and ballads.

559

good reasons for music majors like Sony BMG to also establish retail channels of their own. First, each player of the mobile music value chain claims its share of the pie and by way of direct sales to the consumer Sony BMG could itself collect the retail margin. Additionally, there are further reasons why Sony BMG should try to establish its own retail channels:

- Leverage on own customer contacts. With its websites and newsletters, Sony BMG has nearly 3m unique users and 15m PIs[41].

- Gain experience to better understand retail mechanisms and consumer behavior and thereby improve its own B2B business.

- Achieve uniqueness by launching new services and digital content offers (B2B or B2C).

- Make things happen that either do not happen or happen too late if not done by oneself.

Most of Sony BMG's digital music business is B2B. According to Marc Dimolaidis, there has always been the core question whether to engage in B2C projects or stick to traditional distribution channels. He reconsiders eMedia's resources and capabilities:

> Our sweeping weapon is our excellent content and our immediate access to artists. We can further build on synergies with our general marketing activities. In addition we can count on our know-how in music and on our strengths in category management. Needless to say, our core competence is bringing music to the market.

Sony BMG meets MVNO

Idea

Twice a year, Sony BMG managers from around the world meet at Sony BMG headquarters in New York. In this year (2005), Marc attended the semi-annual conference eager to become acquainted with cutting-edge concepts from around the globe. He reminisces about the first moment he got in touch with MVNO[42] concepts:

> We were sitting in the conference room with more than 20 managers when our French colleague gave a presentation on MVNOs in France. My first impression was: 'WOW, we need one as well.' When I sat on the plane back from New York City my mind was racing. Would such a concept fly in Germany?

Back in Munich, Marc and his team immediately kicked off and started conceptualizing a prospectively viable

MVNO. They were at the same time approached by several consultancies and solution providers including Arvato Mobile and Materna. In order to knit a thorough business case, eMedia scrutinized the idea by:

- Asking Materna and a well-known management consultancy firm for advice.

- Benchmarking a very detailed MVNO case in the USA.

- Contacting prospective partners in the value chain and entering into first negotiations.

The information phase shed some light on the success factors of MVNOs:

> It seems that MVNOs might flood the German market. In all likelihood, MVNOs will capture 10–20% of the market in the long-run. Since MVNO concepts are usually topic-centred, and music is very suitable for this purpose, music is actually predestined to play a role in this emerging market. In my opinion, the most important ingredients for a successful MVNO installation are a compelling concept, attractive content, customer contacts and a strong brand.

Marc Dimolaidis

Product design

In a nutshell, the MVNO concept which made it to the final round is a pre-paid mobile offer comprising a UMTS enabled multimedia handset and premium content scattered around in virtual music worlds (Hip-Hop, etc.).

Marc Dimolaidis comments on the hardware components:

> We need a customized UMTS mobile to have our software and applications preinstalled. Thus, we facilitate fast access to a myriad of Sony BMG content posted on our WAP-Portal.[43] It is obvious that a suitable cellular phone is to have the full arsenal of multimedia functions.

---

41 Page impressions (page views) are requests to load a single page of an Internet site.

42 A Mobile Virtual Network Operator (MVNO) is a mobile operator that does not have its own network infrastructure. Instead, MVNOs have business arrangements with traditional mobile operators to buy minutes of use (MOU) for sale to their own customers. In Germany, see Lidl, Tschibo, etc. On a global scale check out Virgin Mobile/US, UK, Universal Scoop/France, Mobile ESPN/US, etc.

43 WAP (Wireless Application Protocol) is the protocol used for most of the world's mobile internet sites. It enables users to enter the internet from mobile devices.

Besides, we would be a pioneer bundling a pre-paid tariff with a 3G enabled handset. We focus on pre-paid as post-paid offerings would blow our department in terms of administration and marketing investment.

With respect to the content component, eMedia created a concept of virtual lifestyle and music worlds that are based on Sony BMG content. A WAP-portal serves as a gateway to enter these worlds via mobile phone. Compared to its competitors, eMedia would try to differentiate itself on the basis of content, image and moderate prices (Exhibit 10). Marc Dimolaidis defines the customer target group as follows:

> We would focus on circa 15 million 12–29-year-old mobile users who are both content and music affine. We estimate that these users pay about 10€ per month for content and value-added services.

World Concept

The content component of the MVNO concept is labeled 'World Concept'. It is based on four virtual worlds with eight different content components meant to create unique image and content differentiation (Exhibit 11).

The challenge is to create a new differentiated product which appeals to the customer. Therefore, we first conducted marketing surveys. For our prototype, we then defined four virtual worlds building our concept's cornerstones and directly catering to customer needs.

Marc Dimolaidis

- **Hip-Hop world:** During its research, eMedia found out that almost two-thirds in the relevant segment listen to Rap and R'n'B music. All eight building blocks of this specific world are related to Hip-Hop.

- **Latino world:** This virtual Latino-branded music landscape consists of South American and Spanish music and communities. In Germany, more than 15% of 12–40 year-old people are interested in this type of music.

- **Turkish world:** This world addresses the 2.1m Turkish residents in Germany. Ay Yildiz is another MVNO which already operates in this attractive

Exhibit 10 Strategic positioning

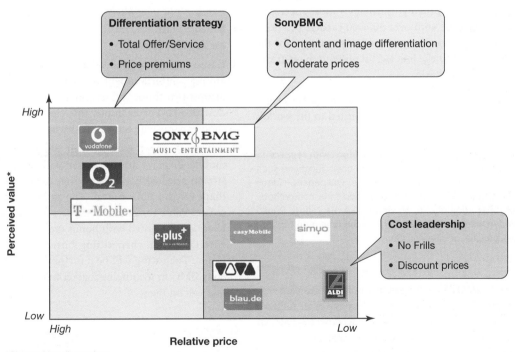

*Only multimedia services.

Exhibit 11 Concept of virtual worlds

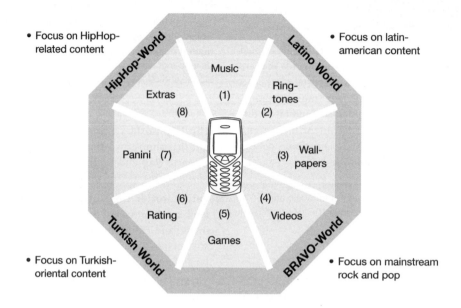

- Focus on HipHop-related content
- Focus on latin-american content
- Focus on Turkish-oriental content
- Focus on mainstream rock and pop

niche. It competes on price by offering international calls Turkey-to-Germany and vice versa for 15 cents/min.

- **Bravo world:** Bravo is Germany's most successful teen magazine with over 500,000 readers per print run. In this case, Bravo is used as a synonym for the 12–19 year old age bracket listening to mainstream rock and pop music.

Again, each of the four virtual worlds consists of eight content components which are adjusted to the world's image, brand and target group.

> To play head-on with our competitors with respect to product range, we have to provide basic functions such as over-the-air fulltracks, ringtones, wallpapers, videos and games. But in order to outperform our competitors, we offer additional applications like our rating, Panini and world-specific extras. This is the cream on top that will provide for differentiation.
>
> **Marc Dimolaidis**

- **Fulltrack OTAs:** Four out of five in the relevant segment show interest and willingness to pay for fulltrack downloads. Users would be able to download almost the entire Sony BMG digital music catalogue.

- **Ringtones:** Almost two-thirds of the potential target users want all state-of-the-art forms of ringtones.

- **Wallpapers[44]:** With 86%, wallpapers seem to be the blockbuster for mobile users in the relevant segment (even though users' readiness to pay for the same is clearly lower than e.g. for ringtones).

- **Videos:** Fulltrack music videos are made available for downloading.

- **Games:** Playing games has rapidly proliferated among entertainment-addicted mobile users. Almost two-thirds will not miss the service of game downloads. For example, this can be a racing or shooter game with Sony BMG background music.

- **Rating:** A short message will pop up on users' mobile displays and any user will be enticed to stream selected newcomer songs for free and rate them on the WAP-portal. The rating component creates value for both sides: Users and Sony BMG. Users are rewarded with bonus credits and get free entertainment when sitting bored on buses and trains. The rating will be a further instrument for Sony BMG in identifying market trends and records that will hit the roof. [45]

---

44 Wallpapers are background images displayed on one's mobile screen; like a background image on the screen of one's PC.
45 The flop rate amounts to 90% industry-wide, saying that only investments in one of ten artists will pay off.

■ **Panini:** Traditionally, Paninis are card collections of specific events such as football world cups for example. Usually collectors are not resistant to epidemic effects and become addicted to completing their albums. In this case, mobile handsets are equipped with pre-installed albums. Collectors purchase via WAP and later trade the cards with peers through Bluetooth-interfaces.

■ **World-specific extra:** There is no general concept behind this component. It will differ from virtual world to virtual world. Hip-hop devotees for example take advantage of a pre-installed musicbox which enables them to 'spit'[46] their own lyrics to non-voice background music.

Customer demand

To excel in the German wireless telecommunications arena, MVNOs should meet at least most of the mobile customer demands. Marc Dimolaidis knows what is expected:

> Today, customers are very discerning and high-maintenance. Not enough that they insist on low prices, they want to purchase anytime and anywhere and as easy as possible. Interaction and community aspects massively gained in importance. The offer needs to capture the spirit of the market.

Revenue model

Generally, there are two kinds of revenue streams from subscribers: first, an upfront fee to the consumer to enter the service plan, e.g. the upfront fee for a handset, and second, monthly average revenues per user (ARPU); ARPU is the monthly payment that a customer spends on voice & data (including SMS) and value-added services like content downloads.

Marc Dimolaidis reflects on their business model:

> Under an MVNO concept, we'd ideally like to participate in both of the aforesaid revenue streams.

Operations

Implementation

> We bear in mind that our core competency is not the provision of telecommunication services but bringing music to the market. Starting up our own MVNO is a big thing. To reduce the manpower bound in the project we would involve a MVNE service provider to come to our

aid. As a result, we only had to tie one or two fulltime employees in the entire project.

> **Marc Dimolaidis**

In general, mobile virtual network enablers (MVNEs) are intermediaries and position themselves between MVNOs and MNOs. In terms of services, MVNEs offer a one-stop shopping solution for MVNOs by providing and selling the infrastructure and a full range of services necessary for MVNOs to launch and run their operations.

> The MVNE is a crux. During the selection process, we go through all possible MVNEs with a fine-tooth comb and check if they meet our multilayer criteria: technical infrastructure, price, flexibility, MNO partner and project references.

> **Marc Dimolaidis**

Big German MVNEs are Vistream, Arvato Mobile, Siemens and Transatel.

The major benefit that a MVNE can provide to the MVNO is to outsource non-core telco functions and in-house only those functions related to their core competency. Thus, they allow the deferral of capital expenditures (risk) and cost reductions while allowing the MVNO to focus on marketing and customer relationship management rather than operations.

> If we were to run our own MVNO, we would want to leverage our competencies and most probably keep in-house only those activities that are related to content/value-added services, marketing and sales.

> **Marc Dimolaidis**

In compliance with its existing resources and capabilities, Sony BMG would most likely adjust its operations to merely develop new products and services and map out its own marketing, communication and sales strategy (Exhibit 12).

MVNEs would team up with wireless operators and provide the residual functions necessary for Sony BMG to run a viable mobile offering.

Revenue sharing is a common method applied to allocate costs and revenues in the mobile music value chain. For their mobile services (including fees for airtime packages bought from mobile network operators), MVNEs charge between 30–50% of value-added-

---

46 'Spit' is Hip-Hop language for composing and performing lyrics.

Exhibit 12 MVNO value chain

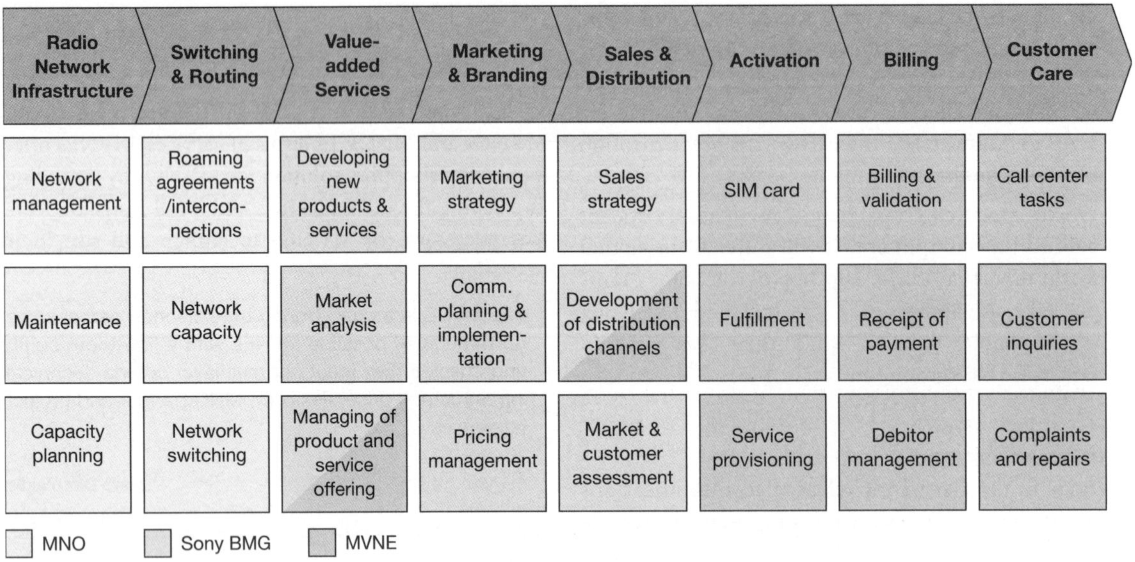

Radio Network Infrastructure	Switching & Routing	Value-added Services	Marketing & Branding	Sales & Distribution	Activation	Billing	Customer Care
Network management	Roaming agreements /interconnections	Developing new products & services	Marketing strategy	Sales strategy	SIM card	Billing & validation	Call center tasks
Maintenance	Network capacity	Market analysis	Comm. planning & implementation	Development of distribution channels	Fulfillment	Receipt of payment	Customer inquiries
Capacity planning	Network switching	Managing of product and service offering	Pricing management	Market & customer assessment	Service provisioning	Debitor management	Complaints and repairs

☐ MNO   ☐ Sony BMG   ☐ MVNE

service revenues and 60–80% of standard service revenues (voice and SMS). Another variable cost pool might be cash paid for each subscriber, namely 0.5€/quarter for example. Depending on the individual arrangements, MVNOs might pay a fixed monthly fee of 50,000€ to 150,000€, too.

Handset purchasing

Mobile phones play a central role for most customers considering the acquisition of a starter package comprising a prepaid card and a handset. Usually, each mobile phone bought with a pre-paid card is subsidized. Determining the amount of subsidization is balancing on a knife's edge. However, total handset purchasing costs are one major cost pool for those MVNOs that do not just distribute SIM-only prepaid cards.

> For a rough approximation of handset wholesale costs, we did consider a retail distribution margin of circa 20% and subtracted a bulk discount of around 25%. At this point of time, we would most likely go for Sony Ericsson or Nokia models because they currently excel in image and multimedia equipment. Retail prices for relevant models lie at around 400€. Since the phones need to be customized and our applications need to be uploaded we calculate with additional costs of 10€/unit plus packaging (2.5€/unit) and handset logistics/aftersales (5€/unit).[47]

> **Marc Dimolaidis**

IT setup/content production

The concept of virtual worlds existed on the drawing board but was not put into practice yet. IT setup costs would include programming the WAP-portal, hosting and updating handsets, monitoring chat rooms and developing applications like Panini, rating, etc. Rough calculation forecasts indicate that costs will be within Euro 300,000 and 400,000 p.a.:

> If we produce games specifically for the MVNO offer, then this will be an important cost driver. According to estimates of mobile entertainment firms, the development of a basic no-frills game costs 10,000€. Assuming that we would create synergies in that we would re-use the 'engine' (e.g. of a music quiz, of a racing game, of a shooting game etc.) and parts of the design of each applicable game for a multitude of further games, then costs for a sufficiently attractive pool of self-produced games would probably run up to Euro 250,000 p.a.

> **Marc Dimolaidis**

---

47 As of 1/2007 VAT in Germany is 19%.

Marketing
Pricing

eMedia considers a starter package priced at 149€ (Exhibit 13) consisting of SIM-card, high-end handset and credits to purchase music content. As mentioned above, traditional or virtual operators subsidize their handsets to push sales. In the case of Sony BMG, moderate priced prepaid packages including 3G enabled handsets are not on the market yet. Notwithstanding that subsidization would be immense, these costs are inevitable. 3G penetration and UMTS-handsets are not prevalent but essential for prospective users to have access to the virtual worlds and the respective content. According to reports of McKinsey & Company, prepaid subsidizations of 25–35€ are customary within the German telecommunications industry. Compared to its peers, Sony BMG would be forced to disburse twice this amount.

> A very simple tariff structure like charging 0.29€/min and 0.19€/SMS would be advantageous for us and our users. We would couple the tariff with two extra features. First, we'd integrate 'budget protection'. Minors won't be able to exceed a certain monthly ARPU which can be pre-set by their parents. As parents will need to approve the purchasing decision, we think that they will appreciate such a tariff feature. Second, we encourage users over 18 to enhanced voice and traffic consumption by rewarding credit recharging with free content.
>
> **Marc Dimolaidis**

Post-paid customers are accustomed to monthly subscriptions; prepaid users are not. Taking this into consideration, eMedia does not opt for unlimited subscription models to price their content products. Instead, they allow customers to consume à la carte, i.e. pay-per-use. This pricing model applies to single products, bundles and short-term subscriptions.

> As to pricing, we don't try to reinvent the wheel. Our prices and price models would be close to our competitors. (Exhibit 14)
>
> **Marc Dimolaidis**

Distribution

Rolling out the MVNO entails a threefold distribution strategy; i.e. for starter packages (incl. handset and SIM), (recharging) vouchers and content (Exhibit 15). Since the aim of the MVNO is to establish its own distribution channel, content will be distributed 100% over-the-air via UMTS and the WAP-portal. eMedia will not rely on any indirect distribution channels to spread its content. The opposite scenario applies to handset purchasing and voucher recharging. Marc Dimolaidis explains:

> As a rule of thumb 90% of our handset and voucher sales will run through traditional retail channels (as opposed to sales through a website). Our service plans will sell best in brick-and-mortar stores as customers want to touch the

Exhibit 13 Pricing

Handset	Content
Starter-package	**A la carte**
• Mobile phone + credits for content consumption • Retail price 149€	• Unit prices in line with industry price levels (wallpaper 1.99€)
Tariff	**Subscription**
• Uniform tariff (29 Cent/Min.) • Budget protection (optional installation of a monthly max. spending) • Bonus for recharging (credits for content purchase) • Target group related incentives	• Monthly fee (duration restricted to 6 months) • Monthly genre-related subscriptions (15 Jazz-songs for 14.99€) • Free-choice (discounted monthly credits used for free-choice)
	Bundles
	• Content packages (2 wallpapers & 2 ringtones for 4.99€ e.g.)

Exhibit 14 **Sample competitor content prices**

Content	Competitors	Pay-per-use	Subscription
Music file	Vodafone-Live	1.49€	14.99€
Wallpaper	Jamba!, Zed, RTLHandyfun.de	1.99€	4.99€ (10/month)
Game	Jamba!, Zed, RTLHandyfun.de	4.99€	4.99€ (2/month)
Realtone	Jamba!, Zed, RTLHandyfun.de	2.99€	4.99€ (3/month)
Video	Jamba!, i-tunes, RTLHandyfun.de	2.49€–2.99€	4.99€ (5/month)

Source: http://www.jamba.de, http://www.zed.de, http://www.apple.de, www.vodafone-live.de, http://www.rtlhandyfun.de.

phone and also because a lot of them are minors. The lion share of our handsets will be sold through the dense network of our MNO partner's branches. Selling vouchers is a slightly different task. To pass vouchers to our customers, we would team up with a partner like Lekkerland. Lekkerland is responsible for 90% of German prepaid market sales through its 20,000 terminals in gas stations, supermarkets and kiosks. Customers will either recharge electronically (78%) or purchase old-fashioned physical prepaid vouchers (22%).

eMedia would try to distribute the remaining 10% handsets and vouchers through its direct channels including website, hotline, over-the-air voucher recharging, etc. Costs thereby incurred are only 2% of voucher value compared to 6% with retail e-loading and 12% with physical retail vouchers. Calculating distribution commissions for handset sales is a lot easier as Marc Dimolaidis admits:

> According to consultant estimates accrued costs are 25–35€/package for indirect sales and 15€/package for direct sales.

Exhibit 15 **Distribution channels**

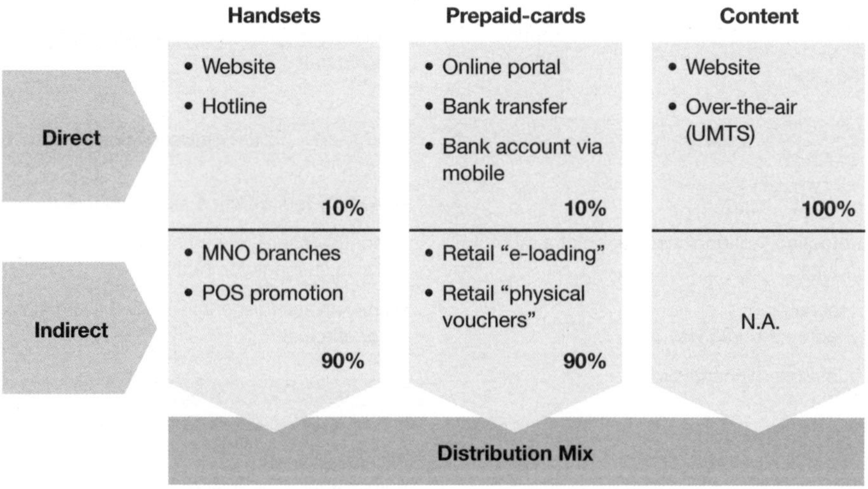

Promotion (marketing)

Marketing is the most important lever for a successful premium MVNO based on content. Usually, we contribute licences instead of cash investments to our conjoint projects. By doing this, we keep project risks within a limit because our maximum loss is a zero royalty payoff. If we were to launch the MVNO our risk profile would be enormous since it highly correlates with necessary cash expenses for marketing activities. Therefore, if launching an MVNO on our own, we maybe should share the cost and risk by way of cooperation with a TV-station, Internet-Portal or print magazine that has high impact in our target group.

Marc Dimolaidis

To create awareness in the relevant customer segment, i.e. 12–29-year-old music devotees, eMedia would focus on print, TV and online marketing. Music channels MTV and VIVA are predestined to divulge spots promoting a premium music MVNO.[48] An effective TV campaign would require eMedia to daily air at least three minutes of 10-second spots on VIVA and MTV respectively. Three minutes of 10-second spots on VIVA accrue total costs of 10,576€. MTV charges almost the same namely 10,598€. Annual running TV costs are calculated off 10% bulk discount.

Additional major costs will come from print advertising. Marc comments on possible target journals for their marketing campaigns:

The German market is full of fashion and music magazines for young people. However, Bravo, YAM, Mädchen, Musikexpress and Rolling Stones outnumber their peers in terms of print runs (magazines sold)[49].

Bravo is the German blockbuster teenage magazine with more than 500,000 copies sold weekly. If eMedia wanted to post its MVNO ads on three-eighths of a page, Bravo would charge eMedia 14,700€. Multiplied with 13 weeks (per quarter) totals 191,100€ on a quarterly basis. YAM and Mädchen charge 13,790€ for a blank half-pager (per weekly edition). Musikexpress and Rolling Stones are released once a month and charge 7,880€.

Creating awareness and reaching five million people through online marketing accrues additional costs of approximately 250,000€ per month.

Competitors

We do not look for competitors in our neighborhood [music majors]. Our direct competitors are other wireless operators, be it virtual or not, which compete on premium content and differentiation, too. In consequence, I would not consider no-frills MVNOs as competitors fighting for the same turf.

Marc Dimolaidis

No-frills MVNOs offer no value-added services or content in any kind or form. In addition, Tchibo[50] is the only no-frills provider which even includes handsets in its starter packages (these handsets are very basic though). Other no-frills players only offer SIM-cards and charge on average 19c/min. No-frills MVNOs are predominantly large retailers which capitalize on their customer range and distribution channels (i.e., dense network of branches).

At the end of 2005, music channel VIVA started running its own MVNO in cooperation with E-Plus.[51] It was the first hybrid MVNO which attempted a miscellaneous strategy. On the one hand, they focused on moderate prices for voice (29c/min) and low prices for SMS (9c/min). On the other hand, they leveraged what they consider their core assets: brand and image. With this combination VIVA aimed at gaining about 300,000 customers within its first 12 months of operations. The offering, however, only comprises ringtones and not fulltracks.

Among the remaining competitors are the four established mobile network operators that command their own network infrastructure (GPRS, UMTS, etc.) and offer pre-paid services as well (Exhibit 16); T-Mobile, Vodafone, E-Plus and O2. Their major strength is their control of network infrastructure as a gateway to any kind of value-added services.

- **E-Plus** can be poorly ranked in terms of value-added services compared to its competitors. It does not include over-the-air fulltrack downloads in its service portfolio, nor does it have fertile content cooperation for its own distribution. Instead, according to its CEO Thorsten Dirks, E-Plus is

---

48 Germany's first domestic music channel is nowadays market leader with MTV and owned by American media giant Viacom.
49 Bravo, YAM and Mädchen (German for 'girl') are teenage magazines. Musikexpress and Rolling Stones are music journals.
50 Tchibo is a huge German retailer selling coffee and non-food products through its dense net of branches. Tchibo has a brand awareness of 99% in Germany.
51 E-Plus owns more than 200 branches in Germany.

Exhibit 16 Competitor prices for prepaid handsets

Competitor	Brand	Price Range	UMTS Mobile
Vodafone	CallYa	49.50–299.50€	>199.50€
E-Plus	Free&Easy	29.90–149.90€	N.A.
T-Mobile	Xtra	19.95–229.95€	N.A.
O2	Loop	49.99–199.99€	N.A.

Source: www.vodafone.de, www.eplus.de, www.t-mobile.de, www.o2.de.

always on the look-out for potential MVNO cooperation to gain overall market share and increase profitability[52] (Exhibit 17).

■ **T-Mobile** is the wireless business unit of former German monopolist Deutsche Telekom. T-Mobile has a relatively strong competency in Mobile TV. In mobile music, it merely concentrates on single events like for instance a pre-release of Robbie Williams' songs or a video of Robbie live in concert. Nevertheless, access to mobile music content is available only via two specific handsets.

---

52 Taken from a speech 'Erfahrungen eines Pioniers in MVNO-Segment' held by Thorsten Dirks on 18/11/2005.

Exhibit 17 European MNO strategies

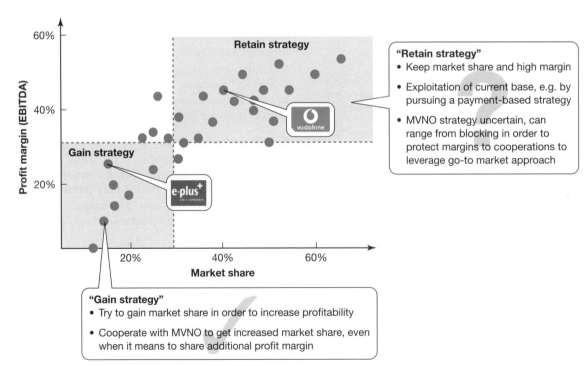

Source: McKinsey.

■ **O2** builds on a strong brand reputation in the target customer segment and has an extensive mobile juke-box available to download. However, O2 still has to overcome cumbersome technical roadblocks.

■ **Vodafone** outperforms its peers and its value-added service portfolio is best-in-class. Its portal, labeled Vodafone Live!, allows customers to access a vast catalogue of music downloads as well as mobile TV and newspaper services. The flip side of Vodafone's sophisticated service portfolio is its relatively high price level.

Outlook

Forecasts of digital music all predict ramping digital music revenues. Wolfgang Orthmayer reflects on Sony BMG:

> Digital music is going to be the industry's bread-and-butter business. Among the four music majors, we are probably the most successful and most advanced in digital music. Maybe by 2010, one-third of our revenues will come from digital music.

Nevertheless, when it comes to mobile music, experts are not sure whether to have bearish or bullish expectations on mobile music future developments and especially over-the-air fulltrack downloads. In Germany, adoptions of technological advances are very slow by nature and relevant penetration rates have not reached a critical mass yet. Most research institutes take an optimistic stance on mobile music developments and predict steady growth though (Exhibit 18). However, the question still remains whether mobile music turns out to be the next mobile killer application.

Leaning back in his chair Marc Dimolaidis folds his arms and watches out of his office window. It was early evening and the sun was sinking slowly in front of him, just about to slip behind the shadows of the Sony BMG headquarters. It has been a long day; however, right now he reflects on the last weeks and contemplates the success chances of a prospective Sony BMG music MVNO. Marc asks himself whether such a project is the right choice for Sony BMG.

Exhibit 18 Mobile music* forecast

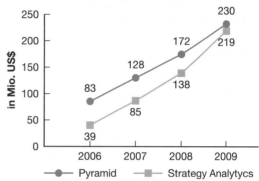

*All music download and streaming services excl. all forms of ringtones.

Source: Pyramid Research; Strategy Analytycs.

GLOSSARY

3G (Third generation technology) Standard that displays texts and graphics phones

ARPU Average revenue per user

B2B Business to business

B2C Business to consumer

DRM (Digital rights management) System for protecting the *copyrights* of digital data by enabling secure distribution and disabling illegal distribution of data

EBIT Earnings before interest and taxes

FMC (Fixed mobile convergence) Integration of wireline and wireless technologies and services to create a single network foundation.

GPRS (General packet radio services) Mobile data transmission service based on packets

HSDPA (High speed downlink packet access) UMTS mobile telephony protocol that allows higher data transfer speeds

IFPI International Federation of the Phonographic Industry

Indies Independent labels

IP Internet protocol

Kbps Kilobytes per second

m Million

MNO (Mobile network operator) Also known as wireless service provider, wireless carrier or mobile phone operator. A telephone company that owns an underlying network and provides wireless services to customers

MVNE (Mobile virtual network enabler) Intermediaries which position themselves between MVNOs and MINUs. MVNEs offer a one stop shopping solution by providing the infrastructure and a full range of services necessary to launch and operate a MVNO

MVNO (Mobile virtual network operator) Companies launching mobile service offerings using the network infrastructure of traditional carriers

OTA (Over the air) Over the air distribution of data and services

P1 (Page impression) Request to load a single page of an Internet site

P2P Peer to peer

SD Secure digital

SIM (Subscriber identity module) Chip card for mobile phones with registration and telephone number

Triple Play Combination of telephone, broadband and entertainment services (such as TV and Video on demand)

UMTS (Universal mobile telecommunication system) Third generation broadband, packet based transmission of text, digitized voice, video, and multimedia at data rates up to 2 megabits per second

VAS (Value added services) Mobile services beyond voice and SMS

VAT Value added tax

WAP (Wireless application protocol) Standard that displays texts and graphics on mobile phones

NTT DoCoMo (Japan)

Moving from a mobile phone operator to a lifestyle service provider

On March 7th 2007, Yuichi Kato, President and CEO of NTT DoCoMo, and his management team were reflecting in their European headquarters in Paris on the history of NTT DoCoMo, the mobile telecom business of Nippon Telegraph and Telephone. Since its beginning, NTT DoCoMo has been focusing on its Japanese home market and offering innovative and value-adding mobile phone services. Mr. Kato has recently announced to a rather surprised audience that

> our goal is to serve our clients as a lifestyle service provider[1].

Company background

NTT, Japan's former telecommunication monopoly, was privatized in 1985 with 46% of its shares held by the Japanese government. Soon after the 1992 deregulation of the Telecom market in Japan, it spun off its mobile telephony division, became its majority stakeholder and appointed Kouji Ohboshi first CEO of NTT DoCoMo. The name DoCoMo was an acronym for 'Do Communications over the Mobile Network' and also a homonym of the Japanese word 'anywhere'.

With more than 52 million customers, NTT DoCoMo is the world's second largest and Japan's leading mobile communications company. With the launch of its wireless Internet service 'i-mode' in February 1999, it evolved from a mobile telecom and 'wireless-infrastructure' (mobile voice) operator to an 'IT-infrastructure' (mobile data) one. Introducing in July 2004 the 'Osaifu-Keitai' service which transforms the handset into a mobile digital wallet, the company fostered its shift towards becoming a lifestyle service provider (see Exhibit 1).

The shift from 1G to 2G mobile communications technology

Over the last decade, mobile communications technology has made giant strides, rapidly moving from first-generation (1G) analog voice-only service to second-generation (2G) digital voice and data communications. The year 1979 was the start of the analog cellular era with NTT's introduction of the first mobile phone network in Tokyo. The mobile phone was only affordable to wealthy business people because of the high service fee that was charged. Services were especially tailored for in-car use and became available only on a rental basis. Users were charged a deposit of ¥200,000[2], a ¥72,000 subscription fee, a ¥26,000 monthly fee and a call charge of ¥280 for every three minutes of usage. These high charges led to an unsuccessful launch.

---

1 Excerpt from an invited speech to the first World Congress of the ENPC MBA Alumni held on March 2nd and 3rd 2007 in Marrakech (Morocco).

2 In January 1979, the monthly average exchange rate was: $1=¥201.40; in April 2007, it was: $1=¥118.64.

This case study was prepared by André Achtstätter, MBA participant at the ENPC MBA Paris, and W. Henning Blarr, Research Assistant under the supervision of Tawfik Jelassi, Dean and Professor of e-Business and IT at the School of International Management of Ecole Nationale des Ponts et Chaussées (ENPC, Paris). It is intended to be used as the basis for class discussion rather than to illustrate effective or ineffective handling of a management situation.

This case study is made possible thanks to the cooperation of Mr. Yuichi Kato, President & Chief Executive Officer of NTT DoCoMo Europe.

Exhibit 1 Evolution of NTT DoCoMo subscribers and mobile phone services

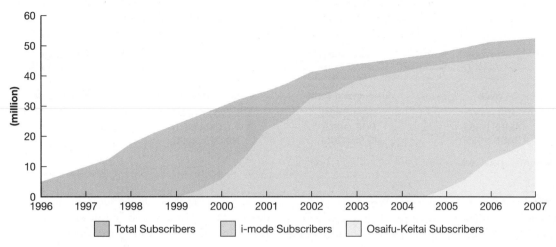

Source: NTT DoCoMo, 2007

Second Generation (2G) mobile communications technology included D-AMPS[3] in the U.S., GSM[4] in Europe and PDC[5] in Japan. NTT DoCoMo started operations in a highly competitive environment, characterized by an overregulated mobile phone market, poor transmission quality, costly subscription fees, and heavy handsets. The company established in 1993 its PDC service, named 'mova', including voice services, call waiting, voice mail, three-way calling, call forwarding, data service (up to 9.6 Kbit/s[6]), and packet-switched wireless data (up to 28.8 Kbit/s) (see Exhibit 2).

NTT DoCoMo charged for voice calls ¥95 per minute and basic subscription plans started at ¥8,000 per month. By introducing the PDC service, it was the first to provide customers with a high transmission quality. This new service brought clearer communications, less background noise and fewer call interruptions. Within months, PDC became the standard in Japan and was adopted by competitors, whereas demand was artificially held back by regulators.

Creating wireless internet services

Network infrastructure close to collapse

During the 15 years that followed the 1979 launch of the world's first commercial cellular service, only 2.1 million subscribers signed up for this service. In the mid 1990s, several factors, including 2G mobile services, market deregulation, as well as lower subscription fees and

handset costs, led to a rapid customer uptake. For the first three years after deregulation, the number of mobile phone subscribers doubled every year. In 1997, NTT DoCoMo's competitor KDD announced an alliance with DDI, forming the KDDI group. Two years later, the merger between Digital Phone Group (DPG) and Digital TU-KA Group led to the creation of J-Phone Co. Ltd.

Due to the rapid growth of cellular phones in Japan, NTT DoCoMo's network was by 1997 close to collapse, suffering from dropped calls and poor transmission quality. The company knew that if it could entice subscribers to use through the existing network more data than voice, it would postpone investing in a completely new infrastructure. It noticed that Japanese mobile phone users frequently changed their handset – on average, every eight months. Handset features were one factor that the company could control, due to the leverage it had over cell phone manufacturers. However, in Japan dial-up Internet access was too expensive for most users and PC penetration was very low.

---

3 IS-54 and IS-136 are second-generation mobile phone systems, known as Digital AMPS (D-AMPS), used throughout the Americas, particularly in the United States and Canada.

4 The Global System for Mobile Communications (GSM) is the most popular standard for mobile phones in the world. GSM service is used by over 2 billion people across more than 212 countries and territories.

5 Personal Digital Cellular (PDC) is a 2G mobile phone standard developed and used exclusively in Japan.

6 A kilobit per second (Kbit/s) is a unit of data transfer rate.

Exhibit 2 **Different generations of mobile phone services**

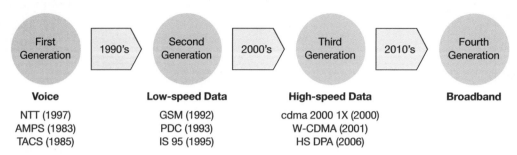

First Generation	1990's	Second Generation	2000's	Third Generation	2010's	Fourth Generation
Voice		**Low-speed Data**		**High-speed Data**		**Broadband**
NTT (1997)		GSM (1992)		cdma 2000 1X (2000)		
AMPS (1983)		PDC (1993)		W-CDMA (2001)		
TACS (1985)		IS 95 (1995)		HS DPA (2006)		

Source: NTT DoCoMo, 2007.

Developing and launching i-mode

Until 1997, although most of its wireless data services were not very successful, NTT DoCoMo believed in their future market potential. In October 1998, right after the Asian financial crisis, it went for its Initial Public Offering (IPO) at the Tokyo Stock Exchange and became listed in the Nikkei 225 Index. In December 1998, it acquired the Personal Handyphone System (PHS) business from NTT Personal Group.

In January 1997, Kouji Ohboshi asked Keiichi Enoki to design, develop and launch a new mobile data communication service to be delivered over a single handset and target the mass market. The new service was called 'i-mode', with 'i' standing for interactive, Internet and information.

At first, the i-mode team thought of launching SMS and information services similar to those offered by their competitor, J-Phone (J-Sky Web services). It also looked at new business models developed in the PC-Internet environment and tried to understand the correlation between the number of sites and the number of Internet users. The more content was available on the Net, the greater the number of users, and vice-versa. However, some team members did not believe that simply putting information on the mobile network would differentiate i-mode from the existing PC-based Internet. They thought that users would need some guidance and selective information for the new service to be truly useful. The idea was then to offer a user-friendly menu that customers could prompt through a single click of the 'i' button of the handset. This main menu, showing simple information categories and made easy to navigate, enabled accessing a large number of useful sites.

Based on the above design ideas, the i-mode team developed an innovative business model. NTT DoCoMo collaborated closely with equipment manufacturers, content providers and other operators to ensure that wireless technology, content quality and user experience evolve in parallel. This synchronization guaranteed that customers, partners, and shareholders had converging objectives, thus enabling all parties to maximize value and improve the quality of the products and services accessed through i-mode.

> From cell phones for talking to cell phones for using, this is where the cell phone market is going. Voice-less communication is sure to exceed voice communication in the future![7]

On February 22nd 1999 the i-mode service was launched and attracted 17.2 million subscribers by the end of 2000, 30.2 million by the end of 2001 and 47.6 million subscribers by the end of March 2007 (see Exhibit 3).

The i-mode technology

i-mode websites are created with 'i-mode Compatible HTML', a subset of the standard HTML[8]. Converting existing HTML websites to the i-mode format requires only minor changes, making it fast and easy to create new content. As a result, the number of i-mode sites is high and still rising.

In order to provide users with an 'always-on' network access, the i-mode team designed a packet-switched communications technology, eliminating the need to log on or log off. This meant that no dedicated radio

---

7 Kouji Ohboshi, in Computing, Japan, Vol. 6, Issue 4, April 1999.
8 Hypertext Markup Language (HTML) is the predominant markup language for the creation of web pages.

Exhibit 3 Evolution of i-mode services and number of subscribers

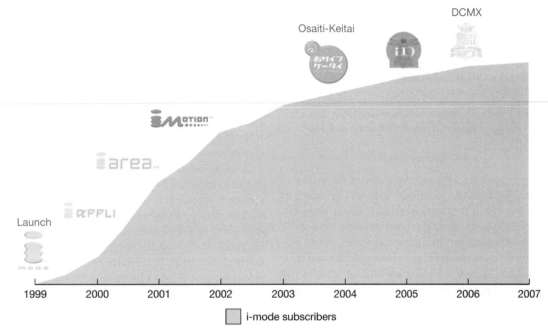

i-mode subscribers

Source: NTT DoCoMo, 2007.

channel is required for accessing i-mode sites, thus lowering costs for customers since they are only billed for the data volume which they send and receive. During all the development phases, NTT DoCoMo pursued a policy of open technology exchange with the world's leading research organizations, mobile communication operators, and equipment manufacturers.

The first i-mode handsets looked like mobile phones of that time, but had a larger LCD[9] screen and the distinctive 'i' button. The screens were able to display up to 48 Japanese characters (corresponding to 6 lines of text). Retail prices for the handsets, still heavily subsidized by the operator, ranged from ¥35,900 to ¥42,800, an increase of about 25% over regular mobile phones. Users were charged a ¥300 monthly fee to subscribe to the i-mode service, between ¥100 and ¥300 for each site they subscribe to, plus the voice and data transmission fees based on usage volume.

Expanding the i-mode services
Since they used 2G technology mova, the first i-mode services that NTT DoCoMo offered (including e-mail or text-based push-information) had a small amount of

data usage. However, the transfer of Java technologies[10] from the PC to the mobile phone was the starting point for the company to offer in January 2001 'i-appli' services which consisted of software (programs) that can be used with i-mode compatible phones. By downloading an i-appli service, users can broaden the functions of their mobile phone. For example a game portal site is available at the iMenu with a monthly charge of ¥525 per game used.

To get quick and easy area information, i-area was introduced in July 2001 and integrated into the iMenu. This service automatically selects and displays i-mode content that is related to the geographical location of the user. The latter does not select service areas since base stations recognize his/her location and offer location-based content such as weather, restaurants, town information, maps, nearby ATM[11], etc. With the

---

9 A liquid crystal display (LCD) is a thin, flat display device made up of any number of color or monochrome pixels arrayed in front of a light source or reflector.
10 Java technology, which was developed by Sun Microsystems, is a system for developing and deploying cross-platform applications.
11 ATM stands for Automatic Teller Machines.

'imadoco-search' (¥210 per month), the user can pinpoint the position of the people that he/she cares about, or set up a scheduled search.

Setting up the IT infrastructure

Third-generation mobile communication technology

Voice communication services decreased but data communication increased. It makes stabilizing total ARPU.[12]

Tatsuro Hayakawa, Director, DoCoMo Europe

Before i-mode became successful, Kouji Ohboshi had to struggle to develop this new data service. Since its costs threatened the financial stability of the company, some opponents of the project thought that NTT DoCoMo was wasting its time and money.

However, the company was first to market and its i-mode service enjoyed a few months of competitive lead. By exploiting its first mover's advantage, NTT DoCoMo was able to minimize the threat of new entrants and take advantage of the market expansion. Right after the launch, several other wireless Internet offerings became available and some of them offered enhanced services.

In October 2001, NTT DoCoMo became the world's first carrier to launch a W-CDMA[13]-based 3G service, called 'FOMA[14].' The 3G technology enabled shifting the use of mobile phones from data and voice communication only to enhanced and highly differentiated services (see Exhibit 3). Deployed in the 2 GHz frequency band, FOMA transmitted data on the downlink ranging from 64 Kbit/s to 384 Kbit/s, compared to 28.8 Kbit/s with the 2G standard PDC. High handset prices and technical problems, such as short battery life and poor reception within buildings, reduced the demand for 3G devices. KDDI launched its next-generation service in April 2002 using the CDMA2000-1X[15] standard, a 2.5G technology. Although the downlink of 144 Kbit/s was slower than NTT DoCoMo's FOMA, the company was able to offer at lower prices better-equipped phones, using the existing network. SoftBank, the third mobile communications provider in Japan, introduced in December 2002 its W-CDMA-based 3G services.

Mobile multimedia

Three years after i-mode's launch, NTT DoCoMo offered several highly differentiated services, aligned with the i-Menu that went beyond the traditional mobile phone functions. Just as important as the enhancements of the net-infrastructure was the continuous improvement of the handset, moving from being a telephone to becoming a miniaturized entertainment device.

Digital camera technology integrated in mobile phones enabled the offering in June 2002 of the 'i-shot' service. i-mode users could send pictures taken with their phone to other DoCoMo phones, non-DoCoMo phones and even to personal computers. The maximum size authorized for i-shots increased from 100kb[16] to 500kb, thus allowing users to send high-quality (megapixel) images.

To send videos taken with the mobile phone, NTT DoCoMo introduced in January 2003 the 'i-motion mail' service. Compared to similar competing services, i-motion mail provides a consistent frame rate[17] of 15 fps[18], allowing a fluid and smooth rendering. Since videos were converted to the size (or format) supported by the receiving terminal, this service offers an exchange of videos between FOMA phones, non-FOMA phones and personal computers. To offer this compatibility, videos sent via i-motion were first temporarily stored on a server, while the receiver gets an e-mail with the link, allowing him/her to download the video within 10 days. Charges for the i-shot and i-motion mail services vary depending on the data volume used through each service.

Launched in January 2005, 'i-channel' enables users to connect to a wide range of channels, such as news, sports, entertainment, or fortune. It is a push-service that updates its content every two hours from morning to night. In order to foster its uptake, new handsets included a special i-channel button. The displayed information, comparable to RSS-Feeds[19], is free of communication charges but additional packet charges of about ¥157.50 apply when detailed content is viewed. By the end of 2007, DoCoMo had more than 10 million i-channel users.

---

12 Statement made during a meeting held in Paris on March 7th 2007 with the case study authors.
13 Wideband Code Division Multiple Access (W-CDMA) is a type of 3G cellular network.
14 Freedom of Mobile Multimedia Access (FOMA) is the brand name for NTT DoCoMo's 3G services and compatible with standard UMTS.
15 CDMA2000 is a hybrid 2.5G/3G protocol of mobile telecommunications standards.
16 A kilobyte (kb) is a unit of data storage on a computer.
17 The frame rate is the measurement of how quickly an imaging device produces unique consecutive images called frames.
18 The frame rate is most often expressed in frames per second (fps).
19 Really Simple Syndication (RSS) is a web feed format which is used to publish frequently updated digital content.

Beyond the mobile frontier

In 1999, Kouji Ohboshi and Keiji Tachikawa initiated a project called 'Vision 2010' and carried out by the Corporate Strategy Planning Department of NTT DoCoMo. The aim was to stimulate further growth of the mobile communications market through the use of mobile multimedia. The project was based on five key concepts nicknamed MAGIC (Mobile Multimedia; Anytime, Anywhere, Anyone; Global Mobility Support; Integrated Wireless Solutions and Customized Personal Service).

In 2002, NTT DoCoMo produced a video illustrating its 2010 vision of mobile multimedia services and the opportunities they offer to customers, enriching personal lives and supporting global corporate activities. According to this vision, mobile data services will play a greater role in people's life and focus on the needs of women, children, senior citizens and handicapped people.

A 'Mobile Remote Learning System,' which enables the transmission of 3D optic sensitive touch over the air and can be used for network community schools, is one of the new services illustrating Vision 2010. Other services include a mobile digital wallet that fosters e-commerce purchases and enables customers to pay merchants online even for micro charges. Customer's input information ensures an optimized and smooth handling at delivery points. A 'Mobile Town Monitoring System' provides customers with information like seat availability at restaurants, real-time data on urban situations, traffic jams, etc. 'Mobile Medical Examination Systems' enable online examinations; hospital databases are linked through the network with doctors and patients to allow remote and speedy medical diagnosis. The 'Mobile Virtual Laboratory' links the mobile network with large-volume databases 24 hours a day permitting environmental monitoring in places difficult to access. Furthermore, the mobile network combines personal data in an all-in-one terminal for daily situations like passport control in airports or contact-less flight check in (the latter service is called 'One-Stop Boarding System'). Public transport traffic systems and user terminals are linked to buses enabling efficient route planning and allowing users to select boarding times (this service is called 'Bus-On-Demand System').

The Vision 2010 project is aligned with NTT DoCoMo's corporate social responsibility; it ultimately aims at contributing to a healthier and more secure society while strengthening the company's brand in a highly competitive and globalized market. The technology underpinning Vision 2010 is expected to lead the strategy of NTT DoCoMo into the future, creating a new generation of wireless services and positioning the company as a lifestyle service provider.

The mobile phone as a 'lifestyle infrastructure' tool

Increasing rivalry in the marketplace

> If NTT DoCoMo sticks with simply carrying voice and data, it ll have no way to go but down![20]
>
> **Philip Sugai**, Marketing researcher at the International University of Japan in Niigata

By December 2006, Japan had a population of 128 million people inculding 95 million mobile phone subscribers, representing a penetration rate of 74% (see Exhibit 4). NTT DoCoMo leads the market and is followed respectively by KDDI and SoftBank; the latter took over the business of Vodafone KK (see Exhibit 5).

As of March 2007 NTT DoCoMo had 52.6 million subscribers divided into 17.1 million subscribers to the 2G service (mova) and 35.5 million subscribers to the 3G service (FOMA). Among the 52.6 million subscribers, 47.6 million are i-mode subscribers and 21 million are Osaifu-Keitai subscribers. Its operating revenues for the Financial Year 2006 were 33.6 billion Euros. In March 2005, its market share was 56.12%; it dropped to 55.72% by December 2006 and to 54.41% by March 2007 (see Exhibit 5).

KDDI offers 2G (cdmaOne) and 3G (CDMA2000-1X) network types and had, by December 2006, 26.6 million subscribers (corresponding to 27.8% market share) and operating revenues of €16 billion. SoftBank also offers 2G (PDC) and 3G (W-CDMA) network types (see Exhibit 6 for a technical comparison of mobile telecommunication operators in Japan) and had, by December 2006, 15.8 million subscribers (corresponding to 16.3% market share) but its operating revenues were not disclosed. SoftBank bought in the spring of 2005 the mobile phone business of Vodafone, which left Japan after its market share declined from 17.6% in 2002 to 16.6% in 2006.

---

20 Quoted in Business Week, June 2005.

Exhibit 4 Performance in Japan

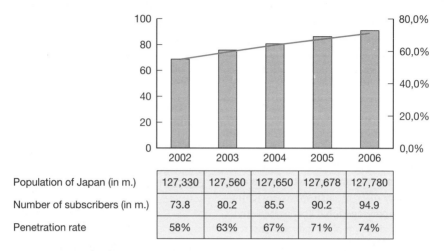

	2002	2003	2004	2005	2006
Population of Japan (in m.)	127,330	127,560	127,650	127,678	127,780
Number of subscribers (in m.)	73.8	80.2	85.5	90.2	94.9
Penetration rate	58%	63%	67%	71%	74%

Source: Statistics Bureau, Ministry of Internal Affairs & Communication/Telecommunication Carriers Association.

After the struggle and subsequent sale of the Vodafone operations in Japan, foreign companies were cautious to enter the Japanese mobile phone market.[21]

Tatsuro Hayakawa, Director, DoCoMo Europe

Strong competition within the nearly saturated market led to the decline of the industry's average revenue per unit (ARPU) for voice services from ¥6,320 per month in December 2002 to an estimated ¥4,720 per month in 2007. All three mobile network providers have reported a customer migration from 2G to 3G services. To attract customers, mobile network providers introduced flat-rate pricing (which include voice and data

---

21 Statement made during a meeting held in Paris on March 7th 2007 with the case study authors.

Exhibit 5 Competitiors' share of the mobile telecommunications market in Japan

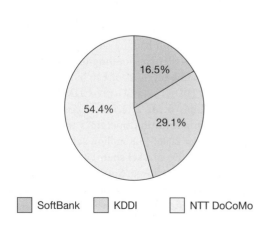

NTT DoCoMo	Operating Revenues	33.6 Billion €
	Subscribers	52.2 millions
	ARPU	42.72 €
	Churn rate	0.93% / month
KDDI	Operating Revenues	16.08 Billion €
	Subscribers	27.2 millions
	ARPU	42.27 €
	Churn rate	1% / month
SoftBank	Operating Revenues	N.A.
	Subscribers	15.5 millions
	ARPU	35.61 €
	Churn rate	1.6% / month

Legend: ■ SoftBank □ KDDI □ NTT DoCoMo

Source: NTT DoCoMo, KDDI, Softbank, 2007.

Exhibit 6 **Technical comparison of mobile telecommunication operators in Japan**

		NTT DoCoMo	KDDI	SoftBank
Network	2G	PDC	PDC, CDMA	PDC
	3G	W-CDMA	CDMA 2000	W-CDMA
	3.5 G	HSDPA	EV-DO Rev.A	HSDPA
Handset	Brand	Own Brand	Own Brand	Own Brand
	One-Segment TV	✓	✓	✓
	GPS	✓	✓	✓
Portal		i-mode	EZ-Web	Yahoo!Keitai
Services	Video-Conferencing	✓	✓	✓
	Full Music Downloads	✓	✓	✓
	E-Wallet (FeliCa)	✓	✓	✓
	Data Flat Rate	✓	✓	✓
Credit Business		i-mode	✗	✗
International Roaming (Handset Roaming)		149 Countries and Regions	22 Countries and Regions	173 Countries and Regions

Source: NTT DoCoMo, KDDI, SoftBank, 2007.

services); however, these pricing models made revenue and ARPU growth even more difficult.

The competition is expected to increase, since two new companies have entered the market in spring 2007. Offering attractive deals and promotions, EMOBILE plans to acquire 5 million subscribers and IP Mobile aims at reaching 11.6 million subscribers within the next five years (see Exhibit 7).

Responding to new challenges

NTT DoCoMo serves its customers with an integrated service model.[22]

Yuichi Kato, President & CEO, DoCoMo Europe

The strategy of NTT DoCoMo is to achieve sustained growth by focusing on a customer-oriented management policy. In 2004, under the leadership of Masao Nakamura and in order to be more competitive, the company implemented this policy which called for a drastic reform of operations with respect to the rate structure, handset lineup, network quality and after-

sales support. As a result of these efforts, the churn rate (subscriber termination rate) was reduced to 0.77% (which was the lowest figure ever) but increased in the 3rd Quarter of 2006 to 0.93%. However, NTT DoCoMo still has today the lowest churn rate in the market. Furthermore, it achieved in 2005 the largest market

---

22 Statement made during a meeting held in Paris on March 7th 2007 with the case study authors.

Exhibit 7 **New entrants into the mobile telecommunications market in Japan**

New Entrant	E MOBILE	IP Mobile
Network	W-CDMA	TDD/TD-CDMA
Launch Date	March 31, 2007	Spring, 2007
Planned number of subscribers after 5 years from launch	5.05 million	11.6 million

Source: EMobile, IP Mobile, 2007.

Exhibit 8 mova and FOMA subscribers in Japan

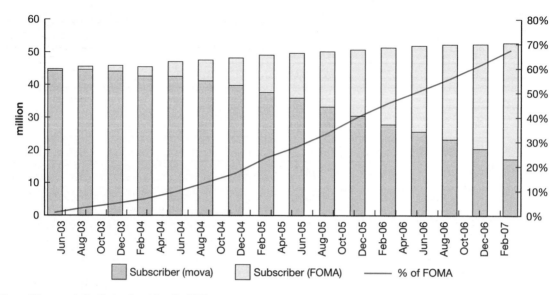

Source: Telecommunication Carriers Association, May 2007.

share of net additional subscriptions, which was 48.7%, but this figure dropped during the first 9 months of 2006 to 34%. Its main competitor KDDI increased its market share of net additional subscriptions from 14.2% in 2002 to 48.1% in 2006. In 2006 the migration from mova services to FOMA services led to this increase. The total number of FOMA subscribers increased to 32.11 million, representing 61.5% of total subscribers (see Exhibit 8).

The first priority of the customer-oriented management policy is to strengthen the core business by improving the quality of the FOMA network and expanding the number of base stations. The creation of new revenue streams was aimed at compensating the slowdown of the mobile phone market and helping to achieve sustained growth. NTT DoCoMo expected that national and international equity and business alliances to be critical for generating new revenue sources and creating synergies with the core mobile phone business. These alliances cover the following five areas: payments and commercial transactions, broadcasting, content and Internet, global services, and mobile phone peripheral technology. Yuichi Kato said:

> The mobile phone industry is driven by innovation. NTT DoCoMo's strategy is to be the first-mover in the market with new services. In Japan we are one month ahead of the competition. However, between Japan and the inter-

national market, there is a technology gap of about one year.[23]

Between 2002 and 2006, NTT DoCoMo's net profit margin was volatile: it was –2.49% in 2002, 4.42% in 2003, 12.88% in 2004, 15.43% in 2005 and 12.81% in 2006.[24] The financial performance of NTT DoCoMo provided returns to shareholders and Standard & Poor's rated it AA- with a stable outlook.

Strengthening the core business

> We will continue to offer and promote new services aggressively![25]

Masao Nakamura, President & CEO, NTT DoCoMo

The mobile phone has become an integral element of consumers' daily life and its use shifted from being just a communication and information tool (as it was in the 1990s) to becoming a mode of self-expression. Thus NTT

---

23 Statement made during a meeting held in Paris on March 7th 2007 with the case study authors.
24 Regarding the ROE analysis of NTT DoCoMo, the net profit margin was the only ratio that was very volatile. The Asset Turnover ratio as well as the leverage did not drastically change. The ROE in 2002 was –3.53%, 6.11% in 2003, 17.55% in 2004, 19.13% in 2005 and 15.07% in 2006. It was driven by the volatile net profit margin.
25 Quoted in Telecommunications International, January 2005.

DoCoMo diversified its range of services and handsets in order to meet new customers' needs and expectations.

Handsets tailored to customers' needs

DoCoMo focused on expanding its standard handset models in order to make them suitable for the core customer segment. It also developed special models that meet various user needs. Handsets are manufactured by several well-known companies, but all bear the NTT DoCoMo brand name.

Firstly, DoCoMo defines the product lineup, commercial launch date and required functions for each handset series which includes several models. Secondly, a detailed plan for a specific handset is discussed and finalized by DoCoMo and each manufacturer. Lastly, the handset is developed according to the specifications also provided by DoCoMo.

> Japanese customers only trust good brands![26]
>
> **Yuichi Kato**, President & CEO, DoCoMo Europe

Standard handset models offer a wealth of up-to-date choices and primarily target the core segment of mobile phone users whose age ranges between teens and mid-thirties. There is on the one hand the '9 series', which is equipped with advanced features, and on the other hand the '7 series', which offers a balance between design and functionality.

In September 2004, DoCoMo introduced its FOMA 'RAKU RAKU Phone', the first model in the easy-to-use Raku Raku phone series that is compatible with the 3G network. Current Raku Raku phones, including the one designed by Kenya Hara (a renowned graphic designer and art director of the popular goods manufacturer Muji), offer special features like 'Slow Voice' and 'Clear Voice'. The former feature improves comprehensibility through embedded software that slows the other person's voice speed, while the later one automatically adjusts voice and ringtone volume according to the surrounding noise level. Enhanced 'Read Aloud' audibly announces the name of the caller or e-mail sender and provides audio readouts of i-mode pages, while 'Simple Mail Generation' offers pre-set messages for quick replies to e-mails. The Raku-Raku PHONE Basic is compatible with i-channel and the text can be displayed in large letters for easy reading. Besides the above standard series, DoCoMo offers a range of handsets targeting the various needs and preferences of special customer groups.

Innovative mobile services

> Knowing how horrible it is for a kid to get snatched, at least someone is trying something. However, there is not a single company that does things without thinking of a profit margin.
>
> **An NTT DoCoMo customer**, Tokyo, November 2005

In Japan, the increase in crime against school children led NTT DoCoMo to introduce in March 2005 the 'Kids' PHONE', which the company considered as part of its corporate social responsibility. This handset includes a GPS function, providing the user's geographical location and a crime prevention buzzer interlinked with the functions of the phone and sending a mail even when the handset is switched off. A battery lock prevents the battery destruction by a third party. Using the imodoco search service, the handset has additional functions such as the confirmation about the user's whereabouts (including date and time), retrieval of location information when the device is turned off, and a mail notification of the user's location to its guardian when the crime prevention buzzer is triggered. Four months after the Kids' PHONE was launched, 170,000 units of it were sold.

NTT DoCoMo also launched in April 2006 the 'SIMPURE series', which simplified the handset by narrowing down its functions. This model targeted cost-conscious customers. In April 2007, it launched a new 3G FOMA handset developed with award-winning designer Stefano Giovannoni (the creator of highly acclaimed designs for world-famous companies such as Alessi) and the collaboration of the handset manufacturer NEC Corporation. Giovannoni also designed the new exhibition booth of the company, entitled 'DoCoMo: New Vibes from Stefano Giovannoni – design for cellular phones.' This move enabled DoCoMo to enter the market of designer handsets, a move also made by Motorola with Dolce&Gabbana and LG with Prada.

Upgrading the network

> Higher speed and larger capacity are the characteristics of future networks.[27]
>
> **Shinsuke Kuroda**, Manager, DoCoMo Europe

---

26 Statement made during a meeting held in Paris on March 7th 2007 with the case study authors.

27 Statement made during a meeting held in Paris on March 7th 2007 with the case study authors.

In December 2005, NTT DoCoMo was the first mobile telecom operator in Japan to introduce the 'push-to-talk' walkie-talkie features. Using handsets made by manufacturers such as Mitsubishi, Matsushita and NEC, users were able to simultaneously talk to several people by pressing a button on the i-phone. Customers pay ¥5 per 'push' or ¥1,000 per month if they subscribe to the 'all-you-can-use' plan, while users wishing to speak to up to 20 people at once need to sign up to an upgraded plan for ¥2,000 per month. In addition, NTT DoCoMo offered a wireless LAN[28] service (called 'MZone'), using Wi-Fi[29] to provide high-speed data transmission at up to 11 Mbit/s for PDAs and mobile PCs. As part of the transition from 3.5G to 4G, NTT DoCoMo's R&D effort aims at creating a network with even a higher speed and larger capacity. Introduced in August 2006, HSDPA (3.5G) can achieve a speed of up to 14 Mbit/s even when using the same 5 MHz frequency band as W-CDMA (3G) (see Exhibit 11).

Setting up new partnerships in Japan

By expanding the applications of mobile phones beyond communication, we are promoting the creation of a 'lifestyle infrastructure.' We consider that collaboration with businesses in various sectors will be even more essential than before.[30]

Masao Nakamura, President & CEO, NTT DoCoMo

In July 2004, NTT DoCoMo launched the i-mode FeliCa service for mobile wallet applications (see Exhibit 9). FeliCa is a contactless RFID[31] microprocessor-based smart card system by Sony, primarily used in electronic money cards. First used in the Octopus card system[32] in Hong Kong, the technology is also integrated in a variety of cards in countries such as Singapore and Japan. FeliCa is externally powered; i.e., it does not need a battery to operate. The card uses power supplied from the special FeliCa card reader when the card comes within its range. When the data transfer is completed, the reader stops supplying power.

Mobile FeliCa is an adaptation of FeliCa for use in mobile phones by FeliCa Networks, a subsidiary company of both NTT DoCoMo and Sony. NTT DoCoMo developed a wallet phone concept, called 'Osaifu-Keitai', based on mobile FeliCa and set up a wide network of business partnerships. Sony started shipping the FeliCa cards in 1996 and has since shipped approximately 160 million micro-processors for use in FeliCa-based cards (such as 'Suica[33]' and 'Edy[34]') and over 40 million

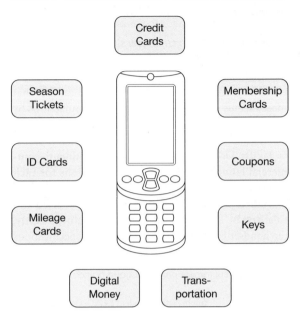

Exhibit 9 The mobile wallet: i-mode FeliCa services

Source: NTT DoCoMo, 2007.

Mobile FeliCa chips (used in Osaifu-Keitai mobile phones with digital wallet functions). Handsets equipped with the FeliCa chip can be used for a variety of functions, including train pass, debit card (digital wallet), credit card and personal identification card. FeliCa-enabled touch-and-go payments work over a distance of a few centimeters and take 0.1 second to complete a transaction.

The mobile wallet service

The first Osaifu-Keitai wallet service 'Edy', provided by bitWallet Inc., made the mobile phone a pre-paid rechargeable smart card. Activated via i-appli, the e-money could be loaded onto the handset and the

---

28 A local area network (LAN) is a computer network.
29 Wi-Fi is a brand to describe the underlying technology of wireless local area networks (WLAN).
30 Quoted in Telecommunications International, Japan, February 2006.
31 Radio-frequency identification (RFID) is an automatic identification method, relying on storing and remotely retrieving data using devices called RFID tags or transponders.
32 The Octopus card is a rechargeable contactless stored value smart card used to transfer electronic payments in online or offline systems in Hong Kong.
33 Suica is a rechargeable contactless smart card used as a fare card on train lines in Japan, launched in November 2001.
34 Edy is a prepaid rechargeable contactless smart card.

customer could pay simply by waving the handset across a reader/writer at participating stores or vending machines. In addition to the terminal's cost, merchants are charged a transaction fee ranging from 2% to 3% of the transaction value.

Complementary to Edy, NTT DoCoMo introduced in November 2005 the 'ToruCa'[35] service. ToruCa enables customers to obtain information by simply waving their phones in front of a dedicated reader/writer installed at restaurants, theaters, music stores, arcades and other establishments. For example, when users buy a CD at a store using Osaifu-Keitai, they can wave their DoCoMo phone in front of the store's reader/writer to retrieve extra information about the CD, artist, etc., and possibly a promotional coupon offered by the artist's recording label. Information obtained from readers/writers are available at i-mode sites. Moreover, users could perform customized searches to receive the information they are looking for (see Exhibit 10).

In January 2006, East Japan Railway Company (JR East) launched a service named Mobile Suica[36] enabling users through their mobile Suica handset to 'touch and go' by just holding the mobile phone near the sensor of the automatic fare gate and be on their way. The new service also enabled mobile phone users to conduct all ticket-related transactions such as reservations, purchases and fare collection. Moreover, Mobile Suica-ready phones can be used to pay for purchases at JR East railway stations and other stores that support the service.

NTT DoCoMo merges its credit card and mobile phone businesses

We consider that the market has extremely high potential for growth by improving infrastructure and services, and promoting the use of credit via the phone. In specific terms, we expect sales revenue to reach about ¥100 billion, but regarding the specific time when such a figure will be achieved, we cannot as yet say.

Masao Nakamura, President & CEO, NTT DoCoMo

In April 2005, NTT DoCoMo agreed to invest about ¥98 billion in Sumitomo Mitsui Card Co. to promote a new payment service through Osaifu-Keitai. This investment led to the launch of the mobile credit platform 'iD' and the consumer credit service 'DCMX'. The idea to enter the credit business resulted from two market trends: the increasing number of Osaifu-Keitai users, and the expanding Japanese credit card market. Moreover, the domestic credit card market had a strong potential in the small-account payment (less than ¥3,000) market, which NTT DoCoMo estimated to be worth ¥57 million annually.

NTT DoCoMo's first stage of participation in the credit business was the provision in December 2005 of the credit platform iD. Users could complete their payments quickly by waiving their Osaifu-Keitai device,

---

35 ToruCa is a term coined from two Japanese words, 'Toru' (pronounced 'toe-roo') meaning capture and 'Ca' (pronounced 'kah') is the first sound of the word for card.
36 Suica stands for 'Super Urban Intelligent Card'.

Exhibit 10 **NTT DoCoMo press release**

McDonald's and DoCoMo to Jointly Promote e-Marketing based on Osaifu-Keitai Partnerships

TOKYO, JAPAN, February 26, 2007 --- McDonald's Holdings Company (Japan), Ltd. and NTT DoCoMo, Inc. today announced they have agreed to jointly promote e-marketing based on DoCoMo Osaifu-Keitai™ e-wallet services. The undertaking will include the establishment of a joint venture company to plan and manage e-marketing promotions to McDonald's newly planned membership club, and the introduction of DoCoMo's iD™ platform for mobile-phone credit cards and ToruCa™ information-capture service at McDonald's stores.

McDonald's plans to establish the membership club by October 2007 to offer enhanced membership services and to strengthen customer loyalty. Members of a current membership club will be invited to join the new club. Mobile services for iD credit-card payments and ToruCa information capture will be introduced in McDonald's stores throughout Japan beginning in October 2007. The joint venture company will aim to quickly launch services by integrating the massive customer bases comprised of McDonald's 1.4 billion annual customers and DoCoMo's 52 million mobile phone subscribers, as well as their respective brands and know-how. The company will be established in July 2007 with paid-in capital of 300 million yen, 70% coming from McDonald's and 30% from DoCoMo.

Source: NTT DoCoMo, 2007.

like using Edy. In addition, iD is an open model platform, which allows various credit card companies to provide their mobile credit service via iD. To expand the number of places where iD can be used, DoCoMo secured cooperation with Sumitomo Mitsui Card Co. and UC Card Co., reaching 320,000 installed iD terminals by April 2006.

The launch of NTT DoCoMo's credit card service is the second stage of participation in the credit business. Since April 2006, DoCoMo has been offering the consumer credit service 'DCMX Mini' to customers over 12 years of age and applying for it through the i-mode website, and 'DCMX' as a normal credit card to customers over 18 years of age. DCMX Mini offers a monthly credit line of ¥10,000, and DCMX offers a monthly credit line of ¥200,000. The service of DCMX Mini can be made available through the pre-installed i-appli software. Payments of DCMX Mini are billed at the end of each month together with the user's phone bill.

> I don't think these types of services represent a global trend. They are going to be strictly in Japan![37]
>
> **Kirk Boodry**, telecoms analyst at Dresdner Kleinwort Wasserstein

Since the start of Osaifu-Keitai in 2004, the number of subscribers has quadrupled. By February 2007, NTT DoCoMo had 19 million customers using their handset as a digital wallet.

DoCoMo's international network and alliances

> Our basic international strategies are to expand i-mode alliances, enhance user convenience by global roaming and increase earning opportunities through investments in and partnerships with mobile operators and related businesses.[38]
>
> **Masao Nakamura**, President & CEO, NTT DoCoMo

In order to foster its international activities, NTT DoCoMo was in 2002 first listed on the London Stock Exchange and then on the New York Stock Exchange. In June 2004, Masao Nakamura was appointed DoCoMo President and CEO; prior to that he worked for both DoCoMo and NTT for 35 years and served as Senior Executive Vice-President since June 2002. Masao Nakamura said:

> The total number of subscriptions among our i-mode partners overseas had already exceeded six million as of December 2005. We will continue to consider potential new partners in markets where there are no i-mode services.[39]

NTT DoCoMo has been offering its i-mode service all over the world and has today outside of Japan more than 6 million i-mode subscribers in 25 countries. It has a cooperation agreement in Germany with e-plus since March 2002, in France with Bouygues Telecom since November 2002, and in Russia with MTC since September 2005. Furthermore, i-mode services were launched in several countries including Australia, Greece, Israel, Spain, Italy, Netherlands, Hong Kong, Philippines, Belgium, U.K., Taiwan and Singapore. The international strategy of NTT DoCoMo is to provide in each country the i-mode services through a strategic alliance with a local mobile network operator. Another important strategic issue is that NTT DoCoMo invested in international operators like HTCL in Hong Kong, FET in Taiwan, KTF in Korea and PLDT in the Philippines, Guam & Northern Mariana Islands.

NTT DoCoMo also invested in companies that are its main suppliers like Sumitomo Mitsui Card Co. or Lawson in the payment and commercial transactions business, and Fuji Television Network in the broadcasting sector. Through these investments, NTT DoCoMo hopes to be able to influence its suppliers' products.

> We select our partners according to our strategy and the strategy of our suppliers to create a win-win situation[40].
>
> **Yuichi Kato**, President and CEO, DoCoMo Europe

Internationally, NTT DoCoMo has offices in London where DoCoMo's European strategy is developed, in Paris where surveys of European regulations and markets are conducted, and in Amsterdam where the European expansion of the i-mode service is managed. Through its New York City office, NTT DoCoMo coordinates the company's strategy in the USA. DoCoMo's supporting center for world roaming is located in Hawaii. In China, NTT DoCoMo's offices in Beijing and Shanghai serve as liaison with the Chinese government and its related agencies and also for assessing opportunities for new business in China. In Singapore, DoCoMo's office collects data concerning mobile communications in India and the ten ASEAN countries.

NTT DoCoMo runs two overseas R&D centers in California: one center (DoCoMo Communications

---

37 Quoted in the Economist magazine, 2005.
38 Quoted in Telecom Asia, June 2006.
39 Quoted in Telecom Asia, June 2006.
40 Statement made during a meeting held in Paris on March 7th 2007 with the case study authors.

Laboratories USA, Inc.) which focuses on next-generation Internet technology and international standardization; the other center (DoCoMo Capital, Inc.) searches for and invests in venture companies with innovative state-of-the-art technology applicable to mobile communications services. DoCoMo Communications Laboratory in Munich (Germany), staffed with 35 researchers, focuses on next generation platform technologies and participates in research/standardization projects in Europe. The DoCoMo Beijing Communications Laboratory focuses on cutting-edge wireless technology aimed at the next generation of mobile communications and participates in standardization activities in China.

The know-how and technology transfers take place both ways between NTT DoCoMo's headquarters in Tokyo and its overseas offices. Patents and new technologies are imported to Japan to be implemented in new innovative products.

As of the end of March 2007, international services (like the roaming-out service) were expanded to 149 countries and regions for voice calls and short message services (SMS), packet communications to 98 countries and videophone calls to 36 countries.

A strong focus on R&D

NTT DoCoMo is determined to continue leading the way in the global mobile communications industry. In fiscal year 2005, NTT DoCoMo spent over ¥110 billion on R&D activities through its research laboratories and development centers in Japan and overseas. It continues exploring the new potential of mobile communications.

Human beings and mobile phones will merge

A new technology, which is already operational today, uses the human hand as part of the receiver. The Finger Whisper handset 'Yubi-Wa' being developed at the NTT DoCoMo Yokosuka R&D center is a quest for future communication possibilities and a new kind of wearable telephone handset. Worn on the wrist, this watch-like terminal converts voice to vibration through an actuator and channels this vibration through the bones to the tip of the index finger. By inserting this finger into the ear canal, the vibration can be heard as voice.

Another approach, named Mime Speech Recognition, enables handsets to recognize vowels from muscle activities around the mouth. Speech recognition is accomplished by electrodes on the face that detect electromyography in the underlying muscles. Currently,

the five vowel sounds in Japanese language (a, i, u, e, o) can already be recognized by this technique and consonants are currently in the works. Furthermore, the analysis of physiological information such as brainwaves, body temperature, and electromyography has a strong potential depending on what information is acquired and how it is utilized.

For Nayeem Islam, Vice President of NTT DoCoMo Inc.'s mobile software lab in San Jose (California),

> the future is in the software; the hardware is a commodity.[41]

Reaching a new level

By 2010, NTT DoCoMo plans to upgrade its network to the 'Super 3G' network for less than one-tenth of what it costs to roll out the existing infrastructure. The new network will enable uploads and downloads at up to 260 times the speed that is used in 2007 by FOMA. Initial investments will be around ¥100 to ¥200 billion.

NTT DoCoMo is currently carrying out research into the infrastructure required for the fourth generation mobile communications (4G). A key focus of this research is VSF-OFCDM (Variable Spreading Factor – Orthogonal Frequency and Code Division Multiplexing) technology, offering transmission at an extremely high speed of up to 100 Mbit/s outdoors and 1 Gbit/s[42] indoors. The basic functionality of this groundbreaking technology has already been confirmed and NTT DoCoMo is now conducting field tests and experiments. In fact, in a 4G field experiment conducted in December 2005, NTT DoCoMo achieved a maximum packet transmission speed of 2.5 Gbit/s, which is a world record. In December 2006, the company announced that it achieved a maximum packet transmission rate of approximately 5 Gbit/s in the downlink using 100 MHz frequency bandwidth to a mobile station moving at 10 km/h. The field experiment of fourth-generation (4G) radio access took place in Yokosuka, Kanagawa. As compared with the December 2005 test, the frequency spectrum efficiency, or the ratio of data transmission rate to channel bandwidth, was also doubled from 25 bit/s/Hz to 50 bit/s/Hz. Through its ongoing R&D activities, NTT DoCoMo aims at contributing significantly to the global standardization of 4G technology (see Exhibit 11).

---

41 Quoted in RCR Wireless News, 2004.
42 A gigabit per second (Gbit/s) is a unit of data transfer rate equal to 1,000 megabits per second.

Exhibit 11 NTT DoCoMo's planned network evolution

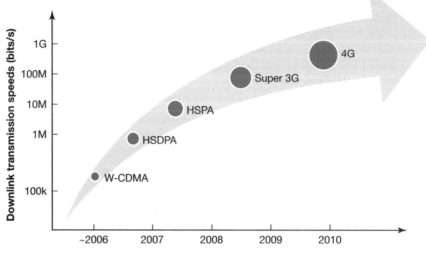

Source: NTT DoCoMo, 2007.

An uncertain future

We always keep our eyes on potential future technologies and markets.[43]

Yuichi Kato, President & CEO, DoCoMo Europe

With the launch of i-mode and Osaifu-Keitai, NTT DoCoMo shifted the purpose of mobile phones from voice-only to a multi-utility device and the company has been transforming itself from initially being a mobile network operator to becoming a lifestyle service provider.

In light of this new market positioning and the increasingly fierce competition, Yuichi Kato and his management team wondered what NTT DoCoMo should do in order to maintain its market lead. More specifically, what additional products and services should the company consider offering in order to sus-

tain its first-mover advantage in Japan and internationally? How can it leverage new technological advances (such as 4G and wearable technology) to create new customer value? How can it educate customers and generate demand in overseas markets where the technology gap with Japan is quite significant and NTT DoCoMo relies on its local partners for rolling out its mobile services? In further developing its innovation capability and marketing its high-tech products and services along its new 'life-style provider' positioning, NTT DoCoMo needs to properly determine the timing of its value delivery in Japan and overseas and assess the risk involved with its strategy.

---

43 Statement made during a meeting held in Paris on March 7th 2007 with the case study authors.

GLOSSARY

0G Mobile radio telephone systems preceded modern cellular mobile telephony technology. Since they were the predecessors of the first generation of cellular telephones, these systems are sometimes retroactively referred to as 0G (zero generation) systems.

1G First generation wireless telephone technology (1G) is a collective term for the analog mobile phone standards that were introduced in the 1980s.

2G Second generation wireless telephone technology (2G) is a collective term for the digital mobile standards that were introduced in the 1990s.

2.5G 2.5G is a stepping stone between 2G and 3G cellular wireless technologies. The term is used to describe 2G systems that have implemented a packet switched domain in addition to the circuit

switched domain. While the terms 2G and 3G are officially defined, 2.5G is not. It was invented for marketing purposes only.

3G Third generation technology (3G) is a collective term for mobile standards with the ability to transfer simultaneously both voice data (a telephone call) and non voice data (such as downloading information, exchanging email, and instant messaging).

3.5G High Speed Downlink Packet Access (HSDPA) is a 3G mobile telephony protocol which provides a roadmap for UMTS based networks to increase their data transfer speeds and capacity.

4G There is no definition yet for fourth generation technology (4G). However, the 4G will be a fully IP based integrated system capable of providing 100 Mbitls and IGbitis.

Source: Wikipedia.com.

YOC AG

Integrating the mobile phone into the marketing mix

YOC AG[1] – Integrating the mobile phone into the marketing mix

Fifty-nine year-old Geof Pearson cheers into the camera. He has just won £10,000 for himself and a massive £250,000 for his beloved football club, Hull City, to spend on a new player for the next season. 'I've been a Hull City fan all my life, so to personally win this huge transfer fund for the club makes me so proud. It's amazing to see how far we've come and hopefully this money can help us build for the future with a great new signing.'[2]

Geof had participated in one of Coca-Cola's Buy-a-Player campaigns through which a total of £600,000 has been given to clubs to fund the buying of new players. He was selected randomly from all participants in the draw who had entered an SMS code found under Coca-Cola bottle caps. Integrating the mobile phone, the Buy-a-Player campaign has become one of the most innovative sponsorship campaigns masterminded by YOC since its beginnings in the year 2000.

YOC and the beginnings of mobile marketing

A colleague of mine and I worked in the restructuring team of Roland Berger Strategy Consultants taking care of the very old economy. We had definitely nothing to do with the new economy, but of course we read the newspapers and it was hard for us to see that all these crazy ideas got

financed. So we thought that we could also start a business, and we were totally convinced of our idea.

Dirk Kraus, CEO, YOC AG

Dirk Kraus and his colleague came up with the idea of using the mobile phone as a marketing channel in April/May 2000, when the dot-com bubble had already burst. They had been observing the scene since 1999 and were astonished to see how often absurd ideas attracted enormous amounts of money from venture capitalists. Although they sometimes wondered how companies could make money with their often shady business models, they also saw a lot of interesting web-based business applications. However, they decided it would be difficult to come up with just another web-based idea because everything seemed to have already been done.

Yet their desire to set up their own business was strong. Even as more and more companies ran out of cash and finally went bankrupt in 2000, the two kept on

1 YOC is one of the leading mobile marketing providers in Europe, with branded goods producers from the consumer industry, trading and services sector as well as the automobile industry as its clients. YOC integrates the mobile phone into the media mix of clients and realizes technologically innovative and intelligent made-to-measure mobile marketing concepts that allow companies to increase sales and awareness, lead the consumer to the point of sale, generate dialogue-marketing contacts or enable customer loyalty programs. YOC stands for 'your opinion counts'.

2 http://www.coca-cola.co.uk/football/buyaplayer/winners.aspx.

This case was written by Matthias Promny, Research Associate at INSEAD (Fontainebleau), under the supervision of Tawfik Jelassi, Professor of e-Business and IT at the School of International Management at the Ecole Nationale des Ponts et Chaussées, Paris, Albrecht Enders, Assistant Professor at the School of Management at Friedrich Alexander University, Nürnberg and Charles Waldman, Senior Affiliate Professor of Marketing at INSEAD. It is intended to be used as a basis for class discussion rather than to illustrate either effective or ineffective handling of an administrative situation.

This case study was made possible by the cooperation of Dirk Kraus (CEO, YOC AG) and Stefanis Fehse (Head of Corporate Communication, YOC AG).

screening the market for feasible business models. When, in parallel to the developments on the Internet, they saw the number of text messages continue to rise from month to month, Kraus and Challier decided that the mobile phone as a new marketing channel could be of interest to them. The penetration rate of mobile phones was already higher than that of fixed-line Internet connections. Furthermore, they realized that the mobile handset was not only easy to use but was also very close to the user, thus allowing for more efficient and personal interaction with consumers than any other medium. Kraus remembers:

> At that time, we saw that marketing companies were looking for new approaches to get in contact with consumers. [...] We knew that we would have to start with 160 character text messages, but we also knew that this would not be the end.

Kraus had been studying marketing and corporate finance at the WHU in Koblenz, Germany,[3] and had a keen interest in new marketing approaches. Now that he could see the penetration rate rising from month to month, it became clear to him that sooner or later everybody would have a mobile phone. The auctioning of the UMTS licenses further underscored the assumption that transfer volumes would increase over time, along with the capacity of each mobile phone to show movies, display pictures or play sound. With a vision in mind to use the mobile phone as a rich marketing tool, the two entrepreneurs started to look for investors, as Kraus elaborates:

> When other companies went bankrupt, the attitude of VCs towards new ideas changed a lot. They became much more critical; however, at the end of the day, there were five VCs who wanted to invest into our idea. Although this was a very comfortable situation, we had to accept that the conditions had changed. Half a year before, we could have gotten twice the amount of capital for the same equity share.

The founders finally signed the contract on December 18th 2000. The team received €3.6 million in 2000. 80% of the capital was mezzanine capital[4], saddling the young company with a high interest rate burden of around 7.14% per year. The remaining 20% of the capital consisted of real equity. In exchange for the start-up money, 35% of the company went to the VCs, while 65% stayed with the founders.

Kraus recalls the start-up phase:

> We had 7 months from the first idea to the signing of the contract. If I would do the same thing again, I am quite sure that you could reduce the time from 7 months down to 4 or 5 months. The first 3 months, we were remodelling the idea and writing the business plan. We could have skipped that. It would have been better, if we had just done a very good presentation, communicated a clear view on the idea and afterwards gone through the process of writing the business plan together with the VCs, because we had to do so anyway. Since a VC wanted us to rewrite the business plan, we kind of did double work, but that's OK. That is experience, if you do something like this for the first time.

YOC finally started operating in January 2001. It had an office in Berlin, five people, and an ambition to make the mobile phone a feasible marketing tool.

YOC's business model and full service approach

Today, YOC is one of the leading mobile marketing providers in Europe, with branded goods producers from the consumer industry, the trading and services sector, and the automobile industry as its clients. In addition to its headquarters in Berlin, the company has offices in Vienna, London and Madrid and a workforce of approximately 75 employees. YOC's business (Exhibit 1) comprises three pillars: Mobile Marketing, Mobile B2C-Services and Affiliate Marketing.

- **Mobile Marketing**: YOC integrates the mobile phone into the media mix and realizes technologically innovative and intelligent, made-to-measure mobile marketing concepts. These concepts allow companies to increase sales and awareness, lead the consumer to the point of sale, generate dialogue-marketing contacts or enable customer loyalty programs. YOC deems itself as a full service provider, covering the whole value chain in mobile marketing since it offers its clients the full range from campaign design to reporting including creation, development and technical implementation.

- **Mobile B2C-Services:** YOC also offers a portfolio of self-developed or licensed mobile content such as logos, animation, themes and ring-tones. In

---

3 WHU – Otto Beisheim School of Management is a private international business school based in Koblenz, Germany; http://www.whu.edu.

Exhibit 1 **YOC business units**

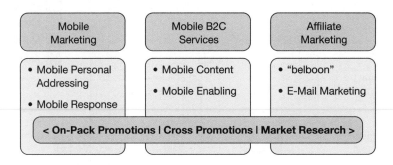

Source: YOC AG website.

addition, YOC has applications for mobile shipping and billing, and therefore also functions as an enabler in the B2C business.

- **Affiliate Marketing:** YOC's affiliate marketing platform 'belboon'[5] also functions as a marketplace connecting online advertisers with publishers. While advertisers provide the actual ads for their products and services, affiliates such as private or commercial website owners incorporate these, for instance, as text links or banners in websites or e-mails. The affiliate is rewarded by the merchant, in the form of commission, for every visitor, subscriber, customer or sale provided through the affiliate's efforts. Although belboon does not contribute to mobile marketing at the moment, it allows YOC to position itself for the future of mobile advertising (see 'Future Outlook' section).

Furthermore, YOC already uses the YOC.de community,[6] and its members for e-mail marketing. 1.175 million out of the 3.6 million members have declared their willingness to receive advertising e-mails on the basis of permission marketing. Members give their consent to this, which YOC verifies, using a so-called double opt-in process.[7] Having exclusively expressed their desire to take part, the yoc.de members are deemed particularly attentive to a client's campaign. Response rates are three to four times higher, on average, than with comparable offline campaigns.

Exhibit 2 shows YOC's sales mix and its source of revenues. Mobile marketing is dominant, accounting for 80% of sales. Affiliate marketing is becoming more relevant and leaving B2C-Services behind, indicating the trend towards new online advertising concepts.

Jump-starting the yoc.de community

The yoc.de community allows its members to meet other people and individually express what they feel, like, and think through digital content. Members share music, pictures or videos and can create a profile or write a blog. The community came into existence long before the term 'web 2.0' was coined, and user-generated content, hyped to be 'the next big thing', has been growing ever since. YOC has so far made over 500 campaigns interactive with mobile marketing using this permission-based approach.

At the beginning, however, it was difficult to convince potential clients of the benefits of mobile marketing and a community like yoc.de. Dirk Kraus remembers:

Mobile marketing was a totally new channel to them. They realized that they had spent too much money on the web without effect. The bubble burst and everything that had to do with the new economy and new media was banned. There was a total switch back to classic marketing channels, and that made it really difficult for us. [...] At the very beginning, mobile marketing was so special. There were media agencies that thought of it as cars driving through cities displaying some kind of banner. They were definitely not aware.

---

4 Mezzanine capital refers to financing through a combination of debt and equity. Due to an increased credit risk, interest rates are higher. However, a company can achieve less dilution compared to exclusive financing through equity.
5 http://www.belboon.de.
6 http://www.yoc.de.
7 A commonly used analogy is to consider when you give a waiter your lunch order ('first opt-in'); when the waiter reads back your order and asks if it is right, this is confirming your lunch order. Accepting this confirmed first order ('second opt-in') completes the double opt-in process.

Exhibit 2 YOC's sales mix by source of revenue and region (2006 in thousand Euro)

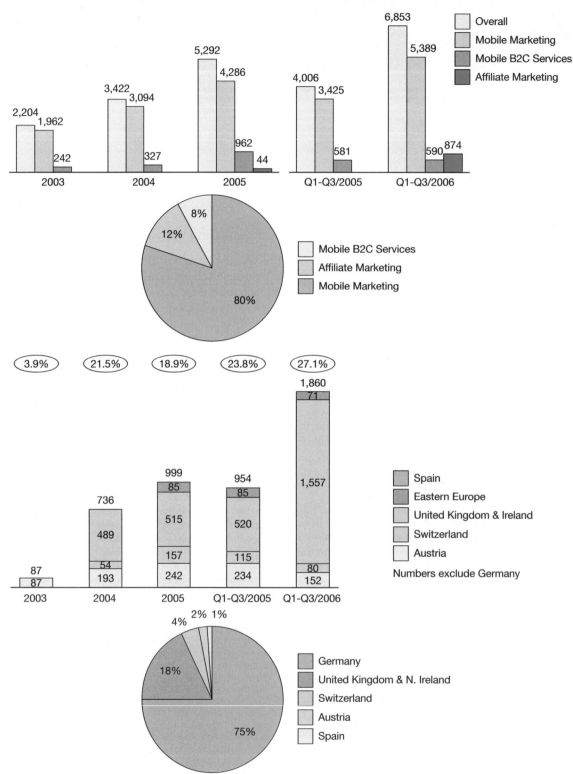

Source: YOC AG company report, Deutsches Eigenkapitalforum 2006.

The founders believed that mobile marketing would have to work in two directions. One of these directions would be the response-oriented mobile marketing, or pull mobile marketing, and the other direction would have to be push mobile marketing. This belief proved to be right. In a pull campaign, it is the user who initiates communications. Campaigns can be set up to collect consumer profiles through the mobile media channel or to enrich information on existing consumers with mobile data. In push campaigns, marketing services are delivered directly to the user on the mobile device. In this case, a list of targeted users is addressed with a message that is compelling and preferably interactive.

YOC stands for 'your opinion counts'.[8] From the beginning, the company aimed to engage its users in a dialogue by making them an integral part of its campaigns. YOC's community, in combination with push mobile marketing, complements classic communication channels and allows clients to reach their target group on the mobile phone directly and without divergence losses. Therefore, mobile marketing presents great opportunities for managing customer relationships through excellent reach, highly targeted campaigns and depth in customer intimacy.

But in order to convince marketers of the effectiveness of mobile marketing, YOC needed to get established and create a brand reputation, as Dirk Kraus points out:

> Our idea was to generate our own database with profiles that we could use as a media range. For push marketing, it is very crucial to have your own database of profiles, and we were very lucky that we could build up this user base in the first 12 months to 800,000 users. [....] We wanted to interact with consumers, and by participating in our campaigns, you can influence things. That was the reason why we came up with this crazy idea of crashing a Porsche in the 'cash-or-crash' campaign.

'Cash-or-Crash' – Destroying a Porsche 911

To create publicity and spread the word about the company, the founder team conceived the 'cash-or-crash' campaign. Hanging a Porsche 911 50 meters above the ground on Potsdamer Platz in Berlin and asking people to vote whether to crash the car or not created a highly emotionalizing 'buzz'. People could either text in 'crash' in order to see the car fall and hit the ground, or text in 'cash' in order to have a chance of winning the car. To

promote the campaign, YOC was partnering with BILD, Germany's biggest tabloid newspaper, on a national basis, and also with Radio Energy in Berlin on a local basis. While BILD published the story four days in advance in the nationwide newspaper, Radio Energy told the story 120 times a day, and was asking the audience to text in 'cash' or 'crash', therefore mentioning YOC's short code[9] 120 times on air.

Initially YOC contacted several event agencies, which offered to carry out highly expensive campaigns on their behalf. Given the prohibitive price they were asking, the founders decided that they would do it on their own. This unconventional approach[10] seemed just right for a low budget in order to establish the brand. In total, YOC spent 350,000 DM (around €180,000), a price they would have easily paid for a campaign organized by an agency.

> The Porsche campaign was important to jump-start the service. Everybody knew this story. There were critical people asking how we could destroy a car which was worth more than €50,000. On the other hand, everybody understood what we had been doing: attracting nearly 80,000 users within 6 days.

To participate, people had to opt in by texting in age, gender and 'cash' or 'crash'. As a telecommunications company, YOC had to follow special opt-in procedures. It held lengthy talks with the national authority for the telecom industry, which had to agree to this procedure, allowing people to opt in over the mobile phone. Later on, YOC switched the opt-in procedure to the web, which made people register online first.

'Crashing' the car turned out to be the preferred option. The slim probability (one out of 80,000) of winning the car drove most people to the 100% certainty of seeing the car crash. The campaign created huge awareness for YOC. Many of the very first users who participated in the cash-or-crash campaign are still registered with YOC and continue to participate in other campaigns, as Kraus explains:

> 80,000 participants was a huge success. People voted for seeing the car crash to the ground, and that is the

---

8 A short three-letter name contained in a 160-character text-message seemed to be an ideal name for a mobile marketing company.

9 Short codes – also known as short number or Common Short Codes (CSC) – are special telephone numbers, significantly shorter than full telephone numbers, which can also be used to addres SMS and MMS messages from mobile phones or fixed phones.

10 Compare 'guerilla marketing'.

point: 'Influencing the world, your opinion counts.' We said our users want to see the car falling and that is what we will do. [...] Actually, we were happy to see the car crashing. Every single German TV station was there, Sat1, RTL, even CNN was there. They said the Germans must have become crazy, so it was in the European news, and of course we had written YOC on the car.

'Schummelhilfe' – helping students cheat

The cash-or-crash campaign was very successful in establishing YOC as a brand, creating awareness and fuelling its database. By June 2001 YOC already had 500,000 registered users, but the team recognized that they lacked users of a very low age. YOC was aimed at creating a marketing community of 12 to 18 year-olds but the average age of registered users was 24. To attract more youngsters the founders came up with an idea called 'Schummelhilfe',[11] which was marketed as a cheating aid for students and comprised a translation service for Latin, English and French words. By texting in a foreign word via the mobile phone, students would be supplied with the translation.

> For exams in schools, this was a way of supporting people to cheat, Dirk Kraus remembers and adds: 'As you can imagine, you can't do something like that in Germany. You will have at least 100,000 people who want to stop you. The side-effect is that you have a lot of media coverage. Every single newspaper reported this funny story and even described how the whole thing worked.

Even Tagesthemen, Germany's prime daily television news magazine, covered YOC's campaign. In addition, 60 radio stations contacted headquarters in Berlin asking how it worked. Only a small percentage of users were actually tempted to cheat and try out the service, but YOC won a lot of users in a very efficient way:

> From an efficiency point of view, it was the best thing we have done. At that time, we had several campaigns, so it was hard to estimate the exact number of new users, but it was a 6-digit number only from 'Schummelhilfe'. For the cheating service, we hired three teachers, which was the hook to get the press into our office, because they wanted to see the teachers sitting in front of our computers answering text messages. It cost us €5,000 to €10,000. Again, from this perspective it was excellent.

'Birth-Control' – Reminding women to take their pill

A third unconventional jump-starting strategy involved attracting more women to the platform, since there was a small excess of males in the database. A new service was set up that reminded women to take their birth control pill. After registering with YOC, participants were asked to type in the first day of taking the pill and the exact time at which the pill was taken. Thereafter, the service sent out a message for 21 days reminding the user to take the pill. After a seven day break another text message was sent asking whether to start another month or not. Between 50,000 to 60,000 women registered with YOC and used the service. Numerous women's magazines covered the story.

> At the end of the day, we had to pay a lot of text messages, because 50,000 women and 21 text messages a month means even more than 1 million dispatched text messages per month, and the whole campaign was run for 2 or 3 months. For us, it was pure marketing. We wanted to install our own database in order to be able to offer a certain kind of media range to our potential clients. Today, we have 3.6 million users through various opt-in campaigns.

YOC not only managed to grow their database; more importantly they created a brand name. It even got them nominated at the Cannes Lions International Advertising Festival, which is generally regarded as the most prestigious in the industry.

> We made the short list in Cannes and we got down to the five last companies in line to win. It was amazing. There was Ogilvy Paris, McCann Erickson New York and all these companies, and then there was YOC from Berlin. We didn't win but we were among the last five companies. That was in 2002, and helped us again, since we could tell our clients about it, and of course, they were deeply impressed.

Making YOC profitable and going public

The €3.6 million venture capital enabled YOC to establish themselves by developing the technical infrastructure, setting up profiles and acquiring the first clients. Since raising further funds appeared to be difficult in the light of a weak economy and low growth expectations, YOC had to become profitable soon. In

11 Schummelhilfe': 'Cheating – Support'.

Exhibit 3 YOC's EBIT development

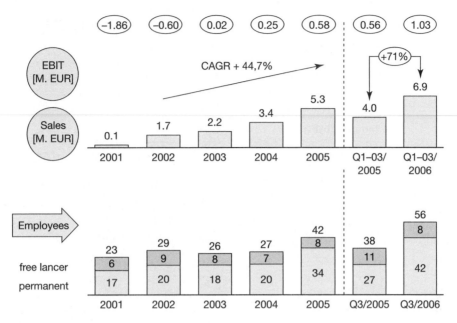

Source: YOC AG company report, Deutsches Eigenkapitalforum 2006.

2003, the company became cash-flow positive (Exhibit 3), which was important not only to keep the company alive and growing, but also to facilitate interest payments on its mezzanine capital, which amounted to €200,000 per year.

In order to trigger further growth and to facilitate the exit of the venture capitalists, YOC and its investors unanimously decided to conduct an IPO in 2005. After checking with banks, YOC was confident enough to go public and initiated the process. Nine months later, on 2 June 2006, YOC was listed as the first pure play mobile marketing company on Germany's Entry Standard at the Frankfurt Stock Exchange. With the support of investment bank Sal Oppenheim, YOC could sell major shares to investment funds. The share issue price was settled at €18, with the closing price on 27 July of €19.50. 53% of shares are in free float.

Results in 2006 showed increased turnover and operating profits. YOC boosted its turnover from €5.3 million to €9.1 million in the fiscal year 2006 (compared with fiscal year 2005), representing a growth rate of 72%. The mobile marketing business showed a significant growth in turnover of 71%, reaching €7.3 million, compared to €4.3 million in 2005. The affiliate marketing business even had an increase of over 100%

in 2006 (Exhibit 4). One-off costs amounting to €1.1 million were incurred by the preparation and realization of the IPO. Excluding these costs, company profits were up 250%.

The competitive landscape of mobile marketing

Mobile marketing may still be a small market and a niche on the advertising scene but competition is strong. 12Snap and Mindmatics, both located in Munich, are YOC's key competitors. The three are roughly equal in size in terms of their mobile marketing revenues in 2005. Then there is Sponge in the UK and Enpocket, as well as some smaller suppliers in every single country. YOC and 12Snap, however, are closest in terms of their strategy.[12]

Although YOC, Mindmatics and 12Snap are expected to continue to dominate the mobile marketing sector in Germany,[13] recent new entrants include multimedia agencies attempting to transfer their competence in digital marketing to mobile marketing. Kraus observes:

---

12 Sal Oppenheim, Oppenheim Research.
13 Sal Oppenheim, Oppenheim Research.

Exhibit 4 YOC turnover and EBIT

	2006	2005	Change	Change
Total Turnover [EUR]*	9.090	5.292	3.798	72%
Turnover Germany [EUR]*	6.948	4.294	2.654	62%
Turnover Foreign Countries [EUR]*	2.142	998	1.144	115%
Total Turnover [EUR]*	9.090	5.292	3.798	72%
Mobile Marketing [EUR]*	7.312	4.286	3.027	71%
B2C-Services [EUR]*	703	962	−259	−27%
Affiliate Marketing [EUR]*	1.075	44	1.031	> 100%
EBIT [EUR]*	1.193	579	614	106%
EBIT Margin	13.1%	10.9%		

* in thousand Euro.

Source: YOC AG annual report 2006.

What we have seen is that these agencies lack experience, and we have seen a lot of campaigns failing because of basic mistakes. Furthermore, these multimedia agencies lack the technical background. YOC has only 24 people working in the technical department, taking care of programming JAVA applications and WAP portals, managing the database and the connectivity with telecom operators. We have 75 people in total, with 24 persons working in the technical department it is our largest unit with the highest growth rate. All the multimedia companies don't have such a backbone; they still believe that mobile marketing is about running campaigns by putting a short code in place. I think this represents 5% of mobile marketing since it is more important how to actually contact consumers. We have six years of experience in how to contact them and to get the maximum response rate.

For Kraus, the value chain begins with the conceptualization of campaigns and ends with the reporting of campaigns: YOC covers all activities from campaign design, to development, to implementation, all the way to reporting (Exhibit 5):

Our USP is that we are able to offer our clients the full service, the whole value chain just from one single supplier. Furthermore, YOC is able to offer both directions of mobile marketing: push and pull. We can combine them and we can also offer each direction separately. I don't know of another company in Europe which is able to offer push and pull and the whole value chain at the same time.

YOC's full-service approach for mobile marketing constitutes its main competitive advantage. According to Kraus, 12Snap lacks the technical backbone since it has no database of its own, but it makes up on the creative side with marketing experience. Mindmatics, in contrast, is strong on the technical side, but lacks creativity and marketing experience. In 2002, 12Snap even used YOC's database in order to conduct push campaigns, and paid royalties for the use. It was a comfortable situation for YOC, but eventually led to 12Snap's complete withdrawal from push campaigns. Mindmatics, in its role as a technical enabler, offers premium SMS services and message termination for TV votings, for instance. Kraus comments:

We decided three years ago that it was crucial in order to survive to offer technical services for our clients and to combine this with our marketing experience. From my point of view, this is the reason why we were able to increase our turnover and relationships with our main customers. We could offer our clients more and more simultaneously, increasing the average project volume tremendously.

The technical complexity involved in creating and managing mobile marketing campaigns favors specialists such as YOC over in-house groups and is a key factor in the company's sustainability.

Exhibit 5 **YOC: A full service provider for mobile marketing**

Activities	Concept Development	Creation	Technical Realization of Mobile Applications	Provision of Technical Infrastructure	Planning and Activation of Target Audience	Project-management	Reporting
YOC	Yes	Yes	Yes	partly	Yes	Yes	Yes
Cost-driver	10%			60%		25%	5%
Description	– Concept Development of Mobile Phone Integration into a Client's Marketing Mix – Consulting	– Creation of Mobile Artwork (SMS, MMS, JAVA, WAP) – Coordination with client	– Programming of Mobile Application – Integration into a Client's Technical Infrastructure	Provision of: – System Architecture – Short Codes – Contingents	– Selecting and Contacting Profiles – Permission Marketing	– Maintenance of Mobile Applications – Customer Support	– Real-time Reporting – Evaluation – Market Research

Source: YOC AG company report, Deutsches Eigenkapitalforum 2006.

Sustaining YOC's competitive position

For YOC, sustainability is based on two core aspects: (1) high product and project quality, and (2) high technological competence (Exhibit 6). Based on these core competencies, YOC aims at:

- retaining established customers,
- attracting new customers through its full-service approach,
- intensifying relationships with established customers, and
- supporting clients in entering foreign markets.

YOC's approach has proven to be a successful path to sustainability, as Kraus affirms:

> What we have realized is that our clients stick with us. This is first of all the most important point, since we are able to increase budgets with our existing clients. We are also able to expand into new regions, with the same clients. Furthermore, YOC is very strong in acquiring new clients. Last year, we acquired a lot of companies from the automotive industry like Ford, Land Rover, Volvo and Renault. Furthermore, YOC has never lost one client in the past. We are really proud of it, since it is a very important step towards sustainability.

In addition to its marketing experience, YOC's technological competence is a crucial pillar of its sustainability, as Kraus stresses:

> We are heavily concentrating on things that are do-able when it comes to technology. This is very important. At the very beginning, YOC was only able to send and receive text messages and to further cluster and analyze these messages. That was our initial technological capability. Right now, we are able to bring newspapers on mobile phones. That's really a heavy development that was only possible by analyzing the market, realizing what the newest technology was and how it could be applied. I think it holds true for every individual company to focus on technological developments. If you don't do so, you will be out of the game.

YOC's technological competence drives its innovation and therefore allows for higher customer orientation in the long run. The company also benefits from a growing acceptance of mobile marketing in the media mix of advertising campaigns, and from its own marketing experience, as Kraus points out:

> It is very important in every aspect to really aim at reaching customers' marketing objectives. Our clients love us because we are focussing on bringing in marketing experience, and at the end of the day reaching the marketing objectives, whether it is awareness, sales or an enhanced image.

Exhibit 6 YOC growth strategies

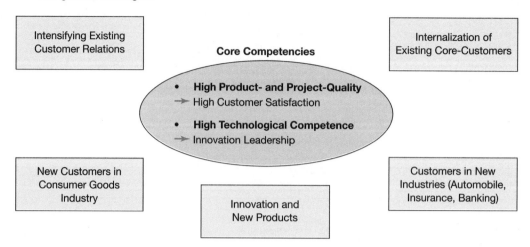

Source: YOC AG company report, Deutsches Eigenkapitalforum 2006.

While YOC's technology orientation and speed of innovation in the mobile marketing space are important factors that help to explain its customer attraction and retention in general, its business unit strategies warrant further explanation:

■ In mobile marketing, YOC tries to realize scale effects by leveraging the technical and R&D base in Berlin. YOC's infrastructure allows the company to make connections with networks in multiple countries. Accompanying existing clients into foreign markets helps YOC to increase its international presence and allows the company to win new customers through the opening of new sales representations in these countries. Its offices in London, Madrid and Vienna became profitable soon after their opening. Approaching the US market with clients such as Nike and Coca-Cola, would appear to be a logical move, as well as the acquisition of new customers from industry and service sectors which have not yet used mobile marketing (insurance, automobile, banking).

■ By entering the market of B2C mobile content distribution and performance-based (online) marketing, YOC has managed to diversify and go beyond pure mobile marketing.

■ In light of mobile and online convergence, YOC has built its own affiliate marketing platform at the request of its existing customers. Belboon positions YOC well, should performance-based marketing extend to mobile phones in the future.[14]

International expansion

In accordance with its growth strategy, YOC has already managed to leverage its brand and go international. Since clients want to run Europe-wide campaigns, YOC helps clients entering foreign markets. So far the company has opened up offices in Vienna (2003), Madrid and London (2005), facilitating its expansion mainly by organic growth or acquisition. Kraus explains the advantages of starting business in a foreign country through organic growth:

> What is very important in that perspective is that it isn't that difficult for us to enter a new market, because all of the technological activities such as software development, database management, and connectivity to operators or enablers are done here in Berlin (see Exhibit 7). Furthermore, we have hired locals for every single market, which are also working at the headquarters in Berlin. That allows us to open very small sales offices in a new country because our organization helps us a lot to achieve scale effects. On the one hand, our employees are able to realize what the client really wants to have, and on the other hand, it is very easy for them to explain these wants to our technical department.

In Germany, YOC has bi-directional links to mobile telecom operators, while in smaller foreign markets YOC connects through an enabler, a company that has links to every single foreign operator, as Kraus explains:

---

14 Sal Oppenheim, Oppenheim Research.

Exhibit 7 YOC's IT infrastructure

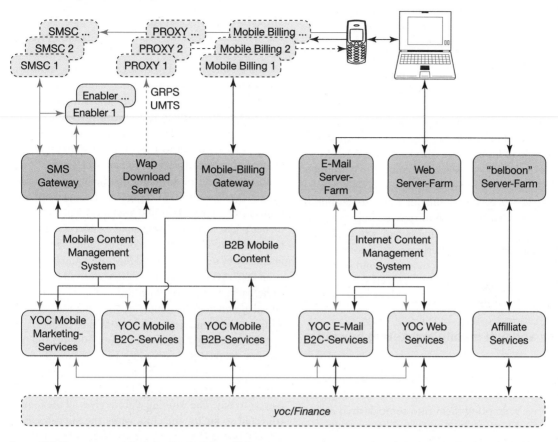

Source: YOC AG company report, Deutsches Eigenkapitalforum 2006.

We can connect to that company and then work with every single operator in a foreign country. It's important to note that this ensures only the connectivity. From my point of view, it is the mobile marketing application behind it, which is definitely much more important, meaning the software and content you are transferring through that line. And again, this is done here in Berlin.

It was in this way that YOC started doing business in Vienna, Madrid and London. In the UK, where they set up their own office without making any acquisition, YOC is one of the suppliers to choose from when it comes to mobile marketing. As Kraus insists, organic growth is needed in order to provide quality in mobile marketing, and therefore it takes time to achieve sustainable growth.

YOC is also eager to grow organically in the French market, since the acquisition of an established incumbent appears too expensive. Although YOC is doing business for Nike and Masterfoods in Spain on a profitable basis, the Spanish market appears to be more reluctant to mobile marketing than other markets. YOC is also in the process of entering the Polish market – although they don't have an office there yet, YOC has started doing business (see Exhibit 2).

Dirk Kraus elaborates on the expansion into the US market:

We are also thinking about North America, which is a very difficult market. I don't believe that we can just open up offices in New York City or San Francisco. We definitely need to have locals and they not only cost a lot of money, you also need to trust them. It can happen that you have paid a salary for one and a half years and nothing has happened, so it is very difficult. We still have the option to buy a company. The IPO proceeds are still with us.

In order to set up their own B2C business, YOC bought their first company in February 2007, putting another pillar into place. Brussels-based Moustik allows YOC to sell mobile content such as music downloads to consumers. The B2C business is important for YOC to generate additional turnover. A crucial aspect of the B2C business is that it allows YOC to generate sales on a continuous basis. It is not only profitable, but also a quite stable business unit. YOC had already started their B2C activities in 2004 in Germany, although 'unlabeled' in order to avoid pushing YOC (yoc.de) as a cost-free community in the area of paid content. The integration of Moustik was seamless, since YOC already had the technology to deliver the content to consumers. According to Dirk Kraus, it is pretty much the same if you dispatch a WAP push link for a Java application or if you dispatch a WAP push to receive a ring-tone. The same things apply to the billing system, which YOC has set up in Germany. Furthermore, YOC knows what type of content is relevant to consumers and is combining its expertise in market knowledge with its technological competence.

Push and pull mobile marketing beyond SMS

Mobile marketing is still dominated by text messaging and used as a means of enticing consumers to a point of sale or prompting them into some desired action. From a technical point of view, on-pack promotion – a very common mobile marketing campaign – is simple to install. What adds complexity is the mass of people participating. More advanced mobile marketing campaigns include WAP portals or Java applications. Kraus comments on the technological developments in the mobile domain:

> It became clear to us that sending text messages is a commodity. This is how mobile marketing started in 2001, but we should not leave text messaging out of our activities. We have clients that want to approach, for instance, 400,000 people in Germany or Spain via text messages, so it is still a highly demanded channel. But of course the technology development has become much more advanced. We are talking about Java applications and WAP portals. Our newest project will bring newspapers on the mobile phone. That shows you that SMS is still very important today, but other things become relevant too, in some respect they become even more relevant.

SMS on-pack promotions – Coca-Cola

The cash-or-crash campaign helped to push YOC into the market and to establish a brand name. Although push campaigns, carried out on the basis of a database, are still an integral part of mobile marketing, YOC prioritizes selling response-oriented campaigns or pull campaigns, which do not require a permission-based approach. Particularly in foreign countries, such as the UK or Spain, where YOC does not have its own database, when it comes to push mobile marketing, the company has to partner with somebody else.

In addition to push mobile marketing, pull mobile marketing allows clients to engage in a dialogue with consumers and increase sales and awareness. The use of the mobile phone as a response channel enables classic advertising such as TV, print, outdoor or radio, to be made interactive by sending SMS and MMS post purchase.

In 2007, YOC ran a promotion on around 60 million Coke packs in the UK. The 'Buy-a-Player' campaign aimed at enticing consumers to send in a text message with a code found under the bottle cap. Codes had a certain denomination ranging from 50p to £100,000 and fans banked their winnings to their favorite football club. The winner of the draw among participants was invited to decide with the club manager which players to buy. The winning club receives all the money collected so far for the club, while the fan received a £10,000 bonus (Exhibit 8). Kraus describes the participation levels for this typical on-pack promotion:

> If such a campaign is prepared very well, and if the incentives for users are sufficient enough to participate, clients can achieve response rates of 1.5% up to 2.5% counted on the total number of units, and this is massive.

Two marketing objectives can be achieved with on-pack promotions: creating awareness and creating image. While the former helps to attract new customers, the latter binds consumers to the brand and creates loyalty. In the case of the Buy-a-Player campaign, Coke sought to reiterate its dedication to sports in general and soccer in particular, while keeping up its image as a lifestyle brand.

Running a pull campaign like on-pack promotions, Kraus believes, increases the speed at which product units are shifted out of the market. A lot of people decide only at the point of sale whether to buy the blue or the red cola – an important factor as attracting impulse buyers is key to accelerating sales. Additionally, what makes these

Exhibit 8 YOC's campaign for Coca-Cola

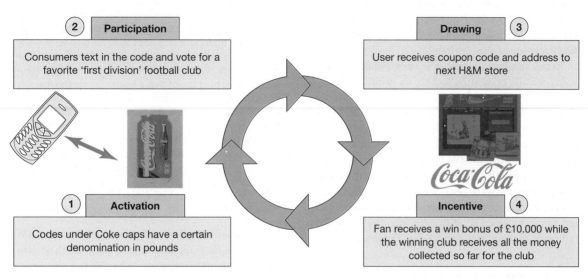

Source: YOC AG company report, Deutsches Eigenkapitalforum, 2006.

campaigns so valuable to clients is that marketers can measure the success of a campaign by their own sales figures. Obviously this is crucial in convincing marketers of the benefits of mobile marketing.

Although text messaging generates a lot of revenue for telecom operators, YOC receives no kickbacks, and it appears to be very difficult to negotiate discounts. YOC gets special rates for dispatching text messages and are allowed to use the telecom's infrastructure and short codes. As Dirk Kraus points out, time is better spent on acquiring new deals with clients than on negotiating kickbacks, an admission which shows the dominance of telecom operators and YOC's depencence on them.

WAP portals – BILD newspaper

YOC's latest project brings BILD, Germany's biggest tabloid newspaper, to the mobile phone. Users access BILD through a WAP portal by following a link sent to the mobile phone. The difficult part is to make such a portal viewable on the screen of every single device available. Given the vast number of different handsets on the market, many of which can run multimedia applications and have state-of-the-art connectivity, there is tremendous complexity involved, as Kraus elaborates:

That makes mobile marketing so different and so complex. There was a time when people were discussing how to converge the two formats of Internet Explorer and Netscape so that every single website could be viewed by anybody worldwide. In mobile marketing, we are dealing with much more complexity. There is a Samsung handset with Vodafone and then there is a Nokia handset with T-Mobile. BILD must be viewable clearly on every mobile phone. YOC is one of the few companies that are able to realize such complex things.

YOC not only provides the technical resources for such campaigns, it also delivers its service rapidly. One important factor for closing the deal with BILD was the speed of innovation:

The BILD campaign was really a challenge for us, but we were the first who could offer a working service to the client and simultaneously guarantee a high quality. That was the reason why we could win this order.

Java applications – Ford Motor Company

YOC created a Java portal for the Ford Motor Company in a campaign launched in 2006 for the new Ford S-MAX. Users could download the software by texting in a certain keyword, which they had seen in TV spots or on print ads. The Java application allowed people to download a product catalogue on the mobile phone using an intuitive navigation similar to the one on the web. Users were able to see how the car looked from inside and outside, and were even able to switch it around in 3D on their mobile phones. Furthermore, they could get information on the design, comfort and safety features of the car (Exhibit 9).

Kraus emphasizes that it is very important when doing mobile marketing to keep in mind that people want to be entertained. Therefore, the application allows users to download wallpapers, videos and screensavers. What moves the customer from being a prospect to almost a buyer is the dealer look-up. The sales tool implemented in the Java application makes the user type in the postal code of the area of residence so that the software will automatically display the names of dealers in close proximity. In this way the customer can make an appointment with the dealer for a test drive, moving the prospect to the point of sale.

Toward location-based services – H&M fashion retailing

There are potentially countless ideas for using the mobile phone: identifying the user's location to push specific location-sensitive offers to the customer is one of them. Prototypes indicate that the technology is ready but Kraus is hesitant when it comes to location-based services (LBS):

People need to express their specific wish to receive location-sensitive messages, which would require having a database of company-specific profiles. On the one hand, I doubt that people want to get automatic text messages offering a 10% discount for buying two Big Macs when they are close to the next McDonald's. Off course, there will be people interested in having a service like that, but I doubt that it holds true for the majority of consumers. On the other hand, we will see things like mobile search, and this is where LBS will become more relevant. The difference is that people by themselves want to get information and they will love it if they get localized information. When it comes to that, I believe that LBS will become very relevant. It is obvious to everybody that Google is going in that direction already. They want to combine LBS with their search engine, and this will be a functionality that will be used quite heavily.

For companies interested in developing their own CRM program, the first step might be to build up their own database out of which they would be able to contact customers in the future. However, this requires a commitment to invest heavily in maintaining the database or pay a company like YOC for it. Kraus doubts that department stores are ready or willing to take on this investment:

From our perspective, we need to see if that is really becoming a business case for us, because I really doubt that clients are willing to spend money on a constant

Exhibit 9 **FYOC's campaign for Ford Motor Company**

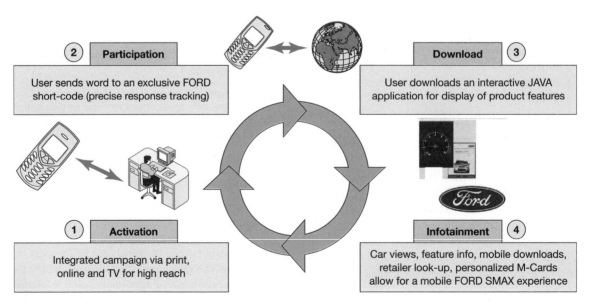

Source: YOC AG company report, Deutsches Eigenkapitalforum 2006.

basis for a company like YOC to generate this database and to work with it. At the end of the day potential clients have to compare costs and additional revenues, and if this is a positive balance they will do it.

For the opening of H&M flagship stores in Cologne, Hamburg and Berlin, YOC conducted campaigns which represented a first step in evolving a company-specific database for CRM activities. YOC contacted people from their own database and asked them to text H&M to receive a coupon for a free T-shirt. People who did so received a bi-dimensional matrix code on their mobile phone which would be scanned by a machine in the store. The machine then printed out a coupon carrying a bar code which, in turn, could be read by the cashier handing out the free T-shirt (Exhibit 10).

YOC contacted 100,000 people with an initial response rate of 4.5%. Of these 4,500 users, 2,000 (2%) actually came to the store opening. Not only was the bar code reader connected via GPRS with YOC's database in order to prevent a code from being used twice, it also allowed them to analyze who actually used the code, and whether the person lived locally (within a 10km radius). Since the system was also connected to the cash system, it was possible to state who only went to the shop to get a free T-shirt, and who bought two pairs of jeans, for instance.

Trust in mobile marketing

In the light of spam and dubious ring tone sellers, privacy issues are a concern. There have been cases of companies dispatching unsolicited text messages. However, since it costs money to send text messages (unlike e-mails), and since it is easier than on the web to track who has sent these messages, this kind of mobile spam has declined considerably.

As a member of the mobile marketing association (MMA Global), YOC has to abide by international, and especially European law, and to follow the association's guidelines. Kraus feels it is reassuring for the industry to have these laws because people have to double opt in and give their active permission to be contacted via the mobile phone. In the rare case that a user has forgotten that he has registered an account with YOC, the exact registration and permission date can be given.

Although it is easy to opt out – texting 'STOP' to YOC deletes the user's profile – YOC have a low churn rate.[15] Their biggest loss occurs, in fact, because users regularly change their mobile phone number and do not update their profile information. Every single year YOC is losing around 300,000 to 400,000 profiles in this way.

---

15 Churn rate, as applied to a customer base, refers to the proportion of contractual customers or subscribers who leave a supplier during a given time period.

Exhibit 10 H&M store opening: Moving customers to the POS through mobile couponing

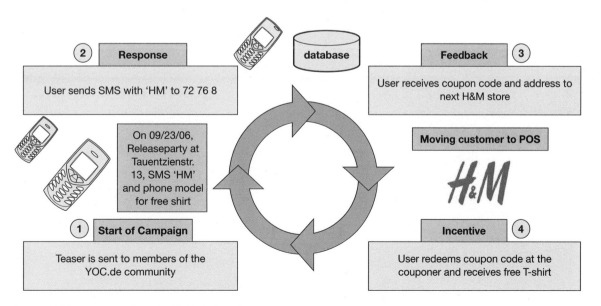

Source: YOC AG company report, Deutsches Eigenkapitalforum 2006.

599

Future outlook

With a positive profit and European expansion underway, YOC have made the first step toward a sustainable future. When asked about his vision for YOC and potential expansion possibilities, Dirk Kraus says:

> We are concentrating heavily on marketing mobile advertising. This is the newest tendency in mobile marketing. We all are aware of online advertising and we all know the classic online advertising means such as banners, skyscrapers and content ads. All that stuff is getting integrated on WAP portals, for instance, on the WAP portal for BILD. We will see that these WAP portals will be used on a constant basis. The download figures are increasing already. This is a very interesting development.

Furthermore, he sticks by the decision to function as a full service provider offering the full range of services to its B2B clients:

> Like DoubleClick for the Internet, we have a mobile ad server technology in order to bring ads to the portals and adapt it to every single handset, because again, you have the complexity that every mobile phone is different. Furthermore, we will be selling ads. Mobile news portals, such as the one for BILD or Die Welt, are becoming a massive market that will push mobile marketing and the whole scenery a lot. Of course, we will see new entrants; I assume that players such as Yahoo! will be entering the market, starting to market their own portals first. Our strategy will be to bundle portals. Therefore, we are working together with TV stations and news magazines in order to use their portals. We are just in the phase of building up these relationships. Our software will let clients choose which type of portal they want to have their ad served to, and these six to seven clusters range from entertainment to sports and news.

Finally, Kraus remarks that the convergence of the mobile and fixed-line Internet will make it easier for YOC to communicate their value proposition:

> Our clients will be able to automatically place their advertisement. This makes the whole matter very interesting. Furthermore, you don't need to explain how mobile marketing functions because all these companies are aware of how Internet or web-based online marketing/advertising is working – they know that they have to pay a price for a thousand clicks on their online banners and they are aware of the effects. It is easy to explain to them that you can just put it on mobile phones too, so you don't need to explain the whole story, and this will facilitate the sales process tremendously.

Paybox.net (Germany)

A mobile payment service

> Our goal is to establish the international standard for paying via the mobile phone.
>
> **Mathias Entenmann**, Chief Executive Officer, paybox.net AG

With these words, Mathias Entenmann addressed the journalists who had gathered in Hannover (Germany) for CeBIT 2001, which is the world's largest information technology trade fair. Prior to his address, Entenmann was awarded the CeBIT Innovation Prize for his payment solution, a prestigious industry award which, before paybox.net, went to other innovative companies such as Microsoft and Napster.

Six months later, the board of paybox.net met at the company headquarters near Frankfurt to decide whether to market paybox to business customers as a B2B2C (business to business to consumer) product called PIA (Paybox Intelligent Architecture). The PIA business model would be similar to that of credit cards: companies would license the paybox brand name and have their payment service operated by paybox employees and technology. Selling the PIA could, in the short run, mean improved revenues for the fledgling company, and, in the longer term, stimulate the European m-payment market, which has, so far, been slow to materialize. However, on the negative side, paybox would allow other companies to capitalize on its technological capabilities and surrender end customer relationships to their new partners.

Paybox.net: The initial idea

In July 1999, Mathias Entenmann left his management consultancy job to found paybox.net AG, with the help of a recent graduate and two university students. The company focused on developing a secure and convenient mobile payment service for online and offline transactions. Entenmann had the idea for such a service during a trip he made to Finland in 1998. He read about an experiment that took place there where one could buy a drink from a vending machine and pay for it with the mobile phone. The buyer would, on their mobile phone, dial a number printed on the vending machine for a particular drink, which would then dispense the beverage. The call charge for the dialled number would include the price of the drink.

Entenmann thought that the use of such a system could be expanded. 'That's great for a simple purchase of a beverage, but think of all the phone numbers you would need [to assign to the different books] for a moderately sized bookstore.' His paybox.net start-up would be built on this idea, but would be more versatile.

The system matches a special personal identification number (PIN) with the caller's mobile phone ID ('caller-ID'). To initiate a standard transaction, the payee dials the paybox.net transaction phone number and is identified via the caller-ID, which is automatically transmitted by the calling phone. The payee then enters the phone number of the payer as well as the amount to be paid. An interactive voice response (IVR)

This case study was written by Philipp Leutiger, MBA graduate of the Leipzig Graduate School of Business, Germany, and Tawfik Jelassi, Affiliate Professor of Technology Management at INSEAD. It is intended to be used as the basis for class discussion rather than to illustrate an effective or ineffective handling of a management situation.

The case was made possible by the co-operation of paybox.net (Germany).

then transmits this information to the paybox.net server, which immediately calls the designated payer. The latter is asked to confirm the payment via a four-digit PIN. The server then confirms the payment to the payee, thus completing the transaction. Afterwards, paybox.net initiates a money transfer from the payer's account to the payee's account. 'The beauty is', says Entenmann, 'that paybox works with any mobile phone network, any phone, and any bank account. Our focus is the market, not a specific technology.'

In May 2000, paybox.net released its mobile payment ('m-payment') service in Germany. It was a proactive move to seize the business opportunities that lay ahead. Indeed, according to a May 2001 Forrester poll, bricks-and-mortar companies, as well as online retailers, expected that, in three years' time, 10% of their transactions would be paid for via mobile phones.

By April 2002, paybox.net had 750 000 customers in Europe, and successfully launched its operations in Austria, Spain, Sweden and the UK. A total of 10 000 merchants accepted the payment service. Further international expansion was considered and planned.

Launching paybox.net

To implement his business plan, Mathias Entenmann persuaded four friends, some from his previous management consultancy, to join him. They took over the responsibilities for the product development, finance, marketing and operations activities of paybox.net. Entenmann also sought funding from some financial institutions and venture capitalists, but no deal was in sight. Nevertheless, he decided not to approach telecommunications operators so as to avoid becoming a proprietary m-payment system for a single network. He thought that such a dependency would limit the business potential of his m-payment solution.

Despite the lack of financial investors, Eckhard Ortwein, paybox.net's Chief Technology Officer, forged ahead and built a prototype of the system, with the help of two small software companies, financed by the personal funds of the paybox.net board members. The trial test ran on a Compaq desktop computer with the use of a computer telephony integration (CTI) card that received and placed the voice calls required. The system became operational in December 1999.

'It proved to be a breakthrough', recalls Entenmann. 'We could simply walk up to a potential investor and say, "just take this phone, Sir, and let's assume I want you to

pay me some money". We'd punch in some numbers, and the person's phone would ring, prompting him for a PIN. People were quite amazed!'

A number of potential investors then became interested in paybox.net. After some consideration, the company decided to turn down the venture capitalists' offers and instead struck a deal with Deutsche Bank in February 2000. The bank paid for a 50% stake in the start-up, with the option to participate in any additional capital offering, so as to maintain its equity share. In addition, the bank agreed to handle the 'back office' billing and money transfer operations of paybox.net.

In March 2000, the funding enabled the company to move to larger offices in nearby Wiesbaden and to employ 25 people, in addition to involving several outside IT systems integrators. Product development began in earnest with the development team working hard to build a scalable and reliable payment solution. In April 2000, the first transactions using the new paybox.net system were made. At the same time, a marketing campaign was launched aiming at winning merchants and especially online retailers. Stefano Nepute, then Chief Marketing Officer of paybox.net, explains:

> The reason [for this focus] is quite simple: you would need thousands of bricks-and-mortar shops to gain a national coverage; yet you will only have a minimal selection of products. But on the Internet, merchants who sell the goods you want and who are willing to accept the paybox.net payment service are only a click away from you.

The initial reaction to the paybox.net product was positive, with the new payment service being presented in several national newscasts. In June 2000, *Business Week* named, in its international edition, Mathias Entenmann one of the '50 Stars of Europe'. Mathias Entenmann and Jochen Schwiersch, Chief Financial Officer of paybox.net, started building a network of alliances and partnerships, laying the groundwork for the internalization of the payment system. At the same time, paybox was restructured, with paybox.net becoming a holding organization and national paybox companies being founded for each market. The company sought sales and infrastructure co-operation partners in every market, with mobile telecommunications network re-seller, Debitel, taking the lead as sales partner for paybox.de, the German subsidiary (see Exhibit 1 for the company structure).

However, the paybox team also suffered some setbacks. It was hard to convince major anchor clients to

Exhibit 1 **Paybox ownership structure**

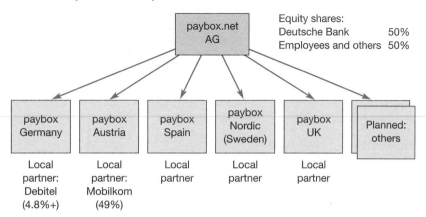

join the system. Many merchants required 'split billing' (for example, if a customer bought several books online but not all of these were delivered, only a partial sum would be billed). Also, some alliances to gain customers took longer to implement than initially thought, or were not as effective as expected. Furthermore, in December 2000, Stefano Nepute left the company.

Still, the service roll-out continued; it included mobile merchants like taxi drivers and pizza delivery personnel. By December 2000, paybox.net served 4 300 merchants and 120 000 customers. The company moved again to larger offices near Frankfurt and employed a total of 100 people, including those working in national offices.

Paybox.net service offering: A variety of online payment systems

The current paybox.net service is quite different from Entenmann's original idea. In March 2001, the company identified the following types of online payment transactions (see Exhibits 2–6):

Internet-to-paybox (I2P)

This type of transaction is designed for all sorts of online purchases. A consumer first selects items at an online store in much the same way as with any other payment system. At checkout, however, they select 'pay with paybox' instead of any other regular payment

Exhibit 2 **Internet-to-paybox payment process**

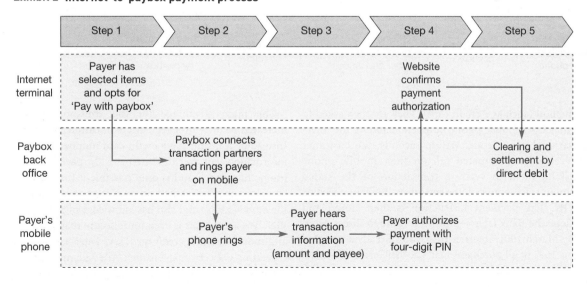

Exhibit 3 Paybox-to-paybox payment process

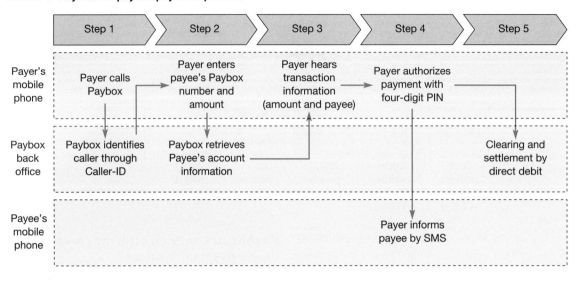

Exhibit 4 Mobile-to-paybox payment process

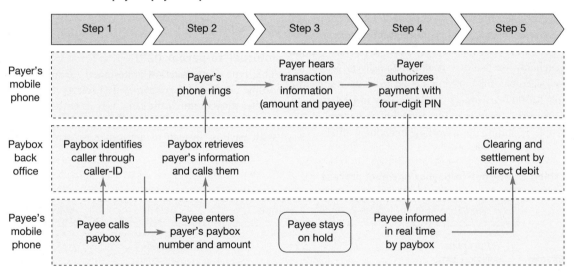

method (such as a credit card). They are then asked to enter their mobile phone number, including the international access code. Within seconds, the customer receives an automated call on their mobile phone asking them to verify a transaction of the stated amount. To approve it, the customer enters their paybox PIN. The payment instruction is then stored and Deutsche Bank later completes it through direct debit. By March 2001, Internet-to-paybox already accounted for 10% of all purchases made at the German Internet bookstore buch.de.

The main advantage for the consumer is the increased security over regular credit card transactions. Instead of transmitting a credit card number, the only information sent over the Internet is the payer's mobile phone number. Fraud is only possible if the offender has access to the switched-on mobile phone (or knows the mobile's PIN) and also has knowledge of the paybox PIN. 'We believe this is even more secure than a bricks-and-mortar use of a credit card', says Peter Seipp, Chief Operating Officer of paybox.net. 'After all, most people use their credit card only once every couple of days, so

Exhibit 5 Money transfer with paybox

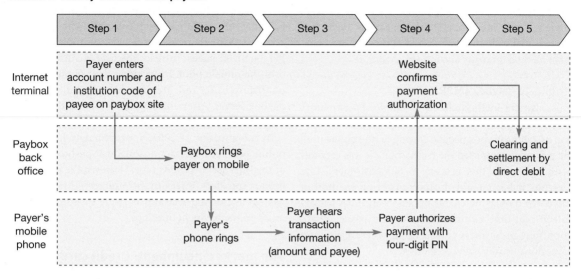

Exhibit 6 Debitel cashline

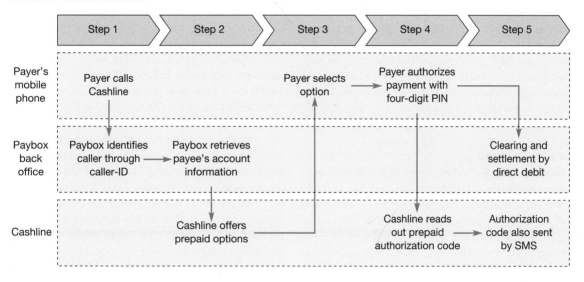

stealing one could go unnoticed for a while. But everyone notices immediately when they lose their mobile phone, because it is viewed as a personal item.' According to online surveys in Germany, approximately 90% of the visits to Internet merchants, where shopping carts were filled, did not result in any sales, because of consumers' security concerns.

Paybox-to-paybox (P2P)

This service allows users to transfer money among themselves. The payer calls the paybox server through their

mobile phone. The system automatically identifies them due to the caller-ID. The payer then enters the paybox number of the payee as well as the amount involved. Paybox asks for the PIN in order to validate the transaction. Then, within seconds, the payee is informed about the transaction via SMS (short message system). 'Unlike any credit card, paybox-to-paybox is a peer-to-peer service', says Joerg Ziesche, responsible for consumer marketing at paybox.de. 'In addition, you can use it to transfer money to a mobile phone that is currently not paybox enabled. The owner of the phone can then leave his account information with us or sign up as a payboxer (i.e. a paybox customer) and have the money transferred to his account.' In October 2001, the paybox-to-paybox mode was already well established as the preferred payment method for many auctioneers at eBay.de.

Mobile-to-paybox (M2P)

This payment method closely resembles Entenmann's original concept, with the payee triggering the transaction by calling paybox.net and staying on the phone until the payer has completed the transaction. 'It was very difficult to explain this process to our customers', says Ziesche. 'It has remained our transaction method of choice for mobile merchants because it includes a guaranteed real-time confirmation for the payee. That's important in business transactions, where payer and payee don't usually know each other.'

Money transfers over the Web

Paybox.net users can also visit the company's website to make money transfers. In addition to their phone number, they key in either the payee's phone number or the standard bank information (account number and institution code). After entering the amount to be paid, the payer is called on their mobile phone to validate the transaction. Thus, money transfers can be made over the Internet without the complicated use of transaction numbers (TAN), the current standard for online banks.

Debitel Cashline

Debitel Cashline is a service with which Debitel prepaid phone customers can recharge their prepaid cards by using paybox, without having to go into a store. Users call the Cashline phone number, order an increase on their spending limit, and authorize a payment over this amount with their PIN. Then, the prepaid code is read out by the paybox call server and sent to the user via SMS. The user can then call the regular recharge hotline and enter the code the same way the code bought on a card would be entered. Since the complete transaction with the customer is done over the mobile phone, paybox markets this service as the first m-commerce solution.

Additional services

Paybox.net users who are concerned about their privacy can get a paybox alias on the website. This number can be entered for any paybox transaction instead of providing the user's cellular phone number. The paybox database matches the phone number and the alias. Also,

paybox users have access to the 'myPaybox' personal site, which includes a history of transactions and the personal information of each customer. The site is not accessed through a password, as is common for other personalized pages. Instead, the user is authenticated over the mobile phone: they enter their phone number on the website and are immediately called by the paybox server. After entering their PIN on the phone, the personal page is displayed.

In the autumn of 2001, approximately half of the online payment transactions made at paybox.net were of the Internet-to-paybox type. However, the number of money transfers, a service introduced in March 2001, has been growing fast and is likely to dominate the other online payment offerings.

The market incumbent: Credit card companies

The credit card industry was thought to be a duopoly between the two largest players, Visa and Mastercard. A firm like Visa is actually a co-operation between all card-issuing banks, called member banks. A typical transaction between a consumer and a merchant in Europe is depicted in Exhibit 7. The consumer would present their card upon purchase, with which the merchant would create a credit card receipt either with an online terminal, or, where no online connection is available, imprint a carbon copy of the card information using a special manual press. The payer would sign the receipt, thereby confirming the amount and validating the transaction. The merchant would hand the transaction information to its bank, which would identify the consumer's card-issuing bank and inform it about the payment. The card-issuing bank would collect all incoming receipts and send the consumer a monthly statement of their payments. It would then withdraw the required funds from the consumer's bank account. This money, less a commission (called *disagio*), which the card-issuing bank retains, would be transferred to the merchant's bank, which would credit the money to the merchant (minus a commission).

In addition, the card-issuing bank charges the consumer an annual card membership fee, while the merchant's bank charges the merchant a subscription fee as well as a service fee. In return, consumers benefit from the convenience offered and a later debit date. For the merchant, the card-issuing bank guarantees payment if the card was physically present at the time of purchase.

Exhibit 7 Regular credit card transaction

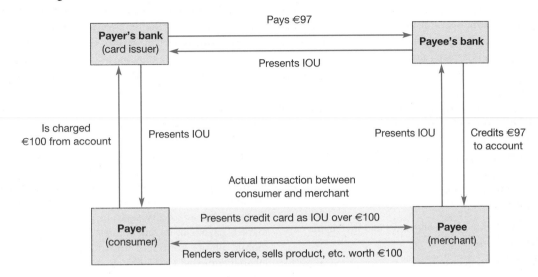

Although they are a considerable force in the market now, credit card companies had faced an uphill struggle over many years in the European markets. After their launch in the early 1970s, it took the credit card industry a full 22 years to attract 500 000 customers in Germany.

The paybox.net business model

The paybox.net revenue model is similar to that of a credit card company, described above. Paybox charges consumers an annual fee of €5. Merchants usually pay a fee for the integration of the payment system (€500 to €2 500 for Internet shops) and are charged a yearly fee. This fee is €100 for the basic transaction functionality, which requires manual payment requests from the merchant at the time it ships its goods. For premium service, which includes automated billing, the annual fee is €300. Moreover, for every transaction, the company charges merchants a *disagio* in the single digit percentage range. The minimum charge per transaction is €0.25, which enables the company to break even on a payment. Anchor merchants, as well as launch merchants, pay less. For paybox-to-paybox transactions, the company charges €0.25 for each €25 of transaction volume. The company competes with credit card companies on the payment guarantee dimension. As paybox does not have a banking licence, it is legally not allowed to promise guaranteed fulfilment. The contractual basis is that merchants 'can expect payment', coupled with the understanding of both paybox as well as the merchant that paybox would bear the burden of customer insolvency. Paybox payment days for merchants are every 14 days, which is slightly shorter than the monthly cycles of credit cards. For all transactions, paybox.net uses direct debits operated by Deutsche Bank.

Establishing a mobile payment solution

Five market segments for a mobile payment system can be identified. The first distinction is between micro-payments (amounts of €10 or less for parking tickets, bus fares, vending machines, or online content) and macro-payments (e.g. for books, petrol, groceries, etc.). This classification is important because transaction costs are relative to the total cost of goods sold, and many payment methods used for macro-payments are too expensive or too time-consuming for smaller amounts. Micro-payments can be made either for mobile content (such as location-based services), online purchases (Internet content), or offline purchases (e.g. from vending machines). Since it is unlikely that mobile content applications will charge more than €10, the two possibilities for macro-payments include online purchases and offline purchases.

CEO Entenmann identifies the following six key factors for the success of an m-payment system:

■ All user groups must have access to the payment method – using any phone, over any network. Systems using proprietary technical solutions in handsets will fail because of the required upgrade of all handsets. Systems focusing on the users of a single network operator will not attract merchants who would need four to six payment systems serving customers in Germany alone.

- The payment system must have universal applications for m-commerce products as well as online and offline stores. This increases the versatility of the system and thus the customer benefit derived from it.

- The payment system must be easy and convenient to use. The steps required to trigger a transaction (i.e. entering a PIN for authentification), should follow a procedure that consumers and merchants alike are familiar with.

- Security concerns of consumers and merchants have to be addressed.

- The transaction cost of the payment system must be priced attractively for the consumer.

- The system must be internationally accepted.

Interest in mobile payment is generally high, especially among merchants. They cite enhanced customer service, increased sales and reduced cash handling as the main advantages of m-payment. Internet merchants, in particular, are desperately searching for a payment method that could convince their customers of its security features. Many Internet merchants fear dependence on credit card transactions and would prefer an alternative, strong and efficient payment method. However, common fears concerning m-payment are high transaction costs due to the relatively high call charges of mobile phones.

Consumers, on the other hand, having already resisted other radically new payment methods, seem unlikely to join m-payment solutions in droves. The challenge is to dispel their worries over data privacy and security issues in order to attract customers beyond the initial early adopters.

Driving customers' adoption

We have the coolest product. I've never met anyone who didn't get enthusiastic about it once I explained to him how paybox works. The problem is [that] I don't have the time to speak to everyone in person.

Mathias Entenmann

Paybox.net has been focusing on online macro-payments, since its minimum charge of €0.25 is not suited

for micro-payments. 'We provide the service for those who want to offer it, but it doesn't really make sense to promote it', says Ralph Westenburger, Head of Merchant Acquisition at paybox Germany. 'When you are selling a new ring tone for a cell phone for €1, you don't want to pay that much just to have the transaction confirmed.' Nonetheless, to achieve a critical mass of customers, paybox started several alliances, referral programmes and advertisements.

Partnership with Debitel

In September 2000, paybox forged its partnership with Debitel, a telecommunications network re-seller. In exchange for an equity stake in paybox.net, Debitel markets paybox in its retail outlets in conjunction with mobile phone contracts. In addition, paybox and Debitel launched Cashline, which enables all prepaid customers to reload their accounts via paybox. The equity stake could be increased depending on the number of paybox customers acquired by Debitel. Mobilkom Austria, a major player in the Austrian mobile phone market, also bought a stake (49%) in paybox Austria. Paybox is actively searching for similar co-operation partners in its other national subsidiaries. The current ownership structure of paybox.net is depicted in Exhibit 1.

Co-branding and referrals

To gain consumers quickly, paybox co-branded its payment system with a number of alliance partners. For this, the paybox registration and payment processes are integrated in the current offering of an online partner, or contracts and information brochures are made available at the partner's offline locations. Online partnerships include the German portal web.de, Ciao.com, as well as the mobile portal jamba!. Paybox was also advertised as a mobile wallet at AOL Germany, on eBay.de, and on the website of Deutsche Bank 24 (which is Deutsche Bank's retail arm). In the offline world, paybox alliances include the students' magazine *Unicum*, MTV and Debitel. Paybox usually pays its partners a customer acquisition fee per registered paybox consumer and co-brands the product. Eckhard Ortwein says:

The success of the co-branding effort relies heavily on the integration efforts of both partners. Web.de, for example, was exemplary in incorporating paybox into their unique look and feel, and including our payment options on their website.

To instigate referral links on private websites and word-of-mouth between friends, paybox also paid consumers a €5 referral fee per signed up customer. Word-of-mouth referral was especially powerful when paybox-to-paybox enabled consumers to send money to any phone. 'Repay your debt to someone conveniently and earn €5 as soon as that person signs on, how good is that?' says Ziesche, a consumer marketing firm.

Another agreement was drawn up with Norisbank, whose bank account E@sy Mobile Giro now features Internet brokerage, home banking and a paybox registration. 'This was possible with Norisbank because they are one of the smaller retail banks, and are thus under higher competitive pressure in over-banked Germany', says Ortwein.

Merchant integration and reselling

Paybox.net set up several alliances aimed at getting merchants to accept its m-payment system. In partnerships with e-commerce platform providers and merchant associations, the company standardized its system integration process with that of the merchants.

This integration was especially successful with online stores. Paybox.net set up an alliance with Pago and launched its payment solution to Pago merchants in February 2000 (three months before the actual launch). Similar agreements were made with other online hosting providers, such as Brodos.de. Furthermore, a software cartridge was developed in co-operation with Intershop and other e-commerce software providers to allow the easy integration of the paybox system. 'A partnership that is really going well in this regard is the hosting provider 3C Systems', says Westenburger. 'Some hosting providers simply don't have a stable hosting environment. And things then do not run well. In general, the hosting providers are our main partners for rolling out the system. We would never have the resources by ourselves to integrate so many merchants.'

A similar partnership was implemented with taxi companies. However, the mobile-to-paybox solution proved to be a major stumbling block. 'We have showered those cab drivers with tapes [containing usage instructions] and stickers. Product awareness was certainly boosted; however, only one third of the taxi drivers offering paybox are fervent missionaries. The mobile-to-paybox solution still requires a lot of data entry from the taxi driver', says Westenburger. To improve this situation, the paybox team tried to integrate the payment system into information terminals already existing in taxis. However, as Ortwein puts it: 'There is room for improvement.'

Until a solution with a stronger value proposition for all involved can be implemented, paybox.net has scaled down the taxi driver acquisition effort and used the currently integrated taxis to raise awareness of its payment method. 'This is what we call the "lighthouse concept"', says Westenburger.

Innovation and image

Paybox is pursuing its drive to establish its brand with merchants and end users. The first aspect of this was innovative new product designs. At Munich's Systems in November 2000, CTO Ortwein unveiled a cigarette vending machine without a coin slot. Cigarettes could only be bought through the mobile phone. 'The system could potentially prevent teenagers from buying cigarettes, because paybox could check the age of the payer', says Ortwein. A new WAP-based 'push-paybox' was also unveiled at Munich's Systems, in co-operation with the mobile portal jamba!. The system was built to demonstrate micro-payments for mobile content. At CeBIT 2001, paybox presented two bricks-and-mortar cashier systems that were paybox enabled. 'In general, these are great products that create some buzz. But the tech industry is very short-lived. You need to follow up immediately to gain the most of these inventions', is Westenburger's experience.

The second important factor that paybox emphasizes is its security image. Prior to the launch of its payment solution, paybox partnered with Experian, a real-time customer scoring system. The company was also proud of obtaining, in May 2000, the certification for its Trusted Shop money back guarantee.

Third, paybox highlights its growing acceptance network by presenting anchor clients such as eBay.de, Karstadt Reisebüro (a bricks-and-mortar travel agency) and Kinowelt (a movie-theatre chain). 'These opinion leaders are really central to any product establishment', comments Westenburger. 'Get one of the big names and they all come. However, negotiating a workable contract with these fellows takes time. In the beginning, large companies would turn you back and say: "come back when you have shown that it works." Well, they don't say that any longer.' A major coup in this regard was the

Madonna Greeting Campaign launched in September 2000, when the online demo of the paybox system included a teaser of a Madonna song launched in Germany at that time. Ziesche remembers: 'That was when people out there realized: paybox is a company to reckon with.'

Advertisements and promotions

Paybox also started regular advertising campaigns. In June 2000, a TV campaign on MTV was launched, combined with a paybox–MTV lottery. Conventional print media advertisements followed, as well as a second campaign on national TV stations in April 2001. Promotional activity included a Loveparade lottery, where payboxers (paybox users) could win a ride on the paybox truck at the Berlin Loveparade 2000, as well as free business cards for paybox users at Web.de and flower vouchers at online flower service Valentins.de. 'In general, I find that European customers are a bit suspicious of cash offers, like our €5 referral fee. Our promotions with Valentins.de or Web.de better match their tastes', says Ortwein.

In addition, paybox has a number of continuous offers. For example, it dropped its €5 annual fee for the first year of membership and switched, in autumn 2000, all incoming phone calls to free call numbers. Soon afterwards, it dropped all transaction charges for consumers, making merchant fees the major revenue source. 'The *disagio* is our cash generator', says Jochen Schwiersch.

End users' perspective

For end users, the widespread availability of the paybox solution (across computer networks and phone systems), Deutsche Bank's backing and support of paybox, and the security system underlying the paybox offering are important features of the product. However, they think that the system also has some shortcomings:

- In the Internet-to-paybox payment mode, it is the merchant who decides when the charged amount should be withdrawn from the payer's account, while credit card companies typically execute the actual debit at a later date than the merchant does.

- Sometimes, the system cannot be used due to bad phone connections or low battery power of the mobile phone. Also, in some peak periods, the mobile

telecommunications network is very congested and, therefore, the paybox system cannot be used. (One consumer reported that he could not pay a taxi driver one New Year's Eve due to the above problem.)

- Consumers argue that they would need to have two mobile phones if they wanted to enjoy the convenience they are used to from corporate and personal credit cards.

- The internationalization of Internet merchants has not progressed as much as online customers would have wished, especially since the latter shop at international sites such as Amazon.com or eBay.com.

Technology factors

The paybox payment infrastructure is presented in Exhibit 8. Paybox does everything to ensure safe and reliable transactions. The payment servers, which consist of several Hewlett Packard Unix machines, are hosted by Lufthansa Systems at their Frankfurt data centre, where many other data centres of banks are also managed. The IT department remains an integral part of the paybox.net parent company. Although marketing, sales and operations offices are also set up in the other European countries where paybox is to be launched, the complete technological backbone is developed, hosted and administrated in the company headquarters in Raunheim and the nearby data center. Calls are routed from the paybox call servers via voice-over IP to the respective countries where the transactions are actually made. The company is in close contact with its database vendor, Oracle, as well as the provider of the computer–telephone interface, Envox, that manages the voice calls.

Although over 99% of the transactions confirmed by paybox are processed by Deutsche Bank, around one in seven transactions fail to be confirmed in the first place because the connection to one of the transaction partners is lost during the transaction. Ortwein says: 'Of course, we don't know for sure whether someone just hung up or had a technical problem.' The reason for this is the technological set-up of the telephone network: it does not differentiate between lost connections and normally finished calls.

In addition, transaction times are fairly long. While the phone call to the payer (in Internet-to-paybox payment mode, for example) averages 25 seconds, calls by

Exhibit 8 Regular paybox transaction

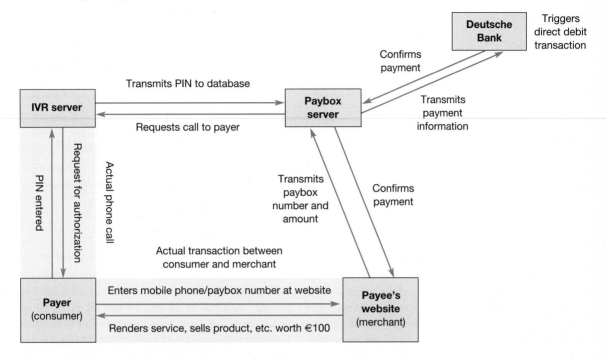

payees average 90 seconds. This is, of course, partly due to the fact that users are not yet very familiar with the system and require more time than necessary to enter the data correctly. The cost of these calls adds to the paybox cost per transaction, and makes it higher than that of a credit card processing company, if fraud is not taken into account.

Ortwein is unfazed by these apparent limitations:

> That may be the current state of affairs, but technology is advancing quickly. We will not stop at authentication over voice calls. With the always-on data functionality of mobile phones, which will be possible, starting with GRPS-networks, we will only need to send a short data packet. We will be faster, more convenient and cheaper than a credit card.

Competition

> We are no longer a regular start-up. We are a fledgling company on its way to becoming an international player. Exceptionally qualified and professional employees[1] are just as important for our success as the quality of our paybox products.

Mathias Entenmann

During the launch preparations, paybox employees were debating the success in the US of PayPal, a pay-

ment system that enables peer-to-peer transactions using e-mail or personal digital assistants (PDA). PayPal is a free system that has financed itself since a couple of days after float, and from charging, like paybox, a €5 referral fee. Two years after its launch, PayPal had 5 000 000 users, and became the number-one method of payment at eBay.com. Ortwein admits: 'So far, we haven't made a breakthrough similar to that of PayPal' (see Exhibit 9). 'However,' added Entenmann:

> PayPal's value proposition in the US is very different from whatever existed there before. People relied on postal mail to send cheques, with transaction times peaking at 14 days. PayPal was therefore launched to meet an urgent market need. Obviously, this situation in the US, where wireless transfers are also virtually unknown, doesn't compare with the one in Europe.

Paybox is not very worried by the possible entry in Europe of PayPal. 'PayPal, like most US products, is PC-centred', says Peter Seipp. 'European consumers are mobile phone-centred. Besides, PayPal's service in Europe would be far less convincing because the banking system here is only slightly less convenient than PayPal.'

---

1 By April 2002, paybox.net employed in its Raunheim headquarters 80 people, representing 25 nationalities.

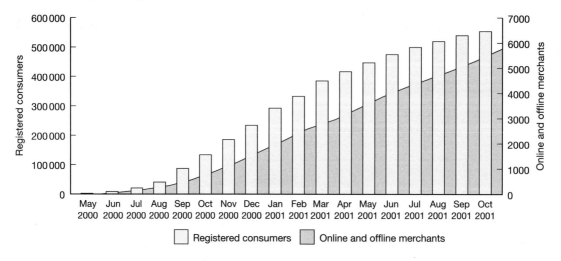

Recently, numerous m-payment systems have been introduced in Germany. These include prepaid cards (such as PaySafeCard) and SMS-based solutions (like PayItMobile). Like paybox, these systems can operate over any mobile phone, any telecommunications network, and via any bank account. However, the PaySafeCard solution would require recharging the account as is already the case with prepaid phones. SMS-based systems are triggered via a website to send an SMS to the consumer's phone, which is then entered at the website by the consumer. These systems are cheaper to operate than paybox, but the SMS is not guaranteed to arrive within a specific time frame. Furthermore, unlike paybox, the use of SMS-based systems does not require a PIN; therefore, anyone with access to the phone could trigger the payment transaction.

More sophisticated ideas include storing credit card information on the cell phone's SIM[2] card. This solution, heralded by some credit card companies, is still in its testing phase. However, it is hampered by the cost of integrating the system into the telecommunications network and exchanging users' mobile phones and SIM cards.

In March 2001, Durlacher research categorized different international m-payment services along two dimensions: the strength of the payment service and the stage of development, implementation and acceptance (see Exhibit 10). Although PayPal scored higher in the second dimension, the report emphasized the strong market position of paybox.

In general, possible entrants include the major telecommunications operators, banks and credit card companies. However, nearly all of the rival systems are still in the test or launch phase. 'Large telecommunications companies have underestimated the complexity of the online payment process', says Entenmann. 'Credit card companies, instead of worrying about m-payments, have been busy trying to make their cards safer for the online world', states Ortwein. 'Banks have been content to fund small start-ups, like PayPal or paybox', adds Seipp.

With directly competing m-payment systems still to come, the real competitors may prove to be the entrenched market incumbents. In the Internet-to-paybox transaction mode, paybox is similar to credit card companies. 'Merchants asked us to match the [business] terms they had from credit card companies. When we did that, they were happy since they didn't want to rely too much on a single payment system; plus many merchants liked the security of our solution. But when we didn't, they just walked away', says Ralph Westenburger. In the offline world, the main competitor of paybox is the EC banking card. 'This card has 55 million users in Germany alone. That's a huge critical mass', says Westenburger.

Although cash is the only competing system for the paybox-to-paybox transaction mode, the main barrier to entry is customers' awareness of the m-payment system.

---

2 SIM stands for subscriber's identification memory.

Exhibit 10 **Comparison of macro-payment solutions**

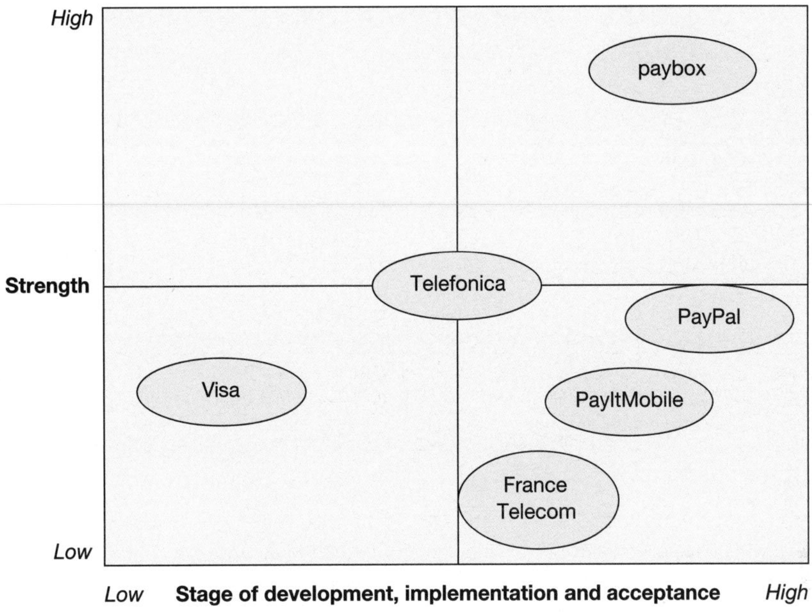

Source: UMTS Report, Durlacher Research, March 2000.

'We have to ensure that people think of paybox the next time they need to pay someone. The idea is just too new and will take some time to make its way through', says Eckhard Ortwein. 'Overall', explains Entenmann, 'I think that a bunch of dauntless [m-payment] competitors could help us spread the word and educate consumers. After all, competition is good for business!'

The PIA proposal

The Paybox Intelligent Architecture (or PIA) proposal is about creating these 'dauntless competitors', although they would also use the paybox technology platform. The architecture is planned to be a modular, global application infrastructure comprising all parts of the paybox service and its various applications. Paybox.net would wholly or partially license the technology to interested parties and sell consulting services on the implementation, operation and management of the m-payment service. Paybox could also help integrate its payment system into the customers' existing technology infrastructure.

The above services could interest banks, service companies and major corporations for which the paybox system may complement their existing customer loyalty programmes. They could also appeal to telecommunications companies, especially to second- or third-generation mobile network operators. They could all leverage the PIA technology to create co-branded paybox products.

'With our existing base of 750 000 consumers using the paybox solution every day, we have proved that our system works', says CTO Ortwein. 'Other companies have failed to create a mass-market system. With PIA, they can buy the most successful, off-the-shelf [m-payment] solution. So why wait?'

Paybox has invested heavily in its consumer business and intends to keep this operation:

We have a strong customer base and are growing steadily. However, with the functionality to submit standard payment transfers, we have finally found a killer application; we have established backward compatibility … In the last few months, we have driven growth by taking only small fees or no fees at all, especially where consumers are concerned. Our main challenge now is how to make money from the paybox-to-paybox transaction mode and from money transfers.

INDEX